CCNP TSHOOT 642-832

Official Certification Guide

Kevin Wallace, CCIE No. 7945

Cisco Press

800 East 96th Street

Indianapolis, IN 46240

CCNP TSHOOT 642-832 Official Certification Guide

Kevin Wallace, CCIE No. 7945

Copyright © 2010 Pearson Education, Inc.

Published by:
Cisco Press
800 East 96th Street
Indianapolis, IN 46240 USA

Printed in the United States of America

Third Printing September 2010

Library of Congress Cataloging-in-Publication Data:

Wallace, Kevin, CCNP.
    CCNP TSHOOT 642-832 official certification guide / Kevin Wallace.
      p. cm.
    Includes index.
    ISBN-13: 978-1-58705-844-8
    ISBN-10: 1-58705-844-8
  1. Computer networks—Management—Examinations—Study guides. 2. Telecommunications engineers—Certification. 3. Cisco Systems, Inc.—Examinations—Study guides. I. Title.
    TK5105.8.C57W35 2010
    004.6076—dc22

Warning and Disclaimer

This book is designed to provide information about the CCNP TSHOOT Exam (Exam 642-832) for the CCNP Routing and Switching certification. Every effort has been made to make this book as complete and as accurate as possible, but no warranty or fitness is implied.

The information is provided on an "as is" basis. The authors, Cisco Press, and Cisco Systems, Inc. shall have neither liability nor responsibility to any person or entity with respect to any loss or damages arising from the information contained in this book or from the use of the discs or programs that may accompany it.

The opinions expressed in this book belong to the author and are not necessarily those of Cisco Systems, Inc.

Trademark Acknowledgments

All terms mentioned in this book that are known to be trademarks or service marks have been appropriately capitalized. Cisco Press or Cisco Systems, Inc., cannot attest to the accuracy of this information. Use of a term in this book should not be regarded as affecting the validity of any trademark or service mark.

Corporate and Government Sales

The publisher offers excellent discounts on this book when ordered in quantity for bulk purchases or special sales, which may include electronic versions and/or custom covers and content particular to your business, training goals, marketing focus, and branding interests. For more information, please contact: **U.S. Corporate and Government Sales**   1-800-382-3419   corpsales@pearsontechgroup.com

For sales outside the United States please contact: **International Sales**   international@pearsoned.com

Feedback Information

At Cisco Press, our goal is to create in-depth technical books of the highest quality and value. Each book is crafted with care and precision, undergoing rigorous development that involves the unique expertise of members from the professional technical community.

Readers' feedback is a natural continuation of this process. If you have any comments regarding how we could improve the quality of this book, or otherwise alter it to better suit your needs, you can contact us through e-mail at feedback@ciscopress.com. Please make sure to include the book title and ISBN in your message.

We greatly appreciate your assistance.

Publisher: Paul Boger

Associate Publisher: Dave Dusthimer

Executive Editor: Brett Bartow

Managing Editor: Patrick Kanouse

Senior Project Editor: Tonya Simpson

Senior Development Editor: Christopher Cleveland

Editorial Assistant: Vanessa Evans

Book Designer: Louisa Adair

Composition: Mark Shirar

Indexer: Tim Wright

Business Operation Manager, Cisco Press: Anand Sundaram

Manager Global Certification: Erik Ullanderson

Copy Editors: Gill Editorial Services and Water Crest Publishing, Inc.

Technical Editor: Elan Beer

Proofreader: Williams Woods Publishing Services, LLC

CISCO

Americas Headquarters
Cisco Systems, Inc.
San Jose, CA

Asia Pacific Headquarters
Cisco Systems (USA) Pte. Ltd.
Singapore

Europe Headquarters
Cisco Systems International BV
Amsterdam, The Netherlands

Cisco has more than 200 offices worldwide. Addresses, phone numbers, and fax numbers are listed on the Cisco Website at **www.cisco.com/go/offices**.

CCDE, CCENT, Cisco Eos, Cisco HealthPresence, the Cisco logo, Cisco Lumin, Cisco Nexus, Cisco StadiumVision, Cisco TelePresence, Cisco WebEx, DCE, and Welcome to the Human Network are trademarks; Changing the Way We Work, Live, Play, and Learn and Cisco Store are service marks; and Access Registrar, Aironet, AsyncOS, Bringing the Meeting To You, Catalyst, CCDA, CCDP, CCIE, CCIP, CCNA, CCNP, CCSP, CCVP, Cisco, the Cisco Certified Internetwork Expert logo, Cisco IOS, Cisco Press, Cisco Systems, Cisco Systems Capital, the Cisco Systems logo, Cisco Unity, Collaboration Without Limitation, EtherFast, EtherSwitch, Event Center, Fast Step, Follow Me Browsing, FormShare, GigaDrive, HomeLink, Internet Quotient, IOS, iPhone, iQuick Study, IronPort, the IronPort logo, LightStream, Linksys, MediaTone, MeetingPlace, MeetingPlace Chime Sound, MGX, Networkers, Networking Academy, Network Registrar, PCNow, PIX, PowerPanels, ProConnect, ScriptShare, SenderBase, SMARTnet, Spectrum Expert, StackWise, The Fastest Way to Increase Your Internet Quotient, TransPath, WebEx, and the WebEx logo are registered trademarks of Cisco Systems, Inc. and/or its affiliates in the United States and certain other countries.

All other trademarks mentioned in this document or website are the property of their respective owners. The use of the word partner does not imply a partnership relationship between Cisco and any other company. (0812R)

About the Author

Kevin Wallace, CCIE No. 7945, is a certified Cisco instructor who holds multiple Cisco certifications, including CCSP, CCVP, CCNP, and CCDP, in addition to multiple security and voice specializations. With Cisco experience dating back to 1989 (beginning with a Cisco AGS+ running Cisco IOS 7.x), Kevin has been a network design specialist for the Walt Disney World Resort, a senior technical instructor for SkillSoft/Thomson NETg/KnowledgeNet, and a network manager for Eastern Kentucky University. Kevin holds a bachelor of science degree in electrical engineering from the University of Kentucky. Kevin has authored multiple books for Cisco Press, including *Routing Video Mentor* and *TSHOOT Video Mentor*, both of which target the current CCNP Routing and Switching certification. Kevin lives in central Kentucky with his wife (Vivian) and two daughters (Stacie and Sabrina).

About the Technical Reviewer

Elan Beer, CCIE No. 1837, CCSI No. 94008, is a senior consultant and Certified Cisco Instructor. His internetworking expertise is recognized internationally through his global consulting and training engagements. As one of the industry's top internetworking consultants and Cisco instructors, Elan has used his expertise for the past 17 years to design, implement, and deploy multiprotocol networks for a wide international clientele. As a senior instructor and course developer, Elan has designed and presented public and implementation-specific technical courses spanning many of today's top technologies. Elan specializes in MPLS, BGP, QoS, and other Internetworking technologies.

Dedications

This book is dedicated to my family. To my beautiful wife Vivian, you have an unbelievably giving spirit. To my daughter Sabrina, you have a keen business mind at only 12 years of age. You're destined for big things. To my daughter Stacie, at the age of 14, you radiate happiness and are maturing into a wonderful young lady.

Acknowledgments

My thanks go out to the team of professionals at Cisco Press. I'm proud to be associated with such a respected organization.

My family is unbelievably supportive of my writing efforts. Thank you to my wife, Vivian, and my daughters, Sabrina and Stacie. You all have been very understanding when I seclude myself to write. Also, I'm grateful to God for surrounding me with such quality people, both personally and professionally.

Contents at a Glance

CD-Only Appendixes

Contents

Icons Used in This Book

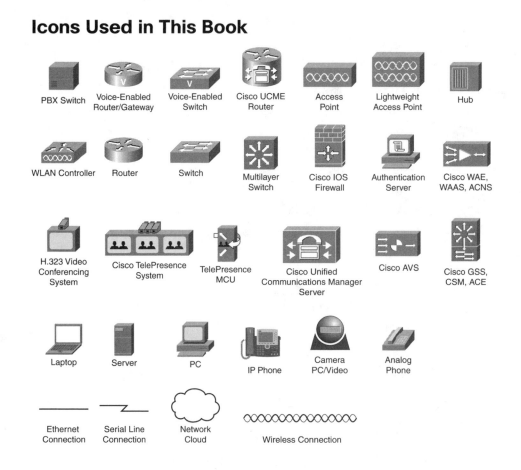

Command Syntax Conventions

The conventions used to present command syntax in this book are the same conventions used in the IOS Command Reference. The Command Reference describes these conventions as follows:

- **Boldface** indicates commands and keywords that are entered literally as shown. In actual configuration examples and output (not general command syntax), boldface indicates commands that are manually input by the user (such as a **show** command).

- *Italic* indicates arguments for which you supply actual values.

- Vertical bars (|) separate alternative, mutually exclusive elements.

- Square brackets ([ ]) indicate an optional element.

- Braces ({ }) indicate a required choice.

- Braces within brackets ([{ }]) indicate a required choice within an optional element.

Foreword

CCNP TSHOOT 642-832 Official Certification Guide is an excellent self-study resource for the CCNP TSHOOT exam. Passing this exam is a crucial step to attaining the valued CCNP Routing and Switching certification.

Gaining certification in Cisco technology is key to the continuing educational development of today's networking professional. Through certification programs, Cisco validates the skills and expertise required to effectively manage the modern enterprise network.

Cisco Press Certification Guides and preparation materials offer exceptional—and flexible—access to the knowledge and information required to stay current in your field of expertise or to gain new skills. Whether used as a supplement to more traditional training or as a primary source of learning, these materials offer users the information and knowledge validation required to gain new understanding and proficiencies.

Developed in conjunction with the Cisco certifications and training team, Cisco Press books are the only self-study books authorized by Cisco and offer students a series of exam practice tools and resource materials to help ensure that learners fully grasp the concepts and information presented.

Additional authorized Cisco instructor-led courses, e-learning, labs, and simulations are available exclusively from Cisco Learning Solutions Partners worldwide. To learn more, visit http://www.cisco.com/go/training.

I hope that you find these materials to be an enriching and useful part of your exam preparation.

Erik Ullanderson
Manager, Global Certifications
Learning@Cisco
January 2010

Introduction: Overview of Certification and How to Succeed

Professional certifications have been an important part of the computing industry for many years and will continue to become more important. Many reasons exist for these certifications, but the most popularly cited reason is that of credibility. All other considerations held equal, the certified employee/consultant/job candidate is considered more valuable than one who is not.

Objectives and Methods

The most important and somewhat obvious objective of this book is to help you pass the Cisco CCNP TSHOOT exam (Exam 642-832). In fact, if the primary objective of this book were different, the book's title would be misleading; however, the methods used in this book to help you pass the TSHOOT exam are designed to also make you much more knowledgeable about how to do your job. Although this book and the accompanying CD-ROM have many exam preparation tasks and example test questions, the method in which they are used is not to simply make you memorize as many questions and answers as you possibly can.

The methodology of this book helps you discover the exam topics about which you need more review, fully understand and remember exam topic details, and prove to yourself that you have retained your knowledge of those topics. So this book helps you pass not by memorization, but by helping you truly learn and understand the topics. The TSHOOT exam is just one of the foundation topics in the CCNP Routing and Switching certification, and the knowledge contained within is vitally important to consider yourself a truly skilled routing and switching engineer or specialist. This book would do you a disservice if it did not attempt to help you learn the material. To that end, the book can help you pass the TSHOOT exam by using the following methods:

- Covering all of the exam topics and helping you discover which exam topics you have not mastered

- Providing explanations and information to fill in your knowledge gaps

- Supplying multiple troubleshooting case studies with diagrams and diagnostic output that enhance your ability to resolve trouble tickets presented in the exam environment, in addition to real-world troubleshooting issues you might encounter

- Providing practice exercises on exam topics, presented in each chapter and on the enclosed CD-ROM

Who Should Read This Book?

This book is not designed to be a general networking topics book, although it can be used for that purpose. This book is intended to tremendously increase your chances of passing the Cisco TSHOOT exam. Although other objectives can be achieved from using this book, the book is written with one goal in mind: to help you pass the exam.

The TSHOOT exam is primarily based on the content of the Cisco TSHOOT course. You should have either taken the course, read through the TSHOOT course material or this book, or have a couple of years of troubleshooting experience.

Cisco Certifications and Exams

Cisco offers four levels of routing and switching certification, each with an increasing level of proficiency: Entry, Associate, Professional, and Expert. These are commonly known by their acronyms CCENT (Cisco Certified Entry Networking Technician), CCNA (Cisco Certified Network Associate), CCNP (Cisco Certified Network Professional), and CCIE (Cisco Certified Internetworking Expert). There are others as well, but this book focuses on the certifications for enterprise networks.

For the CCNP Routing and Switching certification, you must pass exams on a series of CCNP topics, including the SWITCH, ROUTE, and TSHOOT exams. For most exams, Cisco does not publish the scores needed for passing. You need to take the exam to find that out for yourself.

To see the most current requirements for the CCNP Routing and Switching certification, go to cisco.com and click Training and Events. There you can find out other exam details such as exam topics and how to register for an exam.

The strategy you use to prepare for the TSHOOT exam might be slightly different than strategies used by other readers, mainly based on the skills, knowledge, and experience you have already obtained. For example, if you have attended the TSHOOT course, you might take a different approach than someone who learned troubleshooting through on-the-job training. Regardless of the strategy you use or the background you have, this book is designed to help you get to the point where you can pass the exam with the least amount of time required.

How This Book Is Organized

Although this book can be read cover to cover, it is designed to be flexible and enable you to easily move between chapters to cover only the material that you need more work with. The chapters can be covered in any order, although some chapters are related and build upon each other. If you do intend to read them all, the order in the book is an excellent sequence to use.

Each core chapter covers a subset of the topics on the CCNP TSHOOT exam. The chapters are organized into parts, covering the following topics:

- **Chapter 1, "Introduction to Network Maintenance":** This chapter discusses the importance of proactive maintenance tasks, as opposed to the reactive maintenance required to address a problem. Also discussed in this chapter is a collection of commonly used maintenance approaches.

  Next, this chapter lists common maintenance tasks, emphasizes the importance of regularly scheduled maintenance, and summarizes critical areas of network performance. Finally, this chapter identifies how to compile a set of network maintenance tools that complement your network maintenance plan.

- **Chapter 2, "Introduction to Troubleshooting Processes":** This chapter addresses troubleshooting fundamentals, discusses the benefits of having a structured troubleshooting model, and discusses several popular troubleshooting models.

  Also discussed is each subprocess in a structured troubleshooting approach. Finally, this chapter shows how maintenance processes and troubleshooting process can work in tandem to complement one another.

- **Chapter 3, "The Maintenance and Troubleshooting Toolbox":** This chapter shows how a few readily accessible Cisco IOS commands can be used to quickly gather information, as part of a structured troubleshooting process.

  This chapter also introduces a collection of specialized features, such as SPAN, RSPAN, SMTP, NetFlow, and EEM, which can be used to collect information about a problem.

- **Chapter 4, "Basic Cisco Catalyst Switch Troubleshooting":** This chapter reviews the basics of Layer 2 switch operation and demonstrates a collection of Cisco Catalyst **show** commands that can be used to quickly gather information, as part of a structured troubleshooting process.

  Also, this chapter introduces spanning tree protocol (STP), which allows a Layer 2 topology to have redundant links while avoiding the side effects of a looped Layer 2 topology, such as a broadcast storm. You then learn strategies for troubleshooting an STP issue.

  Finally, troubleshooting an EtherChannel connection is addressed. This chapter concludes with a trouble ticket and an associated topology. You are also given **show** command output (baseline output and output collected after the reported issue occurred). Based on the information provided, you hypothesize an underlying cause for the reported issue and develop a solution. You can then compare your solution with a suggested solution.

- **Chapter 5, "Advanced Cisco Catalyst Switch Troubleshooting":** This chapter begins by contrasting Layer 3 switches and routers. Troubleshooting procedures are also compared for these platforms. Two approaches for routing packets using Layer 3 switches are also discussed. These approaches are using routed ports and using switched virtual interfaces (SVIs).

  Next, this chapter discusses three approaches to providing first-hop router redundancy. Options include HSRP, VRRP, and GLBP. Troubleshooting strategies are discussed for HSRP with suggestions on how to modify those strategies for troubleshooting VRRP and GLBP. Examined next is the architecture of a Cisco Catalyst switch and the different architectural components that could become troubleshooting targets. You are presented with a series of **show** commands used to gather information about different aspects of a switch's performance.

  Finally, this chapter presents you with a trouble ticket and an associated topology. You are also given **show** and **debug** command output (baseline output and output collected after a reported issue occurred). Based on the information provided, you hypothesize an underlying cause for the reported issue and develop a solution. You can then compare your solution with a suggested solution.

- **Chapter 6, "Introduction to Troubleshooting Routing Protocols":** This chapter begins by reviewing basic routing concepts. For example, you examine the changes to a frame's header as that frame's data is routed from one network to another. You see how Layer 2 information can be learned and stored in a router. Cisco Express Forwarding (CEF) is also discussed. Additionally, you are presented with a collection of **show** commands, useful for troubleshooting IP routing.

  Next, this chapter generically reviews how an IP routing protocol's data structures interact with a router's IP routing table. Then, EIGRP's data structures are considered, followed by a review of basic EIGRP operation. Again, you are presented with a collection of **show** and **debug** commands useful for troubleshooting various EIGRP operations.

  Finally, this chapter challenges you with a trouble ticket and an associated topology. You are also given **show** command output. Based on the information provided, you hypothesize an underlying cause for the reported issue and develop a solution. You can then compare your solution with a suggested solution.

- **Chapter 7, "OSPF and Route Redistribution Troubleshooting":** This chapter begins by introducing you to OSPF's routing structures, followed by a review of OSPF operation. You are then presented with a collection of **show** and **debug** commands useful for troubleshooting OSPF operations.

  This chapter next presents you with a trouble ticket and an associated topology. You are also given **show** command output. Based on the information provided, you hypothesize an underlying cause for the reported issues and develop solutions. You can then compare your solutions with the suggested solutions.

  This chapter also introduces the concept of route redistribution and discusses how a route from one routing process can be injected into a different routing process. Common route redistribution troubleshooting targets are identified, along with strategies for troubleshooting route redistribution.

  Finally, this chapter challenges you with another trouble ticket and an associated topology. You are also given **show** command output. Based on the information provided, you hypothesize an underlying cause for the reported issue and develop a solution. You can then compare your solution with a suggested solution.

- **Chapter 8, "Troubleshooting BGP and Router Performance Issues":** This chapter begins by introducing you to BGP's data structures, followed by a review of BGP operation. You are then presented with a collection of **show** and **debug** commands useful for troubleshooting BGP operations.

  This chapter next presents you with a trouble ticket and an associated topology. You are given **show** command output. Based on the information provided, you hypothesize an underlying cause for the reported issue and develop a solution. You can then compare your solutions with the suggested solutions.

  Finally, this chapter discusses how to troubleshoot performance issues on a router, focusing on CPU utilization, packet-switching modes, and memory utilization.

- **Chapter 9, "Security Troubleshooting":** This chapter begins by reviewing various security measures that might be put in place on Cisco routers and switches to protect three different planes of network operation. These planes are the management plane, the control plane, and the data plane. Once you review these security measures, this chapter considers how your troubleshooting efforts might be impacted by having various layers of security in place.

  Next, this chapter describes the basic operation and troubleshooting tips for Cisco IOS firewalls and AAA services. Although complete configuration details for Cisco IOS firewalls and AAA is beyond the scope of the TSHOOT curriculum, as a reference, this chapter does provide a couple of basic configuration examples with an explanation of the syntax used.

  Finally, this chapter presents you with a trouble ticket and an associated topology. You are also given **show** command output and a syntax reference. Based on the information provided, you hypothesize how to correct the reported issues. You can then compare your solutions with the suggested solutions.

- **Chapter 10, "IP Services Troubleshooting":** This chapter begins by reviewing the purpose and basic operation of Network Address Translation (NAT). As a reference, sample topologies are provided, along with their configurations. Common NAT troubleshooting targets are identified, and a syntax reference is provided to aid in troubleshooting NAT issues.

  Next, this chapter reviews Dynamic Host Configuration Protocol (DHCP) operation and various types of DHCP messages. You are given three configuration examples corresponding to the three roles a router might play in a DHCP environment: DHCP relay agent, DHCP client, and DHCP server. Common DHCP troubleshooting targets are reviewed, along with recommended DHCP troubleshooting practices. This section also presents a collection of commands that could prove to be useful in troubleshooting a suspected DHCP issue.

  Finally, this chapter presents you with a trouble ticket and an associated topology. You are also given **show** and **debug** command output, which confirms the reported issue. Then, you are challenged to hypothesize how to correct the reported issue. You can then compare your solution with a suggested solution.

- **Chapter 11, "IP Communications Troubleshooting":** This chapter begins by introducing you to design and troubleshooting considerations that arise when adding voice traffic to a data network. Several protocols are involved when a Cisco IP Phone registers with its call agent in order to place and receive voice calls. You review the function of these protocols along with recommendations for troubleshooting voice issues. One of the major troubleshooting targets for voice networks involves quality of service. Therefore, this chapter provides overview of quality of service configuration, verification, and troubleshooting commands. Additionally, this chapter considers video traffic in an IP network, including video's unique design and troubleshooting challenges.

Also, video-based networks often rely on an infrastructure that supports IP multicasting. Because multicasting has not been addressed in any depth thus far in this book, this chapter serves as a primer to multicast technologies. Included in this primer are commands used to configure, monitor, and troubleshoot multicast networks. The chapter next considers common video troubleshooting issues and recommends resolutions for those issues.

Finally, this chapter presents you with two trouble tickets focused on unified communications. You are presented with a topology used by both trouble tickets, in addition to a collection of **show** command output. For each trouble ticket, you are challenged to hypothesize how to correct the reported issue. You can also compare your solutions with suggested solutions.

- **Chapter 12, "IPv6 Troubleshooting":** This chapter introduces the purpose and structure of IP version 6 (IPv6) addressing. You consider the various types of IPv6 addresses, routing protocols supporting IPv6, and basic syntax for enabling a router to route IPv6 traffic. A sample configuration is provided to illustrate the configuration of a router to support IPv6. Additionally, as an organization is migrating from IPv4 to IPv6, there might be portions of the network that are still running IPv4 with other portions of the network running IPv6. For IPv6 traffic to span an IPv4 portion of the network, one option is to create a tunnel spanning the IPv4 network. Then, IPv6 traffic can travel inside the tunnel to transit the IPv4 network. This section discusses the syntax and provides an example of tunneling IPv6 over an IPv4 tunnel.

This chapter also contrasts the characteristics of two versions of OSPF, specifically OSPFv2 and OSPFv3. OSPFv3 can support the routing of IPv6 networks, whereas OSPFv2 cannot. OSPFv3 configuration syntax is presented, along with a sample configuration. You are also provided with a collection of verification troubleshooting commands and a listing of common OSPFv3 issues.

Next, this chapter presents you with a trouble ticket addressing a network experiencing OSPF adjacency issues. You are presented with a collection of **show** and **debug** command output and challenged to resolve a series of misconfigurations. Suggested solutions are provided.

Also, this chapter contrasts the characteristics of RIP next generation (RIPng) with RIPv2. You are given a set of RIPng configuration commands along with a sample configuration. From a troubleshooting perspective, you compare RIPng troubleshooting commands with those commands used to troubleshoot RIPv1 and RIPv2. This chapter also discusses some of the more common RIPng troubleshooting issues you might encounter.

Finally, this chapter challenges you to resolve a couple of RIPng issues being observed in a network. Specifically, load balancing and default route advertisements are not behaving as expected. To assist in your troubleshooting efforts, you are armed with a collection of **show** and **debug** command output. Your proposed solutions can then be compared with suggested solutions.

- **Chapter 13, "Advanced Services Troubleshooting":** This chapter introduces you to Cisco's Application Network Services (ANS) architecture. Cisco ANS includes multiple pieces of dedicated equipment aimed at optimizing the performance of network-based applications (for example, improving the response time of a corporate web server for users at a remote office). Although this chapter introduces a collection of Cisco ANS components, the primary focus is on Cisco IOS features that can improve application performance. Specifically, the Cisco IOS features addressed are NetFlow, IP SLAs, NBAR, and QoS.

  Also, this chapter addresses the troubleshooting of wireless networks, and it begins by contrasting autonomous and split-MAC wireless network architectures. Wired network issues that could impact wireless networks are then highlighted. These issues include power, VLAN, security, DHCP, and QoS issues.

- **Chapter 14, "Large Enterprise Network Troubleshooting":** This chapter begins by identifying a collection of technologies that might become troubleshooting targets for a remote office network. The primary technologies focused on are Virtual Private Network (VPN) technologies. Sample syntax is provided for a VPN using IPsec and GRE. Also, several useful **show** commands are provided as a troubleshooting reference.

  Finally, this chapter discusses the troubleshooting of complex networks, and begins by identifying how multiple network technologies map to the seven layers of the OSI model. Also, you are given a list of resources a troubleshooter should have prior to troubleshooting a complex enterprise network. Finally, this chapter reviews key points from all trouble tickets previously presented.

- **Chapter 15, "Final Preparation":** This chapter identifies tools for final exam preparation and helps you develop an effective study plan.

Appendix A has the answers to the "Do I Know This Already" quizzes and an online appendix tells you how to find any updates should there be changes to the exam.

Each chapter in the book uses several features to help you make the best use of your time in that chapter. The features are as follows:

- **Assessment:** Each chapter begins with a "Do I Know This Already?" quiz that helps you determine the amount of time you need to spend studying each topic of the chapter. If you intend to read the entire chapter, you can save the quiz for later use. Questions are all multiple-choice, to give a quick assessment of your knowledge.

- **Foundation Topics:** This is the core section of each chapter that explains the protocols, concepts, configuration, and troubleshooting strategies for the topics in the chapter.

- **Exam Preparation Tasks:** At the end of each chapter, this section collects key topics, references to memory table exercises to be completed as memorization practice, key terms to define, and a command reference that summarizes any relevant commands presented in the chapter.

Finally, the companion CD-ROM contains practice CCNP TSHOOT questions to reinforce your understanding of the book's concepts. Be aware that the TSHOOT exam will primarily be made up of trouble tickets you need to resolve. Mastery of the topics covered by the CD-based questions, however, will help equip you with the tools needed to effectively troubleshoot the trouble tickets presented on the exam.

The CD also contains the Memory Table exercises and answer keys.

How to Use This Book for Study

Retention and recall are the two features of human memory most closely related to performance on tests. This exam-preparation guide focuses on increasing both retention and recall of the topics on the exam. The other human characteristic involved in successfully passing the exam is intelligence; this book does not address that issue!

This book is designed with features to help you increase retention and recall. It does this in the following ways:

■ By providing succinct and complete methods of helping you determine what you recall easily and what you do not recall at all.

■ By referencing the portions of the book that review those concepts you most need to recall, so you can quickly be reminded about a fact or concept. Repeating information that connects to another concept helps retention, and describing the same concept in several ways throughout a chapter increases the number of connectors to the same pieces of information.

■ Finally, accompanying this book is a CD-ROM that has questions covering troubleshooting theory, tools, and methodologies. Familiarity with these troubleshooting resources can help you be more efficient when diagnosing and resolving a reported network issue.

When taking the "Do I Know This Already?" assessment quizzes in each chapter, make sure that you treat yourself and your knowledge fairly. If you come across a question that makes you guess at an answer, mark it wrong immediately. This forces you to read through the part of the chapter that relates to that question and forces you to learn it more thoroughly.

If you find that you do well on the assessment quizzes, it still might be wise to quickly skim through each chapter to find sections or topics that do not readily come to mind. Look for the Key Topics icons. Sometimes even reading through the detailed table of contents will reveal topics that are unfamiliar or unclear. If that happens to you, mark those chapters or topics, and spend time working through those parts of the book.

CCNP TSHOOT Exam Topics

Carefully consider the exam topics Cisco has posted on its website as you study, particularly for clues to how deeply you should know each topic. Also, you can develop a broader knowledge of the subject matter by reading and studying the topics presented in this book. Remember that it is in your best interest to become proficient in each of the CCNP subjects. When it is time to use what you have learned, being well rounded counts more than being well tested.

Table I-1 shows the official exam topics for the TSHOOT exam, as posted on cisco.com. Note that Cisco has occasionally changed exam topics without changing the exam number, so do not be alarmed if small changes in the exam topics occur over time. When in doubt, go to cisco.com and click Training and Events.

Table I-1   *CCNP TSHOOT Exam Topics*

Exam Topics	Chapters Where Exam Topics Are Covered
Maintain and monitor network performance	
Develop a plan to monitor and manage a network Perform network monitoring using IOS tools Perform routine IOS device maintenance Isolate sub-optimal internetwork operation at the correctly defined OSI Model layer	Chapters 1–3 and 14
Troubleshooting IPv4 and IPv6 routing protocols and IP services in a multiprotocol system network	
Troubleshoot EIGRP Troubleshoot OSPF Troubleshoot eBGP Troubleshoot routing redistribution solution Troubleshoot a DHCP client and server solution Troubleshoot NAT Troubleshoot first-hop redundancy protocols Troubleshoot IPv6 routing Troubleshoot IPv6 and IPv4 interoperability	Chapters 5–8, 10, and 12
Troubleshoot switch-based features	
Troubleshoot switch-to-switch connectivity for a VLAN-based solution Troubleshoot loop prevention for a VLAN-based solution Troubleshoot access ports for a VLAN-based solution Troubleshoot private VLANS Troubleshoot port security Troubleshoot general switch security Troubleshoot VACL and PACL Troubleshoot switch virtual interfaces (SVIs) Troubleshoot switch supervisor redundancy Troubleshoot switch support of advanced services Troubleshoot a VoIP support solution Troubleshoot a video support solution	Chapters 4–5, 11, and 13

Table I-1 *CCNP TSHOOT Exam Topics* *(Continued)*

Exam Topics	Chapters Where Exam Topics Are Covered
Troubleshoot Cisco router and switch device hardening	
Troubleshoot Layer 3 security Troubleshoot issues related to ACLs used to secure access to Cisco routers Troubleshoot configuration issues related to accessing an AAA server for authentication purposes Troubleshoot security issues related to IOS services	Chapters 9 and 10

For More Information

If you have any comments about the book, you can submit those via the ciscopress.com website. Just go to the website, select Contact Us, and type your message. Cisco might make changes that affect the CCNP Routing and Switching certification from time to time. You should always check cisco.com for the latest details. Also, you can look to www.ciscopress.com/title/1587058448, where we publish any information pertinent to how you might use this book differently in light of Cisco's future changes. For example, if Cisco decided to remove a major topic from the exam, it might post that on its website; Cisco Press will make an effort to list that information as well via an online updates appendix.

This chapter covers the following subjects:

Understanding Maintenance Methods: This section discusses the importance of proactive maintenance tasks, as opposed to reactive maintenance, required to address a problem in a network. Also discussed in this section is a collection of commonly used maintenance approaches.

Identifying Common Maintenance Procedures: This section lists common maintenance tasks, emphasizes the importance of regularly scheduled maintenance, and summarizes critical areas of network performance.

The Network Maintenance Toolkit: This section identifies how to compile a set of network maintenance tools that complement your network maintenance plan.

CHAPTER 1

Introduction to Network Maintenance

Business operations are becoming increasingly dependent upon the reliable operation of business data networks (which might also carry voice and video traffic). A structured and systematic maintenance approach significantly contributes to the uptime for such networks.

Consider the purchase of a new car. Many excited owners of a new car peruse the owner's manual to find the recommended maintenance schedule and vow to perform the routine recommended maintenance. They instinctively know that adhering to a documented maintenance plan can reduce the occurrence of issues with their car. Similarly, the number of issues in a network can be reduced by following a documented schedule of maintenance.

This chapter discusses the importance of having a maintenance plan and introduces several popular models that can be adapted to your network. Next, you are introduced to specific maintenance tasks. Finally in this chapter, you identify the tools (for example, network monitoring and disaster recovery tools) you need in your virtual toolbox.

"Do I Know This Already?" Quiz

The "Do I Know This Already?" quiz helps you determine your level of knowledge on this chapter's topics before you begin. Table 1-1 details the major topics discussed in this chapter and their corresponding quiz sections.

Table 1-1   *"Do I Know This Already?" Section-to-Question Mapping*

Foundation Topics Section	Questions
Understanding Maintenance Methods	1–4
Identifying Common Maintenance Procedures	5–10
The Network Maintenance Toolkit	11–14

1. Which of the following are considered network maintenance tasks? (Choose the three best answers.)

    a.   Troubleshooting problem reports

    b.   Attending training on emerging network technologies

    c.   Planning for network expansion

    d.   Hardware installation

2. Network maintenance tasks can be categorized into one of which two categories? (Choose two.)

   a. Recovery tasks

   b. Interrupt-driven tasks

   c. Structured tasks

   d. Installation tasks

3. Identify the network maintenance model defined by the ITU-T for maintaining telecommunications networks.

   a. FCAPS

   b. ITIL

   c. TMN

   d. Cisco Lifecycle Services

4. Which letter in the FCAPS acronym represents the maintenance area responsible for billing end users?

   a. F

   b. C

   c. A

   d. P

   e. S

5. The lists of tasks required to maintain a network can vary widely, depending on the goals and characteristics of that network. However, some network maintenance tasks are common to most networks. Which of the following would be considered a common task that should be present in any network maintenance model?

   a. Performing database synchronization for a network's Microsoft Active Directory

   b. Making sure digital certificates used for PKI are renewed in advance of their expiration

   c. Using CiscoWorks to dynamically discover network device changes

   d. Performing scheduled backups

6. Which of the following statements is true regarding scheduled maintenance?

   a. Scheduled maintenance helps ensure that important maintenance tasks are not overlooked.

   b. Scheduled maintenance is not recommended for larger networks, because of the diversity of maintenance needs.

   c. Maintenance tasks should only be performed based on a scheduled maintenance schedule, in order to reduce unexpected workflow interruptions.

   d. Scheduled maintenance is more of a reactive approach to network maintenance, as opposed to a proactive approach.

7. Which of the following questions are appropriate when defining your change management policies? (Choose two.)

    a. What version of operating system is currently running on the device to be upgraded?

    b. What is the return on investment (ROI) of an upgrade?

    c. What measureable criteria determine the success or failure of a network change?

    d. Who is responsible for authorizing various types of network changes?

8. Which three of the following components would you expect to find in a set of network documentation? (Choose three.)

    a. Logical topology diagram

    b. Listing of interconnections

    c. License files

    d. IP address assignments

9. Which three of the following are components that would be most useful when recovering from a network equipment outage? (Choose three.)

    a. Backup of device configuration information

    b. Physical topology

    c. Duplicate hardware

    d. Operating system and application software (along with any applicable licensing) for the device

10. What type of agreement exists between a service provider and one of their customers, which specifies performance metrics for the link interconnecting the customer with the service provider?

    a. MTBF

    b. GoS

    c. TOS

    d. SLA

11. Which command would you use to view archival copies of a router's startup configuration?

    a. show backup

    b. show archive

    c. show flash: | begin backup

    d. show ftp: | begin archive

12. Which of the following would be appropriate for a collaborative web-based documentation solution?

    a. blog

    b. vlog

    c. wiki

    d. podcast

13. CiscoWorks Resource Manager Essentials (RME) is a component of what CiscoWorks product?

    a. LMS

    b. RWAN

    c. QPM

    d. IPM

14. Which of the following is a Cisco IOS technology that uses a collector to take data from monitored devices and present graphs, charts, and tables to describe network traffic patterns?

    a. NBAR

    b. Netflow

    c. QDM

    d. IPS

Foundation Topics

Understanding Maintenance Methods

Network maintenance is an inherent component of a network administrator's responsibilities. However, that network administrator might be performing maintenance tasks in response to a reported problem. This reactive approach is unavoidable, because unforeseen issues do arise. However, the occurrence of these interrupt-driven maintenance tasks can be reduced by proactively performing regularly scheduled maintenance tasks.

You could think of regularly scheduled tasks, such as performing backups and software upgrades, as *important* but not *urgent*. Spending more time on the important tasks can help reduce time spent on the urgent tasks (for example, responding to user connectivity issues or troubleshooting a network outage).

This section begins by identifying several network maintenance tasks. Common network maintenance models are discussed. However, an off-the-shelf network maintenance model might not be a perfect fit for your organization. So, this section concludes by discussing how a well-known model can be adapted to your needs.

Introducing Network Maintenance

Before discussing approaches to network maintenance, let us first spend a few moments defining network maintenance. Network maintenance, at its essence, is doing whatever is required to keep the network functioning and meeting the business needs of an organization.

Some examples of the tasks that fall under the umbrella of network maintenance are as follows:

- Hardware and software installation and configuration

- Troubleshooting problem reports

- Monitoring and tuning network performance

- Planning for network expansion

- Documenting the network and any changes made to the network

- Ensuring compliance with legal regulations and corporate policies

- Securing the network against internal and external threats

Obviously, this listing is only a sampling of network maintenance tasks. Also, keep in mind that the list of tasks required to maintain your network could be quite different from the list of tasks required to maintain another network.

Proactive Versus Reactive Network Maintenance

Network maintenance tasks can be categorized as one of the following:

- **Structured tasks:** Performed as a predefined plan.

- **Interrupt-driven tasks:** Involve resolving issues as they are reported.

As previously mentioned, interrupt-driven tasks can never be completely eliminated; however, their occurrence can be lessened through a strategic structured approach.

Not only does a structured maintenance approach offer reduced downtime (by fixing problems before they occur), it also proves to be more cost effective. Specifically, unplanned network outages can be resolved more quickly. Fewer resources are consumed responding to problems, because fewer problems occur. Also, because a structured maintenance approach includes planning for future network capacity, appropriate hardware and software purchases can be made early on, reducing obsolescence of relatively new purchases.

Because a structured approach considers underlying business goals, resources can be allocated that complement business drivers. Also, security vulnerabilities are more likely to be discovered through ongoing network monitoring, which is another component of a structured maintenance approach.

Well-Known Network Maintenance Models

The subtleties of each network should be considered when constructing a structured network maintenance model. However, rather than starting from scratch, you might want to base your maintenance model on one of the well-known maintenance models and make adjustments as appropriate.

The following is a sampling of some of the more well-known maintenance models:

- **FCAPS:** FCAPS (which stands for Fault management, Configuration management, Accounting management, Performance management, and Security management) is a network maintenance model defined by the International Organization for Standardization (ISO).

- **ITIL:** An IT Infrastructure Library (ITIL) defines a collection of best-practice recommendations that work together to meet business goals.

- **TMN:** The Telecommunications Management Network (TMN) network management model is the Telecommunications Standardization Sector's (ITU-T) variation of the FCAPS model. Specifically, TMN targets the management of telecommunications networks.

- **Cisco Lifecycle Services:** The Cisco Lifecycle Services maintenance model defines distinct phases in the life of a Cisco technology in a network. These phases are Prepare, Plan, Design, Implement, Operate, and Optimize. As a result, the Cisco Lifecycle Services model is often referred to as the PPDIOO model.

Adapting a Well-Known Network Maintenance Model

The maintenance model you use in your network should reflect business drivers, resources, and expertise unique to your network. Your maintenance model might, however, be based on one of the previously discussed well-known maintenance models.

As an example, imagine you have selected the ISO FCAPS model as the foundation for your maintenance model. To adapt the FCAPS model for your environment, for each element of the FCAPS model, you should identify specific tasks to perform on your network. Table 1-2 provides a sampling of tasks that might be categorized under each of the FCAPS management areas.

Table 1-2 *FCAPS Management Tasks*

Type of Management	Examples of Management Tasks
Fault management	Use network management software to collect information from routers and switches. Send an e-mail alert when processor utilization or bandwidth utilization exceeds a threshold of 80 percent. Respond to incoming trouble tickets from the help desk.
Configuration management	Require logging of any changes made to network hardware or software configurations. Implement a change management system to alert relevant personnel of planned network changes.
Accounting management	Invoice IP telephony users for their long distance and international calls.
Performance management	Monitor network performance metrics for both LAN and WAN links. Deploy appropriate quality of service (QoS) solutions to make the most efficient use of relatively limited WAN bandwidth, while prioritizing mission critical traffic.
Security management	Deploy firewall, virtual private network (VPN), and intrusion prevention system (IPS) technologies to defend against malicious traffic. Create a security policy dictating rules of acceptable network use. Use an Authorization, Authentication, and Accounting (AAA) server to validate user credentials, assign appropriate user privileges, and log user activity.

Key
Topic

By clearly articulating not just a theoretical methodology but actionable and measurable processes, you can reduce network downtime and more effectively perform interrupt-driven tasks. This structured approach to network management helps define what tools are needed in a toolkit prior to events requiring the use of those tools.

Identifying Common Maintenance Procedures

Although the listings of procedures contained in various network maintenance models vary, some procedures are common to nearly all network maintenance models. This section identifies common network maintenance tasks, discusses the importance of regularly scheduled maintenance, and summarizes critical network maintenance areas.

Routine Maintenance Tasks

Some routine maintenance tasks should be present in a listing of procedures contained in a network maintenance model. Following is a listing of such common maintenance tasks:

■   **Configuration changes:** Businesses are dynamic environments, where relocation of users from one office space to another, the addition of temporary staffers, and new hires are commonplace. In response to organizational changes, network administrators need to respond by performing appropriate reconfigurations and additions to network hardware and software. These processes are often referred to as moves, adds, and changes.

■   **Replacement of older or failed hardware:** As devices age, their reliability and comparable performance tend to deteriorate. Therefore, a common task is the replacement of older hardware, typically with better performing and more feature-rich devices. Occasionally, production devices fail, thus requiring immediate replacement.

■   **Scheduled backups:** Recovery from a major system failure can occur much quicker if network data and device configurations have been regularly backed up. Therefore, a common network maintenance task is to schedule, monitor, and verify backups of selected data and configuration information. These backups can also be useful in recovering important data that were deleted.

■   **Updating software:** Updates to operating system software (for servers, clients, and even network devices) are periodically released. The updates often address performance issues and security vulnerabilities. New features are also commonly offered in software upgrades. Therefore, performing routine software updates becomes a key network maintenance task.

■   **Monitoring network performance:** The collection and interpretation of traffic statistics, bandwidth utilization statistics, and resource utilization statistics for network devices are common goals of network monitoring. Through effective network monitoring (which might involve the collection and examination of log files or the implementation of a high-end network management server), you can better plan for future expansion (that is, *capacity planning*), anticipate potential issues before they arise, and better understand the nature of the traffic flowing through your network.

Benefits of Scheduled Maintenance

After defining the network maintenance tasks for your network, those tasks can be ranked in order of priority. Some task will undoubtedly be urgent in nature and need a quick response (for example, replacing a failed router that connects a business to the Internet). Other tasks can be scheduled. For example, you might schedule weekly full backups of your network's file servers, and you might have a monthly maintenance window, during which time you apply software patches.

By having such a schedule for routine maintenance tasks, network administrators are less likely to forget an important task, because they were busy responding to urgent tasks. Also, users can be made aware of when various network services will be unavailable, due to maintenance windows, thus minimizing the impact on workflow.

Managing Network Changes

Making changes to a network often has the side effect of impacting the productivity of users relying on network resources. Additionally, a change to one network component might create a problem for another network component. For example, perhaps a firewall was installed to provide better security for a server farm. However, in addition to common protocols that were allowed to pass through the firewall (for example, DNS, SMTP, POP3, HTTP, HTTPS, and IMAP), one of the servers in the server farm acted as an FTP server, and the firewall configuration did not consider that server. Therefore, the installation of a firewall to better secure a server farm resulted in a troubleshooting issue, where users could no longer reach their FTP server.

The timing of network changes should also be considered. Rather than taking a router down in order to upgrade its version of Cisco IOS during regular business hours, such an operation should probably be performed during off hours.

Making different organization areas aware of upcoming maintenance operations can also aid in reducing unforeseen problems associated with routine maintenance. For example, imagine that one information technology (IT) department within an organization is responsible for maintaining WAN connections that interconnect various corporate offices, whereas another IT department is charged with performing network backups. If the WAN IT department plans to upgrade the WAN link between a couple of offices at 2:00 AM next Tuesday, the IT department in charge of backups should be made aware of that planned upgrade, because a backup of remote data (that is, data accessible over the WAN link to be upgraded) might be scheduled for that same time period.

Some organizations have a formalized change management process, where one department announces online their intention to perform a particular maintenance task during a specified time period. Other departments are then notified of this upcoming change, and determine if the planned change will conflict with that department's operations. If a conflict is identified, the departments can work together to accommodate one another's needs.

Of course, some network maintenance tasks are urgent (for example, a widespread network outage). Those tasks need timely response, without going through a formalized change management notification process and allowing time for other departments to respond.

When defining a change management system for your organization, consider the following:

- Who is responsible for authorizing various types of network changes?

- Which tasks should only be performed during scheduled maintenance windows?

- What procedures should be followed prior to making a change (for example, backing up a router's configuration prior to installing a new module in the router)?

- What measureable criteria determine the success or failure of a network change?

- How will a network change be documented, and who is responsible for the documentation?

- How will a rollback plan be created, such that a configuration can be restored to its previous state if the changes resulted in unexpected problems?

Key
Topic

■ Under what circumstances can formalized change management policies be overridden, and what (if any) authorization is required for an override?

Maintaining Network Documentation

Network documentation typically gets created as part of a network's initial design and installation. However, keeping that documentation current, reflecting all changes made since the network's installation, should be part of any network maintenance model. Keeping documentation current helps more effectively isolate problems when troubleshooting. Additionally, accurate documentation can prove to be valuable to designers who want to scale the network.

At a basic level, network documentation could consist of physical and logical network diagrams, in addition to a listing of network components and their configurations. However, network documentation can be much more detailed, including such components as formalized change management procedures, a listing of contact information (for example, for service providers and points of contact in an organization's various IT groups), and the rationale for each network change made.

While the specific components in a set of network documentation can vary, just as the procedures in a network maintenance model vary, the following list outlines common elements found in a set of network documentation:

■ **Logical topology diagram:** A logical topology diagram shows the interconnection of network segments, the protocols used, and how end users interface with the network. However, this diagram is not concerned with the physical locations of network components.

■ **Physical topology diagram:** Unlike a logical topology diagram, a physical topology diagram shows how different geographical areas (for example, floors within a building, buildings, or entire sites) interconnect. The diagram reflects where various network components are physically located.

■ **Listing of interconnections:** A listing of interconnections could be, for example, a spreadsheet that lists which ports on which devices are used to interconnect network components, or connect out to service provider networks. Circuit IDs for service provider circuits might be included in this documentation.

■ **Inventory of network equipment:** An inventory of network equipment would include such information as the equipment's manufacturer, model number, version of software, information about the licensing of the software, serial number, and an organization's asset tag number.

■ **IP address assignments:** An organization might use private IP address space internally and use network address translation (NAT) to translate those private IP address space numbers into publicly routable IP addresses. Alternately, an organization might have public IP addresses assigned to some or all of their internal devices. A classful IP address space (either public or private) might be subdivided within an organization, resulting in subnets with a non-default subnet mask. These types of IP addressing specifications would be included in a set of network documentation.

- **Configuration information:** When a configuration change is made, the current configuration should be backed up. With a copy of current configuration information, a device could be replaced quicker, in the event of an outage. Beyond having a backup of current configuration information, some network administrators also maintain archival copies of previous configurations. These older configurations could prove to be useful when attempting to roll back to a previous configuration state or when trying to duplicate a previous configuration in a new location. It is a good practice to name archival copies of previous configurations based on a certain format that makes sense to you. For example, some companies name their archival copies by date, others by function, and still others by a combination of both.

- **Original design documents:** Documents created during the initial design of a network might provide insight into why certain design decisions were made, and how the original designers envisioned future network expansion.

Larger network environments often benefit from having step-by-step guidelines for troubleshooting a given network issue. Such a structured approach to troubleshooting helps ensure that all troubleshooting personnel use a common approach. Although a network issue might be successfully resolved through various means, if different personnel troubleshoot using different approaches, at some point those approaches might conflict with one another, resulting in further issues.

For example, consider one network administrator that configures IEEE 802.1Q trunking on Cisco Catalyst switches by disabling Dynamic Trunk Protocol (DTP) frames and forcing a port to act as a trunk port. Another network administrator within the same company configures 802.1Q trunking by setting a port's trunk state to *desirable*, which creates a trunk connection only if it receives a DTP frame from the far end of the connection. These two approaches are not compatible, and if each of these two network administrators configured different ends of what they intended to be an 802.1Q trunk, the trunk connection would never come up. This example illustrates the criticality of having clear communication among IT personnel and a set of standardized procedures to ensure consistency in network configuration and troubleshooting practices.

Restoring Operation After Failure

Although most modern network hardware is very reliable, failures do occur from time to time. Aside from hardware failures, environmental factors could cause a network outage. As a few examples, the failure of an air conditioner unit could cause network equipment to overheat; water leakage due to flooding or plumbing issues could cause hardware failures; or a fire could render the network equipment unusable.

Planning and provisioning hardware and software for such outages before they occur can accelerate recovery time. To efficiently replace a failed (or damaged) device, you should be in possession of the following:

- Duplicate hardware

- Operating system and application software (along with any applicable licensing) for the device

- Backup of device configuration information

Measuring Network Performance

Network monitoring is a proactive approach to network maintenance, enabling you to be alerted to trends and utilization statistics (as a couple of examples), which can forecast future issues. Also, if you work for a service provider, network performance monitoring can ensure that you are providing an appropriate service level to a customer. Conversely, if you are a customer of a service provider, network monitoring can confirm that the service provider is conforming to the SLA for which you are paying.

The Network Maintenance Toolkit

After selecting the processes, and their corresponding tasks, that make up your network maintenance model, you next need to identify the tools required to carry out your maintenance processes. These tools should be targeted toward your specific processes and tasks, helping you focus your troubleshooting efforts without having to wade through reams of irrelevant information. This section provides examples of a few indispensible elements you should have in your network maintenance toolkit.

Basic Network Maintenance Tools

Network maintenance tools often range in expense from free to tens of thousands of dollars. Similarly, these tools vary in their levels of complexity and usefulness for troubleshooting specific issues. You need to select tools that balance your troubleshooting needs and budgetary constraints.

Regardless of budget, nearly all network maintenance toolkits can contain the command-line interface (CLI) commands executable from a router or switch prompt. Many network devices have a graphical user interface (GUI) to assist network administrators in their configuration and monitoring tasks. External servers (for example, backup servers, logging servers, and time servers) can also collect, store, or provide information useful for day-to-day network operation and for troubleshooting.

CLI Tools

Cisco IOS offers a wealth of CLI commands, which can be invaluable when troubleshooting a network issue. For example, a **show** command can display router configuration information and the routes that have been learned by a routing process. The **debug** command can provide real-time information about router or switch processes. To illustrate, consider Example 1-1, which shows router R2 receiving Open Shortest Path First (OSPF) link state updates from its OSPF neighbors as those updates occur.

Example 1-1   *Sample* debug *Output*

```
R2# debug ip ospf events
OSPF events debugging is on
R2#
*Mar  1 00:06:06.679: OSPF: Rcv LS UPD from 10.4.4.4 on Serial1/0.2 length 124
  LSA count 1
*Mar  1 00:06:06.691: OSPF: Rcv LS UPD from 10.3.3.3 on Serial1/0.1 length 124
  LSA count 1
```

```
*Mar  1 00:06:06.999: OSPF: Rcv LS UPD from 10.4.4.4 on Serial1/0.2 length 124
  LSA count 1
*Mar  1 00:06:07.067: OSPF: Rcv LS UPD from 10.3.3.3 on Serial1/0.1 length 156
  LSA count 2
```

A newer Cisco IOS feature, which allows a router to monitor events and automatically respond to a specific event (such as a defined threshold being reached) with a predefined action, is called Cisco IOS Embedded Event Manager (EEM). EEM policies can be created using Cisco's tool command language (Tcl).

GUI Tools

Although Cisco has some GUI tools, such as CiscoWorks, that can manage large enterprise networks, several device-based GUI tools are freely available. Examples of these free tools from Cisco are the following:

■ Cisco Configuration Professional (CCP)

■ Cisco Configuration Assistant (CCA)

■ Cisco Network Assistant (CNA)

■ Cisco Security Device Manager (SDM)

Figure 1-1 shows the home screen of Cisco SDM.

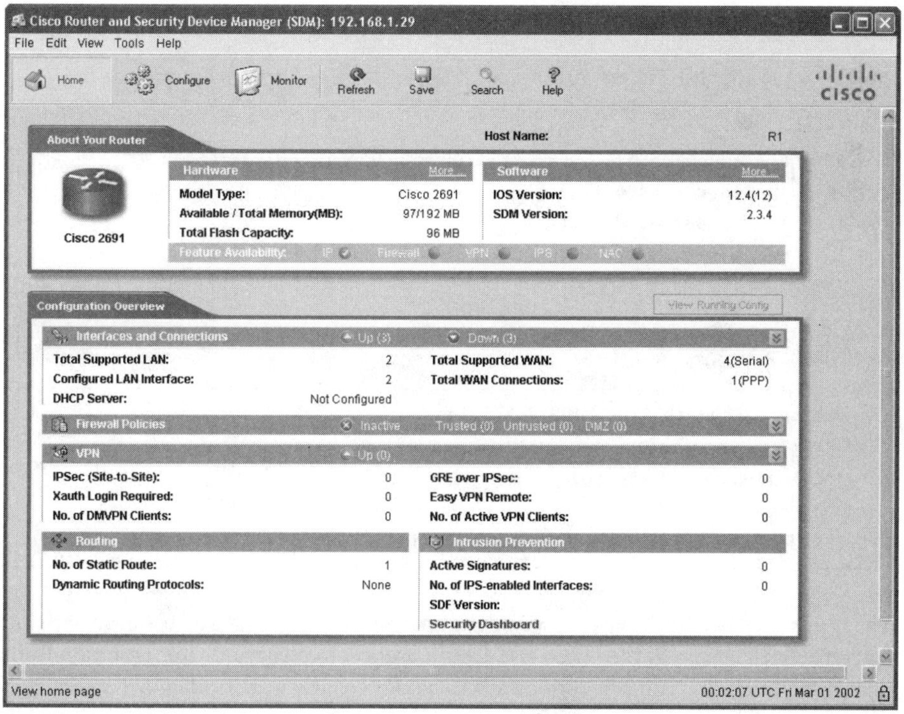

Figure 1-1 *Cisco Security Device Manager*

Backup Tools

External servers are often used to store archival backups of a device's operating system (for example, a Cisco IOS image) and configuration information. Depending on your network device, you might be able to back up your operating system and configuration information to a TFTP, FTP, HTTP, or SCP server. To illustrate, consider Example 1-2.

Example 1-2 *Backing Up a Router's Startup Configuration to an FTP Server*

```
R1# copy startup-config ftp://kevin:cisco@192.168.1.74
Address or name of remote host [192.168.1.74]?
Destination filename [r1-confg]?
Writing r1-confg !
1446 bytes copied in 3.349 secs (432 bytes/sec)
```

In Example 1-2, router R1's startup configuration is being copied to an FTP server with an IP address of 192.168.1.74. Notice that the login credentials (that is, username=kevin and password=cisco) for the FTP server are specified in the **copy** command.

If you intend to routinely copy backups to an FTP server, you can avoid specifying the login credentials each time (for security purposes), by adding those credentials to the router's configuration. Example 1-3 shows how to add username and password credentials to the router's configuration, and Example 1-4 shows how the startup configuration can be copied to an FTP server without explicitly specifying those credentials in the **copy** command.

Example 1-3 *Adding FTP Server Login Credentials to a Router's Configuration*

```
R1# conf term
Enter configuration commands, one per line.  End with CNTL/Z.
R1(config)# ip ftp username kevin
R1(config)# ip ftp password cisco
R1(config)# end
```

Example 1-4 *Backing Up a Router's Startup Configuration to an FTP Server Without Specifying Login Credentials*

```
R1# copy startup-config ftp://192.168.1.74
Address or name of remote host [192.168.1.74]?
Destination filename [r1-confg]?
Writing r1-confg !
1446 bytes copied in 3.389 secs (427 bytes/sec)
```

The process of backing up a router's configuration can be automated using an archiving feature, which is part of the Cisco IOS Configuration Replace and Configuration Rollback feature. Specifically, you can configure a Cisco IOS router to periodically (that is, at intervals specified in minutes) back up a copy of the startup configuration to a specified location (for example, the router's flash or an FTP server). Also, the archive feature can be configured to create an archive every time you copy a router's running configuration to the startup configuration.

Example 1-5 illustrates a router configured to back up its startup configuration every day (that is, every 1440 minutes) to an FTP server (with an IP address of 192.168.1.74, where the login credentials have already been configured in the router's configuration). In addition to regular daily backups, the **write-memory** command causes the router to archive a copy of the startup configuration whenever the router's running configuration is copied to the startup configuration.

Example 1-5 *Automatic Archive Configuration*

```
R1#show run
Building configuration...
...OUTPUT OMITTED...
ip ftp username kevin
ip ftp password cisco
!
archive
 path ftp://192.168.1.74/R1-config
 write-memory
 time-period 1440
...OUTPUT OMITTED...
```

Key Topic

You can view the files stored in a configuration archive by issuing the **show archive** command, as demonstrated in Example 1-6.

Example 1-6 *Viewing a Configuration Archive*

```
R1# show archive
The next archive file will be named ftp://192.168.1.74/R1-config-3
 Archive #  Name
   0
   1         ftp://192.168.1.74/R1-config-1
   2         ftp://192.168.1.74/R1-config-2 <- Most Recent
   3
   4
   5
   6
   7
   8
   9
   10
   11
   12
   13
   14
```

Key Topic

Example 1-7 shows the execution of the **copy run start** command, which copies a router's running configuration to the router's startup configuration. The **show archive** command is then reissued, and the output confirms that an additional configuration archive (named R1-config-3) has been created on the FTP server.

Example 1-7   *Confirming Automated Backups*

```
R1# copy run start
Destination filename [startup-config]?
Building configuration...
[OK]
Writing R1-config-3 !
R1# show archive
The next archive file will be named ftp://192.168.1.74/R1-config-4
 Archive #  Name
   0
   1         ftp://192.168.1.74/R1-config-1
   2         ftp://192.168.1.74/R1-config-2
   3         ftp://192.168.1.74/R1-config-3 <- Most Recent
   4
   5
   6
   7
   8
   9
   10
   11
   12
   13
   14
```

You can restore a previously archived configuration using the **configure replace** command. This command does not merge the archived configuration with the running configuration, but rather completely replaces the running configuration with the archived configuration. Example 1-8 shows the restoration of an archived configuration to a router. Notice that the router's hostname changes after the configuration restoration.

Example 1-8   *Restoring an Archived Configuration*

```
Router# configure replace ftp://192.168.1.74/R1-config-3
This will apply all necessary additions and deletions
to replace the current running configuration with the
contents of the specified configuration file, which is
assumed to be a complete configuration, not a partial
configuration. Enter Y if you are sure you want to proceed. ? [no]: Y
Loading R1-config-3 !
[OK - 3113/4096 bytes]
```

```
Total number of passes: 1
Rollback Done

R1#
```

Logging Tools

Device logs often offer valuable information when troubleshooting a network issue. Many events that occur on a router are automatically reported to the router's console. For example, if a router interface goes down, a message is written to the console. However, this feedback is not provided to you, by default, if you are connected to a router via Telnet. If you are connected to a router via Telnet and want to see console messages, you can enter the command **terminal monitor**.

A downside of solely relying on console messages is that those messages can scroll off the screen, or you might close your terminal emulator, after which those messages would no longer be visible. Therefore, a step beyond console messages is logging those messages to a router's buffer (that is, in the router's RAM). To cause messages to be written to a router's buffer, you can issue the **logging buffered** command. As part of that command, you can specify how much of the router's RAM can be dedicated to logging. After the buffer fills to capacity, older entries will be deleted to make room for newer entries. This buffer can be viewed by issuing the **show logging history** command.

You might only want to log messages that have a certain level of severity. Severity levels range from 0–7, with corresponding names, as shown in Table 1-3. Notice that lower severity levels produce less logging output.

Table 1-3 *Severity Levels*

Key
Topic

Severity Level	Name
0	Emergencies
1	Alerts
2	Critical
3	Errors
4	Warnings
5	Notifications
6	Informational
7	Debugging

You might want to log messages of one severity level to a router's console and messages of another severity level to the router's buffer. That is possible, by using the **logging console** *severity_level* and **logging buffered** *severity_level* commands.

Another logging option is to log messages to an external syslog server. By sending log messages to an external server, you are able to keep a longer history of logging messages. You can direct your router's log output to a syslog server's IP address using the **logging** *ip_address* command.

Example 1-9 illustrates several of the logging configurations discussed here.

Key Topic

Example 1-9 *Logging Configuration*

```
R1# show run
...OUTPIT OMITTED...
Building configuration...
!
logging buffered 4096 warnings
logging console warnings
!
logging 192.168.1.50
...OUTPUT OMITTED...
```

In Example 1-9, events with a security level of *warning* (that is, 4) or less (that is, 0–3) are logged to the router's buffer. This buffer can be viewed with the **show logging history** command. The router can use a maximum of 4096 bytes of RAM for the buffered logging. The console is configured for logging events of the same severity level. Additionally, the router is configured to log messages to a syslog server with an IP address 192.168.1.50. Figure 1-2 shows logging messages being collected by a Kiwi Syslog Server (available from www.kiwisyslog.com).

Network Time Protocol

Imagine that you are reviewing device logs collected in a router's buffer and are attempting to correlate the events in the device logs with an issue you are troubleshooting. To make that correlation, the logged events need to have accurate timestamps.

Although you could individually set the clock on each of your routers, those clocks might drift over time and not agree. You might have heard the saying that a man with one watch always knows what time it is, whereas a man with two watches is never sure. This implies that devices need to have a common point of reference for their time. Such a reference point is made possible by Network Time Protocol (NTP), which allows routers to point to a device acting as an NTP server. Because the NTP server might be referenced by devices in different time zones, each device has its own time zone configuration, which indicates how many hours its time zone differs from Greenwich Mean Time (GMT).

Example 1-10 shows an NTP configuration entered on a router located in the Eastern time zone, which is five hours behind GMT when daylight savings time is not in effect. The **clock summer-time** command defines when daylight savings time begins and ends. In this example, daylight savings time begins at 2:00 AM on the second Sunday in March and ends at 2:00 AM on the first Sunday in November. The **ntp server** command is used to point to an NTP server. Note that a configuration can have more than one **ntp server** command, for redundancy.

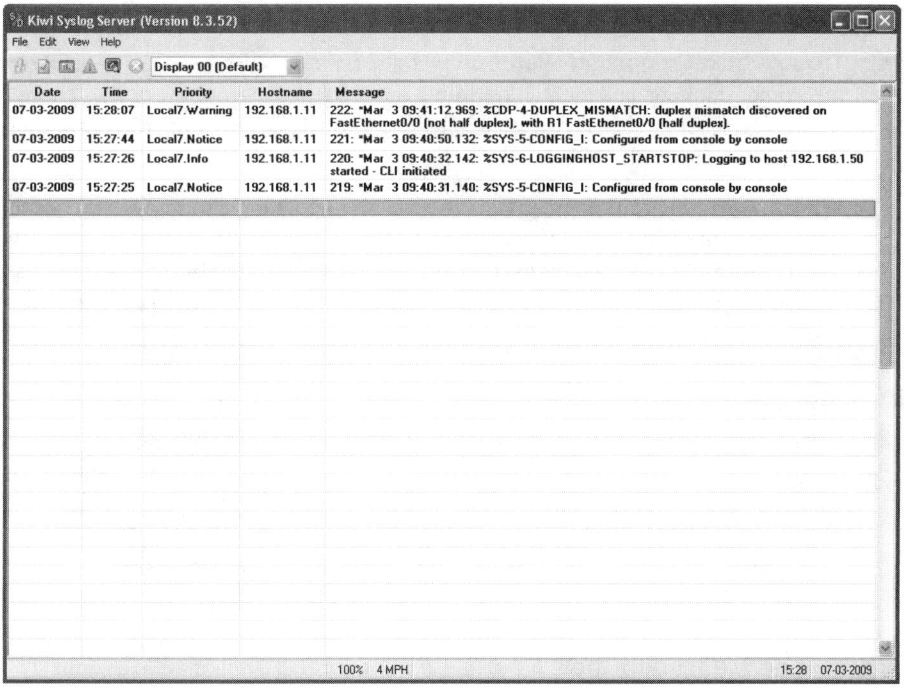

Figure 1-2 *Syslog Server*

Example 1-10 *Configuring a Router to Point to an NTP Server*

```
R1# conf term
Enter configuration commands, one per line.  End with CNTL/Z.
R1(config)# clock timezone EST -5
R1(config)# clock summer-time EDT recurring 2 Sun Mar 2:00 1 Sun Nov 2:00
R1(config)# ntp server 192.168.1.150
R1(config)# end
```

Key
Topic

Cisco Support Tools

Cisco has several other troubleshooting and maintenance tools available on its website:

http://www.cisco.com/en/US/support/tsd_most_requested_tools.html

Some of the tools available at this website require login credentials with appropriate privilege levels.

Network Documentation Tools

Earlier, we discussed the importance of network documentation. For this documentation to truly add value, however, it should be easy to retrieve and be current. To keep the documentation current, it should be easy to update.

A couple of documentation management system examples are as follows:

- **Trouble ticket reporting system:** Several software applications are available for recording, tracking, and archiving trouble reports (that is, trouble tickets). These applications are often referred to as help desk applications. However, their usefulness extends beyond the help desk environment.

- **Wiki:** A wiki can act as a web-based collaborative documentation platform. A popular example of a wiki is Wikipedia (www.wikipedia.com), an Internet-based encyclopedia that can be updated by users. This type of wiki technology can also be used on your local network to maintain a central repository for documentation that is both easy to access and easy to update.

Incident Recovery Tools

This section demonstrated how to automatically archive and manually restore router configurations using Cisco IOS commands. However, higher-end tools are available for automating backups, tracking configuration or hardware changes, and pushing out a centralized configuration to multiple devices. An example of such an application is CiscoWorks Resource Manager Essentials (RME). RME is a component of CiscoWorks LAN Management Solutions (LMS).

Monitoring and Measuring Tools

Keeping an eye on network traffic patterns and performance metrics can help you anticipate problems before they occur. As a result, you can address those issues proactively, rather than taking a reactive stance where you continually respond to problem reports.

Beyond basic **show** and **debug** commands, more advanced utilities are available for traffic and performance monitoring. For example, Cisco IOS Netflow can provide you with tremendous insight into your network traffic patterns. Several companies market Netflow collectors, which are software applications that can take the Netflow information reported from a Cisco router and convert that raw data into useful graphs, charts, and tables reflecting traffic patterns.

Simple Network Management Protocol (SNMP) allows a monitored device (for example, a router or a switch) to run an SNMP agent. An SNMP server can then query the SNMP agent running on a monitored device to collect data such as utilization statistics or device configuration information.

Reasons to monitor network performance include the following:

- **Assuring compliance with an SLA:** If you work for a service provider or are a customer of a service provider, you might want to confirm that performance levels to and from the service provider's cloud are conforming to the agreed-upon SLA.

- **Trend monitoring:** Monitoring resource utilization on your network (for example, bandwidth utilization and router CPU utilization) can help you recognize trends and forecast when upgrades will be required.

- **Troubleshooting performance issues:** Performance issues can be difficult to troubleshoot in the absence of a baseline. By routinely monitoring network performance, you have a reference point (that is, a *baseline*) against which you can compare performance metrics collected after a user reports a performance issue.

Exam Preparation Tasks

Review All the Key Topics

Review the most important topics from inside the chapter, noted with the Key Topics icon in the outer margin of the page. Table 1-4 lists these key topics and the page numbers where each is found.

Key Topic

Table 1-4 *Key Topics for Chapter 1*

Key Topic Element	Description	Page Number
List	Network maintenance tasks	7
List	Well-known maintenance models	8
Table 1-2	FCAPS management tasks	9
List	Change management considerations	11
List	Common network documentation elements	12
Example 1-2	Backing up a router's startup configuration to an FTP server	16
Example 1-5	Automatic archive configuration	17
Example 1-6	Viewing configuration archive	17
Example 1-8	Restoring an archived configuration	18
Table 1-3	Severity levels	19
Example 1-9	Logging configuration	20
Example 1-10	Configuring a router to point to an NTP server	21

Complete the Tables and Lists from Memory

Print a copy of Appendix B, "Memory Tables" (found on the CD) or at least the section for this chapter, and complete the tables and lists from memory. Appendix C, "Memory Tables Answer Key," also on the CD, includes completed tables and lists to check your work.

Definition of Key Terms

Define the following key terms from this chapter, and check your answers in the Glossary:

interrupt-driven task, structured maintenance task, FCAPS, ITIL, TMN, Cisco Lifecycle Services, SLA, wiki

Command Reference to Check Your Memory

This section includes the most important configuration commands (see Table 1-5) and EXEC commands (see Table 1-6) covered in this chapter. To determine how well you have memorized the commands as a side effect of your other studies, cover the left side of the table with a piece of paper; read the descriptions on the right side; and see whether you remember the command.

Table 1-5   *Chapter 1 Configuration Command Reference*

Command	Description
archive	Global configuration mode command, used to enter archive configuration mode.
path ftp://*IP_address/ filename_prefix*	Archive configuration mode command that specifies the IP address of an FTP server and filename prefix a router uses to write its archival configuration files.
write-memory	Archive configuration mode command that causes an archival backup of a router's configuration to be written each time the router's running configuration is copied to its startup configuration.
time-period *seconds*	Archive configuration mode command that specifies the interval used by a router to automatically back up its configuration.
ip ftp username *username*	Global configuration mode command used to specify an FTP username credential, which no longer necessitates the user entering the username.
ip ftp password *password*	Global configuration mode command used to specify an FTP password credential, which no longer necessitates the user entering the password.
logging buffered [*max_buffer_size*] [*minimum_severity_level*]	Global configuration mode command used to log events to a router's internal buffer, optionally with a maximum number of bytes to be used by the buffer and optionally the minimum severity level of an event to be logged.
logging console [*minimum_severity_level*]	Global configuration mode command used to log events to a router's console, optionally with a minimum severity level of an event to be logged.
logging *IP_address*	Global configuration mode command used to specify the IP address of a syslog server to which a router's log files are written.

Table 1-5 *Chapter 1 Configuration Command Reference*   (*Continued*)

Command	Description
clock timezone *time_zone_name* {+ | -} *hours*	Global configuration mode command used to specify a router's local time zone and number of hours the time zone varies from Greenwich Mean Time (GMT).
clock summer-time *time_zone_name* recurring {1-4} *beginning_day beginning_month time* {1-4} *ending_day ending_month time*	Global configuration mode command used to specify a router's time zone when daylight savings time is in effect, and when daylight savings time begins and ends.
ntp server *IP_address*	Global configuration mode command used to specify the IP address of an NTP server.

Table 1-6 *Chapter 1 EXEC Command Reference*

Command	Description
copy startup-config ftp://*username:password@IP_address*	Performs a backup of a router's startup configuration to an FTP server at the specified IP address, where the login credentials are provided by the username and password parameters.
copy startup-config ftp://*IP_address*	Performs a backup of a router's startup configuration to an FTP server at the specified IP address, where the login credentials have previously been added to the router's configuration.
show archive	Displays files contained in a router's configuration archive.
configure replace ftp://*IP_address/filename*	Replaces (as opposed to merges) a router's running configuration with a specified configuration archive.

This chapter covers the following subjects:

Troubleshooting Methods: This section addresses troubleshooting fundamentals, discusses the benefits of having a structured troubleshooting model, and discusses several popular troubleshooting models.

Using Troubleshooting Procedures: This section discusses each subprocess in a structured troubleshooting approach.

Including Troubleshooting in Routine Network Maintenance: This section shows how maintenance processes and troubleshooting processes can work in tandem to complement one another.

CHAPTER 2

Introduction to Troubleshooting Processes

Workflow within an organization can be severely impacted because of network problems. Therefore, troubleshooting those problems must be done efficiently, rather than haphazardly trying one potential solution after another.

As the size of a network increases, so does the complexity facing a network administrator attempting to resolve a network problem. Therefore, a structured troubleshooting process can help troubleshooters better focus their efforts, avoid duplication of efforts, and help other IT personnel to better assist in troubleshooting an issue.

This chapter defines troubleshooting and identifies the steps involved in a structured troubleshooting process. Additionally, this chapter emphasizes that network maintenance and network troubleshooting are not independent tasks, but rather overlap in several areas.

"Do I Know This Already?" Quiz

The "Do I Know This Already?" quiz helps you determine your level of knowledge of this chapter's topics before you begin. Table 2-1 details the major topics discussed in this chapter and their corresponding quiz questions.

Table 2-1   *"Do I Know This Already?" Section-to-Question Mapping*

Troubleshooting Methods	Questions
Understanding Troubleshooting Methods	1–4
Using Troubleshooting Procedures	5–11
Including Troubleshooting in Routine Network Maintenance	12–16

1. Identify the three steps in a simplified troubleshooting model. (Choose three.)

    a. Problem replication

    b. Problem diagnosis

    c. Problem resolution

    d. Problem report

2. Experienced troubleshooters with in-depth comprehension of a particular network might skip the *examine information* and *eliminate potential causes* steps in a structured troubleshooting model, instead relying on their own insight to determine the

most likely cause of a problem. This illustrates what approach to network troubleshooting?

    a. Ad hoc

    b. Shoot from the hip

    c. Crystal ball

    d. Independent path

3. Which of the following troubleshooting models requires access to a specific application?

    a. Bottom-up

    b. Divide and conquer

    c. Comparing configurations

    d. Top-down

4. Based on your analysis of a problem report and the data collected, you want to use a troubleshooting model that can quickly eliminate multiple layers of the OSI model as potential sources of the reported problem. Which of the following troubleshooting methods would be most appropriate?

    a. Following the traffic path

    b. Bottom-up

    c. Top-down

    d. Component swapping

5. Which of the following is the best statement to include in a problem report?

    a. The network is broken.

    b. User A cannot reach the network.

    c. User B recently changed his PC's operating system to Microsoft Windows 7.

    d. User C is unable to attach to an internal share resource of \\10.1.1.1\Budget, although he can print to all network printers, and he can reach the Internet.

6. What troubleshooting step should you perform after a problem has been reported and clearly defined?

    a. Hypothesize underlying cause

    b. Collect information

    c. Eliminate potential causes

    d. Examine collected information

7. What are the two primary goals of troubleshooters as they are collecting information? (Choose two answers.)

    a. Eliminate potential causes from consideration.

    b. Identify indicators pointing to the underlying cause of the problem.

    c. Hypothesize the most likely cause for a problem.

    d. Find evidence that can be used to eliminate potential causes.

8. When performing the *eliminate potential causes* troubleshooting step, which caution should the troubleshooter be aware of?

    a. The danger of drawing an invalid conclusion from the observed data

    b. The danger of troubleshooting a network component over which the troubleshooter does not have authority

    c. The danger of causing disruptions in workflow by implementing the proposed solution

    d. The danger of creating a new problem by implementing the proposed solution

9. A troubleshooter is hypothesizing a cause for an urgent problem, and her hypothesis involves a network device that she is not authorized to configure. The person who is authorized to configure the network device is unavailable. What should the troubleshooter do?

    a. Wait for authorized personnel to address the issue.

    b. Attempt to find a temporary workaround for the issue.

    c. Override corporate policy, based on the urgency, and configure the network device independently because authorized personnel are not currently available.

    d. Instruct the user to report the problem to the proper department that is authorized to resolve the issue.

10. What are two reasons why troubleshooters should document their steps as they attempt to verify their hypothesis? (Choose the two best answers.)

    a. The steps can be submitted to the proper authority prior to their implementation.

    b. The steps serve as a rollback plan if the attempted solution does not resolve the problem.

    c. The steps help ensure the troubleshooters do not skip a step in their solution.

    d. The steps help reduce duplication of efforts.

11. What two steps should be taken after a problem has been resolved? (Choose two answers.)

    a. For consistency, the same configuration should be implemented on all equipment of the same type.

    b. To accidentally prevent their reuse, previously archived configurations of the repaired device should be deleted from the archive server.

    c. Confirm that the user who reported the problem agrees that the problem is resolved.

    d. Make sure the implemented solution is integrated into the network's routine maintenance model.

12. What is the ideal relationship between network maintenance and troubleshooting?

    a. Networking maintenance and troubleshooting efforts should be isolated from one another.

    b. Networking maintenance and troubleshooting efforts should complement one another.

    c. Networking maintenance and troubleshooting efforts should be conducted by different personnel.

    d. Networking maintenance is a subset of network troubleshooting.

13. Which three of the following suggestions can best help troubleshooters keep in mind the need to document their steps? (Choose three.)

    a. Require documentation.

    b. Routinely back up documentation.

    c. Schedule documentation checks.

    d. Automate documentation.

14. What command can you use to display a router's CPU utilization averages?

    a. show processes cpu

    b. show cpu processes

    c. show cpu util

    d. show util cpu

15. Which three troubleshooting phases require clear communication with end users? (Choose three answers.)

    a. Problem report

    b. Information collection

    c. Hypothesis verification

    d. Problem resolution

16. What are two elements of a change management system? (Choose two answers.)

    a. Determine when changes can be made.

    b. Determine potential causes for the problem requiring the change.

    c. Determine who can authorize a change.

    d. Determine what change should be made.

Foundation Topics

Troubleshooting Methods

Troubleshooting network issues is implicit in the responsibilities of a network administrator. Such issues could arise as a result of human error (for example, a misconfiguration), equipment failure, a software bug, or traffic patterns (for example, high utilization or a network being under attack by malicious traffic).

Network issues can be successfully resolved using a variety of approaches. However, having a formalized troubleshooting method can prove more efficient than a haphazard approach to troubleshooting. A troubleshooter can select from several formalized troubleshooting approaches. Although these approaches vary in their effectiveness, based on the issue being addressed, a troubleshooter should have knowledge of several approaches to troubleshooting.

This section begins by introducing you to the basics of troubleshooting. Next, you learn the benefits of having a structured troubleshooting model, and then you are introduced to several popular troubleshooting models. Finally, this section provides guidance to help you select an appropriate combination of approaches for a given troubleshooting issue.

Defining Troubleshooting

The process of troubleshooting at its essence is the process of responding to a problem report (sometimes in the form of a trouble ticket), diagnosing the underlying cause of the problem, and resolving the problem. Although you normally think of the troubleshooting process beginning when a user reports an issue, realize that through effective network monitoring, you might detect a situation that could become a troubleshooting issue and resolve that situation before users are impacted.

After an issue is reported, the first step toward resolution is clearly defining the issue. When you have a clearly defined troubleshooting target, you can begin gathering information related to that issue. Based on the information collected, you might be able to better define the issue. Then you hypothesize likely causes of the issue. Evaluation of these likely causes leads to the identification of the suspected underlying root cause of the issue.

After you identify a suspected underlying cause, you next define approaches to resolving the issue and select what you consider to be the best approach. Sometimes the best approach to resolving an issue cannot be implemented immediately. For example, a piece of equipment might need replacing, or a business's workflow might be disrupted by implementing such an approach during working hours. In such situations, a troubleshooter might use a temporary fix until a permanent fix can be put in place.

As a personal example, when troubleshooting a connectivity issue for a resort hotel at a major theme park, we discovered that the supervisor engine in a Cisco Catalyst switch had an issue causing Spanning Tree Protocol (STP) to fail, resulting in a Layer 2 topological loop. This loop flooded the network with traffic, preventing the hotel from issuing keycards for guest rooms. The underlying cause was clear. Specifically, we had a bad supervisor engine. However, the time was about 4:00 PM, a peak time for guest registration. So, instead of immediately replacing the supervisor engine, we disconnected one of the redundant links, thus breaking the Layer 2 loop. The logic was that it was better to have the network function at this time without STP than for the network to experience an even longer outage while the supervisor engine was replaced. Late that night, someone came back to the switch and swapped out the supervisor engine, resolving the underlying cause while minimizing user impact.

Consider Figure 2-1, which depicts a simplified model of the troubleshooting steps previously described.

Figure 2-1   *Simplified Troubleshooting Flow*

Key Topic

This simplified model consists of three steps:

Step 1.   Problem report

Step 2.   Problem diagnosis

Step 3.   Problem resolution

Of these three steps, the majority of a troubleshooter's efforts are spent in the problem diagnosis step. Table 2-2 describes key components of this problem diagnosis step.

Key Topic

Table 2-2   *Steps to Diagnose a Problem*

Step	Description
Collect information	Because a typical problem report lacks sufficient information to give a troubleshooter insight into a problem's underlying cause, the troubleshooter should collect additional information, perhaps using network maintenance tools or by interviewing impacted users.
Examine collected information	After collecting sufficient information about a problem, the troubleshooter then examines that information, perhaps comparing the information against previously collected baseline information.
Eliminate potential causes	Based on the troubleshooter's knowledge of the network and his interrogation of collected information, he can begin to eliminate potential causes for the problem.
Hypothesize underlying cause	After the troubleshooter eliminates multiple potential causes for the problem, he is left with one or more causes that are more likely to have resulted in the problem. The troubleshooter hypothesizes what he considers to be the most likely cause of the problem.

Table 2-2   *Steps to Diagnose a Problem*   *(Continued)*

Step	Description
Verify hypothesis	The troubleshooter then tests his hypothesis to confirm or refute his theory about the problem's underlying cause.

The Value of a Structured Troubleshooting Approach

Troubleshooting skills vary from administrator to administrator. Therefore, although most troubleshooting approaches include collection and analysis of information, elimination of potential causes, hypothesizing of likely causes, and testing of the suspected cause, troubleshooters might spend different amounts of time performing these tasks.

If a troubleshooter does not follow a structured approach, the temptation is to move between the previously listed troubleshooting tasks in a fairly random way, often based on instinct. Although such an approach might lead to a problem resolution, it can become confusing to remember what you have tried and what you have not. Also, if another administrator comes to assist you, communicating to that other administrator the steps you have already gone through could be a challenge. Therefore, following a structured troubleshooting approach not only can help reduce the possibility of trying the same resolution more than once and inadvertently skipping a task, but aid in communicating to someone else possibilities you have already eliminated.

A structured troubleshooting method might look like the approach depicted in Figure 2-2.

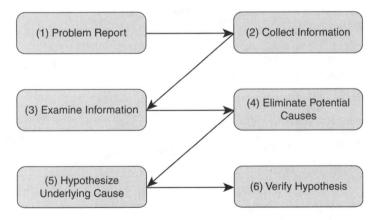

Figure 2-2   *Structured Troubleshooting Approach*

Some experienced troubleshooters, however, might have seen similar issues before and might be extremely familiar with the subtleties of the network they are working on. In such instances, spending time methodically examining information and eliminating potential causes might actually be less efficient than immediately hypothesizing a cause after they collect information about the problem. This method, illustrated in Figure 2-3, is often called the *shoot from the hip* method.

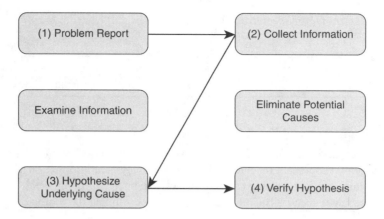

Figure 2-3   *Shoot from the Hip Troubleshooting Approach*

Notice that the major distinction between a structured approach and a shoot from the hip approach is examining information and eliminating potential causes based on that information. The danger with the shoot from the hip method is that if the troubleshooter's instincts are incorrect, valuable time is wasted. Therefore, a troubleshooter needs the perceptual acuity to know when to revert to a structured approach.

Popular Troubleshooting Methods

As noted previously, the elimination of potential causes is a key step in a structured troubleshooting approach. You can use several common approaches to narrow the field of potential causes:

- The Top-Down Method

- The Bottom-Up Method

- The Divide and Conquer Method

- Following the Traffic Path

- Comparing Configurations

- Component Swapping

The Top-Down Method

The top-down troubleshooting method begins at the top layer of the Open Systems Interconnection (OSI) seven-layer model, as shown in Figure 2-4. The top layer is numbered Layer 7 and is named the application layer.

The top-down method first checks the application residing at the application layer and moves down from there. The theory is, when the troubleshooter encounters a layer that is functioning, the assumption can be made that all lower layers are also functioning. For example, if you can ping a remote IP address, because ping uses Internet Control Message Protocol (ICMP), which is a Layer 3 protocol, you can assume that Layers 1–3 are functioning properly. Otherwise, your ping would have failed. A potential downside to this approach is that the troubleshooter needs access to the specific application experiencing a problem to test Layer 7.

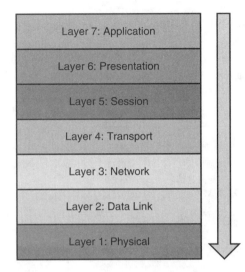

Figure 2-4   *Top-Down Troubleshooting Method*

The Bottom-Up Method

The reciprocal of the top-down method is the bottom-up method, as illustrated in Figure 2-5. The bottom-up method seeks to narrow the field of potential causes by eliminating OSI layers beginning at Layer 1, the physical layer.

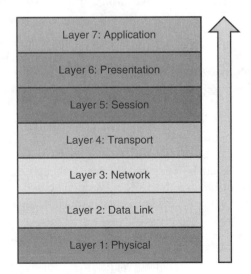

Figure 2-5   *Bottom-Up Troubleshooting Method*

Although this is a highly effective method, the bottom-up approach might not be efficient in larger networks because of the time required to fully test lower layers of the OSI model. Therefore, the bottom-up method is often used after employing some other method to narrow the scope of the problem.

The Divide and Conquer Method

After analyzing the information collected for a problem, you might not see a clear indication as to whether the top-down or bottom-up approach would be most effective. In such a situation, you might select the divide and conquer approach, which begins in the middle of the OSI stack, as shown in Figure 2-6.

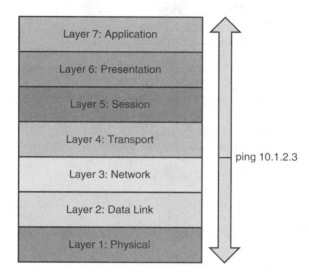

Figure 2-6   *Divide and Conquer Troubleshooting Method*

In the example shown in Figure 2-6, the network administrator issued the **ping 10.1.2.3** command. If the result was successful, the administrator could conclude that Layers 1–3 were operational, and a bottom-up approach could begin from that point. However, if the ping failed, the administrator could begin a top-down approach at Layer 3.

Following the Traffic Path

Another useful troubleshooting approach is to follow the path of the traffic experiencing a problem. For example, if the client depicted in Figure 2-7 is unable to reach its server, you could first check the link between the client and switch SW1. If everything looks good on that link, you could then check the connection between the switch SW1 and router R1. Next, you would check the link between router R1 and switch SW2 and finally the link between switch SW2 and the server.

Comparing Configurations

Did you ever go to the dentist as a kid and find yourself looking through a *Highlights* magazine? This magazine often featured two similar pictures, and you were asked to spot the differences. This childhood skill can also prove valuable when troubleshooting some network issues.

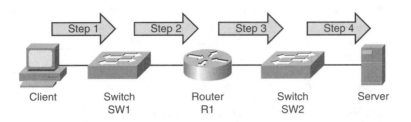

Figure 2-7   *Following the Path of Traffic*

For example, imagine you have multiple remote offices, each running the same model of Cisco router. Clients at one of those remote offices cannot obtain an IP address via DHCP. One troubleshooting approach is to compare that site's router configuration with the router configuration of another remote site that is working properly. This methodology is often an appropriate approach for a less experienced troubleshooter not well versed in the specifics of the network. However, the problem might be resolved without a thorough understanding of what caused the problem. Therefore, the problem is more likely to reoccur.

Component Swapping

Yet another approach to narrowing the field of potential causes of a problem is to physically swap out components. If a problem's symptoms disappear after swapping out a particular component (for example, a cable or a switch), you can conclude that the old component was faulty (either in its hardware or its configuration).

As an example, consider Figure 2-8. A problem report states that the connection between laptop A and switch SW1 is not bringing up a link light on either the laptop or the switch.

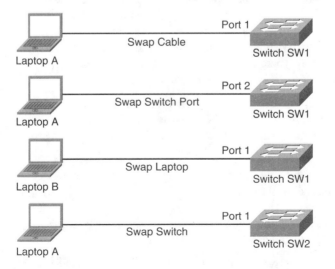

Figure 2-8   *Component Swapping*

As a first step, you might swap out the cable interconnecting these two devices with a known working cable.

If the problem persists, you will want to undo the change you made and then move the cable from switch port 1 to switch port 2. As a next step, you could connect a different laptop to switch SW1. If the problem goes away, you could conclude that the issue is with laptop A. However, if the problem continues, you could swap out switch SW1 with another switch: SW2 in this example. As you test each component and find it is not the problem, undo the change.

Although swapping out components in this fashion might not provide great insight into the specific problem, it could help focus your troubleshooting efforts. For example, if swapping out the switch resolved the issue, you could start to investigate the configuration of the original switch, checking for configuration or hardware issues.

Practice Exercise: Selecting a Troubleshooting Approach

As a troubleshooter, you might use one of the previously discussed troubleshooting methods or perhaps a combination of methods. To illustrate how you might select an appropriate troubleshooting approach, consider the following problem report:

> A computer lab at a university contains 48 PCs. Currently, 24 of the PCs cannot access the Internet, whereas the other 24 PCs can. The 24 PCs that cannot currently access the Internet were able to access the Internet yesterday.

Consider which of the previously discussed troubleshooting models might be appropriate for an issue such as the one reported. After you reach your own conclusions regarding which method or methods would be most appropriate, consider the following rationale:

- **Top-down:** Because the application is working on some PCs in the same location, starting at the application layer will probably not be effective. Although it is possible that 24 of the PCs have some setting in their Internet browser (for example, a proxy configuration) that prevents them from accessing the Internet, these PCs were working yesterday. Therefore, it is unlikely that these 24 PCs were all recently reconfigured with an incorrect application configuration.

- **Bottom-up:** Based on the symptom reported, it is reasonable to guess that there might be an issue with an Ethernet switch (perhaps with a port density of 24). Therefore, a bottom-up approach stands a good chance of isolating the problem quickly.

- **Divide and conquer:** The problem seems to be related to a block of PCs, and the problem is probably not application related. Therefore, a divide and conquer approach could be useful. Starting at Layer 3 (that is, the network layer), you could issue a series of pings to determine if a next-hop gateway is reachable. If the next-hop gateway is not reachable, you could start to troubleshoot Layer 2, checking the Cisco Catalyst switch to which these 24 PCs are attached.

- **Following the traffic path:** The symptom seems to indicate that these 24 PCs might share a common switch. Therefore, following the traffic path to the other end of the cabling (that is, to a switch) could prove useful. Perhaps the switch has lost power resulting in this connectivity issue for the 24 PCs.

■ **Comparing configurations:** If a previous troubleshooting method (for example, bottom-up, divide and conquer, or following the traffic path) reveals that the 24 PCs that are not working are connected to one Cisco Catalyst switch, and the 24 PCs that are working are connected to another Cisco Catalyst switch, comparing the configuration of those two switches could be helpful.

■ **Component swapping:** Because the 24 PCs are experiencing the same problem within a short time frame (since yesterday), it is unlikely that swapping cables would be useful. However, if these 24 PCs connect to the same Cisco Catalyst switch, swapping out the switch could help isolate the problem.

Using Troubleshooting Procedures

No single collection of troubleshooting procedures is capable of addressing all conceivable network issues, because too many variables (for example, user actions) are in play. However, having a structured troubleshooting approach can help ensure that an organization's troubleshooting efforts are following a similar flow, thus allowing one troubleshooter to more efficiently take over for or assist another troubleshooter.

The previous section, "Troubleshooting Methods," introduced a three-step troubleshooting flow consisting of the following:

Step 1.   Problem report

Step 2.   Problem diagnosis

Step 3.   Problem resolution

As mentioned, most troubleshooting efforts occur in the *problem diagnosis* step, which can again be dissected into its subcomponents:

A.   Collect information

B.   Examine collected information

C.   Eliminate potential causes

D.   Hypothesize underlying cause

E.   Verify hypothesis

By combining these components, you get the following listing of all subprocesses in the structured troubleshooting procedure:

Step 1.   Problem report

Step 2.   Collect information

Step 3.   Examine collected information

Key Topic

Step 4.   Eliminate potential causes

Step 5.   Hypothesize underlying cause

Step 6.   Verify hypothesis

Step 7.   Problem resolution

This section examines each of these subprocesses in more detail.

Problem Report

A problem report from a user often lacks sufficient detail for you to take that problem report and move on to the next troubleshooting process (that is, collect information). For example, a user might report, "The network is broken." If you receive such a vague report, you probably need to contact the user and ask him exactly what aspect of the network is not functioning correctly.

After your interview with the user, you should be able to construct a more detailed problem report that includes statements such as, when the user does X, she observes Y. For example, "When the user attempts to connect to a website on the Internet, her browser reports a 404 error. However, the user can successfully navigate to websites on her company's intranet."

After you have a clear articulation of the issue, you might need to determine who is responsible for working on the hardware or software associated with that issue. For example, perhaps your organization has one IT group tasked with managing switches and another IT group charged with managing routers. Therefore, as the initial point of contact, you might need to decide whether this issue is one you are authorized to address or if you need to forward the issue to someone else.

Collect Information

When you are in possession of a clear problem report, the next step is gathering relevant information pertaining to the problem. Efficiently and effectively gathering information involves focusing information gathering efforts on appropriate network entities (for example, routers, servers, switches, or clients) from which information should be collected. Otherwise, the troubleshooter could waste time wading through reams of irrelevant data.

Perhaps a troubleshooter is using a troubleshooting model where he follows the path of the affected traffic, and information needs to be collected from a network device over which he has no access. At that point, the troubleshooter might need to work with appropriate personnel who *do* have access to that device. Alternatively, the troubleshooter might switch troubleshooting models. For example, instead of following the traffic's path, he might swap components or use a bottom-up troubleshooting model.

Examine Collected Information

After collecting information regarding the problem report (for example, collecting output from **show** or **debug** commands, or performing packet captures), the next structured troubleshooting process is the analysis of the collected information.

A troubleshooter has two primary goals while examining the collected information:

■ Identify indicators pointing to the underlying cause of the problem.

■ Find evidence that can be used to eliminate potential causes.

To achieve these two goals, the troubleshooter attempts to find a balance between two questions:

■ What *is* occurring on the network?

■ What *should be* occurring on the network?

The delta between the responses to these questions might give the troubleshooter insight into the underlying cause of a reported problem. A challenge, however, is for the troubleshooter to know what currently should be occurring on the network.

If the troubleshooter is experienced with the applications and protocols being examined, she might be able to determine what is occurring on the network and how that differs from what should be occurring. However, if the troubleshooter lacks knowledge of specific protocol behavior, she still might be able to effectively examine her collected information by contrasting that information with baseline data.

Baseline data might contain, for example, the output of **show** and **debug** commands issued on routers when the network was functioning properly. By contrasting this baseline data with data collected after a problem occurred, even an inexperienced troubleshooter might be able to see the difference between the data sets, thus giving him a clue as to the underlying cause of the problem under investigation. This implies that as part of a routine network maintenance plan, baseline data should periodically be collected when the network is functioning properly.

Eliminate Potential Causes

Following an examination of collected data, a troubleshooter can start to form conclusions based on that data. Some conclusions might suggest a potential cause for the problem, whereas other conclusions eliminate certain causes from consideration.

A caution to be observed when drawing conclusions is not to read more into the data than what is actually there. As an example, a troubleshooter might reach a faulty conclusion based on the following scenario:

A problem report indicates that PC A cannot communicate with server A, as shown in Figure 2-9. The troubleshooter is using a troubleshooting method where she follows the path of traffic through the network. The troubleshooter examines output from the **show cdp neighbor** command on routers R1 and R2. Because those routers recognize each other as Cisco Discovery Protocol (CDP) neighbors, the troubleshooter leaps to the conclusion that these two routers see each other as OSPF neighbors and have mutually formed OSPF adjacencies. However, the **show cdp neighbor** output is insufficient to conclude that OSPF adjacencies have been formed between routers R1 and R2.

Figure 2-9 *Scenario Topology*

If time permits, explaining the rationale for your conclusions to a coworker can often help reveal faulty conclusions. Continuing your troubleshooting efforts based on a faulty conclusion can dramatically increase the time required to resolve a problem.

Hypothesize Underlying Cause

By eliminating potential causes of a reported problem, as described in the previous process, a troubleshooter should be left with one (or a few) potential cause. The troubleshooter should then select the potential cause she believes is most likely to be the underlying one for the reported problem. Her efforts then focus on addressing this hypothesized cause.

After hypothesizing an underlying cause, the troubleshooter might realize that he is not authorized to access a network device that needs to be accessed to resolve the problem report. In such a situation, the troubleshooter needs to assess whether the problem can wait until authorized personnel have an opportunity to resolve the issue. If the problem is urgent and no authorized administrator is currently available, the troubleshooter might attempt to at least alleviate the symptoms of the problem by creating a temporary workaround. Although this approach does not solve the underlying cause, it might help business operations continue until the main cause of the problem can be appropriately addressed.

Verify Hypothesis

After the troubleshooter has proposed what he believes to be the most likely cause of a problem, he needs to develop a plan to address the suspected cause. Alternatively, if the troubleshooter decided to implement a workaround, he needs to come up with a plan for deploying it.

Often, implementing a plan to resolve a network issue causes a temporary network outage for other users. Therefore, the troubleshooter must balance the urgency of the problem with the potential productivity impact resulting from deploying a planned solution at that time and network regulations regarding when and how changes can be made. If the impact on workflow outweighs the urgency of the problem, the troubleshooter might wait until after business hours to execute the plan.

A key component in deploying a solution is to have the steps documented. Not only does a documented list of steps help ensure the troubleshooter does not skip any, but such a document can serve as a rollback plan if the implemented solution fails to resolve the problem.

If the problem is not resolved after the troubleshooter implements the plan, or if the execution of the plan resulted in one or more additional problems, the troubleshooter should execute the rollback plan. After the network is returned to its previous state (that is, the state prior to deploying the proposed solution), the troubleshooter can then reevaluate her hypothesis.

Perhaps the troubleshooter still believes the underlying cause has been identified, even though the original solution failed to resolve that cause. In that case, the troubleshooter could create a different plan to address that cause. Alternatively, if the troubleshooter still knows of other potential causes that have not yet been ruled out, he can identify which of those causes is most likely resulting in the problem and create an action plan to resolve that cause.

This process can repeat itself until the troubleshooter has exhausted the list of potential causes. At that point, she might need to gather additional information or enlist the aid of a coworker or the Cisco Technical Assistance Center (TAC).

Problem Resolution

After the reported problem is resolved, the troubleshooter should make sure the solution becomes a documented part of the network. This implies that routine network maintenance will maintain the implemented solution. For example, if the solution involved reconfiguring a Cisco IOS router, a backup of that new configuration should be made part of routine network maintenance practices.

As a final task, the troubleshooter should report the problem resolution to the appropriate party or parties. Beyond simply notifying a user that a problem has been resolved, however, the troubleshooter should get user confirmation that the observed symptoms are now gone. This task confirms that the troubleshooter resolved the specific issue reported in the problem report, rather than a tangential issue.

Including Troubleshooting in Routine Network Maintenance

Troubleshooting occurs not only in response to a problem report, but as part of routine network maintenance. Similarly, ongoing network maintenance processes (for example, updating network documentation) often help troubleshoot future problems. This section addresses the mutually beneficial relationship between troubleshooting and maintenance.

The Relationship Between Maintenance and Troubleshooting Tasks

Chapter 1, "Introduction to Network Maintenance," pointed out that network maintenance is composed of multiple processes and tasks. Interestingly, network maintenance tasks often include troubleshooting tasks, and vice versa. For example, when installing a new network component as part of ongoing network maintenance, an installer is often required to troubleshoot the installation until the new network component is functioning properly. Also, when troubleshooting a network issue, the troubleshooter might use network documentation (for example, a physical topology diagram created as part of a network maintenance task) to help isolate a problem.

This interrelationship between maintenance and troubleshooting suggests that the effectiveness of your troubleshooting efforts is influenced by the effectiveness of your routine network management tasks. Because these tasks are so interrelated, you might want to take proactive measures to ensure your structured maintenance and troubleshooting processes complement one another. For example, both network troubleshooting and maintenance include a documentation component. Therefore, the value of a centralized repository of documentation increases as a result of its use for both maintenance and troubleshooting efforts.

Maintaining Current Network Documentation

A set of current network documentation can dramatically improve the efficiency of troubleshooting efforts. For example, if a troubleshooter is following the path that specific traffic takes through a network, a physical network topology diagram could help in quickly determining the next network component to check.

A danger with relying on documentation, however, is that if the documentation is dated, the troubleshooter could be led down an incorrect path because of her reliance on that documentation. Such a scenario is often worse than not having documentation at all, because in the absence of documentation, a troubleshooter is aware of the need to collect updated and appropriate data.

Although few argue with the criticality of maintaining current documentation, in practice, documenting troubleshooting efforts often falls by the wayside. The lack of follow-through when it comes to documenting what happened during a troubleshooting scenario is understandable. The troubleshooter's focus is on resolving a reported issue in a timely manner (that is, an *urgent* task) rather than documenting what they are doing at the time (that is, an *important* task). Following are a few suggestions to help troubleshooters keep in mind the need to document their steps:

- **Require documentation:** By making documentation a component in the troubleshooting flow, troubleshooters know that before a problem report or a trouble ticket can be closed out, they must generate appropriate documentation. This knowledge often motivates troubleshooters to perform some level of documentation (for example, scribbling notes on the back of a piece of paper) as they are performing their tasks as opposed to later trying to recall what they did from memory, thus increasing the accuracy of the documentation.

- **Schedule documentation checks:** A structured maintenance plan could include a component that routinely requires verification of network documentation.

- **Automate documentation:** Because manual checks of documentation might not be feasible in larger environments, automated processes could be used to, for example, compare current and backup copies of device configurations. Any difference in the configurations indicates that someone failed to update the backup configuration of a device after making a configuration change to that device. To assist with the automation of backups, Cisco IOS offers the Configuration Archive and Rollback feature and the Embedded Event Manager.

Establishing a Baseline

As previously mentioned, troubleshooting involves knowing what should be happening on the network, observing what is currently happening on the network, and determining the difference between the two. To determine what should be happening on the network, a baseline of network performance should be measured as part of a routine maintenance procedure.

For example, a routine network maintenance procedure might require that a **show processes cpu** command be periodically issued on all routers in a network, with the output logged and archived. As shown in Example 2-1, the **show processes cpu** command demonstrates the 5-second, 1-minute, and 5-minute CPU utilization averages. When troubleshooting a performance problem on a router, you could issue this command to determine how a router is currently operating. However, without a baseline as a reference before troubleshooting, you might not be able to draw a meaningful conclusion based on the command output.

Example 2-1 *Monitoring Router CPU Utilization*

```
R1# show processes cpu
CPU utilization for five seconds: 18%/18%; one minute: 22%; five minutes: 22%

 PID Runtime(ms)     Invoked      uSecs  5Sec   1Min   5Min TTY Process
   1           0           1          0  0.00%  0.00%  0.00%   0 Chunk Manager
   2           4         167         23  0.00%  0.00%  0.00%   0 Load Meter
   3         821         188       4367  0.00%  0.13%  0.14%   0 Exec
   4           4           1       4000  0.00%  0.00%  0.00%   0 EDDRI_MAIN
   5       43026        2180      19736  0.00%  4.09%  4.03%   0 Check heaps
...OUTPUT OMITTED...
```

Communicating Throughout the Troubleshooting Process

Each of the troubleshooting phases described in the previous section, "Using Troubleshooting Procedures," requires clear communication. Table 2-3 describes how communication plays a role in each troubleshooting phase.

Table 2-3 *Importance of Clear Communication During Troubleshooting*

Troubleshooting Phase	The Role of Communication
Problem report	When a user reports a problem, clear communication with that user helps define the problem. For example, the user can be asked exactly what is not working correctly, if she made any recent changes, or when the problem started.

continues

Table 2-3   *Importance of Clear Communication During Troubleshooting*   *(Continued)*

Troubleshooting Phase	The Role of Communication
Collect information	Some information collected might come from other parties (for example, a service provider). Clearly communicating with those other parties helps ensure collection of the proper data.
Examine collected information	Because a troubleshooter is often not fully aware of all aspects of a network, collaboration with other IT personnel is often necessary.
Eliminate potential causes	The elimination of potential causes might involve consultation with others. This consultation could provide insight leading to the elimination of a potential cause.
Hypothesize underlying cause	The consultation a troubleshooter conducts with other IT personnel when eliminating potential causes might also help the troubleshooter more accurately hypothesize a problem's underlying cause.
Verify hypothesis	Temporary network interruptions often occur when verifying a hypothesis; therefore, the nature and reason for an interruption should be communicated to the users impacted.
Problem resolution	After a problem is resolved, the user originally reporting the problem should be informed, and the user should confirm that the problem has truly been resolved.

Also, depending on the severity of an issue, multiple network administrators could be involved in troubleshooting a problem. Because these troubleshooters might be focused on different tasks at different times, it is possible that no single administrator can report on the overall status of the problem. Therefore, when managing a major outage, those involved in troubleshooting the outage should divert user inquiries to a manager who is in frequent contact with the troubleshooting personnel. As a side benefit, being able to quickly divert user requests for status reports to a manager helps minimize interruptions from users.

Change Management

Managing when changes can be made and by whose authority helps minimize network downtime. In fact, these two factors (that is, when a change is allowed and who can authorize it) are the distinguishing factors between making a change as part of a routine maintenance plan and making a change as part of a troubleshooting process.

The process of change management includes using policies that dictate rules regarding how and when a change can be made and how that change is documented. Consider the following scenario, which illustrates how a maintenance change could be a clue while troubleshooting a problem report:

> Last week, a network administrator attempted to better secure a Cisco Catalyst switch by administratively shutting down any ports that were in the down/down state (that is, no physical layer connectivity to a device). This morning a user reported that her PC could not access network resources. After clearly defining the problem, the troubleshooter asked if anything had changed, as part of the collect information troubleshooting phase. Even though the user was unaware of any changes, she mentioned that she had just returned from vacation, thus leading the troubleshooter to wonder if any network changes had occurred while the user was on vacation. Thanks to the network's change management system, the troubleshooter was able to find in the documentation that last week an administrator had administratively shut down this user's switch port.

The previous illustration points out the need for a troubleshooter to ask the question "Has anything changed?" By integrating a documentation requirement in a change management policy, someone troubleshooting a problem can leverage that documented change information.

Exam Preparation Tasks

Review All the Key Topics

Key Topic

Review the most important topics from inside the chapter, noted with the Key Topics icon in the outer margin of the page. Table 2-4 lists these key topics and the page numbers where each is found.

Table 2-4   *Key Topics for Chapter 2*

Key Topic Element	Description	Page Number
List	Simplified troubleshooting model	32
Table 2-2	Steps to diagnose a problem	32
List	Common approaches to troubleshooting	34
List	Structured troubleshooting procedure	39
List	Primary goals when collecting information	41
Example 2-1	Monitoring router CPU utilization	45
Table 2-3	The importance of clear communication	45

Complete the Tables and Lists from Memory

Print a copy of Appendix B, "Memory Tables," (found on the CD) or at least the section for this chapter, and complete the tables and lists from memory. Appendix C, "Memory Tables Answer Key," also on the CD, includes completed tables and lists to check your work.

Definition of Key Terms

Define the following key terms from this chapter, and check your answers in the Glossary:

shoot from the hip, top-down method, bottom-up method, divide and conquer method, following the traffic path, comparing configurations, component swapping, baseline

Command Reference to Check Your Memory

This section includes the EXEC command covered in this chapter. To determine how well you have memorized this command as a side effect of your other studies, cover the left side of the table with a piece of paper; read the description on the right side; and see whether you remember the command.

Table 2-5   *Chapter 2 EXEC Command Reference*

Command	Description
show processes cpu	Displays 5-second, 1-minute, and 5-minute CPU utilization statistics

This chapter covers the following subjects:

Cisco IOS Diagnostic Tools: This section shows how a few readily accessible Cisco IOS Software commands can be used to quickly gather information as part of a structured troubleshooting process.

Specialized Diagnostic Tools: This section introduces a collection of specialized features, such as Switched Port Analyzer (SPAN), Remote SPAN (RSPAN), Simple Mail Transfer Protocol (SMTP), NetFlow, and Embedded Event Manager (EEM), which can be used to collect information about a problem.

CHAPTER 3

The Maintenance and Troubleshooting Toolbox

Key to maintaining and troubleshooting a network is the collection of information about that network. Fortunately, Cisco IOS offers many commands that can be used for information gathering. Mastery of these basic tools can dramatically reduce the time a troubleshooter spends isolating the specific information needed for a troubleshooting task.

Beyond basic Cisco IOS commands, many network devices support features targeted toward the collection of information. Perhaps an event occurs on a network device, such as a router's processor utilization exceeding a defined threshold. The network device could report the occurrence of such an event. Alternatively, network devices might be periodically queried by a network management system for device and traffic statistics.

This chapter covers several basic Cisco IOS commands, in addition to specialized information collection features. These features not only help a troubleshooter collect information about a problem, but they can create a baseline of network performance. This baseline data can then be contrasted with data collected when a problem is occurring. The comparison of these two data sets often provides insight into the underlying cause of a problem.

"Do I Know This Already?" Quiz

The "Do I Know This Already?" quiz helps you determine your level of knowledge of this chapter's topics before you begin. Table 3-1 details the major topics discussed in this chapter and their corresponding quiz questions.

Table 3-1   *"Do I Know This Already?" Section-to-Question Mapping*

Foundation Topics Section	Questions
Cisco IOS Diagnostic Tools	1–3
Specialized Diagnostic Tools	4–7

1. Which of the following commands displays a router's running configuration, starting where the routing protocol configuration begins?

    a. show running-config | tee router

    b. show running-config | begin router

    c. show running-config | redirect router

    d. show running-config | append router

2. Which of the following is the ping response to a transmitted ICMP Echo datagram that needed to be fragmented when fragmentation was not permitted?

   a. U

   b. .

   c. M

   d. D

3. Which portion of the **show interfaces** command output indicates that a router received information faster than the information could be processed by the router?

   a. input queue drops

   b. output queue drops

   c. input errors

   d. output errors

4. The types of information collection used in troubleshooting fall into which three broad categories? (Choose three.)

   a. Troubleshooting information collection

   b. Baseline information collection

   c. QoS information collection

   d. Network event information collection

5. What features available on Cisco Catalyst switches allow you to connect a network monitor to a port on one switch to monitor traffic flowing through a port on a different switch?

   a. RSTP

   b. SPAN

   c. RSPAN

   d. SPRT

6. Which two of the following are characteristics of the NetFlow feature? (Choose the two best answers.)

   a. Collects detailed information about traffic flows

   b. Collects detailed information about device statistics

   c. Uses a pull model

   d. Uses a push model

7. Identify the Cisco IOS feature that allows you to create your own event definition for a network device and specify the action that should be performed in response to that event.

   a. SNMP

   b. EEM

   c. NetFlow

   d. syslog

Foundation Topics

Cisco IOS Diagnostic Tools

After a problem has been clearly defined, the first step in diagnosing that problem is collecting information, as described in Chapter 2, "Introduction to Troubleshooting Processes." Because the collection of information can be one of the most time consuming of the troubleshooting processes, the ability to quickly collect appropriate information becomes a valuable troubleshooting skill. This section introduces a collection of basic Cisco IOS commands useful in gathering information and discusses the filtering of irrelevant information from the output of those commands. Also included in this section are commands helpful in diagnosing connectivity and hardware issues.

Filtering the Output of **show** Commands

Cisco IOS offers multiple **show** commands useful for gathering information. However, many of these **show** commands produce a large quantity of output.

Consider the output shown in Example 3-1. The output from the **show processes cpu** command generated approximately 180 lines of output, making it challenging to pick out a single process.

Example: **show processes cpu** Command

Example 3-1   show processes cpu *Command Output*

Key Topic

```
R1# show processes cpu
CPU utilization for five seconds: 0%/0%; one minute: 0%; five minutes: 0%
 PID  Runtime(ms)    Invoked      uSecs  5Sec   1Min   5Min TTY Process
   1            4          3       1333  0.00%  0.00%  0.00%   0 Chunk Manager
   2         7245       1802       4020  0.08%  0.08%  0.08%   0 Load Meter
   3           56       2040         27  0.00%  0.00%  0.00%   0 OSPF Hello 1
   4            4          1       4000  0.00%  0.00%  0.00%   0 EDDRI_MAIN
   5        21998       1524      14434  0.00%  0.32%  0.25%   0 Check heaps
   6            0          1          0  0.00%  0.00%  0.00%   0 Pool Manager
   7            0          2          0  0.00%  0.00%  0.00%   0 Timers
   8            0          1          0  0.00%  0.00%  0.00%   0 Crash writer
   9            0        302          0  0.00%  0.00%  0.00%   0 Environmental mo
  10          731       1880        388  0.00%  0.00%  0.00%   0 ARP Input
...OUTPUT OMITTED...
 171            0          1          0  0.00%  0.00%  0.00%   0 lib_off_app
 172            4          2       2000  0.00%  0.00%  0.00%   0 Voice Player
 173            0          1          0  0.00%  0.00%  0.00%   0 Media Record
 174            0          1          0  0.00%  0.00%  0.00%   0 Resource Measure
 175           12          6       2000  0.00%  0.00%  0.00%   0 Session Applicat
 176           12        151         79  0.00%  0.00%  0.00%   0 RTPSPI
```

```
  177         4      17599        0   0.00%   0.00%  0.00%     0  IP NAT Ager
  178         0          1        0   0.00%   0.00%  0.00%     0  IP NAT WLAN
  179         8        314       25   0.00%   0.00%  0.00%     0  CEF Scanner
```

Perhaps you were only looking for CPU utilization statistics for the *Check heaps* process. Because you know that the content of the one line you are looking for contains the text **Check heaps,** you could take the output of the **show processes cpu** command and *pipe* that output (that is, use the | character) to the **include Check heaps** statement. The piping of the output causes the output to be filtered to only include lines that include the text **Check heaps,** as demonstrated in Example 3-2. This type of filtering can help troubleshooters more quickly find the data they are looking for.

Example 3-2 *Filtering the* **show processes cpu** *Command Output*

```
R1# show processes cpu | include Check heaps
   5       24710      1708      14467  1.14%   0.26%  0.24%     0  Check heaps
```

Example: **show ip interfaces brief** Command

Similar to piping output to the **include** option, you could alternatively pipe output to the **exclude** option. The **exclude** option can display all lines of the output *except* lines containing the string you specify. For example, the **show ip interfaces brief** command can display IP address and status information for all interfaces on a router, as shown in Example 3-3.

Example 3-3 **show ip interface brief** *Command Output*

```
R1# show ip interface brief
Interface          IP-Address       OK?   Method   Status                 Protocol
FastEthernet0/0    192.168.1.11     YES   NVRAM    up                     up
Serial0/0          unassigned       YES   NVRAM    administratively down  down

FastEthernet0/1    192.168.0.11     YES   NVRAM    up                     up

Serial0/1          unassigned       YES   NVRAM    administratively down  down

NVI0               unassigned       YES   unset    up                     up

Loopback0          10.1.1.1         YES   NVRAM    up                     up
```

Notice in Example 3-3 that some of the interfaces have an IP address of **unassigned.** If you want to only view information pertaining to interfaces with assigned IP addresses, you can pipe the output of the **show ip interface brief** command to **exclude unassigned,** as illustrated in Example 3-4.

Example 3-4   *Filtering Output from the* **show ip interface brief** *Command*

```
R1# show ip interface brief | exclude unassigned
Interface             IP-Address      OK?     Method    Status    Protocol
FastEthernet0/0       192.168.1.11    YES     NVRAM     up        up

FastEthernet0/1       192.168.0.11    YES     NVRAM     up        up

Loopback0             10.1.1.1        YES     NVRAM     up        up
```

Example: Jumping to the First Occurrence of a String in **show** Command Output

As another example, you might be troubleshooting a routing protocol issue and want to see the section of your running configuration where the routing protocol configuration begins. Piping the output of the **show running-config** command to **begin router**, as shown in Example 3-5, skips the initial portion of the **show running-config** output and begins displaying the output where the routing protocol configuration begins.

Example 3-5   *Filtering the Output from the* **show running-config** *Command*

```
R1# show running-config | begin router
router ospf 1
 log-adjacency-changes
 network 0.0.0.0 255.255.255.255 area 0
...OUTPUT OMITTED...
```

Example: The **show ip route** Command

Another command that often generates a lengthy output, especially in larger environments, is the **show ip route** command. As an example, consider the **show ip route** output presented in Example 3-6.

Example 3-6   *Sample* **show ip route** *Command Output*

```
R1# show ip route
Codes: C - connected, S - static, R - RIP, M - mobile, B - BGP
       D - EIGRP, EX - EIGRP external, O - OSPF, IA - OSPF inter area
       N1 - OSPF NSSA external type 1, N2 - OSPF NSSA external type 2
       E1 - OSPF external type 1, E2 - OSPF external type 2
       i - IS-IS, su - IS-IS summary, L1 - IS-IS level-1, L2 - IS-IS level-2
       ia - IS-IS inter area, * - candidate default, U - per-user static route
       o - ODR, P - periodic downloaded static route

Gateway of last resort is not set

     172.16.0.0/30 is subnetted, 2 subnets
O       172.16.1.0 [110/65] via 192.168.0.22, 00:50:57, FastEthernet0/1
```

```
O          172.16.2.0 [110/65] via 192.168.0.22, 00:50:57, FastEthernet0/1
        10.0.0.0/8 is variably subnetted, 6 subnets, 3 masks
O          10.2.2.2/32 [110/2] via 192.168.0.22, 00:50:57, FastEthernet0/1
O          10.1.3.0/30 [110/129] via 192.168.0.22, 00:50:57, FastEthernet0/1
O          10.3.3.3/32 [110/66] via 192.168.0.22, 00:50:57, FastEthernet0/1
O          10.1.2.0/24 [110/75] via 192.168.0.22, 00:50:58, FastEthernet0/1
C          10.1.1.1/32 is directly connected, Loopback0
O          10.4.4.4/32 [110/66] via 192.168.0.22, 00:50:58, FastEthernet0/1
C      192.168.0.0/24 is directly connected, FastEthernet0/1
C      192.168.1.0/24 is directly connected, FastEthernet0/0
```

Although the output shown in Example 3-6 is relatively small, some IP routing tables contain hundreds or even thousands of entries. If, for example, you wanted to determine if a route for network 172.16.1.0 were present in a routing table, you could issue the command **show ip route 172.16.1.0**, as depicted in Example 3-7.

Perhaps you were looking for all subnets of the 172.16.0.0/16 address space. In that event, you could specify the subnet mask and the **longer-prefixes** argument as part of your command. Such a command, as demonstrated in Example 3-8, shows all subnets of network 172.16.0.0/16, including the major classful network of 172.16.0.0/16.

Example 3-7 *Specifying a Specific Route with the* show ip route *Command*

```
R1# show ip route 172.16.1.0
Routing entry for 172.16.1.0/30
  Known via "ospf 1", distance 110, metric 65, type intra area
  Last update from 192.168.0.22 on FastEthernet0/1, 00:52:08 ago
  Routing Descriptor Blocks:
  * 192.168.0.22, from 10.2.2.2, 00:52:08 ago, via FastEthernet0/1
      Route metric is 65, traffic share count is 1
```

Example 3-8 *Filtering Output from the* show ip route *Command with the* **longer-prefixes** *Option*

```
R1#show ip route 172.16.0.0 255.255.0.0 longer-prefixes
Codes: C - connected, S - static, R - RIP, M - mobile, B - BGP
       D - EIGRP, EX - EIGRP external, O - OSPF, IA - OSPF inter area
       N1 - OSPF NSSA external type 1, N2 - OSPF NSSA external type 2
       E1 - OSPF external type 1, E2 - OSPF external type 2
       i - IS-IS, su - IS-IS summary, L1 - IS-IS level-1, L2 - IS-IS level-2
       ia - IS-IS inter area, * - candidate default, U - per-user static route
       o - ODR, P - periodic downloaded static route

Gateway of last resort is not set
```

```
     172.16.0.0/30 is subnetted, 2 subnets
O       172.16.1.0 [110/65] via 192.168.0.22, 00:51:39, FastEthernet0/1
O       172.16.2.0 [110/65] via 192.168.0.22, 00:51:39, FastEthernet0/1
```

Redirecting **show** Command Output to a File

Imagine that you are working with Cisco Technical Assistance Center (TAC) to troubleshoot an issue, and they want a file containing output from the **show tech-support** command issued on your router. Example 3-9 shows how you can use the **| redirect** option to send output from the **show tech-support** command to a file on a TFTP server.

Notice that directing output to a file suppresses the onscreen output. If you wanted both (that is, for the output to be displayed onscreen and stored to a file), you could pipe the output to the **tee** option, as demonstrated in Example 3-10.

Example 3-9   *Redirecting Output to a TFTP Server*

```
R1# show tech-support | redirect tftp://192.168.1.50/tshoot.txt
!
R1#
```

Example 3-10   *Redirecting Output While Also Displaying the Output Onscreen*

```
R1# show tech-support | tee tftp://192.168.1.50/tac.txt
!

-------------------show version-------------------

Cisco IOS Software, C2600 Software (C2600-IPVOICE_IVS-M), Version 12.4(3b), RELE
ASE SOFTWARE (fc3)
Technical Support: http://www.cisco.com/techsupport
Copyright (c) 1986-2005 by Cisco Systems, Inc.
Compiled Thu 08-Dec-05 17:35 by alnguyen
...OUTPUT OMITTED...
```

If you already have an output file created and you want to append the output of another **show** command to your existing file, you can pipe the output of your **show** command to the **append** option. Example 3-11 shows how to use the **append** option to append the output of the **show ip interface brief** command to a file named **baseline.txt**.

Example 3-11   *Appending Output to an Existing File*

```
R1# show ip interface brief | append tftp://192.168.1.50/baseline.txt
!
R1#
```

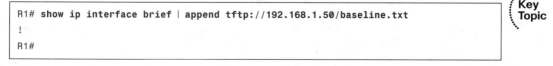

Troubleshooting Connectivity

In addition to **show** command output, you can use many other Cisco IOS commands to troubleshoot network conditions. A common command, which can be used to check network connectivity, is the **ping** command. A basic **ping** command sends Internet Control Message Protocol (ICMP) Echo messages to a specified destination; for every ICMP Echo Reply received from that specified destination, an exclamation point appears in the output, as shown in Example 3-12.

Example 3-12   *Basic* ping *Command*

```
R1# ping 10.4.4.4


Type escape sequence to abort.
Sending 5, 100-byte ICMP Echos to 10.4.4.4, timeout is 2 seconds:
!!!!!
```

The **ping** command does have several options that can prove useful during troubleshooting. For example:

- **size:** Specifies the number of bytes per datagram

- **repeat:** Specifies the number of ICMP Echo messages sent (defaults to 5)

- **timeout:** Specifies the number of seconds to wait for an ICMP Echo Reply

- **source:** Specifies the source of the ICMP Echo datagrams

- **df-bit:** Sets the *do not fragment* bit in the ICMP Echo datagram

Not only can a **ping** command indicate that a given IP address is reachable, but the response to a **ping** command might provide insight into the nature of a problem. For example, if the **ping** results indicate alternating failures and successes (that is, **!.!.!**), a troubleshooter might conclude that traffic is being load-balanced between the source and destination IP addresses. Traffic flowing across one path is successful, whereas traffic flowing over the other path is failing.

You can also use the **ping** command to create a load on the network to troubleshoot the network under heavy use. Specifically, you can specify a datagram size of 1500 bytes, along with a large byte count and a timeout of zero seconds, as shown in Example 3-13.

Notice that all the pings failed. These failures occurred because of the zero-second timeout. Specifically, the router did not wait for any amount of time before considering the ping to have failed and sending another ICMP Echo message.

Example 3-13   *Creating a Heavy Load on the Network*

```
R1# ping 10.4.4.4 size 1500 repeat 9999 timeout 0


Type escape sequence to abort.
```

```
Sending 9999, 1500-byte ICMP Echos to 10.4.4.4, timeout is 0 seconds:
.............................................................
.............................................................
.............................................................
...OUTPUT OMITTED...
```

Perhaps you suspect that an interface has a nondefault maximum transmission unit (MTU) size. You could send ICMP Echo messages across that interface using the **df-bit** and **size** options of the **ping** command to specify the size of the datagram to be sent. The **df-bit** option instructs a router to drop this datagram rather than fragmenting it if fragmentation is required.

Example 3-14 shows the sending of pings with the do not fragment bit set. Notice the **M** in the ping responses. An **M** indicates that fragmentation was required but could not be performed because the do not fragment bit was set. Therefore, you can conclude that a link between the source and destination is using a nonstandard MTU (that is, an MTU less than 1500 bytes).

Example 3-14 *Pinging with the Do Not Fragment Bit Set*

```
R1# ping 10.4.4.4 size 1500 df-bit
Type escape sequence to abort.
Sending 5, 1500-byte ICMP Echos to 10.4.4.4, timeout is 2 seconds:
Packet sent with the DF bit set
M.M.M
```

The challenge is how to determine the nondefault MTU size without multiple manual attempts. An extended ping can help with such a scenario. Consider Example 3-15, which issues the **ping** command without command-line parameters. This invokes the extended ping feature. The extended ping feature allows you to granularly customize your pings. For example, you could specify a range of datagram sizes to use in your pings to help determine the size of a nondefault MTU. Specifically, in Example 3-15, you could determine that the MTU across at least one of the links from the source to the destination IP address was set to 1450 bytes, because the **M** ping responses begin after 51 ICMP Echo datagrams were sent (with datagram sizes in the range of 1400 to 1450 bytes).

Example 3-15 *Extended Ping Performing a Ping Sweep*

> **Key Topic**

```
R1# ping
Protocol [ip]:
Target IP address: 10.4.4.4
Repeat count [5]: 1
Datagram size [100]:
Timeout in seconds [2]:
Extended commands [n]: y
```

```
Source address or interface:
Type of service [0]:
Set DF bit in IP header? [no]: yes
Validate reply data? [no]:
Data pattern [0xABCD]:
Loose, Strict, Record, Timestamp, Verbose[none]:
Sweep range of sizes [n]: y
Sweep min size [36]: 1400
Sweep max size [18024]: 1500
Sweep interval [1]:
Type escape sequence to abort.
Sending 101, [1400..1500]-byte ICMP Echos to 10.4.4.4, timeout is 2 seconds:
Packet sent with the DF bit set
!!!!!!!!!!!!!!!!!!!!!!!!!!!!!!!!!!!!!!!!!!!!!!!!!!!!!!!!!!M.M.M.M.M.M.M.M.M.M
.M.M.M.M.M.M.M.M.M.M.M.M.M.M.M.M
Success rate is 50 percent (51/101), round-trip min/avg/max = 60/125/232 ms
```

Although the **ping** command can be useful for testing Layer 3 (that is, the network layer) connectivity, the **telnet** command is useful for troubleshooting Layer 4 (that is, the transport layer). Specifically, although Telnet typically uses TCP port 23, you can specify an alternate port number to see if a particular Layer 4 service is running on a destination IP address. Such an approach might be useful if you are using a divide and conquer approach, starting at Layer 3 (which was determined to be operational as a result of a successful ping), or a bottom-up approach (which has also confirmed Layer 3 to be operational).

To illustrate, notice the **telnet 192.168.1.50 80** command issued in Example 3-16. This command causes router R1 to attempt a TCP connection with 192.168.1.50 using port 80 (that is, the HTTP port). The response of **Open** indicates that 192.168.1.50 is indeed running a service on port 80.

Example 3-16   *Using Telnet to Connect to a Nondefault Port*

```
R1#telnet 192.168.1.50 80
Trying 192.168.1.50, 80 ... Open
```

Troubleshooting Hardware

In addition to software configurations, a network's underlying hardware often becomes a troubleshooting target. As a reference, Table 3-2 offers a collection of Cisco IOS commands used to investigate hardware performance issues.

Table 3-2 *Cisco IOS Commands for Hardware Troubleshooting*

Command	Description
show processes cpu	Provides 5-second, 1-minute, and 5-minute CPU utilization statistics, in addition to a listing of processes running on a platform along with each process's utilization statistics
show memory	Displays summary information about processor and I/O memory, followed by a more comprehensive report of memory utilization
show interfaces	Shows Layer 1 and Layer 2 interface status, interface load information, and error statistics including the following: ■ **input queue drops:** Indicates a router received information faster than the information could be processed by the router ■ **output queue drops:** Indicates a router received information faster than the information could be sent out of the outgoing interface (perhaps because of an input/output speed mismatch) ■ **input errors:** Indicates frames were not received correctly (for example, a cyclic redundancy check (CRC) error occurred), perhaps indicating a cabling problem or a duplex mismatch ■ **output errors:** Indicates frames were not transmitted correctly, perhaps due to a duplex mismatch NOTE: Prior to collecting statistics, interface counters can be reset using the **clear counters** command.
show controllers	Displays statistical information for an interface (for example, error statistics), where the information varies for different interface types (for example, the type of connected cable might be displayed for a serial interface)
show platform	Provides detailed information about a router or switch hardware platform

Specialized Diagnostic Tools

The collection of network information occurs not just as part of a structured troubleshooting process but when gathering baseline data. Additionally, the occurrence of certain network events (for example, processor utilization on a network server exceeding a specified threshold) might be configured to trigger the writing of log information (for example, to a syslog server). Cisco offers network maintenance and troubleshooting tools targeted toward this type of data collection. This section introduces you to a sampling of these specialized tools, which can supplement the Cisco IOS commands used for data collection as discussed in the section "Cisco IOS Diagnostic Tools," earlier in this chapter.

Using Specialized Tools in the Troubleshooting Process

Chapter 2 introduced you to a series of processes (and subprocesses) that can work together in a structured troubleshooting process. Several of these processes involve the collection of information:

- **Difficulty report:** By proactively monitoring network devices, you might be alerted to impending performance issues before users are impacted.

- **Collect information:** The collection of information when troubleshooting a problem can often be made more efficient through the use of specialized maintenance and troubleshooting tools.

- **Examine collected information:** As troubleshooters investigate the information they collected while troubleshooting a problem, they need to know what normal network behavior looks like. They can then contrast that normal (that is, baseline) behavior against what they are observing in their collected data. Specialized maintenance and troubleshooting tools can be used in a network to collect baseline data on an ongoing basis.

- **Verify hypothesis:** Specialized maintenance and troubleshooting tools help a troubleshooter roll back an attempted fix, if that fix proves unsuccessful.

Most of the information collection tasks performed in the previous processes fall into one of three categories:

- **Troubleshooting information collection:** This information collection is conducted as part of troubleshooting a reported problem.

- **Baseline information collection:** This information collection is conducted when the network is operating normally, to form a frame of reference against which other data can be compared.

- **Network event information collection:** Some network devices can be configured to automatically generate alerts in response to specific conditions (for example, configured utilization levels on a switch, router, or server being exceeded).

Performing Packet Captures

You can use dedicated appliances or PCs running packet capture software to collect and store packets flowing across a network link. When troubleshooting, analysis of captured packets can provide insight into how a network is treating traffic flow. For example, a packet capture data file can show if packets are being dropped or if sessions are being reset. You can also look inside Layer 2, 3, and 4 headers using a packet capture application. For example, you can view a packet's Layer 3 header to determine that packet's Layer 3 quality of service (QoS) priority marking. An example of a popular and free packet capture utility you can download is Wireshark (www.wireshark.org), as shown in Figure 3-1.

Capturing and analyzing packets, however, presents two major obstacles. First, the volume of data collected as part of a packet capture can be so large that finding what you are looking for can be a challenge. Therefore, you should understand how to use your packet capture application's filtering features.

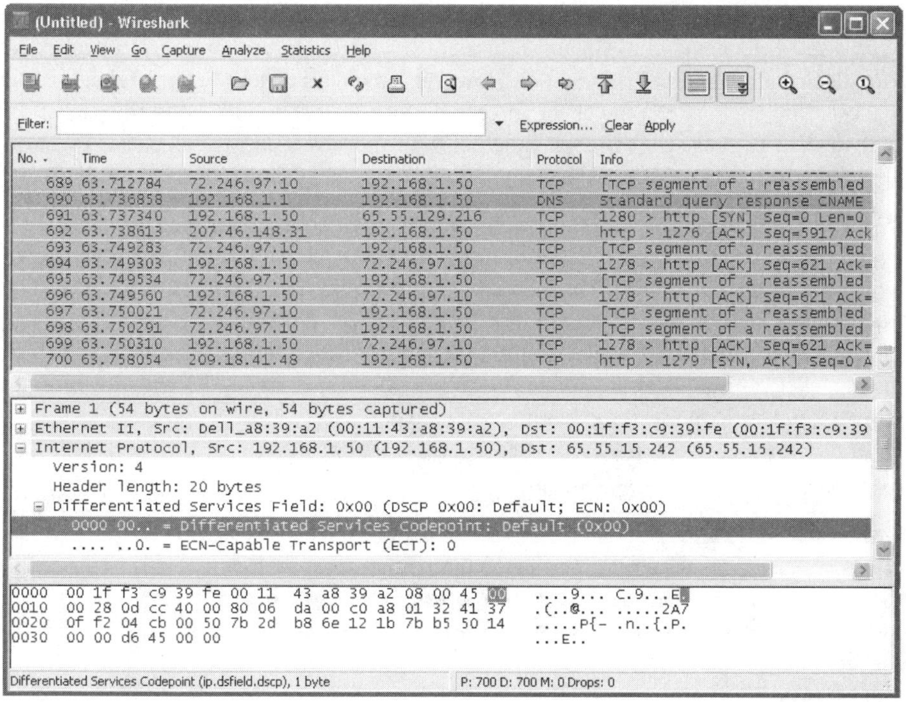
(Untitled) - Wireshark
File Edit View Go Capture Analyze Statistics Help
Filter:
Expression... Clear Apply
No. Time Source Destination Protocol Info
689 63.712784 72.246.97.10 192.168.1.50 TCP [TCP segment of a reassembled
690 63.736858 192.168.1.1 192.168.1.50 DNS Standard query response CNAME
691 63.737340 192.168.1.50 65.55.129.216 TCP 1280 > http [SYN] Seq=0 Len=0
692 63.738613 207.46.148.31 192.168.1.50 TCP http > 1276 [ACK] Seq=5917 Ack
693 63.749283 72.246.97.10 192.168.1.50 TCP [TCP segment of a reassembled
694 63.749303 192.168.1.50 72.246.97.10 TCP 1278 > http [ACK] Seq=621 Ack=
695 63.749534 72.246.97.10 192.168.1.50 TCP [TCP segment of a reassembled
696 63.749560 192.168.1.50 72.246.97.10 TCP 1278 > http [ACK] Seq=621 Ack=
697 63.750021 72.246.97.10 192.168.1.50 TCP [TCP segment of a reassembled
698 63.750291 72.246.97.10 192.168.1.50 TCP [TCP segment of a reassembled
699 63.750310 192.168.1.50 72.246.97.10 TCP 1278 > http [ACK] Seq=621 Ack=
700 63.758054 209.18.41.48 192.168.1.50 TCP http > 1279 [SYN, ACK] Seq=0 A
Frame 1 (54 bytes on wire, 54 bytes captured)
Ethernet II, Src: Dell_a8:39:a2 (00:11:43:a8:39:a2), Dst: 00:1f:f3:c9:39:fe (00:1f:f3:c9:39
Internet Protocol, Src: 192.168.1.50 (192.168.1.50), Dst: 65.55.15.242 (65.55.15.242)
Version: 4
Header length: 20 bytes
Differentiated Services Field: 0x00 (DSCP 0x00: Default; ECN: 0x00)
0000 00.. = Differentiated Services Codepoint: Default (0x00)
.... ..0. = ECN-Capable Transport (ECT): 0
0000 00 1f f3 c9 39 fe 00 11 43 a8 39 a2 08 00 45 00 ....9... C.9...E.
0010 00 28 0d cc 40 00 80 06 da 00 c0 a8 01 32 41 37 .(..@... .....2A7
0020 0f f2 04 cb 00 50 7b 2d b8 6e 12 1b 7b b5 50 14 .....P{- .n..{.P.
0030 00 00 d6 45 00 00 ...E..
Differentiated Services Codepoint (ip.dsfield.dscp), 1 byte
P: 700 D: 700 M: 0 Drops: 0

Figure 3-1 *Wireshark Packet Capture Application*

A second challenge is that if you want to monitor, for example, traffic flow between two network devices connected to a switch, the packets traveling between those two devices will not appear on your packet capture device's switch port. Fortunately, Cisco IOS supports a feature known as SPAN. SPAN instructs a switch to send copies of packets seen on one port (or one VLAN) to another port. You can connect your packet capture device to this other port, as shown in Figure 3-2.

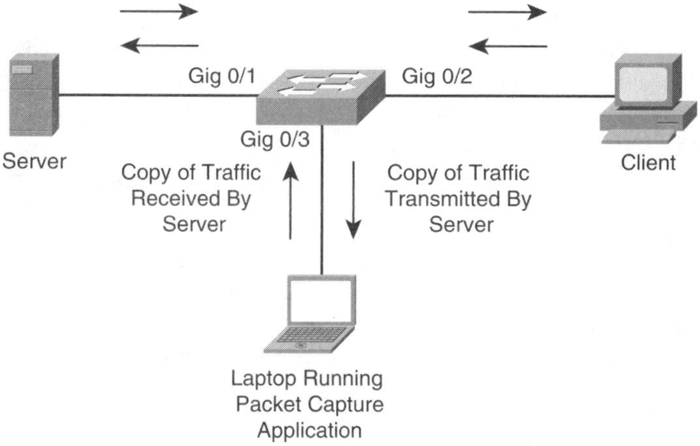
Gig 0/1
Gig 0/2
Gig 0/3
Server
Client
Copy of Traffic Received By Server
Copy of Traffic Transmitted By Server
Laptop Running Packet Capture Application

Figure 3-2 *Cisco Catalyst Switch Configured for SPAN*

Notice that Figure 3-2 depicts a client (connected to Gigabit Ethernet 0/2) communicating with a server (connected to Gigabit Ethernet 0/1). A troubleshooter inserts a packet capture device into Gigabit Ethernet 0/3. However, a switch's default behavior does not send packets flowing between the client and server out the port connected to the packet capture device. To cause port Gigabit Ethernet 0/3 to receive a copy of all packets sent or received by the server, SPAN is configured on the switch, as shown in Example 3-17.

Notice that Example 3-17 uses the **monitor session** *id* **source interface** *interface_id* command to indicate that a SPAN monitoring session with a locally significant identifier of **1** will copy packets crossing (that is, entering and exiting) port Gigabit Ethernet 0/1. Then the **monitor session** *id* **destination interface** interface_id command is used to specify port Gigabit Ethernet 0/3 as the destination port for those copied packets. A laptop running packet capture software connected to port Gigabit Ethernet 0/3 will now receive a copy of all traffic the server is sending or receiving.

Key Topic

Example 3-17   *SPAN Configuration*

```
Cat3550# conf term
Enter configuration commands, one per line.  End with CNTL/Z.
Cat3550(config)# monitor session 1 source interface gig 0/1
Cat3550(config)# monitor session 1 destination interface gig 0/3
Cat3550(config)# end
Cat3550# show monitor
Session 1
- - - - - - - - - - - -
Type                   : Local Session
Source Ports           :
    Both               : Gi0/1
Destination Ports      : Gi0/3
    Encapsulation      : Native
        Ingress : Disabled
```

In larger environments, a network capture device connected to one switch might need to capture packets flowing through a different switch. *Remote SPAN* (RSPAN) makes such a scenario possible. Consider Figure 3-3, where a troubleshooter has her laptop running a packet capture application connected to port Fast Ethernet 5/2 on switch SW2. The traffic that needs to be captured is traffic coming from and going to the server connected to port Gigabit Ethernet 0/1 on switch SW1.

A VLAN is configured whose purpose is to carry captured traffic between the switches. Therefore, a trunk exists between switches SW1 and SW2 to carry the SPAN VLAN in addition to a VLAN carrying user data. Example 3-18 shows the configuration on switch SW1 used to create the SPAN VLAN (that is, VLAN 20) and to specify that RSPAN should monitor port Gigabit Ethernet 0/1 and send packets sent and received on that port out of Gigabit Ethernet 0/3 on VLAN 20. The **show monitor** command is then used to verify the RSPAN source and destination. Also, note that by default the **monitor session** *id* **source** command monitors both incoming and outgoing traffic on the monitored port.

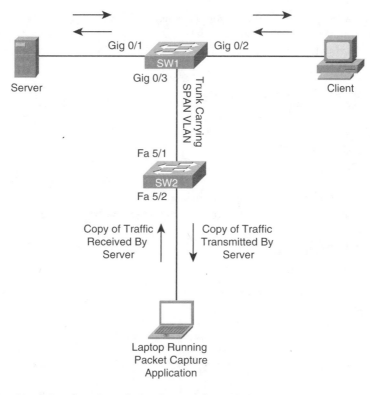

Figure 3-3 *Cisco Catalyst Switch Configured for RSPAN*

Example 3-18 *RSPAN Configuration on Switch SW1*

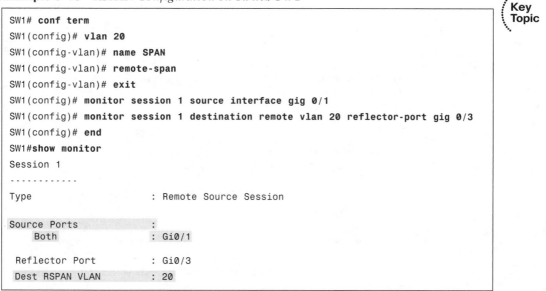

```
SW1# conf term
SW1(config)# vlan 20
SW1(config-vlan)# name SPAN
SW1(config-vlan)# remote-span
SW1(config-vlan)# exit
SW1(config)# monitor session 1 source interface gig 0/1
SW1(config)# monitor session 1 destination remote vlan 20 reflector-port gig 0/3
SW1(config)# end
SW1#show monitor
Session 1
------------
Type                    : Remote Source Session

Source Ports            :
    Both                : Gi0/1

 Reflector Port         : Gi0/3
 Dest RSPAN VLAN        : 20
```

Example 3-19 shows the configuration on switch SW2 used to create the SPAN VLAN (which is not necessary if the switches belong to the same VTP domain), to specify that RSPAN should receive captured traffic from VLAN 20 and send it out port Fast Ethernet 5/2.

Example 3-19 *RSPAN Configuration on Switch SW2*

```
SW2# conf term
SW2(config)# vlan 20
SW2(config-vlan)# name SPAN
SW2(config-vlan)# remote-span
SW2(config-vlan)# exit
SW2(config)# monitor session 2 source remote vlan 20
SW2(config)# monitor session 2 destination interface fa 5/2
SW2(config)# end
SW2# show monitor
Session 2
-----------
Type               : Remote Destination Session
Source RSPAN VLAN : 20
Destination Ports : Fa5/2
```

Creating a Baseline with SNMP and NetFlow

Simple Network Management Protocol (SNMP) and NetFlow are two technologies available on some Cisco IOS platforms that can automate the collection statistics. These statistics can be used, for example, to establish a baseline in a troubleshooting scenario. Table 3-3 contrasts these two technologies.

Key Topic

Table 3-3 *Comparing SNMP and NetFlow*

Technology	Characteristics
SNMP	Collects device statistics (for example, platform resource utilization, traffic counts, and error counts)
	Uses a pull model (that is, statistics pulled from monitored device by a network management station [NMS])
	Available on nearly all enterprise network devices
NetFlow	Collects detailed information about traffic flows
	Uses a push model (that is, statistics pushed from the monitored device to a NetFlow collector)
	Available on routers and high-end switches

Although both SNMP and NetFlow are useful for statistical data collection, they target different fundamental functions. For example, SNMP is primarily focused on device statistics, whereas NetFlow is primarily focused on traffic statistics.

SNMP

A device being managed by SNMP runs a process called an *SNMP agent*. A Network Management System (NMS) can then query the agent for information, using the SNMP protocol. SNMP version 3 (that is, SNMPv3) supports encryption and authentication of SNMP messages; however, the most popular SNMP version deployed today is SNMPv2c. SNMPv2c uses *community strings* for security. Specifically, for an NMS to be allowed to read data from a device running an SNMP agent, the NMS must be configured with a community string that matches the managed device's read-only community string. For the NMS to change the information on the managed device, the NMS must be configured with a community string that matches the managed device's read-write community string. To enhance the security available with SNMPv2c, you can create an access list that determines valid IP addresses or network addresses for NMS servers.

Figure 3-4 shows a topology using SNMP. In the topology, router R1 is running an SNMP agent that the NMS server can query.

NMS   Managed Device
                                        Running an SNMP
                                        Agent

Figure 3-4 *SNMP Sample Topology*

Example 3-20 illustrates the SNMP configuration on router R1. The **snmp-server community** *string* [**ro** | **rw**] commands specify a read-only (that is, **ro**) community string of **CISCO** and a read-write (that is, **rw**) community string of **PRESS**. Contact and location information for the device is also specified. Finally, notice the **snmp-server ifindex persist** command. This command ensures that the SNMP interface index stays consistent during data collection, even if the device is rebooted. This consistency is important when data is being collected for baselining purposes.

Example 3-20 *SNMP Sample Configuration*

```
R1# conf term
R1(config)# snmp-server community CISCO ro
R1(config)# snmp-server community PRESS rw
R1(config)# snmp-server contact demo@ciscopress.local
R1(config)# snmp-server location 3rd Floor of Wallace Building
R1(config)# snmp-server ifindex persist
```

Key
Topic

NetFlow

Unlike SNMP, NetFlow can distinguish between different traffic flows. A *flow* is a series of packets, all of which have shared header information such as source and destination IP addresses, protocols numbers, port numbers, and Type of Service (TOS) field information. NetFlow can keep track of the number of packets and bytes observed in each flow. This information is stored in a *flow cache*. Flow information is removed from a flow cache if the flow is terminated, times out, or fills to capacity.

You can use the NetFlow feature as a standalone feature on an individual router. Such a standalone configuration might prove useful for troubleshooting because you can observe flows being created as packets enter a router. However, rather than using just a standalone implementation of NetFlow, entries in a router's flow cache can be exported to a *NetFlow collector* prior to the entries expiring. After the NetFlow collector has received flow information over a period of time, analysis software running on the NetFlow collector can produce reports detailing traffic statistics.

Figure 3-5 shows a sample topology in which NetFlow is enabled on router R4, and a NetFlow collector is configured on a PC at IP address 192.168.1.50.

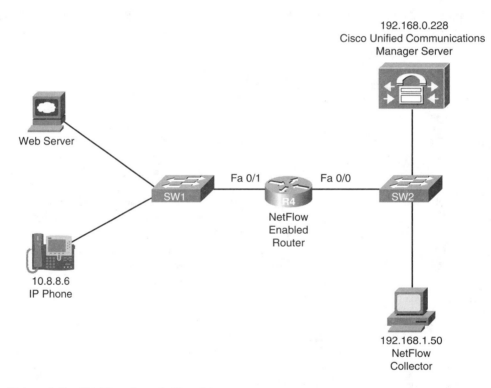

Figure 3-5   *NetFlow Sample Topology*

Example 3-21 illustrates the NetFlow configuration on router R4. Notice that the **ip flow ingress** command is issued for both the Fast Ethernet 0/0 and Fast Ethernet 0/1 interfaces. This ensures that all flows passing through the router, regardless of direction, can be monitored. Although not required, router R4 is configured to report its NetFlow information to a NetFlow collector at IP address 192.168.1.50. The **ip flow-export source lo 0** command indicates that all communication between router R4 and the NetFlow collector will be via interface Loopback 0. A NetFlow version of **5** was specified. Note that although version 5 is the most widely deployed, you should check the documentation for your

NetFlow collector software to confirm which version to configure. Finally, the **ip flow-export destination 192.168.1.50 5000** command is issued to specify that the NetFlow collector's IP address is **192.168.1.50**, and communication to the NetFlow collector should be done over UDP port **5000**. Because NetFlow does not have a standardized port number, please check your NetFlow collector's documentation when selecting a port.

Example 3-21 *NetFlow Sample Configuration*

Key Topic

```
R4# conf term
R4(config)# int fa 0/0
R4(config-if)# ip flow ingress
R4(config-if)# exit
R4(config)# int fa 0/1
R4(config-if)# ip flow ingress
R4(config-if)# exit
R4(config)# ip flow-export source lo 0
R4(config)# ip flow-export version 5
R4(config)# ip flow-export destination 192.168.1.50 5000
R4(conig)# end
```

Although an external NetFlow collector is valuable for longer-term flow analysis, you can issue the **show ip cache flow** command at a router's CLI prompt to produce a summary of flow information, as shown in Example 3-22. A troubleshooter can look at the output displayed in Example 3-22 and be able to confirm, for example, that traffic is flowing between IP address 10.8.8.6 (a Cisco IP Phone) and 192.168.0.228 (a Cisco Unified Communications Manager server).

Both syslog (discussed in Chapter 1, "Introduction to Network Maintenance") and SNMP (introduced in this section) are protocols that can report the occurrence of specific events on a network device. Although these protocols by themselves lack a mechanism to alert a network administrator (for example, via e-mail) when a network event is logged, third-party software is available that can selectively alert appropriate personnel when specific events are logged.

Earlier, this section discussed how a network device running an SNMP agent can be queried for information from an NMS. However, a network device running an SNMP agent can also initiate communication with an NMS. If an interface goes down, for example, the SNMP agent on a managed network device can send a message containing information about the interface state change to an NMS. Such notifications that a managed device sends to an NMS are called *traps*. These traps require an NMS to be interpreted because they are not in a readable format.

Example 3-22 *Viewing NetFlow Information*

Key Topic

```
R4# show ip cache flow
...OUTPUT OMITTED...
Protocol        Total     Flows   Packets   Bytes  Packets  Active(Sec)  Idle(Sec)
```

```
----------       Flows     /Sec    /Flow   /Pkt    /Sec         /Flow      /Flow
TCP-Telnet          12      0.0       50      40     0.1          15.7       14.2
TCP-WWW             12      0.0       40     785     0.1           7.1        6.2
TCP-other          536      0.1        1      55     0.2           0.3       10.5
UDP-TFTP           225      0.0        4      59     0.1          11.9       15.4
UDP-other          122      0.0      114     284     3.0          15.9       15.4
ICMP                41      0.0       13      91     0.1          49.9       15.6
IP-other             1      0.0      389      60     0.0        1797.1        3.4
Total:             949      0.2       18     255     3.8           9.4       12.5


SrcIf       SrcIPaddress    DstIf        DstIPaddress   Pr    SrcP  DstP  Pkts
Fa0/0       10.3.3.1        Null         224.0.0.10     58    0000  0000  62
Fa0/1       10.8.8.6        Fa0/0        192.168.0.228  06    C2DB  07D0  2
Fa0/0       192.168.0.228   Fa0/1        10.8.8.6       06    07D0  C2DB  1
Fa0/0       192.168.1.50    Fa0/1        10.8.8.6       11    6002  6BD2  9166
Fa0/1       10.8.8.6        Fa0/0        192.168.1.50   11    6BD2  6002  9166
Fa0/0       10.1.1.2        Local        10.3.3.2       06    38F2  0017  438
```

Providing Notifications for Network Events

Whereas responding to problem reports from users is a reactive form of troubleshooting, monitoring network devices for significant events and responding to those events is a proactive form of troubleshooting. For example, before a user loses connectivity with the Internet, a router that is dual-homed to the Internet might report the event of one of its Internet connections going down. The redundant link can then be repaired, in response to the notification, thus resolving the problem without users being impacted.

Example 3-23 demonstrates how to enable a router to send SNMP traps to an NMS. The **snmp-server host 192.168.1.50 version 2c CISCOPRESS** command points router R4 to an SNMP server (that is, an NMS) at IP address 192.168.1.50. The SNMP server is configured for SNMP version **2c** and a community string of **CISCOPRESS**. The **snmp-server enable traps** command attempts to enable all traps. Notice from the output, however, that a couple of the traps are mutually exclusive, causing one of the traps to not be enabled. You can view the enabled traps by using the **show run | include traps** command. Rather than enabling all possible traps with the **snmp-server enable traps** command, you can selectively enable traps using the **snmp-server enable traps** *trap-name* command.

Key Topic

Example 3-23   *Enabling SNMP Traps*

```
R4# conf term
R4(config)# snmp-server host 192.168.1.150 version 2c CISCOPRESS
R4(config)# snmp-server enable traps
% Cannot enable both sham-link state-change interface traps.
% New sham link interface trap not enabled.
R4(config)# end
R4# show run | include traps
```

```
snmp-server enable traps snmp authentication linkdown linkup coldstart warmstart
snmp-server enable traps vrrp
snmp-server enable traps ds1
snmp-server enable traps gatekeeper
snmp-server enable traps tty
snmp-server enable traps eigrp
snmp-server enable traps xgcp
snmp-server enable traps ds3
...OUTPUT OMITTED...
```

The messages received via syslog and SNMP are predefined within Cisco IOS. This large collection of predefined messages accommodates most any network management requirement; however, Cisco IOS supports a featured called EEM that allows you to create your own event definitions and specify custom responses to those events. An event can be defined based on syslog messages, SNMP traps, and entering specific Cisco IOS commands, as just a few examples. In response to a defined event, EEM can perform various actions, including sending an SNMP trap to an NMS, writing a log message to a syslog server, executing specified Cisco IOS commands, sending an e-mail to an appropriate party, or executing a tool command language (Tcl) script.

To illustrate the basic configuration steps involved in configuring EEM, consider Example 3-24. The purpose of the configuration is to create a syslog message, which will be displayed on the router console, when someone clears the router's interface counters using the **clear counters** command. The message should remind the administrator to update the network documentation, listing the rationale for clearing the interface counters.

Example 3-24 *EEM Sample Configuration*

```
R4# conf term
R4(config)# event manager applet COUNTER-RESET
R4(config-applet)# event cli pattern "clear counters" sync no skip no occurs 1
R4(config-applet)# action A syslog priority informational msg "Please update
  network documentation to record why the counters were reset."
R4(config-applet)# end
```

Key
Topic

The **event manager applet COUNTER-RESET** command creates an EEM applet named **COUNTER-RESET** and enters applet configuration mode. The **event** command specifies what you are looking for in your custom-defined event. In this example, you are looking for the CLI command **clear counters**. Note that the **clear counters** command would be detected even if a shortcut (for example, **cle co**) were used. The **sync no** parameter says that the EEM policy will run asynchronously with the CLI command. Specifically, the EEM policy will not be executed before the CLI command executes. The **skip no** parameter says that the CLI command will not be skipped (that is, the CLI command will be executed). Finally, the **occurs 1** parameter indicates that the EEM event is triggered by a single occurrence of the **clear counters** command being issued.

The **action** command is then entered to indicate what should be done in response to the defined event. In Example 3-24, the action is given a locally significant name of **A** and is assigned a syslog priority level of **informational**. The specific action to be taken is producing an informational message saying, **"Please update network documentation to record why the counters were reset."**

To verify the operation of the EEM configuration presented in Example 3-24, the **clear counters** command is executed in Example 3-25. Notice that entering the **clear counters** command triggers the custom-defined event, resulting in generation of a syslog message reminding an administrator to document the reason he cleared the interface counters.

Example 3-25   *Testing EEM Configuration*

```
R4# clear counters
Clear "show interface" counters on all interfaces [confirm]
R4#
*Mar  3 08:41:00.582: %HA_EM-6-LOG: COUNTER-RESET: Please update network docu-
  mentation to record why the counters were reset.
```

Exam Preparation Tasks

Review All the Key Topics

Review the most important topics from inside the chapter, noted with the Key Topics icon in the outer margin of the page. Table 3-4 lists these key topics and the page numbers where each is found.

Table 3-4 *Key Topics for Chapter 3*

Key Topic · Element	Description	Page Number
Example 3-1	The **show processes cpu** command	53
Example 3-8	Filtering **show** output with the **longer-prefixes** option	56
Example 3-9	Redirecting output using the **redirect** option	57
Example 3-10	Redirecting output using the **tee** option	57
Example 3-11	Redirecting output using the **append** option	57
Example 3-15	Extended Ping performing a Ping sweep	59
Example 3-16	Using **telnet** to connect to a nondefault port	60
Table 3-2	Cisco IOS commands for hardware troubleshooting	61
List	How information collection plays a role in troubleshooting	62
List	Three categories of information collection	62
Example 3-17	SPAN configuration	64
Example 3-18	RSPAN configuration	65
Table 3-3	Comparing SNMP and NetFlow	66
Example 3-20	SNMP sample configuration	67
Example 3-21	NetFlow sample configuration	69
Example 3-22	Viewing NetFlow information	69
Example 3-23	Enabling SNMP traps	70
Example 3-24	EEM Sample configuration	71

Complete Tables and Lists from Memory

Print a copy of Appendix B, "Memory Tables" (found on the CD), or at least the section for this chapter, and complete the tables and lists from memory. Appendix C, "Memory Tables Answer Key," also on the CD, includes completed tables and lists to check your work.

Define Key Terms

Define the following key terms from this chapter, and check your answers in the Glossary:

input queue drops, output queue drops, input errors, output errors, SPAN, RSPAN, trap, NMS, NetFlow, EEM

Command Reference to Check Your Memory

This section includes the most important configuration and EXEC commands covered in this chapter. To determine how well you have memorized the commands as a side effect of your other studies, cover the left side of the table with a piece of paper; read the descriptions on the right side; and see whether you remember the command.

Table 3-5 *Chapter 3 Configuration Command Reference*

Command	Description
monitor session *id* {source | destination} interface *interface_id*	Global configuration mode command that configures SPAN, which specifies the source or destination interface for traffic monitoring
remote-span	VLAN configuration mode command that indicates a VLAN is to be used as an RSPAN VLAN
monitor session *id* destination remote vlan *VLAN_id* reflector-port *port_id*	Global configuration mode command that configures RSPAN on a monitored switch, where the RSPAN VLAN is specified in addition to the port identifier for the port being used to flood the monitored traffic to the monitoring switch
monitor session *id* source remote vlan *VLAN_id*	Global configuration mode command that configures RSPAN on a monitoring switch, where the RSPAN VLAN is specified
snmp-server community *community_string* {ro | rw}	Global configuration mode command that defines a read-only (**ro**) or read-write (**rw**) SNMP community string
snmp-server contact *contact_info*	Global configuration mode command that specifies SNMP contact information

Table 3-5 *Chapter 3 Configuration Command Reference* *(Continued)*

Command	Description
snmp-server location *location*	Global configuration mode command that specifies SNMP location information
snmp-server ifindex persist	Global configuration mode command that forces an SNMP interface index to stay consistent during data collection, even if a device is rebooted
ip flow ingress	Interface configuration mode command that enables NetFlow for that interface
ip flow-export source *interface_id*	Global configuration mode command that specifies the interface used to communicate with an external NetFlow collector
ip flow-export version {1 | 5 | 9}	Global configuration mode command that specifies the NetFlow version used by a device
ip flow-export destination *IP_address port*	Global configuration mode command that specifies the IP address and port number of an external NetFlow collector
snmp-server host *IP_address* version {1 | 2c | 3} *community_string*	Global configuration mode command that specifies the IP address, SNMP version, and community string of an NMS
snmp-server enable traps	Global configuration mode command that enables all possible SNMP traps
event manager applet *name*	Global configuration mode command that creates an embedded event manager applet and enters applet configuration mode

Table 3-6 *Chapter 3 EXEC Command Reference*

Command	Description
show processes cpu	Displays 5-second, 1-minute, and 5-minute CPU utilization averages, in addition to a listing of running processes with their CPU utilization
show ip route *network_address subnet_mask* longer-prefixes	Shows all subnets within the specified address space

continues

Table 3-6   *Chapter 3 EXEC Command Reference   (Continued)*

Command	Description
ping *IP_address* **size** [*bytes*] **repeat** [*number*] **timeout** [*seconds*] [**df-bit**]	Sends ICMP Echo packets to the specified IP address, with options that include these: **size:** The number of bytes in the ICMP Echo packet **repeat:** The number of ICMP Echo packets sent **timeout:** The number of seconds the router waits for an ICMP Echo Reply packet after sending an ICMP Echo packet **df-bit:** Sets the do-not-fragment bit in the ICMP Echo packet
telnet IP_address [port]	Connects to a remote IP address via Telnet using TCP port 23 by default or optionally via a specified TCP port
show memory	Displays summary information about processor and I/O memory, followed by a more comprehensive report of memory utilization
show interfaces	Shows Layer 1 and Layer 2 interface status, interface load information, and error statistics including these: **input queue drops:** Indicates a router received information faster than the information could be processed by the router **output queue drops:** Indicates a router received information faster than the information could be sent out of the outgoing interface (perhaps because of an input/output speed mismatch) **input errors:** Indicates frames were not received correctly (for example, a CRC error occurred), perhaps indicating a cabling problem or a duplex mismatch **output errors:** Indicates frames were not transmitted correctly, perhaps due to a duplex mismatch **NOTE:** Prior to collecting statistics, interface counters can be reset using the **clear counters** command.
show controllers	Displays statistical information for an interface (for example, error statistics) where the information varies for different interface types (for example, the type of connected cable might be displayed for a serial interface)
show platform	Provides detailed information about a router or switch hardware platform

This chapter covers the following subjects:

VLAN Troubleshooting: This section reviews the basics of Layer 2 switching operation and shows how a few readily accessible Cisco IOS commands can be used to quickly gather information as part of a structured troubleshooting process.

Spanning Tree Protocol Troubleshooting: This section introduces Spanning Tree Protocol (STP), which allows a Layer 2 topology to have redundant links while avoiding the side effects of a looped Layer 2 topology, such as a broadcast storm. You then learn strategies for troubleshooting an STP issue. Finally, this section addresses troubleshooting an EtherChannel connection.

Trouble Ticket STP: This section presents you with a trouble ticket and an associated topology. You are also given **show** command output (baseline output and output collected after the reported issue occurred). Based on the information provided, you hypothesize an underlying cause for the reported issue and develop a solution. You can then compare your solution with a suggested solution.

CHAPTER 4

Basic Cisco Catalyst Switch Troubleshooting

Most enterprise LANs rely on some flavor of Ethernet technology (for example, Ethernet, Fast Ethernet, or Gigabit Ethernet). Therefore, an understanding of Ethernet switch operation at Layer 2 is critical to troubleshooting many issues. This chapter reviews basic Layer 2 switch operation. Beyond a review of basic operation, this chapter discusses potential troubleshooting issues involving Layer 2 switches and steps to troubleshoot these issues.

Maintaining high availability for today's enterprise networks is a requirement for many applications, such as voice and e-commerce, which can impact a business' bottom line if these applications are unavailable for even a short period. To improve availability, many enterprise networks interconnect Layer 2 switches with redundant connections, allowing a single switch or a single link to fail while still maintaining connectivity between any two network endpoints. Such a redundant topology, however, can result in Layer 2 loops, which can cause frames to endlessly circle a LAN (for example, broadcast frames creating a broadcast storm). Therefore, STP is frequently used to logically break these Layer 2 topological loops by strategically blocking ports, while being able to detect a link failure and bring up a previously blocked switch port to restore connectivity. This chapter reviews the operation of STP and focuses on troubleshooting STP issues.

Finally, you are introduced to the first in a series of trouble tickets, which provides a reported issue and its associated topology. Various **show** command output is provided to help you hypothesize the underlying cause of the issue being reported. This chapter's trouble ticket focuses on troubleshooting an STP issue.

"Do I Know This Already?" Quiz

The "Do I Know This Already?" quiz helps you determine your level of knowledge of this chapter's topics before you begin. Table 4-1 details the major topics discussed in this chapter and their corresponding quiz questions.

Table 4-1 *"Do I Know This Already?" Section-to-Question Mapping*

Foundation Topics Section	Questions
VLAN Troubleshooting	1–2
Spanning Tree Protocol Troubleshooting	3–6

1. Which two of the following statements are true of a Layer 2 switch? (Choose two.)

   a. Each switch port is in its own collision domain.

   b. Each switch port is in its own broadcast domain.

   c. Each VLAN is its own collision domain.

   d. Each VLAN is its own broadcast domain.

2. Which two Cisco Catalyst switch commands display to which VLAN each switch port belongs? (Choose two.)

   a. show mac address-table

   b. show interfaces trunk

   c. show vlan

   d. traceroute mac

3. What is the STP port type for all ports on a root bridge?

   a. Designated port

   b. Root port

   c. Nondesignated port

   d. Nonroot port

4. Which two of the following commands are most helpful in determining STP information for a Layer 2 switch? (Choose two.)

   a. show spanning-tree vlan

   b. debug spanning-tree state

   c. show spanning-tree interface

   d. show port span

5. What are two common issues that could result from an STP failure? (Choose two.)

   a. Tagged frames being sent into a native VLAN

   b. Broadcast storms

   c. MAC address table filling to capacity

   d. MAC address table corruption

6. Which switch feature allows multiple physical links to be bonded into a logical link?

   a. FRF.12

   b. EtherChannel

   c. Jumbo frames

   d. RPF

Foundation Topics

VLAN Troubleshooting

To effectively troubleshoot Ethernet-based LAN environments, you should be familiar with the basics of Layer 2 switch operation. Therefore, this section reviews switch fundamentals, including how a switch's MAC address table is populated, as well as the characteristics of VLANs and trunks. After a review of basic switch operation, this section highlights common issues in a switched environment and how to use Cisco IOS to troubleshoot such issues.

Reviewing Layer 2 Switching

Unlike Ethernet hubs, which take bits in one port and send those same bits out all other ports, Ethernet switches learn the devices connected to their ports. Therefore, when an Ethernet switch sees a frame destined for a particular MAC address, the switch can consult its MAC address table to determine out of which port to forward the newly arrived frame. This behavior results in more efficient bandwidth utilization on a LAN and eliminates the concern of collisions. Specifically, in a hubbed environment, if two endpoints each transmitted a data frame on the wire at the same time, those two frames would collide, resulting in both frames being corrupted. This collision would require each endpoint to retransmit its data frame. Every port on an Ethernet switch, however, is its own collision domain, whereas all ports on a hub are in a common collision domain.

Ethernet switches can dynamically learn the MAC addresses attached to various switch ports by looking at the source MAC address on frames coming into a port. For example, if switch port Gigabit Ethernet 1/1 received a frame with a source MAC address of DDDD.DDDD.DDDD, the switch could conclude that MAC address DDDD.DDDD.DDDD resided off of port Gigabit Ethernet 1/1. In the future, if the switch received a frame destined for a MAC address of DDDD.DDDD.DDDD, the switch would only send that frame out of port Gigabit Ethernet 1/1.

Initially, however, a switch is unaware of what MAC addresses reside off of which ports (unless MAC addresses have been statically configured). Therefore, when a switch receives a frame destined for a MAC address not yet present in the switch's MAC address table, the switch floods that frame out of all the switch ports, other than the port on which the frame was received. Similarly, broadcast frames (that is, frames with a destination MAC address of FFFF.FFFF.FFFF) are always flooded out all switch ports except the port on which the frame was received. The reason broadcast frames are always flooded is that no endpoint will have a MAC address of FFFF.FFFF.FFFF, meaning that the FFFF.FFFF.FFFF MAC address will never be learned in the MAC address table of a switch.

To illustrate how a switch's MAC address table becomes populated, consider an endpoint named PC1 that wants to form a Telnet connection with a server as shown in Figure 4-1. Also, assume that PC1 and its server reside on the same subnet (that is, no routing is required to get traffic between PC1 and its server). Before PC1 can send a Telnet segment to its server, PC1 needs to know the IP address (that is, the Layer 3 address) and the MAC address (that is, the Layer 2 address) of the server. The IP address of the server is typically known or is resolved via a Domain Name System (DNS) lookup. In this example, assume the server's IP address is known. To properly form a Telnet segment, however, PC1 needs to know the server's Layer 2 MAC address. If PC1 does not already have the server's MAC address in its ARP cache, PC1 can send an Address Resolution Protocol (ARP) request in an attempt to learn the server's MAC address.

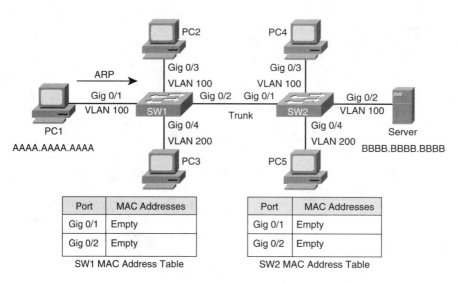

Figure 4-1   *Endpoint Sending an ARP Request*

When switch SW1 sees PC1's ARP request enter port Gigabit 0/1, the PC1 MAC address of AAAA.AAAA.AAAA is added to the MAC address table of switch SW1. Also, because the ARP request is a broadcast, its destination MAC address is FFFF.FFFF.FFFF. Because the MAC address of FFFF.FFFF.FFFF is unknown to switch SW1's MAC address table, switch SW1 floods a copy of the incoming frame out all switch ports except the port on which the frame was received, with one exception. Notice that port Gig 0/1 on switch SW1 belongs to VLAN 100, whereas port Gig 0/4 belongs to VLAN 200. Because a broadcast is constrained to a VLAN, this broadcast frame originating in VLAN 100 is not flooded out Gig 0/4 because Gig 0/4 is a member of a different VLAN. Port Gig 0/2, however, is a trunk port, and a trunk can carry traffic for multiple VLANs. Therefore, the ARP request is flooded out of port Gig 0/2, as illustrated in Figure 4-2.

When switch SW2 receives the ARP request over its Gig 0/1 trunk port, the source MAC address of AAAA.AAAA.AAAA is added to switch SW2's MAC address table. Also, similar to the behavior of switch SW1, switch SW2 floods the broadcast frame out of port Gig 0/3 (a member of VLAN 100) and out of port Gig 0/2 (also a member of VLAN 100), as depicted in Figure 4-3.

The server receives the ARP request and responds with an ARP reply, as seen in Figure 4-4. Unlike the ARP request, however, the ARP reply frame is not a broadcast frame. The ARP reply in this case has a destination MAC address of AAAA.AAAA.AAAA.

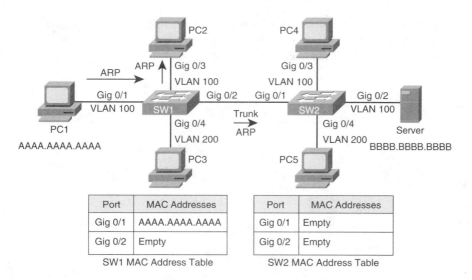

Figure 4-2 *Switch SW1 Flooding the ARP Request*

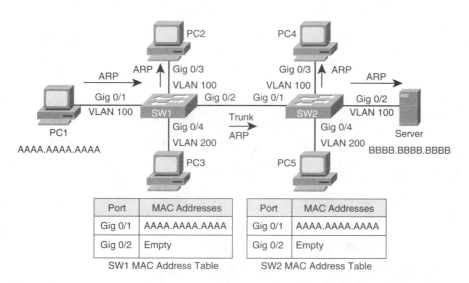

Figure 4-3 *Switch SW2 Flooding the ARP Request*

Upon receiving the ARP reply from the server, switch SW2 adds the server's MAC address of BBBB.BBBB.BBBB to its MAC address table, as shown in Figure 4-5. Also, the ARP reply is only sent out port Gig 0/1 because switch SW1 knows that the destination MAC address of AAAA.AAAA.AAAA is available off of port Gig 0/1.

When receiving the ARP reply in its Gig 0/2 port, switch SW1 adds the server's MAC address of BBBB.BBBB.BBBB to its MAC address table. Also, like switch SW2, switch SW1 now has an entry in its MAC address table for the frame's destination MAC address of AAAA.AAAA.AAAA. Therefore, switch SW1 forwards the ARP reply out port Gig 0/1 to the endpoint of PC1, as illustrated in Figure 4-6.

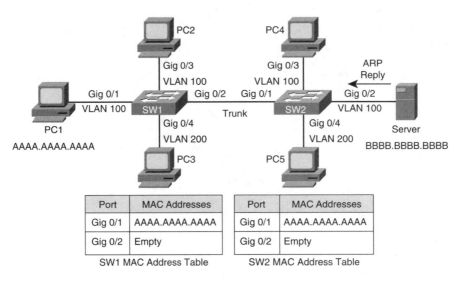

Figure 4-4   *ARP Reply Sent from the Server*

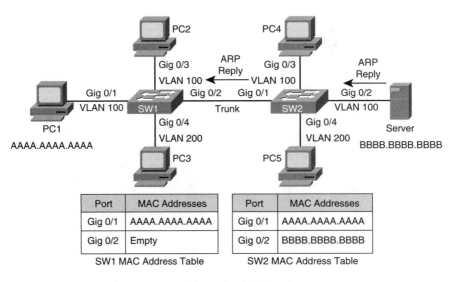

Figure 4-5   *Switch SW2 Forwarding the ARP Reply*

After receiving the server's ARP reply, PC1 now knows the MAC address of the server. Therefore, PC1 can now send a properly constructed Telnet segment destined for the server, as depicted in Figure 4-7.

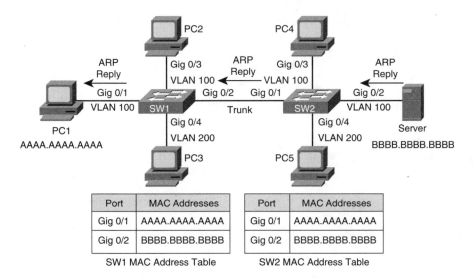

Figure 4-6   *Switch SW1 Forwarding the ARP Reply*

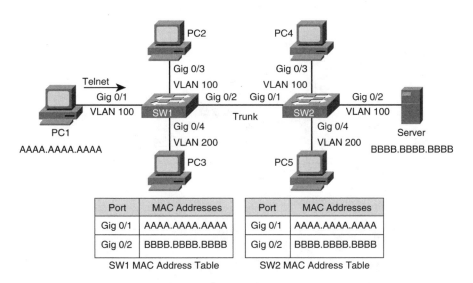

Figure 4-7   *PC1 Sending a Telnet Segment*

Switch SW1 has the server's MAC address of BBBB.BBBB.BBBB in its MAC address table. Therefore, when switch SW1 receives the Telnet segment from PC1, that segment is forwarded out of the Gig 0/2 port of switch SW1, as seen in Figure 4-8.

Similar to the behavior of switch SW1, switch SW2 forwards the Telnet segment out its Gig 0/2 port. This forwarding, shown in Figure 4-9, is possible because switch SW2 has an entry for the segment's destination MAC address of BBBB.BBBB.BBBB in its MAC address table.

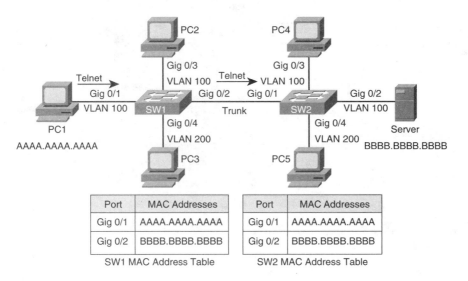

Figure 4-8   *Switch SW1 Forwarding the Telnet Segment*

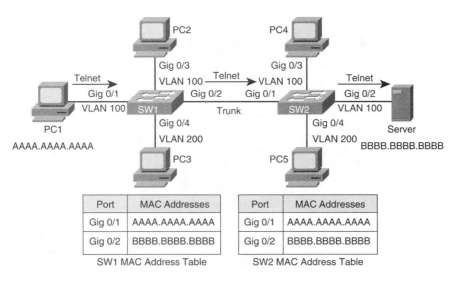

Figure 4-9   *Switch SW2 Forwarding the Telnet Segment*

Finally, the server responds to PC1, and a bidirectional Telnet session is established between the PC and the server, as illustrated in Figure 4-10. Because PC1 learned the MAC address of the server as a result of its earlier ARP request and stored that result in its local ARP cache, the transmission of subsequent Telnet segments does not require additional ARP requests. If unused for a period of time, however, entries in a PC's ARP cache can time out.

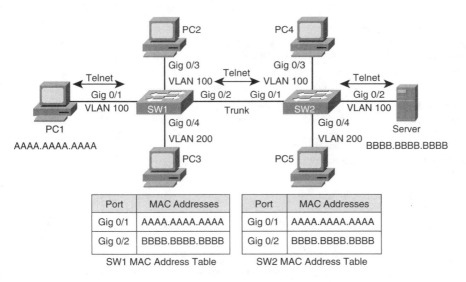

Figure 4-10   *Bidirectional Telnet Session Between PC1 and the Server*

When troubleshooting an issue involving Layer 2 switch communication, a thorough understanding of the preceding steps can help you identify potential problems. If you were troubleshooting an issue similar to the previous example, where a PC is attempting to communicate with a server on a common VLAN, you might consider possibilities such as the following:

■ **Hardware issues:** Potential hardware problems include the cabling interconnecting devices and the devices themselves. For example, one switch port might be faulty. You could eliminate that possibility by moving a cable to a known good switch port.

■ **VLAN configuration:** For traffic to move from one VLAN to another, that traffic must be routed. Therefore, you might want to confirm that the PC and server in such a scenario are connected to ports in a common VLAN.

■ **Trunk configuration:** Switches are often interconnected via an Ethernet trunk (for example, an IEEE 802.1Q trunk). A trunk has the unique capability to carry traffic for multiple VLANs over a single link. When troubleshooting an issue like the one in the preceding scenario, you might want to confirm that the trunk is configured identically on each switch. For example, each switch should be using the same trunking encapsulation (for example, 802.1Q or ISL). Also, if you are using an 802.1Q trunk, each switch should have a common native VLAN (that is, the VLAN on an 802.1Q trunk, which does not add tag bytes to the frames in that VLAN). One other possibility is that traffic for one or more VLANs has been excluded on a trunk.

Layer 2 Troubleshooting Techniques

After you understand how a frame should flow through a Layer 2 portion of the network (that is, through Layer 2 switches), you can begin to troubleshoot a communications issue by following the path of a frame. For example, you can examine the first switch along the path of a frame. If that switch has not learned the MAC address of the sender, you might need to check hardware and software (for example, the configuration and cabling of a PC) upstream from the switch. Perhaps the first-hop switch did learn the MAC address of the sender, but that MAC address was learned on an inappropriate VLAN. This result could prompt you to check the VLAN configuration of the switch. Alternatively, the switch might have learned the sender's MAC address but not on the port that connects to the sender. This unusual symptom suggests you have a duplicate MAC address.

As a reference, Table 4-2 provides a collection of Cisco Catalyst switch commands that can assist you in troubleshooting basic Layer 2 switch-related issues.

Table 4-2 *Cisco Catalyst Switch Troubleshooting Commands*

Command	Description
clear mac address-table dynamic	Clears dynamically learned MAC addresses from a switch's MAC address table; this can help a troubleshooter determine if a previously learned MAC address is relearned
	NOTE: On some versions of Cisco IOS running on Cisco Catalyst switches, the **clear mac address-table** command contains a hyphen between **mac** and **address** (that is, **clear mac-address-table**).
show mac address-table	Displays MAC addresses learned by a switch along with each associated port and VLAN of the MAC address
	NOTE: On some versions of Cisco IOS running on Cisco Catalyst switches, the **show mac address-table** command contains a hyphen between **mac** and **address** (that is, **show mac-address-table**).
show vlan	Shows to which VLANs the ports of a switch belong
show interfaces trunk	Displays which VLANs are permitted on the trunk ports of a switch and which switch ports are configured as trunks
show interfaces switchport	Displays summary information for the ports on a switch, including VLAN and trunk configuration information

Key Topic

Table 4-2 *Cisco Catalyst Switch Troubleshooting Commands*   (*Continued*)

Command	Description
traceroute mac source_MAC_address destination_MAC_address	Uses Cisco Discovery Protocol (CDP) information to produce a list of switches to be transited for traffic traveling from a specified source MAC address to a specified destination MAC address

Examples 4-1, 4-2, and 4-3 provide sample output from a few of the commands described in Table 4-2.

Example 4-1   show mac address-table *Command Output*

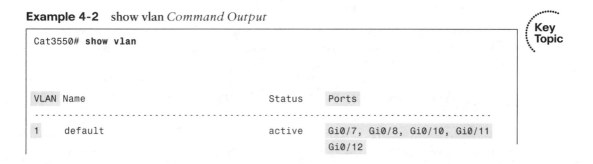

```
Cat3550# show mac address-table
          Mac Address Table
-------------------------------------------

Vlan    Mac Address     Type       Ports
----    -----------     -----      -----
...OUTPUT OMITTED...
   1    0000.865c.7fc2  DYNAMIC    Gi0/7
   1    0009.1260.0aee  DYNAMIC    Gi0/9
   1    0009.b7fa.d1e1  DYNAMIC    Gi0/9
  10    0009.1260.0aee  DYNAMIC    Gi0/9
 261    0004.27d4.0b21  DYNAMIC    Gi0/3
 261    0008.a3b8.945e  DYNAMIC    Gi0/1
 261    0008.a3b8.95c4  DYNAMIC    Gi0/4
 261    0008.a3d1.fbaa  DYNAMIC    Gi0/2
 261    0009.1260.0aee  DYNAMIC    Gi0/9
 262    0004.27d4.0b21  DYNAMIC    Gi0/3
 262    0008.a3b8.945e  DYNAMIC    Gi0/1
 262    0008.a3b8.95c4  DYNAMIC    Gi0/4
 262    0008.a3d1.fbaa  DYNAMIC    Gi0/2
 262    0009.1260.0aee  DYNAMIC    Gi0/9
Total Mac Addresses for this criterion: 48
```

Example 4-2   show vlan *Command Output*

```
Cat3550# show vlan


VLAN Name                             Status    Ports
---------------------------------------------------------------------------
1    default                          active    Gi0/7, Gi0/8, Gi0/10, Gi0/11
                                                Gi0/12
```

```
10    VLAN0010                          active
20    SPAN                             active
261   VLAN0261                         active    Gi0/1, Gi0/2, Gi0/3, Gi0/4
                                                 Gi0/5, Gi0/6
262   VLAN0262                         active    Gi0/1, Gi0/2, Gi0/3, Gi0/4
...OUTPUT OMITTED...
```

Example 4-3   show interfaces trunk *Command Output*

```
Cat3550# show interfaces trunk


Port           Mode          Encapsulation   Status        Native vlan
Gi0/9          desirable     n-isl           trunking      1


Port           Vlans allowed on trunk
Gi0/9                 1-4094


Port                 Vlans allowed and active in management domain
Gi0/9                 1,10,20,261-262


Port                 Vlans in spanning tree forwarding state and not pruned
Gi0/9                 1,10,20,261-262
```

Spanning Tree Protocol Troubleshooting

Administrators of corporate telephone networks often boast about their telephone system (that is, a PBX system) having the *five nines* of availability. If a system has five nines of availability, it is available 99.999 percent of the time, which translates to about five minutes of downtime per year.

Traditionally, corporate data networks struggled to compete with corporate voice networks in terms of availability. Today, however, many networks that traditionally carried only data now carry voice, video, and data. Therefore, availability becomes an even more important design consideration.

To improve network availability at Layer 2, many networks have redundant links between Layer 2 switches. However, unlike Layer 3 packets, Layer 2 frames lack a time-to-live (TTL) field. As a result, a Layer 2 frame can circulate endlessly through a looped Layer 2 topology. Fortunately, IEEE 802.1D STP allows a network to physically have Layer 2 loops while strategically blocking data from flowing over one or more switch ports to prevent the looping of traffic.

This section reviews how an STP topology is dynamically formed. Additionally, this section discusses commands useful in troubleshooting STP issues. Finally, the section concludes with a discussion of troubleshooting EtherChannel technology, which can bond multiple physical connections into a single logical connection.

Reviewing STP Operation

STP prevents Layer 2 loops from occurring in a network, because such an occurrence could result in a broadcast storm or a corruption of a switch's MAC address table. Switches in an STP topology are classified as one of the following:

■ **Root bridge:** The root bridge is a switch elected to act as a reference point for a spanning tree. The switch with the lowest bridge ID (BID) is elected as the root bridge. The BID is made up of a priority value and a MAC address.

■ **Nonroot bridge:** All other switches in the STP topology are considered nonroot bridges.

Figure 4-11 illustrates the root bridge election in a network. Notice that because both bridge priorities are 32768, the switch with the lowest MAC address (that is, SW1) is elected as the root bridge.

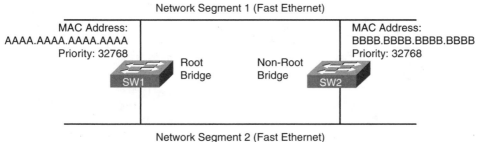

Figure 4-11 *Root Bridge Election*

Ports that interconnect switches in an STP topology are categorized as one of the port types described in Table 4-3 and illustrated in Figure 4-12.

Table 4-3 *STP Port Types*

Port Type	Description
Root port	Every nonroot bridge has a single root port, which is the port on that switch that is closest to the root bridge, in terms of cost.
Designated port	Every network segment has a single designated port, which is the port on that segment that is closest to the root bridge, in terms of cost. Therefore, all ports on a root bridge are designated ports.
Nondesignated port	Nondesignated ports block traffic to create a loop-free topology.

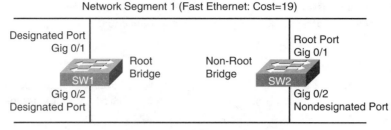

Figure 4-12 *STP Port Types*

Notice the root port for switch SW2 is selected based on the lowest port ID, because the costs of both links are equal. Specifically, each link has a cost of 19, because both links are Fast Ethernet links.

Figure 4-13 shows a similar topology to Figure 4-12. In this figure, however, the top link is running at a speed of 10 Mbps, whereas the bottom link is running at a speed of 100 Mbps. Because switch SW2 seeks to get back to the root bridge (that is, switch SW1) with the least cost, port Gig 0/2 on switch SW2 is selected as the root port.

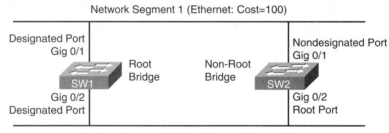

Figure 4-13 *STP with Different Port Costs*

Specifically, port Gig 0/1 has a cost of 100, and Gig 0/2 has a cost of 19. Table 4-4 shows the port costs for various link speeds.

Table 4-4 *Port Costs*

Link Speed	STP Port Cost
10 Mbps (Ethernet)	100
100 Mbps (Fast Ethernet)	19
1 Gbps (Gigabit Ethernet)	4
10 Gbps (Ten Gig Ethernet)	2

Nondesignated ports do not forward traffic during normal operation but do receive bridge protocol data units (BPDUs). BPDU packets contain information on ports, addresses, priorities, and costs and ensure that the data ends up where it was intended to go. BPDU messages are exchanged across bridges to detect loops in a network topology. The loops are then removed by shutting down selected bridge interfaces and placing redundant switch ports in a backup, or blocked, state. If a link in the topology goes down, the nondesignated port detects the link failure and determines whether it needs to transition to the forwarding state.

If a nondesignated port does need to transition to the forwarding state, it does not do so immediately. Rather, it transitions through the following states:

1. **Blocking:** The port remains in the blocking state for 20 seconds by default. During this time the nondesignated port evaluates BPDUs in an attempt to determine its role in the spanning tree.

2. **Listening:** The port moves from the blocking state to the listening state and remains in this state for 15 seconds by default. During this time, the port sources BPDUs, which inform adjacent switches of the port's intent to forward data.

3. **Learning:** The port moves from the listening state to the learning state and remains in this state for 15 seconds by default. During this time, the port begins to add entries to its MAC address table.

4. **Forwarding:** The port moves from the learning state to the forwarding state and begins to forward frames.

Collecting Information About an STP Topology

Some Layer 2 topologies dynamically form a spanning tree using default port costs and bridge priorities. Other Layer 2 topologies have been configured with nondefault port costs or bridge priorities. For example, a network administrator might want to influence a particular switch to become a root bridge to ensure optimal pathing through a Layer 2 topology. The administrator can reduce the bridge priority on the switch he wants to become the root bridge, thus influencing that switch to assume the role of root bridge.

When troubleshooting an STP topology, one of the first tasks is to learn which switch is acting as the root bridge, in addition to learning the port roles on the various switches in the topology. Not only is this information important in understanding how frames are currently flowing through the topology, but comparing the current STP state of a topology to a baseline state can provide clues as to the underlying cause of an issue.

The **show spanning-tree [vlan** *vlan_id*] command can display information about the STP state of a switch. Consider Example 4-4, which shows the output from the **show spanning-tree vlan 1** command. The VLAN is specified because Cisco Catalyst switches, by default, use per-VLAN spanning tree (PVST). PVST allows a switch to run a separate STP instance for each VLAN. The output in Example 4-4 shows that switch SW2 is not the root bridge for the spanning tree of VLAN1, because the MAC address of the root bridge is different from the MAC address of switch SW2. The Gig 0/9 port of switch SW2 is the root port of the switch, whereas port Gig 0/10 is a nondesignated port. (That is, it is a blocking port.) Note that the port cost of Gig 0/9 is 19, whereas the port cost of Gig 0/10 is 100.

Key Topic

Example 4-4   show spanning-tree vlan *Command Output*

```
SW2# show spanning-tree vlan 1



VLAN0001
  Spanning tree enabled protocol ieee
  Root ID    Priority    32768
             Address     0009.122e.4181
             Cost        19
             Port        9 (GigabitEthernet0/9)
             Hello Time  2 sec  Max Age 20 sec  Forward Delay 15 sec

  Bridge ID  Priority    32769  (priority 32768 sys-id-ext 1)
             Address     000d.28e4.7c80
             Hello Time  2 sec  Max Age 20 sec  Forward Delay 15 sec
             Aging Time 300


Interface           Role Sts Cost      Prio.Nbr Type
------------------------------------------------------------------------

Gi0/9               Root FWD 19        128.9    P2p
Gi0/10              Altn BLK 100       128.10   Shr
```

The **show spanning-tree interface** *interface_id* **detail** command shows information contained in BPDUs. Also, as shown in Example 4-5, this command displays the number of BPDUs sent and received.

Example 4-5   show spanning-tree interface *Command Output*

```
SW2# show spanning-tree interface gig 0/9 detail
 Port 9 (GigabitEthernet0/9) of VLAN0001 is root forwarding
   Port path cost 19, Port priority 128, Port Identifier 128.9.
   Designated root has priority 32768, address 0009.122e.4181
   Designated bridge has priority 32768, address 0009.122e.4181
   Designated port id is 128.303, designated path cost 0
   Timers: message age 2, forward delay 0, hold 0
   Number of transitions to forwarding state: 1
   Link type is point-to-point by default
   BPDU: sent 1, received 1245
```

STP Troubleshooting Issues

If STP fails to operate correctly, Layer 2 frames can endlessly circulate through a network. This behavior can lead to a couple of major issues: MAC address table corruption and broadcast storms.

Corruption of a Switch's MAC Address Table

The MAC address table of a switch can dynamically learn what MAC addresses are available off of its ports; however, in the event of an STP failure, the MAC address table of a switch can become corrupted. To illustrate, consider Figure 4-14. PC1 is transmitting traffic to PC2. When the frame sent from PC1 is transmitted on segment A, the frame is seen on the Gig 0/1 ports of switches SW1 and SW2, causing both switches to add an entry to their MAC address tables associating a MAC address of AAAA.AAAA.AAAA with port Gig 0/1. Because STP is not functioning, both switches then forward the frame out segment B. As a result, PC2 receives two copies of the frame. Also, switch SW1 sees the frame forwarded out the Gig 0/2 port of switch SW2. Because the frame has a source MAC address of AAAA.AAAA.AAAA, switch SW1 incorrectly updates its MAC address table indicating that a MAC address of AAAA.AAAA.AAAA resides off port Gig 0/2. Similarly, switch SW2 sees the frame forwarded onto segment B by switch SW1 on its Gig 0/2 port. Therefore, switch SW2 also incorrectly updates its MAC address table.

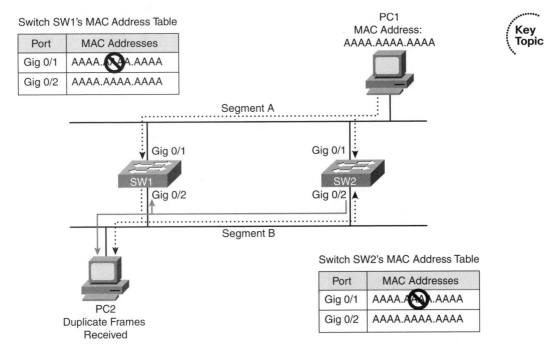

Figure 4-14 *MAC Address Table Corruption*

Broadcast Storms

As previously mentioned, when a switch receives a broadcast frame (that is, a frame destined for a MAC address of FFFF.FFFF.FFFF), the switch floods the frame out all switch ports except the port on which the frame was received. Because a Layer 2 frame does not have a TTL field, a broadcast frame endlessly circulates through the Layer 2 topology, consuming resources on both switches and attached devices (for example, user PCs).

Figure 4-15 illustrates how a broadcast storm can form in a Layer 2 topology when STP is not functioning correctly.

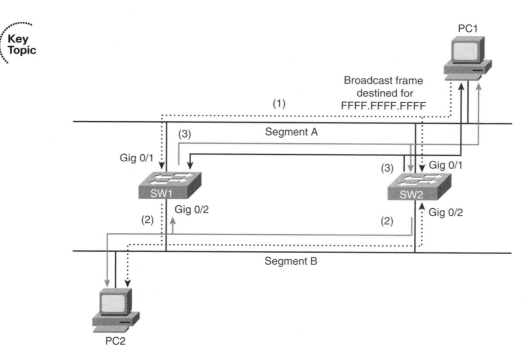

Figure 4-15 *Broadcast Storm*

1. PC1 sends a broadcast frame onto Segment A, and the frame enters each switch on port Gig 0/1.

2. Both switches flood a copy of the broadcast frame out of their Gig 0/2 ports (that is, onto Segment B), causing PC2 to receive two copies of the broadcast frame.

3. Both switches receive a copy of the broadcast frame on their Gig 0/2 ports (that is, from Segment B) and flood the frame out of their Gig 0/1 ports (that is, onto Segment A), causing PC1 to receive two copies of the broadcast frame.

This behavior continues, as the broadcast frame copies continue to loop through the network. The performance of PC1 and PC2 is impacted, because they also continue to receive copies of the broadcast frame.

Troubleshooting EtherChannel

An exception to STP operation can be made if two switches are interconnected via multiple physical links and those links are configured as an *EtherChannel*. An EtherChannel logically combines the bandwidth of multiple physical interfaces into a logical connection between switches, as illustrated in Figure 4-16. Specifically, Figure 4-16 shows four Gigabit Ethernet links logically bonded into a single EtherChannel link.

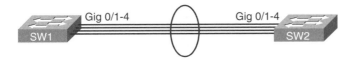

Figure 4-16   *EtherChannel*

When multiple ports are combined into a logical EtherChannel, STP treats the logical bundle as a single port for STP calculation purposes. Following are common troubleshooting targets to consider when troubleshooting an EtherChannel issue:

- **Mismatched port configurations:** The configurations of all ports making up an EtherChannel, on both switches, should be identical. For example, all ports should have the same speed, duplex, trunk mode, and native VLAN configurations.

- **Mismatched EtherChannel configuration:** Both switches forming the EtherChannel should be configured for the same EtherChannel negotiation protocol. The options are Link Aggregation Control Protocol (LACP) and Port Aggregation Protocol (PAgP).

- **Inappropriate EtherChannel distribution algorithm:** EtherChannel determines which physical link to use to transmit frames based on a hash calculation. The hashing approach selected should distribute the load fairly evenly across all physical links. For example, a hash calculation might be based only on the destination MAC address of a frame. If the frames are destined for only a few different MAC addresses, the load distribution could be uneven.

Trouble Ticket: STP

This trouble ticket is the first of a series of trouble tickets presented throughout the remainder of the book. All the trouble tickets are based on the same basic network topology, although addressing and links might vary for some trouble tickets.

All trouble tickets begin with a problem report and a network topology diagram. Some of the trouble tickets provide you with baseline data, and all the trouble tickets offer output from appropriate verification commands (for example, **show** or **debug** commands) that you can examine.

After you hypothesize the underlying cause of the network issue and formulate a solution, you can check the *Suggested Solution* comments to confirm your hypothesis. Realize, however, that some trouble tickets might be resolvable by more than one method. Therefore, your solution might be different from the suggested solution.

Trouble Ticket #1

You receive the following trouble ticket:

> Users on network 192.168.1.0/24 are experiencing latency or no connectivity when attempting to reach network 10.1.2.0/24.

This trouble ticket references the topology shown in Figure 4-17.

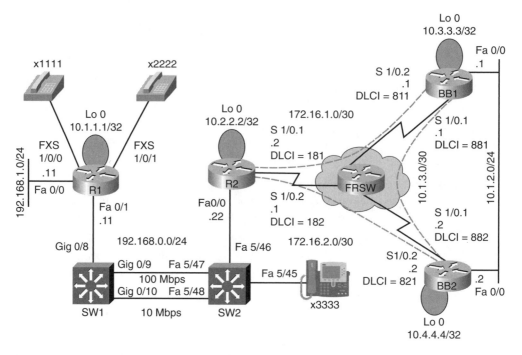

Figure 4-17   *Topology for Trouble Ticket #1*

As you follow the path of the traffic from network 192.168.1.0/24 to 10.1.2.0/24, you notice high port utilization levels on switches SW1 and SW2. Therefore, you decide to investigate these switches further.

You have previously issued **show** commands on these switches as part of your baseline collection process. A selection of the **show** command output is presented in Examples 4-6 and 4-7.

Example 4-6   *Baseline* show *Output from Switch SW1*

```
SW1# show spanning-tree vlan 1

VLAN0001
  Spanning tree enabled protocol ieee
  Root ID    Priority    32768
             Address     0009.122e.4181
             Cost        19
             Port        9 (GigabitEthernet0/9)
             Hello Time  2 sec  Max Age 20 sec  Forward Delay 15 sec
  Bridge ID  Priority    32769  (priority 32768 sys-id-ext 1)
             Address     000d.28e4.7c80
             Hello Time  2 sec  Max Age 20 sec  Forward Delay 15 sec
             Aging Time 300
```

```
Interface          Role Sts Cost      Prio.Nbr Type
------------------------------------------------------------------------
Gi0/8              Desg FWD 19        128.8    P2p
Gi0/9              Root FWD 19        128.9    P2p
Gi0/10             Altn BLK 100       128.10   Shr


SW1# show spanning-tree summary
Switch is in pvst mode
Root bridge for: none
Extended system ID            is enabled
Portfast Default              is disabled
PortFast BPDU Guard Default   is disabled
Portfast BPDU Filter Default  is disabled
Loopguard Default             is disabled
EtherChannel misconfig guard  is enabled
UplinkFast                    is disabled
BackboneFast                  is disabled
Configured Pathcost method used is short


Name                    Blocking Listening Learning Forwarding STP Active
----------------------------------------------------------------------
VLAN0001                     1       0        0         2          3
----------------------------------------------------------------------
1 vlan                       1       0        0         2          3
SW1# show spanning-tree interface gig 0/10 detail
 Port 10 (GigabitEthernet0/10) of VLAN0001 is alternate blocking
   Port path cost 100, Port priority 128, Port Identifier 128.10.
   Designated root has priority 32768, address 0009.122e.4181
   Designated bridge has priority 32768, address 0009.122e.4181
   Designated port id is 128.304, designated path cost 0
   Timers: message age 1, forward delay 0, hold 0
   Number of transitions to forwarding state: 0
   Link type is shared by default
   BPDU: sent 1, received 276
```

Example 4-7 *Baseline* show *Output from Switch SW2*

```
SW2# show spanning-tree vlan 1

VLAN0001
  Spanning tree enabled protocol ieee
  Root ID    Priority    32768
             Address     0009.122e.4181
```

```
                        This bridge is the root
                        Hello Time    2 sec  Max Age 20 sec  Forward Delay 15 sec


        Bridge ID  Priority    32768
                   Address     0009.122e.4181
                   Hello Time    2 sec  Max Age 20 sec  Forward Delay 15 sec
                   Aging Time 300


  Interface            Role Sts Cost      Prio.Nbr Type
  ------------------------------------------------------------------------------
  Fa5/46               Desg FWD 19        128.302  Shr
  Fa5/47               Desg FWD 19        128.303  P2p
  Fa5/48               Desg FWD 100       128.304  Shr
```

When you connect to the console of switch SW1, you receive the console messages displayed in Example 4-8.

Example 4-8 *Console Messages on Switch SW1*

```
SW1#
00:15:45: %SW_MATM-4-MACFLAP_NOTIF: Host 0009.b7fa.d1e1 in vlan 1 is flapping
  between port Gi0/8 and port Gi0/9
SW1#
00:16:35: %SW_MATM-4-MACFLAP_NOTIF: Host 0009.b7fa.d1e1 in vlan 1 is flapping
  between port Gi0/8 and port Gi0/9
SW1#
00:16:37: %SW_MATM-4-MACFLAP_NOTIF: Host c001.0e8c.0000 in vlan 1 is flapping
  between port Gi0/9 and port Gi0/10
SW1#
00:16:41: %SW_MATM-4-MACFLAP_NOTIF: Host 0009.b7fa.d1e1 in vlan 1 is flapping
  between port Gi0/8 and port Gi0/9
```

You also issue the **show spanning-tree vlan 1** command on switches SW1 and SW2, as shown in Examples 4-9 and 4-10.

Example 4-9 show spanning-tree vlan 1 *Command Output on Switch SW1*

```
SW1# show spanning-tree vlan 1

Spanning tree instance(s) for vlan 1 does not exist.
```

Example 4-10   show spanning-tree vlan 1 *Command Output on Switch SW2*

```
SW2# show spanning-tree vlan 1

Spanning tree instance(s) for vlan 1 does not exist.
```

Take a moment to look through the baseline information, the topology, and the **show** command output. Then hypothesize the underlying cause for the connectivity issue reported in the trouble ticket. Finally, on a separate sheet of paper, write out a proposed action plan for resolving the reported issue.

Suggested Solution

The %SW_MATM-4-MACFLAP_NOTIF console message appearing on switch SW1 indicates that the port of a MAC address in the MAC address table of switch SW1 is flapping between a couple of ports. This is the MAC address table corruption issue discussed previously. The underlying cause of such an issue was STP not functioning correctly.

This suspicion is confirmed from the output in the **show spanning-tree vlan 1** command, issued on switches SW1 and SW2, which indicates that there is no STP instance for VLAN 1 on either switch. Therefore, as a solution, STP could be enabled for VLAN 1 on both switches, which is depicted in Examples 4-11 and 4-12.

Example 4-11   *Enabling STP for VLAN 1 on Switch SW1*

```
SW1# conf term
Enter configuration commands, one per line.   End with CNTL/Z.
SW1(config)# spanning-tree vlan 1
SW1(config)# end
```

Example 4-12   *Enabling STP for VLAN 1 on Switch SW2*

```
SW2# conf term
Enter configuration commands, one per line.   End with CNTL/Z.
SW2(config)# spanning-tree vlan 1
SW2(config)# end
```

After giving STP sufficient time to converge, after the enabling of STP for VLAN 1, the **show spanning-tree vlan 1** is once again issued on switches SW1 and SW2, as illustrated in Examples 4-13 and 4-14. The output in these examples confirms that STP is now functioning correctly.

Example 4-13   *Checking the STP Status for VLAN 1 on Switch SW1*

```
SW1# show spanning-tree vlan 1
...OUTPUT OMITTED...
```

```
Interface         Role Sts Cost      Prio.Nbr Type
----------------------------------------------------------------------
Gi0/8             Desg FWD 19        128.8    P2p
Gi0/9             Root FWD 19        128.9    P2p
Gi0/10            Altn BLK 100       128.10   Shr
```

Example 4-14   *Checking the STP Status for VLAN 1 on Switch SW2*

```
SW2# show spanning-tree vlan 1
...OUTPUT OMITTED...
Interface         Role Sts Cost      Prio.Nbr Type
----------------------------------------------------------------------
Fa5/46            Desg FWD 19        128.302  Shr
Fa5/47            Desg FWD 19        128.303  P2p
Fa5/48            Desg FWD 100       128.304  Shr
```

Exam Preparation Tasks

Review All the Key Topics

Review the most important topics from inside the chapter, noted with the Key Topics icon in the outer margin of the page. Table 4-5 lists these key topics and the page numbers where each is found.

Key Topic

Table 4-5   *Key Topics for Chapter 4*

Key Topic Element	Description	Page Number
List	Possible reasons for a Layer 2 issue	87
Table 4-2	Cisco Catalyst switch troubleshooting commands	88
Example 4-1	The **show mac address-table** command	89
Example 4-2	The **show vlan** command	89
Example 4-3	The **show interfaces trunk** command	90
List	STP bridge types	91
Table 4-3	STP port types	91
Table 4-4	STP port costs	92
List	STP forwarding states	93
Example 4-4	The **show spanning-tree vlan** command	94
Figure 4-14	MAC address table corruption	95
Figure 4-15	Broadcast storm	96
List	Common EtherChannel issues	97

Complete Tables and Lists from Memory

Print a copy of Appendix B, "Memory Tables" (found on the CD), or at least the section for this chapter, and complete the tables and lists from memory. Appendix C, "Memory Tables Answer Key," also on the CD, includes completed tables and lists to check your work.

Define Key Terms

Define the following key terms from this chapter, and check your answers in the Glossary:

Media Access Control (MAC) address, virtual LAN (VLAN), Address Resolution Protocol (ARP), trunk, Spanning Tree Protocol (STP), root bridge, root port, designated port, non-designated port, blocking, listening, learning, forwarding, EtherChannel

Command Reference to Check Your Memory

This section includes the most important EXEC commands covered in this chapter. To determine how well you have memorized the commands as a side effect of your other studies, cover the left side of the table with a piece of paper; read the descriptions on the right side; and see whether you remember the command.

Table 4-6   *Chapter 4 EXEC Command Reference*

Command	Description
clear mac address-table dynamic	Clears dynamically learned MAC addresses from the MAC address table of a switch; this can allow a troubleshooter to determine whether a previously learned MAC address is relearned
	NOTE: On some versions of Cisco IOS running on Cisco Catalyst switches, the **clear mac address-table** command contains a hyphen between **mac** and **address** (that is, **clear mac-address-table**).
show vlan	Shows to which VLANs the ports of a switch belong
show interfaces trunk	Displays what VLANs are permitted on the trunk ports of a switch and what switch ports are configured as trunks
show interfaces switchport	Displays summary information for the ports on a switch, including VLAN and trunk configuration information
traceroute mac source_MAC_ address destination_MAC_address	Uses CDP information to produce a list of switches to be transited for traffic traveling from a specified source MAC address to a specified destination MAC address
show spanning-tree [vlan vlan_id]	Displays information about the STP state of a switch
show spanning-tree interface interface_id detail	Shows information contained in BPDUs, in addition to the number of BPDUs sent and received

This chapter covers the following subjects:

Resolving InterVLAN Routing Issues: This section begins by contrasting Layer 3 switches and routers. Troubleshooting procedures are also compared for these platforms. Lastly, this section discusses two approaches for routing packets using Layer 3 switches: routed ports and Switched Virtual Interfaces (SVIs).

Router Redundancy Troubleshooting: This section discusses three approaches to providing first-hop router redundancy. Options include: Hot Standby Routing Protocol (HSRP), Virtual Router Redundancy Protocol (VRRP), and Gateway Load Balancing Protocol (GLBP). Troubleshooting strategies are discussed for HSRP with suggestions on how to modify those strategies for troubleshooting VRRP and GLBP.

Cisco Catalyst Switch Performance Tuning: This section examines the architecture of a Cisco Catalyst switch and points out different architectural components that could become troubleshooting targets. Also, you are presented with a series of **show** commands used to gather information about different aspects of a switch's performance.

Trouble Ticket: HSRP: This section presents you with a trouble ticket and an associated topology. You are also given **show** and **debug** command output (baseline output and output collected after a reported issue occurred). Based on the information provided, you hypothesize an underlying cause for the reported issue and develop a solution. You can then compare your solution with a suggested solution.

CHAPTER 5

Advanced Cisco Catalyst Switch Troubleshooting

This chapter builds on Chapter 4, "Basic Cisco Catalyst Switch Troubleshooting," by continuing to focus on troubleshooting Cisco Catalyst Switch platforms. Although the term *switch* might conjure up the image of a Layer 2 device, many modern switches can also route. Specifically, many switches can make forwarding decisions based on Layer 3 information (for example, IP address information). Therefore, this chapter starts by discussing a couple of ways to make a Layer 3 (or multilayer) switch perform routing.

Next, because many Layer 3 switches reside in a wiring closet, these switches might very well act as the default gateway for endpoints (for example, user PCs). Rather than having this switch (or perhaps a router at the distribution layer) become a single point of failure for endpoints relying on the IP address maintained by that switch (or router), you can take advantage of a first-hop redundancy protocol. A first-hop redundancy protocol allows clients to continue to reach their default gateway's IP address, even if the Layer 3 switch or router that had been servicing that IP address becomes available. This chapter contrasts three first-hop redundancy protocols and discusses the troubleshooting of first-hop redundancy.

Often a trouble reported by a user comes in some variation of, "The network is slow." Although such a description is less than insightful, troubleshooters are likely to encounter network performance issues resulting in a poor user experience. This chapter focuses on troubleshooting performance problems that originate from a Cisco Catalyst switch.

Finally, this chapter presents another trouble ticket. This trouble ticket describes a first-hop redundancy protocol not operating as expected. Given a collection of **show** and **debug** output, you are challenged to determine the underlying cause of the issue and formulate a solution.

"Do I Know This Already?" Quiz

The "Do I Know This Already?" quiz helps you determine your level of knowledge of this chapter's topics before you begin. Table 5-1 details the major topics discussed in this chapter and their corresponding quiz questions.

Table 5-1 *"Do I Know This Already?" Section-to-Question Mapping*

Foundation Topics Section	Questions
Resolving InterVLAN Routing Issues	1–3

continues

Table 5-1 *"Do I Know This Already?" Section-to-Question Mapping   (Continued)*

Foundation Topics Section	Questions
Router Redundancy Troubleshooting	4–7
Cisco Catalyst Switch Performance Troubleshooting	8–10

1. What are two differences between Layer 3 switches and routers? (Choose two.)

   a. Layer 3 switches do not maintain a routing table.

   b. Layer 3 switches usually forward traffic faster than routers.

   c. Layer 3 switches support more interface types than routers.

   d. Layer 3 switches usually support fewer features than routers.

2. What type of special memory is used by Layer 3 switches, and not routers, that supports very rapid route lookups?

   a. NBAR

   b. TCAM

   c. NetFlow

   d. MIB

3. What type of interface can be created on a Layer 3 switch to support routing between VLANs on that switch?

   a. BVI

   b. VPI

   c. SVI

   d. VCI

4. What is the default priority for an HSRP interface?

   a. 0

   b. 100

   c. 256

   d. 1000

5. What is the name for the router in a VRRP virtual router group that is actively forwarding traffic on behalf of the virtual router group?

   a. virtual forwarder

   b. active virtual gateway

   c. virtual router master

   d. active virtual forwarder

6. Which of the following statements is true concerning GLBP?

  a. GLBP is an industry-standard first-hop redundancy protocol.

  b. GLBP allows multiple routers to simultaneously forward traffic for the group of GLBP routers.

  c. The active virtual forwarder in a GLBP group is responsible for responding to ARP requests with different MAC addresses.

  d. A GLBP group has multiple active virtual gateways.

7. Which of the following are Cisco proprietary first-hop router redundancy protocols? (Choose two.)

  a. HSRP

  b. VRRP

  c. GLBP

  d. DSCP

8. What are two components of a switch's control plane? (Choose two.)

  a. Backplane

  b. Memory

  c. CPU

  d. Forwarding logic

9. Which three of the following are situations when a switch's TCAM would punt a packet to the switch's CPU? (Choose the three best answers.)

  a. OSPF sends a multicast routing update.

  b. An administrator Telnets to a switch.

  c. An ACL is applied to a switch port.

  d. A switch's TCAM has reached capacity.

10. The output of a **show processes cpu** command on a switch displays the following in the first line of the output:

```
CPU utilization for five seconds: 10%/7%; one minute: 12%; five minutes: 6%
```

Based on the output, what percent of the switch's CPU is being consumed with interrupts?

  a. 10 percent

  b. 7 percent

  c. 12 percent

  d. 6 percent

Foundation Topics

Resolving InterVLAN Routing Issues

As mentioned in Chapter 4, "Basic Cisco Catalyst Switch Troubleshooting," for traffic to pass from one VLAN to another VLAN, that traffic has to be routed. Several years ago, one popular approach to performing interVLAN routing with a Layer 2 switch was to create a *router on a stick* topology, where a Layer 2 switch is interconnected with a router via a trunk connection, as seen in Figure 5-1.

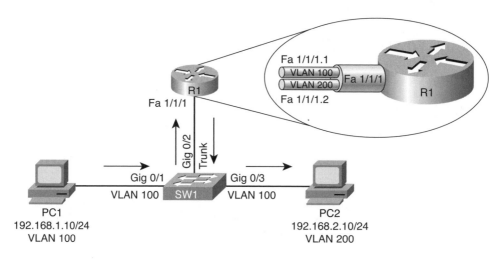

Figure 5-1   *Router on a Stick*

In Figure 5-1, router R1's Fast Ethernet 1/1/1 interface has two subinterfaces, one for each VLAN. Router R1 can route between VLANs 100 and 200, while simultaneously receiving and transmitting traffic over the trunk connection to the switch.

More recently, many switches have risen above their humble Layer 2 beginnings and started to route traffic. Some literature refers to these switches that can route as *Layer 3 switches*. Other sources might call such switches *multilayer switches*, because of the capability of a switch to make forwarding decisions based on information from multiple layers of the OSI model.

This section refers to these switches as Layer 3 switches because the focus is on the capability of the switches to route traffic based on Layer 3 information (that is, IP address information). Specifically, this section discusses troubleshooting Layer 3 switch issues and contrasts troubleshooting a Layer 3 switch versus a router.

Contrasting Layer 3 Switches with Routers

Because a Layer 3 switch performs many of the same functions as a router, it is important for a troubleshooter to distinguish between commonalities and differences in these two platforms.

Table 5-2 lists the characteristics that Layer 3 switches and routers have in common, as well as those characteristics that differ.

Table 5-2 *Layer 3 Switch and Router Characteristics: Compare and Contrast*

Key Topic

Layer 3 Switch/Router Shared Characteristics	Layer 3 Switch/Router Differentiating Characteristics
Both can build and maintain a routing table using both statically configured routes and dynamic routing protocols.	Routers usually support a wider selection of interface types (for example, non-Ethernet interfaces).
Both can make packet forwarding decisions based on Layer 3 information (for example, IP addresses).	Switches leverage application-specific integrated circuits (ASIC) to approach wire speed throughput. Therefore, most Layer 3 switches can forward traffic faster than their router counterparts.
	A Cisco IOS version running on routers typically supports more features than a Cisco IOS version running on a Layer 3 switch, because many switches lack the specialized hardware required to run many of the features available on a router.

Control Plane and Data Plane Troubleshooting

Many router and Layer 3 switch operations can be categorized as control plane or data plane operations. For example, routing protocols operate in a router's control plane, whereas the actual forwarding of data is handled by a router's data plane.

Fortunately, the processes involved in troubleshooting control plane operations are identical on both Layer 3 switch and router platforms. For example, the same command-line interface (CLI) commands could be used to troubleshoot an Open Shortest Path First (OSPF) issue on both types of platforms.

Data plane troubleshooting, however, can vary between Layer 3 switches and routers. For example, if you were troubleshooting data throughput issues, the commands you issued might vary between types of platforms, because Layer 3 switches and routers have fundamental differences in the way traffic is forwarded through the device.

First, consider how a router uses Cisco Express Forwarding (CEF) to efficiently forward traffic through a router. CEF creates a couple of tables that reside at the data plane. These are the *forwarding information base* (FIB) and the *adjacency table*. These tables are constructed from information collected from the router's control plane (for example, the control plane's IP routing table and Address Resolution Protocol [ARP] cache). When troubleshooting a router, you might check control plane operations with commands such as **show ip route**. However, if the observed traffic behavior seems to contradict information shown in the output of control plane verification commands, you might want to examine information contained in the router's CEF Forwarding Information Base (FIB) and adjacency tables. You can use the commands presented in Table 5-3 to view information contained in a router's FIB and adjacency table.

Table 5-3 *Router Data Plan Verification Commands*

Command	Description
show ip cef	Displays the router's Layer 3 forwarding information, in addition to multicast, broadcast, and local IP addresses.
show adjacency	Verifies that a valid adjacency exists for a connected host.

Example 5-1 and Example 5-2 provide sample output from the **show ip cef** and **show adjacency** commands, respectively.

Example 5-1 **show ip cef** *Command Output*

```
R4# show ip cef
Prefix              Next Hop         Interface
0.0.0.0/0           10.3.3.1         FastEthernet0/0
0.0.0.0/32          receive
10.1.1.0/24         10.3.3.1         FastEthernet0/0
10.1.1.2/32         10.3.3.1         FastEthernet0/0
10.3.3.0/24         attached         FastEthernet0/0
10.3.3.0/32         receive
10.3.3.1/32         10.3.3.1         FastEthernet0/0
10.3.3.2/32         receive
10.3.3.255/32       receive
10.4.4.0/24         10.3.3.1         FastEthernet0/0
10.5.5.0/24         10.3.3.1         FastEthernet0/0
10.7.7.0/24         10.3.3.1         FastEthernet0/0
10.7.7.2/32         10.3.3.1         FastEthernet0/0
10.8.8.0/24         attached         FastEthernet0/1
10.8.8.0/32         receive
10.8.8.1/32         receive
10.8.8.4/32         10.8.8.4         FastEthernet0/1
10.8.8.5/32         10.8.8.5         FastEthernet0/1
10.8.8.6/32         10.8.8.6         FastEthernet0/1
10.8.8.7/32         10.8.8.7         FastEthernet0/1
10.8.8.255/32       receive
192.168.0.0/24      10.3.3.1         FastEthernet0/0
224.0.0.0/4         drop
224.0.0.0/24        receive
255.255.255.255/32  receive
```

Example 5-2 show adjacency *Command Output*

```
R4# show adjacency
Protocol  Interface              Address
IP        FastEthernet0/0        10.3.3.1(21)
IP        FastEthernet0/1        10.8.8.6(5)
IP        FastEthernet0/1        10.8.8.7(5)
IP        FastEthernet0/1        10.8.8.4(5)
IP        FastEthernet0/1        10.8.8.5(5)
```

Although many Layer 3 switches also leverage CEF to efficiently route packets, some Cisco Catalyst switches take the information contained in CEF's FIB and adjacency table and compile that information into Ternary Content Addressable Memory (TCAM). This special memory type uses a mathematical algorithm to very quickly look up forwarding information.

The specific way a switch's TCAM operates depends on the switch platform. However, from a troubleshooting perspective, you can examine information stored in a switch's TCAM using the **show platform** series of commands on Cisco Catalyst 3560, 3750, and 4500 switches. Similarly, TCAM information for a Cisco Catalyst 6500 switch can be viewed with the **show mls cef** series of commands.

Comparing Routed Switch Ports and Switched Virtual Interfaces

On a router, an interface often has an IP address, and that IP address might be acting as a default gateway to hosts residing off of that interface. However, if you have a Layer 3 switch with multiple ports belonging to a VLAN, where should the IP address be configured?

You can configure the IP address for a collection of ports belonging to a VLAN under a virtual VLAN interface. This virtual VLAN interface is called a *Switched Virtual Interface* (SVI). Figure 5-2 shows a topology using SVIs, and Example 5-3 shows the corresponding configuration. Notice that two SVIs are created: one for each VLAN (that is, VLAN 100 and VLAN 200). An IP address is assigned to an SVI by going into interface configuration mode for a VLAN. In this example, because both SVIs are local to the switch, the switch's routing table knows how to forward traffic between members of the two VLANs.

Example 5-3 *SVI Configuration*

Key Topic

```
Cat3550# show run
...OUTPUT OMITTED...
!
interface GigabitEthernet0/7
 switchport access vlan 100
 switchport mode access
!
interface GigabitEthernet0/8
 switchport access vlan 100
 switchport mode access
```

```
!
interface GigabitEthernet0/9
 switchport access vlan 200
 switchport mode access
!
interface GigabitEthernet0/10
 switchport access vlan 200
 switchport mode access
!
...OUTPUT OMITTED...
!
interface Vlan100
 ip address 192.168.1.1 255.255.255.0
!
interface Vlan200
 ip address 192.168.2.1 255.255.255.0
```

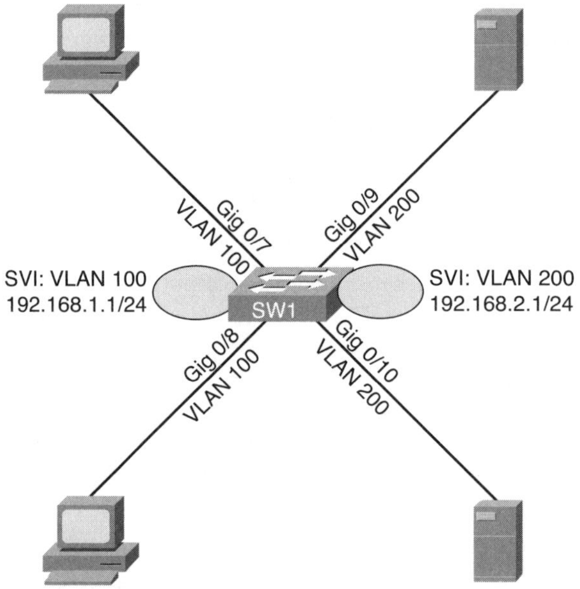

Figure 5-2 *SVI Used for Routing*

Although SVIs can route between VLANs configured on a switch, a Layer 3 switch can be configured to act more as a router (for example, in an environment where you are replacing a router with a Layer 3 switch) by using *routed ports* on the switch. Because the ports on many Cisco Catalyst switches default to operating as switch ports, you can issue the **no switchport** command in interface configuration mode to convert a switch port to a routed port. Figure 5-3 and Example 5-4 illustrate a Layer 3 switch with its Gigabit Ethernet 0/9 and 0/10 ports configured as routed ports.

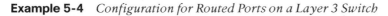

Figure 5-3   *Routed Ports on a Layer 3 Switch*

Example 5-4   *Configuration for Routed Ports on a Layer 3 Switch*

```
Cat3550# show run
...OUTPUT OMITTED...
!
interface GigabitEthernet0/9
 no switchport
 ip address 192.168.1.2 255.255.255.0
!
interface GigabitEthernet0/10
 no switchport
 ip address 192.168.2.2 255.255.255.0
!
...OUTPUT OMITTED...
```

When troubleshooting Layer 3 switching issues, keep the following distinctions in mind between SVIs and routed ports:

■   A routed port is considered to be in the down state if it is not operational at both Layer 1 and Layer 2.

■   An SVI is considered to be in a down state only when none of the ports in the corresponding VLAN are active.

■   A routed port does not run switch port protocols such as Spanning Tree Protocol (STP) or Dynamic Trunking Protocol (DTP).

Router Redundancy Troubleshooting

Many devices, such as PCs, are configured with a *default gateway*. The default gateway parameter identifies the IP address of a next-hop router. As a result, if that router were to become unavailable, devices that relied on the default gateway's IP address would be unable to send traffic off their local subnet.

Fortunately, Cisco offers technologies that provide next-hop gateway redundancy. These technologies include HSRP, VRRP, and GLBP.

This section reviews the operation of these three *first-hop redundancy protocols* and provides a collection of Cisco IOS commands that can be used to troubleshoot an issue with one of these three protocols.

Note that although this section discusses *router* redundancy, keep in mind that the term *router* is referencing a device making forwarding decisions based on Layer 3 information.

Therefore, in your environment, a Layer 3 switch might be used in place of a router to support HSRP, VRRP, or GLBP.

HSRP

Hot Standby Router Protocol (HSRP) uses virtual IP and MAC addresses. One router, known as the *active router*, services requests destined for the virtual IP and MAC addresses. Another router, known as the *standby router*, can service such requests in the event the active router becomes unavailable. Figure 5-4 illustrates a basic HSRP topology.

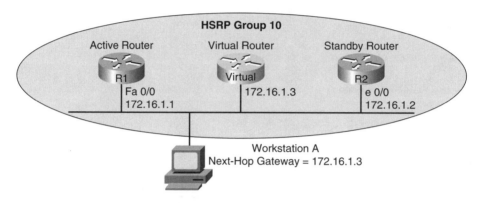

Figure 5-4 *Basic HSRP Operation*

Examples 5-5 and 5-6 show the HSRP configuration for routers R1 and R2.

Example 5-5 *HSRP Configuration on Router R1*

```
R1# show run
...OUTPUT OMITTED...
interface FastEthernet0/0
 ip address 172.16.1.1 255.255.255.0
 standby 10 ip 172.16.1.3
 standby 10 priority 150
 standby 10 preempt
...OUTPUT OMITTED...
```

Example 5-6 *HSRP Configuration on Router R2*

```
R2# show run
...OUTPUT OMITTED...
interface Ethernet0/0
 ip address 172.16.1.2 255.255.255.0
 standby 10 ip 172.16.1.3
...OUTPUT OMITTED...
```

Notice that both routers R1 and R2 have been configured with the same virtual IP address of 172.16.1.3 for an HSRP group of 10. Router R1 is configured to be the active router with the **standby 10 priority 150** command. Router R2 has a default HSRP priority of 100 for group 10, and with HSRP, higher priority values are more preferable. Also, notice that router R1 is configured with the **standby 10 preempt** command, which means that if router R1 loses its active status, perhaps because it is powered off, it will regain its active status when it again becomes available.

Converging After a Router Failure

By default, HSRP sends hello messages every three seconds. Also, if the standby router does not hear a hello message within ten seconds by default, the standby router considers the active router to be down. The standby router then assumes the active role.

Although this ten-second convergence time applies for a router becoming unavailable for a reason such as a power outage or a link failure, convergence happens more rapidly if an interface is administratively shut down. Specifically, an active router sends a *resign* message if its active HSRP interface is shut down.

Also, consider the addition of another router to the network segment whose HSRP priority for group 10 is higher than 150. If it were configured for preemption, the newly added router would send a *coup* message, to inform the active router that the newly added router was going to take on the active role. If, however, the newly added router were not configured for preemption, the currently active router would remain the active router.

HSRP Verification and Troubleshooting

When verifying an HSRP configuration or troubleshooting an HSRP issue, you should begin by determining the following information about the HSRP group under inspection:

■ Which router is the active router

■ Which routers, if any, are configured with the preempt option

■ What is the virtual IP address

■ What is the virtual MAC address

The **show standby brief** command can be used to show a router's HSRP interface, HSRP group number, and preemption configuration. Additionally, this command identifies the router that is currently the active router, the router that is currently the standby router, and the virtual IP address for the HSRP group. Examples 5-7 and 5-8 show the output from the **show standby brief** command issued on routers R1 and R2, where router R1 is currently the active router.

Example 5-7   show standby brief *Command Output on Router R1*

```
R1# show standby brief
                     P indicates configured to preempt.
                     |
Interface   Grp Prio P State    Active       Standby      Virtual IP
Fa0/0       10  150  P Active   local        172.16.1.2   172.16.1.3
```

Example 5-8   show standby brief *Command Output on Router R2*

```
R2# show standby brief
                    P indicates configured to preempt.
                    |
Interface   Grp Prio P State    Active       Standby      Virtual IP
Et0/0       10  100    Standby  172.16.1.1   local        172.16.1.3
```

In addition to an interface's HSRP group number, the interface's state, and the HSRP group's virtual IP address, the **show standby** *interface_id* command also displays the HSRP group's virtual MAC address. Issuing this command on router R1, as shown in Example 5-9, shows that the virtual MAC address for HSRP group 10 is **0000.0c07.ac0a**.

Example 5-9   show standby fa 0/0 *Command Output on Router R1*

```
R1# show standby fa 0/0
FastEthernet0/0 - Group 10
  State is Active
    1 state change, last state change 01:20:00
  Virtual IP address is 172.16.1.3
  Active virtual MAC address is 0000.0c07.ac0a
    Local virtual MAC address is 0000.0c07.ac0a (v1 default)
  Hello time 3 sec, hold time 10 sec
    Next hello sent in 1.044 secs
  Preemption enabled
  Active router is local
  Standby router is 172.16.1.2, priority 100 (expires in 8.321 sec)
  Priority 150 (configured 150)
  IP redundancy name is "hsrp-Fa0/0-10" (default)
```

The default virtual MAC address for an HSRP group, as seen in Figure 5-5, is based on the HSRP group number. Specifically, the virtual MAC address for an HSRP group begins with a vendor code of **0000.0c**, followed with a well-known HSRP code of **07.ac**. The last two hexadecimal digits are the hexadecimal representation of the HSRP group number. For example, an HSRP group of 10 yields a default virtual MAC address of **0000.0c07.ac0a**, because **10** in decimal equates to **0a** in hexadecimal.

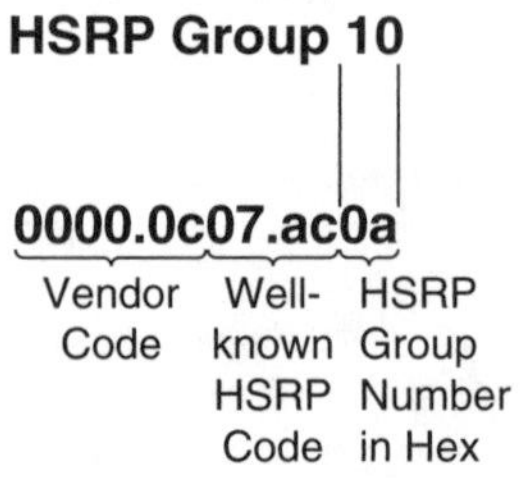

HSRP Group 10

0000.0c07.ac0a

Vendor	Well-	HSRP
Code	known	Group
	HSRP	Number
	Code	in Hex

Figure 5-5   *HSRP Virtual MAC Address*

Once you know the current HSRP configuration, you might then check to see if a host on the HSRP virtual IP address' subnet can ping the virtual IP address. Based on the topology previously shown in Figure 5-4, Example 5-10 shows a successful ping from Workstation A.

Example 5-10 *Ping Test from Workstation A to the HSRP Virtual IP Address*

```
C:\>ping 172.16.1.3

Pinging 172.16.1.3 with 32 bytes of data:

Reply from 172.16.1.3: bytes=32 time=2ms TTL=255
Reply from 172.16.1.3: bytes=32 time=1ms TTL=255
Reply from 172.16.1.3: bytes=32 time=1ms TTL=255
Reply from 172.16.1.3: bytes=32 time=1ms TTL=255

Ping statistics for 172.16.1.3:
    Packets: Sent = 4, Received = 4, Lost = 0 (0% loss),
Approximate round trip times in milli-seconds:
    Minimum = 1ms, Maximum = 2ms, Average = 1ms
```

A client could also be used to verify the appropriate virtual MAC address learned by the client corresponding to the virtual MAC address reported by one of the HSRP routers. Example 5-11 shows Workstation A's ARP cache entry for the HSRP virtual IP address of 172.16.1.3. Notice in the output that the MAC address learned via ARP does match the HSRP virtual MAC address reported by one of the HSRP routers.

Example 5-11 *Workstation A's ARP Cache*

```
C:\>arp -a


Interface: 172.16.1.4 --- 0x4
  Internet Address      Physical Address      Type
   172.16.1.3            00-00-0c-07-ac-0a     dynamic
```

You can use the **debug standby terse** command to view important HSRP changes, such as a state change. Example 5-12 shows this **debug** output on router R2 because router R1's Fast Ethernet 0/0 interface is shut down. Notice that router R2's state changes from Standby to Active.

Example 5-12   **debug standby terse** *Command Output on Router R2: Changing HSRP to Active*

```
R2#
*Mar  1 01:25:45.930: HSRP: Et0/0 Grp 10 Standby: c/Active timer expired
  (172.16.1.1)
```

```
*Mar  1 01:25:45.930: HSRP: Et0/0 Grp 10 Active router is local, was 172.16.1.1
*Mar  1 01:25:45.930: HSRP: Et0/0 Grp 10 Standby router is unknown, was local
*Mar  1 01:25:45.930: HSRP: Et0/0 Grp 10 Standby -> Active
*Mar  1 01:25:45.930: %HSRP-6-STATECHANGE: Ethernet0/0 Grp 10 state Standby ->
  Active
*Mar  1 01:25:45.930: HSRP: Et0/0 Grp 10 Redundancy "hsrp-Et0/0-10" state Standby
  -> Active
*Mar  1 01:25:48.935: HSRP: Et0/0 Grp 10 Redundancy group hsrp-Et0/0-10 state
  Active -> Active
*Mar  1 01:25:51.936: HSRP: Et0/0 Grp 10 Redundancy group hsrp-Et0/0-10 state
  Active -> Active
```

When router R1's Fast Ethernet 0/0 interface is administratively brought up, router R1 reassumes its previous role as the active HSRP router for HSRP group 10, because router R1 is configured with the preempt option. The output shown in Example 5-13 demonstrates how router R2 receives a coup message, letting router R2 know that router R1 is taking back its active role.

Example 5-13 debug standby terse *Command Output on Router R2: Changing HSRP to Standby*

```
R2#
*Mar  1 01:27:57.979: HSRP: Et0/0 Grp 10 Coup    in  172.16.1.1 Active  pri 150
  vIP 172.16.1.3
*Mar  1 01:27:57.979: HSRP: Et0/0 Grp 10 Active: j/Coup rcvd from higher pri
  router (150/172.16.1.1)
*Mar  1 01:27:57.979: HSRP: Et0/0 Grp 10 Active router is 172.16.1.1, was local
*Mar  1 01:27:57.979: HSRP: Et0/0 Grp 10 Active -> Speak
*Mar  1 01:27:57.979: %HSRP-6-STATECHANGE: Ethernet0/0 Grp 10 state Active -> Speak
*Mar  1 01:27:57.979: HSRP: Et0/0 Grp 10 Redundancy "hsrp-Et0/0-10" state Active
  -> Speak
*Mar  1 01:28:07.979: HSRP: Et0/0 Grp 10 Speak: d/Standby timer expired (unknown)
*Mar  1 01:28:07.979: HSRP: Et0/0 Grp 10 Standby router is local
*Mar  1 01:28:07.979: HSRP: Et0/0 Grp 10 Speak -> Standby
*Mar  1 01:28:07.979: HSRP: Et0/0 Grp 10 Redundancy "hsrp-Et0/0-10" state Speak
  -> Standby
```

VRRP

Virtual Router Redundancy Protocol (VRRP), similar to HSRP, allows a collection of routers to service traffic destined for a single IP address. Unlike HSRP, the IP address serviced by a VRRP group does not have to be a virtual IP address. The IP address can be the address of a physical interface on the *virtual router master*, which is the router responsible for forwarding traffic destined for the VRRP group's IP address. A VRRP group can have multiple routers acting as *virtual router backups*, as shown in Figure 5-6, any of which could take over in the event of the virtual router master becoming unavailable.

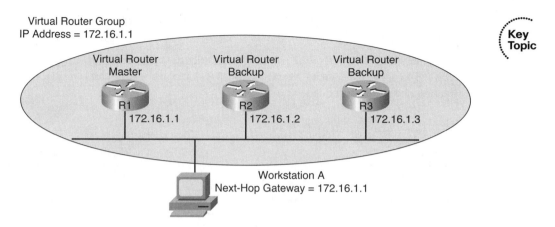

Figure 5-6 *Basic VRRP Operation*

GLBP

Global Load Balancing Protocol (GLBP) can load balance traffic destined for a next-hop gateway across a collection of routers, known as a *GLBP group*. Specifically, when a client sends an Address Resolution Protocol (ARP) request, in an attempt to determine the MAC address corresponding to a known IP address, GLBP can respond with the MAC address of one member of the GLBP group. The next such request would receive a response containing the MAC address of a different member of the GLBP group, as depicted in Figure 5-7. Specifically, GLBP has one *active virtual gateway* (AVG), which is responsible for replying to ARP requests from hosts. However, multiple routers acting as *active virtual forwarders* (AVFs) can forward traffic.

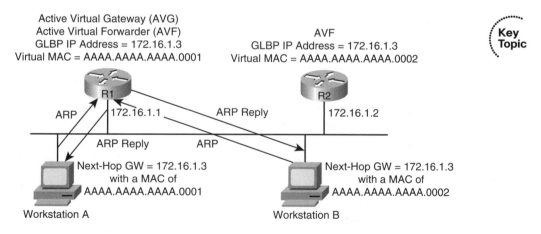

Figure 5-7 *Basic GLBP Operation*

Troubleshooting VRRP and GLBP

Because VRRP and GLBP perform a similar function to HSRP, you can use a similar troubleshooting philosophy. Much like HSRP's **show standby brief** command, similar information can be gleaned for VRRP operation with the **show vrrp brief** command and for GLBP operation with the **show glbp brief** command.

Although HSRP, VRRP, and GLBP have commonalities, it is important for you as a troubleshooter to understand the differences. Table 5-4 compares several characteristics of these first-hop router redundancy protocols.

Table 5-4   *Comparing HSRP, VRRP, and GLBP*

Characteristic	HSRP	VRRP	GLBP
Cisco proprietary	Yes	No	Yes
Interface IP address can act as virtual IP address	No	Yes	No
More than one router in a group can simultaneously forward traffic for that group	No	No	Yes
Hello timer default value	3 seconds	1 second	3 seconds

Cisco Catalyst Switch Performance Troubleshooting

Switch performance issues can be tricky to troubleshoot, because the problem reported is often subjective. For example, if a user reports that the network is running "slow," the user's perception might mean that the network is slow compared to what he expects. However, network performance might very well be operating at a level that is hampering productivity and at a level that is indeed below its normal level of operation. At that point, as part of the troubleshooting process, you need to determine what network component is responsible for the poor performance. Rather than a switch or a router, the user's client, server, or application could be the cause of the performance issue.

If you do determine that the network performance is not meeting technical expectations (as opposed to user expectations), you should isolate the source of the problem and diagnose the problem on that device. This section assumes that you have isolated the device causing the performance issue, and that device is a Cisco Catalyst switch.

Cisco Catalyst Switch Troubleshooting Targets

Cisco offers a variety of Catalyst switch platforms, with different port densities, different levels of performance, and different hardware. Therefore, troubleshooting one of these switches can be platform dependent. Many similarities do exist, however. For example, all Cisco Catalyst switches include the following hardware components:

■ **Ports:** A switch's ports physically connect the switch to other network devices. These ports (also known as *interfaces*) allow a switch to receive and transmit traffic.

■ **Forwarding logic:** A switch contains hardware that makes forwarding decisions. This hardware rewrites a frame's headers.

■ **Backplane:** A switch's backplane physically interconnects a switch's ports. Therefore, depending on the specific switch architecture, frames flowing through a switch enter via a port (that is, the ingress port), flow across the switch's backplane, and are forwarded out of another port (that is, an egress port).

- **Control plane:** A switch's CPU and memory reside in a control plane. This control plane is responsible for running the switch's operating system.

Figure 5-8 depicts these switch hardware components. Notice that the control plane does not directly participate in frame forwarding. However, the forwarding logic contained in the forwarding hardware comes from the control plane. Therefore, there is an indirect relationship between frame forwarding and the control plane. As a result, a continuous load on the control plane could, over time, impact the rate at which the switch forwards frames. Also, if the forwarding hardware is operating at maximum capacity, the control plane begins to provide the forwarding logic. So, although the control plane does not architecturally appear to impact switch performance, it should be considered when troubleshooting.

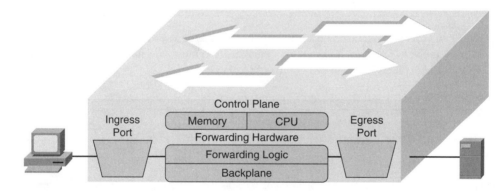

Figure 5-8   *Cisco Catalyst Switch Hardware Components*

The following are two common troubleshooting targets to consider when diagnosing a suspected switch issue:

- Port errors
- Mismatched duplex settings

The sections that follow evaluate these target areas in greater detail.

Port Errors

When troubleshooting a suspected Cisco Catalyst switch issue, a good first step is to check port statistics. For example, examining port statistics can let a troubleshooter know if an excessive number of frames are being dropped. If a TCP application is running slow, the reason might be that TCP flows are going into *TCP slow start*, which causes the window size, and therefore the bandwidth efficiency, of TCP flows to be reduced. A common reason that a TCP flow enters slow start is packet drops. Similarly, packet drops for a UDP flow used for voice or video could result in noticeable quality degradation, because dropped UDP segments are not retransmitted.

Although dropped frames are most often attributed to network congestion, another possibility is that the cabling could be bad. To check port statistics, a troubleshooter could leverage a **show interfaces** command. Consider Example 5-14, which shows the output of the **show interfaces gig 0/9 counters** command on a Cisco Catalyst 3550 switch. Notice that this output shows the number of inbound and outbound frames seen on the specified port.

Example 5-14   show interfaces gig 0/9 counters *Command Output*

```
SW1# show interfaces gig 0/9 counters

Port              InOctets    InUcastPkts    InMcastPkts    InBcastPkts
Gi0/9             31265148          20003           3179              1


Port             OutOctets   OutUcastPkts   OutMcastPkts   OutBcastPkts
Gi0/9            18744149           9126             96              6
```

To view errors that occurred on a port, you could add the keyword of **errors** after the **show interfaces** *interface_id* **counters** command. Example 5-15 illustrates sample output from the **show interfaces gig 0/9 counters errors** command.

Example 5-15   show interfaces gig 0/9 counters errors *Command Output*

```
SW1# show interfaces gig 0/9 counters errors
Port          Align-Err      FCS-Err     Xmit-Err     Rcv-Err UnderSize
Gi0/9                 0            0            0           0         0


Port         Single-Col Multi-Col  Late-Col Excess-Col Carri-Sen     Runts     Giants
Gi0/9              5603         0       5373          0         0         0          0
```

Table 5-5 provides a reference for the specific errors that might show up in the output of the **show interfaces** *interface_id* **counters errors** command.

Table 5-5   *Errors in the* show interfaces interface_id counters errors *Command*

Error Counter	Description
Align-Err	An alignment error occurs when frames do not end with an even number of octets, while simultaneously having a bad Cyclic Redundancy Check (CRC). An alignment error normally suggests a Layer 1 issue, such as cabling or port (either switch port or NIC port) issues.
FCS-Err	A Frame Check Sequence (FCS) error occurs when a frame has an invalid checksum, although the frame has no framing errors. Like the Align-Err error, an FCS-Err often points to a Layer 1 issue.

continues

Table 5-5   *Errors in the* **show interfaces interface_id counters errors** *Command*   *(Continued)*

Error Counter	Description
Xmit-Err	A transmit error (that is, Xmit-Err) occurs when a port's transmit buffer overflows. A speed mismatch between inbound and outbound links often results in a transmit error.
Rcv-Err	A receive error (that is, Rcv-Err) occurs when a port's receive buffer over-flows. Congestion on a switch's backplane could cause the receive buffer on a port to fill to capacity, as frames await access to the switch's backplane. However, most likely, a Rcv-Err is indicating a duplex mismatch.
UnderSize	An undersize frame is a frame with a valid checksum but a size less than 64 bytes. This issue suggests that a connected host is sourcing invalid frame sizes.
Single-Col	A Single-Col error occurs when a single collisions occurs before a port successfully transmits a frame. High bandwidth utilization on an attached link or a duplex mismatch are common reasons for a Single-Col error.
Multi-Col	A Multi-Col error occurs when more than one collision occurs before a port successfully transmits a frame. Similar to the Single-Col error, high band-width utilization on an attached link or a duplex mismatch are common reasons for a Multi-Col error.
Late-Col	A late collision is a collision that is not detected until well after the frame has begun to be forwarded. While a Late-Col error could indicate that the connected cable is too long, this is an extremely common error seen in mis-matched duplex conditions.
Excess-Col	The Excess-Col error occurs when a frame experienced sixteen successive collisions, after which the frame was dropped. This error could result from high bandwidth utilization, a duplex mismatch, or too many devices on a segment.
Carri-Sen	The Carri-Sen counter is incremented when a port wants to send data on a half-duplex link. This is normal and expected on a half-duplex port, because the port is checking the wire, to make sure no traffic is present, prior to sending a frame. This operation is the carrier sense procedure described by the Carrier Sense Multiple Access with Collision Detect (CSMA/CD) opera-tion used on half-duplex connections. Full-duplex connections, however, do not use CSMA/CD.
Runts	A runt is a frame that is less than 64 bytes in size and has a bad CRC. A runt could result from a duplex mismatch or a Layer 1 issue.
Giants	A giant is a frame size greater than 1518 bytes (assuming the frame is not a jumbo frame) that has a bad FCS. Typically, a giant is caused by a problem with the NIC in an attached host.

Mismatched Duplex Settings

As seen in Table 5-5, duplex mismatches can cause a wide variety of port errors. Keep in mind that almost all network devices, other than shared media hubs, can run in full-duplex mode. Therefore, if you have no hubs in your network, all devices should be running in full-duplex mode.

A new recommendation from Cisco is that switch ports be configured to autonegotiate both speed and duplex. Two justifications for this recommendation are as follows:

■ If a connected device only supported half-duplex, it would be better for a switch port to negotiate down to half-duplex and run properly than being forced to run full-duplex which would result in multiple errors.

■ The automatic medium-dependent interface crossover (auto-MDIX) feature can automatically detect if a port needs a crossover or a straight-through cable to interconnect with an attached device and adjust the port to work regardless of which cable type is connected. You can enable this feature in interface configuration mode with the **mdix auto** command on some models of Cisco Catalyst switches. However, the auto-MDIX feature requires that the port autonegotiate both speed and duplex.

In a mismatched duplex configuration, a switch port at one end of a connection is configured for full-duplex, whereas a switch port at the other end of a connection is configured for half-duplex. Among the different errors previously listed in Table 5-5, two of the biggest indicators of a duplex mismatch are a high Rcv-Err counter or a high Late-Col counter. Specifically, a high Rcv-Err counter is common to find on the full-duplex end of a connection with a mismatched duplex, while a high Late-Col counter is common on the half-duplex end of the connection.

To illustrate, examine Examples 5-16 and 5-17, which display output based on the topology depicted in Figure 5-9. Example 5-16 shows the half-duplex end of a connection, and Example 5-17 shows the full-duplex end of a connection.

Figure 5-9   *Topology with Duplex Mismatch*

Example 5-16   *Output from the* **show interfaces gig 0/9 counters errors** *and the* **show interfaces gig 0/9 | include duplex** *Commands on a Half-Duplex Port*

```
SW1# show interfaces gig 0/9 counters errors

Port         Align-Err     FCS-Err     Xmit-Err     Rcv-Err  UnderSize
Gi0/9               0           0            0            0          0


Port      Single-Col Multi-Col  Late-Col Excess-Col Carri-Sen    Runts     Giants
Gi0/9           5603         0      5373          0         0         0          0
```

```
SW1# show interfaces gig 0/9 | include duplex
  Half-duplex, 100Mb/s, link type is auto, media type is 10/100/1000BaseTX
SW1# show interfaces gig 0/9 counters errors
```

Example 5-17   *Output from the* show interfaces fa 5/47 counters errors *and the* show interfaces fa 5/47 | include duplex *Commands on a Full-Duplex Port*

```
SW2# show interfaces fa 5/47 counters errors


Port         Align-Err      FCS-Err    Xmit-Err    Rcv-Err UnderSize OutDiscards
Fa5/47              0          5248          0         5603        27           0


Port     Single-Col Multi-Col Late-Col Excess-Col Carri-Sen      Runts     Giants
Fa5/47            0         0        0          0         0        227          0


Port        SQETest-Err Deferred-Tx IntMacTx-Err IntMacRx-Err Symbol-Err
Fa5/47                0           0            0            0           0

SW2# show interfaces fa 5/47 | include duplex
  Full-duplex, 100Mb/s
SW1# show interfaces gig 0/9 counters errors
```

In your troubleshooting, even if you only have access to one of the switches, if you suspect a duplex mismatch, you could change the duplex settings on the switch over which you do have control. Then, you could clear the interface counters to see if the errors continue to increment. You could also perform the same activity (for example, performing a file transfer) the user was performing when he noticed the performance issue. By comparing the current performance to the performance experienced by the user, you might be able to conclude that the problem has been resolved by correcting a mismatched duplex configuration.

TCAM Troubleshooting

As previously mentioned, the two primary components of forwarding hardware are forwarding logic and backplane. A switch's backplane, however, is rarely the cause of a switch performance issue, because most Cisco Catalyst switches have high-capacity backplanes. However, it is conceivable that in a modular switch chassis, the backplane will not have the throughput to support a fully populated modular chassis, where each card in the chassis supports the highest combination of port densities and port speeds.

The architecture of some switches allows groups of switch ports to be handled by separated hardware. Therefore, you might experience a performance gain by simply moving a cable from one switch port to another. However, to strategically take advantage of this design characteristic, you must be very familiar with the architecture of the switch with which you are working.

A multilayer switch's forwarding logic can impact switch performance. Recall that a switch's forwarding logic is compiled into a special type of memory called ternary content addressable memory (TCAM), as illustrated in Figure 5-10. TCAM works with a switch's CEF feature to provide extremely fast forwarding decisions. However, if a switch's TCAM is unable, for whatever reason, to forward traffic, that traffic is forwarded by the switch's CPU, which has a limited forwarding capability.

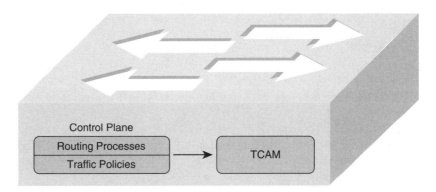

Figure 5-10   *Populating the TCAM*

The process of the TCAM sending packets to a switch's CPU is called *punting*. Consider a few reasons why a packet might be punted from a TCAM to its CPU:

■ Routing protocols, in addition to other control plane protocols such as STP, that send multicast or broadcast traffic will have that traffic sent to the CPU.

■ Someone connecting to a switch administratively (for example, establishing a Telnet session with the switch) will have their packets sent to the CPU.

■ Packets using a feature not supported in hardware (for example, packets traveling over a GRE tunnel) are sent to the CPU.

■ If a switch's TCAM has reached capacity, additional packets will be punted to the CPU. A TCAM might reach capacity if it has too many installed routes or configured access control lists.

From the events listed, the event most likely to cause a switch performance issue is a TCAM filling to capacity. Therefore, when troubleshooting switch performance, you might want to investigate the state of the switch's TCAM. Please be sure to check documentation for your switch model, because TCAM verification commands can vary between platforms.

As an example, the Cisco Catalyst 3550 Series switch supports a collection of **show tcam** commands, whereas Cisco Catalyst 3560 and 3750 Series switches support a series of **show platform tcam** commands. Consider the output from the **show tcam inacl 1 statistics** command issued on a Cisco Catalyst 3550 switch, as shown in Example 5-18. The number **1** indicates TCAM number one, because the Cisco Catalyst 3550 has three TCAMs. The **inacl** refers to access control lists applied in the ingress direction. Notice that fourteen masks are allocated, while 402 are available. Similarly, seventeen entries are currently allocated, and 3311 are available. Therefore, you could conclude from this output that TCAM number one is not approaching capacity.

Example 5-18   show tcam inacl 1 statistics *Command Output on a Cisco Catalyst 3550 Series Switch*

```
Cat3550# show tcam inacl 1 statistics
Ingress ACL TCAM#1: Number of active labels: 3
Ingress ACL TCAM#1: Number of masks    allocated:    14, available:  402
Ingress ACL TCAM#1: Number of entries allocated:    17, available: 3311
```

On some switch models (for example, a Cisco Catalyst 3750 platform), you can use the **show platform ip unicast counts** command to see if a TCAM allocation has failed. Similarly, you can use the **show controllers cpu-interface** command to display a count of packets being forwarded to a switch's CPU.

On most switch platforms, TCAMs cannot be upgraded. Therefore, if you conclude that a switch's TCAM is the source of the performance problems being reported, you could either use a switch with higher-capacity TCAMs or reduce the number of entries in a switch's TCAM. For example, you could try to optimize your access control lists or leverage route summarization to reduce the number of route entries maintained by a switch's TCAM. Also, some switches (for example, Cisco Catalyst 3560 or 3750 Series switches) enable you to change the amount of TCAM memory allocated to different switch features. For example, if your switch ports were configured as routing ports, you could reduce the amount of TCAM space used for storing MAC addresses, and instead use that TCAM space for Layer 3 processes.

High CPU Utilization Level Troubleshooting

The load on a switch's CPU is often low, even under high utilization, thanks to the TCAM. Because the TCAM maintains a switch's forwarding logic, the CPU is rarely tasked to forward traffic. The **show processes cpu** command that you earlier learned for use on a router can also be used on a Cisco Catalyst switch to display CPU utilization levels, as demonstrated in Example 5-19.

Example 5-19   show processes cpu *Command Output on a Cisco Catalyst 3550 Series Switch*

Key Topic

```
Cat3550# show processes cpu
CPU utilization for five seconds: 19%/15%; one minute: 20%; five minutes: 13%
 PID Runtime(ms)   Invoked     uSecs   5Sec    1Min    5Min TTY Process
   1          0         4         0   0.00%   0.00%   0.00%   0 Chunk Manager
```

```
    2              0            610             0   0.00%   0.00%   0.00%     0 Load Meter
    3            128              5         25600   0.00%   0.00%   0.00%     0 crypto sw pk pro
    4           2100            315          6666   0.00%   0.05%   0.05%     0 Check heaps
...OUTPUT OMITTED...
```

Notice in the output in Example 5-19 that the switch is reporting a 19 percent CPU load, with 15 percent of the CPU load used for interrupt processing. The difference between these two numbers is 4, suggesting that 4 percent of the CPU load is consumed with control plane processing.

Although such load utilization values might not be unusual for a router, these values might be of concern for a switch. Specifically, a typical CPU load percentage dedicated to interrupt processing is no more than five percent. A value as high as ten percent is considered acceptable. However, the output given in Example 5-19 shows a fifteen percent utilization. Such a high level implies that the switch's CPU is actively involved in forwarding packets that should normally be handled by the switch's TCAM. Of course, this value might only be of major concern if it varies from baseline information. Therefore, your troubleshooting efforts benefit from having good baseline information.

Periodic spikes in processor utilization are also not a major cause for concern if such spikes can be explained. Consider the following reasons that might cause a switch's CPU utilization to spike:

■   The CPU processing routing updates

■   Issuing a **debug** command (or other processor-intensive commands)

■   Simple Network Management Protocol (SNMP) being used to poll network devices

If you determine that a switch's high CPU load is primarily the result of interrupts, you should examine the switch's packet switching patterns and check the TCAM utilization. If, however, the high CPU utilization is primarily the result of processes, you should investigate those specific processes.

A high CPU utilization on a switch might be a result of STP. Recall that an STP failure could lead to a broadcast storm, where Layer 2 broadcast frames endlessly circulate through a network. Therefore, when troubleshooting a performance issue, realize that a switch's high CPU utilization might be a symptom of another issue.

Trouble Ticket: HSRP

This trouble ticket focuses on HSRP. HSRP was one of three first-hop redundancy protocols discussed in this chapter's "Router Redundancy Troubleshooting" section.

Trouble Ticket #2

You receive the following trouble ticket:

A new network technician configured HSRP on routers BB1 and BB2, where BB1 was the active router. The configuration was initially working; however, now BB2 is acting as the active router, even though BB1 seems to be operational.

This trouble ticket references the topology shown in Figure 5-11.

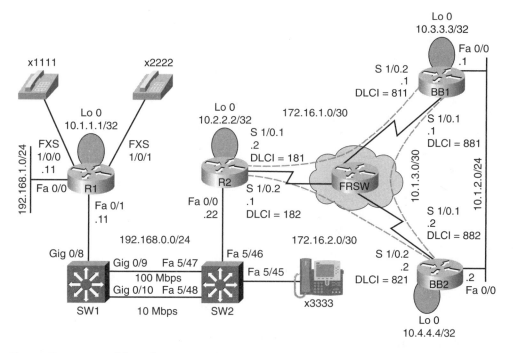

Figure 5-11   *Trouble Ticket #2 Topology*

As you investigate this issue, you examine baseline data collected after HSRP was initially configured. Examples 5-20 and 5-21 provide **show** and **debug** command output collected when HSRP was working properly. Notice that router BB1 was acting as the active HSRP router, whereas router BB2 was acting as the standby HSRP router.

Example 5-20   *Baseline Output for Router BB1*

```
BB1# show standby brief
                        P indicates configured to preempt.
                        |
Interface  Grp Prio P State    Active      Standby       Virtual IP
Fa0/1       1   150   Active    local        172.16.1.3     172.16.1.4

BB1# debug standby
HSRP debugging is on
*Mar  1 01:14:21.487: HSRP: Fa0/1 Grp 1 Hello  in  172.16.1.3 Standby pri 100 vIP
   172.16.1.4
*Mar  1 01:14:23.371: HSRP: Fa0/1 Grp 1 Hello  out 172.16.1.1 Active  pri 150 vIP
   172.16.1.4
```

```
BB1# u all
All possible debugging has been turned off

BB1# show standby fa 0/1 1
FastEthernet0/1 - Group 1
  State is Active
    10 state changes, last state change 00:12:40
  Virtual IP address is 172.16.1.4
  Active virtual MAC address is 0000.0c07.ac01
    Local virtual MAC address is 0000.0c07.ac01 (v1 default)
  Hello time 3 sec, hold time 10 sec
    Next hello sent in 1.536 secs
  Preemption disabled
  Active router is local
  Standby router is 172.16.1.3, priority 100 (expires in 9.684 sec)
  Priority 150 (configured 150)
  IP redundancy name is "hsrp-Fa0/1-1" (default)

BB1# show run
...OUTPUT OMITTED...
hostname BB1
!
interface Loopback0
 ip address 10.3.3.3 255.255.255.255
!
interface FastEthernet0/0
 ip address 10.1.2.1 255.255.255.0
!
interface FastEthernet0/1
 ip address 172.16.1.1 255.255.255.0
 standby 1 ip 172.16.1.4
 standby 1 priority 150
!
router ospf 1
 network 0.0.0.0 255.255.255.255 area 0
```

Example 5-21   *Baseline Output for Router BB2*

```
BB2# show standby brief
                     P indicates configured to preempt.
                   |
```

```
Interface    Grp Prio P State      Active          Standby         Virtual IP
Fa0/1          1  100    Standby   172.16.1.1      local           172.16.1.4

BB2# show run
...OUTPUT OMITTED...
hostname BB2
!
interface Loopback0
 ip address 10.4.4.4 255.255.255.255
!
interface FastEthernet0/0
 ip address 10.1.2.2 255.255.255.0
!
interface FastEthernet0/1
 ip address 172.16.1.3 255.255.255.0
 standby 1 ip 172.16.1.4
!
router ospf 1
 network 0.0.0.0 255.255.255.255 area 0
```

As part of testing the initial configuration, a ping was sent to the virtual IP address of 172.16.1.4 from router R2 in order to confirm that HSRP was servicing requests for that IP address. Example 5-22 shows the output from the **ping** command.

Example 5-22   *PINGing the Virtual IP Address from Router R2*

```
R2# ping 172.16.1.4
Type escape sequence to abort.
Sending 5, 100-byte ICMP Echos to 172.16.1.4, timeout is 2 seconds:
!!!!!
```

As you begin to gather information about the reported problem, you reissue the **show standby brief** command on routers BB1 and BB2. As seen in Examples 5-23 and 5-24, router BB1 is administratively up with an HSRP priority of 150, whereas router BB2 is administratively up with a priority of 100.

Example 5-23   *Examining the HSRP State of Router BB1's FastEthernet 0/1 Interface*

```
BB1# show standby brief
                     P indicates configured to preempt.
                     |
Interface    Grp Prio P State      Active          Standby         Virtual IP
Fa0/1          1  150    Standby   172.16.1.3      local           172.16.1.4
```

Example 5-24 *Examining the HSRP State of Router BB2's FastEthernet 0/1 Interface*

```
BB2# show standby brief
                      P indicates configured to preempt.
                      |
Interface   Grp Prio P State    Active        Standby       Virtual IP
Fa0/1        1   100   Active    local         172.16.1.1    172.16.1.4
```

Take a moment to look through the baseline information, the topology, and the **show** command output. Then, hypothesize the underlying cause, explaining why router BB2 is currently the active HSRP router, even thought router BB1 has a higher priority. Finally, on a separate sheet of paper, write out a proposed action plan for resolving the reported issue.

Suggested Solution

Upon examination of BB1's output, it becomes clear that the preempt feature is not enabled for the Fast Ethernet 0/1 interface on BB1. The absence of the preempt feature explains the reported symptom. Specifically, if BB1 had at one point been the active HSRP router for HSRP group 1, and either router BB1 or its Fast Ethernet 0/1 interface became unavailable, BB2 would have become the active router. Then, if BB1 or its Fast Ethernet 0/1 interface once again became available, BB1 would assume a standby HSRP role, because BB1's FastEthernet 0/1 interface was not configured for the preempt feature.

To resolve this configuration issue, the preempt feature is added to BB1's Fast Ethernet 0/1 interface, as shown in Example 5-25. After enabling the preempt feature, notice that router BB1 regains its active HSRP role.

Example 5-25 *Enabling the Preempt Feature on Router BB1's FastEthernet 0/1 Interface*

```
BB1# conf term
Enter configuration commands, one per line.  End with CNTL/Z.
BB1(config)#int fa 0/1
BB1(config-if)#standby 1 preempt
BB1(config-if)#end
BB1#
*Mar  1 01:17:39.607: %HSRP-5-STATECHANGE: FastEthernet0/1 Grp 1 state Standby ->
  Active

BB1#show standby brief
                      P indicates configured to preempt.
                      |
Interface   Grp Prio P State    Active        Standby       Virtual IP
Fa0/1        1   150 P Active    local         172.16.1.3    172.16.1.4
```

Exam Preparation Tasks

Review All Key Topics

Review the most important topics from inside the chapter, noted with the Key Topics icon in the outer margin of the page. Table 5-6 lists these key topics and the page numbers where each is found.

Key Topic

Table 5-6 *Key Topics for Chapter 5*

Key Topic Element	Description	Page Number
Table 5-2	Similarities and differences between routers and Layer 3 switches	111
Table 5-3	Router data plane verification commands	112
Example 5-3	SVI configuration	113
List	Differences between SVIs and routed ports	115
Examples 5-5 and 5-6	HSRP configuration	116
Figure 5-6	Basic VRRP Operation	121
Figure 5-7	Basic GLBP Operation	121
Table 5-4	Comparing HSRP, VRRP, and GLBP	122
List	Cisco Catalyst hardware components	122
Table 5-5	Errors in the **show interfaces** *interface_id* **counters errors** command	124
List	Reasons why a packet might be punted from a TCAM to its CPU	128
Example 5-19	Output from the **show processes cpu** command on a Cisco Catalyst 3550 Series switch	129

Complete Tables and Lists from Memory

Print a copy of Appendix B, "Memory Tables," (found on the CD) or at least the section for this chapter, and complete the tables and lists from memory. Appendix C, "Memory Tables Answer Key," also on the CD, includes completed tables and lists to check your work.

Define Key Terms

Define the following key terms from this chapter, and check your answers in the Glossary:

Layer 3 switch, switched virtual interface (SVI), Hot Standby Router Protocol (HSRP), Virtual Router Redundancy Protocol (VRRP), Global Load Balancing Protocol (GLBP), control plane, backplane, Ternary Content Addressable Memory (TCAM)

Command Reference to Check Your Memory

This section includes the most important configuration and EXEC commands covered in this chapter. To determine how well you have memorized the commands as a side effect of your other studies, cover the left side of Tables 5-7 and 5-8 with a piece of paper, read the descriptions on the right side, and see whether you remember the command.

Table 5-7   *Chapter 5 Configuration Command Reference*

Command	Description
standby *group ip virtual-ip-address*	Interface configuration mode command, used to specify the virtual IP address to be serviced by an HSRP group.
standby group **priority** priority	Interface configuration mode command, used to configure an interface's HSRP priority (which defaults to 100).
standby group **preempt**	Interface configuration mode command, which causes a previously active HSRP router to regain its active status if it becomes available.
mdix auto	Interface configuration mode command for a switch that allows the switch port to automatically detect and adjust to the connected cable type (that is, either straight-through or cross-over).

Table 5-8 *Chapter 5 EXEC Command Reference*

Command	Description
show standby *interface-id group*	Displays the HSRP configuration applied to a specified interface in a specified HSRP group.
show standby brief	Provides a summary view of a router's HSRP configuration.
debug standby	Shows HSRP state changes and information about sent and received HSRP packets.
show vrrp brief	Provides a summary view of a router's VRRP configuration.
show glbp brief	Provides a summary view of a router's GLBP configuration.
show ip cef	Displays the router's Layer 3 forwarding information, in addition to multicast, broadcast, and local IP addresses.
show adjacency	Verifies that a valid adjacency exists for a connected host.
show tcam inacl *tcam_number* statistics	A Cisco Catalyst 3550 Series switch command that displays the amount of TCAM memory allocated and used for inbound access control lists.
show platform ip unicast counts	A Cisco Catalyst 3750 Series switch command that can be used to see if a TCAM allocation has failed.
show controllers cpu-interface	A Cisco Catalyst 3750 Series switch command that can be used to display a count of packets being forwarded to a switch's CPU.

This chapter covers the following subjects:

Layer 3 Troubleshooting: This section begins by reviewing basic routing concepts. For example, you examine the changes to a frame's header as that frame's data is routed from one network to another. You see how Layer 2 information can be learned and stored in a router. Cisco Express Forwarding (CEF) is also discussed. Finally, this section presents a collection of **show** commands, useful for troubleshooting IP routing.

EIGRP Troubleshooting: This section begins by generically reviewing how an IP routing protocol's data structures interact with a router's IP routing table. Then, EIGRP's data structures are considered, followed by a review of basic EIGRP operation. Finally, this section provides a collection of **show** and **debug** commands useful for troubleshooting various EIGRP operations.

Trouble Ticket: EIGRP: This section presents you with a trouble ticket and an associated topology. You are also given **show** command output. Based on the information provided, you hypothesize an underlying cause for the reported issue and develop a solution. You can then compare your solution with a suggested solution.

CHAPTER 6

Introduction to Troubleshooting Routing Protocols

Enterprise networks (that is, networks containing multiple subnets) depend on routing technologies to move traffic from one subnet to another. Routers, or Layer 3 switches discussed in Chapter 5, "Advanced Cisco Catalyst Switch Troubleshooting," can be configured to route packets using statically configured route entries or using dynamically configured routing protocols. Also, routers can learn about the existence of networks by examining the networks directly connected to the routers' interfaces.

Routing packets is considered to be a Layer 3 process; however, Layer 2 information (for example, MAC address information) is also required to route packets. An understanding of this basic routing process is critical to troubleshooting issues with various routing protocols. Therefore, this chapter begins with a discussion of fundamental routing concepts. Then, a specific routing protocol (that is, Enhanced Interior Gateway Routing Protocol [EIGRP]) is discussed. You also learn techniques for troubleshooting an EIGRP-based network.

Finally, this chapter presents you with a trouble ticket. This trouble ticket describes an EIGRP issue. Given a collection of **show** command output, you are challenged to determine the underlying cause of the issue and formulate a solution.

"Do I Know This Already?" Quiz

The "Do I Know This Already?" quiz helps you to determine your level of knowledge of this chapter's topics before you begin. Table 6-1 details the major topics discussed in this chapter and their corresponding quiz questions.

Table 6-1 *"Do I Know This Already?" Section-to-Question Mapping*

Foundation Topics Section	Questions
Layer 3 Troubleshooting	1–2
EIGRP Troubleshooting	3–6

1. A router is attempting to route a packet over an Ethernet network from a PC with an IP address of 10.1.1.2 to a server with an IP address of 172.16.1.2. If you examined a frame exiting the PC destined for the server, what would be the two MAC addresses found in the frame's header? (Choose two.)

   a. The PC's MAC address

   b. The server's MAC address

   c. The router's MAC address

   d. A broadcast MAC address

2. Identify two data structures maintained by CEF. (Choose two.)

   a. IP routing table

   b. Router ARP cache

   c. FIB

   d. Adjacency table

3. A router is running two routing protocols: EIGRP and RIPv2. Each routing protocol knows of a route for network 10.1.2.0/24. What determines which route will be injected into the router's IP routing table?

   a. The metric of each route

   b. The advertised distance of each routing protocol

   c. The administrative distance of each routing protocol

   d. The feasible distance of each routing protocol

4. Identify three EIGRP data structures. (Choose three.)

   a. EIGRP topology table

   b. EIGRP adjacency table

   c. EIGRP neighbor table

   d. EIGRP interface table

5. Which two distances does EIGRP consider when selecting the best route for a particular network?

   a. Advertised distance

   b. Successor distance

   c. Topological distance

   d. Feasible distance

6. Which command would you use to display all routes known to a router's EIGRP routing process?

   a. show ip eigrp interfaces

   b. show ip eigrp neighbors

   c. show ip eigrp topology

   d. show ip route eigrp

Foundation Topics

Layer 3 Troubleshooting

When troubleshooting connectivity issues for an IP-based network, the network layer (that is, Layer 3) of the OSI reference model is often an appropriate place to begin your troubleshooting efforts. For example, if you are experiencing connectivity issues between two hosts on a network, you could check Layer 3 by pinging between the hosts. If the pings are successful, you can conclude that the issue resides at upper layers of the OSI reference model (that is, Layers 4–7). However, if the pings fail, you can focus your troubleshooting efforts on Layers 1–3. This section discusses fundamental routing concepts and provides you with a collection of Cisco IOS Software commands that could prove to be useful when troubleshooting routing issues.

Basic Routing Processes

To review basic routing processes, consider Figure 6-1. In this topology, PC1 needs to send traffic to Server1. Notice that these hosts are on different networks. So, the question becomes, how does a packet from a source IP address of 192.168.1.2 get routed to a destination IP address of 192.168.3.2?

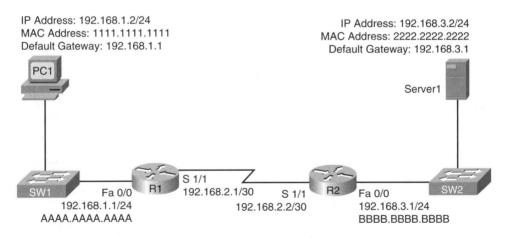

IP Address: 192.168.1.2/24
MAC Address: 1111.1111.1111
Default Gateway: 192.168.1.1

IP Address: 192.168.3.2/24
MAC Address: 2222.2222.2222
Default Gateway: 192.168.3.1

PC1

Server1

SW1   Fa 0/0 R1 S 1/1
             192.168.2.1/30   S 1/1   R2   Fa 0/0   SW2
192.168.1.1/24   192.168.2.2/30   192.168.3.1/24
AAAA.AAAA.AAAA   BBBB.BBBB.BBBB

Figure 6-1 *Basic Routing Topology*

Consider the following walkthrough of this process, step-by-step:

Step 1.   PC1 compares its IP address and subnet mask of 192.168.1.2/24 with the destination IP address and subnet mask of 192.168.3.2/24. PC1 concludes that the destination IP address resides on a remote subnet. Therefore, PC1 needs to send the packet to its default gateway, which could have been manually configured on PC1 or dynamically learned via DHCP. In this example, PC1 has a default gateway of 192.168.1.1 (that is, router R1). In order to construct a

Key
Topic

properly constructed Layer 2 frame, however, PC1 also needs the MAC address of its default gateway. PC1 ARPs for router R1's MAC address. Once PC1 receives an ARP Reply from router R1, PC1 adds router R1's MAC address to its ARP cache. PC1 now sends its data in a frame destined for Server1, as shown in Figure 6-2.

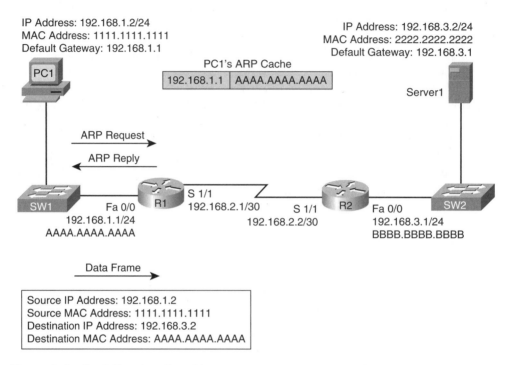

Figure 6-2 *Basic Routing: Step #1*

Step 2.   Router R1 receives the frame sent from PC1 and interrogates the IP header. An IP header contains a Time-to-Live (TTL) field, which is decremented once for each router hop. Therefore, router R1 decrements the packet's TTL field. If the value in the TTL field is reduced to zero, the router discards the frame and sends a *time exceeded* Internet Control Message Protocol (ICMP) message back to the source. Assuming the TTL is not decremented to zero, router R1 checks its routing table to determine the best path to reach network 192.168.3.0/24. In this example, router R1's routing table has an entry stating that network 192.168.3.0/24 is accessible via interface Serial 1/1. Note that ARPs are not required for serial interfaces, because these interface types do not have MAC addresses. Router R1, therefore, forwards the frame out of its Serial 1/1 interface, as depicted in Figure 6-3.

Step 3.   When router R2 receives the frame, it decrements the TTL in the IP header, just as router R1 did. Again, assuming the TTL did not get decremented to zero, router R2 interrogates the IP header to determine the destination network. In this case, the destination network of 192.168.3.0/24 is directly attached to router R2's Fast Ethernet 0/0 interface. Similar to how PC1 sent out an ARP Request to determine the MAC address of its default gateway, router R2 sends an ARP Request to determine the MAC address of Server1. Once an ARP Reply is received from Server1, router R2 forwards the frame out of its Fast Ethernet 0/0 interface to Server1, as illustrated in Figure 6-4.

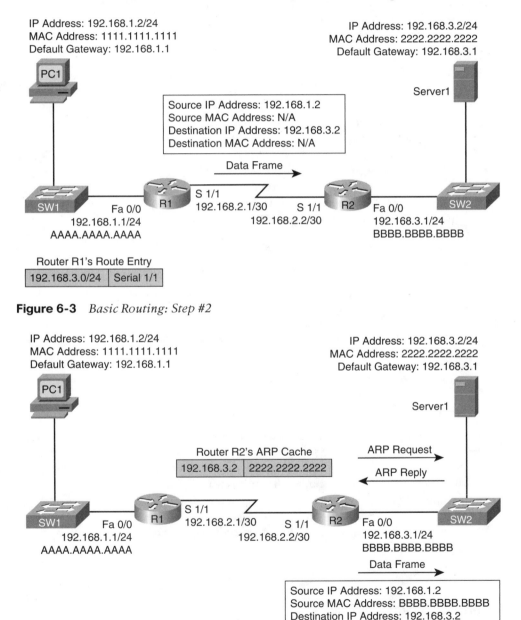

Figure 6-3 *Basic Routing: Step #2*

Figure 6-4 *Basic Routing: Step #3*

The previous steps identified two router data structures:

- **IP routing table:** When a router needed to route an IP packet, it consulted its IP routing table to find the best match. The best match is the route that has the *longest prefix*. Specifically, a route entry with the longest prefix is the most specific network. For example, imagine that a router has an entry for network 10.0.0.0/8 and for network 10.1.1.0/24. Also, imagine that the router is seeking the best match for a destination address of 10.1.1.1/24. The router would select the 10.1.1.0/24 route entry as the best entry, because that route entry has the longest prefix.

- **Layer 3 to Layer 2 mapping:** In the previous example, router R2's ARP cache contained Layer 3 to Layer 2 mapping information. Specifically, the ARP cache had a mapping that said a MAC address of 2222.2222.2222 corresponded to an IP address of 192.168.3.2. While an ARP cache is the Layer 3 to Layer 2 mapping data structure used for Ethernet-based networks, similar data structures are used for Frame Relay and Asynchronous Transfer mode (ATM) point-to-multipoint links. For point-to-point links, however, an egress interface might be shown in the IP routing table, as opposed to a next-hop IP address. For these types of links (for example, point-to-point Frame Relay or ATM Permanent Virtual Circuits [PVC], High-level Data Link Control [HDLC], or Point-to-Point Protocol [PPP] links), the information required to construct an outgoing frame can be gleaned from the egress interface, thus not requiring a next-hop IP address.

Continually querying a router's routing table and its Layer 3 to Layer 2 mapping data structure (for example, an ARP cache) is less than efficient. Fortunately, Cisco Express Forwarding (CEF), as introduced in Chapter 5, makes lookups much more efficient. CEF gleans its information from the router's IP routing table and Layer 3 to Layer 2 mapping tables. Then, CEF's data structures can be referenced when forwarding packets. The two primary CEF data structures are as follows:

- **Forwarding Information Base (FIB):** The FIB contains Layer 3 information, similar to the information found in an IP routing table. Additionally, a FIB contains information about multicast routes and directly connected hosts.

- **Adjacency table:** When a router is performing a route lookup using CEF, the FIB references an entry in the adjacency table. The adjacency table entry contains the frame header information required by the router to properly form a frame. Therefore, an egress interface and a next-hop IP address would be in an adjacency entry for a multipoint interface, whereas a point-to-point interface would require only egress interface information. Note that if a host is *adjacent* to a router, the router can reach that host over a single Layer 2 hop (that is, traffic would not have to be routed to reach an adjacency).

As a reference, Figure 6-5 shows the router data structures previously discussed.

Troubleshooting Basic Routing

When troubleshooting some routing issues, you might want to examine a router's IP routing table. If the traffic's observed behavior is not conforming to information in the IP routing table, however, recall that the IP routing table is maintained by a router's control plane. CEF, however, operates in the data plane. Therefore, you might also want to view CEF information, because CEF's data structures (that is, the FIB and the adjacency table) contain all the information required to make packet forwarding decisions. For your reference, Table 6-2 contains a collection of commands useful for verifying both IP routing table information (that is, control plane information) and CEF information (that is, data plane information).

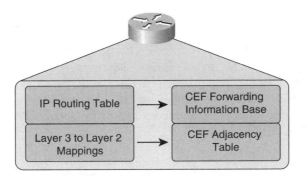

Figure 6-5   *A Router's Data Structures*

Table 6-2   *Troubleshooting Layer 3 Forwarding Information*

Key
Topic

show ip route *ip-address*	Displays a router's best route to the specified IP address.
show ip route *network subnet-mask*	Displays a router's best route to the specified network, if the specific route (with a matching subnet mask length) is found in the router's IP routing table.
show ip route *network subnet-mask* **longer-prefixes**	Displays all routes in a router's IP routing table that are encompassed by the specified network address and subnet mask. (NOTE: This command is often useful when troubleshooting route summarization issues.)
show ip cef *ip-address*	Displays information (for example, next-hop IP address and egress interface) required to forward a packet, similar to the output of the **show ip route** *ip-address* command. (NOTE: The output of this command comes from CEF. Therefore, routing protocol information is not presented in the output.)
show ip cef *network subnet-mask*	Displays information from a router's FIB showing the information needed to route a packet to the specified network with the specified subnet mask.

continues

Table 6-2   *Troubleshooting Layer 3 Forwarding Information*   *(Continued)*

Command	Description
show ip cef exact-route *source-ip-address destination-ip-address*	Displays the adjacency that will be used to forward a packet from the specified source IP address to the specified destination IP address. (NOTE: This command is useful if the router is load balancing across multiple adjacencies, and you want to see which adjacency will be used for a certain combination of source and destination IP addresses.)

Example 6-1 provides sample output from the **show ip route** *ip-address* command. The output shows that the next-hop IP address to reach an IP address of 192.168.1.11 is 192.168.0.11, which is accessible via interface Fast Ethernet 0/0. Because this information is coming from the control plane, it includes information about the routing protocol, which is OSPF in this case.

Example 6-1   show ip route ip-address *Command Output*

```
R2# show ip route 192.168.1.11
Routing entry for 192.168.1.0/24
  Known via "ospf 1", distance 110, metric 11, type intra area
  Last update from 192.168.0.11 on FastEthernet0/0, 00:06:45 ago
  Routing Descriptor Blocks:
  * 192.168.0.11, from 10.1.1.1, 00:06:45 ago, via FastEthernet0/0
      Route metric is 11, traffic share count is 1
```

Example 6-2 provides sample output from the **show ip route** *network subnet-mask* command. The output indicates that network 192.168.1.0/24 is accessible out of interface Fast Ethernet 0/0, with a next-hop IP address of 192.168.0.11.

Example 6-2   show ip route network subnet_mask *Command Output*

```
R2# show ip route 192.168.1.0 255.255.255.0
Routing entry for 192.168.1.0/24
  Known via "ospf 1", distance 110, metric 11, type intra area
  Last update from 192.168.0.11 on FastEthernet0/0, 00:06:57 ago
  Routing Descriptor Blocks:
  * 192.168.0.11, from 10.1.1.1, 00:06:57 ago, via FastEthernet0/0
      Route metric is 11, traffic share count is 1
```

Example 6-3 provides sample output from the **show ip route** *network subnet-mask* [**longer-prefixes**] command, with and without the **longer-prefixes** option. Notice that the router responds that the subnet 172.16.0.0 255.255.0.0 is not in the IP routing table. However, after adding the **longer-prefixes** option, two routes are displayed, because these routes are subnets of the 172.16.0.0/16 network.

Example 6-3   show ip route network subnet-mask [longer-prefixes] *Command Output*

```
R2# show ip route 172.16.0.0 255.255.0.0
% Subnet not in table
R2# show ip route 172.16.0.0 255.255.0.0 longer-prefixes
Codes: C - connected, S - static, R - RIP, M - mobile, B - BGP
       D - EIGRP, EX - EIGRP external, O - OSPF, IA - OSPF inter area
       N1 - OSPF NSSA external type 1, N2 - OSPF NSSA external type 2
       E1 - OSPF external type 1, E2 - OSPF external type 2
       i - IS-IS, su - IS-IS summary, L1 - IS-IS level-1, L2 - IS-IS level-2
       ia - IS-IS inter area, * - candidate default, U - per-user static route
       o - ODR, P - periodic downloaded static route


Gateway of last resort is not set


      172.16.0.0/30 is subnetted, 2 subnets
C        172.16.1.0 is directly connected, Serial1/0.1
C        172.16.2.0 is directly connected, Serial1/0.2
```

Example 6-4 provides sample output from the **show ip cef** *ip-address* command. The output indicates that, according to CEF, an IP address of 192.168.1.11 is accessible out of interface Fast Ethernet 0/0, with a next-hop IP address of 192.168.0.11.

Example 6-4   show ip cef ip-address *Command Output*

```
R2# show ip cef 192.168.1.11
192.168.1.0/24, version 42, epoch 0, cached adjacency 192.168.0.11
0 packets, 0 bytes
  via 192.168.0.11, FastEthernet0/0, 0 dependencies
    next hop 192.168.0.11, FastEthernet0/0
    valid cached adjacency
```

Example 6-5 provides sample output from the **show ip cef** *network subnet_mask* command. The output indicates that network 192.168.1.0/24 is accessible off of interface Fast Ethernet 0/0, with a next-hop IP address of 192.168.0.11.

Example 6-5   show ip cef network subnet-mask *Command Output*

```
R2# show ip cef 192.168.1.0 255.255.255.0
192.168.1.0/24, version 42, epoch 0, cached adjacency 192.168.0.11
0 packets, 0 bytes
  via 192.168.0.11, FastEthernet0/0, 0 dependencies
    next hop 192.168.0.11, FastEthernet0/0
    valid cached adjacency
```

Example 6-6 provides sample output from the **show ip cef exact-route** *source-ip-address destination-ip-address* command. The output indicates that a packet sourced from an IP address of 10.2.2.2 and destined for an IP address of 192.168.1.11 will be sent out of interface Fast Ethernet 0/0 to a next-hop IP address of 192.168.0.11.

Example 6-6   show ip cef exact-route source-ip-address destination-ip-address *Command Output*

```
R2# show ip cef exact-route 10.2.2.2 192.168.1.11
10.2.2.2        -> 192.168.1.11   : FastEthernet0/0 (next hop 192.168.0.11)
```

For a multipoint interface (for example, a point-to-multipoint Frame Relay/ATM PVC or an Ethernet interface), after a router knows the next-hop address for a packet, it needs appropriate Layer 2 information (for example, next-hop MAC address, Data Link Connection Identifier [DLCI], or Virtual Path Identifier/Virtual Circuit Identifier [VPI/VCI]) to properly construct a frame (or a cell, in the case of ATM). Table 6-3 outlines some useful commands for viewing a router's Layer 3 to Layer 2 mapping information.

Key Topic

Table 6-3   *Troubleshooting Layer 3 to Layer 2 Mapping Information*

Command	Description
show ip arp	Displays a router's ARP cache, containing IP address to MAC address mappings. (NOTE: By default, a router's ARP cache stores information for four hours. Therefore, you might need to execute a **clear ip arp** command to allow a router to relearn information after you make a topology change.)
show frame-relay map	Displays Frame Relay DLCIs associated with different next-hop IP addresses.
show adjacency detail	Displays the frame headers in a router's CEF adjacency table used to encapsulate a frame being sent to an adjacency.

Example 6-7 provides sample output from the **show ip arp** command. The output shows the learned or configured MAC addresses along with their associated IP addresses.

Example 6-7   show ip arp *Command Output*

```
R2# show ip arp
Protocol  Address         Age (min)   Hardware Addr   Type    Interface
Internet  192.168.0.11            0   0009.b7fa.d1e1  ARPA    FastEthernet0/0
Internet  192.168.0.22            -   c001.0f70.0000  ARPA    FastEthernet0/0
```

Example 6-8 provides sample output from the **show ip frame-relay map** command. The output shows the Frame Relay subinterfaces that correspond to DLCIs (that is, Frame Relay PVC identifiers) known to the router. Notice that these subinterfaces are point-to-point subinterfaces, meaning that next-hop IP address information is not required to properly construct a frame.

Example 6-8   show frame-relay map *Command Output*

```
R2# show frame-relay map
Serial1/0.2 (up): point-to-point dlci, dlci 182(0xB6,0x2C60), broadcast
          status defined, active
Serial1/0.1 (up): point-to-point dlci, dlci 181(0xB5,0x2C50), broadcast
          status defined, active
```

Example 6-9 provides sample output from the **show adjacency detail** command. The output shows the CEF information used to construct frame headers for the various router interfaces and subinterfaces.

Example 6-9   show adjacency detail *Command Output*

```
R2# show adjacency detail
Protocol Interface              Address
IP       Serial1/0.1           point2point(25)
                               0 packets, 0 bytes
                               2C510800
                               CEF    expires: 00:02:18
                                      refresh: 00:00:19
                               Epoch: 0
IP       Serial1/0.2           point2point(25)
                               0 packets, 0 bytes
                               2C610800
                               CEF    expires: 00:02:18
                                      refresh: 00:00:19
                               Epoch: 0
IP       FastEthernet0/0       192.168.0.11(9)
                               0 packets, 0 bytes
                               0009B7FAD1E1C0010F7000000800
                               ARP        04:02:59
                               Epoch: 0
```

EIGRP Troubleshooting

The Cisco proprietary Enhanced Interior Gateway Routing Protocol (EIGRP) is considered to be a balanced hybrid routing protocol (or an advanced distance-vector routing protocol). Specifically, EIGRP advertises routes to directly attached neighbors, like a distance-vector routing protocol, while using a series of tables, similar to a link-state routing protocol.

EIGRP also offers the benefit of fast convergence after a link failure. Load balancing is supported over both equal-cost paths (a default behavior) and unequal-cost paths (through the *variance* feature).

This section discusses strategies for troubleshooting an EIGRP-based network. Before considering the specifics of EIGRP troubleshooting, however, this section takes a more generic look at how the data structures of various IP routing protocols interact with a router's IP routing table.

Data Structures of IP Routing Protocols

As traffic is routed through a network, the routers encountered along the way from the source to the destination need consistency in how they route traffic. For example, if one router selected the best path based on hop count, and another router selected the best path based on a link's bandwidth, a routing loop could conceivably occur. Fortunately, having a common routing protocol configured on all routers within a topology helps ensure consistency in routing decisions.

That is not to say that a topology could not have more than one routing protocol. You could strategically redistribute routes between routing protocols. Also, you could use static routes in conjunction with dynamic routing protocols. However, you must take care in environments with redundant links and multiple routing protocols to avoid potential routing loops.

To better troubleshoot specific dynamic routing protocols, consider, generically, how dynamic routing protocols' data structures interact with a router's IP routing table.

Figure 6-6 shows the interaction between the data structures of an IP routing protocol and a router's IP routing table. Realize, however, that not all routing protocols maintain their own data structures. For example, Routing Information Protocol (RIP) is a routing protocol that works directly with an IP routing table in a router, rather than maintaining a separate data structure.

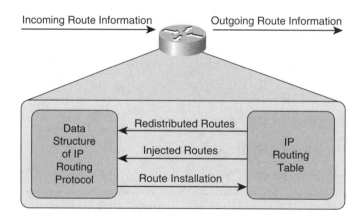

Figure 6-6   *Interaction between IP Routing Protocol Data Structures and IP Routing Tables*

As a router receives route information from a neighboring router, that information is stored in the data structures of the IP routing protocol (if the IP routing protocol uses data structures). A data structure might also be populated by the local router. For example, a router might be configured for route redistribution where route information is redistributed by a routing information source (for example, a dynamic routing protocol, a static route, or a connected route). Also, the router might be configured to have specific interfaces participate in an IP routing protocol.

The data structure analyzes all the information it receives to select the best route to certain networks. This best route is determined by looking for the route with the best metric. The data structure of an IP routing protocol will then inject that best route into the router's IP routing table, if that same route information has not already been learned by a more believable routing source. Specifically, different routing protocols have different *administrative distances*. An administrative distance of a routing protocol can be thought of as the *believability* of that routing protocol. As an example, RIP has an administrative distance of 120, whereas OSPF has an administrative distance of 110. Therefore, if both RIP and OSPF had knowledge of a route to a specific network, the OSPF route would be injected into the router's IP routing table because OSPF has a more believable administrative distance. Therefore, the best route selected by an IP routing protocol's data structure is only a *candidate* to be injected into the router's IP routing table. As a reminder, the following is a list of the administrative distances. The lower the administrative distance, the more preferred the route.

Connected interface	0
Static route	1
Enhanced Interior Gateway Routing Protocol (EIGRP) summary route	5
External Border Gateway Protocol (BGP)	20
Internal EIGRP	90
IGRP	100
OSPF	110
Intermediate System-to-Intermediate System (IS-IS)	115
Routing Information Protocol (RIP)	120
Exterior Gateway Protocol (EGP)	140
On Demand Routing (ODR)	160
External EIGRP	170
Internal BGP	200
Unknown*	255

If an IP routing protocol's data structure identifies more than one route to a destination network, multiple routes might be injected into a router's IP routing table if those multiple routes have an equal metric. In some cases, however, a routing protocol (for example, EIGRP) might support load balancing across unequal-cost paths. In such an instance, multiple routes might be injected into a router's IP routing table, even though those routes have different metrics.

Depending on the IP routing protocol in use, a router will periodically advertise all of its routes, or updates to its routing information, to its neighbors. Also be aware that some routing protocols need to establish a relationship with a neighboring router before exchanging route information with that neighbor. This relationship is called an *adjacency* or a *neighborship*.

Data Structures of EIGRP

Now that you have reviewed, from a generic perspective, how an IP routing protocol's data structure interacts with a router's IP routing table, consider the specific data structures used by EIGRP, as described in Table 6-4.

Table 6-4   *EIGRP Data Structures*

Data Structure	Description
EIGRP interface table	All of a router's interfaces that have been configured to participate in an EIGRP routing process are listed in this table. However, if an interface has been configured as a passive interface (that is, an interface that does not send routing information), that interface does not appear in this table.
EIGRP neighbor table	This table lists a router's EIGRP neighbors (that is, neighboring routers from whom an EIGRP Hello message has been received). A neighbor is removed from this table if the neighbor has not been heard from for a period of time defined as the *hold-time*. Also, if an interface, from which a neighbor is known, is removed from the EIGRP interface table because it goes down, the neighbor is removed from this table unless there is a multiple link and one of the interfaces is still up. In that case, the second interface will still provide the neighborship.
EIGRP topology table	This table contains routes learned by a router's EIGRP routing process. The best route for a network in this table becomes a candidate to be injected into the router's IP routing table. If multiple routes in this table have an equal metric, or if EIGRP's variance feature is configured, more than one route might become candidates for injection into the IP routing table, but only to a maximum of 4 by default.

Key Topic

EIGRP Operation

Like most high-end routing protocols, EIGRP supports variable-length subnet masking (VLSM), and advertisements are sent via multicast (that is, to an address of 224.0.0.10). By default, EIGRP automatically performs route summarization. This could be an issue for a topology containing discontiguous subnets of the same major classful network. To turn off automatic summarization, you can issue the **no auto-summary** command in router configuration mode for an EIGRP autonomous system.

EIGRP also supports load balancing across unequal-cost cost paths using the *variance* feature. By default, the variance value for an EIGRP routing process defaults to a variance of one, meaning the load balancing will only occur over equal-cost paths. You can, however, issue the **variance** *multiplier* command in router configuration mode to specify a range of metrics over which load balancing will occur. For example, imagine that a route had a metric of 200000, and you configured the **variance 2** command for the EIGRP routing process. This would cause load balancing to occur over routes with a metric in the range of 200000 through 400000 (2 * 200000). As you can see, a route could have a metric as high as 400000 (that is, the variance multiplier multiplied by the best metric) and still be used.

Upon learning of a neighbor, due to the receipt of an EIGRP Hello packet, an EIGRP router will perform a full exchange of routing information with the newly established neighbor. Once the neighborship has been formed, however, only updated route information will be exchanged with that neighbor.

Routing information learned from EIGRP neighbors is inserted into the EIGRP topology table. The best route for a specific network in the IP EIGRP topology table becomes a candidate to be injected into the router's IP routing table. If that route is indeed injected into the IP routing table, that route becomes known as the *successor* route. This is the route that is then advertised to neighboring routers.

The following parameters are used to determine the best route:

- **Advertised Distance (AD):** The distance from a neighbor to the destination network

- **Feasible Distance (FD):** The AD plus the metric to reach the neighbor advertising the AD

EIGRP's metric is calculated with the following formula:

EIGRP metric = [K1 * bandwidth + ((K2 * bandwidth) / (256 – load)) + K3 * delay] * [K5 / (reliability + K4)]

By default, the K values are as follows:

- $K1 = 1$

- $K2 = 0$

- $K3 = 1$

- $K4 = 0$

- $K5 = 0$

As a result of these default K values, EIGRP's default metric can be calculated as

default EIGRP metric = bandwidth + delay

where:

- **bandwidth** = 10,000,000 / minimum bandwidth in kbps * 256

- **delay** = sum of delays of all interfaces in path in tens of microseconds * 256

EIGRP Troubleshooting Commands

With an understanding of EIGRP's data structures, and an understanding of how data structures play a role in populating a router's IP routing table, you can now strategically use Cisco IOS **show** and **debug** commands to collect information about specific steps in the routing process. Table 6-5 shows a collection of such commands, along with their description, and the step of the routing process or EIGRP data structure each command can be used to investigate.

Table 6-5 *EIGRP Troubleshooting Commands*

Command	Routing Component or Data Structure	Description
show ip eigrp interfaces	EIGRP interface table	This command displays all of a router's interfaces configured to participate in an EIGRP routing process (with the exception of passive interfaces).
show ip eigrp neighbors	EIGRP neighbor table	This command shows a router's EIGRP neighbors.
show ip eigrp topology	EIGRP topology table	This command displays routes known to a router's EIGRP routing process. These routes are contained in the EIGRP topology table.
show ip route eigrp	IP routing table	This command shows routes known to a router's IP routing table that were injected by the router's EIGRP routing process.
debug ip routing	IP routing table	This command displays updates that occur in a router's IP routing table. Therefore, this command is not specific to EIGRP.
debug eigrp packets	Exchanging EIGRP information with neighbors	This command can be used to display all EIGRP packets exchanged with a router's EIGRP neighbors. However, the focus of the command can be narrowed to only display specific EIGRP packet types (for example, EIGRP Hello packets).
debug ip eigrp	Exchanging EIGRP information with neighbors	This command shows information contained in EIGRP packets and reveals how an EIGRP routing process responds to that information.

Example 6-10 provides sample output from the **show ip eigrp interfaces** command. Although three interfaces are configured to participate in EIGRP autonomous system 100, only two of those interfaces have a peer, because the other interface is a loopback interface.

Example 6-10 show ip eigrp interfaces *Command Output*

```
R2# show ip eigrp interfaces
IP-EIGRP interfaces for process 100
```

Interface	Peers	Xmit Queue Un/Reliable	Mean SRTT	Pacing Time Un/Reliable	Multicast Flow Timer	Pending Routes
Lo0	0	0/0	0	0/1	0	0
Se1/0.1	1	0/0	880	0/15	4155	0
Fa0/0	1	0/0	193	0/2	828	0

Example 6-11 provides sample output from the **show ip eigrp neighbors** command. In the output, notice that two neighbors are known to this router. Also notice that the output shows off of which interface each neighbor resides.

Example 6-11   show ip eigrp neighbors *Command Output*

```
R2# show ip eigrp neighbors
IP-EIGRP neighbors for process 100
H   Address            Interface       Hold Uptime   SRTT RTO    Q    Seq
                                       (sec)         (ms)        Cnt  Num
1   192.168.0.11       Fa0/0           12 00:01:34   193  1158   0    3
0   172.16.1.1         Se1/0.1         12 00:01:39   880  5000   0    23
```

Example 6-12 provides sample output from the **show ip eigrp topology** command. The output displays the routes known to the EIGRP topology table. Also, notice that the output contains the feasible distance (FD) for each route. Recall that the FD is the advertised distance (AD) from a neighbor, plus the metric required to reach that neighbor. Finally, notice that the state of each route is *passive*. This is the desired state. A route that stays in the *active* state, however, could indicate a problem. A state of active means that the router is actively searching for a route. If a route remains in this state, the resulting condition is an EIGRP *stuck-in-active* (SIA) error.

Example 6-12   show ip eigrp topology *Command Output*

```
R2# show ip eigrp topology
IP-EIGRP Topology Table for AS(100)/ID(10.2.2.2)

Codes: P - Passive, A - Active, U - Update, Q - Query, R - Reply,
       r - reply Status, s - sia Status

P 10.1.3.0/30, 1 successors, FD is 2681856
        via 172.16.1.1 (2681856/2169856), Serial1/0.1
P 10.2.2.2/32, 1 successors, FD is 128256
        via Connected, Loopback0
P 10.3.3.3/32, 1 successors, FD is 2297856
        via 172.16.1.1 (2297856/128256), Serial1/0.1
P 10.1.2.0/24, 1 successors, FD is 2195456
        via 172.16.1.1 (2195456/281600), Serial1/0.1
P 10.0.0.0/8, 1 successors, FD is 128256
        via Summary (128256/0), Null0
```

```
P 10.1.1.1/32, 1 successors, FD is 409600
        via 192.168.0.11 (409600/128256), FastEthernet0/0
P 10.4.4.4/32, 1 successors, FD is 2323456
        via 172.16.1.1 (2323456/409600), Serial1/0.1
P 192.168.0.0/24, 1 successors, FD is 281600
        via Connected, FastEthernet0/0
P 192.168.1.0/24, 1 successors, FD is 284160
        via 192.168.0.11 (284160/28160), FastEthernet0/0
P 172.16.0.0/16, 1 successors, FD is 2169856
        via Summary (2169856/0), Null0
P 172.16.1.0/30, 1 successors, FD is 2169856
        via Connected, Serial1/0.1
```

Example 6-13 provides sample output from the **show ip route eigrp** command. The output of this command only shows entries in the IP routing table that were learned via EIGRP.

Example 6-13   show ip route eigrp *Command Output*

```
R2# show ip route eigrp
     172.16.0.0/16 is variably subnetted, 3 subnets, 2 masks
D       172.16.0.0/16 is a summary, 00:01:36, Null0
     10.0.0.0/8 is variably subnetted, 7 subnets, 4 masks
D       10.1.3.0/30 [90/2681856] via 172.16.1.1, 00:01:36, Serial1/0.1
D       10.3.3.3/32 [90/2297856] via 172.16.1.1, 00:01:36, Serial1/0.1
D       10.1.2.0/24 [90/2195456] via 172.16.1.1, 00:01:36, Serial1/0.1
D       10.0.0.0/8 is a summary, 00:01:36, Null0
D       10.1.1.1/32 [90/409600] via 192.168.0.11, 00:01:36, FastEthernet0/0
D       10.4.4.4/32 [90/2323456] via 172.16.1.1, 00:01:36, Serial1/0.1
D    192.168.1.0/24 [90/284160] via 192.168.0.11, 00:01:36, FastEthernet0/0
```

Example 6-14 provides sample output from the **debug ip routing** command. The output shown reflects a loopback interface on a neighboring router being administratively shut down and then brought back up. Specifically, the loopback interface has an IP address of 10.1.1.1, and it is reachable via an EIGRP neighbor with an IP address of 192.168.0.11.

Example 6-14   debug ip routing *Command Output*

```
R2# debug ip routing
IP routing debugging is on
*Mar  1 00:20:11.215: RT: delete route to 10.1.1.1 via 192.168.0.11, eigrp metric
  [90/409600]
*Mar  1 00:20:11.219: RT: SET_LAST_RDB for 10.1.1.1/32
  OLD rdb: via 192.168.0.11, FastEthernet0/0
```

```
*Mar  1 00:20:11.227: RT: no routes to 10.1.1.1
*Mar  1 00:20:11.227: RT: NET-RED 10.1.1.1/32
*Mar  1 00:20:11.231: RT: delete subnet route to 10.1.1.1/32
*Mar  1 00:20:11.235: RT: NET-RED 10.1.1.1/32
*Mar  1 00:20:17.723: RT: SET_LAST_RDB for 10.1.1.1/32
  NEW rdb: via 192.168.0.11
*Mar  1 00:20:17.723: RT: add 10.1.1.1/32 via 192.168.0.11, eigrp metric
 [90/409600]
*Mar  1 00:20:17.723: RT: NET-RED 10.1.1.1/32
```

Example 6-15 provides sample output from the **debug eigrp packets** command. This command can produce a large volume of output by default. However, you can specify specific EIGRP packet types you want to see in the output.

Example 6-15   debug eigrp packets *Command Output*

```
R2# debug eigrp packets
EIGRP Packets debugging is on
    (UPDATE, REQUEST, QUERY, REPLY, HELLO, IPXSAP, PROBE, ACK, STUB, SIAQUERY,
SIAREPLY)
*Mar  1 00:20:48.151: EIGRP: Received HELLO on FastEthernet0/0 nbr 192.168.0.11
*Mar  1 00:20:48.155:   AS 100, Flags 0x0, Seq 0/0 idbQ 0/0 iidbQ un/rely 0/0
 peerQ un/rely 0/0
*Mar  1 00:20:48.187: EIGRP: Sending HELLO on FastEthernet0/0
*Mar  1 00:20:48.191:   AS 100, Flags 0x0, Seq 0/0 idbQ 0/0 iidbQ un/rely 0/0
...OUTPUT OMITTED...
*Mar  1 00:20:59.091: EIGRP: Received QUERY on FastEthernet0/0 nbr 192.168.0.11
*Mar  1 00:20:59.095:   AS 100, Flags 0x0, Seq 6/0 idbQ 0/0 iidbQ un/rely 0/0
 peerQ un/rely 0/0
...OUTPUT OMITTED...
*Mar  1 00:20:59.287: EIGRP: Received REPLY on Serial1/0.1 nbr 172.16.1.1
*Mar  1 00:20:59.291:   AS 100, Flags 0x0, Seq 25/16 idbQ 0/0 iidbQ un/rely 0/0
 peerQ un/rely 0/0
*Mar  1 00:20:59.295: EIGRP: Enqueueing ACK on Serial1/0.1 nbr 172.16.1.1
...OUTPUT OMITTED...
*Mar  1 00:21:06.915: EIGRP: Sending UPDATE on FastEthernet0/0
*Mar  1 00:21:06.915:   AS 100, Flags 0x0, Seq 19/0 idbQ 0/0 iidbQ un/rely 0/0
 serno 17-17
*Mar  1 00:21:06.919: EIGRP: Enqueueing UPDATE on Serial1/0.1 iidbQ un/rely 0/1
 serno 17-17
*Mar  1 00:21:06.923: EIGRP: Enqueueing UPDATE on Serial1/0.1 nbr 172.16.1.1 iidbQ
 un/rely 0/0 peerQ un/rely 0/0 serno 17-17
```

Example 6-16 provides sample output from the **debug ip eigrp** command. This command provides real-time tracking of EIGRP messages, much like the **debug eigrp packets** command. However, the **debug ip eigrp** command focuses more on showing what the EIGRP routing process is doing in response to the messages, as illustrated in the highlighted text.

Example 6-16   debug ip eigrp *Command Output*

```
R2# debug ip eigrp
IP-EIGRP Route Events debugging is on
*Mar  1 00:21:30.123: IP-EIGRP(Default-IP-Routing-Table:100): Processing incoming
  QUERY packet
*Mar  1 00:21:30.127: IP-EIGRP(Default-IP-Routing-Table:100): Int 10.1.1.1/32 M
  4294967295 - 0 4294967295 SM 4294967295 - 0 4294967295
*Mar  1 00:21:30.147: IP-EIGRP(Default-IP-Routing-Table:100): 10.1.1.1/32 - don't
  advertise out Serial1/0.1
*Mar  1 00:21:30.155: IP-EIGRP(Default-IP-Routing-Table:100): Int 10.1.1.1/32
  metric 4294967295 - 0 4294967295
*Mar  1 00:21:30.335: IP-EIGRP(Default-IP-Routing-Table:100): Processing incoming
  REPLY packet
*Mar  1 00:21:30.339: IP-EIGRP(Default-IP-Routing-Table:100): Int 10.1.1.1/32 M
  4294967295 - 0 4294967295 SM 4294967295 - 0 4294967295
*Mar  1 00:21:30.343: IP-EIGRP(Default-IP-Routing-Table:100): 10.1.1.1/32 routing
  table not updated thru 192.168.0.11
*Mar  1 00:21:30.903: IP-EIGRP(Default-IP-Routing-Table:100): 10.1.1.1/32 - not in
  IP routing table
*Mar  1 00:21:30.907: IP-EIGRP(Default-IP-Routing-Table:100): Int 10.1.1.1/32
  metric 4294967295 - 0 4294967295
*Mar  1 00:21:36.739: IP-EIGRP(Default-IP-Routing-Table:100): Processing incoming
  UPDATE packet
*Mar  1 00:21:36.739: IP-EIGRP(Default-IP-Routing-Table:100): Int 10.1.1.1/32 M
  409600 - 256000 153600 SM 128256 - 256 128000
*Mar  1 00:21:36.743: IP-EIGRP(Default-IP-Routing-Table:100): route installed for
  10.1.1.1 ()
*Mar  1 00:21:36.775: IP-EIGRP(Default-IP-Routing-Table:100): Int 10.1.1.1/32
  metric 409600 - 256000 153600
*Mar  1 00:21:36.779: IP-EIGRP(Default-IP-Routing-Table:100): 10.1.1.1/32 - don't
  advertise out Serial1/0.1
```

Trouble Ticket: EIGRP

This trouble ticket focuses on EIGRP. You are presented with baseline data, a trouble ticket, and information collected while investigating the reported issue. You are then challenged to identify the issue and create an action plan to resolve that issue.

Trouble Ticket #3

You receive the following trouble ticket:

EIGRP has just been configured as the routing protocol for the network. After configuring EIGRP on all routers and instructing all router interfaces to participate in EIGRP, router R2 does not appear to be load balancing across its links to BB1 and BB2 when sending traffic to network 10.1.2.0/24.

This trouble ticket references the topology shown in Figure 6-7.

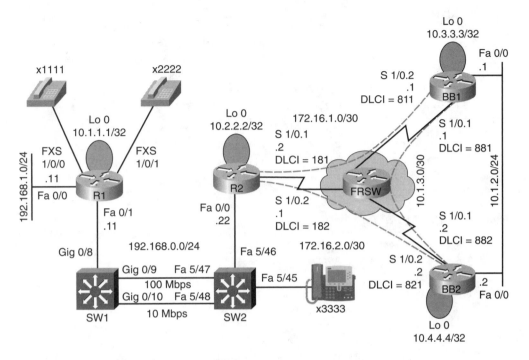

Figure 6-7 *Trouble Ticket #3 Topology*

As you investigate this issue, you examine baseline data collected after EIGRP was initially configured. Example 6-17 confirms that router R2's IP routing table contains only a single path to get to the backbone network of 10.1.2.0/24.

Example 6-17 *Baseline IP Routing Table on Router R2*

```
R2# show ip route
Codes: C - connected, S - static, R - RIP, M - mobile, B - BGP
       D - EIGRP, EX - EIGRP external, O - OSPF, IA - OSPF inter area
       N1 - OSPF NSSA external type 1, N2 - OSPF NSSA external type 2
       E1 - OSPF external type 1, E2 - OSPF external type 2
       i - IS-IS, su - IS-IS summary, L1 - IS-IS level-1, L2 - IS-IS level-2
       ia - IS-IS inter area, * - candidate default, U - per-user static route
       o - ODR, P - periodic downloaded static route

Gateway of last resort is not set

     172.16.0.0/30 is subnetted, 2 subnets
C       172.16.1.0 is directly connected, Serial1/0.1
C       172.16.2.0 is directly connected, Serial1/0.2
     10.0.0.0/8 is variably subnetted, 6 subnets, 3 masks
```

```
C        10.2.2.2/32 is directly connected, Loopback0
D        10.1.3.0/30 [90/3072000] via 172.16.2.2, 00:00:34, Serial1/0.2
D        10.3.3.3/32 [90/2713600] via 172.16.2.2, 00:00:34, Serial1/0.2
D        10.1.2.0/24 [90/2585600] via 172.16.2.2, 00:00:34, Serial1/0.2
D        10.1.1.1/32 [90/409600] via 192.168.0.11, 00:00:46, FastEthernet0/0
D        10.4.4.4/32 [90/2688000] via 172.16.2.2, 00:00:34, Serial1/0.2
C    192.168.0.0/24 is directly connected, FastEthernet0/0
D    192.168.1.0/24 [90/284160] via 192.168.0.11, 00:18:33, FastEthernet0/0
```

You then view the EIGRP topology table on router R2 to see if EIGRP has learned more than one route to reach the 10.1.2.0/24 network. The output, shown in Example 6-18, indicates that the EIGRP topology table knows two routes that could be used to reach the 10.1.2.0/24 network.

Example 6-18 *EIGRP Topology Table on Router R2*

```
R2# show ip eigrp topology
IP-EIGRP Topology Table for AS(1)/ID(10.2.2.2)

Codes: P - Passive, A - Active, U - Update, Q - Query, R - Reply,
       r - reply Status, s - sia Status

P 10.1.3.0/30, 1 successors, FD is 3072000
        via 172.16.2.2 (3072000/2169856), Serial1/0.2
        via 172.16.1.1 (4437248/2169856), Serial1/0.1
P 10.2.2.2/32, 1 successors, FD is 128256
        via Connected, Loopback0
P 10.1.2.0/24, 1 successors, FD is 2585600
        via 172.16.2.2 (2585600/281600), Serial1/0.2
        via 172.16.1.1 (3950848/281600), Serial1/0.1
P 10.3.3.3/32, 1 successors, FD is 2713600
        via 172.16.2.2 (2713600/409600), Serial1/0.2
        via 172.16.1.1 (4053248/128256), Serial1/0.1
P 10.1.1.1/32, 1 successors, FD is 409600
        via 192.168.0.11 (409600/128256), FastEthernet0/0
P 10.4.4.4/32, 1 successors, FD is 2688000
        via 172.16.2.2 (2688000/128256), Serial1/0.2
        via 172.16.1.1 (4078848/409600), Serial1/0.1
P 192.168.0.0/24, 1 successors, FD is 281600
        via Connected, FastEthernet0/0
P 192.168.1.0/24, 1 successors, FD is 284160
        via 192.168.0.11 (284160/28160), FastEthernet0/0
P 172.16.1.0/30, 1 successors, FD is 3925248
        via Connected, Serial1/0.1
P 172.16.2.0/30, 1 successors, FD is 2560000
        via Connected, Serial1/0.2
```

Finally, you examine the EIGRP configuration on router R1, as presented in Example 6-19.

Example 6-19   *EIGRP Configuration on Router R2*

```
R2# show run | begin router
router eigrp 1
 network 10.2.2.2 0.0.0.0
 network 172.16.1.0 0.0.0.3
 network 172.16.2.0 0.0.0.3
 network 192.168.0.0
 auto-summary
```

Take a moment to look through the **show** command output and the topology. Then, hypothesize the underlying cause, explaining why router R2's IP routing table only shows one route to network 10.1.2.0/24, even though the EIGRP topology table knows of two routes to that network. Finally, on a separate sheet of paper, write out a proposed action plan for resolving the reported issue.

Suggested Solution

Upon examination of router R2's EIGRP topology table (as previously shown in Example 6-18), it becomes clear that the reason router R2 is only injecting one of the 10.1.2.0/24 routes into the IP routing table, is that the feasible distances of the two routes are different. By default, EIGRP load balances over routes with equal-cost metrics (that is, equal feasible distances); however, the two routes present in the EIGRP topology table have different metrics.

Examine the two metrics (that is, 2585600 and 3950848), and notice that the metrics differ by less than a factor of two. Specifically, if you took the smallest metric of 2585600 and multiplied it by two, the result would be 5171200, which is greater than the largest metric of 3950848.

Because the metrics for the two routes vary by less than a factor of two, EIGRP's variance feature could be configured to specify a variance of two, as shown in Example 6-20. Specifically, this configuration tells EIGRP on router R2 to not only inject the best EIGRP route into the IP routing table, but rather inject the route with the best metric in addition to any route whose metric is within a factor of two of the best metric (that is, in the range 2585600–5171200). This allows the route with a metric of 3950848 to also be injected into the IP routing table.

Example 6-20   *Enabling the Variance Feature on Router R2*

Key
Topic

```
R2# conf term
Enter configuration commands, one per line.  End with CNTL/Z.
R2(config)# router eigrp 1
R2(config-router)# variance 2
```

To confirm that router R2 can now load balance across routers BB1 and BB2 to reach the 10.1.2.0/24 network, examine the output of the **show ip route** command seen in

Example 6-21. This output confirms that router R2 can now load balance over two un-equal-cost paths to reach the 10.1.2.0/24 network.

Example 6-21   *Examining Router R2's IP Routing Table After Enabling the Variance Feature*

```
R2# show ip route
Codes: C - connected, S - static, R - RIP, M - mobile, B - BGP
       D - EIGRP, EX - EIGRP external, O - OSPF, IA - OSPF inter area
       N1 - OSPF NSSA external type 1, N2 - OSPF NSSA external type 2
       E1 - OSPF external type 1, E2 - OSPF external type 2
       i - IS-IS, su - IS-IS summary, L1 - IS-IS level-1, L2 - IS-IS level-2
       ia - IS-IS inter area, * - candidate default, U - per-user static route
       o - ODR, P - periodic downloaded static route

Gateway of last resort is not set

     172.16.0.0/30 is subnetted, 2 subnets
C       172.16.1.0 is directly connected, Serial1/0.1
C       172.16.2.0 is directly connected, Serial1/0.2
     10.0.0.0/8 is variably subnetted, 6 subnets, 3 masks
C       10.2.2.2/32 is directly connected, Loopback0
D       10.1.3.0/30 [90/3072000] via 172.16.2.2, 00:00:03, Serial1/0.2
                    [90/4437248] via 172.16.1.1, 00:00:03, Serial1/0.1
D       10.3.3.3/32 [90/2713600] via 172.16.2.2, 00:00:03, Serial1/0.2
                    [90/4053248] via 172.16.1.1, 00:00:03, Serial1/0.1
D       10.1.2.0/24 [90/2585600] via 172.16.2.2, 00:00:03, Serial1/0.2
                    [90/3950848] via 172.16.1.1, 00:00:03, Serial1/0.1
D       10.1.1.1/32 [90/409600] via 192.168.0.11, 00:00:03, FastEthernet0/0
D       10.4.4.4/32 [90/2688000] via 172.16.2.2, 00:00:03, Serial1/0.2
                    [90/4078848] via 172.16.1.1, 00:00:03, Serial1/0.1
C    192.168.0.0/24 is directly connected, FastEthernet0/0
D    192.168.1.0/24 [90/284160] via 192.168.0.11, 00:00:04, FastEthernet0/0
```

Exam Preparation Tasks

Review All Key Topics

Review the most important topics from inside the chapter, noted with the Key Topics icon in the outer margin of the page. Table 6-6 lists these key topics and the page numbers where each is found.

Table 6-6 *Key Topics for Chapter 6*

Key Topic Element	Description	Page Number
List	Steps to route traffic from one subnet to another	141
List	Router data structures	144
List	CEF data structures	144
Table 6-2	Troubleshooting Layer 3 forwarding information	145
Table 6-3	Troubleshooting Layer 3 to Layer 2 mapping information	148
Table 6-4	EIGRP data structures	152
Table 6-5	EIGRP troubleshooting commands	154
Example 6-18	Viewing an EIGRP topology table	160
Example 6-20	Enabling the EIGRP variance feature	161

Complete Tables and Lists from Memory

Print a copy of Appendix B, "Memory Tables," (found on the CD) or at least the section for this chapter, and complete the tables and lists from memory. Appendix C, "Memory Tables Answer Key," also on the CD, includes completed tables and lists to check your work.

Define Key Terms

Define the following key terms from this chapter, and check your answers in the Glossary:

Forwarding Information Base (FIB), adjacency table, Data Link Connection Identifier (DLCI), Virtual Path Identifier/Virtual Circuit Identifier (VPI/VCI), administrative distance, EIGRP interface table, EIGRP neighbor table, EIGRP topology table, variance

Command Reference to Check Your Memory

This section includes the most important configuration and EXEC commands covered in this chapter. To determine how well you have memorized the commands as a side effect of your other studies, cover the left side of the table with a piece of paper, read the descriptions on the right side, and see whether you remember the command.

Table 6-7   *Chapter 6 Configuration Command Reference*

Command	Description
router eigrp *autonomous-system-number*	Global configuration mode command that starts the EIGRP routing process. (NOTE: All routers that exchange EIGRP routing information must use the same autonomous system number.)
network *network* [**wildcard-mask**]	Router configuration mode command that specifies a connected network whose interface will participate in the EIGRP routing process.
no auto-summary	Router configuration mode command that disables automatic network summarization.
variance *multiplier*	Router configuration mode command that determines the metric values over which EIGRP will load-balance traffic.

Table 6-8   *Chapter 6 EXEC Command Reference*

Command	Description
show ip route *IP_address*	Displays a router's best route to the specified IP address.
show ip route *network subnet_mask*	Displays a router's best route to the specified network, if the specific route (with a matching subnet mask length) is found in the router's IP routing table.
show ip route *network subnet_mask* **longer-prefixes**	Displays all routes in a router's IP routing table that are encompassed by the specified network address and subnet mask. (NOTE: This command is often useful when troubleshooting route summarization issues.)
show ip cef *ip-address*	Displays information (for example, next-hop IP address and egress interface) required to forward a packet, similar to the output of the **show ip route** *IP_address* command. (NOTE: The output of this command comes from CEF. Therefore, routing protocol information is not presented in the output.)
show ip cef *network subnet_mask*	Displays information from a router's FIB showing the information needed to route a packet to the specified network with the specified subnet mask.
show ip cef exact-route *source-ip-address destination-ip-address*	Displays the adjacency that will be used to forward a packet from the specified source IP address to the specified destination IP address. (NOTE: This command is useful if the router is load balancing across multiple adjacencies, and you want to see which adjacency will be used for a certain combination of source and destination IP addresses.)

Table 6-8   *Chapter 6 EXEC Command Reference   (Continued)*

Command	Description
show ip arp	Displays a router's ARP cache, containing IP address to MAC address mappings. (NOTE: By default, a router's ARP cache stores information for four hours. Therefore, you might need to execute a **clear ip arp** command to allow a router to re-learn information after you make a topology change.)
show frame-relay map	Displays Frame Relay DLCIs associated with different next-hop IP addresses.
show adjacency detail	Displays the frame headers in a router's CEF adjacency table used to encapsulate a frame being sent to an adjacency.
show ip eigrp interfaces	Displays all of a router's interfaces configured to participate in an EIGRP routing process (with the exception of passive interfaces).
show ip eigrp neighbors	Shows a router's EIGRP neighbors.
show ip eigrp topology	Displays routes known to a router's EIGRP routing process. (NOTE: These routes are contained in the EIGRP topology table.)
show ip route eigrp	Displays routes known to a router's IP routing table that were injected by the router's EIGRP routing process.
debug ip routing	Displays updates that occur in a router's IP routing table. (NOTE: This is command is not specific to EIGRP.)
debug eigrp packets	Displays all EIGRP packets exchanged with a router's EIGRP neighbors. (NOTE: The focus of the command can be narrowed to only display specific EIGRP packet types, such as EIGRP Hello packets.)
debug ip eigrp	Displays information contained in EIGRP packets and reveals how an EIGRP routing process responds to that information.

This chapter covers the following subjects:

OSPF Troubleshooting: This section begins by introducing you to OSPF routing structures, followed by a review of OSPF operation. Finally, you are presented with a collection of **show** and **debug** commands useful for troubleshooting OSPF operations.

Trouble Ticket: OSPF: This section presents you with a trouble ticket and an associated topology. You are also given **show** command output. Based on the information provided, you hypothesize an underlying cause for the reported issues and develop solutions. You can then compare your solutions with the suggested solutions.

Route Redistribution Troubleshooting: This section introduces the concept of route redistribution and discusses how a route from one routing process can be injected into a different routing process. Common route redistribution troubleshooting targets are identified, along with strategies for troubleshooting a route redistribution issue.

Trouble Ticket: Route Redistribution with EIGRP and OSPF: This section presents you with a trouble ticket and an associated topology. You are also given **show** command output. Based on the information provided, you hypothesize an underlying cause for the reported issue and develop a solution. You can then compare your solution with a suggested solution.

CHAPTER 7

OSPF and Route Redistribution Troubleshooting

This chapter reviews the characteristics of Open Shortest Path First (OSPF), including OSPF data structures, router types, link-state advertisement (LSA) types, and network types. You also see how an OSPF adjacency is formed. Then you are presented with a collection of commands useful for troubleshooting OSPF networks.

This chapter contains two trouble tickets, the first of which addresses OSPF. Presented with a trouble ticket, a topology, and a collection of **show** command output, you are challenged to resolve the issue (or possibly multiple issues) in an OSPF-based network.

Next, you review the concept of route redistribution, where routes learned via one routing process can be injected into another routing process. Troubleshooting strategies for route redistribution are then presented.

Finally, this chapter challenges you with another trouble ticket. This final trouble ticket focuses on route redistribution.

"Do I Know This Already?" Quiz

The "Do I Know This Already?" quiz helps you determine your level of knowledge of this chapter's topics before you begin. Table 7-1 details the major topics discussed in this chapter and their corresponding quiz questions.

Table 7-1 *"Do I Know This Already?" Section-to-Question Mapping*

Foundation Topics Section	Questions
OSPF Troubleshooting	1–6
Route Redistribution Troubleshooting	7–8

1. Which OSPF data structure contains topological information for all areas in which an OSPF router is participating?

    a. OSPF Routing Information Base

    b. OSPF link-state database

    c. OSPF interface table

    d. OSPF neighbor table

2. What OSPF LSA type is sourced by all OSPF routers?

    a. Type 1

    b. Type 2

    c. Type 3

    d. Type 4

    e. Type 5

3. What type of OSPF router has at least one of its connected networks participating in OSPF area 0?

    a. Internal

    b. ABR

    c. Backbone

    d. ASBR

4. What is the default OSPF network type on LAN interfaces?

    a. Point-to-point

    b. Nonbroadcast

    c. Point-to-multipoint

    d. Broadcast

5. What OSPF adjacency state occurs when two OSPF routers have received Hello messages from each other, and each router saw its own OSPF router ID in the Hello message it received?

    a. Exchange

    b. ExStart

    c. 2-Way

    d. Loading

6. What command displays the LSA headers in a router's OSPF link-state database?

    a. show ip ospf neighbor

    b. show ip ospf database

    c. show ip ospf statistics

    d. show ip ospf interface

7. When performing route redistribution, the destination routing protocol needs a metric to assign to routes being redistributed into that routing protocol. What is this metric called?

    a. External metric

    b. Internal metric

    c. Seed metric

    d. Source metric

8. Which of the following commands would you use to enable the Cisco IOS IP route profiling feature?

    a.   Router(config)#**ip route profile**

    b.   Router(config-if)#**ip route profile**

    c.   Router(config)#**route profiling ip**

    d.   Router(config-if)#**route profiling ip**

Foundation Topics

OSPF Troubleshooting

Chapter 6, "Introduction to Troubleshooting Routing Protocols," began with a discussion on troubleshooting routing protocols from a generic perspective. Chapter 6 also reviewed router and Cisco Express Forwarding (CEF) data structures, as well as Enhanced Interior Gateway Routing Protocol (EIGRP), including EIGRP data structures. Finally, the chapter concluded with coverage of a collection of commands for gathering information from EIGRP data structures.

This section addresses the OSPF routing protocol in a similar fashion to the Chapter 6 treatment of EIGRP. Specifically, this section examines OSPF data structures, reviews OSPF operation, and presents you with commands useful for collecting information from the OSPF data structures.

OSPF is a nonproprietary link-state protocol. Like EIGRP, OSPF offers fast convergence and is a popular enterprise routing protocol.

OSPF Data Structures

Whereas EIGRP has three major data structures (that is, EIGRP interface table, EIGRP neighbor table, and EIGRP topology table), OSPF uses four data structures, as described in Table 7-2.

Table 7-2 *OSPF Data Structures*

Data Structure	Description
OSPF interface table	All the router interfaces that have been configured to participate in an OSPF routing process are listed in this table.
OSPF neighbor table	OSPF neighbors learned via Hello packets are present in this table. A neighbor is removed from this table if Hellos have not been heard from the neighbor within the dead time interval. Additionally, a neighbor is removed from this table if the interface associated with the neighbor goes down.
OSPF link-state database	This data structure contains topology information for all areas in which a router participates, in addition to information about how to route traffic to networks residing in other areas or autonomous systems.
OSPF Routing Information Base	The OSPF Routing Information Base (RIB) stores the results of the OSPF shortest path first (SPF) calculations.

Of the data structures listed in Table 7-2, the OSPF link-state database contains the most comprehensive collection of information. Therefore, the OSPF link-state database is valuable to view for OSPF troubleshooting.

An OSPF link-state database stored in an OSPF router contains comprehensive information about the topology within a specific OSPF area. Note that if a router is participating in more than one OSPF area, the router contains more than one OSPF link-state database (one for each area). Because an OSPF link-state database contains the topology of an OSPF area, all routers participating in that OSPF area should have identical OSPF link-state databases.

In addition to networks residing in OSPF areas, an OSPF router can store information about routes redistributed into OSPF in an OSPF link-state database. Information about these redistributed routes is stored in an area separate from the area-specific OSPF link-state databases.

OSPF Operation

Because OSPF is a link-state protocol, it receives LSAs from adjacent OSPF routers. The Dijkstra SPF algorithm takes the information contained in the LSAs to determine the shortest path to any destination within an area of the network.

Although multiple routers can participate in a single OSPF area, larger OSPF networks are often divided into multiple areas. In a multiarea OSPF network, a backbone area (numbered *area 0*) must exist, and all other areas must connect to area 0. If an area is not physically adjacent to area 0, a *virtual link* can be configured to logically connect the nonadjacent area with area 0.

OSPF Metric

OSPF uses a metric of *cost*, which is a function of bandwidth. Cost can be calculated as follows:

cost = 100,000,000 / bandwidth (in bps)

Designated Router

A multiaccess network can have multiple routers residing on a common network segment. Rather than having all routers form a full mesh of adjacencies with one another, a *designated router* (DR) can be elected, and all other routers on the segment can form an adjacency with the DR, as illustrated in Figure 7-1.

A DR is elected based on router priority, with larger priority values being more preferable. If routers have equal priorities, the DR is elected based on the highest OSPF router ID. An OSPF router ID is determined by the IP address of the loopback interface of the router or by the highest IP address on an active interface, or it can be statically defined if the router is not configured with a loopback interface.

A backup designated router (BDR) is also elected. Routers on the multiaccess network also form adjacencies if the DR becomes unavailable.

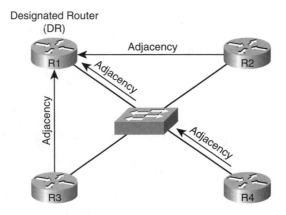

Figure 7-1 *Designated Router Adjacencies*

OSPF Router Types

When an OSPF network grows beyond a single area, you need to be aware of the role played by each OSPF router in a topology. Specifically, four OSPF router types exist:

- **Internal router:** All the networks directly connected to an internal router belong to the same OSPF area. Therefore, an internal router has a single link-state database.

- **Area border router (ABR):** An ABR connects to more than one OSPF area and therefore maintains multiple link-state databases (one for each connected area). A primary responsibility of an ABR is to exchange topological information between the backbone area and other connected areas.

- **Backbone router:** A backbone router has at least one of its connected networks participating in OSPF area 0 (that is, the backbone area). If all the connected networks are participating in the backbone area, the router is also considered to be an internal router. However, if a backbone router has one or more connected networks participating in another area, the backbone router is also considered to be an ABR.

- **Autonomous system boundary router (ASBR):** An ASBR has at least one connected route participating in an OSPF area and at least one connected route participating in a different autonomous system. The primary role of an ASBR is to exchange information between an OSPF autonomous system and one or more external autonomous systems.

As an example, Figure 7-2 illustrates these various OSPF router types.

Table 7-3 lists the OSPF router type or types for each OSPF router in the topology (that is, routers R1, R2, R3, and R4).

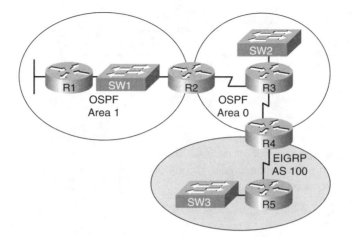

Figure 7-2 *OSPF Router Types*

Table 7-3 *OSPF Router Types in Figure 7-2*

Router	OSPF Router Type(s)
R1	Internal (because all the connected routes of the router belong to the same OSPF area)
R2	ABR (because the connected routes of the router belong to more than one OSPF area)
	Backbone (because the router has at least one connected route participating in OSPF area 0)
R3	Internal (because all the connected routes of the router belong to the same OSPF area)
	Backbone (because the router has at least one connected route participating in OSPF area 0)
R4	Backbone (because the router has at least one connected route participating in OSPF area 0)
	ASBR (because the router has at least one connected route participating in an OSPF area and one connected route participating in a different autonomous system)

OSPF LSA Types

As previously mentioned, an OSPF router receives LSAs from adjacent OSPF neighbors. However, OSPF uses multiple LSA types. Table 7-4 lists the common LSA types you might encounter when troubleshooting a Cisco-based OSPF network.

Table 7-4 *LSA Types*

LSA Type	Description
1	All OSPF routers source Type 1 LSAs. These advertisements list information about directly connected subnets, the OSPF connection types of a router, and the known OSPF adjacencies of a router. A Type 1 LSA is not sent out of its local area.
2	The designated router on a multiaccess network sends a Type 2 LSA for that network if the network contains at least two routers. A Type 2 LSA contains a listing of routers connected to the multiaccess network and, like a Type 1 LSA, is constrained to its local area.
3	A Type 3 LSA is sourced by an ABR. Each Type 3 LSA sent into an area contains information about a network reachable in a different area. Note that network information is exchanged only between the backbone area and a nonbackbone area, as opposed to being exchanged between two nonbackbone areas.
4	Similar to a Type 3 LSA, a Type 4 LSA is sourced by an ABR. However, instead of containing information about OSPF networks, a Type 4 LSA contains information stating how to reach an ASBR.
5	A Type 5 LSA is sourced by an ASBR and contains information about networks reachable outside the ospf domain. A Type 5 LSA is sent to all OSPF areas, except for stub areas. Note: The ABR for a stub area sends default route information into the stub area, rather than the network-specific Type 5 LSAs.
7	A Type 7 LSA is sourced from a router within a not-so-stubby-area (NSSA). Whereas a stub area does not connect to an external autonomous system, an NSSA can. Those external routes are announced by an ABR of the NSSA using Type 7 LSAs. Like a stub area, however, external routes known to another OSPF area are not forwarded into an NSSA.

To illustrate how the database of an OSPF router is populated with these various LSA types, once again consider Figure 7-2. Table 7-5 shows the number of each LSA type present in the OSPF routers of the topology. Note that the topology has no Type 7 LSAs because it does not contain NSSAs.

Table 7-5   *OSPF LSA Types in Figure 7-2*

Router	Type 1 LSAs	Type 2 LSAs	Type 3 LSAs	Type 4 LSAs	Type 5 LSAs
R1	2 (because two routers are in area 1)	1 (because only one of the multiaccess networks of area 1 contains at least two routers)	3 (because the area 1 database contains the three networks in area 0)	1 (because the topology contains only one ASBR)	2 (because the EIGRP AS contains two networks that are external to the OSPF AS)
R2	5 (because area 1 has two routers and area 0 has three routers)	1 (because area 1 contains only one multiaccess network containing at least two routers, while area 0 contains zero multiaccess networks with at least two routers)	5 (because the area 1 database contains the three networks in area 0, and the area 0 database contains the two networks in area 1)	1 (because the topology contains only one ASBR)	2 (because the EIGRP AS contains two networks that are external to the OSPF AS)
R3	3 (because area 0 has three routers)	0 (because area 0 does not contain any multiaccess networks with at least two routers)	2 (because the area 0 database contains the two networks in area 1)	1 (because the topology contains only one ASBR)	2 (because the EIGRP AS contains two networks that are external to the OSPF AS)
R4	3 (because area 0 has three routers)	0 (because area 0 does not contain multiaccess networks with at least two routers)	2 (because the area 0 database contains the two networks in area 1)	1 (because the topology contains only one ASBR)	2 (because the EIGRP AS contains two networks that are external to the OSPF AS)

OSPF Network Types

OSPF can support multiple network types. For example, a multiaccess network such as Ethernet is considered to be an OSPF *broadcast* network. Table 7-6 shows a listing of supported OSPF network types and characteristics of each.

Key
Topic

Table 7-6   *OSPF Network Types and Characteristics*

	Broadcast	Nonbroadcast	Point-to-Point	Point-to-Multipoint
Characteristics	Default OSPF network type on LAN interfaces	Default OSPF network type on Frame Relay serial interfaces	Default OSPF network type on non-Frame Relay serial interfaces	Can be configured on any interface
	Neighbors automatically discovered	Neighbors statically configured	Routers at each end of a link form adjacencies	Neighbors automatically determined
	All routers on same subnet	All routers on same subnet	Each point-to-point link on a separate subnet	All routers on same subnet
	Has a designated router	Has a designated router	Does not have a designated router	Does not have a designated router

Forming an OSPF Adjacency

Although two OSPF routers can form an adjacency (that is, become neighbors) through the exchange of Hello packets, the following parameters in the Hello packets must match:

Key
Topic

■ **Hello timer:** This timer defaults to 10 seconds for broadcast and point-to-point network types. The default is 30 seconds for nonbroadcast and point-to-multipoint network types.

■ **Dead timer:** This timer defaults to 40 seconds for broadcast and point-to-point network types. The default is 120 seconds for nonbroadcast and point-to-multipoint network types.

■ **Area number:** Both ends of a link must be in the same OSPF area.

■ **Area type:** In addition to a normal OSPF area type, an area type could be either stub or NSSA.

■ **Subnet:** Note that this common subnet is not verified on point-to-point OSPF networks.

■ **Authentication information:** If one OSPF interface is configured for authentication, the OSPF interface at the other end of the link should be configured with matching authentication information (for example, authentication type and password).

Adjacencies are not established upon the immediate receipt of Hello messages. Rather, an adjacency transitions through multiple states, as described in Table 7-7.

Table 7-7 *Adjacency States*

State	Description
Down	This state indicates that no Hellos have been received from a neighbor.
Attempt	This state occurs after a router sends a unicast Hello (as opposed to a multicast Hello) to a configured neighbor and has not yet received a Hello from that neighbor.
Init	This state occurs on a router that has received a Hello message from its neighbor; however, the OSPF router ID of the receiving router was not contained in the Hello message. If a router remains in this state for a long period, something is probably preventing that router from correctly receiving Hello packets from the neighboring router.
2-Way	This state occurs when two OSPF routers have received Hello messages from each other, and each router saw its own OSPF router ID in the Hello message it received. The 2-Way state could be a final state for a multiaccess network if the network has already elected a designated router and a backup designated router.
ExStart	This state occurs when the designated and nondesignated routers of a multiaccess network begin to exchange information with other routers in the multiaccess network. If a router remains in this state for a long period, a maximum transmission unit (MTU) mismatch could exist between the neighboring routers, or a duplicate OSPF router ID might exist.
Exchange	This state occurs when the two routers forming an adjacency send one another database descriptor (DBD) packets containing information about a router's link-state database. Each router compares the DBD packets received from the other router to identify missing entries in its own link-state database. Like the ExStart state, if a router remains in the Exchange state for a long period, the issue could be an MTU mismatch or a duplicate OSPF router ID.
Loading	Based on the missing link-state database entries identified in the Exchange state, the Loading state occurs when each neighboring router requests the other router to send those missing entries. If a router remains in this state for a long period, a packet might have been corrupted, or a router might have a memory corruption issue. Alternatively, it is possible that such a condition could result from the neighboring routers having an MTU mismatch.
Full	This state indicates that the neighboring OSPF routers have successfully exchanged their link-state information with one another, and an adjacency has been formed.

Tracking OSPF Advertisements Through a Network

When troubleshooting an OSPF issue, tracking the path of OSPF advertisements can be valuable in determining why certain entries are in a router's RIB.

As an example, notice network 192.168.1.0/24 in the topology provided in Figure 7-3, and consider how this network is entered into the RIB of the other OSPF routers.

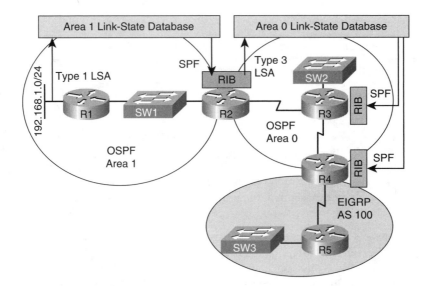

Figure 7-3 *Tracking an OSPF Advertisement*

The following steps describe how network 192.168.1.0/24, which is directly connected to router R1, is learned by the RIB of routers R2, R3, and R4.

Step 1. Router R1 creates an LSA for the 192.168.1.0/24 network in the area 1 link-state database.

Step 2. Router R2, which also has a copy of the area 1 link-state database, runs the SPF algorithm to determine the best path through area 1 to reach the 192.168.1.0/24 network. The result is stored in router R2's RIB.

Step 3. Router R2 informs area 0 routers about this network by injecting a Type 3 LSA into the link-state database of area 0. This LSA includes the cost to reach the 192.168.1.0/24 network, from the perspective of router R2.

Step 4. Each of the other area 0 routers (that is, routers R3 and R4) run the SPF algorithm to determine the cost to reach router R2. This cost is then added to the cost router R2 advertised in its Type 3 LSA, and the result is stored in the RIB for routers R3 and R4.

OSPF Troubleshooting Commands

With an understanding of OSPF's data structures and an understanding of OSPF's router types, network types, LSA types, and adjacency states, you can now strategically use Cisco IOS **show** and **debug** commands to collect information about specific steps in the routing process. Table 7-8 shows a collection of such commands, along with their descriptions, and the step of the routing process or OSPF data structure each command can be used to investigate.

Table 7-8 *OSPF Troubleshooting Commands*

Command	Routing Component or Data Structure	Description
show ip ospf interface [brief]	OSPF interface table	This command displays all of a router's interfaces configured to participate in an OSPF routing process. The **brief** option provides a more concise view of OSPF interface information.
show ip ospf neighbor	OSPF neighbor table	This command displays the state of OSPF neighbors learned off a router's active OSPF interfaces.
show ip ospf database	OSPF link-state database	This command displays the LSA headers contained in a router's OSPF link-state database.
show ip ospf statistics	OSPF RIB	This command provides information about how frequently a router is executing the SPF algorithm. Additionally, this command shows when the SPF algorithm last ran.
debug ip ospf monitor	OSPF RIB	This command provides real-time updates showing when a router's SPF algorithm is scheduled to run.
debug ip routing	IP routing table	This command displays updates that occur in a router's IP routing table. Therefore, this command is not specific to OSPF.
show ip route ospf	IP routing table	This command shows routes known to a router's IP routing table that were learned via OSPF.
debug ip ospf packet	Exchanging OSPF information with neighbors	This command shows the transmission and reception of OSPF packets in real time. This command is useful for monitoring Hello messages.
debug ip ospf adj	Exchanging OSPF information with neighbors	This command provides real-time updates about the formation of an OSPF adjacency.

continues

Table 7-8   *OSPF Troubleshooting Commands*   (*Continued*)

Command	Routing Component or Data Structure	Description
debug ip ospf events	Exchanging OSPF information with neighbors	This command shows real-time information about OSPF events, including the transmission and reception of Hello messages and LSAs. This command might be useful on a router that appears to be ignoring Hello messages received from a neighboring router.
show ip ospf virtual-links	OSPF interface table	This command provides information about the status of OSPF virtual links that are required for areas not physically adjacent to the backbone area (that is, area 0).

Example 7-1 provides sample output from the **show ip ospf interface brief** command. Notice that the output shows summary information about all the router interfaces participating in an OSPF routing process, including the OSPF process ID (PID), the OSPF area, and the network associated with each interface. Additionally, the output contains the OSPF metric of cost, information about the state of an interface, and the number of neighbors that an interface has.

Example 7-1   show ip ospf interface brief *Command Output*

```
R2# show ip ospf interface brief
Interface     PID   Area          IP Address/Mask      Cost    State    Nbrs F/C
Lo0           1     0             10.2.2.2/32          1       LOOP     0/0
Se1/0.2       1     0             172.16.2.1/30        64      P2P      1/1
Se1/0.1       1     0             172.16.1.2/30        64      P2P      1/1
Fa0/0         1     0             192.168.0.22/24      10      DR       1/1
```

Example 7-2 provides sample output from the **show ip ospf neighbor** command. A neighbor's OSPF router ID is shown. For a multiaccess segment (FastEthernet 0/0 in this example), the neighbor's priority, used for designated router election, is shown. The remaining dead time for a neighbor is displayed. Finally, the output contains information about each neighbor's interface (and the IP address of that interface) through which the neighbor is reachable.

Example 7-2   show ip ospf neighbor *Command Output*

```
R2# show ip ospf neighbor
Neighbor ID     Pri    State        Dead Time    Address         Interface
10.4.4.4         0     FULL/  -      00:00:38     172.16.2.2      Serial1/0.2
10.3.3.3         0     FULL/  -      00:00:38     172.16.1.1      Serial1/0.1
10.1.1.1         1     FULL/BDR     00:00:36     192.168.0.11    FastEthernet0/0
```

Example 7-3 provides sample output from the **show ip ospf database** command. The database of the router has been populated with various LSAs, as previously discussed. The *Router Link States* in the database come from Type 1 LSAs, whereas the *Net Link States* come from Type 2 LSAs.

Example 7-3   show ip ospf database *Command Output*

```
R2# show ip ospf database
            OSPF Router with ID (10.2.2.2) (Process ID 1)
        Router Link States (Area 0)
Link ID         ADV Router      Age        Seq#         Checksum   Link count
10.1.1.1        10.1.1.1        969        0x8000000C   0x0092ED   3
10.2.2.2        10.2.2.2        968        0x80000013   0x00FD7D   6
10.3.3.3        10.3.3.3        1598       0x80000007   0x00DAEA   6
10.4.4.4        10.4.4.4        1597       0x80000007   0x0009B1   6
        Net Link States (Area 0)

Link ID         ADV Router      Age        Seq#         Checksum
10.1.2.2        10.4.4.4        1622       0x80000001   0x00CE1D
192.168.0.22    10.2.2.2        968        0x8000000B   0x008AF8
```

Example 7-4 provides sample output from the **show ip ospf statistics** command. Notice that the primary focus of the command is on the SPF algorithm. For example, you can see from the output how many times the SPF algorithm has been executed for a particular OSPF area.

Example 7-4   show ip ospf statistics *Command Output*

```
R2# show ip ospf statistics
            OSPF Router with ID (10.2.2.2) (Process ID 1)
  Area 0: SPF algorithm executed 23 times
  Summary OSPF SPF statistic
  SPF calculation time
Delta T    Intra    D-Intra    Summ     D-Summ    Ext    D-Ext    Total    Reason
00:21:00   12       0          0        0         0      0        16       R, N,
00:20:50   16       0          0        0         0      0        20       R,
00:19:40   12       4          0        0         0      0        20       R, N,
00:19:30   12       0          0        0         0      0        16       R, N,
00:19:20   16       0          0        0         4      0        24       R,
```

```
00:18:09     12      4      0      0      0      0      16     R, N,
00:17:59     12      0      0      0      0      0      16     R, N,
00:17:49     16      0      0      0      0      0      20     N,
00:16:37      4      4      0      0      0      0       8     R, N,
00:16:27     16      0      0      0      0      0      20     R, N,
    RIB manipulation time during SPF (in msec):
Delta T      RIB Update      RIB Delete
00:21:00     3               0
00:20:52     4               0
00:19:42     0               3
00:19:32     3               0
00:19:22     7               0
00:18:10     3               0
00:18:00     7               0
00:17:50     0               0
00:16:39     0               0
00:16:29     0               0
```

Example 7-5 provides sample output from the **debug ip ospf monitor** command. This command provides real-time information about when the SPF algorithm is scheduled to run and when it actually does run.

Example 7-5   debug ip ospf monitor *Command Output*

```
R2# debug ip ospf monitor
OSPF spf monitoring debugging is on
*Mar  1 00:29:11.923: OSPF: Schedule SPF in area 0
       Change in LS ID 10.1.1.1, LSA type R, , spf-type Full
*Mar  1 00:29:11.927: OSPF: reset throttling to 5000ms
*Mar  1 00:29:11.927: OSPF: schedule SPF: spf_time 00:29:11.928 wait_interval 5000ms
*Mar  1 00:29:16.927: OSPF: Begin SPF at 1756.928ms, process time 1132ms
*Mar  1 00:29:16.927:        spf_time 00:29:11.928, wait_interval 5000ms
*Mar  1 00:29:16.947: OSPF: wait_interval 10000ms next wait_interval 10000ms
*Mar  1 00:29:16.947: OSPF: End SPF at 1756.948ms, Total elapsed time 20ms
*Mar  1 00:29:16.951:        Schedule time 00:29:16.948, Next wait_interval 10000ms
*Mar  1 00:29:16.955:        Intra: 12ms, Inter: 0ms, External: 0ms
*Mar  1 00:29:16.955:        R: 4, N: 2, Stubs: 10
*Mar  1 00:29:16.955:        SN: 0, SA: 0, X5: 0, X7: 0
*Mar  1 00:29:16.955:        SPF suspends: 0 intra, 0 total
*Mar  1 00:29:26.175: OSPF: Schedule SPF in area 0
       Change in LS ID 10.1.1.1, LSA type R, , spf-type Full
*Mar  1 00:29:26.947: OSPF: Begin SPF at 1766.948ms, process time 1160ms
*Mar  1 00:29:26.947:        spf_time 00:29:16.948, wait_interval 10000ms
*Mar  1 00:29:26.971: OSPF: wait_interval 10000ms next wait_interval 10000ms
*Mar  1 00:29:26.975: OSPF: End SPF at 1766.972ms, Total elapsed time 28ms
*Mar  1 00:29:26.975:        Schedule time 00:29:26.972, Next wait_interval 10000ms
```

```
*Mar  1 00:29:26.975:          Intra: 16ms, Inter: 0ms, External: 0ms
*Mar  1 00:29:26.975:          R: 4, N: 2, Stubs: 11
*Mar  1 00:29:26.975:          SN: 0, SA: 0, X5: 0, X7: 0
*Mar  1 00:29:26.975:          SPF suspends: 0 intra, 0 total
```

Example 7-6 provides sample output from the **debug ip routing** command. The output reflects a loopback interface (with an IP address of 10.1.1.1) on a neighboring router being administratively shut down and brought back up.

Example 7-6   debug ip routing *Command Output*

```
R2# debug ip routing
IP routing debugging is on
*Mar  1 00:29:58.163: RT: del 10.1.1.1/32 via 192.168.0.11, ospf metric [110/11]
*Mar  1 00:29:58.163: RT: delete subnet route to 10.1.1.1/32
*Mar  1 00:29:58.163: RT: NET-RED 10.1.1.1/32
*Mar  1 00:30:08.175: RT: SET_LAST_RDB for 10.1.1.1/32
  NEW rdb: via 192.168.0.11
*Mar  1 00:30:08.179: RT: add 10.1.1.1/32 via 192.168.0.11, ospf metric [110/11]
*Mar  1 00:30:08.183: RT: NET-RED 10.1.1.1/32
```

Example 7-7 provides sample output from the **show ip route ospf** command. This command produces a subset of the output from the **show ip route** command, showing only those route entries learned via OSPF.

Example 7-7   show ip route ospf *Command Output*

```
R2# show ip route ospf
     10.0.0.0/8 is variably subnetted, 6 subnets, 3 masks
O       10.1.3.0/30 [110/128] via 172.16.2.2, 00:00:20, Serial1/0.2
                    [110/128] via 172.16.1.1, 00:00:20, Serial1/0.1
O       10.3.3.3/32 [110/65] via 172.16.1.1, 00:00:20, Serial1/0.1
O       10.1.2.0/24 [110/74] via 172.16.2.2, 00:00:20, Serial1/0.2
                    [110/74] via 172.16.1.1, 00:00:20, Serial1/0.1
O       10.1.1.1/32 [110/11] via 192.168.0.11, 00:00:20, FastEthernet0/0
O       10.4.4.4/32 [110/65] via 172.16.2.2, 00:00:20, Serial1/0.2
```

Example 7-8 provides sample output from the **debug ip ospf packet** command. The output confirms OSPF packets are being received from specific neighbors and over what interfaces those OSPF packets are being received. For example, the output indicates that an OSPF neighbor with a router ID of 10.1.1.1 sent an OSPF packet, and that packet came into this router on FastEthernet 0/0.

Example 7-8   debug ip ospf packet *Command Output*

```
R2# debug ip ospf packet
OSPF packet debugging is on
*Mar  1 00:30:42.995: OSPF: rcv. v:2 t:1 l:48 rid:10.1.1.1
       aid:0.0.0.0 chk:5422 aut:0 auk: from FastEthernet0/0
*Mar  1 00:30:45.039: OSPF: rcv. v:2 t:4 l:76 rid:10.1.1.1
       aid:0.0.0.0 chk:E9B4 aut:0 auk: from FastEthernet0/0
*Mar  1 00:30:45.179: OSPF: rcv. v:2 t:1 l:48 rid:10.3.3.3
       aid:0.0.0.0 chk:D294 aut:0 auk: from Serial1/0.1
*Mar  1 00:30:45.363: OSPF: rcv. v:2 t:1 l:48 rid:10.4.4.4
       aid:0.0.0.0 chk:D192 aut:0 auk: from Serial1/0.2
*Mar  1 00:30:47.727: OSPF: rcv. v:2 t:5 l:44 rid:10.3.3.3
       aid:0.0.0.0 chk:2EF0 aut:0 auk: from Serial1/0.1
```

Example 7-9 provides sample output from the **debug ip adj** command. This command shows real-time details as a router establishes an adjacency with an OSPF neighbor, including the states through which the adjacency transitions.

Example 7-9   debug ip ospf adj *Command Output*

```
R2# debug ip ospf adj
OSPF adjacency events debugging is on
*Mar  1 00:31:44.719: OSPF: Rcv LS UPD from 10.3.3.3 on Serial1/0.1 length 100
  LSA count 1
*Mar  1 00:31:57.475: OSPF: Cannot see ourself in hello from 10.4.4.4 on
  Serial1/0.2, state INIT
*Mar  1 00:31:57.807: OSPF: 2 Way Communication to 10.4.4.4 on Serial1/0.2,
  state 2WAY
*Mar  1 00:31:57.811: OSPF: Send DBD to 10.4.4.4 on Serial1/0.2 seq 0x7FD opt
  0x52 flag 0x7 len 32
*Mar  1 00:31:57.815: OSPF: Rcv DBD from 10.4.4.4 on Serial1/0.2 seq 0xDF9 opt
  0x52 flag 0x7 len 32   mtu 1500 state EXSTART
*Mar  1 00:31:57.819: OSPF: NBR Negotiation Done. We are the SLAVE
*Mar  1 00:31:57.819: OSPF: Send DBD to 10.4.4.4 on Serial1/0.2 seq 0xDF9 opt
  0x52 flag 0x2 len 152
*Mar  1 00:31:57.983: OSPF: Build router LSA for area 0, router ID 10.2.2.2, seq
  0x80000014
*Mar  1 00:31:58.191: OSPF: Rcv DBD from 10.4.4.4 on Serial1/0.2 seq 0xDFA opt
  0x52 flag 0x3 len 152   mtu 1500 state EXCHANGE
*Mar  1 00:31:58.195: OSPF: Send DBD to 10.4.4.4 on Serial1/0.2 seq 0xDFA opt
  0x52 flag 0x0 len 32
*Mar  1 00:31:58.199: OSPF: Rcv LS UPD from 10.3.3.3 on Serial1/0.1 length 112
  LSA count 1
*Mar  1 00:31:58.455: OSPF: Rcv DBD from 10.4.4.4 on Serial1/0.2 seq 0xDFB opt
  0x52 flag 0x1 len 32   mtu 1500 state EXCHANGE
*Mar  1 00:31:58.459: OSPF: Exchange Done with 10.4.4.4 on Serial1/0.2
*Mar  1 00:31:58.463: OSPF: Synchronized with 10.4.4.4 on Serial1/0.2, state FULL
*Mar  1 00:31:58.463: %OSPF-5-ADJCHG: Process 1, Nbr 10.4.4.4 on Serial1/0.2 from
  LOADING to FULL, Loading Done
```

Example 7-10 provides sample output from the **debug ip ospf events** command. This command produces real-time information about OSPF events, including the transmission and reception of OSPF Hello messages and LSAs.

Example 7-10   debug ip ospf events *Command Output*

```
R2# debug ip ospf events
OSPF events debugging is on
*Mar  1 00:32:23.007: OSPF: Rcv hello from 10.1.1.1 area 0 from FastEthernet0/0
  192.168.0.11
*Mar  1 00:32:23.011: OSPF: End of hello processing
*Mar  1 00:32:25.195: OSPF: Rcv hello from 10.3.3.3 area 0 from Serial1/0.1
  172.16.1.1
*Mar  1 00:32:25.199: OSPF: End of hello processing
*Mar  1 00:32:27.507: OSPF: Rcv hello from 10.4.4.4 area 0 from Serial1/0.2
  172.16.2.2
*Mar  1 00:32:27.511: OSPF: End of hello processing
*Mar  1 00:32:28.595: OSPF: Send hello to 224.0.0.5 area 0 on Serial1/0.1 from
  172.16.1.2
*Mar  1 00:32:28.687: OSPF: Send hello to 224.0.0.5 area 0 on Serial1/0.2 from
  172.16.2.1
*Mar  1 00:32:29.163: OSPF: Send hello to 224.0.0.5 area 0 on FastEthernet0/0
  from 192.168.0.22
*Mar  1 00:32:32.139: OSPF: Rcv LS UPD from 10.3.3.3 on Serial1/0.1 length 100
  LSA count 1
*Mar  1 00:32:33.007: OSPF: Rcv hello from 10.1.1.1 area 0 from FastEthernet0/0
  192.168.0.11
*Mar  1 00:32:33.011: OSPF: End of hello processing
*Mar  1 00:32:35.087: OSPF: Rcv hello from 10.3.3.3 area 0 from Serial1/0.1
  172.16.1.1
*Mar  1 00:32:35.091: OSPF: End of hello processing
```

Example 7-11 provides sample output from the **show ip ospf virtual-links** command. The output indicates that the other end of the virtual link has an OSPF router ID of 10.2.2.2. Also, notice that the transit area (that is, the area between the discontiguous area and area 0) is area 1.

Example 7-11   show ip ospf virtual-links *Command Output*

```
R1# show ip ospf virtual-links
Virtual Link OSPF_VL5 to router 10.2.2.2 is up
  Run as demand circuit
  DoNotAge LSA allowed.
  Transit area 1, via interface FastEthernet0/1, Cost of using 1
  Transmit Delay is 1 sec, State POINT_TO_POINT,
  Timer intervals configured, Hello 10, Dead 40, Wait 40, Retransmit 5
    Hello due in 00:00:00
    Adjacency State FULL (Hello suppressed)
    Index 1/2, retransmission queue length 0, number of retransmission 0
```

```
First 0x0(0)/0x0(0) Next 0x0(0)/0x0(0)
Last retransmission scan length is 0, maximum is 0
Last retransmission scan time is 0 msec, maximum is 0 msec
```

Trouble Ticket: OSPF

This trouble ticket focuses on OSPF. You are presented with baseline data, a trouble ticket, and information collected while investigating the reported issue. You are then challenged to identify the issue (or issues) and create an action plan to resolve that issue(s).

Trouble Ticket #4

You receive the following trouble ticket:

> For vendor interoperability reasons, a company changed its routing protocol from EIGRP to OSPF. The network was divided into areas, and all interfaces were instructed to participate in OSPF. The configuration was initially working. However, now none of the routers have full reachability to all the subnets.

This trouble ticket references the topology shown in Figure 7-4.

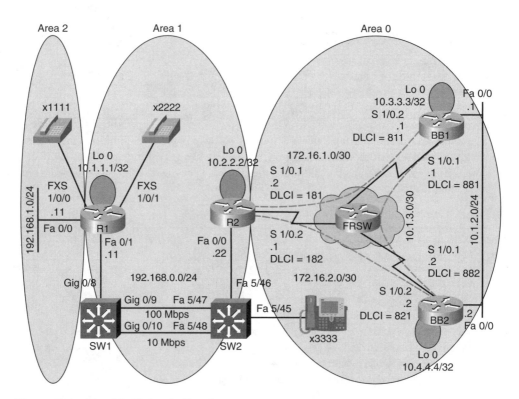

Figure 7-4   *Trouble Ticket #4 Topology*

As you investigate this issue, you examine baseline data collected after OSPF was initially configured. Example 7-12 shows baseline data collected from router R1, when the network was fully operational. Notice that router R1 is configured with a virtual link because it does not physically touch area 0.

Example 7-12 *Baseline Configuration Data from Router R1*

```
R1# show run | begin router
router ospf 1
 area 1 virtual-link 10.2.2.2
 network 10.1.1.1 0.0.0.0 area 1
 network 192.168.0.0 0.0.0.255 area 1
 network 192.168.1.0 0.0.0.255 area 2

R1# show ip ospf neighbor

Neighbor ID     Pri   State      Dead Time    Address         Interface
10.2.2.2        0     FULL/  -      -          192.168.0.22    OSPF_VL2
10.2.2.2        1     FULL/DR    00:00:38     192.168.0.22    FastEthernet0/1

R1# show ip route
Codes: C - connected, S - static, R - RIP, M - mobile, B - BGP
       D - EIGRP, EX - EIGRP external, O - OSPF, IA - OSPF inter area
       N1 - OSPF NSSA external type 1, N2 - OSPF NSSA external type 2
       E1 - OSPF external type 1, E2 - OSPF external type 2
       i - IS-IS, su - IS-IS summary, L1 - IS-IS level-1, L2 - IS-IS level-2
       ia - IS-IS inter area, * - candidate default, U - per-user static route
       o - ODR, P - periodic downloaded static route

Gateway of last resort is not set

     172.16.0.0/30 is subnetted, 2 subnets
O       172.16.1.0 [110/134] via 192.168.0.22, 01:34:44, FastEthernet0/1
O       172.16.2.0 [110/81] via 192.168.0.22, 01:34:44, FastEthernet0/1
     10.0.0.0/8 is variably subnetted, 6 subnets, 3 masks
O       10.2.2.2/32 [110/2] via 192.168.0.22, 02:24:31, FastEthernet0/1
O       10.1.3.0/30 [110/145] via 192.168.0.22, 01:34:44, FastEthernet0/1
O       10.3.3.3/32 [110/92] via 192.168.0.22, 01:34:44, FastEthernet0/1
O       10.1.2.0/24 [110/91] via 192.168.0.22, 01:34:45, FastEthernet0/1
C       10.1.1.1/32 is directly connected, Loopback0
O       10.4.4.4/32 [110/82] via 192.168.0.22, 01:34:45, FastEthernet0/1
C    192.168.0.0/24 is directly connected, FastEthernet0/1
C    192.168.1.0/24 is directly connected, FastEthernet0/0
R1# show ip ospf
```

```
Routing Process "ospf 1" with ID 10.1.1.1
Supports only single TOS(TOS0) routes
Supports opaque LSA
Supports Link-local Signaling (LLS)
Supports area transit capability It is an area border router
Initial SPF schedule delay 5000 msecs
Minimum hold time between two consecutive SPFs 10000 msecs
Maximum wait time between two consecutive SPFs 10000 msecs
Incremental-SPF disabled
Minimum LSA interval 5 secs

Minimum LSA arrival 1000 msecs
LSA group pacing timer 240 secs
Interface flood pacing timer 33 msecs
Retransmission pacing timer 66 msecs
Number of external LSA 0. Checksum Sum 0x000000
Number of opaque AS LSA 0. Checksum Sum 0x000000
Number of DCbitless external and opaque AS LSA 0
Number of DoNotAge external and opaque AS LSA 0
Number of areas in this router is 3. 3 normal 0 stub 0 nssa
Number of areas transit capable is 1
External flood list length 0
    Area BACKBONE(0)
Number of interfaces in this area is 1
    Area has no authentication
    SPF algorithm last executed 01:35:17.308 ago
    SPF algorithm executed 9 times
    Area ranges are
    Number of LSA 12. Checksum Sum 0x063B08
    Number of opaque link LSA 0. Checksum Sum 0x000000
    Number of DCbitless LSA 0
    Number of indication LSA 0
    Number of DoNotAge LSA 7
    Flood list length 0
    Area 1
Number of interfaces in this area is 2 (1 loopback)
    This area has transit capability: Virtual Link Endpoint
    Area has no authentication
    SPF algorithm last executed 02:25:04.377 ago
    SPF algorithm executed 22 times
    Area ranges are
```

```
        Number of LSA 10. Checksum Sum 0x059726
        Number of opaque link LSA 0. Checksum Sum 0x000000
        Number of DCbitless LSA 0
        Number of indication LSA 0
        Number of DoNotAge LSA 0
        Flood list length 0
    Area 2
    Number of interfaces in this area is 1
        Number of indication LSA 0
        Number of DoNotAge LSA 0
        Flood list length 0
        Area has no authentication
        SPF algorithm last executed 02:25:15.880 ago
        SPF algorithm executed 9 times
        Area ranges are
        Number of LSA 10. Checksum Sum 0x05F97B
        Number of opaque link LSA 0. Checksum Sum 0x000000
        Number of DCbitless LSA 0
R1# show ip ospf interface fa0/1
FastEthernet0/1 is up, line protocol is up
    Internet Address 192.168.0.11/24, Area 1
    Process ID 1, Router ID 10.1.1.1, Network Type BROADCAST, Cost: 1
    Transmit Delay is 1 sec, State BDR, Priority 1
    Designated Router (ID) 10.2.2.2, Interface address 192.168.0.22
    Backup Designated router (ID) 10.1.1.1, Interface address 192.168.0.11
    Timer intervals configured, Hello 10, Dead 40, Wait 40, Retransmit 5
        oob-resync timeout 40
        Hello due in 00:00:00
    Supports Link-local Signaling (LLS)
    Index 2/2, flood queue length 0
    Next 0x0(0)/0x0(0)
    Last flood scan length is 1, maximum is 1
    Last flood scan time is 0 msec, maximum is 4 msec
    Neighbor Count is 1, Adjacent neighbor count is 1
        Adjacent with neighbor 10.2.2.2  (Designated Router)
    Suppress hello for 0 neighbor(s)
```

Example 7-13 shows baseline configuration data collected from router R2.

Example 7-13 *Baseline Configuration Data from Router R2*

```
R2# show run | begin router
router ospf 1
 area 1 virtual-link 10.1.1.1
 network 10.2.2.2 0.0.0.0 area 1
 network 172.16.1.0 0.0.0.3 area 0
 network 172.16.2.0 0.0.0.3 area 0
 network 192.168.0.0 0.0.0.255 area 1


R2# show ip ospf neighbor

Neighbor ID    Pri    State        Dead Time   Address        Interface
10.4.4.4       0      FULL/   -    00:00:34    172.16.2.2     Serial1/0.2
10.3.3.3       0      FULL/   -    00:00:37    172.16.1.1     Serial1/0.1
10.1.1.1       0      FULL/   -    -           192.168.0.11   OSPF_VL0
10.1.1.1       1      FULL/BDR     00:00:39    192.168.0.11   FastEthernet0/0


R2# show ip route
Codes: C - connected, S - static, R - RIP, M - mobile, B - BGP
       D - EIGRP, EX - EIGRP external, O - OSPF, IA - OSPF inter area
       N1 - OSPF NSSA external type 1, N2 - OSPF NSSA external type 2
       E1 - OSPF external type 1, E2 - OSPF external type 2
       i - IS-IS, su - IS-IS summary, L1 - IS-IS level-1, L2 - IS-IS level-2
       ia - IS-IS inter area, * - candidate default, U - per-user static route
       o - ODR, P - periodic downloaded static route
Gateway of last resort is not set


     172.16.0.0/30 is subnetted, 2 subnets
C        172.16.1.0 is directly connected, Serial1/0.1
C        172.16.2.0 is directly connected, Serial1/0.2
     10.0.0.0/8 is variably subnetted, 6 subnets, 3 masks
C        10.2.2.2/32 is directly connected, Loopback0
O        10.1.3.0/30 [110/144] via 172.16.2.2, 01:34:50, Serial1/0.2
O        10.3.3.3/32 [110/91] via 172.16.2.2, 01:34:50, Serial1/0.2
O        10.1.2.0/24 [110/90] via 172.16.2.2, 01:34:50, Serial1/0.2
O        10.1.1.1/32 [110/11] via 192.168.0.11, 02:24:36, FastEthernet0/0
O        10.4.4.4/32 [110/81] via 172.16.2.2, 01:34:50, Serial1/0.2
C    192.168.0.0/24 is directly connected, FastEthernet0/0
O IA 192.168.1.0/24 [110/11] via 192.168.0.11, 01:34:50, FastEthernet0/0


R2# show run   begin router
router ospf 1
 area 1 virtual-link 10.1.1.1
 network 10.2.2.2 0.0.0.0 area 1
```

```
network 172.16.1.0 0.0.0.3 area 0
network 172.16.2.0 0.0.0.3 area 0
network 192.168.0.0 0.0.0.255 area 1
```

Example 7-14 shows baseline configuration data collected from router BB1.

Example 7-14 *Baseline Configuration Data from Router BB1*

```
BB1# show run  begin router
router ospf 1
 network 0.0.0.0 255.255.255.255 area 0


BB1# show ip ospf neighbor

Neighbor ID      Pri     State        Dead Time     Address          Interface
10.4.4.4         1       FULL/DR      00:00:38      10.1.2.2         FastEthernet0/
0
10.2.2.2         0       FULL/        00:00:39      172.16.1.2       Serial1/0.2
10.4.4.4         0       FULL/  -     00:00:38      10.1.3.2         Serial1/0.1


BB1# show ip route
Codes: C - connected, S - static, R - RIP, M - mobile, B - BGP
       D - EIGRP, EX - EIGRP external, O - OSPF, IA - OSPF inter area
       N1 - OSPF NSSA external type 1, N2 - OSPF NSSA external type 2
       E1 - OSPF external type 1, E2 - OSPF external type 2
       i - IS-IS, su - IS-IS summary, L1 - IS-IS level-1, L2 - IS-IS level-2
       ia - IS-IS inter area, * - candidate default, U - per-user static route
       o - ODR, P - periodic downloaded static route
Gateway of last resort is not set

     172.16.0.0/30 is subnetted, 2 subnets
C       172.16.1.0 is directly connected, Serial1/0.2
O       172.16.2.0 [110/90] via 10.1.2.2, 01:35:01, FastEthernet0/0
     10.0.0.0/8 is variably subnetted, 6 subnets, 3 masks
O IA    10.2.2.2/32 [110/91] via 10.1.2.2, 01:35:01, FastEthernet0/0
C       10.1.3.0/30 is directly connected, Serial1/0.1
C       10.3.3.3/32 is directly connected, Loopback0
C       10.1.2.0/24 is directly connected, FastEthernet0/0
O IA    10.1.1.1/32 [110/101] via 10.1.2.2, 01:35:01, FastEthernet0/0
O       10.4.4.4/32 [110/11] via 10.1.2.2, 01:35:01, FastEthernet0/0
O IA 192.168.0.0/24 [110/100] via 10.1.2.2, 01:35:01, FastEthernet0/0
O IA 192.168.1.0/24 [110/101] via 10.1.2.2, 01:35:01, FastEthernet0/0
```

Example 7-15 shows baseline configuration data collected from router BB2.

Example 7-15   *Baseline Configuration Data from Router BB2*

```
BB2# show run | begin router
router ospf 1
 network 0.0.0.0 255.255.255.255 area 0


BB2# show ip ospf neighbor
10.2.2.2          0    FULL/  -      00:00:32     172.16.2.1    Serial1/0.2
10.3.3.3          0    FULL/  -      00:00:39     10.1.3.1      Serial1/0.1
10.3.3.3          1    FULL/BDR      00:00:35     10.1.2.1
FastEthernet0/0
Neighbor ID      Pri   State         Dead Time    Address       Interface
BB2# show ip route
Codes: C - connected, S - static, R - RIP, M - mobile, B - BGP
       D - EIGRP, EX - EIGRP external, O - OSPF, IA - OSPF inter area
       N1 - OSPF NSSA external type 1, N2 - OSPF NSSA external type 2
       E1 - OSPF external type 1, E2 - OSPF external type 2
       i - IS-IS, su - IS-IS summary, L1 - IS-IS level-1, L2 - IS-IS level-2
       ia - IS-IS inter area, * - candidate default, U - per-user static route
       o - ODR, P - periodic downloaded static route


Gateway of last resort is not set


     172.16.0.0/30 is subnetted, 2 subnets
O IA 192.168.1.0/24 [110/101] via 10.1.2.2, 01:35:01, FastEthernet0/0
O        172.16.1.0 [110/143] via 10.1.2.1, 01:35:06, FastEthernet0/0
C        172.16.2.0 is directly connected, Serial1/0.2
     10.0.0.0/8 is variably subnetted, 6 subnets, 3 masks
O IA     10.2.2.2/32 [110/81] via 172.16.2.1, 01:35:06, Serial1/0.2
C        10.1.3.0/30 is directly connected, Serial1/0.1
O        10.3.3.3/32 [110/11] via 10.1.2.1, 01:35:06, FastEthernet0/0
C        10.1.2.0/24 is directly connected, FastEthernet0/0
O IA     10.1.1.1/32 [110/91] via 172.16.2.1, 01:35:06, Serial1/0.2
C        10.4.4.4/32 is directly connected, Loopback0
O IA 192.168.0.0/24 [110/90] via 172.16.2.1, 01:35:06, Serial1/0.2
O IA 192.168.1.0/24 [110/91] via 172.16.2.1, 01:35:06, Serial1/0.2
```

Now that you have seen the baseline data, the following examples present you with data collected after the trouble ticket was issued. Example 7-16 shows information collected from router R1. Notice that router R1's routing table can no longer see the Loopback 0 IP address of router BB2 (that is, 10.4.4.4/32). Also, notice that the virtual link between area 2 and area 0 is down.

Example 7-16 *Information Gathered from Router R1 After the Trouble Ticket Was Issued*

```
R1# show ip route
Codes: C - connected, S - static, R - RIP, M - mobile, B - BGP
       D - EIGRP, EX - EIGRP external, O - OSPF, IA - OSPF inter area
       N1 - OSPF NSSA external type 1, N2 - OSPF NSSA external type 2
       E1 - OSPF external type 1, E2 - OSPF external type 2
       i - IS-IS, su - IS-IS summary, L1 - IS-IS level-1, L2 - IS-IS level-2
       ia - IS-IS inter area, * - candidate default, U - per-user static route
       o - ODR, P - periodic downloaded static route

Gateway of last resort is not set

     172.16.0.0/30 is subnetted, 2 subnets
O IA    172.16.1.0 [110/134] via 192.168.0.22, 00:00:31, FastEthernet0/1
O IA    172.16.2.0 [110/81] via 192.168.0.22, 00:00:31, FastEthernet0/1
     10.0.0.0/8 is variably subnetted, 5 subnets, 3 masks
O       10.2.2.2/32 [110/2] via 192.168.0.22, 00:00:51, FastEthernet0/1
O IA    10.1.3.0/30 [110/198] via 192.168.0.22, 00:00:31, FastEthernet0/1
O IA    10.3.3.3/32 [110/135] via 192.168.0.22, 00:00:31, FastEthernet0/1
O IA    10.1.2.0/24 [110/144] via 192.168.0.22, 00:00:32, FastEthernet0/1
C       10.1.1.1/32 is directly connected, Loopback0
C     192.168.0.0/24 is directly connected, FastEthernet0/1
C     192.168.1.0/24 is directly connected, FastEthernet0/0
R1# show run   begin router
router ospf 1
 log-adjacency-changes
 area 2 virtual-link 10.2.2.2
 network 10.1.1.1 0.0.0.0 area 1
 network 192.168.0.0 0.0.0.255 area 1
 network 192.168.1.0 0.0.0.255 area 2
R1# show ip ospf virtual-links
Virtual Link OSPF_VL4 to router 10.2.2.2 is down
  Run as demand circuit
  DoNotAge LSA allowed.
  Transit area 2, Cost of using 65535
  Transmit Delay is 1 sec, State DOWN,
  Timer intervals configured, Hello 10, Dead 40, Wait 40, Retransmit 5
```

Example 7-17 shows the IP routing table on router R2 after the trouble ticket was issued. Notice that the routing table of router R1 can no longer see the Loopback 0 IP address of router BB2 (that is, 10.4.4.4/32). Also, notice that network 192.168.1.0/24, connected to router R1's Fast Ethernet 0/0 interface, is not present in router R2's IP routing table.

Example 7-17   *Router R2's IP Routing Table After the Trouble Ticket Was Issued*

```
R2# show ip route
Codes: C - connected, S - static, R - RIP, M - mobile, B - BGP
       D - EIGRP, EX - EIGRP external, O - OSPF, IA - OSPF inter area
       N1 - OSPF NSSA external type 1, N2 - OSPF NSSA external type 2
       E1 - OSPF external type 1, E2 - OSPF external type 2
       i - IS-IS, su - IS-IS summary, L1 - IS-IS level-1, L2 - IS-IS level-2
       ia - IS-IS inter area, * - candidate default, U - per-user static route
       o - ODR, P - periodic downloaded static route

Gateway of last resort is not set

     172.16.0.0/30 is subnetted, 2 subnets
C       172.16.1.0 is directly connected, Serial1/0.1
C       172.16.2.0 is directly connected, Serial1/0.2
     10.0.0.0/8 is variably subnetted, 5 subnets, 3 masks
C       10.2.2.2/32 is directly connected, Loopback0
O       10.1.3.0/30 [110/197] via 172.16.1.1, 00:00:53, Serial1/0.1
O       10.3.3.3/32 [110/134] via 172.16.1.1, 00:00:53, Serial1/0.1
O       10.1.2.0/24 [110/143] via 172.16.1.1, 00:00:53, Serial1/0.1
O       10.1.1.1/32 [110/11] via 192.168.0.11, 00:00:53, FastEthernet0/0
C    192.168.0.0/24 is directly connected, FastEthernet0/0
```

Before moving forward to investigate the remainder of the network, do you already see an issue that needs to be resolved? The fact that router R2 cannot see network 192.168.1.0/24 off of router R1 is independent of any configuration on routers BB1 or BB2. So, take a few moments to review the information collected thus far, and hypothesize the issue that is preventing router R2 from seeing network 192.168.1.0/24. On a separate sheet of paper, write your solution to the issue you identified.

Issue #1: Suggested Solution

The virtual link configuration on router R1 was incorrect. Specifically, the transit area in the **area** *number* **virtual-link** *router-id* command was configured as area 2. However, the transit area should have been area 1. Example 7-18 shows the commands used to correct this misconfiguration.

Example 7-18   *Correcting the Virtual Link Configuration Router of R1*

```
R1# conf term
Enter configuration commands, one per line.  End with CNTL/Z.
R1(config)#router ospf 1
R1(config-router)#no area 2 virtual-link 10.2.2.2
R1(config-router)#area 1 virtual-link 10.2.2.2
```

After you correct the virtual link configuration on router R1, network 192.168.1.0/24 is present in router R2's IP routing table, as illustrated in Example 7-19. Notice, however, that the Loopback 0 IP address of router BB2 (that is, 10.4.4.4/32) is still not visible in router R2's IP routing table.

Example 7-19 *Router R2's IP Routing Table After Correcting the Virtual Link Configuration*

```
R2# show ip route
Codes: C - connected, S - static, R - RIP, M - mobile, B - BGP
       D - EIGRP, EX - EIGRP external, O - OSPF, IA - OSPF inter area
       N1 - OSPF NSSA external type 1, N2 - OSPF NSSA external type 2
       E1 - OSPF external type 1, E2 - OSPF external type 2
       i - IS-IS, su - IS-IS summary, L1 - IS-IS level-1, L2 - IS-IS level-2
       ia - IS-IS inter area, * - candidate default, U - per-user static route
       o - ODR, P - periodic downloaded static route
Gateway of last resort is not set
     172.16.0.0/30 is subnetted, 2 subnets
C       172.16.1.0 is directly connected, Serial1/0.1
C       172.16.2.0 is directly connected, Serial1/0.2
     10.0.0.0/8 is variably subnetted, 5 subnets, 3 masks
C       10.2.2.2/32 is directly connected, Loopback0
O       10.1.3.0/30 [110/197] via 172.16.1.1, 00:00:18, Serial1/0.1
O       10.3.3.3/32 [110/134] via 172.16.1.1, 00:00:18, Serial1/0.1
O       10.1.2.0/24 [110/143] via 172.16.1.1, 00:00:18, Serial1/0.1
O       10.1.1.1/32 [110/11] via 192.168.0.11, 00:00:18, FastEthernet0/0
C     192.168.0.0/24 is directly connected, FastEthernet0/0
O IA 192.168.1.0/24 [110/11] via 192.168.0.11, 00:00:18, FastEthernet0/0
```

With one issue now resolved, continue to collect information on router R2. Example 7-20 indicates that router R2 has not formed an adjacency with router BB2, which has an OSPF router ID of 10.4.4.4.

Example 7-20 *OSPF Neighbors of Router R2*

```
R2# show ip ospf neighbor
Neighbor ID     Pri   State       Dead Time    Address        Interface
10.3.3.3        0     FULL/  -    00:00:37     172.16.1.1     Serial1/0.1
10.1.1.1        0     FULL/  -        -        192.168.0.11   OSPF_VL1
10.1.1.1        1     FULL/DR     00:00:39     192.168.0.11   FastEthernet0/0
Example 7-20 shows the OSPF configuration of router R2.

R2# show run   begin router
router ospf 2
 log-adjacency-changes
 area 1 virtual-link 10.1.1.1
 network 10.2.2.2 0.0.0.0 area 1
```

```
network 172.16.1.0 0.0.0.3 area 0
network 172.16.2.0 0.0.0.3 area 0
network 192.168.0.0 0.0.0.255 area 1
```

Even though router R2 has not formed an adjacency with router BB2, Example 7-21 shows the output of a **ping** command, verifying that router R2 can reach router BB2.

Example 7-21 *Pinging Router BB2 from Router R2*

```
R2# ping 172.16.2.2
Type escape sequence to abort.
Sending 5, 100-byte ICMP Echos to 172.16.2.2, timeout is 2 seconds:
!!!!!
Success rate is 100 percent (5/5), round-trip min/avg/max = 52/92/144 ms
```

The topology diagram indicates that router R2 connects with router BB2 via subinterface Serial 1/0.2. Therefore, the **show interface s1/0.2** command is issued on router R2. The output provided in Example 7-22 states that the subinterface is up and functional.

Example 7-22 *Serial 1/0.2 Subinterface of Router R2*

```
R2# show interface s1/0.2
Serial1/0.2 is up, line protocol is up
  Hardware is M4T
  Internet address is 172.16.2.1/30
  MTU 1500 bytes, BW 1250 Kbit, DLY 20000 usec,
      reliability 255/255, txload 1/255, rxload 1/255
  Encapsulation FRAME-RELAY
  Last clearing of "show interface" counters never
```

Example 7-23 confirms that router BB2 is adjacent at Layer 2 with router R2.

Example 7-23 *CDP Neighbors of Router R2*

```
R2# show cdp neighbor
Capability Codes: R - Router, T - Trans Bridge, B - Source Route Bridge
                  S - Switch, H - Host, I - IGMP, r - Repeater

Device ID       Local Intrfce     Holdtme    Capability  Platform  Port ID
BB1             Ser 1/0.1         152        R S I       2691      Ser 1/0.2
BB2             Ser 1/0.2         143        R S I       2691      Ser 1/0.2
R1              Fas 0/0           144        R S I       2611XM    Fas 0/1
```

The output of Example 7-24 shows the OSPF status of router R2's Serial 1/0.2 subinterface.

Example 7-24 *OSPF Status of Router R2 on Subinterface Serial 1/0.2*

```
Supports Link-local Signaling (LLS)
Index 3/4, flood queue length 0
Next 0x0(0)/0x0(0)
Last flood scan length is 1, maximum is 4
Last flood scan time is 0 msec, maximum is 4 msec
Neighbor Count is 0, Adjacent neighbor count is 0
Suppress hello for 0 neighbor(s)
```

Now that data has been collected for router R2, the troubleshooting focus moves to router BB1. Notice that BB1 also lacks a route to router BB2's Loopback 0 IP address of 10.4.4.4/32. Also, even though router BB1 has two direct connections to router BB2, router BB1 has not formed an OSPF adjacency with router BB2. Notice that router BB2 is router BB1's Cisco Discovery Protocol (CDP) neighbor, both on interface FastEthernet 0/0 and on subinterface Serial 1/0.1.

Example 7-25 *Data Collected from Router BB1 After the Trouble Ticket*

```
BB1# show ip route
Codes: C - connected, S - static, R - RIP, M - mobile, B - BGP
       D - EIGRP, EX - EIGRP external, O - OSPF, IA - OSPF inter area
       N1 - OSPF NSSA external type 1, N2 - OSPF NSSA external type 2
       E1 - OSPF external type 1, E2 - OSPF external type 2
       i - IS-IS, su - IS-IS summary, L1 - IS-IS level-1, L2 - IS-IS level-2
       ia - IS-IS inter area, * - candidate default, U - per-user static route
       o - ODR, P - periodic downloaded static route
Gateway of last resort is not set
     172.16.0.0/30 is subnetted, 2 subnets
C        172.16.1.0 is directly connected, Serial1/0.2
O        172.16.2.0 [110/213] via 172.16.1.2, 00:01:02, Serial1/0.2
     10.0.0.0/8 is variably subnetted, 5 subnets, 3 masks
O IA     10.2.2.2/32 [110/134] via 172.16.1.2, 00:01:02, Serial1/0.2
C        10.1.3.0/30 is directly connected, Serial1/0.1
C        10.3.3.3/32 is directly connected, Loopback0
C        10.1.2.0/24 is directly connected, FastEthernet0/0
O IA     10.1.1.1/32 [110/144] via 172.16.1.2, 00:01:02, Serial1/0.2
O IA 192.168.0.0/24 [110/143] via 172.16.1.2, 00:01:02, Serial1/0.2
BB1# show ip ospf neighbor

Neighbor ID     Pri   State        Dead Time   Address      Interface
10.2.2.2        0     FULL/  -     00:00:30    172.16.1.2   Serial1/0.2


BB1# show run    begin router
router ospf 1
```

```
 log-adjacency-changes
 network 0.0.0.0 255.255.255.255 area 0


BB1# show cdp neigh
Capability Codes: R - Router, T - Trans Bridge, B - Source Route Bridge
                  S - Switch, H - Host, I - IGMP, r - Repeater


Device ID          Local Intrfce      Holdtme    Capability  Platform  Port ID
BB2                Ser 1/0.1          148        R S I       2691      Ser 1/0.1
BB2                Fas 0/0            148        R S I       2691      Fas 0/0
R2                 Ser 1/0.2          130        R S I       2691      Ser 1/0.1
BB1# show run

...OUTPUT OMITTED...
interface FastEthernet0/0
 ip address 10.1.2.1 255.255.255.0
 ip ospf network non-broadcast
 duplex auto
speed auto
!
interface Serial1/0
 no ip address
 encapsulation frame-relay
!
interface Serial1/0.1 point-to-point
 ip address 10.1.3.1 255.255.255.252
 ip ospf hello-interval 60
 ip ospf dead-interval 200
 frame-relay interface-dlci 881
!
interface Serial1/0.2 point-to-point
 bandwidth 750
 ip address 172.16.1.1 255.255.255.252
 frame-relay interface-dlci 811
...OUTPUT OMITTED...
```

The data collection continues on router BB2. Example 7-26 provides output from several **show** commands. Notice that router BB2 has not learned networks via OSPF.

Based on the preceding **show** command output from routers R2, BB1, and BB2, hypothesize what you consider to be the issue or issues still impacting the network. Then, on a separate sheet of paper, write how you would solve the identified issue or issues.

Example 7-26 *Data Collected from Router BB2 After the Trouble Ticket*

```
BB2# show ip route
Codes: C - connected, S - static, R - RIP, M - mobile, B - BGP
       D - EIGRP, EX - EIGRP external, O - OSPF, IA - OSPF inter area
       N1 - OSPF NSSA external type 1, N2 - OSPF NSSA external type 2
       E1 - OSPF external type 1, E2 - OSPF external type 2
       i - IS-IS, su - IS-IS summary, L1 - IS-IS level-1, L2 - IS-IS level-2
       ia - IS-IS inter area, * - candidate default, U - per-user static route
       o - ODR, P - periodic downloaded static route
Gateway of last resort is not set


     172.16.0.0/30 is subnetted, 1 subnets
C       172.16.2.0 is directly connected, Serial1/0.2
     10.0.0.0/8 is variably subnetted, 3 subnets, 3 masks
C       10.1.3.0/30 is directly connected, Serial1/0.1
C       10.1.2.0/24 is directly connected, FastEthernet0/0
C       10.4.4.4/32 is directly connected, Loopback0


BB2# show run   begin router
router ospf 1
 log-adjacency-changes
 network 0.0.0.0 255.255.255.255 area 0


BB2# show ip ospf interface s1/0.1
Serial1/0.1 is up, line protocol is up
  Internet Address 10.1.3.2/30, Area 0
  Process ID 1, Router ID 10.4.4.4, Network Type POINT_TO_POINT, Cost: 64
  Transmit Delay is 1 sec, State POINT_TO_POINT,
  Timer intervals configured, Hello 10, Dead 40, Wait 40, Retransmit 5
    oob-resync timeout 40
    Hello due in 00:00:09
  Supports Link-local Signaling (LLS)
  Index 2/2, flood queue length 0
  Next 0x0(0)/0x0(0)
  Last flood scan length is 1, maximum is 3
  Last flood scan time is 0 msec, maximum is 4 msec
  Neighbor Count is 0, Adjacent neighbor count is 0
  Suppress hello for 0 neighbor(s)


BB2# show ip ospf interface s1/0.2
Serial1/0.2 is up, line protocol is up
  Internet Address 172.16.2.2/30, Area 0
  Process ID 1, Router ID 10.4.4.4, Network Type NON_BROADCAST, Cost: 80
  Transmit Delay is 1 sec, State DR, Priority 1
  Designated Router (ID) 10.4.4.4, Interface address 172.16.2.2
```

```
            No backup designated router on this network
            Timer intervals configured, Hello 30, Dead 120, Wait 120, Retransmit 5
              oob-resync timeout 120
              Hello due in 00:00:09
            Supports Link-local Signaling (LLS)
            Index 3/3, flood queue length 0
            Next 0x0(0)/0x0(0)
            Last flood scan length is 1, maximum is 1
            Last flood scan time is 0 msec, maximum is 4 msec
            Neighbor Count is 0, Adjacent neighbor count is 0
            Suppress hello for 0 neighbor(s)
!
interface FastEthernet0/0
 ip address 10.1.2.2 255.255.255.0
!
interface Serial1/0
 no ip address
 encapsulation frame-relay
!
interface Serial1/0.1 point-to-point
 ip address 10.1.3.2 255.255.255.252
 frame-relay interface-dlci 882
!
interface Serial1/0.2 point-to-point
 bandwidth 1250
 ip address 172.16.2.2 255.255.255.252
 ip ospf network non-broadcast
 frame-relay interface-dlci 821
!
...OUTPUT OMITTED...
```

Issue #2: Suggested Solution

Subinterface Serial 1/0.1 on router BB1 had nondefault Hello and Dead timers, which did not match the timers at the far end of the Frame Relay link. Example 7-27 illustrates how these nondefault values were reset.

Example 7-27   *Correcting the Nondefault Timer Configuration of Router BB1*

```
BB1# conf term
Enter configuration commands, one per line.  End with CNTL/Z.
BB1(config)#int s1/0.1
BB1(config-subif)#no ip ospf hello-interval 60
BB1(config-subif)#no ip ospf dead-interval 200
```

Issue #3: Suggested Solution

Interface FastEthernet 0/0 on router BB1 was configured with an incorrect OSPF network type of nonbroadcast. Example 7-28 demonstrates how this OSPF interface was reset to its default OSPF network type (that is, the broadcast OSPF network type).

Example 7-28 *Correcting the Incorrect OSPF Network Type Configuration of Router BB1*

```
BB1# conf term
Enter configuration commands, one per line.  End with CNTL/Z.
BB1(config)#int fa 0/0
BB1(config-if)#no ip ospf network non-broadcast
```

Issue #4: Suggested Solution

Similar to the incorrect OSPF network type on router BB1's FastEthernet 0/0 interface, the Serial 1/0.2 subinterface on router BB2 was configured incorrectly. A point-to-point Frame Relay subinterface defaults to an OSPF network type of point-to-point; however, Serial 1/0.2 had been configured as an OSPF network type of nonbroadcast. Example 7-29 reviews how this nondefault OSPF network type configuration was removed.

Example 7-29 *Correcting Router BB2's Incorrect OSPF Network Type Configuration*

```
BB2# conf term
Enter configuration commands, one per line.  End with CNTL/Z.
BB2(config)#int s1/0.2
BB2(config-subif)#no ip ospf network non-broadcast
```

After all of the previous misconfigurations are corrected, all routers in the topology once again have full reachability throughout the network. Examples 7-30, 7-31, 7-32, and 7-33 show output from the **show ip route** and **show ip ospf neighbor** commands issued on all routers, confirming the full reachability of each router.

Example 7-30 *Confirming the Full Reachability of Router R1*

```
R1# show ip route
Codes: C - connected, S - static, R - RIP, M - mobile, B - BGP
       D - EIGRP, EX - EIGRP external, O - OSPF, IA - OSPF inter area
       N1 - OSPF NSSA external type 1, N2 - OSPF NSSA external type 2
       E1 - OSPF external type 1, E2 - OSPF external type 2
       i - IS-IS, su - IS-IS summary, L1 - IS-IS level-1, L2 - IS-IS level-2
       ia - IS-IS inter area, * - candidate default, U - per-user static route
       o - ODR, P - periodic downloaded static route


Gateway of last resort is not set

     172.16.0.0/30 is subnetted, 2 subnets
O       172.16.1.0 [110/134] via 192.168.0.22, 00:00:03, FastEthernet0/1
O       172.16.2.0 [110/81] via 192.168.0.22, 00:00:03, FastEthernet0/1
```

```
      10.0.0.0/8 is variably subnetted, 6 subnets, 3 masks
O        10.2.2.2/32 [110/2] via 192.168.0.22, 00:08:18, FastEthernet0/1
O        10.1.3.0/30 [110/145] via 192.168.0.22, 00:00:03, FastEthernet0/1
O        10.3.3.3/32 [110/92] via 192.168.0.22, 00:00:03, FastEthernet0/1
O        10.1.2.0/24 [110/91] via 192.168.0.22, 00:00:04, FastEthernet0/1
C        10.1.1.1/32 is directly connected, Loopback0
O        10.4.4.4/32 [110/82] via 192.168.0.22, 00:00:04, FastEthernet0/1
C     192.168.0.0/24 is directly connected, FastEthernet0/1
C     192.168.1.0/24 is directly connected, FastEthernet0/0


R1# show ip ospf neighbor

Neighbor ID    Pri    State       Dead Time    Address         Interface
10.2.2.2        0     FULL/  -        -         192.168.0.22    OSPF_VL5
10.2.2.2        1     FULL/BDR    00:00:34      192.168.0.22    FastEthernet0/1
```

Example 7-31 *Confirming the Full Reachability of Router R2*

```
R2# show ip route
Codes: C - connected, S - static, R - RIP, M - mobile, B - BGP
       D - EIGRP, EX - EIGRP external, O - OSPF, IA - OSPF inter area
       N1 - OSPF NSSA external type 1, N2 - OSPF NSSA external type 2
       E1 - OSPF external type 1, E2 - OSPF external type 2
       i - IS-IS, su - IS-IS summary, L1 - IS-IS level-1, L2 - IS-IS level-2
       ia - IS-IS inter area, * - candidate default, U - per-user static route
       o - ODR, P - periodic downloaded static route

Gateway of last resort is not set


     172.16.0.0/30 is subnetted, 2 subnets
C        172.16.1.0 is directly connected, Serial1/0.1
C        172.16.2.0 is directly connected, Serial1/0.2
     10.0.0.0/8 is variably subnetted, 6 subnets, 3 masks
C        10.2.2.2/32 is directly connected, Loopback0
O        10.1.3.0/30 [110/144] via 172.16.2.2, 00:00:15, Serial1/0.2
O        10.3.3.3/32 [110/91] via 172.16.2.2, 00:00:15, Serial1/0.2
O        10.1.2.0/24 [110/90] via 172.16.2.2, 00:00:15, Serial1/0.2
O        10.1.1.1/32 [110/11] via 192.168.0.11, 00:08:29, FastEthernet0/0
O        10.4.4.4/32 [110/81] via 172.16.2.2, 00:00:15, Serial1/0.2
C     192.168.0.0/24 is directly connected, FastEthernet0/0
O IA  192.168.1.0/24 [110/11] via 192.168.0.11, 00:00:15, FastEthernet0/0


R2# show ip ospf neighbor
```

Neighbor ID	Pri	State	Dead Time	Address	Interface
10.4.4.4	0	FULL/ -	00:00:33	172.16.2.2	Serial1/0.2
10.3.3.3	0	FULL/ -	00:00:38	172.16.1.1	Serial1/0.1
10.1.1.1	0	FULL/ -	-	192.168.0.11	OSPF_VL1
10.1.1.1	1	FULL/DR	00:00:30	192.168.0.11	FastEthernet0/0

Example 7-32 *Confirming the Full Reachability of Router BB1*

```
BB1# show ip route
Codes: C - connected, S - static, R - RIP, M - mobile, B - BGP
       D - EIGRP, EX - EIGRP external, O - OSPF, IA - OSPF inter area
       N1 - OSPF NSSA external type 1, N2 - OSPF NSSA external type 2
       E1 - OSPF external type 1, E2 - OSPF external type 2
       i - IS-IS, su - IS-IS summary, L1 - IS-IS level-1, L2 - IS-IS level-2
       ia - IS-IS inter area, * - candidate default, U - per-user static route
       o - ODR, P - periodic downloaded static route


Gateway of last resort is not set


     172.16.0.0/30 is subnetted, 2 subnets
C       172.16.1.0 is directly connected, Serial1/0.2
O       172.16.2.0 [110/90] via 10.1.2.2, 00:00:29, FastEthernet0/0
     10.0.0.0/8 is variably subnetted, 6 subnets, 3 masks
O IA    10.2.2.2/32 [110/91] via 10.1.2.2, 00:00:29, FastEthernet0/0
C       10.1.3.0/30 is directly connected, Serial1/0.1
C       10.3.3.3/32 is directly connected, Loopback0
C       10.1.2.0/24 is directly connected, FastEthernet0/0
O IA    10.1.1.1/32 [110/101] via 10.1.2.2, 00:00:29, FastEthernet0/0
O       10.4.4.4/32 [110/11] via 10.1.2.2, 00:00:29, FastEthernet0/0
O IA 192.168.0.0/24 [110/100] via 10.1.2.2, 00:00:29, FastEthernet0/0
O IA 192.168.1.0/24 [110/101] via 10.1.2.2, 00:00:29, FastEthernet0/0
BB1# show ip ospf neighbor

Neighbor ID     Pri   State           Dead Time   Address         Interface
10.4.4.4         1    FULL/DR         00:00:34    10.1.2.2        FastEthernet0/
10.2.2.2         0    FULL/ -         00:00:39    172.16.1.2      Serial1/0.2
10.4.4.4         0    FULL/ -         00:00:33    10.1.3.2        Serial1/0.1
```

Example 7-33 *Confirming the Full Reachability of Router BB2*

```
BB2# show ip route
Codes: C - connected, S - static, R - RIP, M - mobile, B - BGP
       D - EIGRP, EX - EIGRP external, O - OSPF, IA - OSPF inter area
       N1 - OSPF NSSA external type 1, N2 - OSPF NSSA external type 2
       E1 - OSPF external type 1, E2 - OSPF external type 2
       i - IS-IS, su - IS-IS summary, L1 - IS-IS level-1, L2 - IS-IS level-2
       ia - IS-IS inter area, * - candidate default, U - per-user static route
       o - ODR, P - periodic downloaded static route

Gateway of last resort is not set

     172.16.0.0/30 is subnetted, 2 subnets
O        172.16.1.0 [110/143] via 10.1.2.1, 00:00:42, FastEthernet0/0
C        172.16.2.0 is directly connected, Serial1/0.2
     10.0.0.0/8 is variably subnetted, 6 subnets, 3 masks
O IA    10.2.2.2/32 [110/81] via 172.16.2.1, 00:00:42, Serial1/0.2
C        10.1.3.0/30 is directly connected, Serial1/0.1
O        10.3.3.3/32 [110/11] via 10.1.2.1, 00:00:42, FastEthernet0/0
C        10.1.2.0/24 is directly connected, FastEthernet0/0
O IA    10.1.1.1/32 [110/91] via 172.16.2.1, 00:00:42, Serial1/0.2
C        10.4.4.4/32 is directly connected, Loopback0
O IA 192.168.0.0/24 [110/90] via 172.16.2.1, 00:00:42, Serial1/0.2
O IA 192.168.1.0/24 [110/91] via 172.16.2.1, 00:00:42, Serial1/0.2

BB2# show ip ospf neighbor

Neighbor ID     Pri    State         Dead Time    Address       Interface
10.2.2.2          0    FULL/  -      00:00:38     172.16.2.1    Serial1/0.2
10.3.3.3          0    FULL/  -      00:00:29     10.1.3.1      Serial1/0.1
10.3.3.3          1    FULL/BDR      00:00:34     10.1.2.1      FastEthernet0/0
```

Route Redistribution Troubleshooting

Route redistribution allows routes learned via one method (for example, statically configured, locally connected, or learned via a routing protocol) to be injected into a different
routing protocol. If two routing protocols are mutually redistributed, the routes learned
via each routing protocol are injected into the other routing protocol.

A network might benefit from route redistribution in the following scenarios:

- Transitioning to a more advanced routing protocol

- Merger of companies

- Different areas of administrative control

Route Redistribution Overview

A router that sits at the boundary of the routing domains to be redistributed is known as a *boundary router*, as illustrated in Figure 7-5. A boundary router can redistribute static routes, connected routes, or routes learned via one routing protocol into another routing protocol.

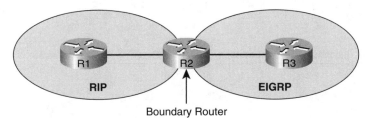
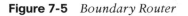

Figure 7-5 *Boundary Router*

Different routing protocols use different types of metrics, as illustrated in Figure 7-6. Therefore, when a route is injected into a routing protocol, a metric used by the destination routing protocol needs to be associated with the route being injected.

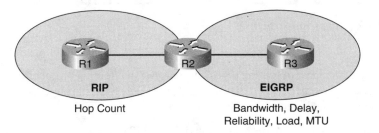

Figure 7-6 *Differing Metric Parameters Between Routing Protocols*

The metric assigned to a route being injected into another routing process is called a *seed metric*. The seed metric is needed to communicate relative levels of reachability between dissimilar routing protocols. A seed metric can be defined in one of three ways:

- The **default-metric** command

- The **metric** parameter in the **redistribute** command

- A route map configuration

If a seed metric is not specified, a default seed metric is used. Keep in mind, however, that RIP and EIGRP have a default metric that is considered unreachable. Therefore, if you do not configure a nondefault seed metric when redistributing routes into RIP or EIGRP, the redistributed route will not be reachable.

Some routing protocols (for example, EIGRP, OSPF, and Intermediate System-to-Intermediate System [IS-IS]) can tag routes as either *internal* (that is, routes locally configured or connected) or *external* (that is, routes learned by another routing process) and give priority to internal routes versus external routes. The capability to distinguish between internal and external routes can help prevent a potential routing loop, where two routing protocols continually redistribute a route into one another.

As described in Chapter 6, a routing protocol can send routes into and learn routes from a router's IP routing table, as depicted in Figure 7-7.

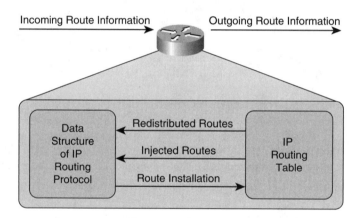

Figure 7-7   *Routing Data Structures*

If a router is running two routing protocols, however, the routing protocols do not exchange routes directly between themselves. Rather, only routes in a router's IP routing table can be redistributed, as seen in Figure 7-8.

Two prerequisites must be met for the routes of one IP routing protocol to be redistributed into another IP routing protocol:

■   A route needs to be installed in a router's IP routing table.

■   The destination IP routing protocol needs a reachable metric to assign to the redistributed routes.

Route Redistribution Troubleshooting Targets

Effective troubleshooting of route redistribution requires knowledge of verification and troubleshooting commands for each routing protocol. Table 7-9 identifies troubleshooting targets to investigate when working to resolve a route redistribution issue.

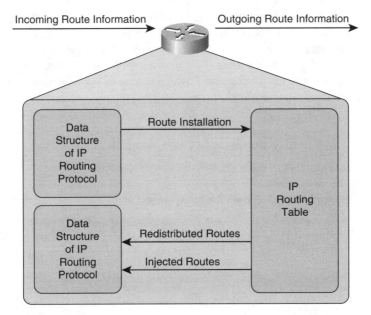

Figure 7-8 *Route Redistribution Between Two IP Routing Protocols*

Table 7-9 *Troubleshooting Targets for Route Redistribution*

Troubleshooting Target	Troubleshooting Recommendation
Source routing protocol	Verify that a route to be redistributed from a routing protocol has been learned by that routing protocol. Therefore, you can issue appropriate **show** commands for the data structures of the source routing protocol to ensure that the source routing protocol has learned the route in question.
Route selection	Because a route must be in a router's IP routing table to be redistributed, you should ensure that the routes of the source routing protocol are indeed being injected into the router's IP routing table.
Redistribution configuration	If a route has been injected into a router's IP routing table from a source routing protocol but not redistributed into the destination routing protocol, you should check the redistribution configuration. This involves checking the metric applied to routes as they are redistributed into the destination routing protocol, checking for any route filtering that might be preventing redistribution, and checking the redistribution syntax to confirm the correct routing process ID or autonomous system number is specified.
Destination routing protocol	If a route has been successfully redistributed into a destination routing protocol but the route has not been successfully learned by neighboring routers, you should investigate the destination routing protocol. You could use traditional methods of troubleshooting a destination routing protocol; however, keep in mind that the redistributed route might be marked as an external route. Therefore, check the characteristics of the destination routing protocol to determine if it treats external routes differently from internal ones.

Although the previously discussed **debug ip routing** command can provide insight into routing loops that might be occurring, you can also use the Cisco IOS IP route profiling feature to troubleshoot route instability. Route profiling can be enabled in global configuration mode with the **ip route profile** command. Example 7-34 provides sample output from the **show ip route profile** command, which is used to view the information collected from the IP route profiling feature.

Example 7-34   show ip route profile *Command Output*

```
R4# show ip route profile
IP routing table change statistics:
Frequency of changes in a 5 second sampling interval
-----------------------------------------------------------------
Change/      Fwd-path    Prefix    Nexthop    Pathcount    Prefix
interval     change      add       change     change       refresh
-----------------------------------------------------------------
0            38          38        41         41           41
1            3           3         0          0            0
2            0           0         0          0            0
3            0           0         0          0            0
4            0           0         0          0            0
5            0           0         0          0            0
10           0           0         0          0            0
15           0           0         0          0            0
20           0           0         0          0            0
25           0           0         0          0            0
30           0           1         0          1            0
55           0           0         0          0            0
80           0           0         0          0            0
105          0           0         0          0            0
130          0           0         0          0            0
155          0           0         0          0            0
280          0           0         0          0            0
405          0           0         0          0            0
530          0           0         0          0            0
655          0           0         0          0            0
780          0           0         0          0            0
1405         0           0         0          0            0
2030         0           0         0          0            0
2655         0           0         0          0            0
3280         0           0         0          0            0
3905         0           0         0          0            0
7030         0           0         0          0            0
10155        0           0         0          0            0
13280        0           0         0          0            0
Overflow     0           0         0          0            0
```

The IP route profiling feature measures the number and type of IP routing table updates every 5 seconds. The left column in the output of the **show ip route profile** command represents the number of changes that occurred during a 5-second interval. As an example, consider the row in the output that has a 30 in the left column. The number 1 under the Prefix Add column indicates that during one 5-second interval, 30–54 prefixes were added to the IP routing table. The range of 30–54 was determined by examining the output. Notice that the next value in the Change/Interval column after 30 is 55. Therefore, a number appearing in the 30 row indicates during how many 5-second timing intervals a particular IP routing update occurred 30–54 times.

Ideally, only numbers in the first row (that is, the 0 row) should change in a stable network. If numbers in other rows change, a routing loop might be occurring.

Trouble Ticket: Route Redistribution with EIGRP and OSPF

This trouble ticket focuses on redistribution of EIGRP and OSPF. You are presented with baseline data, a trouble ticket, a topology, and information collected while investigating the reported issue. You are then challenged to identify the issue and create an action plan to resolve it.

Because different IP routing protocols might exhibit different characteristics when performing route redistribution, you should research the syntax used for your specific protocols. As a reference for this trouble ticket, Table 7-10 provides a collection of commands that might be useful in troubleshooting EIGRP or OSPF route redistribution.

Table 7-10   *Route Redistribution Verification and Troubleshooting Syntax for EIGRP and OSPF*

Key Topic

Command	Description
router ospf *process-id*	Global configuration mode command that enables an OSPF process on a router
redistribute eigrp *autonomous-system-number* [**subnets**]	Router configuration mode command that redistributes routes, including subnets (if the optional **subnets** parameter is specified), from a specified EIGRP autonomous system into OSPF

continues

Table 7-10   *Route Redistribution Verification and Troubleshooting Syntax for EIGRP and OSPF   (Continued)*

default-metric *metric*	Router configuration mode command that specifies the metric used for routes redistributed into OSPF
router eigrp *autonomous-system-number*	Global configuration mode command that enables an EIGRP routing process on a router
redistribute ospf *process-id*	Router configuration mode command that redistributes routes from a specified OSPF process ID into EIGRP
default-metric *bandwidth delay reliability load mtu*	Router configuration mode command that specifies the parameters used to calculate the seed metric for routes being redistributed into EIGRP, using the following EIGRP metric parameters: *bandwidth* (in kbps) *delay* (in tens of microseconds) *reliability* (maximum of 255) *load* (minimum of 1) *mtu* (in bytes)

Trouble Ticket #5

You receive the following trouble ticket:

> Company A has acquired company B. Company A's network (that is, routers R1 and R2) uses EIGRP, whereas Company B's network (that is, routers BB1 and BB2) uses OSPF. Router R2 was configured as a boundary router, and router R2's configuration specifies that EIGRP and OSPF are mutually redistributed. The configuration was originally functional. However, routers R1, BB1, and BB2 do not currently see all the subnets present in the network.

This trouble ticket references the topology shown in Figure 7-9.

You begin your troubleshooting efforts by analyzing baseline information collected when the configuration was working properly. Examples 7-35, 7-36, 7-37, and 7-38 provide output from the **show ip route** command on each router.

Example 7-35   *Baseline Output for Router R1*

```
R1# show ip route
Codes: C - connected, S - static, R - RIP, M - mobile, B - BGP
       D - EIGRP, EX - EIGRP external, O - OSPF, IA - OSPF inter area
       N1 - OSPF NSSA external type 1, N2 - OSPF NSSA external type 2
       E1 - OSPF external type 1, E2 - OSPF external type 2
       i - IS-IS, su - IS-IS summary, L1 - IS-IS level-1, L2 - IS-IS level-2
       ia - IS-IS inter area, * - candidate default, U - per-user static route
```

```
        o - ODR, P - periodic downloaded static route

Gateway of last resort is not set


     172.16.0.0/30 is subnetted, 2 subnets
D EX    172.16.1.0 [170/1734656] via 192.168.0.22, 00:04:39, FastEthernet0/1
D EX    172.16.2.0 [170/1734656] via 192.168.0.22, 00:04:39, FastEthernet0/1
     10.0.0.0/8 is variably subnetted, 6 subnets, 3 masks
D       10.2.2.2/32 [90/156160] via 192.168.0.22, 00:04:39, FastEthernet0/1
D EX    10.1.3.0/30 [170/1734656] via 192.168.0.22, 00:04:39, FastEthernet0/1
D EX    10.3.3.3/32 [170/1734656] via 192.168.0.22, 00:04:39, FastEthernet0/1
D EX    10.1.2.0/24 [170/1734656] via 192.168.0.22, 00:04:40, FastEthernet0/1
C       10.1.1.1/32 is directly connected, Loopback0
D EX    10.4.4.4/32 [170/1734656] via 192.168.0.22, 00:04:40, FastEthernet0/1
C    192.168.0.0/24 is directly connected, FastEthernet0/1
C    192.168.1.0/24 is directly connected, FastEthernet0/0
```

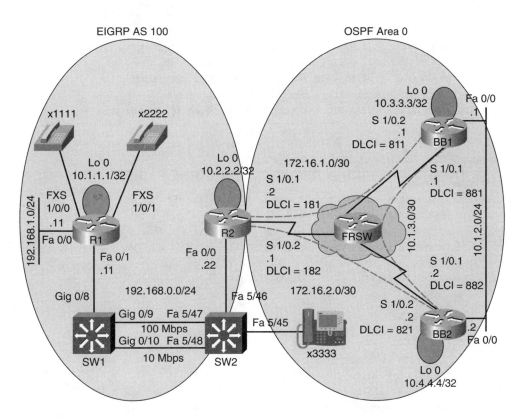

Figure 7-9 *Trouble Ticket #5: Topology*

Example 7-36   *Baseline Output for Router R2*

```
R2# show ip route
Codes: C - connected, S - static, R - RIP, M - mobile, B - BGP
       D - EIGRP, EX - EIGRP external, O - OSPF, IA - OSPF inter area
       N1 - OSPF NSSA external type 1, N2 - OSPF NSSA external type 2
       E1 - OSPF external type 1, E2 - OSPF external type 2
       i - IS-IS, su - IS-IS summary, L1 - IS-IS level-1, L2 - IS-IS level-2
       ia - IS-IS inter area, * - candidate default, U - per-user static route
       o - ODR, P - periodic downloaded static route

Gateway of last resort is not set

     172.16.0.0/30 is subnetted, 2 subnets
C       172.16.1.0 is directly connected, Serial1/0.1
C       172.16.2.0 is directly connected, Serial1/0.2
     10.0.0.0/8 is variably subnetted, 6 subnets, 3 masks
C       10.2.2.2/32 is directly connected, Loopback0
O       10.1.3.0/30 [110/144] via 172.16.2.2, 00:07:12, Serial1/0.2
O       10.3.3.3/32 [110/91] via 172.16.2.2, 00:07:12, Serial1/0.2
O       10.1.2.0/24 [110/90] via 172.16.2.2, 00:07:12, Serial1/0.2
D       10.1.1.1/32 [90/409600] via 192.168.0.11, 00:04:46, FastEthernet0/0
O       10.4.4.4/32 [110/81] via 172.16.2.2, 00:07:12, Serial1/0.2
C     192.168.0.0/24 is directly connected, FastEthernet0/0
D     192.168.1.0/24 [90/284160] via 192.168.0.11, 00:04:46, FastEthernet0/0
```

Example 7-37   *Baseline Output for Router BB1*

```
BB1# show ip route
Codes: C - connected, S - static, R - RIP, M - mobile, B - BGP
       D - EIGRP, EX - EIGRP external, O - OSPF, IA - OSPF inter area
       N1 - OSPF NSSA external type 1, N2 - OSPF NSSA external type 2
       E1 - OSPF external type 1, E2 - OSPF external type 2
       i - IS-IS, su - IS-IS summary, L1 - IS-IS level-1, L2 - IS-IS level-2
       ia - IS-IS inter area, * - candidate default, U - per-user static route
       o - ODR, P - periodic downloaded static route

Gateway of last resort is not set

     172.16.0.0/30 is subnetted, 2 subnets
C       172.16.1.0 is directly connected, Serial1/0.2
O       172.16.2.0 [110/90] via 10.1.2.2, 00:07:08, FastEthernet0/0
     10.0.0.0/8 is variably subnetted, 6 subnets, 3 masks
O E2    10.2.2.2/32 [110/64] via 10.1.2.2, 00:07:08, FastEthernet0/0
C       10.1.3.0/30 is directly connected, Serial1/0.1
C       10.3.3.3/32 is directly connected, Loopback0
```

```
C        10.1.2.0/24 is directly connected, FastEthernet0/0
O E2    10.1.1.1/32 [110/64] via 10.1.2.2, 00:04:49, FastEthernet0/0
O        10.4.4.4/32 [110/11] via 10.1.2.2, 00:07:08, FastEthernet0/0
O E2 192.168.0.0/24 [110/64] via 10.1.2.2, 00:07:08, FastEthernet0/0
O E2 192.168.1.0/24 [110/64] via 10.1.2.2, 00:04:49, FastEthernet0/0
```

Example 7-38   *Baseline Output for Router BB2*

```
BB2# show ip route
Codes: C - connected, S - static, R - RIP, M - mobile, B - BGP
       D - EIGRP, EX - EIGRP external, O - OSPF, IA - OSPF inter area
       N1 - OSPF NSSA external type 1, N2 - OSPF NSSA external type 2
       E1 - OSPF external type 1, E2 - OSPF external type 2
       i - IS-IS, su - IS-IS summary, L1 - IS-IS level-1, L2 - IS-IS level-2
       ia - IS-IS inter area, * - candidate default, U - per-user static route
       o - ODR, P - periodic downloaded static route

Gateway of last resort is not set

     172.16.0.0/30 is subnetted, 2 subnets
O        172.16.1.0 [110/143] via 10.1.2.1, 00:08:48, FastEthernet0/0
C        172.16.2.0 is directly connected, Serial1/0.2
     10.0.0.0/8 is variably subnetted, 6 subnets, 3 masks
O E2    10.2.2.2/32 [110/64] via 172.16.2.1, 00:08:48, Serial1/0.2
C        10.1.3.0/30 is directly connected, Serial1/0.1
O        10.3.3.3/32 [110/11] via 10.1.2.1, 00:08:48, FastEthernet0/0
C        10.1.2.0/24 is directly connected, FastEthernet0/0
O E2    10.1.1.1/32 [110/64] via 172.16.2.1, 00:06:30, Serial1/0.2
C        10.4.4.4/32 is directly connected, Loopback0
O E2 192.168.0.0/24 [110/64] via 172.16.2.1, 00:08:48, Serial1/0.2
O E2 192.168.1.0/24 [110/64] via 172.16.2.1, 00:06:30, Serial1/0.2
```

Router R2, acting as a boundary router, had previously been configured for mutual route redistribution. Example 7-39 illustrates this route redistribution configuration.

Example 7-39   *Mutual Route Redistribution on Router R2*

```
R2# show run | begin router
router eigrp 100
 redistribute ospf 1 metric 1500 100 255 1 1500
 network 10.2.2.2 0.0.0.0
 network 192.168.0.0
 no auto-summary
!
```

```
router ospf 1
 redistribute eigrp 100 metric 64 subnets
 network 172.16.1.0 0.0.0.3 area 0
 network 172.16.2.0 0.0.0.3 area 0
```

To begin the troubleshooting process, you issue the **show ip route** command on all routers to determine exactly what routes are missing from the IP routing table of each router.

Router R1's IP routing table lacks all OSPF-learned routes, as shown in Example 7-40.

Example 7-40 *Router R1's IP Routing Table*

```
R1# show ip route
Codes: C - connected, S - static, R - RIP, M - mobile, B - BGP
       D - EIGRP, EX - EIGRP external, O - OSPF, IA - OSPF inter area
       N1 - OSPF NSSA external type 1, N2 - OSPF NSSA external type 2
       E1 - OSPF external type 1, E2 - OSPF external type 2
       i - IS-IS, su - IS-IS summary, L1 - IS-IS level-1, L2 - IS-IS level-2
       ia - IS-IS inter area, * - candidate default, U - per-user static route
       o - ODR, P - periodic downloaded static route

Gateway of last resort is not set

     10.0.0.0/32 is subnetted, 2 subnets
D       10.2.2.2 [90/156160] via 192.168.0.22, 00:09:44, FastEthernet0/1
C       10.1.1.1 is directly connected, Loopback0
C    192.168.0.0/24 is directly connected, FastEthernet0/1
C    192.168.1.0/24 is directly connected, FastEthernet0/0
```

Router R2, which is acting as the boundary router, is actively participating in both the EIGRP and OSPF routing processes. Therefore, all routes are visible in the IP routing table of router R2, as shown in Example 7-41.

Example 7-41 *IP Routing Table of Router R2*

```
R2# show ip route
Codes: C - connected, S - static, R - RIP, M - mobile, B - BGP
       D - EIGRP, EX - EIGRP external, O - OSPF, IA - OSPF inter area
       N1 - OSPF NSSA external type 1, N2 - OSPF NSSA external type 2
       E1 - OSPF external type 1, E2 - OSPF external type 2
       i - IS-IS, su - IS-IS summary, L1 - IS-IS level-1, L2 - IS-IS level-2
       ia - IS-IS inter area, * - candidate default, U - per-user static route
       o - ODR, P - periodic downloaded static route
```

```
Gateway of last resort is not set

     172.16.0.0/30 is subnetted, 2 subnets
C        172.16.1.0 is directly connected, Serial1/0.1
C        172.16.2.0 is directly connected, Serial1/0.2
     10.0.0.0/8 is variably subnetted, 6 subnets, 3 masks
C        10.2.2.2/32 is directly connected, Loopback0
O        10.1.3.0/30 [110/144] via 172.16.2.2, 00:07:12, Serial1/0.2
O        10.3.3.3/32 [110/91] via 172.16.2.2, 00:07:12, Serial1/0.2
O        10.1.2.0/24 [110/90] via 172.16.2.2, 00:07:12, Serial1/0.2
D        10.1.1.1/32 [90/409600] via 192.168.0.11, 00:04:46, FastEthernet0/0
O        10.4.4.4/32 [110/81] via 172.16.2.2, 00:07:12, Serial1/0.2
C     192.168.0.0/24 is directly connected, FastEthernet0/0
D     192.168.1.0/24 [90/284160] via 192.168.0.11, 00:04:46, FastEthernet0/0
```

Router BB1, which is running OSPF, has some routes that originated in EIGRP. However, the 10.1.1.1/32 and the 10.2.2.2/32 networks, which are the IP addresses of the Loopback 0 interfaces on routers R1 and R2, are missing from the IP routing table of router BB1, as illustrated in Example 7-42.

Example 7-42   *IP Routing Table of Router BB1*

```
BB1# show ip route
Codes: C - connected, S - static, R - RIP, M - mobile, B - BGP
       D - EIGRP, EX - EIGRP external, O - OSPF, IA - OSPF inter area
       N1 - OSPF NSSA external type 1, N2 - OSPF NSSA external type 2
       E1 - OSPF external type 1, E2 - OSPF external type 2
       i - IS-IS, su - IS-IS summary, L1 - IS-IS level-1, L2 - IS-IS level-2
       ia - IS-IS inter area, * - candidate default, U - per-user static route
       o - ODR, P - periodic downloaded static route

Gateway of last resort is not set

     172.16.0.0/30 is subnetted, 2 subnets
C        172.16.1.0 is directly connected, Serial1/0.2
O        172.16.2.0 [110/90] via 10.1.2.2, 00:13:00, FastEthernet0/0
     10.0.0.0/8 is variably subnetted, 4 subnets, 3 masks
C        10.1.3.0/30 is directly connected, Serial1/0.1
C        10.3.3.3/32 is directly connected, Loopback0
C        10.1.2.0/24 is directly connected, FastEthernet0/0
O        10.4.4.4/32 [110/11] via 10.1.2.2, 00:13:00, FastEthernet0/0
O E2 192.168.0.0/24 [110/64] via 10.1.2.2, 00:01:14, FastEthernet0/0
O E2 192.168.1.0/24 [110/64] via 10.1.2.2, 00:01:14, FastEthernet0/0
```

The IP routing table of router BB2, as depicted in Example 7-43, is similar to the IP routing table of router BB1.

Example 7-43   *IP Routing Table of Router BB2*

```
BB2# show ip route
Codes: C - connected, S - static, R - RIP, M - mobile, B - BGP
       D - EIGRP, EX - EIGRP external, O - OSPF, IA - OSPF inter area
       N1 - OSPF NSSA external type 1, N2 - OSPF NSSA external type 2
       E1 - OSPF external type 1, E2 - OSPF external type 2
       i - IS-IS, su - IS-IS summary, L1 - IS-IS level-1, L2 - IS-IS level-2
       ia - IS-IS inter area, * - candidate default, U - per-user static route
       o - ODR, P - periodic downloaded static route

Gateway of last resort is not set

     172.16.0.0/30 is subnetted, 2 subnets
O       172.16.1.0 [110/143] via 10.1.2.1, 00:13:39, FastEthernet0/0
C       172.16.2.0 is directly connected, Serial1/0.2
     10.0.0.0/8 is variably subnetted, 4 subnets, 3 masks
C       10.1.3.0/30 is directly connected, Serial1/0.1
O       10.3.3.3/32 [110/11] via 10.1.2.1, 00:13:39, FastEthernet0/0
C       10.1.2.0/24 is directly connected, FastEthernet0/0
C       10.4.4.4/32 is directly connected, Loopback0
O E2 192.168.0.0/24 [110/64] via 172.16.2.1, 00:01:53, Serial1/0.2
O E2 192.168.1.0/24 [110/64] via 172.16.2.1, 00:01:53, Serial1/0.2
```

Because router R2 is acting as the boundary router, you examine its redistribution configuration, as shown in 7-44.

Example 7-44   *Redistribution Configuration on Router R2*

```
R2# show run | begin router
router eigrp 100
 redistribute ospf 1
 network 10.2.2.2 0.0.0.0
 network 192.168.0.0
 no auto-summary
!
router ospf 1
 log-adjacency-changes
 redistribute eigrp 100 metric 64
 network 172.16.1.0 0.0.0.3 area 0
 network 172.16.2.0 0.0.0.3 area 0
```

Take a moment to look through the baseline configuration information, the topology, the **show** command output collected after the issue was reported, and the syntax reference presented in Table 7-10. Then hypothesize the underlying cause or causes of the reported issue, explaining why routers R1, BB1, and BB2 do not see all the networks in the topology, even though mutual redistribution does appear to be configured on router R2.

Suggested Solution

After examining the redistribution configuration on router R2, you might have noticed the following issues:

- The EIGRP routing process on router R2 lacked a default metric, which would be assigned to routes being redistributed into the EIGRP routing process. Example 7-45 shows the commands used to correct this misconfiguration.

Example 7-45   *Adding a Default Metric for Router R2's EIGRP Routing Process*

```
R2# conf term
Enter configuration commands, one per line.  End with CNTL/Z.
R2(config)#router eigrp 100
R2(config-router)#default-metric 1500 100 255 1 1500
R2(config-router)#end
```

- The OSPF routing process lacked the **subnets** parameter at the end of the **redistribute** command. The **subnets** parameter is required to allow nonclassful networks to be redistributed into OSPF. Example 7-46 illustrates how this configuration can be corrected.

Example 7-46   *Redistributing Subnets into Router R2's OSPF Routing Process*

```
R2# conf term
Enter configuration commands, one per line.  End with CNTL/Z.
R2(config)#router ospf 1
R2(config-router)#no redistribute eigrp 100 metric 64
R2(config-router)#redistribute eigrp 100 metric 64 subnets
R2(config-router)#end
```

After making the suggested corrections, all routers in the topology have IP routing tables that contain all advertised networks. Examples 7-47, 7-48, 7-49, and 7-50 illustrate the IP routing tables of these routers.

Example 7-47   *IP Routing Table of Router R1*

```
R1# show ip route
Codes: C - connected, S - static, R - RIP, M - mobile, B - BGP
       D - EIGRP, EX - EIGRP external, O - OSPF, IA - OSPF inter area
       N1 - OSPF NSSA external type 1, N2 - OSPF NSSA external type 2
```

```
          E1 - OSPF external type 1, E2 - OSPF external type 2
          i - IS-IS, su - IS-IS summary, L1 - IS-IS level-1, L2 - IS-IS level-2
          ia - IS-IS inter area, * - candidate default, U - per-user static route
          o - ODR, P - periodic downloaded static route

Gateway of last resort is not set


     172.16.0.0/30 is subnetted, 2 subnets
D EX     172.16.1.0 [170/1734656] via 192.168.0.22, 00:04:39, FastEthernet0/1
D EX     172.16.2.0 [170/1734656] via 192.168.0.22, 00:04:39, FastEthernet0/1
     10.0.0.0/8 is variably subnetted, 6 subnets, 3 masks
D        10.2.2.2/32 [90/156160] via 192.168.0.22, 00:18:05, FastEthernet0/1
D EX     10.1.3.0/30 [170/1734656] via 192.168.0.22, 00:04:39, FastEthernet0/1
D EX     10.3.3.3/32 [170/1734656] via 192.168.0.22, 00:04:39, FastEthernet0/1
D EX     10.1.2.0/24 [170/1734656] via 192.168.0.22, 00:04:40, FastEthernet0/1
C        10.1.1.1/32 is directly connected, Loopback0
D EX     10.4.4.4/32 [170/1734656] via 192.168.0.22, 00:04:40, FastEthernet0/1
C     192.168.0.0/24 is directly connected, FastEthernet0/1
C     192.168.1.0/24 is directly connected, FastEthernet0/0
```

Example 7-48 *IP Routing Table of Router R2*

```
R2# show ip route
Codes: C - connected, S - static, R - RIP, M - mobile, B - BGP
       D - EIGRP, EX - EIGRP external, O - OSPF, IA - OSPF inter area
       N1 - OSPF NSSA external type 1, N2 - OSPF NSSA external type 2
       E1 - OSPF external type 1, E2 - OSPF external type 2
       i - IS-IS, su - IS-IS summary, L1 - IS-IS level-1, L2 - IS-IS level-2
       ia - IS-IS inter area, * - candidate default, U - per-user static route
       o - ODR, P - periodic downloaded static route


Gateway of last resort is not set


     172.16.0.0/30 is subnetted, 2 subnets
C        172.16.1.0 is directly connected, Serial1/0.1
C        172.16.2.0 is directly connected, Serial1/0.2
     10.0.0.0/8 is variably subnetted, 6 subnets, 3 masks
C        10.2.2.2/32 is directly connected, Loopback0
O        10.1.3.0/30 [110/144] via 172.16.2.2, 00:21:04, Serial1/0.2
O        10.3.3.3/32 [110/91] via 172.16.2.2, 00:21:04, Serial1/0.2
O        10.1.2.0/24 [110/90] via 172.16.2.2, 00:21:04, Serial1/0.2
D        10.1.1.1/32 [90/409600] via 192.168.0.11, 00:18:38, FastEthernet0/0
O        10.4.4.4/32 [110/81] via 172.16.2.2, 00:21:04, Serial1/0.2
C     192.168.0.0/24 is directly connected, FastEthernet0/0
D     192.168.1.0/24 [90/284160] via 192.168.0.11, 00:18:38, FastEthernet0/0
```

Example 7-49 *IP Routing Table of Router BB1*

```
BB1# show ip route
Codes: C - connected, S - static, R - RIP, M - mobile, B - BGP
       D - EIGRP, EX - EIGRP external, O - OSPF, IA - OSPF inter area
       N1 - OSPF NSSA external type 1, N2 - OSPF NSSA external type 2
       E1 - OSPF external type 1, E2 - OSPF external type 2
       i - IS-IS, su - IS-IS summary, L1 - IS-IS level-1, L2 - IS-IS level-2
       ia - IS-IS inter area, * - candidate default, U - per-user static route
       o - ODR, P - periodic downloaded static route

Gateway of last resort is not set

     172.16.0.0/30 is subnetted, 2 subnets
C       172.16.1.0 is directly connected, Serial1/0.2
O       172.16.2.0 [110/90] via 10.1.2.2, 00:21:08, FastEthernet0/0
     10.0.0.0/8 is variably subnetted, 6 subnets, 3 masks
O E2    10.2.2.2/32 [110/64] via 10.1.2.2, 00:04:44, FastEthernet0/0
C       10.1.3.0/30 is directly connected, Serial1/0.1
C       10.3.3.3/32 is directly connected, Loopback0
C       10.1.2.0/24 is directly connected, FastEthernet0/0
O E2    10.1.1.1/32 [110/64] via 10.1.2.2, 00:04:44, FastEthernet0/0
O       10.4.4.4/32 [110/11] via 10.1.2.2, 00:21:08, FastEthernet0/0
O E2 192.168.0.0/24 [110/64] via 10.1.2.2, 00:04:44, FastEthernet0/0
O E2 192.168.1.0/24 [110/64] via 10.1.2.2, 00:04:44, FastEthernet0/0
```

Example 7-50 *IP Routing Table of Router BB2*

```
BB2# show ip route
Codes: C - connected, S - static, R - RIP, M - mobile, B - BGP
       D - EIGRP, EX - EIGRP external, O - OSPF, IA - OSPF inter area
       N1 - OSPF NSSA external type 1, N2 - OSPF NSSA external type 2
       E1 - OSPF external type 1, E2 - OSPF external type 2
       i - IS-IS, su - IS-IS summary, L1 - IS-IS level-1, L2 - IS-IS level-2
       ia - IS-IS inter area, * - candidate default, U - per-user static route
       o - ODR, P - periodic downloaded static route

Gateway of last resort is not set

     172.16.0.0/30 is subnetted, 2 subnets
O       172.16.1.0 [110/143] via 10.1.2.1, 00:21:13, FastEthernet0/0
C       172.16.2.0 is directly connected, Serial1/0.2
     10.0.0.0/8 is variably subnetted, 6 subnets, 3 masks
O E2    10.2.2.2/32 [110/64] via 172.16.2.1, 00:04:50, Serial1/0.2
C       10.1.3.0/30 is directly connected, Serial1/0.1
O       10.3.3.3/32 [110/11] via 10.1.2.1, 00:21:13, FastEthernet0/0
```

```
C        10.1.2.0/24 is directly connected, FastEthernet0/0
O E2     10.1.1.1/32 [110/64] via 172.16.2.1, 00:04:50, Serial1/0.2
C        10.4.4.4/32 is directly connected, Loopback0
O E2 192.168.0.0/24 [110/64] via 172.16.2.1, 00:04:50, Serial1/0.2
O E2 192.168.1.0/24 [110/64] via 172.16.2.1, 00:04:50, Serial1/0.2
```

Exam Preparation Tasks

Review All the Key Topics

Review the most important topics from inside the chapter, noted with the Key Topics icon in the outer margin of the page. Table 7-11 lists these key topics and the page numbers where each is found.

Table 7-11 *Key Topics for Chapter 7*

Key Topic Element	Description	Page Number
Table 7-2	OSPF data structures	170
List	OSPF router types	172
Table 7-3	OSPF router types in Figure 7-2	173
Table 7-4	LSA types	174
Table 7-5	OSPF LSA types in Figure 7-2	175
Table 7-6	OSPF Network Types and Characteristics	176
List	OSPF Hello packet parameters that must match for an adjacency to form	176
Table 7-7	Adjacency states	177
Table 7-8	OSPF troubleshooting commands	179
List	Reasons a network might benefit from route redistribution	205
List	Ways to define a seed metric	205
List	Prerequisites for IP route redistribution	206
Table 7-9	Troubleshooting targets for route redistribution	207
Example 7-34	Output from the **show ip route** profile command	208
Table 7-10	Route redistribution verification and troubleshooting syntax	209

Complete Tables and Lists from Memory

Print a copy of Appendix B, "Memory Tables" (found on the CD), or at least the section for this chapter, and complete the tables and lists from memory. Appendix C, "Memory Tables Answer Key," also on the CD, includes completed tables and lists to check your work.

Define Key Terms

Define the following key terms from this chapter, and check your answers in the Glossary:

OSPF interface table, OSPF neighbor table, OSPF link-state database, OSPF Routing Information Base (RIB), link-state advertisement (LSA), Dijkstra shortest path first (SPF) algorithm, virtual link, OSPF internal router, OSPF area border router (ABR), OSPF backbone router, OSPF Autonomous System Boundary Router (ASBR), route redistribution, boundary router

Command Reference to Check Your Memory

This section includes the most important configuration and EXEC commands covered in this chapter. To determine how well you have memorized the commands as a side effect of your other studies, cover the left side of the table with a piece of paper; read the descriptions on the right side; and see whether you remember the command.

Table 7-12 *Chapter 7 Configuration Command Reference*

Command	Description
ip route profile	Global configuration mode command that enables the Cisco IOS IP route profiling feature, which collects information regarding the frequency of IP routing table updates
router ospf *process-id*	Global configuration mode command that enables an OSPF process on a router
redistribute eigrp *autonomous-system-number* [subnets]	Router configuration mode command that redistributes routes, including subnets (if the optional **subnets** parameter is specified), from a specified EIGRP autonomous system into OSPF
default-metric *metric*	Router configuration mode command that specifies the metric used for routes redistributed into OSPF
router eigrp *autonomous-system-number*	Global configuration mode command that enables an EIGRP routing process on a router
redistribute ospf *process-id*	Router configuration mode command that redistributes routes from a specified OSPF process ID into EIGRP
default-metric *bandwidth delay reliability load mtu*	Router configuration mode command that specifies the parameters used to calculate the seed metric for routes being redistributed into EIGRP, using the following EIGRP metric parameters: *bandwidth* (in kbps) *delay* (in tens of microseconds) *reliability* (maximum of 255) *load* (minimum of 1) *mtu* (in bytes)

Table 7-13 *Chapter 7 EXEC Command Reference*

Command	Description
show ip ospf interface [brief]	Displays all of a router's interfaces configured to participate in an OSPF routing process (Note: The **brief** option provides a more concise view of OSPF interface information.)
show ip ospf neighbor	Displays the state of OSPF neighbors learned off of the active OSPF interfaces of a router
show ip ospf database	Displays the LSA headers contained in the OSPF link-state database of a router
show ip ospf statistics	Provides information about how frequently a router is executing the SFP algorithm. (Note: This command also shows when the SPF algorithm last ran.)
debug ip ospf monitor	Provides real-time updates showing when the SPF algorithm of a router is scheduled to run
debug ip routing	Displays updates that occur in an IP routing table (Note: This command is not specific to OSPF.)
show ip route ospf	Shows routes known to a router's IP routing table that were learned via OSPF
debug ip ospf packet	Shows the transmission and reception of OSPF packets in real time (Note: This command is useful for monitoring Hello messages.)
debug ip ospf adj	Provides real-time updates about the formation of an OSPF adjacency
debug ip ospf events	Shows real-time information about OSPF events, including the transmission and reception of Hello messages and LSAs (Note: This command might be useful on a router that appears to be ignoring Hello messages received from a neighboring router.)
show ip ospf virtual-links	Provides information about the status of OSPF virtual links, which are required for areas not physically adjacent to the backbone area (that is, area 0)
show ip route profile	Displays information collected by the Cisco IOS IP route profiling feature, which shows the frequency of IP routing table updates

This chapter covers the following subjects:

BGP Troubleshooting Issues: This section begins by introducing you to the Border Gateway Protocol (BGP) data structures, followed by a review of BGP operation. Finally, you are presented with a collection of **show** and **debug** commands useful for troubleshooting BGP operations.

Trouble Ticket: BGP: This section presents you with a trouble ticket and an associated topology. You are also given **show** command output. Based on the information provided, you hypothesize an underlying cause for the reported issue and develop a solution. You can then compare your solutions with those that have been suggested.

Router Performance Issues: This section discusses how to troubleshoot performance issues on a router, focusing on CPU utilization, packet switching modes, and memory utilization.

CHAPTER 8

Troubleshooting BGP and Router Performance Issues

This chapter begins by discussing Border Gateway Protocol (BGP). You will see how to use BGP between autonomous systems. Additionally, you will be equipped with a collection of **show** and **debug** commands, which can prove useful when troubleshooting a BGP issue.

To reinforce the theory of BGP troubleshooting, you are presented with a trouble ticket. The trouble ticket deals with a suboptimal path selection that BGP makes. You are then challenged to determine the cause of this path selection and reconfigure BGP to select a more appropriate path.

At that point, you will have covered troubleshooting approaches for multiple IP routing protocols (that is, Enhanced Interior Gateway Routing Protocol [EIGRP], Open Shortest Path First [OSPF], and BGP). Finally in this chapter, you review from a more generic perspective the troubleshooting of router performance issues. These issues can stem from a lack of available router memory, a lack of available buffers, or perhaps the packet switching mode of the router.

"Do I Know This Already?" Quiz

The "Do I Know This Already?" quiz helps you determine your level of knowledge of this chapter's topics before you begin. Table 8-1 details the major topics discussed in this chapter and their corresponding quiz questions.

Table 8-1 *"Do I Know This Already?" Section-to-Question Mapping*

Foundation Topics Section	Questions
BGP Troubleshooting Issues	1–2
Router Performance Issues	3–5

1. Identify two BGP data structures. (Choose the two best answers.)

    a. BGP table

    b. link-state database

    c. interface table

    d. neighbor table

2. Which command displays the network prefixes present in the BGP table?

    a.   show ip bgp neighbors

    b.   show ip bgp

    c.   show ip route bgp

    d.   show ip bgp summary

3. Which router process is in charge of handling interface state changes?

    a.   TCP Timer process

    b.   IP Background process

    c.   Net Background process

    d.   ARP Input process

4. Which of the following is the least efficient (that is, the most CPU intensive) of a router's packet switching modes?

    a.   Fast switching

    b.   CEF

    c.   Optimum switching

    d.   Process switching

5. Identify two common reasons a router displays a MALLOCFAIL error. (Choose the two best answers.)

    a.   Cisco IOS bug

    b.   Security issue

    c.   QoS issue

    d.   BGP filtering

Foundation Topics

BGP Troubleshooting Issues

Chapter 6, "Introduction to Troubleshooting Routing Protocols," and Chapter 7, "OSPF and Route Redistribution Troubleshooting," focused on interior gateway protocols (IGP). An IGP is used within an autonomous system (AS), where an *autonomous system* is defined as a network under a single administrative control. This chapter, however, focuses on an exterior gateway protocol (EGP)—specifically BGP.

An EGP, like BGP, is a routing protocol typically used between autonomous systems. For example, if your enterprise network connects to more than one Internet service provider (ISP), you might be running BGP between your network (that is, your AS) and each ISP (each of which is a separate AS).

This section examines BGP data structures, reviews BGP operation, and presents commands useful for collecting information from the BGP data structures.

BGP Data Structures

Figure 8-1 reviews how the data structures of an IP routing protocol interact with an IP routing table.

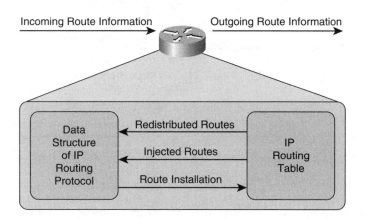

Figure 8-1   *Data Structure and IP Routing Table Interaction*

Table 8-2 describes how BGP operates within this framework.

Key Topic

Table 8-2   *Interaction Between the Data Structures of a BGP and an IP Routing Table*

Component of Routing Process	Description
Incoming Route Information	A BGP router receives BGP updates from a BGP neighbor. Unlike OSPF and EIGRP neighbors, BGP neighbors do not need to be directly connected. Rather, BGP neighbors can be multiple hops away from one another. Therefore, BGP neighbors are often referred to as *peers*.
Data Structure of IP Routing Protocol	BGP maintains two data structures: the neighbor table and the BGP table. The neighbor table contains status information about BGP neighbors, whereas the BGP table contains network prefixes learned from BGP neighbors.
Injecting and Redistributing Routes	Routes can be inserted in the BGP table by advertisements received from BGP neighbors or by locally injected routes. For a route to be locally injected (either through a manual configuration or through a redistribution configuration), it must be present in the IP routing table.
Route Installation	Similar to OSPF and EIGRP, BGP might have more than one route to a network prefix in its BGP table. BGP then selects what it considers to be the best route to that network prefix; that best route becomes a candidate to be inserted into the IP routing table.
Outgoing Route Information	Routes in a router's BGP table that are considered the best routes to their network prefixes are advertised to the router's BGP peers. BGP offers several features to limit routes advertised to BGP peers or received from BGP peers.

Figure 8-2 illustrates BGP's two data structures, which are described in the list that follows.

Key Topic

■ **Neighbor table:** The BGP neighbor table contains a listing of all BGP neighbors configured for a router, including each neighbor's IP address, AS number, the state of the neighborship, and several other statistics.

■ **BGP table:** The BGP table, sometimes referred to as the BGP Routing Information Base (RIB), contains routes learned from BGP peers and routes locally injected into the BGP table of a router.

Unlike OSPF and EIGRP, BGP does not consider a link's bandwidth when making a routing decision. Instead, BGP uses the following criteria when deciding how to forward a packet. The criteria are listed in the order in which BGP prioritizes each criterion.

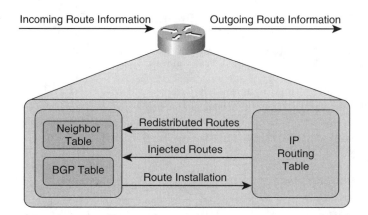

Figure 8-2 *BGP Data Structures*

1. BGP prefers the path with the highest weight. Note that the BGP **weight** parameter is a Cisco-specific parameter.

2. BGP prefers the path with the highest local preference value.

3. BGP prefers the path originated by BGP on the local router.

4. BGP prefers the path with the shortest autonomous system.

5. BGP prefers the path with the lowest origin type. (**NOTE:** IGP < EGP < INCOMPLETE.)

6. BGP prefers the path with the lowest multi-exit discriminator (MED).

7. BGP prefers eBGP paths over iBGP paths.

8. BGP prefers the path with the lowest IGP metric to the BGP next-hop.

9. BGP prefers the path that points to a BGP router with the lowest BGP router ID.

A BGP router always learns its neighbors through manual configuration of those neighbors as opposed to dynamically learning about neighbors. This manual configuration requirement makes sense when you consider that BGP neighbors do not have to be physically adjacent. When a BGP neighbor is statically configured, the AS number of the neighbor is specified.

A BGP router attempts to establish a session with its configured neighbors using TCP port 179. After a session has been established, BGP OPEN messages are exchanged to communicate each neighbor's BGP characteristics.

The following are reasons why the peering of two BGP routers might fail:

■ The AS numbers must match between the AS number in messages received from a neighbor and the AS number a router has configured for that neighbor. If the AS numbers fail to match, the session is reset.

■ TCP establishes a BGP session. Therefore, a lack of IP connectivity between two BGP routers prevents a peering relationship from forming between those routers.

■   A BGP router might have multiple active IP addresses configured across its various in-terfaces. A router might send a BGP message from one of its IP addresses that does not match the IP address configured for that router on its peer. If the peer does not recognize the source IP address of the BGP message, the peering relationship fails.

After initially establishing a peering relationship, two BGP peers exchange information in their BGP tables. Incremental updates are sent thereafter. If a network prefix is re-moved from the BGP table of a router, that router sends a WITHDRAW message to ap-propriate peers.

BGP Troubleshooting Commands

With an understanding of BGP's data structures and path selection criteria, you can now strategically use Cisco IOS **show** and **debug** commands to collect information about spe-cific steps in the BGP routing process. Table 8-3 shows a collection of such commands, along with their descriptions, and the step of the routing process or BGP data structure that each command can be used to investigate.

Key Topic

Table 8-3   *BGP Troubleshooting Commands*

Command	Routing Component or Data Structure	Description
show ip bgp summary	Neighbor table	This command displays a router's BGP router ID, AS number, information about the BGP's memory usage, and summary information about BGP neighbors.
show ip bgp neighbors	Neighbor table	This command displays the detailed informa-tion about all the BGP neighbors of a router.
show ip bgp	BGP table	This command displays the network prefixes present in the BGP table.
debug ip routing	IP routing table	This command displays updates that occur in a router's IP routing table. Therefore, this command is not specific to BGP.
show ip route bgp	IP routing table	This command shows routes known to a router's IP routing table that were learned via BGP.
debug ip bgp	Exchanging BGP in-formation with neigh-bors	Although this command does not show the contents of BGP updates, the output does provide real-time information about BGP events, such as the establishment of a peer-ing relationship.

Table 8-3 *BGP Troubleshooting Commands* *(Continued)*

Command	Routing Component or Data Structure	Description
debug ip bgp updates	Exchanging BGP information with neighbors	This command shows real-time information about BGP updates sent and received by a BGP router.

Example 8-1 provides sample output from the **show ip bgp summary** command. Notice that the output shows that the BGP router ID is 10.2.2.2, and the router is in AS 65001. You can also determine how much memory is being used by the BGP network entries and see summary information about the BGP neighbors of this router.

Example 8-1   show ip bgp summary *Command Output*

```
R2#show ip bgp summary
 BGP router identifier 10.2.2.2, local AS number 65001
BGP table version is 11, main routing table version 11
 10 network entries using 1170 bytes of memory
14 path entries using 728 bytes of memory
6/5 BGP path/bestpath attribute entries using 744 bytes of memory
2 BGP AS-PATH entries using 48 bytes of memory
0 BGP route-map cache entries using 0 bytes of memory
0 BGP filter-list cache entries using 0 bytes of memory
BGP using 2690 total bytes of memory
BGP activity 10/0 prefixes, 14/0 paths, scan interval 60 secs

Neighbor        V    AS   MsgRcvd  MsgSent  TblVer  InQ OutQ  Up/Down   State/PfxRcd
172.16.1.1    4   65002       11       15      11    0    0  00:07:45              4
172.16.2.2    4   65003        8       12      11    0    0  00:03:19              4
```

Example 8-2 provides sample output from the **show ip bgp neighbors** command. The output from this command provides detailed information about each neighbor. The truncated output shown here is for a neighbor with a BGP router ID of 10.3.3.3. Among the large number of statistics shown is information about the BGP session with this neighbor. For example, you can see that the BGP state of the session is Established, and the two TCP ports being used for the session are 52907 and 179.

Example 8-2   show ip bgp neighbors *Command Output*

```
R2#show ip bgp neighbors
BGP neighbor is 172.16.1.1,  remote AS 65002, external link
  BGP version 4, remote router ID 10.3.3.3
  BGP state = Established, up for 00:10:05
  Last read 00:00:04, last write 00:00:05, hold time is 180, keepalive interval
```

```
 is 60 seconds
   Neighbor capabilities:
     Route refresh: advertised and received(old & new)
     Address family IPv4 Unicast: advertised and received
   Message statistics:
     InQ depth is 0
     OutQ depth is 0
                       Sent        Rcvd
     Opens:            1           1
     Notifications:    0           0
     Updates:          5           2
     Keepalives:       12          12
     Route Refresh:    0           0
     Total:            18          15
   Default minimum time between advertisement runs is 30 seconds


  For address family: IPv4 Unicast
   BGP table version 11, neighbor version 11/0
  Output queue size : 0
   Index 1, Offset 0, Mask 0x2
   1 update-group member
                       Sent        Rcvd
   Prefix activity:    - - - -     - - - -
     Prefixes Current: 10          5 (Consumes 260 bytes)
     Prefixes Total:   10          5
     Implicit Withdraw: 0          0
     Explicit Withdraw: 0          0
     Used as bestpath:  n/a        3
     Used as multipath: n/a        0

                       Outbound    Inbound
   Local Policy Denied Prefixes:  - - - - - - - - -   - - - - - - - -
     Total:                       0           0
   Number of NLRIs in the update sent: max 3, min 1


   Connections established 1; dropped 0
   Last reset never
  Connection state is ESTAB, I/O status: 1, unread input bytes: 0
  Connection is ECN Disabled, Minimum incoming TTL 0, Outgoing TTL 1
  Local host: 172.16.1.2, Local port: 52907
  Foreign host: 172.16.1.1, Foreign port: 179
  Enqueued packets for retransmit: 0, input: 0  mis-ordered: 0 (0 bytes)
```

```
Event Timers (current time is 0x1268DC):
Timer          Starts    Wakeups          Next
Retrans            16         0           0x0
TimeWait            0         0           0x0
AckHold            14        12           0x0
SendWnd             0         0           0x0
KeepAlive           0         0           0x0
GiveUp              0         0           0x0
PmtuAger            0         0           0x0
DeadWait            0         0           0x0

iss:    43311306  snduna:    43311857  sndnxt:    43311857    sndwnd:    15834
irs: 2939679566   rcvnxt: 2939679955   rcvwnd:       15996  delrcvwnd:     388

SRTT: 279 ms, RTTO: 504 ms, RTV: 225 ms, KRTT: 0 ms
minRTT: 48 ms, maxRTT: 488 ms, ACK hold: 200 ms
Flags: active open, nagle
IP Precedence value : 6

Datagrams (max data segment is 1460 bytes):
Rcvd: 18 (out of order: 0), with data: 14, total data bytes: 388
Sent: 29 (retransmit: 0, fastretransmit: 0, partialack: 0, Second Congestion: 0),
with data: 15, total data bytes: 550
...OUTPUT OMITTED...
```

Example 8-3 provides sample output from the **show ip bgp** command. The output from this command shows the network prefixes present in the BGP table, along with information such as the next-hop IP addresses to reach those networks. Notice that some network prefixes are reachable via more than one path. For example, the 10.1.2.0/24 network is reachable via a next-hop IP address of 172.16.2.2 or 172.16.1.1. The **>** sign indicates which path BGP has selected as the best path. In this case, the path BGP selected as the best path has a next-hop IP address of 172.16.1.1.

Example 8-3   show ip bgp *Command Output*

```
R2#show ip bgp
BGP table version is 11, local router ID is 10.2.2.2
Status codes: s suppressed, d damped, h history, * valid, > best, i - internal,
              r RIB-failure, S Stale
Origin codes: i - IGP, e - EGP, ? - incomplete

   Network          Next Hop          Metric LocPrf Weight Path
*> 10.1.1.1/32      192.168.0.11          11          32768 ?
*  10.1.2.0/24      172.16.2.2             0              0 65003 i
*>                  172.16.1.1             0              0 65002 i
*  10.1.3.0/30      172.16.2.2             0              0 65003 i
```

*>		172.16.1.1	0	0 65002 i
*>	10.2.2.2/32	0.0.0.0	0	32768 ?
*	10.3.3.3/32	172.16.2.2		0 65003 65002 i
*>		172.16.1.1	0	0 65002 i
*	10.4.4.4/32	172.16.1.1		0 65002 65003 i
*>		172.16.2.2	0	0 65003 i
*	172.16.1.0/30	172.16.1.1	0	0 65002 i
*>		0.0.0.0	0	32768 i
*	172.16.2.0/30	172.16.2.2	0	0 65003 i
*>		0.0.0.0	0	32768 i
*>	192.168.0.0	0.0.0.0	0	32768 ?
*>	192.168.1.0	192.168.0.11	11	32768 ?

Example 8-4 provides sample output from the **debug ip routing** command. The output from this command shows updates to a router's IP routing table. In this example, the Loopback 0 interface (with an IP address of 10.3.3.3) of a neighboring router was administratively shut down and then administratively brought back up. As the 10.3.3.3/32 network became unavailable and then once again became available, you can see that the 10.3.3.3/32 route was deleted and then added to this router's IP routing table. Notice that this output is not specific to BGP. Therefore, you can use the **debug ip routing** command with routing processes other than BGP.

Example 8-4   debug ip routing *Command Output*

```
R2#debug ip routing
IP routing debugging is on
*Mar  1 00:20:55.707: RT: 10.3.3.3/32 gateway changed from 172.16.1.1 to
172.16.2.2
*Mar  1 00:20:55.711: RT: NET-RED 10.3.3.3/32
*Mar  1 00:20:55.735: RT: del 10.3.3.3/32 via 172.16.2.2, bgp metric [20/0]
*Mar  1 00:20:55.739: RT: delete subnet route to 10.3.3.3/32
*Mar  1 00:20:55.743: RT: NET-RED 10.3.3.3/32
*Mar  1 00:21:25.815: RT: SET_LAST_RDB for 10.3.3.3/32
  NEW rdb: via 172.16.1.1

*Mar  1 00:21:25.819: RT: add 10.3.3.3/32 via 172.16.1.1, bgp metric [20/0]
*Mar  1 00:21:25.823: RT: NET-RED 10.3.3.3/32
```

Example 8-5 provides sample output from the **show ip route bgp** command. This command displays a subset of a router's IP routing table. Specifically, only routes in the IP routing table which have been learned via BGP are displayed.

Example 8-5   show ip route bgp *Command Output*

```
R2#show ip route bgp
     10.0.0.0/8 is variably subnetted, 6 subnets, 3 masks
B       10.1.3.0/30 [20/0] via 172.16.1.1, 00:11:26
```

```
B        10.3.3.3/32 [20/0] via 172.16.1.1, 00:00:34
B        10.1.2.0/24 [20/0] via 172.16.1.1, 00:11:26
B        10.4.4.4/32 [20/0] via 172.16.2.2, 00:07:35
```

Example 8-6 provides sample output from the **debug ip bgp** command. The output of this command does not show the contents of BGP updates; however, this command can be useful in watching real-time state changes for BGP peering relationships. In this example, you can see a peering session being closed for the neighbor with an IP address of 172.16.1.1.

Example 8-6   debug ip bgp *Command Output*

```
R2#debug ip bgp
BGP debugging is on for address family: IPv4 Unicast
*Mar  1 00:23:26.535: BGP: 172.16.1.1 remote close, state CLOSEWAIT
*Mar  1 00:23:26.535: BGP: 172.16.1.1 -reset the session
*Mar  1 00:23:26.543: BGPNSF state: 172.16.1.1 went from nsf_not_active to
  nsf_not_active
*Mar  1 00:23:26.547: BGP: 172.16.1.1 went from Established to Idle
*Mar  1 00:23:26.547: %BGP-5-ADJCHANGE: neighbor 172.16.1.1 Down Peer closed the
  session
*Mar  1 00:23:26.547: BGP: 172.16.1.1 closing
*Mar  1 00:23:26.651: BGP: 172.16.1.1 went from Idle to Active
*Mar  1 00:23:26.663: BGP: 172.16.1.1 open active delayed 30162ms (35000ms max,
  28% jitter)
```

Example 8-7 provides sample output from the **debug ip bgp updates** command. This command produces more detailed output than the **debug ip bgp** command. Specifically, you can see the content of BGP updates. In this example, you see a route of 10.3.3.3/32 being added to a router's IP routing table.

Example 8-7   debug ip bgp updates *Command Output*

```
R2#debug ip bgp updates
BGP updates debugging is on for address family: IPv4 Unicast
*Mar  1 00:24:27.455: BGP(0): 172.16.1.1 NEXT_HOP part 1 net 10.3.3.3/32, next
  172.16.1.1
*Mar  1 00:24:27.455: BGP(0): 172.16.1.1 send UPDATE (format) 10.3.3.3/32, next
  172.16.1.1, metric 0, path 65002
*Mar  1 00:24:27.507: BGP(0): 172.16.1.1 rcv UPDATE about 10.3.3.3/32 — withdrawn
*Mar  1 00:24:27.515: BGP(0): Revise route installing 1 of 1 routes for
  10.3.3.3/32 -> 172.16.2.2(main) to main IP table
*Mar  1 00:24:27.519: BGP(0): updgrp 1 - 172.16.1.1 updates replicated for
  neighbors: 172.16.2.2
*Mar  1 00:24:27.523: BGP(0): 172.16.1.1 send UPDATE (format) 10.3.3.3/32, next
  172.16.1.2, metric 0, path 65003 65002
```

```
*Mar  1 00:24:27.547: BGP(0): 172.16.2.2 rcvd UPDATE w/ attr: nexthop 172.16.2.2,
   origin i, path 65003 65002
*Mar  1 00:24:27.551: BGP(0): 172.16.2.2 rcvd 10.3.3.3/32...duplicate ignored
*Mar  1 00:24:27.555: BGP(0): updgrp 1 - 172.16.1.1 updates replicated for
   neighbors: 172.16.2.2
*Mar  1 00:24:27.675: BGP(0): 172.16.2.2 rcv UPDATE w/ attr: nexthop 172.16.2.2,
   origin i, originator 0.0.0.0, path 65003 65001 65002, community , extended
   community
*Mar  1 00:24:27.683: BGP(0): 172.16.2.2 rcv UPDATE about 10.3.3.3/32 — DENIED
   due to: AS-PATH contains our own AS;
...OUTPUT OMITTED...
```

Trouble Ticket: BGP

This trouble ticket focuses on BGP. You are presented with baseline data, a trouble ticket, and information collected while investigating the reported issue. You are then challenged to identify the underlying issue and create an action plan to resolve that issue.

Trouble Ticket #6

You receive the following trouble ticket:

> Company A (that is, routers R1 and R2) has connections to two service providers (that is, BB1 and BB2). Router R2 is running BGP and is peering with routers BB1 and BB2. The bandwidth between routers R2 and BB2 is greater than the bandwidth between routers R2 and BB1. Therefore, company A wants to use the R2-to-BB2 link as the primary link to the backbone network (that is, a default route). However, company A noticed that the R2-to-BB1 link is being used.

This trouble ticket references the topology shown in Figure 8-3.

You begin by examining the baseline data collected after company A was dual-homed to its two ISPs. Example 8-8 shows the output from the **show ip route** command on router R1. Notice that router R1 has a default route in its IP routing table. This default route was learned via OSPF from router R2.

Example 8-8 *Baseline Output for Router R1*

```
R1#show ip route
Codes: C - connected, S - static, R - RIP, M - mobile, B - BGP
       D - EIGRP, EX - EIGRP external, O - OSPF, IA - OSPF inter area
       N1 - OSPF NSSA external type 1, N2 - OSPF NSSA external type 2
       E1 - OSPF external type 1, E2 - OSPF external type 2
       i - IS-IS, su - IS-IS summary, L1 - IS-IS level-1, L2 - IS-IS level-2
       ia - IS-IS inter area, * - candidate default, U - per-user static route
       o - ODR, P - periodic downloaded static route
```

```
Gateway of last resort is 192.168.0.22 to network 0.0.0.0


      10.0.0.0/32 is subnetted, 2 subnets
O        10.2.2.2 [110/2] via 192.168.0.22, 00:05:33, FastEthernet0/1
C        10.1.1.1 is directly connected, Loopback0
C     192.168.0.0/24 is directly connected, FastEthernet0/1
C     192.168.1.0/24 is directly connected, FastEthernet0/0
O*E2 0.0.0.0/0 [110/1] via 192.168.0.22, 00:05:33, FastEthernet0/1
```

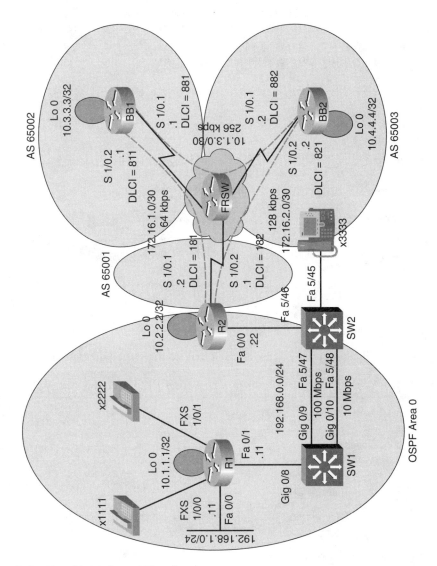

Figure 8-3   *Trouble Ticket #6 Topology*

Router R2 was configured for both OSPF and BGP, with the BGP-learned default route being injected into OSPF, and with OSPF-learned routes being redistributed into BGP. Example 8-9 shows the initial IP routing table for router R2. Notice that the next-hop router for the default route is 172.16.1.1 (that is, router BB1).

Example 8-9   *Baseline IP Routing Table on Router R2*

```
R2#show ip route
Codes: C - connected, S - static, R - RIP, M - mobile, B - BGP
       D - EIGRP, EX - EIGRP external, O - OSPF, IA - OSPF inter area
       N1 - OSPF NSSA external type 1, N2 - OSPF NSSA external type 2
       E1 - OSPF external type 1, E2 - OSPF external type 2
       i - IS-IS, su - IS-IS summary, L1 - IS-IS level-1, L2 - IS-IS level-2
       ia - IS-IS inter area, * - candidate default, U - per-user static route
       o - ODR, P - periodic downloaded static route

Gateway of last resort is 172.16.1.1 to network 0.0.0.0

     172.16.0.0/30 is subnetted, 2 subnets
C       172.16.1.0 is directly connected, Serial1/0.1
C       172.16.2.0 is directly connected, Serial1/0.2
     10.0.0.0/8 is variably subnetted, 6 subnets, 3 masks
C       10.2.2.2/32 is directly connected, Loopback0
B       10.1.3.0/30 [20/0] via 172.16.1.1, 00:01:40
B       10.3.3.3/32 [20/0] via 172.16.1.1, 00:01:40
B       10.1.2.0/24 [20/0] via 172.16.1.1, 00:01:40
O       10.1.1.1/32 [110/11] via 192.168.0.11, 00:08:17, FastEthernet0/0
B       10.4.4.4/32 [20/0] via 172.16.2.2, 00:01:40
C    192.168.0.0/24 is directly connected, FastEthernet0/0
O    192.168.1.0/24 [110/11] via 192.168.0.11, 00:08:17, FastEthernet0/0
B*   0.0.0.0/0 [20/0] via 172.16.1.1, 00:01:40
```

Example 8-10 illustrates the initial OSPF and BGP configuration on router R2.

Example 8-10   *Initial Router Configuration on Router R2*

```
R2#show run | begin router
router ospf 1
 log-adjacency-changes
 network 10.2.2.2 0.0.0.0 area 0
 network 192.168.0.0 0.0.0.255 area 0
 default-information originate
!
router bgp 65001
 no synchronization
 bgp log-neighbor-changes
 network 172.16.1.0 mask 255.255.255.252
```

```
network 172.16.2.0 mask 255.255.255.252
redistribute ospf 1
neighbor 172.16.1.1 remote-as 65002
neighbor 172.16.2.2 remote-as 65003
no auto-summary
```

Example 8-11 shows the output of the **show ip bgp summary** command on router R2, which confirms that router R2 resides in BGP AS 65001. The output also confirms BGP adjacencies have been formed with routers BB1 and BB2.

Example 8-11 *BGP Configuration Summary on Router R2*

```
R2#show ip bgp summary
BGP router identifier 10.2.2.2, local AS number 65001
BGP table version is 18, main routing table version 18
11 network entries using 1287 bytes of memory
20 path entries using 1040 bytes of memory
8/5 BGP path/bestpath attribute entries using 992 bytes of memory
4 BGP AS-PATH entries using 96 bytes of memory
0 BGP route-map cache entries using 0 bytes of memory
0 BGP filter-list cache entries using 0 bytes of memory
BGP using 3415 total bytes of memory
BGP activity 38/27 prefixes, 75/55 paths, scan interval 60 secs

Neighbor        V    AS MsgRcvd MsgSent   TblVer  InQ OutQ Up/Down  State/PfxRcd
172.16.1.1      4 65002     102      97       18    0    0 00:02:47        7
172.16.2.2      4 65003     100      97       18    0    0 00:02:47        7
```

Router BB1 is configured for BGP and is sourcing a default route advertisement. Example 8-12 shows the IP routing table of router BB1.

Example 8-12 *Initial IP Routing Table on Router BB1*

```
BB1#show ip route
Codes: C - connected, S - static, R - RIP, M - mobile, B - BGP
       D - EIGRP, EX - EIGRP external, O - OSPF, IA - OSPF inter area
       N1 - OSPF NSSA external type 1, N2 - OSPF NSSA external type 2
       E1 - OSPF external type 1, E2 - OSPF external type 2
       i - IS-IS, su - IS-IS summary, L1 - IS-IS level-1, L2 - IS-IS level-2
       ia - IS-IS inter area, * - candidate default, U - per-user static route
       o - ODR, P - periodic downloaded static route

Gateway of last resort is 0.0.0.0 to network 0.0.0.0

     172.16.0.0/30 is subnetted, 2 subnets
```

```
C          172.16.1.0 is directly connected, Serial1/0.2
B          172.16.2.0 [20/0] via 10.1.3.2, 00:03:01
        10.0.0.0/8 is variably subnetted, 6 subnets, 3 masks
B          10.2.2.2/32 [20/0] via 172.16.1.2, 00:01:59
C          10.1.3.0/30 is directly connected, Serial1/0.1
C          10.3.3.3/32 is directly connected, Loopback0
C          10.1.2.0/24 is directly connected, FastEthernet0/0
B          10.1.1.1/32 [20/11] via 172.16.1.2, 00:01:59
B          10.4.4.4/32 [20/0] via 10.1.3.2, 00:40:10
B       192.168.0.0/24 [20/0] via 172.16.1.2, 00:01:59
B       192.168.1.0/24 [20/11] via 172.16.1.2, 00:01:59
S*      0.0.0.0/0 is directly connected, Null0
```

Router BB2's IP routing table, as shown in Example 8-13, is similar to router BB1's IP routing table. Notice that router BB2 is also sourcing a default route and is advertising it via BGP to router R2. Therefore, router R2 has two paths to reach a default route in its BGP table.

Example 8-13 *Initial IP Routing Table on Router BB2*

```
BB2#show ip route
Codes: C - connected, S - static, R - RIP, M - mobile, B - BGP
        D - EIGRP, EX - EIGRP external, O - OSPF, IA - OSPF inter area
        N1 - OSPF NSSA external type 1, N2 - OSPF NSSA external type 2
        E1 - OSPF external type 1, E2 - OSPF external type 2
        i - IS-IS, su - IS-IS summary, L1 - IS-IS level-1, L2 - IS-IS level-2
        ia - IS-IS inter area, * - candidate default, U - per-user static route
        o - ODR, P - periodic downloaded static route

Gateway of last resort is 0.0.0.0 to network 0.0.0.0

        172.16.0.0/30 is subnetted, 2 subnets
B          172.16.1.0 [20/0] via 10.1.3.1, 00:03:11
C          172.16.2.0 is directly connected, Serial1/0.2
        10.0.0.0/8 is variably subnetted, 6 subnets, 3 masks
B          10.2.2.2/32 [20/0] via 172.16.2.1, 00:02:09
C          10.1.3.0/30 is directly connected, Serial1/0.1
B          10.3.3.3/32 [20/0] via 10.1.3.1, 00:40:10
C          10.1.2.0/24 is directly connected, FastEthernet0/0
B          10.1.1.1/32 [20/11] via 172.16.2.1, 00:02:09
C          10.4.4.4/32 is directly connected, Loopback0
B       192.168.0.0/24 [20/0] via 172.16.2.1, 00:02:09
B       192.168.1.0/24 [20/11] via 172.16.2.1, 00:02:09
S*      0.0.0.0/0 is directly connected, Null0
```

As shown earlier, in Example 8-9, router R2 preferred the 64-kbps link to router BB1 to reach a default route, as opposed to the 128-kbps link to router BB2. Therefore, the outbound routing from router R2 is suboptimal.

Also, the inbound routing, coming into the enterprise via router R2, is suboptimal. To illustrate this point, consider Example 8-14, which shows the BGP table on router BB1. Notice that router BB1 prefers a next-hop router of router R2 to reach the 10.1.1.1/32 network, which resides inside the enterprise network (that is, the network comprised of routers R1 and R2). Using a next-hop router of R2 would force traffic over the 64-kbps link rather than sending traffic from router BB1 over the 256-kbps link to router BB2, and then over the 128-kbps link to router R2, and finally across the FastEthernet connection to router R1.

Example 8-14   *BGP Forwarding Table on Router BB1*

```
BB1#show ip bgp
BGP table version is 130, local router ID is 10.3.3.3
Status codes: s suppressed, d damped, h history, * valid, > best, i - internal,
              r RIB-failure, S Stale
Origin codes: i - IGP, e - EGP, ? - incomplete

   Network          Next Hop            Metric LocPrf Weight Path
*  0.0.0.0          10.1.3.2                 0             0 65003 i
*> 	                0.0.0.0                  0         32768 i
*  10.1.1.1/32      10.1.3.2                               0 65003 65001 ?
*>                  172.16.1.2              11             0 65001 ?
*  10.1.2.0/24      10.1.3.2                 0             0 65003 i
*>                  0.0.0.0                  0         32768 i
*  10.1.3.0/30      10.1.3.2                 0             0 65003 i
*>                  0.0.0.0                  0         32768 i
*  10.2.2.2/32      10.1.3.2                               0 65003 65001 ?
*>                  172.16.1.2               0             0 65001 ?
*> 10.3.3.3/32      0.0.0.0                  0         32768 i
*  10.4.4.4/32      172.16.1.2                             0 65001 65003 i
*>                  10.1.3.2                 0             0 65003 i
*  172.16.1.0/30    172.16.1.2               0             0 65001 i
*>                  0.0.0.0                  0         32768 i
*  172.16.2.0/30    172.16.1.2               0             0 65001 i
*>                  10.1.3.2                 0             0 65003 i
*  192.168.0.0      10.1.3.2                               0 65003 65001 ?
*>                  172.16.1.2               0             0 65001 ?
*  192.168.1.0      10.1.3.2                               0 65003 65001 ?
*>                  172.16.1.2              11             0 65001 ?
```

As you formulate your solution to correct the inbound and outbound path selection issues, you should limit your configuration to router R2. The reason for this limitation is that routers BB1 and BB2 are acting as ISP routers. In a real-world environment, the administrator of an enterprise network would probably not have privileges to configure the ISP routers.

BGP has multiple attributes that can be manipulated to influence path selection. The suggested solution, however, focuses on how the BGP local preference attribute can influence the outbound path selection and how the BGP ASPATH attribute can influence the inbound path selection. You can configure route maps to set these BGP attributes. If you choose to base your solution on local preference and ASPATH attributes, Table 8-4 provides a syntax reference that might be helpful.

Key Topic

Table 8-4   *Configuring ASPATH and Local Preference BGP Attributes*

Command	Description
Router(config)# **route-map** *tag* [**permit** | **deny**] [*seq-num*]	Creates a route map
Router(config-route-map)# **set local-preference** *local-preference*	Sets the local preference BGP attribute for routes matched by a route map
Router(config-route-map)# **set as-path prepend** *autonomous-system-number-1* [...*autonomous-system-number-n*]	Defines an autonomous system path to prepend to an autonomous system path known by the BGP forwarding table
Router(config)# **router bgp** *as-number*	Enables a BGP process for a specific autonomous system
Router(config-router)# **neighbor** *ip-address* **route-map** *route-map-name* [**in** | **out**]	Applies a specified route map to routes received from or advertised to a specified BGP neighbor

Take a moment to look through the provided **show** command output. Then, on a separate sheet of paper, create a plan for correcting the suboptimal path selection.

Suggested Solution

Local preference values can be applied to routes coming into a router. This can cause that router to make its outbound routing decisions based on those local preference values. Higher local preference values are preferred over lower local preference values.

An AS path (that is, a listing of the autonomous systems that must be transited to reach a specific destination network) advertised to a neighbor can influence the BGP path selection of that neighbor. Specifically, BGP can make routing decisions based on the smallest number of autonomous systems that must be crossed to reach a destination network. Using a route map, you can prepend one or more additional instances of your local AS to the ASPATH advertised to a router's neighbor, thereby making that path appear less attractive to your neighbor.

Therefore, the suggested solution configures local preference values for routes advertised into router R2 from routers BB1 and BB2 to prefer routes being advertised via router BB2. Example 8-15 shows this configuration, which influences outbound path selection.

Example 8-15   *Local Preference Configuration on Router R2*

```
R2(config)#route-map LOCALPREF-BB1
R2(config-route-map)#set local-preference 100
R2(config-route-map)#exit
R2(config)#route-map LOCALPREF-BB2
R2(config-route-map)#set local-preference 200
R2(config-route-map)#exit
R2(config)#router bgp 65001
R2(config-router)#neighbor 172.16.1.1 route-map LOCALPREF-BB1 in
R2(config-router)#neighbor 172.16.2.2 route-map LOCALPREF-BB2 in
R2(config-router)#exit
```

To influence inbound path selection, this suggested solution configured a route map to prepend two additional instances of AS 65001 to routes being advertised via BGP from router R2 to router BB1. Example 8-16 shows this configuration, which causes router BB1 to use router BB2 as a next-hop router when sending traffic into the enterprise network. It does this because the path via router BB2 appears to be fewer AS hops away from the enterprise networks.

Example 8-16   *ASPATH Configuration on Router R2*

```
R2(config)#route-map ASPATH 10
R2(config-route-map)#set as-path prepend 65001 65001
R2(config-route-map)#exit
R2(config)#router bgp 65001
R2(config-router)#neighbor 172.16.1.1 route-map ASPATH out
R2(config-router)#end
```

Example 8-17 confirms that router R2 now prefers router BB2 (that is, a next-hop IP address of 172.16.2.2) to reach the default network.

Example 8-17   *Preferred Path of Router R2 to Backbone Networks*

```
R2#show ip bgp
BGP table version is 16, local router ID is 10.2.2.2
Status codes: s suppressed, d damped, h history, * valid, > best, i - internal,
              r RIB-failure, S Stale
Origin codes: i - IGP, e - EGP, ? - incomplete

   Network          Next Hop          Metric LocPrf Weight Path
*  0.0.0.0          172.16.1.1             0    100      0 65002 i
*>                  172.16.2.2             0    200      0 65003 i
*> 10.1.1.1/32      192.168.0.11          11           32768 ?
```

```
 *   10.1.2.0/24    172.16.1.1         0   100      0 65002 i
 *>                 172.16.2.2         0   200      0 65003 i
 *   10.1.3.0/30    172.16.1.1         0   100      0 65002 i
 *>                 172.16.2.2         0   200      0 65003 i
 *>  10.2.2.2/32    0.0.0.0           0        32768 ?
 *   10.3.3.3/32    172.16.1.1        0   100      0 65002 i
 *>                 172.16.2.2            200      0 65003 65002 i
 *   10.4.4.4/32    172.16.1.1            100      0 65002 65003 i
 *>                 172.16.2.2        0   200      0 65003 i
 *>  172.16.1.0/30  0.0.0.0           0        32768 i
 *                  172.16.1.1        0   100      0 65002 i
 *                  172.16.2.2            200      0 65003 65002 i
 *>  172.16.2.0/30  0.0.0.0           0        32768 i
 *                  172.16.1.1            100      0 65002 65003 i
 *                  172.16.2.2        0   200      0 65003 i
 *>  192.168.0.0    0.0.0.0           0        32768 ?
 *>  192.168.1.0    192.168.0.11     11        32768 ?
```

Example 8-18 confirms that router BB1 will not prefer to send traffic to the enterprise network (that is, to routers R1 and R2) via router R2, but rather via router BB2. Notice from the output that more AS hops appear to be required to reach enterprise networks via router R2 (that is, 172.16.1.2) compared to router BB2 (that is, 10.1.3.2). Therefore, router BB1 prefers to send traffic into the enterprise network via router BB2, as opposed to router R2.

Example 8-18 *Preferred Path of Router BB1 to Enterprise Networks*

```
BB1#show ip bgp
BGP table version is 142, local router ID is 10.3.3.3
Status codes: s suppressed, d damped, h history, * valid, > best, i - internal,
              r RIB-failure, S Stale
Origin codes: i - IGP, e - EGP, ? - incomplete

    Network         Next Hop      Metric LocPrf Weight Path
 *  0.0.0.0         172.16.1.2                   0 65001 65001 65001 65003 i
 *                  10.1.3.2          0          0 65003 i
 *>                 0.0.0.0           0      32768 i
 *> 10.1.1.1/32     10.1.3.2                     0 65003 65001 ?
 *                  172.16.1.2       11          0 65001 65001 65001 ?
 *  10.1.2.0/24     172.16.1.2                   0 65001 65001 65001 65003 i
 *                  10.1.3.2          0          0 65003 i
 *>                 0.0.0.0           0      32768 i
 *  10.1.3.0/30     172.16.1.2                   0 65001 65001 65001 65003 i
 *                  10.1.3.2          0          0 65003 i
 *>                 0.0.0.0           0      32768 i
```

```
*> 10.2.2.2/32      10.1.3.2                      0 65003 65001 ?
*                   172.16.1.2        0           0 65001 65001 65001 ?
*> 10.3.3.3/32      0.0.0.0           0       32768 i
*  10.4.4.4/32      172.16.1.2                    0 65001 65001 65001 65003 i
*>                  10.1.3.2          0           0 65003 i
*  172.16.1.0/30    172.16.1.2        0           0 65001 65001 65001 i
*>                  0.0.0.0           0       32768 i
*  172.16.2.0/30    172.16.1.2        0           0 65001 65001 65001 i
*>                  10.1.3.2          0           0 65003 i
*> 192.168.0.0      10.1.3.2                      0 65003 65001 ?
*                   172.16.1.2        0           0 65001 65001 65001 ?
*> 192.168.1.0      10.1.3.2                      0 65003 65001 ?
*                   172.16.1.2        11          0 65001 65001 65001 ?
```

Router Performance Issues

Chapter 5, "Advanced Cisco Catalyst Switch Troubleshooting," discussed how performance issues on a Cisco Catalyst switch can be the source of network problems. Similarly, a
router performance issue can impact user data flowing through the network.

Also, as an administrator you might notice sluggish response to Telnet sessions you attempt to establish with a router or longer-than-normal ping response times. Such symptoms might indicate a router performance issue.

This section investigates three potential router issues, each of which might result in poor
router performance. These three issues are

- Excessive CPU utilization

- The packet switching mode of a router

- Excessive memory utilization

Excessive CPU Utilization

A router's processor (that is, CPU) utilization escalating to a high level but only remaining
at that high level for a brief time could represent normal behavior. However, if a router's
CPU utilization continually remains at a high level, network performance issues might result. Aside from latency that users and administrators can experience, a router whose CPU
is overtaxed might not send routing protocol messages to neighboring routers in a timely
fashion. As a result, routing protocol adjacencies can fail, resulting in some networks becoming unreachable.

Processes That Commonly Cause Excessive CPU Utilization

One reason that the CPU of a router might be overloaded is that the router is running a process that is taking up an unusually high percentage of its CPU resources. Following are four such processes that can result in excessive CPU utilization.

- **ARP Input process:** The ARP Input process is in charge of sending Address Resolution Protocol (ARP) requests. This process can consume an inordinate percentage of CPU resources if the router has to send numerous ARP requests.

  One configuration that can cause such a high number of ARP requests is having a default route configured that points to a broadcast network. For example, perhaps a router had the **ip route 0.0.0.0 0.0.0.0 fa 0/1** command entered in global configuration mode. Such a configuration can cause an ARP to be sent to all IP addresses available off of that broadcast interface that are not reachable via a better route. From a security perspective, numerous ARP requests can result from an attacker performing a ping sweep of a subnet.

- **Net Background process:** An interface has a certain number of buffers available to store packets. These buffers are sometimes referred to as the queue of an interface. If an interface needs to store a packet in a buffer but all the interface buffers are in use, the interface can pull from a main pool of buffers that the router maintains. The process that allows an interface to allocate one of these globally available buffers is Net Background. If the *throttles*, *ignored*, and *overrun* parameters are incrementing on an interface, the underlying cause might be the Net Background process consuming too many CPU resources.

- **IP Background process:** The IP Background process handles an interface changing its state. A state change might be an interface going from an Up state to a Down state, or vice versa. Another example of state change is an interface's IP address changing. Therefore, anything that can cause repeated state changes, such as bad cabling, might result in the IP Background process consuming a high percentage of CPU resources.

- **TCP Timer process:** The TCP Timer process runs for each TCP router connection. Therefore, many connections can result in a high CPU utilization by the TCP Timer process.

Cisco IOS Commands Used for Troubleshooting High Processor Utilization

Table 8-5 offers a collection of **show** commands that can be valuable when troubleshooting high CPU utilization on a router.

Table 8-5 *Commands for Troubleshooting High CPU Utilization*

Command	Description
show arp	Displays the ARP cache for a router. If several entries are in the Incomplete state, you might suspect a malicious scan (for example, a ping sweep) of a subnet.
show interface *interface-id*	Displays a collection of interface statistics. If the throttles, overruns, or ignore counters continually increment, you might suspect that the Net Background process is attempting to allocate buffer space for an interface from the main buffer pool of the router.
show tcp statistics	Provides information about the number of TCP segments a router sends and receives, including the number of connections initiated, accepted, established, and closed. A high number of connections can explain why the TCP Timer process might be consuming excessive CPU resources.
show processes cpu	Displays average CPU utilization over 5-second, 1-minute, and 5-minute intervals, in addition to listing all the router processes and the percentage of CPU resources consumed by each of those processes.
show processes cpu history	Displays a graphical view of CPU utilization over the past 60 seconds, 1 hour, and 3 days. This graphical view can indicate if an observed high CPU utilization is a temporary spike in utilization or if the high CPU utilization is an ongoing condition.

Example 8-19 shows sample output from the **show arp** command. In the output, only a single instance exists of an Incomplete ARP entry. However, a high number of such entries can suggest the scanning of network resources, which might indicate malicious reconnaissance traffic.

Example 8-19 show arp *Command Output*

```
R2#show arp
Protocol  Address          Age (min)  Hardware Addr   Type   Interface
Internet  10.3.3.2                61  0009.b7fa.d1e0  ARPA   Ethernet0/0
Internet  10.3.3.1                 -  00d0.06fe.9ea0  ARPA   Ethernet0/0
Internet  192.168.1.50             0  Incomplete      ARPA
```

Example 8-20 shows sample output from the **show interface** *interface-id* command. Note the throttles, overrun, and ignored counters. If these counters continue to increment, the Net Background process might be consuming excessive CPU resources while it allocates buffers from the main buffer pool of the router.

Example 8-20   show interface interface-id *Command Output*

```
R2#show interface e0/0
Ethernet0/0 is up, line protocol is up
  Hardware is AmdP2, address is 00d0.06fe.9ea0 (bia 00d0.06fe.9ea0)
  Internet address is 10.3.3.1/24
  MTU 1500 bytes, BW 10000 Kbit, DLY 1000 usec,
      reliability 255/255, txload 1/255, rxload 1/255
  Encapsulation ARPA, loopback not set
  Keepalive set (10 sec)
  ARP type: ARPA, ARP Timeout 04:00:00
  Last input 00:00:02, output 00:00:02, output hang never
  Last clearing of "show interface" counters never
  Input queue: 0/75/0/0 (size/max/drops/flushes); Total output drops: 0
  Queueing strategy: fifo
  Output queue: 0/40 (size/max)
  5 minute input rate 0 bits/sec, 1 packets/sec
  5 minute output rate 0 bits/sec, 0 packets/sec
     2156 packets input, 164787 bytes, 0 no buffer
     Received 861 broadcasts, 0 runts, 0 giants, 0 throttles
     0 input errors, 0 CRC, 0 frame, 0 overrun, 0 ignored
     0 input packets with dribble condition detected
     2155 packets output, 212080 bytes, 0 underruns
     0 output errors, 0 collisions, 7 interface resets
     0 babbles, 0 late collision, 0 deferred
     0 lost carrier, 0 no carrier
     0 output buffer failures, 0 output buffers swapped out
```

Example 8-21 shows sample output from the **show tcp statistics** command. If the output indicates numerous connections, the TCP Timer process might be consuming excessive CPU resources while simultaneously maintaining all those connections.

Example 8-21   show tcp statistics *Command Output*

```
R2#show tcp statistics
Rcvd: 689 Total, 0 no port
       0 checksum error, 0 bad offset, 0 too short
       474 packets (681 bytes) in sequence
       0 dup packets (0 bytes)         .
       0 partially dup packets (0 bytes)
       0 out-of-order packets (0 bytes)
       0 packets (0 bytes) with data after window
       0 packets after close
       0 window probe packets, 0 window update packets
       1 dup ack packets, 0 ack packets with unsend data
       479 ack packets (14205 bytes)
Sent: 570 Total, 0 urgent packets
```

```
        1 control packets (including 0 retransmitted)
        562 data packets (14206 bytes)
        0 data packets (0 bytes) retransmitted
        0 data packets (0 bytes) fastretransmitted
        7 ack only packets (7 delayed)
        0 window probe packets, 0 window update packets
0 Connections initiated, 1 connections accepted, 1 connections established
0 Connections closed (including 0 dropped, 0 embryonic dropped)
0 Total rxmt timeout, 0 connections dropped in rxmt timeout
0 Keepalive timeout, 0 keepalive probe, 0 Connections dropped in keepalive
```

Example 8-22 shows sample output from the **show processes cpu** command. The output in this example indicates a 34 percent CPU utilization in the past 5 seconds, with 13 percent of CPU resources being spent on interrupts. The output also shows the 1-minute CPU utilization average as 36 percent and the 5-minute average as 32 percent. Individual processes running on the router are also shown, along with their CPU utilization levels. Note the ARP Input, Net Background, TCP Timer, and IP Background processes referred to in this section.

Example 8-22   show processes cpu *Command Output*

```
R2#show processes cpu
CPU utilization for five seconds: 34%/13%; one minute: 36%; five minutes: 32%
PID Runtime(ms)    Invoked    uSecs   5Sec    1Min    5Min    TTY Process
...OUTPUT OMITTED...
  12          4         69       57   0.00%   0.00%   0.00%     0 ARP Input
  13          0          1        0   0.00%   0.00%   0.00%     0 HC Counter Timer
  14          0          5        0   0.00%   0.00%   0.00%     0 DDR Timers
  15         12          2     6000   0.00%   0.00%   0.00%     0 Entity MIB API
  16          4          2     2000   0.00%   0.00%   0.00%     0 ATM Idle Timer
  17          0          1        0   0.00%   0.00%   0.00%     0 SERIAL A'detect
  18          0       3892        0   0.00%   0.00%   0.00%     0 GraphIt
  19          0          2        0   0.00%   0.00%   0.00%     0 Dialer event
  20          0          1        0   0.00%   0.00%   0.00%     0 Critical Bkgnd
  21        132        418      315   0.00%   0.00%   0.00%     0 Net Background
  22          0         15        0   0.00%   0.00%   0.00%     0 Logger
...OUTPUT OMITTED...
  46          0        521        0   0.00%   0.00%   0.00%     0 SSS Test Client
  47         84        711      118   0.00%   0.00%   0.00%     0 TCP Timer
  48          4          3     1333   0.00%   0.00%   0.00%     0 TCP Protocols
  49          0          1        0   0.00%   0.00%   0.00%     0 Socket Timers
  50          0         15        0   0.00%   0.00%   0.00%     0 HTTP CORE
```

```
 51         12        5      2400  0.00%  0.00%  0.00%    0 PPP IP Route
 52          4        5       800  0.00%  0.00%  0.00%    0 PPP IPCP
 53        273      157      1738  0.00%  0.00%  0.00%    0 IP Background
 54          0       74         0  0.00%  0.00%  0.00%    0 IP RIB Update
...OUTPUT OMITTED...
```

Example 8-23 shows sample output from the **show processes cpu history** command. The graphical output produced by this command is useful in determining if a CPU spike is temporary or if it is an ongoing condition.

Example 8-23   show processes cpu history *Command Output*

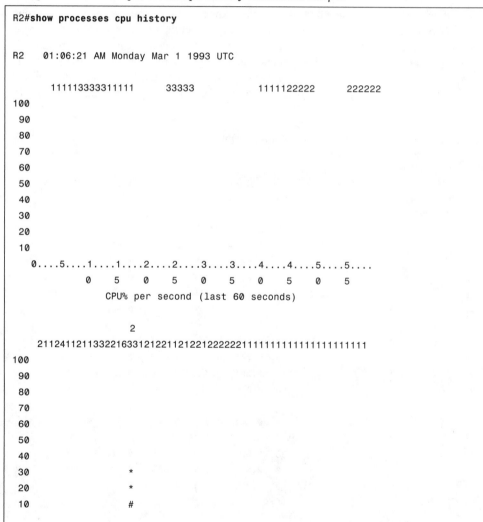

```
R2#show processes cpu history


R2   01:06:21 AM Monday Mar 1 1993 UTC


       111113333311111     33333        1111122222    222222
100
 90
 80
 70
 60
 50
 40
 30
 20
 10
   0....5....1....1....2....2....3....3....4....4....5....5....
           0    5    0    5    0    5    0    5    0    5
              CPU% per second (last 60 seconds)


                   2
   211241121133221633121221121221222222211111111111111111111111
100
 90
 80
 70
 60
 50
 40
 30               *
 20               *
 10               #
```

```
     0....5....1....1....2....2....3....3....4....4....5....5....
          0    5    0    5    0    5    0    5    0    5
               CPU% per minute (last 60 minutes)
              * = maximum CPU%   # = average CPU%


      8
      0
 100
  90
  80 *
  70 *
  60 *
  50 *
  40 *
  30 *
  20 *
  10 *
     0....5....1....1....2....2....3....3....4....4....5....5....6....6....7.
          0    5    0    5    0    5    0    5    0    5    0    5    0
               CPU% per hour (last 72 hours)
              * = maximum CPU%   # = average CPU%
```

Understanding Packet Switching Modes

In addition to the high CPU utilization issues previously discussed, a router's packet switching mode can impact router performance. Before discussing the most common switching modes, realize that the way a router handles packets (or is capable of handling packets) largely depends on the router's architecture. Therefore, for real-world troubleshooting, please consult the documentation for your router to determine how it implements packet switching.

In general, however, Cisco routers support the following three primary modes of packet switching:

- Process switching

- Fast switching

- Cisco Express Forwarding

Key
Topic

Packet switching involves the router making a decision about how a packet should be forwarded and then forwarding that packet out of the appropriate router interface.

Operation of Process Switching

When a router routes a packet (that is, performs packet switching), the router removes the packet's Layer 2 header, examines the Layer 3 addressing, and decides how to forward the packet. The Layer 2 header is then rewritten (which involves changing the source and destination MAC addresses and computing a new cyclic redundancy check [CRC]), and the packet is forwarded out of the appropriate interface. With process switching, as illustrated in Figure 8-4, the router's CPU becomes directly involved with packet switching decisions. As a result, the performance of a router configured for process switching can suffer significantly.

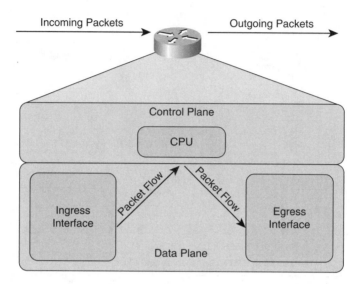

Figure 8-4 *Data Flow with Process Switching*

An interface can be configured for process switching by disabling fast switching on that interface. The interface configuration mode command used to disable fast switching is **no ip route-cache**.

Operation of Fast Switching

Fast switching uses a fast cache maintained in a router's data plane. The fast cache contains information about how traffic from different data flows should be forwarded. As seen in Figure 8-5, the first packet in a data flow is process-switched by a router's CPU. After the router determines how to forward the first frame of a data flow, that forwarding information is stored in the fast cache. Subsequent packets in that same data flow are forwarded based on information in the fast cache, as opposed to being process-switched. As a result, fast switching reduces a router's CPU utilization more than process switching does.

Fast switching can be configured in interface configuration mode with the command **ip route-cache**.

Operation of Cisco Express Forwarding

As described in Chapter 5, Cisco Express Forwarding (CEF) maintains two tables in the data plane. Specifically, the Forwarding Information Base (FIB) maintains Layer 3 forwarding information, whereas the Adjacency Table maintains Layer 2 information for next hops listed in the FIB.

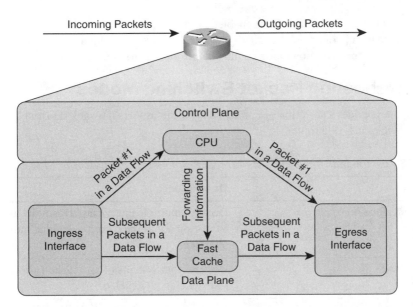

Figure 8-5 *Data Flow with Fast Switching*

Using these tables, populated from a router's IP routing table and ARP cache, CEF can efficiently make forwarding decisions. Unlike fast switching, CEF does not require the first packet of a data flow to be process-switched. Rather, an entire data flow can be forwarded at the data plane, as seen in Figure 8-6.

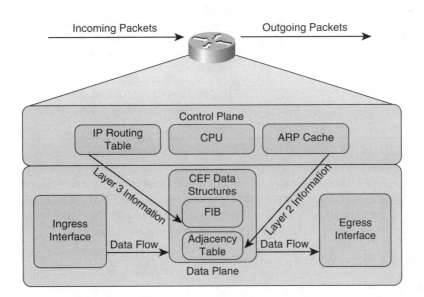

Figure 8-6 *Data Flow with Cisco Express Forwarding*

On many router platforms, CEF is enabled by default. If it is not, you can globally enable it with the **ip cef** command. Alternatively, you can enable CEF for a specific interface with the interface configuration mode command **ip route-cache cef**.

Troubleshooting Packet Switching Modes

Table 8-6 provides a selection of commands you can use when troubleshooting the packet switching modes of a router.

Key Topic

Table 8-6 *Commands for Troubleshooting a Router's Packet Switching Modes*

Command	Description
show ip interface *interface_id*	Displays multiple interface statistics, including information about the packet switching mode of an interface.
show ip cache	Displays the contents of fast cache from a router if fast switching is enabled.
show processes cpu | include IP Input	Displays information about the IP input process on a router. The CPU utilization for this process might show a high value if the CPU of a router is actively engaged in process-switching traffic.
show ip cef	Displays the contents of a router FIB.
show ip cef adjacency *egress-interface-id next-hop-ip-address* **detail**	Displays destinations reachable via the combination of the specified egress interface and next-hop IP address.
show adjacency detail	Provides information contained in the adjacency table of a router, including protocol and timer information.
show cef not-cef-switched	Displays information about packets the router forwards using a packet switching mechanism other than CEF.

Example 8-24 shows sample output from the **show ip interface** *interface-id* command. The output indicates that fast switching is enabled on interface Fast Ethernet 0/0. The reference to flow switching being disabled refers to the Cisco IOS NetFlow feature, which you can use to collect traffic statistics. CEF switching is also enabled.

Example 8-24 show ip interface interface-id *Command Output*

```
R4#show ip interface fa 0/0
FastEthernet0/0 is up, line protocol is up
...OUTPUT OMITTED...
```

```
     ICMP mask replies are never sent
     IP fast switching is enabled
     IP fast switching on the same interface is disabled
     IP Flow switching is disabled
     IP CEF switching is enabled
     IP CEF Fast switching turbo vector
     IP multicast fast switching is enabled
     IP multicast distributed fast switching is disabled
     IP route-cache flags are Fast, CEF
...OUTPUT OMITTED...
```

Example 8-25 shows sample output from the **show ip cache** command. If fast switching is enabled and CEF is disabled, a router begins to populate its fast cache. This command shows the contents of a router's fast cache.

Example 8-25   show ip cache *Command Output*

```
R4#show ip cache
IP routing cache 3 entries, 588 bytes
   12 adds, 9 invalidates, 0 refcounts
Minimum invalidation interval 2 seconds, maximum interval 5 seconds,
   quiet interval 3 seconds, threshold 0 requests
Invalidation rate 0 in last second, 0 in last 3 seconds
Last full cache invalidation occurred 04:13:57 ago

Prefix/Length           Age         Interface        Next Hop
10.8.8.4/32             00:00:07    FastEthernet0/1  10.8.8.4
10.8.8.6/32             00:00:10    FastEthernet0/1  10.8.8.6
192.168.0.0/24          00:00:10    FastEthernet0/0  10.3.3.1
```

Example 8-26 shows sample output from the **show processes cpu | include ip input** command. In the output, the IP input process was using only 0.08 percent of its router's CPU capacity during the last 5-second interval. However, a high percentage value might indicate that a router was performing process switching, where the CPU was directly involved in packet switching.

Example 8-26   show processes cpu | include IP Input *Command Output*

```
R4#show processes cpu | include IP Input
  63       3178      7320       434  0.08%  0.06%  0.04%     0 IP Input
```

Example 8-27 shows sample output from the **show ip cef** command. The output contains the contents of the FIB for a router. Note that if a next-hop of the network prefix is set to *receive*, that network is local to the router, whereas *attached* indicates that the network is directly connected to the router.

Example 8-27   show ip cef *Command Output*

```
R4#show ip cef
Prefix                    Next Hop           Interface
0.0.0.0/0                 drop               Null0 (default route handler entry)
0.0.0.0/32                receive
10.1.1.0/24               10.3.3.1           FastEthernet0/0
10.1.1.2/32               10.3.3.1           FastEthernet0/0
10.3.3.0/24               attached           FastEthernet0/0
10.3.3.0/32               receive
10.3.3.1/32               10.3.3.1           FastEthernet0/0
10.3.3.2/32               receive
10.3.3.255/32             receive
10.4.4.0/24               10.3.3.1           FastEthernet0/0
10.5.5.0/24               10.3.3.1           FastEthernet0/0
10.7.7.0/24               10.3.3.1           FastEthernet0/0
10.7.7.2/32               10.3.3.1           FastEthernet0/0
10.8.8.0/24               attached           FastEthernet0/1
10.8.8.0/32               receive
10.8.8.1/32               receive
10.8.8.4/32               10.8.8.4           FastEthernet0/1
10.8.8.5/32               10.8.8.5           FastEthernet0/1
10.8.8.6/32               10.8.8.6           FastEthernet0/1
10.8.8.7/32               10.8.8.7           FastEthernet0/1
10.8.8.255/32             receive
192.168.0.0/24            10.3.3.1           FastEthernet0/0
224.0.0.0/4               drop
224.0.0.0/24              receive
255.255.255.255/32        receive
```

Example 8-28 shows sample output from the **show ip cef adjacency** *egress-interface-id next-hop-IP-address* **detail** command. This command shows the IP addresses that the router knows how to reach using the specified combination of next-hop IP address and egress interface. In this example, 10.8.8.6 is the IP address of a host and not a router. Therefore, no other IP addresses are known to have a next-hop IP address of 10.8.8.6 with an egress interface of Fast Ethernet 0/1.

Example 8-28   show ip cef adjacency egress-interface-id next-hop-IP-address detail *Command Output*

```
R4#show ip cef adjacency fa 0/1 10.8.8.6 detail
IP CEF with switching (Table Version 25), flags=0x0
  25 routes, 0 reresolve, 0 unresolved (0 old, 0 new), peak 0
  25 leaves, 21 nodes, 25640 bytes, 90 inserts, 65 invalidations
  0 load sharing elements, 0 bytes, 0 references
  universal per-destination load sharing algorithm, id 24360DB1
```

```
   5(2) CEF resets, 1 revisions of existing leaves
   Resolution Timer: Exponential (currently 1s, peak 1s)
   0 in-place/0 aborted modifications
   refcounts:  5702 leaf, 5632 node

   Table epoch: 0 (25 entries at this epoch)

Adjacency Table has 5 adjacencies
10.8.8.6/32, version 10, epoch 0, cached adjacency 10.8.8.6
0 packets, 0 bytes
   via 10.8.8.6, FastEthernet0/1, 0 dependencies
     next hop 10.8.8.6, FastEthernet0/1
     valid cached adjacency
```

Example 8-29 shows sample output from the **show adjacency detail** command. When you see a particular adjacency listed in the FIB, you can issue this command to confirm the router has information about how to reach that adjacency.

Example 8-29   show adjacency detail *Command Output*

```
R4#show adjacency detail
Protocol Interface              Address
IP        FastEthernet0/0        10.3.3.1(19)
                                   32 packets, 1920 bytes
                                   00D006FE9EA00009B7FAD1E00800
                                   ARP          03:53:01
                                   Epoch: 0
IP        FastEthernet0/1        10.8.8.6(5)
                                   4 packets, 264 bytes
                                   0008A3B895C40009B7FAD1E10800
                                   ARP          03:53:35
                                   Epoch: 0
...OUTPUT OMITTED...
```

Example 8-30 shows sample output from the **show cef not-cef-switched** command. Even though CEF is enabled, some traffic might still be switched through another packet-switching path, perhaps because a feature was enabled that required the processor of the router (identified as *RP* in the output) to handle specific traffic types. The **show cef not-cef-switched** command shows information about such traffic that was not CEF-switched.

Example 8-30   show cef not-cef-switched *Command Output*

```
R4#show cef not-cef-switched
CEF Packets passed on to next switching layer
Slot   No_adj No_encap Unsupp'ted Redirect  Receive  Options   Access    Frag
RP       0        0         0         0       6676       0         0        0
```

Now that you have reviewed the different packet-switching options for a router, you can better analyze how a router is forwarding specific traffic. Following is a list of troubleshooting steps you can follow if you suspect that network traffic is being impacted by a performance problem on one of the routers along the path from the source to the destination.

Step 1. Use the **traceroute** command to determine which router along the path is causing excessive delay.

Step 2. After you identify a router that is causing unusually high delay, use the **show processes cpu** command to see the CPU utilization of that router and identify any processes that might be consuming an unusually high percentage of the CPU.

Step 3. Use the **show ip route** *ip-address* command to verify that the router has a route to the destination IP address.

Step 4. Use the **show ip cef** command to determine whether all the router interfaces are configured to use CEF.

Step 5. Use the **show ip cef** *ip-address* **255.255.255.255** command to verify that CEF has an entry in its FIB that can reach the specified IP address. Part of the output from this command will be the next-hop adjacency to which traffic should be forwarded, along with the egress interface used to send traffic to that next-hop.

Step 6. Issue the **show adjacency** *interface-id* **detail** command to verify that CEF has an entry in its adjacency table for the egress interface identified in Step 5.

Step 7. With the **show ip arp** command, you can then confirm that the router knows the MAC address associated with the next-hop IP address shown in the output from Step 6.

Step 8. You can then connect to the next-hop device and verify that the MAC address identified in Step 7 is indeed correct.

You can repeat these steps on the next-hop device or on another router whose response time displayed in the output from Step 1 is suspect.

Excessive Memory Utilization

Much like a PC, router performance can suffer if it lacks sufficient available memory. For example, perhaps you install a version of Cisco IOS on a router, and that router does not have the minimum amount of memory required to support that specific Cisco IOS image. Even though the router might load the image and function, its performance might be sluggish.

Common Memory Troubleshooting Targets

Assuming a router *does* have the recommended amount of memory for its installed Cisco IOS image, consider the following as potential memory utilization issues:

- **Memory leak:** When a router starts a process, that process can allocate a block of memory. When the process completes, the process should return its allocated memory to the router's pool of memory. If not all the allocated memory is returned to the router's main memory pool, a memory leak occurs. Such a condition usually results from a bug in the Cisco IOS version running on the router, requiring an upgrade of the router's Cisco IOS image.

Example 8-31 shows sample output from the **show memory allocating-process totals** command. This command can help identify memory leaks. The output shows information about memory availability on a router after the Cisco IOS image of the router has been decompressed and loaded.

Example 8-31   show memory allocating-process totals *Command Output*

```
R4#show memory allocating-process totals
                Head     Total(b)     Used(b)     Free(b)     Lowest(b)
Largest(b)
Processor    83D27480    67463064    15347168    52115896    50311080    50127020
      I/O    7C21800      4057088     2383016     1674072     1674072     1674044


Allocator PC Summary for: Processor

    PC         Total    Count  Name
0x809D7A30    1749360     180  Process Stack
0x80A7F664     918024      10  Init
0x81CEF6A0     882576       4  pak subblock chunk
0x81C04D9C     595344      54  TCL Chunks
0x800902A4     490328       6  MallocLite
...OUTPUT OMITTED...
```

The *Head* column in the output refers to the address (in hexadecimal) of the memory allocation chain. The *Total* column is the total of used bytes and free bytes, which are individually shown in their own columns. The *Lowest* column shows the lowest amount of free memory (in bytes) that has been available since the router last booted. The *Largest* column indicates the largest block of available memory. Following this summary information, the output shows detailed memory allocation information for each process running on a router.

- **Memory allocation failure:** A memory allocation failure (which produces a MALLOCFAIL error message) occurs when a process attempts to allocate a block of memory and fails to do so. One common cause for a MALLOCFAIL error is a security issue. For example, a virus or a worm that has infested the network can result in a MALLOCFAIL error. Alternatively, a MALLOCFAIL error might be the result of a bug in the router's version of Cisco IOS. You can use the Cisco Bug Toolkit (available from http://www.cisco.com/cgi-bin/Support/Bugtool/launch_bugtool.pl) to research any such known issues with the version of Cisco IOS running on a router.

- **Buffer leak:** Similar to a memory leak, in which a process does not return all of its allocated memory to the router upon terminating, a buffer leak occurs when a process does not return a buffer to the router when the process has finished using the buffer. Consider the output of the **show interfaces** command seen in Example 8-32.

Example 8-32   *Identifying a Wedged Interface*

```
R4#show interfaces
...OUTPUT OMITTED...
  Input queue: 76/75/780/0 (size/max/drops/flushes); Total output drops: 0
  Queueing strategy: fifo
  Output queue: 0/40 (size/max)
...OUTPUT OMITTED...
```

Notice the numbers 76 and 75 highlighted in the output. These values indicate that an input queue of the interface has a capacity of 75 packets, and that queue currently has 76 packets. This is an oversubscription of the queue space. An interface in this condition is called a *wedged interface*. In such a condition, the router does not forward traffic coming into the wedged interface.

The **show buffers** command can also be helpful in diagnosing a buffer leak. To illustrate, consider the output of the **show buffers** command shown in Example 8-33.

Key Topic

Example 8-33   show buffers *Command Output*

```
R4#show buffers
Buffer elements:
       1118 in free list (500 max allowed)
       570 hits, 0 misses, 1119 created

Public buffer pools:
Small buffers, 104 bytes (total 71, permanent 50, peak 71 @ 00:21:43):
       53 in free list (20 min, 150 max allowed)
       317 hits, 7 misses, 0 trims, 21 created
       0 failures (0 no memory)
Middle buffers, 600 bytes (total 49, permanent 25, peak 49 @ 00:21:43):
       5 in free list (10 min, 150 max allowed)
       122 hits, 8 misses, 0 trims, 24 created
...OUTPUT OMITTED...
```

This output indicates that the router has 49 middle buffers, but only 5 of those 49 buffers are available. Such a result might indicate a process allocating buffers but failing to deallocate them. Like a memory leak, a buffer leak might require updating the Cisco IOS image of a router.

Excessive BGP Memory Use

Earlier in this chapter you learned about troubleshooting BGP. If a router is running BGP, be aware that BGP runs multiple processes and can consume significant amounts of router memory. The **show processes memory | include BGP** command, as shown in Example 8-34, can show you how much memory is being consumed by the various BGP processes of a router. If BGP is consuming a large percentage of your router memory, you might consider filtering out unneeded BGP routes, upgrading the memory on that router, or running BGP on a different platform that has more memory.

Example 8-34   show processes memory | include BGP *Command Output*

```
R1#show processes memory | include BGP
   77   0     16960       0     10068       0       0 BGP Router
  108   0         0       0      6892       0       0 BGP I/O
  112   0         0       0      9892       0       0 BGP Scanner
```

Depending on the router platform, your router might have multiple line cards with different amounts of memory available on each line card. The **show diag** command can help you isolate a specific line card that is running low on memory, perhaps because that line card is running BGP.

Exam Preparation Tasks

Review All the Key Topics

Review the most important topics from inside the chapter, noted with the Key Topics icon in the outer margin of the page. Table 8-7 lists these key topics and the page numbers where each is found.

Table 8-7 *Key Topics for Chapter 8*

Key Topic Element	Description	Page Number
Table 8-2	Interaction between BGP's data structures and a router's IP routing table	228
List	BGP data structures	228
Numbered List	BGP path selection criteria	229
List	Common reasons for failure of BGP peering	229
Table 8-3	BGP troubleshooting commands	230
Table 8-4	Configuring ASPATH and local preference BGP attributes	242
List	Reasons for poor router performance	245
List	Four processes that can cause excessive CPU utilization	246
Table 8-5	Commands for troubleshooting high CPU utilization	247
List	Packet-switching modes	251
Table 8-6	Commands for troubleshooting the packet-switching modes of a router	254
Steps	Steps for troubleshooting a router performance issue	258
List	Common memory utilization issues	258
Example 8-33	Sample output from the **show buffers** command	260

Complete Tables and Lists from Memory

Print a copy of Appendix B, "Memory Tables" (found on the CD), or at least the section for this chapter, and complete the tables and lists from memory. Appendix C, "Memory Tables Answer Key," also on the CD, includes completed tables and lists to check your work.

Define Key Terms

Define the following key terms from this chapter, and check your answers in the Glossary:

autonomous system (AS), BGP's neighbor table, BGP table, ASPATH, local preference, ARP Input process, Net Background process, IP Background process, TCP Timer process, process switching, fast switching, Cisco Express Forwarding (CEF), memory leak, memory allocation failure, buffer leak

Command Reference to Check Your Memory

This section includes the most important configuration and EXEC commands covered in this chapter. To determine how well you have memorized the commands as a side effect of your other studies, cover the left side of the table with a piece of paper; read the descriptions on the right side; and see whether you remember the command.

Table 8-8 *Chapter 8 Configuration Command Reference*

Command	Description
route-map *tag* [permit | deny] [*seq-num*]	Global configuration mode command that creates a route map
set local-preference *local-preference*	Route map configuration mode command that sets the local preference BGP attribute for routes matched by a route map
set as-path prepend *autonomous-system-number-1* [...*autonomous-system-number-n*]	Route map configuration mode command that defines an autonomous system path to prepend to an autonomous system path known by the BGP forwarding table
router bgp *as-number*	Global configuration mode command that enables a BGP process for a specific autonomous system
neighbor *ip-address* route-map *route-map-name* [in | out]	Router configuration mode command that applies a specified route map to routes received from or advertised to a specified BGP neighbor
[no] ip route-cache	Interface configuration mode utility used to enable fast switching (or disable fast switching with the **no** option)
ip cef	Global configuration mode command used to globally enable CEF
ip route-cache cef	Interface configuration mode command used to enable CEF for an interface

Table 8-9   *Chapter 8 EXEC Command Reference*

Command	Description
show ip bgp summary	Displays the router BGP router ID, AS number, information about the BGP memory usage, and summary information about BGP neighbors
show ip bgp neighbors	Displays detailed information about all the BGP neighbors of a router
show ip bgp	Displays the network prefixes present in the BGP table
debug ip routing	Displays updates that occur in the IP routing table
show ip route bgp	Shows routes known to a routing table that were learned via BGP
debug ip bgp	Provides real-time information about BGP events, such as the establishment of a peering relationship (Note: This command does not show the contents of BGP updates.)
debug ip bgp updates	Shows real-time information about BGP updates sent and received by a BGP router, including the contents of those BGP updates
show arp	Displays a router's ARP cache (Note: If a large number of the entries are in the Incomplete state, you might suspect a malicious scan [for example, a ping sweep] of a subnet.)
show interface *interface-id*	Shows a collection of interface statistics (Note: If the throttles, overruns, or ignore counters continually increment, you might suspect that the Net Background process is attempting to allocate buffer space for an interface from the router's main buffer pool.)
show tcp statistics	Provides information about the number of TCP segments a router sends and receives, including the number of connections initiated, accepted, established, and closed (Note: A high number of connections might explain why the TCP Timer process is consuming excessive CPU resources.)
show processes cpu	Displays average CPU utilization over 5-second, 1-minute, and 5-minute intervals, in addition to listing all of the router processes and the percentage of CPU resources consumed by each of those processes

Table 8-9   *Chapter 8 EXEC Command Reference   (Continued)*

Command	Description
show processes cpu history	Shows a graphical view of CPU utilization over the past 60 seconds, 1 hour, and 3 days (Note: This graphical view can indicate if an observed high CPU utilization is a temporary spike in utilization or if the high CPU utilization is an ongoing condition.)
show ip interface *interface-id*	Displays multiple interface statistics, including information about the packet switching mode of an interface
show ip cache	Shows the contents of the fast cache for a router if fast switching is enabled
show processes cpu | include IP Input	Displays information about the IP Input process on a router (Note: The CPU utilization for this process might show a high value if the CPU of a router is actively engaged in process-switching traffic.)
show ip cef	Shows the contents of the FIB for a router
show ip cef adjacency *egress-interface-id next-hop-ip-address* **detail**	Displays destinations reachable via the combination of the specified egress interface and next-hop IP address
show adjacency detail	Provides information contained in a router's adjacency table, including protocol and timer information
show cef not-cef-switched	Displays information about packets forwarded by the router using a packet-switching mechanism other than CEF
show memory allocating-process totals	Shows information about memory availability on a router after the router's Cisco IOS image has been decompressed and loaded (Note: This command can help identify memory leaks.)
show buffer	Shows how many buffers (of various types) are currently free (Note: This command can be helpful in diagnosing a buffer leak.)
show processes memory | include bgp	Shows how much memory is being consumed by the various BGP processes of a router
show diag	Shows the memory available on the line cards of a router

This chapter covers the following subjects:

Introduction to Cisco IOS Security: This section begins by reviewing various security measures that might be put in place on Cisco routers and switches to protect three different planes of network operation. These planes are: the management plane, the control plane, and the data plane. Once you review these security measures, this section considers how your troubleshooting efforts might be impacted by having various layers of security in place.

Security Troubleshooting Targets: This section describes the basic operation and troubleshooting tips for Cisco IOS firewalls and AAA services. Although complete configuration details for Cisco IOS firewalls and AAA is beyond the scope of the TSHOOT course, as a reference, this section does provide a couple of basic configuration examples with an explanation of the syntax used.

Trouble Ticket: Cisco IOS Security: This section presents you with a trouble ticket and an associated topology. You are also given **show** command output and a syntax reference. Based on the information provided, you hypothesize how to correct the reported issues. You can then compare your solutions with the suggested solutions.

CHAPTER 9

Security Troubleshooting

This chapter begins by reviewing various security solutions you might deploy on Cisco routers and switches. Some of these solutions are designed to protect the routers and switches themselves. Other solutions protect data flowing over the network and other network devices in the network.

Adding security to a network can complicate your efforts to troubleshoot a reported issue. So, this chapter provides suggestions for carrying out your troubleshooting efforts in a secured network.

Although some networks might have dedicated firewall appliances, a Cisco IOS router, running an appropriate feature set, can also act as a firewall. This chapter reviews the two types of Cisco IOS firewalls supported on many of today's router platforms, including a basic configuration example and troubleshooting tips.

In larger networks, a dedicated security server might be used to, for example, authenticate user logins on a router. Having a centralized server can make password and user updates much more efficient than having to manually apply such updates to each individual router in a topology. This centralized server is often referred to as a AAA server. This chapter discusses popular authentication, authorization, and accounting (AAA) protocols, along with techniques for troubleshooting issues that might arise in a AAA environment.

"Do I Know This Already?" Quiz

The "Do I Know This Already?" quiz helps you determine your level of knowledge of this chapter's topics before you begin. Table 9-1 details the major topics discussed in this chapter and their corresponding quiz questions.

Table 9-1 *"Do I Know This Already?" Section-to-Question Mapping*

Foundation Topics Section	Questions
Introduction to Cisco IOS Security	1–6
Security Troubleshooting Targets	7–8

1. What are the three planes of router and switch operation that should be secured? (Choose the three best answers.)

   a. Management plane

   b. Architectural plane

   c. Data plane

   d. Control plane

2. What command can you use to prevent an attacker from performing password recovery on some platforms?

   a. config-reg 0x2124

   b. service password-encryption

   c. no service password-recovery

   d. enable secret 5

3. What alternative to Telnet provides secure access to a router's command-line interface? (Choose the best answer.)

   a. TACACS+

   b. SSL

   c. HTTPS

   d. SSH

4. Identify two Cisco Catalyst switch features that can mitigate the introduction of a rogue switch into a network by an attacker, where the attacker attempts to make the newly added rogue switch become the root bridge for the topology. (Choose the two best answers.)

   a. Root Guard

   b. Backbone Fast

   c. Uplink Fast

   d. BPDU Guard

5. What Cisco IOS feature, available on some router platforms, can recognize the signature of well-known attacks, and prevent traffic from those attacks from entering the network?

   a. VPN

   b. IPS

   c. Cisco IOS firewall

   d. ACL

6. Which of the following steps should be performed first when troubleshooting a secured network environment? (Choose the best answer.)

    a. Disable the network security features to eliminate them as potential sources of the reported issue.

    b. Begin your troubleshooting at Layer 1, and work your way up to the levels where the security features reside.

    c. Determine whether the reported behavior is actually appropriate behavior, based on the network's security policy.

    d. Begin your troubleshooting at Layer 7, and work your way down to the levels where the security features reside.

7. What are two types of Cisco IOS firewalls? (Choose the two best answers.)

    a. MQC-Based Policy Firewall

    b. Classic Cisco IOS Firewall

    c. Zone-Based Policy Firewall

    d. Basic Cisco IOS Firewall

8. Which two of the following are true concerning TACACS+ but not true concerning RADIUS? (Choose the two best answers.)

    a. TCP-based

    b. Encrypts the entire packet

    c. Standards-based

    d. Offers robust accounting features

Foundation Topics

Introduction to Cisco IOS Security

As the number of security threats continues to grow and the level of required sophistication for an attacker continues to decline, strategically securing today's production networks is a necessity. Adding security features to a network, however, can make troubleshooting that network more difficult.

For example, in addition to troubleshooting basic Layer 2 and Layer 3 connectivity, you also need to check such things as firewall, intrusion prevention system (IPS), and virtual private network (VPN) configurations. Also, a network's security policy might limit what you as a troubleshooter are allowed to do while troubleshooting. For example, you might not be allowed to remove certain access control lists (ACL), even though removing them might simplify your troubleshooting efforts.

This section focuses on securing the different planes of operation on routers and switches. Following are these three planes of operation:

- **Management plane:** The management plane of operation is used to manage a router or a switch. This management involves, for example, accessing and configuring a device.

- **Control plane:** The control plane of operation encompasses protocols used between routers and switches. These protocols include, for example, routing protocols and Spanning Tree Protocol (STP).

- **Data plane:** The data plane is the plane of operation in charge of forwarding data through a router or switch.

The sections that follow also provide you with tips for troubleshooting network security issues.

Securing the Management Plane

When you connect to a router or a switch for management purposes (for example, to make a configuration change), you are accessing the management plane. As shown in Figure 9-1, the data plane can be accessed in several ways, and from a security perspective, each of these access methods should be secured.

Modes of Access

The methods of accessing the data plane illustrated in Figure 9-1 allow three primary modes of access, as described in the list that follows:

- **Command-line interface (CLI) access:** A router or switch's CLI can be accessed via a serial connection, known as a console connection. This connection enables an administrator to directly connect into the managed device. Although a console connection can be password protected, physical security is also a requirement. For example, if attackers gained physical access to a router or switch, they could connect to the console connection and perform a password recovery procedure, thus granting them access.

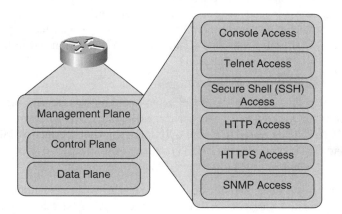

Figure 9-1 *Methods of Accessing the Data Plane*

To prevent a potentially malicious user from performing password recovery on a device, some platforms support the disabling of the password recovery service. The global configuration mode command to disable the password recovery service is **no service password-recovery**.

The ability to disable password recovery, however, does not provide complete protection from an attacker. For example, although attackers that gained physical access to a device would not be able to recover the password of the device, they could wipe out the configuration. Also, if they had gained sufficient information about the network, its protocols, and addressing schemes, they could conceivably recreate a working configuration. They could then add to that working configuration a backdoor for them to gain access to the device and potentially monitor, intercept, or alter traffic flowing through that device. Therefore, physical security remains a critical aspect of overall network security.

CLI access can also be gained over a network connection using protocols such as Telnet and Secure Shell (SSH). Telnet is not considered secure, because its packets are sent in clear text. Conversely, SSH encrypts its traffic, preventing an eavesdropper from interpreting any intercepted traffic.

■ **Web access:** Many network devices can be monitored and configured via a web-based interface (for example, the Cisco Configuration Professional [CCP] or Cisco Security Device Manager [SDM] applications). Although either HTTP or HTTPS can be used to access these web-based administrative interfaces, HTTPS is more secure. For example, if an attacker were to intercept HTTP traffic between an administrator's workstation and a managed router, the attacker might be able to interpret configurations being performed on the router. If HTTPS where used instead, an attacker would not be able to interpret any intercepted configuration information, because HTTPS encrypts its transmissions.

■ **SNMP access:** As discussed in Chapter 3, "The Maintenance and Troubleshooting Toolbox," Simple Network Management Protocol (SNMP) is commonly used to monitor network devices. Devices enabled to support SNMP can be configured to support read-only access or read-write access. SNMP versions 1 and 2c use community strings that must match between the monitoring device and the managed device. SNMP version 3, however, offers enhanced security through encryption and authentication.

Protecting Management Plane Access

Other than the previously mentioned requirement for physical security, network security can be used to limit access to a device's management plane over a network connection. For example, ACLs can be created to permit only specific protocols (such as SSH as opposed to Telnet and HTTPS as opposed to HTTP) coming from specific sources (for example, the IP addresses of administrators) to access a device's management plane.

Once a connection is made with the device to be managed, the connecting user should then be authenticated. Cisco devices support authentication via a single password, or via a username and password combination. If you choose to use usernames and passwords, those credentials could be locally configured on a device. However, for scalability, you might want to have those credentials stored centrally on a server (for example, a Remote Authentication Dial In User Service [RADIUS] or Terminal Access Controller Access-Control System Plus [TACACS+] server). By centrally locating a common user database accessible by multiple network devices, you eliminate the need to maintain a separate user database on each network device.

From a troubleshooting perspective, you should understand how to access a device. For example, a device might be accessible via SSH with username and password credentials. Also, you might need physical access to a device. If so, you should understand how you can be granted physical access of that secured device.

Securing the Control Plane

Control plane protocols include routing protocols (for example, Enhanced Interior Gateway Routing Protocol [EIGRP], Open Shortest Path First [OSPF], and Border Gateway Protocol [BGP]), STP, and Address Resolution Protocol (ARP). These protocols often create data structures that are used directly or indirectly for packet-forwarding decisions by a device. Therefore, such protocols should be secured. Additionally, the control plane itself should be protected from a denial-of-service (DoS) attack, where all of a control plane's resources are consumed by malicious traffic.

Securing Routing Protocols

Although routing protocols can differ in their implementation of authentication methods, most enterprise routing protocols support some sort of authentication. This authentication allows adjacent routers to authenticate one another, thereby preventing an attacker from inserting a rogue router into a network, in an attempt to influence routing decisions. Similar authentication methods are available for router redundancy protocols (that is, Hot Standby Routing Protocol [HSRP], Virtual Router Redundancy Protocol [VRRP], and Gateway Load Balancing Protocol [GLBP]).

Securing STP

Chapter 4, "Basic Cisco Catalyst Switch Troubleshooting," discussed how STP could be used to add redundancy to a network, while preventing problems which could stem from Layer 2 topological loops. STP achieves this loop-free topology by electing one switch as the *root bridge*. The network administrator can influence which switch becomes the root bridge through the manipulation of a switch's bridge priority, where the switch with the lowest bridge priority becomes the root bridge. Every other switch in the network designates a *root port*, which is the port on the switch that is closest to the root bridge, in terms of cost. The bridge priorities of switches are learned through the exchange of Bridge Protocol Data Units (BPDU). After the election of a root bridge, all the switch ports in the topology are either in the *blocking* state (where user data is not forwarded) or in the *forwarding* state (where user data is forwarded).

If the root bridge fails, the STP topology will reconverge by electing a new root bridge. If an attacker has access to two switch ports (each from a different switch), they might be able to introduce a rogue switch into the network. The rogue switch can then be configured with a lower bridge priority than the bridge priority of the root bridge. After the rogue switch announces its *superior BPDUs*, the STP topology reconverges, where all traffic traveling from one switch to another switch now passes through the rogue switch, thus allowing the attacker to capture that traffic.

As an example, consider the topology shown in Figure 9-2. Data traveling from PC1 to Server1 passes through SW2 and SW3 (the root bridge).

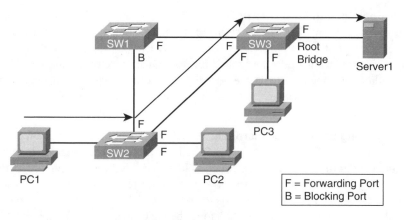

Figure 9-2 *Converged STP Topology*

Notice PC2 and PC3. If an attacker gains access to the switch ports of these two PCs, the attacker could introduce a rogue switch that advertised superior BPDUs, causing the rogue switch to be elected as the new root bridge. The new data path between PC1 and Server1, as illustrated in Figure 9-3, now passes through the attacker's rogue switch. The attacker can configure one of the switch ports as a Switch Port Analyzer (SPAN) port. A SPAN port can receive a copy of traffic crossing another port or VLAN. In this example, the attacker could use the SPAN port to send a copy of traffic crossing the switch to the attacker's PC.

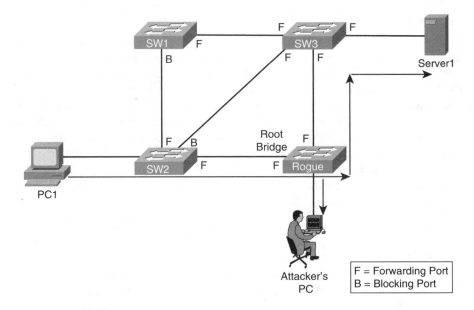

Figure 9-3   *Introduction of a Rogue Switch*

Consider two approaches for protecting a network from this type of STP attack:

■ **Protecting with Root Guard:** The Root Guard feature can be enabled on all switch ports in the network off of which the root bridge should not appear (that is, every port that is not a *root port*, the port on each switch that is considered to be closest to the root bridge). If a port configured for Root Guard receives a superior BPDU, instead of believing the BPDU, the port goes into a *root-inconsistent* state. While a port is in the root-inconsistent state, no user data is sent across the port. However, after the superior BPDUs stop, the port returns to the forwarding state.

■ **Protecting with BPDU Guard:** The BPDU Guard feature is enabled on ports configured with Cisco's PortFast feature. The PortFast feature is enabled on ports that connect out to end-user devices, such as PCs, and it reduces the amount of time required for the port to go into the forwarding state after being connected. The logic of PortFast is that a port that connects to an end-user device does not have the potential to create a topology loop. Therefore, the port can go active sooner by skipping STP's Listening and Learning states, which by default take 15 seconds each. Because these PortFast ports are connected to end-user devices, these ports should never receive a BPDU. Therefore, if a port enabled for BPDU Guard receives a BPDU, the port is disabled.

Securing DHCP and ARP

On today's networks, most clients obtain their IP address information dynamically, using Dynamic Host Configuration Protocol (DHCP), rather than having their IP address information statically configured. To dynamically obtain IP address information, a client (for example, a PC) dynamically discovers a DHCP server via a broadcast and sends out a DHCP request; the DHCP server sees the request; and a DHCP response (including such information as an IP address, subnet mask, and default gateway) is sent to the requesting client.

However, if an attacker connects a rogue DHCP server to the network, the rogue DHCP server can respond to a client's DHCP discovery request. Even though both the rogue DHCP server and the actual DHCP server respond to the request, the rogue DHCP server's response will be used by the client if it reaches the client before the response from the actual DHCP server, as illustrated in Figure 9-4.

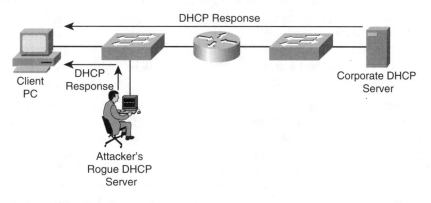

Figure 9-4   *DHCP Server Spoofing*

The DHCP response from an attacker's DHCP server might assign the attacker's IP address as the client's default gateway. As a result, the client sends traffic to the attacker's IP address. The attacker can then capture the traffic and then forward the traffic to an appropriate default gateway. From the client's perspective, everything is functioning correctly, so this type of DHCP server spoofing attack can go undetected for a long period of time.

The *DHCP snooping* feature on Cisco Catalyst switches can be used to combat a DHCP server spoofing attack. This option is off on most Catalyst switches by default. With this solution, Cisco Catalyst switch ports are configured in either the *trusted* or *untrusted* state. If a port is trusted, it is allowed to receive DHCP responses (for example, DHCPOFFER, DHCPACK, or DHCPNAK). Conversely, if a port is untrusted, it is not allowed to receive DHCP responses, and if a DHCP response does attempt to enter an untrusted port, the port is disabled. Fortunately, not every switch port needs to be configured to support DHCP snooping, because if a port is not explicitly configured as a trusted port, it is implicitly considered to be an untrusted port.

Another type of DHCP attack is more of a DoS attack against the DHCP server. Specifically, the attacker can repeatedly request IP address assignments from the DHCP server, thus depleting the pool of addresses available from the DHCP server. The attacker can accomplish this by making the DHCP requests appear to come from different MAC addresses. To mitigate such a DoS attack, you can use the previously mentioned DHCP snooping feature to limit the number of DHCP messages per second that are allowed on an interface, thus preventing a flood of spoofed DHCP requests.

The DHCP snooping feature dynamically builds a DHCP binding table, which contains the MAC addresses associated with specific IP addresses. This DHCP binding table can be used by the *Dynamic ARP Inspection* (DAI) feature to help prevent Address Resolution Protocol (ARP) spoofing attacks.

Recall the purpose of ARP requests. When a network device needs to determine the MAC address that corresponds to an IP address, the device can send out an ARP request. The target device replies to the requesting device with an ARP reply. The ARP reply contains the requested MAC address.

Attackers can attempt to launch an attack by sending gratuitous ARP (GARP) replies. These GARP messages can tell network devices that the attacker's MAC address corresponds to specific IP addresses. For example, the attacker might be able to convince a PC that the attacker's MAC address is the MAC address of the PC's default gateway. As a result, the PC starts sending traffic to the attacker. The attacker captures the traffic and then forwards the traffic on to the appropriate default gateway.

To illustrate, consider Figure 9-5. PC1 is configured with a default gateway of 192.168.0.1. However, the attacker sent GARP messages to PC1, telling PC1 that the MAC address corresponding to 192.168.0.1 is BBBB.BBBB.BBBB, which is the attacker's MAC address. Similarly, the attacker sent GARP messages to the default gateway, claiming that the MAC address corresponding to PC1's IP address of 192.168.0.2 was BBBB.BBBB.BBBB. This *ARP cache poisoning* causes PC1 and Router1 to exchange traffic via the attacker's PC. Therefore, this type of ARP spoofing attack is considered to be a *man-in-the-middle* attack.

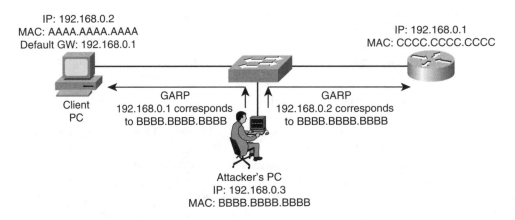

Figure 9-5   *ARP Spoofing*

Networks can be protected from ARP spoofing attacks using the DAI feature. DAI works similarly to DHCP snooping by using *trusted* and *untrusted* ports. ARP replies are allowed into the switch on trusted ports. However, if an ARP reply enters the switch on an untrusted port, the contents of the ARP reply are compared against the DHCP binding table to verify its accuracy. If the ARP reply is not consistent with the DHCP binding table, the ARP reply is dropped, and the port is disabled.

Securing Against a DoS Attack

Rather than intercepting or manipulating traffic, an attacker's goal might be to make a network device unusable. For example, an attacker might launch a DoS attack against a router's control plane.

To protect against flooding of a router's control plane, you could configure Cisco's control plane policing (CoPP) or control plane protection (CPP) feature. Although both features can limit specific traffic types entering the control plane, CPP offers finer control of the policing action.

Table 9-2 summarizes the previously discussed mitigations for control plane threats.

Table 9-2   *Mitigations for Control Plane Threats*

Target	Mitigations
Routing protocols	Authentication of routing protocols
STP	Root Guard
	BPDU Guard
DHCP and ARP	DHCP Snooping
	Dynamic ARP Inspection (DAI)
Control Plane Resources	Control Plane Policing (CoPP)
	Control Plane Protection (CPP)

Key
Topic

Securing the Data Plane

Protecting the management and control planes focuses on protecting a network device (for example, a router or a switch). Protecting the data plane, however, focuses on protecting the actual data flowing through a network and protecting other devices (for example, hosts) on the network.

ACLs (or VLAN access maps on Cisco Catalyst switches) offer a fundamental approach to restricting traffic allowed on a network. For example, an ACL can permit or deny traffic based on source and destination IP address and port number information, in addition to time-of-day restrictions.

Although some networks have a firewall appliance, such as the Cisco Adaptive Security Appliance (ASA), a Cisco IOS router can also perform firewalling features, as shown in Figure 9-6. In the diagram, the Cisco IOS firewall allows Telnet traffic into the campus network from a host on the Internet, if the Telnet session originated from the campus network. If a user on the Internet attempted to establish a Telnet connection with a host inside the campus network, however, the Cisco IOS firewall would block the inbound Telnet traffic.

Similar to firewalling, intrusion prevention can be accomplished via a dedicated intrusion prevention system (IPS) appliance or through the Cisco IOS IPS feature. Figure 9-7 shows a Cisco IOS router configured with the IPS feature. The router is configured with a database of signatures that can recognize a collection of well-known attacks. Therefore, while non-malicious HTTP traffic is allowed to pass through the router, malicious traffic (for example, a SYN flood attack) is not permitted through the router.

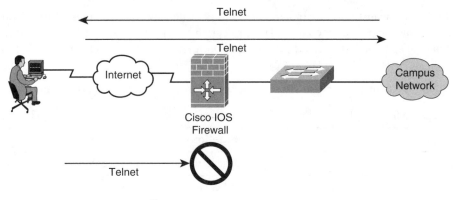

Figure 9-6 *Cisco IOS Firewall*

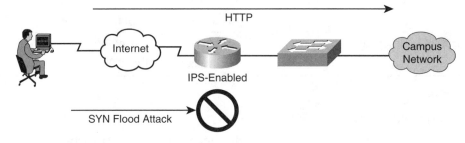

Figure 9-7 *Cisco IOS IPS Feature*

If unencrypted traffic flowing over an unprotected network is intercepted by an attacker, that attacker might be able to glean valuable information (for example, login credentials or account codes) from the intercepted traffic. This type of attack is known as a *man-in-the-middle attack*. Figure 9-8 illustrates an example of such an attack.

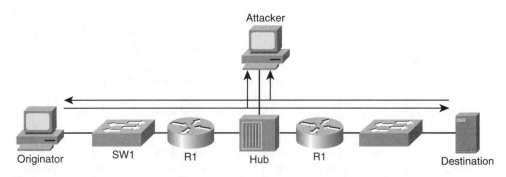

Figure 9-8 *Man-in-the-Middle Attack*

To prevent a man-in-the-middle attack, a secure virtual private network (VPN) tunnel can be constructed between the originator and destination, as illustrated in Figure 9-9. Because the traffic traveling over the logical VPN tunnel can be encrypted, a man-in-the-middle attacker would not be able to interpret any packets they intercepted. Although multiple VPN protocols exist, IPsec is one of the most popular approaches used to protect traffic flowing over a VPN tunnel.

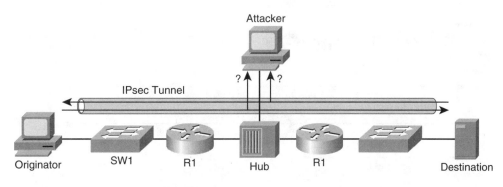

Figure 9-9 *Securing Traffic with a VPN*

As a few other examples of how a Cisco IOS router can protect network traffic and other network devices, consider the Unicast Reverse Path Forwarding (uRPF) feature. This feature allows a router to examine the source IP address of an incoming packet and, based on the router's IP routing table, determine how traffic would be routed back to that source address. If the router notices that the traffic came in on an interface that is different than the interface the router would use to send traffic back to that source IP address, the router can drop the traffic. The rationale for the router dropping this traffic is that this behavior could reflect an IP spoofing attack, where an attacker was impersonating a trusted IP address.

Routers can also play a role in granting users access to the network. For example, consider the IEEE 802.1X technology, as depicted in Figure 9-10.

An 802.1X network requires a client to authenticate before communicating on the network. Once the authentication occurs, a key is generated that is shared between the client and the device to which it attaches (for example, a wireless LAN controller or a Layer 2 switch). The key is then used to encrypt traffic coming from and being sent to the client. In the figure, you see the three primary components of an 802.1X network:

- **Supplicant:** The supplicant is the device that wants to gain access to the network.

Key Topic

- **Authenticator:** The authenticator forwards the supplicant's authentication request on to an authentication server. Once the authentication server has authenticated the supplicant, the authenticator receives a key that is used to communicate securely during a session with the supplicant.

- **Authentication Server:** The authentication server (for example, a RADIUS server) checks the supplicant's credentials. If the credentials are acceptable, the authentication server notifies the authenticator that the supplicant is allowed to communicate on the network. The authentication server also gives the authenticator a key that can be used to securely transmit data during the authenticator's session with the supplicant.

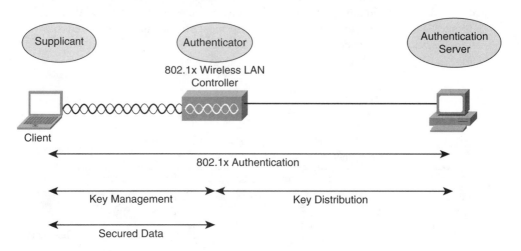

Figure 9-10   *Granting Network Access Using 802.1X*

An even more sophisticated approach to admission control is the Network Admission Control (NAC) feature. Beyond just checking credentials, NAC can check characteristics of the device seeking admission to the network. The client's operating system and version of anti-virus software are examples of these characteristics.

Troubleshooting Network Security Issues

Now that you have reviewed several security measures that networks might have in place to protect their management, control, and data planes, consider how these layers of security might impact your troubleshooting efforts. For example, troubleshooting is often concerned with establishing connectivity between two devices, whereas security features often strategically limit connectivity. Therefore, to effectively troubleshoot a network, you should clearly understand what security features are in place, in addition to the desired behavior of these features.

To begin your troubleshooting efforts in a secure network, you might first determine if the issue being reported is related to the network's security policy or if there is an underlying network problem.

If you determine that there is indeed a network problem, your troubleshooting steps might be limited to actions that conform to the network's security policy. For example, you might want to remove an IPsec configuration from a link between two offices. You should balance that action against the severity of the problem, the likelihood of a security incident occurring during the window of time the IPsec tunnel is deactivated, and the corporate security policy.

Security Troubleshooting Targets

Because adding security to a network can complicate your troubleshooting efforts, you should have an understanding of basic security configurations which you might encounter on a router. Therefore, this section addresses the basic configuration and troubleshooting of two of the more complex Cisco IOS security features: the Cisco IOS Firewall feature and the Authentication, Authorization, and Accounting (AAA) feature.

Configuring and Troubleshooting the Cisco IOS Firewall Feature

Table 9-3 summarizes the two categories of firewalls supported on Cisco IOS routers.

Table 9-3   *Types of Cisco IOS Firewalls*

Target	Mitigations
Classic Cisco IOS Firewall	This firewalling feature was previously known as Context-Based Access Control (CBAC). The Classic Cisco IOS Firewall inspects traffic flowing from a trusted network to an untrusted network, and returning flows from the untrusted network can be permitted into the trusted network. However, if someone attempted to initiate a session from the untrusted network into the trusted network, that session would be denied.
Zone-Based Policy Firewall	This firewalling feature allows various router interfaces to be assigned to a zone. Interzone policies can then be configured to dictate what traffic is permitted between these defined zones.

As an example of a basic Classic Cisco IOS Firewall configuration, consider Figure 9-11. In this example, the campus network is considered the trusted network, whereas the Internet is considered the untrusted network. The goal of the configuration is to allow a user on the trusted network to communicate with a web server on the Internet. Therefore, return traffic from the web server should be allowed back into the trusted network. However, web traffic (that is, HTTP traffic) should not be allowed into the trusted network from the untrusted network if the web traffic is not return traffic from an already established session.

Example 9-1 shows the configuration of the Classic Cisco IOS Firewall depicted.

Example 9-1   *Classic Cisco IOS Firewall Configuration on Router R4*

```
R4# show run
...OUTPUT OMITTED...
 inspect name WEB http
!
interface FastEthernet0/1
 ip address 10.8.8.1 255.255.255.0
 ip access-group 100 in
 ip inspect WEB out
```

```
!
...OUTPUT OMITTED...
!
access-list 100 deny ip any any
...OUTPUT OMITTED...
```

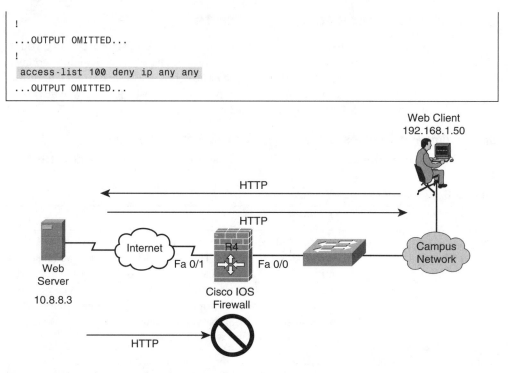

Figure 9-11 *Classic Cisco IOS Firewall Topology*

Notice that ACL 100 has been created to deny all IP traffic. This ACL has been applied in the inbound direction to interface Fast Ethernet 0/1. This blocks all IP traffic sourced from the untrusted network destined for the trusted network.

Also notice that an inspection rule named WEB has been created to inspect HTTP traffic, using the **inspect name WEB http** command. This inspection rule is then applied in the outbound direction to the Fast Ethernet 0/1 interface, using the **ip inspect WEB out** command.

When HTTP traffic leaves the trusted network destined for the untrusted network, via interface Fast Ethernet 0/1, the router inspects those HTTP traffic flows. As a result, when return HTTP comes back from the untrusted network, interface Fast Ethernet 0/1 allows that return traffic back into the router, even though an ACL has been applied to block all inbound IP traffic.

You can use the **show ip inspect session** [**detail**] [**all**] command to troubleshoot such a configuration. By itself, the **show ip inspect session** command shows current sessions being inspected by the Cisco IOS Firewall feature. The **detail** option provides additional details about the current sessions. The **all** option provides information about the way the router is performing its inspection.

Example 9-2 shows sample output from the **show ip inspect session** command. The output indicates that a trusted host with an IP address of 192.168.1.50 has opened two HTTP sessions with a host having an IP address of 10.8.8.3.

Example 9-2   show ip inspect session *Command Output*

```
R4#show ip inspect session
Established Sessions
 Session 84638E80 (192.168.1.50:1832)=>(10.8.8.3:80) http SIS_OPEN
 Session 84638BA8 (192.168.1.50:1830)=>(10.8.8.3:80) http SIS_OPEN
```

Example 9-3 provides sample output from the **show ip inspect session detail** command. The output shows the number of bytes sent by both the session initiator and the session responder. Also indicated in the output is that ACL 100 has been matched 116 times.

Example 9-3   show ip inspect session detail *Command Output*

```
R4#show ip inspect session detail
Established Sessions
 Session 84638E80 (192.168.1.50:1832)=>(10.8.8.3:80) http SIS_OPEN
  Created 00:01:54, Last heard 00:01:32
  Bytes sent (initiator:responder) [408:166394]
  In  SID 10.8.8.3[80:80]=>192.168.1.50[1832:1832] on ACL 100  (116 matches)
 Session 84638BA8 (192.168.1.50:1830)=>(10.8.8.3:80) http SIS_OPEN
  Created 00:02:52, Last heard 00:01:33
  Bytes sent (initiator:responder) [1262:333173]
  In  SID 10.8.8.3[80:80]=>192.168.1.50[1830:1830] on ACL 100  (253 matches)
```

Example 9-4 provides sample output from the **show ip inspect session all** command. This output contains information about the interface's inspection configuration.

Example 9-4   show ip inspect all *Command Output*

```
R4#show ip inspect all
Session audit trail is enabled
Session alert is enabled
one-minute (sampling period) thresholds are [unlimited : unlimited] connections
max-incomplete sessions thresholds are [unlimited : unlimited]
max-incomplete tcp connections per host is unlimited. Block-time 0 minute.
tcp synwait-time is 30 sec — tcp finwait-time is 5 sec
tcp idle-time is 3600 sec — udp idle-time is 30 sec
tcp reassembly queue length 16; timeout 5 sec; memory-limit 1024 kilo bytes
dns-timeout is 5 sec
Inspection Rule Configuration
 Inspection name WEB
    http alert is on audit-trail is on timeout 3600

Interface Configuration
 Interface FastEthernet0/1
  Inbound inspection rule is not set
  Outgoing inspection rule is WEB
```

```
    http alert is on audit-trail is on timeout 3600
  Inbound access list is 100
  Outgoing access list is not set

Established Sessions
 Session 84638E80 (192.168.1.50:1832)=>(10.8.8.3:80) http SIS_OPEN
 Session 84638BA8 (192.168.1.50:1830)=>(10.8.8.3:80) http SIS_OPEN
```

To see real-time updates about the sessions being monitored by a router, you can enter the **ip inspect audit-trail** global configuration mode command. This command causes syslog messages to be created whenever a router creates a new stateful inspection session. Example 9-5 shows sample syslog output (which is sent to a router's console by default) reflecting a new stateful inspection session. The syslog output shows that a new HTTP inspection session began, with an IP address of 192.168.1.50 acting as the initiator and an IP address of 10.8.8.3 acting as the responder. When 192.168.1.50 sends traffic to 10.8.8.3, it does so using TCP port 80 (that is, the default HTTP port). However, when 10.8.8.3 responds to 192.168.1.50, it does so using TCP port 1841.

Example 9-5 *Syslog Output Generated Due to the* **ip inspect audit-trail** *Command*

```
R4#
*Mar  3 12:46:32.465: %SYS-5-CONFIG_I: Configured from console by console
*Mar  3 12:47:10.115: %FW-6-SESS_AUDIT_TRAIL_START: Start http session: initiator
  (192.168.1.50:1841) — responder (10.8.8.3:80)
```

For even more detailed information, you could use the **debug ip inspect object-creation** command. As Example 9-6 demonstrates, the debug output can provide information such as the initiator's and responder's IP addresses, the ACL being used, and the Layer 4 protocol (for example, TCP or UDP) in use. Interestingly, the debug output references Context-Based Access Control (CBAC), the feature that has been renamed as Classic Cisco IOS Firewall.

Example 9-6 **debug ip inspect object-creation** *Command Output*

```
*Mar  3 14:17:55.794: CBAC* OBJ_CREATE: Pak 83A830FC sis 84638BA8 initiator_addr
  (192.168.1.50:1979) responder_addr (10.8.8.3:80)
initiator_alt_addr (192.168.1.50:1979) responder_alt_addr (10.8.8.3:80)
*Mar  3 14:17:55.798: CBAC OBJ-CREATE: sid 846524D4 acl 100 Prot: tcp
*Mar  3 14:17:55.798:  Src 10.8.8.3 Port [80:80]
*Mar  3 14:17:55.798:  Dst 192.168.1.50 Port [1979:1979]
*Mar  3 14:17:55.798: CBAC OBJ_CREATE: create host entry 84641108 addr 10.8.8.3
  bucket 9 (vrf 0:0) insp_cb 0x83EBD140
*Mar  3 14:17:56.251: CBAC* OBJ_CREATE: Pak 83A830FC sis 84638E80 initiator_addr
  (192.168.1.50:1980) responder_addr (10.8.8.3:80)
initiator_alt_addr (192.168.1.50:1980) responder_alt_addr (10.8.8.3:80)
*Mar  3 14:17:56.255: CBAC OBJ-CREATE: sid 84652528 acl 100 Prot: tcp
*Mar  3 14:17:56.255:  Src 10.8.8.3 Port [80:80]
```

```
*Mar  3 14:17:56.255:  Dst 192.168.1.50 Port [1980:1980]
*Mar  3 14:17:56.255: CBAC OBJ_CREATE: create host entry 84641108 addr 10.8.8.3
 bucket 9 (vrf 0:0) insp_cb 0x83EBD140
```

Configuring and Troubleshooting AAA

Enforcing router login security in larger networks can be challenging if you have to manage multiple user databases (for example, having a separate user database locally configured on each router of your network). Fortunately, with AAA services, you can have a single repository for user credentials. Then, when a network administrator attempts to log into, for example, a router, the credentials they supply can be authenticated against a centralized AAA database.

Another advantage of giving different network administrators their own login credentials, as opposed to an enable secret password used on all routers, is that users can quickly be added and deleted from the database without the need to touch each router. Not only can AAA services serve administrative logins connecting to a router, AAA services can also control connections passing through a router to, for example, resources inside a network.

Three services are offered by a AAA server, as follows:

- **Authentication:** The authentication service can check user credentials to confirm they are who they claim to be.

- **Authorization:** Once authenticated, the authorization service determines what that user is allowed to do.

- **Accounting:** The accounting service can collect and store information about a user's login. This information can be used, for example, to keep an audit trail of what was performed on a network.

Figure 9-12 shows a AAA topology where only authentication is being performed. The user at an IP address of 192.168.1.50 is attempting to establish a Telnet session with a router at an IP address of 10.3.3.2. The router's configuration causes the router to prompt the user for username and password credentials and to check those credentials against a AAA server (a TACACS+ server in this example, as opposed to a RADIUS server). If the provided credentials match the database being referenced by the AAA server, the user is permitted to log in to the router.

The Cisco IOS implementation of AAA services includes multiple configuration options, and discussing a complete AAA configuration is beyond the scope of the TSHOOT course. However, Example 9-7 provides a basic configuration example. For more information on AAA configuration, please consult the Cisco IOS Security Configuration Guide available at the following URL: http://tinyurl.com/3ufo6j.

Example 9-7 *AAA Configuration for Authenticating Remote Logins*

```
R4#show run
...OUTPUT OMITTED...
 aaa new-model
 aaa authentication login ADMIN group tacacs+
```

```
!
tacacs-server host 192.168.0.40 key cisco
!
line vty 0 4
 password cisco
 login authentication ADMIN
!
...OUTPUT OMITTED...
```

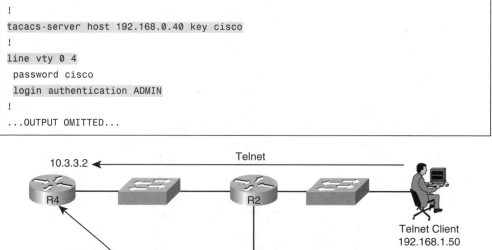

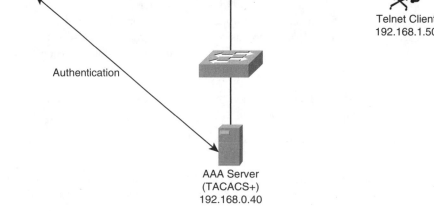

Figure 9-12   *AAA Sample Topology*

In the previous example, the **aaa new-model** command is used to enable AAA services on the router. The **aaa authentication login ADMIN group tacacs+** command defines a method list named **ADMIN**, which requires authentication via a TACACS+ server for logins. The TACACS+ server is defined as having an IP address of **192.168.0.40** with a shared secret key of **cisco**. The method list of **ADMIN** is then applied as the authentication method list for connections coming into the router over VTY lines 0 through 4. Therefore, when someone attempts to Telnet into this router, they are challenged to provide valid username and password credentials, which are then validated by the TACACS+ server.

From a troubleshooting perspective, you can view real-time information about authentication attempts using the **debug aaa authentication** command, as demonstrated in Example 9-8.

Example 9-8   debug aaa authentication *Command Output*

```
*Mar  3 14:39:39.435: AAA/BIND(0000000E): Bind i/f
*Mar  3 14:39:39.435: AAA/AUTHEN/LOGIN (0000000E): Pick method list 'ADMIN'
*Mar  3 14:39:59.211: AAA: parse name=tty66 idb type=-1 tty=-1
```

```
*Mar  3 14:39:59.211: AAA: name=tty66 flags=0x11 type=5 shelf=0 slot=0 adapter=0
  port=66 channel=0
*Mar  3 14:39:59.211: AAA/MEMORY: create_user (0x83C938B4) user='kevin'
  ruser='NULL' ds0=0 port='tty66' rem_addr='192.168.1.50' authen_type=ASCII
  service=ENABLE priv=15 initial_task_id='0', vrf= (id=0)
*Mar  3 14:39:59.211: AAA/AUTHEN/START (4286245615): port='tty66' list=''
  action=LOGIN service=ENABLE
*Mar  3 14:39:59.211: AAA/AUTHEN/START (4286245615): non-console enable - default
  to enable password
*Mar  3 14:39:59.215: AAA/AUTHEN/START (4286245615): Method=ENABLE
*Mar  3 14:39:59.215: AAA/AUTHEN(4286245615): Status=GETPASS
*Mar  3 14:40:00.710: AAA/AUTHEN/CONT (4286245615): continue_login
  (user='(undef)')
*Mar  3 14:40:00.710: AAA/AUTHEN(4286245615): Status=GETPASS
*Mar  3 14:40:00.710: AAA/AUTHEN/CONT (4286245615): Method=ENABLE
*Mar  3 14:40:00.770: AAA/AUTHEN(4286245615): Status=PASS
*Mar  3 14:40:00.770: AAA/MEMORY: free_user (0x83C938B4) user='NULL' ruser='NULL'
  port='tty66' rem_addr='192.168.1.50' authen_type=ASCII service=ENABLE priv=15
  vrf= (id=0)
```

From the preceding output, you can see that the **ADMIN** method list was used, that the username was **kevin**, and that the IP address of the client was **192.168.1.50**. To gather similar types of information for AAA's authorization and accounting features, you can use the **debug aaa authorization** and **debug aaa accounting** commands.

The two most popular AAA protocols used for communicating between a network device and a AAA server are TACACS+ and RADIUS. Table 9-4 contrasts these two protocols.

Table 9-4   *Contrasting the TACACS+ and RADIUS Protocols*

> Key Topic

Characteristic	TACACS+	RADIUS
Transport Layer Protocol	TCP	UDP
Modularity	Provides separate services for authentication, authorization, and accounting	Combines authentication and authorization functions
Encryption	Encrypts entire packet	Only encrypts the password
Accounting Functionality	Offers basic accounting features	Offers robust accounting features
Standards-based	No (Cisco proprietary)	Yes

When troubleshooting a TACACS+ configuration, consider the following common error conditions:

- **The TACACS+ server is offline:** This condition might be indicated by the text "Connection refused by remote host" appearing in the output of the **debug aaa authentication** command.

- **The shared secret key configured on the AAA client doesn't match the key configured on the AAA server:** This condition might be indicated by the text "Invalid AUTHEN/START packet (check keys)" appearing in the output of the debug aaa authentication command.

- **An invalid username/password combination was provided by the AAA client:** This condition might be indicated by the text "Authentication failure" appearing in the output of the debug aaa authentication command.

When troubleshooting a RADIUS configuration, consider the following common error conditions:

- **The RADIUS server is offline:** This condition might be indicated by the text "No response from server" appearing in the output of the **debug radius** command.

- **The shared secret key configured on the AAA client doesn't match the key configured on the AAA server:** This condition might be indicated by the text "Reply for *id* fails decrypt" appearing in the output of the debug radius command.

- **A user is attempting to use a service for which they are not authorized:** This condition might be indicated by the text "No appropriate authorization type for user" appearing in the output of the debug radius command.

- **An invalid username/password combination was provided by the AAA client:** This condition might be indicated by the text "Received from id *id* IP_address:*port_number*. Access-Reject" appearing in the output of the debug radius command.

Although multiple TACACS+ and RADIUS servers are available on the market today, be aware of the Cisco product offering in this area—Cisco Secure ACS. Figure 9-13 shows the web-based console view of Cisco Secure ACS.

By clicking the Reports and Activity button, you can access a collection of valuable troubleshooting information. For example, you can retrieve reports about successful and unsuccessful authentication attempts.

Trouble Ticket: Cisco IOS Security

This trouble ticket focuses on Cisco IOS security. You are presented with a trouble ticket detailing three issues that need resolution. You are given sample **show** command output and are then challenged to identify resolutions for each issue described.

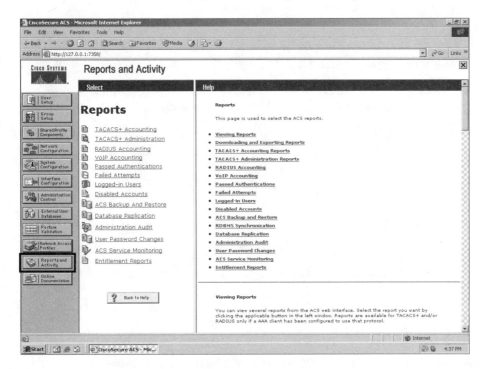

Figure 9-13 *Cisco Secure ACS Web-Based Console*

Trouble Ticket #7

You receive the following trouble ticket:

> A new administrator for Company A has forgotten the enable secret password assigned to router R1 and can no longer log in. Also, when this administrator connects to router R2 via Telnet, the connection is timed out after only one second. The administrator reports this short timeout does not give him sufficient time to correct the configuration. Also, the administrator configured an access list on router R2 to prevent anyone on the backbone (that is, connections coming in to router R2 via the Frame Relay network) from connecting to the Loopback 0 interfaces on routers R1 or R2 via Telnet. However, the access list does not seem to be working.

This trouble ticket references the topology shown in Figure 9-14.

Because a plethora of Cisco IOS security troubleshooting and configuration commands exist, this trouble ticket illustrates verification and configuration commands relevant to the issues described. Table 9-5 presents the syntax for these commands.

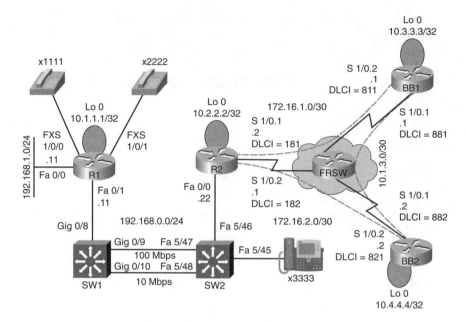

Figure 9-14   *Trouble Ticket #7 Topology*

Table 9-5   *Sampling of Cisco IOS Security Troubleshooting Syntax*

Command	Description
Router(config-line)# **exec-timeout** *minutes* [*seconds*]	Specifies how long the EXEC process running on a line waits for user input before timing out the connection (defaults to 10 minutes)
Router(config)# **access-list** *number* {**deny** | **permit**} *protocol source wildcard-mask destination wildcard-mask* [**eq** *port-number*] [**log**]	Creates an extended IP access list, where the access list number is in the range 100–199
rommon> confreg 0x2142	Configures a router in ROM Monitor configuration mode to ignore its startup configuration when it boots
rommon> **reset**	Causes a router in ROM Monitor configuration mode to reboot
Router(config)# **config-register 0x2102**	Configures a router to uses its startup configuration the next time the router boots
Router(config)# **enable secret** *password*	Configures a router's privileged mode password
Router# **show access-lists**	Displays access lists configured on a router
Router# **show logging**	Displays output collected from logged access list entries

The trouble ticket identified the following three issues:

1. A forgotten enable secret password.

2. An **exec-timeout** parameter set too low.

3. An ACL misconfiguration.

The sections that follow address each issue individually.

Issue #1: Forgotten Enable Secret Password

The first issue to be addressed by this trouble ticket is password recovery. The administrator reportedly forgot the enable secret password on to router R1, which is a Cisco 2611XM router.

On a separate sheet of paper, write out the steps you would go through to perform password recovery on this router. If you are not familiar with password recovery steps, you might need to research password recovery at Cisco.com.

Issue #1: Suggested Solution

To begin the password recovery process on router R1, the router was rebooted, and during the first few seconds of the router booting up, a **Break** was sent from the terminal emulator to the router. The **Break** caused the ROM Monitor prompt (that is, *rommon*) to appear on router R1's console.

The configuration register was set to 0x2142 with the command **confreg 0x2142**. Setting the configuration register to this value causes the router to ignore its startup configuration when the router boots. The router was then rebooted by issuing the **reset** command at the rommon prompt.

Because the router ignored the startup configuration, after the router booted, a prompt was presented, asking the administrator if he wanted to go through the setup dialog. A **no** was entered at this prompt. The **enable** command was entered to go into privileged configuration mode. From privileged mode, the startup configuration, stored in the router's NVRAM, was merged with the existing running configuration using the command **copy star run**. This command does not *replace* the running configuration with the startup configuration. Rather, these two configurations are *merged*. After this merger, all the physical interfaces were administratively shut down. Therefore, the **no shutdown** command was entered for interfaces Fast Ethernet 0/0 and Fast Ethernet 0/1.

The enable secret password was reset to **cisco** using the command **enable secret cisco**. Next, the configuration register was set back to its normal value of 0x2102 with the command **config-register 0x2102**. The running configuration was copied to the startup configuration with the command **copy run star**. The router was then rebooted with the **reload** command. After the router rebooted, the administrator could access the router's privileged mode using an enable secret password of **cisco**. Example 9-9 demonstrates this password recovery procedure.

Example 9-9   *Performing Password Recovery on Router R1*

```
System Bootstrap, Version 12.2(7r) [cmong 7r], RELEASE SOFTWARE (fc1)
Copyright (c) 2002 by cisco Systems, Inc.
C2600 platform with 131072 Kbytes of main memory
...BREAK SEQUENCE SENT...
monitor: command "boot" aborted due to user interrupt
rommon 1 > confreg 0x2142
You must reset or power cycle for new config to take effect
rommon 2 > reset
...OUTPUT OMITTED...
         ---- System Configuration Dialog ----
Would you like to enter the initial configuration dialog? [yes/no]: no
Press RETURN to get started!
...OUTPUT OMITTED...
Router>enable
Router#copy star run
Destination filename [running-config]?
...OUTPUT OMITTED...
R1(config)# enable secret cisco
R1(config)# config-register 0x2102
R1(config)# end
*Mar  3 12:43:26.016: %SYS-5-CONFIG_I: Configured from console by console
R1# copy run star
Destination filename [startup-config]?
Building configuration...
[OK]
R1# reload
Proceed with reload? [confirm]
...OUTPUT OMITTED...
Press RETURN to get started!
R1>
R1>enable
Password:cisco
R1#
```

Issue #2: An exec-timeout Parameter Set Too Low

The second issue addressed in this trouble ticket is recovering from a misconfiguration on router R2, which causes a Telnet session to timeout after only one second of inactivity. The challenge with such a misconfiguration is that when an administrator Telnets to the router to correct the configuration, he might be logged out if he pauses for as little as a single second.

Example 9-10 shows router R2's misconfiguration. Note the **exec-timeout 0 1** command. This command causes a user that connected via a VTY line to be timed out after only one second of inactivity.

Example 9-10 *Incorrect exec-timeout Configuration on Router R2*

```
R2#show run | begin line vty 0 4
line vty 0 4
 exec-timeout 0 1
 password cisco
 login
```

On a separate sheet of paper, write out how you would approach this seemingly paradoxical situation, where you have to log in to the router to correct the configuration, while you will be logged out of the router with only a single second's pause.

Issue #2: Suggested Solution

One fix to this issue is to continuously tap on the keyboard's down arrow with one hand, while using the other hand to enter the commands required to correct the **exec-timeout** misconfiguration. Example 9-11 shows the commands entered to set the **exec-timeout** parameter such that a Telnet session never times out. You could also attach to the console or aux port on the device and change these parameters for the telnet session.

Example 9-11 *Correcting an exec-timeout Misconfiguration*

```
R2#conf term
R2(config)#line vty 0 4
R2(config-line)#exec-timeout 0 0
```

Issue #3: ACL Misconfiguration

This trouble ticket's final troubleshooting issue was an ACL misconfiguration. The goal of the ACL on router R2 was to prevent Telnet traffic coming in from the backbone (that is, coming in over subinterfaces Serial 1/0.1 or Serial 1/0.2) destined for the loopback interface on router R1 or R2 (that is, IP addresses 10.1.1.1 or 10.2.2.2). Example 9-12 shows the ACL configuration on router R2.

Example 9-12 *Baseline ACL Configuration on Router R2*

```
R2#show run
...OUTPUT OMITTED...
interface s1/0.1
 ip access-group 100 out
!
interface s1/0.2
 ip access-group 100 out
!
access-list 100 deny tcp any host 10.1.1.1 eq telnet
access-list 100 deny tcp any host 10.2.2.2 eq telnet
access-list 100 permit ip any any
```

Based on the trouble ticket and the proceeding **show** command output, on a separate sheet of paper, formulate your strategy for resolving the reported issue.

Issue #3: Suggested Solution

Upon examination, the ACL (an extended IP ACL numbered 100) on router R2 appears to be configured correctly. However, ACL 100 was applied in the outbound direction on router R2's Frame Relay subinterfaces. ACL 100 should have been applied in the incoming direction on these subinterfaces. This suggested solution replaces the incorrect **ip access-group** commands, as shown in Example 9-13.

Example 9-13   *Correcting the Application of ACL 100 on Router R2*

```
R2#conf term
R2(config)#interface s1/0.1
R2(config-if)#no ip access-group 100 out
R2(config-if)#ip access-group 100 in
R2(config-if)#interface s1/0.2
R2(config-if)#no ip access-group 100 out
R2(config-if)#ip access-group 100 in
```

After making the previous update, Telnet connections destined for the Loopback interfaces on routers R1 and R2, coming into router R2 over its Frame Relay subinterfaces are now denied.

Exam Preparation Tasks

Review All Key Topics

Review the most important topics from inside the chapter, noted with the Key Topics icon in the outer margin of the page. Table 9-6 lists these key topics and the page numbers where each is found.

Key Topic

Table 9-6   *Key Topics for Chapter 9*

Key Topic Element	Description	Page Number
List	Three planes of operation	270
List	Three modes of router access	270
List	Ways to protect a network from an STP attack	274
Table 9-2	Mitigations for control plane threats	277
List	Three primary components of an 802.1X network	279
Table 9-3	Types of Cisco IOS firewalls	281
List	Three services offered by a AAA server	285
Table 9-4	Contrasting the TACACS+ and RADIUS protocols	287
List	Troubleshooting common TACACS+ issues	288
List	Troubleshooting common RADIUS issues	288
Table 9-5	Sampling of Cisco IOS security troubleshooting syntax	290

Complete the Tables and Lists from Memory

Print a copy of Appendix B, "Memory Tables," (found on the CD) or at least the section for this chapter, and complete the tables and lists from memory. Appendix C, "Memory Tables Answer Key," also on the CD, includes completed tables and lists to check your work.

Define Key Terms

Define the following key terms from this chapter, and check your answers in the Glossary:

intrusion prevention system (IPS), intrusion detection system (IDS), virtual private network (VPN), access control list (ACL), management plane, control plane, data plane, Root Guard, BPDU Guard, DHCP snooping, Dynamic ARP Inspection (DAI), Classic Cisco IOS Firewall, Zone-Based Policy Firewall, authentication, authorization, accounting

Command Reference to Check Your Memory

This section includes the most important configuration and EXEC commands covered in this chapter. To determine how well you have memorized the commands as a side effect of your other studies, cover the left side of the table with a piece of paper, read the descriptions on the right side, and see whether you remember the command.

Table 9-7 *Chapter 9 Configuration Command Reference*

Command	Description
ip inspect audit-trail	Global configuration mode command that causes a router to generate syslog messages whenever the router creates a new stateful inspection session.
aaa new-model	Global configuration mode command used to enable AAA services on a router.
aaa authentication login *method-list* **group tacacs+**	Global configuration mode command that defines a method list that requires authentication via a TACACS+ server for logins.
tacacs-server host *ip-address* **key** *key*	Global configuration mode command that specifies the IP address of a TACACS+ server for a AAA router to use, along with a key that must match a key configured on the specified TACACS+ server.
login authentication *method-list*	Line configuration mode command that specifies what AAA method list should be used for login authentication for a line (for example, a console line or a VTY line).
exec-timeout *minutes* [*seconds*]	Line configuration mode command that specifies how long the EXEC process running on a line waits for user input before timing out the connection (defaults to 10 minutes).
access-list number {**deny** | **permit**} *protocol source wildcard-mask destination wildcard-mask* [**eq** **port-number**] [**log**]	Global configuration mode command that creates an extended IP access list, where the access list number is in the range 100–199.
confreg 0x2142	ROM Monitor command that configures a router to ignore its startup configuration when it boots.
reset	ROM Monitor command that causes a router to reboot.

Table 9-7   *Chapter 9 Configuration Command Reference   (Continued)*

Command	Description
config-register 0x2102	Global configuration mode command that configures a router to use its startup configuration the next time the router boots.
enable secret *password*	Global configuration mode command that configures a router's privileged mode password.

Table 9-8   *Chapter 9 EXEC Command Reference*

Command	Description
show ip inspect session	Displays the IP addresses, port numbers, and protocol that make up an inspection session.
show ip inspect session detail	Displays information such as the number of bytes sent and received by both the inspection session initiator and responder.
show ip inspect session all	Displays information about an interface's inspection configuration.
debug ip inspect object-creation	Displays information such as the initiator's and responder's IP addresses, the ACL being used, and the Layer 4 protocol (for example, TCP or UDP) in use.
debug aaa authentication	Displays real-time information for authentication attempts on a router configured for AAA authentication.
debug aaa authorization	Displays real-time information for authorization requests on a router configured for AAA authorization.
debug aaa accounting	Displays real-time accounting information for a router configured for AAA accounting.
show access-lists	Displays access lists configured on a router.
show logging	Displays output collected from logged access list entries.

This chapter covers the following subjects:

NAT Troubleshooting: This section begins by reviewing the purpose and basic operation of Network Address Translation (NAT). As a reference, sample topologies are provided, along with their configurations. Common NAT troubleshooting targets are identified, and a syntax reference is provided to aid in troubleshooting NAT issues.

DHCP Troubleshooting: This section reviews basic Dynamic Host Configuration Protocol (DHCP) operation and various types of DHCP messages. You are given three configuration examples corresponding to the three roles a router can play in a DHCP environment: DHCP relay agent, DHCP client, and DHCP server. Common DHCP troubleshooting targets are reviewed, along with recommended DHCP troubleshooting practices. Finally, this section presents a collection of commands that might prove useful in troubleshooting a suspected DHCP issue.

Trouble Ticket: NAT: This section presents you with a trouble ticket and an associated topology. You are also given **show** and **debug** command output that confirms the reported issue. Then you are challenged to hypothesize how to correct the reported issue. At that point you can compare your solution against a suggested one.

CHAPTER 10

IP Services Troubleshooting

This chapter begins by reviewing a common IP service found at the boundary of many networks: NAT. The NAT service allows a company to use as many private IP addresses as they need for devices inside of their network and then translate those addresses into publicly routable IP addresses. This translation is possible even if the number of a company's private IP addresses is greater than the number of its allocated public IP addresses. Although NAT does a great job of IP address conservation by using private IP address space, adding NAT to a network does introduce potential troubleshooting concerns. Not every application coexists peacefully with NAT, and adding a NAT configuration to a router comes with the possibility that there will be one or more errors in that configuration. Therefore, this chapter discusses common NAT troubleshooting issues and provides a syntax guide for effectively troubleshooting those issues.

Another common IP service addressed in this chapter is DCHP. Realize that a router might be a DHCP client, where one (or more) of its interfaces obtains an IP address from an external DHCP server. Alternatively, a router can be configured to act as a DHCP server. A router can also serve as a DHCP relay agent, which allows DHCP client broadcast traffic (that is, broadcast traffic a DHCP client sends in an attempt to dynamically discover a DHCP server) to be forwarded through the router, even though a router typically blocks broadcast traffic. DHCP troubleshooting issues and tips are provided along with monitoring, troubleshooting, and configuration syntax for DHCP.

Finally, this chapter challenges you with a trouble ticket addressing NAT. You are guided through a data collection process that confirms a reported issue. Based on the information collected, you identify a probable cause for the issue and construct a plan to resolve the issue. A suggested solution is provided, which you can compare against your own solution.

"Do I Know This Already?" Quiz

The "Do I Know This Already?" quiz helps you determine your level of knowledge of this chapter's topics before you begin. Table 10-1 details the major topics discussed in this chapter and their corresponding quiz questions.

Table 10-1 *"Do I Know This Already?" Section-to-Question Mapping*

Foundation Topics Section	Questions
NAT Troubleshooting	1–5
DHCP Troubleshooting	6–9

1. What type of NAT uses a one-to-one mapping of private internal IP addresses to public external IP addresses?

   a. Static NAT

   b. Dynamic NAT

   c. NAT Overloading

   d. Overlapping NAT

2. What NAT IP address is a public IP address that references an inside device?

   a. Inside Local

   b. Inside Global

   c. Outside Local

   d. Outside Global

3. Which three of the following are potential NAT troubleshooting issues? (Choose the three best answers.)

   a. Using NAT over a VPN

   b. NAT being incompatible with the version of Cisco IOS used on a router

   c. NAT hiding true IP address information

   d. Applications that are not NAT compatible

4. Which two of the following interface operations occur after NAT performs its translation of a global address to an inside address, as traffic comes into an interface? (Choose the two best answers.)

   a. Decryption of IPsec traffic

   b. Output ACL applied

   c. Input ACL applied

   d. Cisco IOS Firewall inspection performed

5. Which command removes all dynamic entries from a router's NAT translation table?

   a. erase ip nat *

   b. clear ip nat translation *

   c. write erase ip nat *

   d. clear nat all

6. Identify the four DHCP messages that are exchanged between a DHCP client and server as the client is obtaining an IP address. (Choose the four best answers.)

    a. DHCPREQUEST

    b. DHCPDISCOVER

    c. DHCPOFFER

    d. DHCPRELEASE

    e. DHCPACK

7. Which two of the following protocols are forwarded by a DCHP relay agent, in addition to DHCP? (Choose the two best answers.)

    a. TFTP

    b. FTP

    c. DNS

    d. NTP

8. Which of the following is most likely a DHCP troubleshooting issue? (Choose the best answer.)

    a. A router not forwarding multicasts

    b. A router not forwarding broadcasts

    c. The DHCP server service not manually started

    d. Switches in the topology not configured to support IGMP snooping

9. Which of the following commands releases all current DHCP leases?

    a. erase ip dhcp binding *

    b. clear ip dhcp binding *

    c. clear ip dhcp mapping *

    d. delete ip dhcp binding *

Foundation Topics

NAT Troubleshooting

Some IP addresses are routable through the public Internet, whereas others are considered private and are intended for use within an organization. Because these private IP addresses might need to communicate outside of their local networks, NAT allows private IP addresses (as defined in RFC 1918) to be translated into Internet-routable IP addresses (that is, public IP addresses).

Types of NAT

Table 10-2 identifies four types of NAT.

Table 10-2   *Types of NAT*

Type of NAT	Description
Static NAT	A one-to-one mapping of private internal IP addresses to public external IP addresses
Dynamic NAT	A dynamic mapping of private internal IP addresses to a pool of public external IP addresses
NAT Overloading	Allows multiple private internal IP addresses to use a single public external IP address by keeping track of Layer 4 port numbers, which make each session unique (that is, Port Address Translation [PAT])
Overlapping NAT	Used when private internal IP addresses at one location overlap destination private internal IP addresses at another location

Key Topic

Sample NAT Topology

Consider Figure 10-1, which shows a basic NAT topology. Note that even though the IP addresses of 172.16.1.1 and 192.168.1.1 are actually private IP addresses, for the purpose of this discussion, assume they are publicly routable IP addresses. The reason for the use of these private IP addresses to represent public IP addresses is to avoid using an entity's registered IP address in the example.

In the topology, a client with a private IP address of 10.1.1.1 wants to communicate with a server on the public Internet. The IP address of the server is 192.168.1.1. Router R1 is configured for NAT. Router R1 takes packets coming from 10.1.1.1 destined for 192.168.1.1 and changes the source IP address in the packet headers to 172.16.1.1 (which is assumed to be a publicly routable IP address for the purposes of this discussion). When the server at IP address 192.168.1.1 receives traffic from the client, the return traffic of the server is sent to a destination address of 172.16.1.1. When router R1 receives traffic from the outside network destined for 172.16.1.1, the router translates the destination IP address to 10.1.1.1 and forwards the traffic to the inside network, where the client receives the traffic.

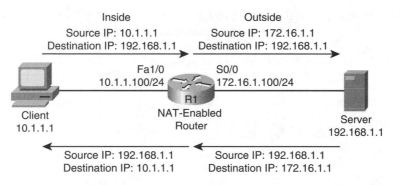

Figure 10-1 *Basic NAT Topology*

To effectively troubleshoot a NAT configuration, you should be familiar with the terminology describing the various IP addresses involved in a translation, as outlined in Table 10-3.

Table 10-3 *Names of NAT IP Addresses*

Advantage	Definition
Inside Local	A private IP address referencing an inside device
Inside Global	A public IP address referencing an inside device
Outside Local	A private IP address referencing an outside device
Outside Global	A public IP address referencing an outside device

As a memory aid, remember that *inside* always refers to an inside device, whereas *outside* always refers to an outside device. Also, think of the word *local* as being similar to the Spanish word *loco*, which means crazy. That is what a local address could be thought of. It is a crazy made-up address (that is, a private IP address not routable on the Internet). Finally, let the *g* in *global* remind you of the *g* in *good*, because a global address is a good (that is, routable on the Internet) IP address.

Based on these definitions, Table 10-4 categorizes the IP addresses previously shown in Figure 10-1.

Table 10-4 *Classifying the NAT IP Addresses in Figure 10-1*

Advantage	NAT IP Address Type
Inside Local	10.1.1.1
Inside Global	172.16.1.1
Outside Local	None
Outside Global	192.168.1.1

Again, refer to Figure 10-1. Example 10-1 shows how router R1 in that figure can be configured for dynamic NAT to support the translation shown.

Example 10-1 *Dynamic NAT Sample Configuration*

```
R1# show run
...OUTPUT OMITTED...
interface FastEthernet1/0
 ip address 10.1.1.100 255.255.255.0
 ip nat inside
!
interface Serial 0/0
 ip address 172.16.1.100 255.255.255.0
 ip nat outside
!
ip nat pool OUTSIDE_POOL 172.16.1.1 172.16.1.10 netmask 255.255.255.0
ip nat inside source list 1 pool OUTSIDE_POOL
!
access-list 1 permit 10.0.0.0 0.0.0.255
...OUTPUT OMITTED...
```

In the example, ACL 1 identifies the inside addresses (the 10.1.1.0/24 network in this example) to be translated. A pool of addresses named **OUTSIDE_POOL** is defined as IP addresses in the range 172.16.1.1 to 172.16.1.10. **The ip nat inside source list 1 pool OUTSIDE_POOL** command associates the internal range of addresses defined by ACL **1** with the range of outside addresses defined by the **OUTSIDE_POOL** pool. Finally, you need to indicate what router interface is acting as the inside interface and what interface is acting as the outside interface. Note that you can have multiple interfaces acting as inside or outside interfaces. The **ip nat inside** command is issued for interface Fast Ethernet 1/0, and the **ip nat outside** command is issued for Serial 0/0.

Potential NAT Troubleshooting Issues

From a troubleshooting perspective, adding NAT into a network introduces potential troubleshooting issues. Consider the following situations in which NAT might cause an issue for end users:

■ **Using NAT over a VPN:** Some VPN protocols check the checksum of a packet to verify its integrity. The checksum calculated for a packet before NAT is different from a checksum calculated for that same packet after NAT (because performing NAT on a packet changes IP address information). Therefore, a VPN protocol (for example, IPsec) might reject such a packet because it appears to have been altered. Workarounds are available, including NAT Traversal, NAT Transparency, and IPsec over TCP/UDP.

■ **NAT hiding true IP address information:** Because NAT translates an inside IP address to an outside IP address, tracing a data flow from end to end for troubleshooting purposes can be challenging. You can start troubleshooting by using the **show ip**

nat translation command to verify whether the translation does exist in the translation table.

■ **Applications that are not NAT compatible:** When some applications initialize, they randomly determine what ports are going to be used for communication, which might be incompatible with how NAT handles incoming traffic. Some Voice over IP (VoIP) protocols face such an issue, as they select the User Datagram Protocol (UDP) port numbers to be used for their Real-time Transport Protocol (RTP) media streams. Also, when setting up communication with a remote device, an application might include IP address information in the payload of a packet. If the remote device attempted to return traffic to the IP address embedded in that payload, that IP address might be unreachable because of the NAT translation. Therefore, you should avoid NAT for some applications; use NAT-aware applications, or configure NAT to work with NAT-unaware applications.

■ **Delays experienced due to NAT's processing:** Because NAT manipulates Layer 3 information of packets, the packets are subject to a bit more delay than they would otherwise experience. This delay might become more evident on routers performing numerous NAT translations.

Order of Operations for an Interface

Also critical for troubleshooting is an understanding of when NAT performs its translation in relation to other interface operations, such as evaluating an ACL. This order of operations depends on the direction of the traffic flow (that is, flowing from the inside network to the outside network or vice versa). Following is a listing of the order of interface operations for traffic flowing from the inside network into the outside network:

1. Decryption of IPsec traffic

2. Input ACL applied

3. Input policing applied

4. Input accounting applied

5. Policy-based routing (PBR)

6. Redirecting traffic to a web cache

7. NAT translating local to global addresses

8. Crypto map application

9. Output ACL applied

10. Cisco IOS Firewall inspection performed

11. TCP intercept feature applied

12. Encryption performed

Following is a listing of the order of interface operations for traffic flowing from the outside network into the inside network. Notice, for example, that an output ACL might need

**Key
Topic**

to reference a translated IP address for a packet as opposed to the original IP address of the packet.

1. Decryption of IPsec traffic

2. Input ACL applied

3. Input policing applied

4. Input accounting applied

5. NAT translating global to local addresses

6. Policy Based Routing (PBR)

7. Redirecting traffic to a web cache

8. Crypto map application

9. Output ACL applied

10. Cisco IOS Firewall inspection performed

11. TCP intercept feature applied

12. Encryption performed

Now that you have reviewed the basic operation of NAT, consider some of the most common causes for a NAT issue:

Key Topic

■ An ACL referenced by a NAT configuration is incorrect.

■ Inside and outside interfaces are not correctly assigned.

■ Incorrect IP addresses (or address ranges) are referenced by a NAT configuration.

■ Applications are not NAT aware.

■ A routing loop occurs as a result of a NAT address translation.

NAT Troubleshooting Syntax

Table 10-5 provides a reference table of commands that could be useful in troubleshooting a NAT configuration.

Key Topic

Table 10-5   *NAT Troubleshooting Commands*

Command	Description
clear ip nat translation *	Removes all dynamic entries from a router's NAT translation table
show ip nat translations	Used to see all entries in a router's NAT translation table

Table 10-5 *NAT Troubleshooting Commands* (*Continued*)

Command	Description
show ip nat statistics	Used to display NAT configuration and statistical information on a router, such as inside and outside interfaces, total translations, number of expired translations, inside address ACL, and outside address pool information
debug ip nat	Provides real-time information about NAT translations as they occur, including the IP address being translated and the IP identification number that can be used to match packets in the output with packets captured with a protocol analyzer
ip nat pool *pool-name start-ip end-ip* {**netmask** *subnet-mask* | **prefix-length** *prefix-length*}	Global configuration mode command that defines a pool of inside global addresses into which inside local addresses can be translated
ip nat inside source list *access-list* **pool** *pool-name* [**overload**]	Global configuration mode command that associates an ACL defining an inside local address space with the specified pool of inside global addresses (Note: The **overload** keyword enables PAT, which allows multiple inside addresses to share a common outside address.)
ip nat translation max-entries *number*	Global configuration mode command that specifies the maximum number of entries permitted in a router's NAT table
ip nat {inside | outside}	Interface configuration mode command that identifies an interface as an inside or outside NAT interface

Example 10-2 provides sample output from the **show ip nat translations** command and how to change this output with the **clear ip nat translation** * command. Initially, the **show ip nat translations** command shows three statically configured NAT translations and one dynamically learned translation (which is highlighted in the output). Then, after issuing the **clear ip nat translation** * command, the dynamically learned NAT entry is deleted from the IP NAT table, leaving the three statically configured NAT entries.

Example 10-2 show ip nat translations *and* clear ip nat translation * *Command Output*

```
R1# show ip nat translations
Pro Inside global      Inside local      Outside local      Outside global
--- 192.168.1.12       192.168.0.1       ---                ---
--- 192.168.1.13       192.168.0.2       ---                ---
tcp 192.168.1.27:23    192.168.0.27:23   192.168.1.50:1158  192.168.1.50:1158
--- 192.168.1.27       192.168.0.27      ---                ---
```

```
R1# clear ip nat translation *
R1# show ip nat translations
Pro Inside global      Inside local      Outside local      Outside global
--- 192.168.1.12       192.168.0.1       - - -              - - -
--- 192.168.1.13       192.168.0.2       - - -              - - -
--- 192.168.1.27       192.168.0.27      - - -              - - -
```

Example 10-3 provides sample output from the **show ip nat statistics** command. The output shows which interfaces are acting as the inside and outside interfaces and the current number of static and dynamic translations.

Example 10-3   show ip nat statistics *Command Output*

```
R1#show ip nat statistics
Total active translations: 4 (3 static, 1 dynamic; 1 extended)
Outside interfaces:
  FastEthernet0/0
Inside interfaces:
  FastEthernet0/1
Hits: 10  Misses: 0
CEF Translated packets: 5, CEF Punted packets: 0
Expired translations: 0
Dynamic mappings:
Appl doors: 0
Normal doors: 0
Queued Packets: 0
```

Example 10-4 provides sample output from the **debug ip nat** command. The output shows that when a source IP address of 192.168.1.50 is attempting to communicate with a destination IP address of 192.168.1.27, the router translates the destination IP address into 192.168.0.27. Also, when a source IP address of 192.168.1.11 is attempting to communicate with a destination IP address of 192.168.1.50, the router translates the source IP address of 192.168.1.11 into an IP address of 192.168.1.27.

Example 10-4   debug ip nat *Command Output*

```
R1#debug ip nat
IP NAT debugging is on
*Mar  3 13:01:28.162: NAT*: s=192.168.1.50, d=192.168.1.27->192.168.0.27 [10202]
*Mar  3 13:01:28.162: NAT: s=192.168.1.11->192.168.1.27, d=192.168.1.50 [210]
*Mar  3 13:01:30.991: NAT*: s=192.168.1.50, d=192.168.1.27->192.168.0.27 [10370]
```

```
*Mar  3 13:01:30.991: NAT: s=192.168.1.11->192.168.1.27, d=192.168.1.50 [211]
*Mar  3 13:01:37.025: NAT*: s=192.168.1.50, d=192.168.1.27->192.168.0.27 [10540]
*Mar  3 13:01:37.029: NAT: s=192.168.1.11->192.168.1.27, d=192.168.1.50 [214]
```

DHCP Troubleshooting

DHCP serves as one of the most common methods of assigning IP address information to a network host. Specifically, DHCP allows a DHCP client to obtain an IP address, subnet mask, default gateway IP address, DNS server IP address, and other types of IP address information from a DHCP server.

If you have a cable modem or DSL connection in your home, your cable modem or DSL router might obtain its IP address from your service provider via DHCP. In many corporate networks, when a PC boots up, that PC receives its IP address configuration information from a corporate DHCP server.

Basic DHCP Operation

Figure 10-2 illustrates the exchange of messages that occur as a DHCP client obtains IP address information from a DHCP server.

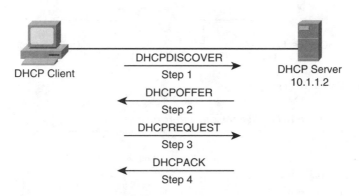

Figure 10-2 *Obtaining IP Address Information from a DHCP Server*

Step 1. When a DHCP client initially boots, it has no IP address, default gateway, or other such configuration information. Therefore, the way a DHCP client initially communicates is by sending a broadcast message (that is, a DHCPDISCOVER message) to a destination address of 255.255.255.255 in an attempt to discover a DHCP server.

Step 2. When a DHCP server receives a DHCPDISCOVER message, it can respond with a DHCPOFFER message. Because the DHCPDISCOVER message is sent as a broadcast, more than one DHCP server might respond to this discover request. However, the client typically selects the server that sent the first DHCPOFFER response it received.

Key Topic

Step 3. The DHCP client communicates with this selected server by sending a DHCPREQUEST message asking the DHCP server to provide IP configuration parameters.

Step 4. Finally, the DHCP server responds to the client with a DHCPACK message. This DHCPACK message contains a collection of IP configuration parameters.

Notice that in Step 1, the DHCPDISCOVER message was sent as a broadcast. By default, a broadcast cannot cross a router boundary. Therefore, if a client resides on a different network than the DHCP server, the next-hop router of the client should be configured as a DHCP relay agent. You can use the **ip helper-address** *ip-address* interface configuration mode command to configure a router interface to relay DHCP requests to either a unicast IP address or a directed broadcast address.

DHCP Configurations

To illustrate the configuration of DHCP, consider Figure 10-3 and Example 10-5. In the figure, the DHCP client belongs to the 172.16.1.0/24 network, whereas the DHCP server belongs to the 10.1.1.0/24 network. Router R1 is configured as a DHCP relay agent, using the syntax shown in Example 10-5.

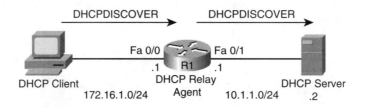

Figure 10-3 *DHCP Relay Agent*

Example 10-5 *DHCP Relay Agent Configuration*

> **Key Topic**

```
R1# conf term
Enter configuration commands, one per line.  End with CNTL/Z.
R1(config)# service dhcp
R1(config)# interface fa 0/0
R1(config-if)# ip helper-address 10.1.1.1
```

In the configuration, notice the **service dhcp** command. This command enables the DHCP service on the router, which must be enabled for the DHCP relay agent feature to function. This command is typically not required, because the DHCP service is enabled by default; however, when troubleshooting a DHCP relay agent issue, you might want to confirm that the service is enabled. Also, the **ip helper-address 10.1.1.1** command specifies the IP address of the DHCP server, although the **ip helper-address 10.1.1.255** command could have been used instead. Specifically, 10.1.1.255 is the directed broadcast IP address for the 10.1.1.0/24 network. Although using a directed broadcast address might enable you to reach all DHCP servers on a particular subnet, Cisco recommends that you use a specific IP address as opposed to a directed broadcast. One reason for this recommendation is that a directed broadcast causes all hosts on the target subnet to examine the DHCPDISCOVER packet, even if those hosts are not DHCP servers. Yet another rationale for this recommendation is that some routers block directed broadcasts (because of a potential security risk).

When you configure a router to act as a DHCP relay agent, realize that it relays a few other broadcast types in addition to a DHCP message. Some other protocols that are forwarded by a DHCP relay agent include the following:

- TFTP
- Domain Name System (DNS)
- Internet Time Service (ITS)
- NetBIOS name server
- NetBIOS datagram server
- BootP
- TACACS

As a reference, Table 10-6 provides a comprehensive listing of DHCP message types you might encounter while troubleshooting a DHCP issue.

Table 10-6 *DHCP Message Types*

Key
Topic

DHCP Message	Description
DHCPDISCOVER	A client sends this message in an attempt to locate a DHCP server. This message is sent to a broadcast IP address of 255.255.255.255 using UDP port 67.
DHCPOFFER	A DHCP server sends this message in response to a DHCPDISCOVER message using UDP port 68.
DHCPREQUEST	This message is a request for IP configuration parameters sent from a client to a specific DHCP server.
DHCPDECLINE	This message is sent from a client to a DHCP server to inform the server that an IP address is already in use on the network.
DHCPACK	A DHCP server sends this message to a client and includes IP configuration parameters.
DHCPNAK	A DHCP server sends this message to a client and informs the client that the DHCP server declines to provide the client with the requested IP configuration information.
DHCPRELEASE	A client sends this message to a DHCP server and informs the DHCP server that the client has released its DHCP lease, thus allowing the DHCP server to reassign the client IP address to another client.
DHCPINFORM	This message is sent from a client to a DHCP server and requests IP configuration parameters. Such a message might be sent from an access server requesting IP configuration information for a remote client attaching to the access server.

In addition to acting as a DHCP relay agent, a router might act as a DHCP client. Specifically, the interface of a router might obtain its IP address from a DHCP server. Also, a router can act as a DHCP server. The text that follows considers each scenario.

Figure 10-4 shows a router acting as a DHCP client, where the router's Fast Ethernet 0/0 interface obtains its IP address from a DHCP server. Example 10-6 provides the configuration for the router in the topology (that is, router R1). Notice the **dhcp** option used in the **ip address** command, instead of the usual IP address and subnet mask information.

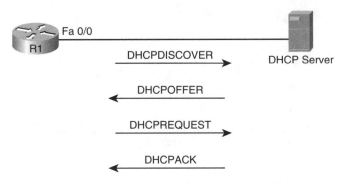

Figure 10-4 *Router Acting as a DHCP Client*

Example 10-6 *DHCP Client Configuration*

```
R1#conf term
R1(config)#int fa 0/0
R1(config-if)#ip address dhcp
```

Figure 10-5 shows a router acting as a DHCP server, and Example 10-7 shows the router configuration. The **ip dhcp excluded-address 10.8.8.1** command prevents DHCP from assigning the 10.8.8.1 IP address to a client. This exclusion occurs because this IP address is one of the interfaces of the router. The **ip dhcp pool POOL-A** command creates a DHCP pool named **POOL-A**. This pool can hand out IP addresses from the 10.8.8.0/24 network, with a default gateway of 10.8.8.1, a DNS server of 192.168.1.1, and a WINS server of 192.168.1.2.

Example 10-7 *DHCP Server Configuration*

```
R1#show run
...OUTPUT OMITTED...
ip dhcp excluded-address 10.8.8.1
!
ip dhcp pool POOL-A
   network 10.8.8.0 255.255.255.0
   default-router 10.8.8.1
   dns-server 192.168.1.1
   netbios-name-server 192.168.1.2
...OUTPUT OMITTED...
```

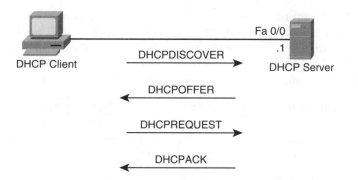

Figure 10-5 *Router Acting as a DHCP Server*

Potential DHCP Troubleshooting Issues

When troubleshooting what you suspect might be a DHCP issue, consider the following potential issues:

- **A router not forwarding broadcasts:** By default, a router does not forward broadcasts, including DHCPDISCOVER broadcast messages. Therefore, a router needs to be explicitly configured to act as a DHCP relay agent if the DHCP client and DHCP server are on different subnets.

- **DHCP pool out of IP addresses:** A DHCP pool contains a finite number of addresses. Once a DCHP pool becomes depleted, new DHCP requests are rejected.

- **Misconfiguration:** The configuration of a DHCP server might be incorrect. For example, the range of network addresses to be given out by a particular pool might be incorrect, or the exclusion of addresses statically assigned to routers or DNS servers might be incorrect.

- **Duplicate IP addresses:** A DHCP server might hand out an IP address to a client that is already statically assigned to another host on the network. These duplicate IP addresses can cause connectivity issues for both the DHCP client and the host that had been statically configured for the IP address.

- **Redundant services not communicating:** Some DHCP servers can coexist with other DHCP servers for redundancy. For this redundancy to function, these DHCP servers need to communicate with one another. If this interserver communication fails, the DHCP servers can hand out overlapping IP addresses to their clients.

- **The "pull" nature of DHCP:** When a DHCP client wants an IP address, it can request an IP address from a DHCP server. However, the DHCP server has no ability to initiate a change in the client IP address after the client obtains an IP address. In other words, the DHCP client pulls information from the DHCP server, but the DHCP server cannot push information to the DHCP client.

At this point in this section, you have reviewed basic DHCP operations and potential DHCP troubleshooting targets. When you begin your troubleshooting efforts, you might want to collect the following information to help you better isolate the underlying cause of the DHCP issue you are investigating.

Key Topic

- **The configuration of the DHCP server:** For example, confirm that the pools are correctly defined with appropriate network addresses, default gateways, and other relevant IP address information.

- **The configuration of the DHCP relay agent:** For example, determine if the target addresses a unicast IP address or a directed broadcast address.

- **Determine the size of a DHCP pool:** Because a pool in a DHCP server accommodates only a limited number of IP addresses, determine how many IP addresses (if any) are still available from a given DHCP pool.

DHCP Troubleshooting Syntax

Table 10-7 provides a collection of commands that can be useful in troubleshooting a DHCP issue.

Key Topic

Table 10-7 *DHCP Troubleshooting Commands*

Command	Description
show ip dhcp conflict	Identifies any IP address conflicts a router identifies, along with the method the router used to identify the conflicts (this is, via ping or gratuitous ARP)
show ip dhcp binding	Displays IP addresses that an IOS DHCP server assigns, their corresponding MAC addresses, and lease expirations
clear ip dhcp binding *	Releases all current DHCP leases
clear ip dhcp conflict *	Clears all currently identified DHCP conflicts
debug ip dhcp server events	Provides real-time information about DHCP address assignments and database updates
debug ip dhcp server packet	Displays real-time decodes of DHCP packets

Table 10-7   *DHCP Troubleshooting Commands*

Command	Description
ip helper-address *ip-address*	Interface configuration mode command that causes an interface to forward specific received UDP broadcasts to the destination IP address, which can be either a specific IP address or a directed broadcast address
ip dhcp excluded-address *beginning-ip-address* [*ending-ip-address*]	Specifies a range of IP addresses not to be assigned to DHCP clients
ip dhcp pool *pool-name*	Creates a DHCP pool
network *network-address subnet-mask*	Identifies a subnet to be used by a DHCP pool
default-router *ip-address*	Specifies the IP address of a default gateway to be given to a DHCP client
dns-server *ip-address*	Configures the IP address of a DNS server to be given to a DHCP client
netbios-name-server *ip-address*	Defines the IP address of a WINS server to be given to a DHCP client
lease {*days hours minutes* | *infinite*}	Determines the duration of a DHCP lease given to a DHCP client

Example 10-8 provides sample output from the **show ip dhcp conflict** command. The output indicates a duplicate 172.16.1.3 IP address on the network, which the router discovered via a ping. You can resolve this conflict by issuing the **clear ip dhcp conflict** * command.

Example 10-8   show ip dhcp conflict *Command Output*

```
R1#show ip dhcp conflict
IP address          Detection method    Detection time
172.16.1.3          Ping                Oct 15 2009 8:56 PM
```

Example 10-9 shows sample output from the **show ip dhcp binding** command. The output indicates that an IP address of 10.1.1.2 was assigned to a DHCP client with a MAC address of 3030.312e.3066.3163. You can release this DHCP lease with the **clear ip dhcp binding** * command.

Example 10-9   show ip dhcp binding *Command Output*

```
R1#show ip dhcp binding
Bindings from all pools not associated with VRF:
IP address Client-ID/          Lease expiration       Type       Hardware address/
User name
10.1.1.2   0063.6973.636f.2d63.Oct 03 2009 12:03 PM Automatic 3030.312e.3066.3163.
  0e30.3030.302d.4661.
```

Example 10-10 shows sample output from the **debug ip dhcp server events** command. The output shows updates to the DHCP database.

Example 10-10   debug ip dhcp server events *Command Output*

```
R1#debug ip dhcp server events
*Mar  1 00:06:47.427: DHCPD: Seeing if there is an internally specified pool class:
*Mar  1 00:06:47.431:    DHCPD: htype 1 chaddr c001.0f1c.0000
*Mar  1 00:06:47.431:    DHCPD: remote id 020a00000a01010101000000
*Mar  1 00:06:47.435:    DHCPD: circuit id 00000000
*Mar  1 00:06:49.415: DHCPD: Seeing if there is an internally specified pool class:
*Mar  1 00:06:49.419:    DHCPD: htype 1 chaddr c001.0f1c.0000
*Mar  1 00:06:49.419:    DHCPD: remote id 020a00000a01010101000000
*Mar  1 00:06:49.423:    DHCPD: circuit id 00000000
*Mar  1 00:06:52.603: DHCPD: no subnet configured for 192.168.1.238.
```

Example 10-11 shows sample output from the **debug ip dhcp server packet** command. The output shows a DHCPRELEASE message being received when a DHCP client with an IP address of 10.1.1.3 is shut down. You can also see the four-step process of a DHCP client obtaining an IP address of 10.1.1.4 with the following messages: DHCPDISCOVER, DHCPOFFER, DHCPREQUEST, and DHCPACK.

Example 10-11   debug ip dhcp server packet *Command Output*

```
R1#debug ip dhcp server packet
*Mar  1 00:07:39.867: DHCPD: DHCPRELEASE message received from client
  0063.6973.636f.2d63.3030.312e.3066.3163.2e30.3030.302d.4661.302f.30 (10.1.1.3).
*Mar  1 00:07:41.855: DHCPD: DHCPRELEASE message received from client
  0063.6973.636f.2d63.3030.312e.3066.3163.2e30.3030.302d.4661.302f.30 (10.1.1.3).
*Mar  1 00:07:41.859: DHCPD: Finding a relay for client
  0063.6973.636f.2d63.3030.312e.3066.3163.2e30.3030.302d.4661.302f.30 on interface
  FastEthernet0/1.
*Mar  1 00:07:54.775: DHCPD: DHCPDISCOVER received from client
  0063.6973.636f.2d63.3030.312e.3066.3163.2e30.3030.302d.4661.302f.30 on interface
  FastEthernet0/1.
*Mar  1 00:07:54.779: DHCPD: Allocate an address without class information
  (10.1.1.0)
*Mar  1 00:07:56.783: DHCPD: Sending DHCPOFFER to client
  0063.6973.636f.2d63.3030.312e.3066.3163.2e30.3030.302d.4661.302f.30 (10.1.1.4).
*Mar  1 00:07:56.787: DHCPD: broadcasting BOOTREPLY to client c001.0f1c.0000.
```

```
*Mar  1 00:07:56.879: DHCPD: DHCPREQUEST received from client
  0063.6973.636f.2d63.3030.312e.3066.3163.2e30.3030.302d.4661.302f.30.
*Mar  1 00:07:56.887: DHCPD: No default domain to append - abort update
*Mar  1 00:07:56.887: DHCPD: Sending DHCPACK to client
  0063.6973.636f.2d63.3030.312e.3066.3163.2e30.3030.302d.4661.302f.30 (10.1.1.4).
*Mar  1 00:07:56.891: DHCPD: broadcasting BOOTREPLY to client c001.0f1c.0000.
```

Trouble Ticket: NAT

This trouble ticket focuses on the previously discussed IP service of NAT. You are presented with a trouble ticket detailing an issue that needs resolution. You are given sample **show** and **debug** command output and are then challenged to identify a resolution for the issue described.

Trouble Ticket #8

You receive the following trouble ticket:

> Company A is dual-homed out to the Internet (that is, routers BB1 and BB2, where each router represents a different ISP). Inside IP addresses in the 192.168.0.0/24 subnet should be translated into the IP address of interface Serial 1/0.1 on router R2, whereas inside IP addresses in the 192.168.1.0/24 subnet should be translated into the IP address of interface Serial 1/0.2 on router R2. Router R2's NAT translation table shows two active translations. The configuration, therefore, seems to be partially working. However, no additional NAT translations can be set up.

This trouble ticket references the topology shown in Figure 10-6.

Because router R2 is the one configured to perform NAT, the following **show** and **debug** command output collects information about the NAT configuration of router R2. Initially, notice the output of the **show ip nat translations** command issued on router R2, as shown in Example 10-12.

Example 10-12 show ip nat translations *Command Output on Router R2*

```
R2#show ip nat translations
Pro Inside global     Inside local      Outside local      Outside global
icmp 172.16.1.2:7     192.168.0.11:7    10.4.4.4:7         10.4.4.4:7
icmp 172.16.2.1:512   192.168.1.50:512  10.1.3.2:512       10.1.3.2:512
```

The **debug ip nat** command is issued next. The output provided in Example 10-13 shows NAT translations as they occur.

Example 10-13 debug ip nat *Command Output on Router R2*

```
R2#debug ip nat
IP NAT debugging is on
*Mar  1 00:34:16.651: NAT*: s=10.4.4.4, d=172.16.1.2->192.168.0.11 [4092]
*Mar  1 00:34:16.711: NAT*: s=192.168.0.11->172.16.1.2, d=10.4.4.4 [4093]
*Mar  1 00:34:16.843: NAT*: s=10.4.4.4, d=172.16.1.2->192.168.0.11 [4093]
```

```
*Mar  1 00:34:16.939: NAT*: s=192.168.0.11->172.16.1.2, d=10.4.4.4 [4094]
*Mar  1 00:34:16.963: NAT*: s=192.168.1.50->172.16.2.1, d=10.1.3.2 [13977]
*Mar  1 00:34:17.115: NAT*: s=10.4.4.4, d=172.16.1.2->192.168.0.11 [4094]
*Mar  1 00:34:17.163: NAT*: s=192.168.0.11->172.16.1.2, d=10.4.4.4 [4095]
*Mar  1 00:34:17.187: NAT*: s=10.1.3.2, d=172.16.2.1->192.168.1.50 [13977]
*Mar  1 00:34:17.315: NAT*: s=10.4.4.4, d=172.16.1.2->192.168.0.11 [4095]
```

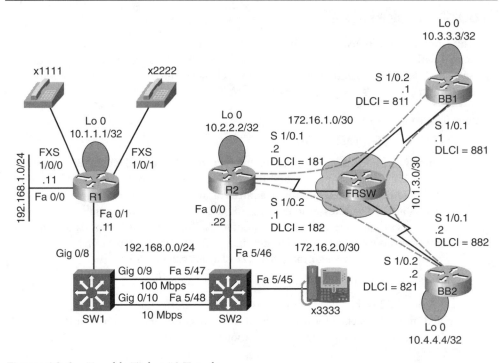

Figure 10-6   *Trouble Ticket #8 Topology*

The trouble ticket indicated that no more than two active translations can be supported at any time. To verify that symptom, Example 10-14 shows an attempt to send a ping from router R1. Notice that the ping response indicates that 10.4.4.4 is unreachable.

Example 10-14   *Attempting to Ping 10.4.4.4 from Router R1*

```
R1#ping 10.4.4.4

Type escape sequence to abort.
Sending 5, 100-byte ICMP Echos to 10.4.4.4, timeout is 2 seconds:
U.U.U
Success rate is 0 percent (0/5)
```

To determine whether the inability to ping 10.4.4.4 is a result of NAT or some other issue, the NAT translation table on router R2 is cleared with the **clear ip nat translation *** command. Then, with the NAT translation table of router R2 cleared, Example 10-15 shows the result of another ping from router R1 to 10.4.4.4. This time, the ping is successful.

Example 10-15   *Reattempting to Ping 10.4.4.4 from Router R1*

```
R1#ping 10.4.4.4

Type escape sequence to abort.
Sending 5, 100-byte ICMP Echos to 10.4.4.4, timeout is 2 seconds:
!!!!!
Success rate is 100 percent (5/5), round-trip min/avg/max = 72/137/240 ms
```

Example 10-16 shows the NAT translation table of router R2 after R1 performs a ping to 10.4.4.4.

Example 10-16   *NAT Translation Table of Router R2*

```
R2#show ip nat translations
Pro Inside global      Inside local       Outside local      Outside global
icmp 172.16.1.2:10     192.168.0.11:10    10.4.4.4:10        10.4.4.4:10
```

The output from the previous commands confirms that router R2 is capable of supporting only two simultaneous NAT translations. This symptom often indicates that a router's NAT pool (or pools in this case) is depleted, perhaps because the NAT configuration did not use the **overload** option in the **ip nat inside source** command. Recall that the **overload** option enables PAT, which allows multiple inside local IP addresses to share a common inside global IP address.

Example 10-17 shows the running configuration of router R2. Interestingly, both the **ip nat inside source** commands have the **overload** option, thus eliminating that as a potential cause for the reported issue.

Example 10-17   *Running Configuration of Router R2*

```
R2# show run
...OUTPUT OMITTED...
hostname R2
!
interface Loopback0
 ip address 10.2.2.2 255.255.255.255
!
interface FastEthernet0/0
 ip address 192.168.0.22 255.255.255.0
```

```
 ip nat inside
!
interface Serial1/0
 no ip address
 encapsulation frame-relay
!
interface Serial1/0.1 point-to-point
 ip address 172.16.1.2 255.255.255.252
 ip nat outside
 frame-relay interface-dlci 181
!
interface Serial1/0.2 point-to-point
 ip address 172.16.2.1 255.255.255.252
 ip nat outside
 ip virtual-reassembly
 frame-relay interface-dlci 182
!
router ospf 1
 network 0.0.0.0 255.255.255.255 area 0
!
ip nat translation max-entries 2
ip nat inside source list 1 interface Serial1/0.2 overload
ip nat inside source list 2 interface Serial1/0.1 overload
!
access-list 1 permit 192.168.1.0 0.0.0.255
access-list 2 permit 192.168.0.0 0.0.0.255
!
...OUTPUT OMITTED...
```

Based on the output of the previous **show** and **debug** commands, on a separate sheet of paper, write out what you believe to be the underlying issue and how you would resolve it.

Suggested Solution

In the running configuration of router R2, you might have noticed the **ip nat translation max-entries 2** command. This command limits the maximum number of NAT translations on router R2 to only two.

To resolve this issue, this configuration command is removed, as shown in Example 10-18.

Example 10-18   *Removing the ip nat translation max-entries 2 Command of Router R2*

```
R2#conf term
Enter configuration commands, one per line.  End with CNTL/Z.
R2(config)#no ip nat translation max-entries 2
R2(config)#end
```

To demonstrate that the removal of the **ip nat translation max-entries 2** command did indeed resolve the reported issue, three NAT translations were established across router R2, as confirmed in Example 10-19.

Example 10-19 *Confirming That Router R2 Supports Multiple NAT Translations*

```
R2#show ip nat translations
Pro Inside global      Inside local       Outside local      Outside global
icmp 172.16.1.2:12     192.168.0.11:12    10.4.4.4:12        10.4.4.4:12
icmp 172.16.2.1:13     192.168.1.11:13    10.3.3.3:13        10.3.3.3:13
icmp 172.16.2.1:512    192.168.1.50:512   10.1.3.2:512       10.1.3.2:512
```

Exam Preparation Tasks

Review All the Key Topics

Key Topic

Review the most important topics from inside the chapter, noted with the Key Topics icon in the outer margin of the page. Table 10-8 lists these key topics and the page numbers where each is found.

Table 10-8 *Key Topics for Chapter 10*

Key Topic Element	Description	Page Number
Table 10-2	Types of NAT	302
Table 10-3	Names of NAT IP addresses	303
Table 10-4	Classifying the NAT IP addresses in Figure 10-1	303
Example 10-1	Dynamic NAT sample configuration	304
List	Potential NAT troubleshooting issues	304
List	Order of operations for an interface	305
List	Common causes for a NAT issue	306
Table 10-5	Table 10-5 NAT troubleshooting commands	306
Steps	Obtaining an IP address from a DHCP server	309
Example 10-5	DHCP relay agent configuration	310
Table 10-6	DHCP message types	311
Example 10-6	DHCP client configuration	312
Example 10-7	DHCP server configuration	312
List	Potential DHCP troubleshooting issues	313
List	Information to collect when investigating a DHCP issue	314
Table 10-7	DHCP troubleshooting commands	314

Complete Tables and Lists from Memory

Print a copy of Appendix B, "Memory Tables" (found on the CD), or at least the section for this chapter, and complete the tables and lists from memory. Appendix C, "Memory Tables Answer Key," also on the CD, includes completed tables and lists to check your work.

Define Key Terms

Define the following key terms from this chapter, and check your answers in the Glossary:

Network Address Translation (NAT), static NAT, dynamic NAT, NAT overloading, overlapping NAT, Dynamic Host Configuration Protocol (DHCP)

Command Reference to Check Your Memory

This section includes the most important configuration and EXEC commands covered in this chapter. To determine how well you have memorized the commands as a side effect of your other studies, cover the left side of the table with a piece of paper; read the descriptions on the right side; and see whether you remember the command.

Table 10-9   *Chapter 10 Configuration Command Reference*

Command	Description
ip nat {**inside** | **outside**}	Interface configuration mode command that identifies an interface as an inside or outside NAT interface
ip nat pool *pool-name start-ip end-ip* {**netmask** *subnet-mask* | **prefix-length** *prefix-length*}	Global configuration mode command that defines a pool of inside global addresses into which inside local addresses can be translated
ip nat inside source list *access-list* **pool** *pool-name* [**overload**]	Global configuration mode command that associates an ACL defining an inside local address space with the specified pool of inside global addresses (Note: The overload keyword enables PAT, which allows multiple inside addresses to share a common outside address.)
ip nat translation max-entries *number*	Global configuration mode command that specifies the maximum number of entries permitted in the NAT table of a router
ip helper-address *ip-address*	Interface configuration mode command that causes an interface to forward specific received UDP broadcasts to the destination IP address, which can be either a specific IP address or a directed broadcast address
ip dhcp excluded-address *beginning-ip-add*ress [*ending-ip-address*]	Global configuration mode command that specifies a range of IP addresses not to be assigned to DHCP clients

continues

Table 10-9   *Chapter 10 Configuration Command Reference (Continued)*

Command	Description
ip dhcp pool *pool-name*	Global configuration mode command that creates a DHCP pool
network *network-address subnet-mask*	DHCP configuration mode command that identifies a subnet to be used by a DHCP pool
default-router *ip-address*	DHCP configuration mode command that specifies the IP address of a default gateway to be given to a DHCP client
dns-server *ip-address*	DHCP configuration mode command that configures the IP address of a DNS server to be given to a DHCP client
netbios-name-server *ip-address*	DHCP configuration mode command that defines the IP address of a WINS server to be given to a DHCP client
lease {*days hours minutes* | **infinite**}	DHCP configuration mode command that determines the duration of a DHCP lease given to a DHCP client
ip address *dhcp*	Interface configuration mode command that tells an interface to obtain its IP address via DHCP

Table 10-10   *Chapter 10 EXEC Command Reference*

Advantage	Limitation
clear ip nat translation *	Removes all dynamic entries from the NAT translation table of a router
show ip nat translations	Shows all entries in the NAT translation table of a router
show ip nat statistics	Displays NAT configuration and statistical information on a router, such as inside and outside interfaces, total translations, number of expired translations, inside address ACL, and outside address pool information
debug ip nat	Provides real-time information about NAT translations as they occur, including the IP address being translated and an IP identification number that can match packets in the output with packets captured with a protocol analyzer
show ip dhcp conflict	Displays any IP address conflicts that a router identifies, along with the method the router used to identify the conflicts (this is, via ping or gratuitous ARP)

Table 10-10 *Chapter 10 EXEC Command Reference   (Continued)*

Advantage	Limitation
show ip dhcp binding	Displays IP addresses assigned by an IOS DHCP server, their corresponding MAC addresses, and lease expirations
clear ip dhcp binding *	Releases all current DHCP leases
clear ip dhcp conflict *	Clears all currently identified DHCP conflicts
debug ip dhcp server events	Provides real-time information about DHCP address assignments and database updates
debug ip dhcp server packet	Displays real-time decodes of DHCP packets

This chapter covers the following subjects:

Voice Troubleshooting: This section introduces you to design and troubleshooting considerations that arise when adding voice traffic to a data network. Several protocols are involved when a Cisco IP Phone registers with its call agent to place and receive voice calls. This section reviews the function of these protocols along with recommendations for troubleshooting voice issues. One of the major troubleshooting targets for voice networks involves quality of service. Therefore, this section concludes by providing an overview of quality of service (QoS) configuration, verification, and troubleshooting commands.

Video Troubleshooting: This section considers video traffic in an IP network, including unique design and troubleshooting challenges. Also, unlike voice, video-based networks often rely on an infrastructure that supports IP multicasting. Because multicasting has not been addressed in any depth thus far in this book, this section serves as a primer to multicast technologies. Included in this primer are commands used to configure, monitor, and troubleshoot multicast networks. Finally, this section considers common video troubleshooting issues and recommends resolutions for those issues.

Trouble Tickets: Unified Communications: This section presents you with two trouble tickets focused on unified communications. You are presented with a topology used by both trouble tickets, in addition to a collection of **show** command output. For each trouble ticket, you are challenged to hypothesize how to correct the reported issue. You can also compare your solutions with suggested solutions.

CHAPTER 11

IP Communications Troubleshooting

Data networks, as the name suggests, were once relegated to being a transmission medium for data; however, network designers have seen the wisdom in combining voice, video, and data on the same network. This type of network, called a *converged network*, can be far more cost effective than maintaining separate networks for each of these media types. This chapter considers the troubleshooting of both voice and video networks.

This chapter begins by introducing voice networks, along with a discussion of how adding voice to a network impacts design decisions. You are also introduced to the roles played by a variety of protocols that allow a Cisco IP Phone to place and receive calls. Common troubleshooting issues for voice networks are addressed, one of which is quality of service.

Because voice traffic is latency-sensitive, the underlying network needs to be able to recognize voice traffic and treat it with high priority. Although a full discussion of quality of service technologies is well beyond the scope of the TSHOOT curriculum, this chapter does provide fundamental configuration, verification, and troubleshooting commands that can get you started in your configuration or troubleshooting of quality of service configurations.

Other than voice, another aspect of IP communications involves sending video over IP networks. For example, you might have an IP-based video conference system, or you might have a video server that sends out a video stream to multiple recipients. This chapter introduces you to some of the video solutions you might encounter, along with unique design and troubleshooting challenges that accompany video networks.

Interestingly, many video networks heavily rely on IP multicast technologies. Therefore, this chapter offers you a mini-course on multicasting, which discusses the theory, configuration, monitoring, and troubleshooting of multicasting.

This chapter concludes with two trouble tickets focused on unified communications. The first trouble ticket addresses an IP phone registration issue, whereas the second trouble ticket addresses a quality of service issue.

"Do I Know This Already?" Quiz

The "Do I Know This Already?" quiz helps you determine your level of knowledge of this chapter's topics before you begin. Table 11-1 details the major topics discussed in this chapter and their corresponding quiz questions.

Table 11-1   *"Do I Know This Already?" Section-to-Question Mapping*

Foundation Topics Section	Questions
Voice Troubleshooting	1–5
Video Troubleshooting	6–9

1. What IP telephony component provides translation between VoIP and non-VoIP networks?

   a. Gatekeeper

   b. Gateway

   c. Call agent

   d. MCU

2. What protocol does a Cisco Catalyst switch use to inform an attached Cisco IP Phone of the VLAN to which the phone belongs?

   a. NTP

   b. DHCP

   c. CDP

   d. TFTP

3. What DHCP option corresponds to the IP address of a TFTP server?

   a. Option 66

   b. Option 80

   c. Option 110

   d. Option 150

4. Which four of the following are common voice troubleshooting targets? (Choose the four best answers.)

   a. Security

   b. IP services

   c. Power

   d. NAT

   e. QoS

5. Identify three valid types of the Cisco AutoQoS feature. (Choose the three best answers.)

   a. AutoQoS Enterprise on a Cisco Catalyst switch

   b. AutoQoS VoIP on a Cisco Catalyst switch

   c. AutoQoS VoIP on a Cisco IOS router

   d. AutoQoS Enterprise on a Cisco IOS router

6. Which video conferencing product offers CD-quality audio and high definition video? (Choose the best answer.)

    a. Cisco Presence Server

    b. Cisco Unified Video Advantage

    c. Cisco TelePresence

    d. Cisco Video Advantage

7. What is the Cisco recommended maximum one-way delay for a video surveillance application?

    a. 150ms

    b. 200ms

    c. 214ms

    d. 500ms

8. What command could be used to display a router's IP multicast routing table?

    a. show ip mroute

    b. show multicast route

    c. show ip route multicast

    d. show mroute

9. Which four of the following are common video troubleshooting targets? (Choose the four best answers.)

    a. Bandwidth

    b. Pervasiveness of video applications

    c. NTP

    d. QoS

    e. Multicast

Foundation Topics

Voice Troubleshooting

Modern enterprise network designs need to support the transmission of voice traffic. This voice traffic can come from both analog phones (much like the phones typically found in homes) and IP phones, which are Ethernet devices that transmit voice IP packets. Because the analog phones cannot generate IP packets, they connect to analog gateways (such as Cisco routers), which convert the analog waveforms into IP packets.

The term *Voice over IP* (VoIP) is used to describe the transmission of voice over an IP network using voice-enabled routers. However, the term *IP telephony* refers to the use of IP phones and a call-processing server (for example, Cisco Unified Communications Manager). More recently, Cisco began using the term *Unified Communications*, which encompasses more than just voice. Unified communications includes a collection of applications and technologies that enhance user collaboration. This section, however, focuses on the IP telephony component of unified communications.

Overview of IP Telephony

An IP telephony network not only duplicates the features offered in traditional corporate Private Branch Exchange (PBX) systems, but IP telephony expands on those features. Figure 11-1 shows the basic components of an IP telephony network, which are described in greater detail in the list that follows:

Key Topic

■ **IP phone:** An IP phone provides IP voice to the desktop.

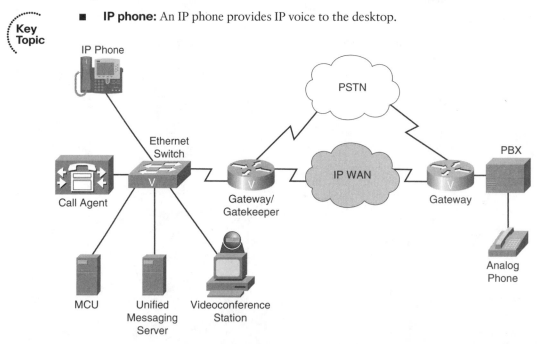

Figure 11-1 *IP Telephony Components*

- **Gatekeeper:** A gatekeeper provides call admission control (CAC), bandwidth control and management, and address translation features.

- **Gateway:** A gateway provides translation between VoIP and non-VoIP networks, such as the *Public Switched Telephone Network* (PSTN). A gateway also provides physical access for local analog and digital voice devices, such as telephones, fax machines, key sets, and PBXs.

- **Multipoint control unit (MCU):** An MCU mixes audio and/or video streams, thus allowing participants in multiple locations to attend the same conference.

- **Call agent:** A call agent provides call control for IP phones, Call Admission Control (CAC), bandwidth control and management, and address translation. Although a call agent could be server-based, Cisco also supports a router-based call agent, known as *Cisco Unified Communications Manager Express* (UCME).

- **Application server:** An application server provides services such as voice mail, unified messaging, and presence information (which can show the availability of another user).

- **Videoconference station:** A videoconference station provides access for end-user participation in videoconferencing. The videoconference station contains a video capture device for video input and a microphone for audio input. The user can view video streams and hear audio originating at a remote user station. Cisco targets its Cisco Unified Video Advantage product at desktop videoconferencing applications.

Design Considerations for Voice Networks

Successfully transmitting voice traffic over an IP network involves more than merely superimposing voice packets on an existing data network. Voice traffic needs to be treated in a special way, where it has higher priority than many other traffic types. Other design considerations include the availability of the voice network, securing the voice network, and a collection of other voice-related services. First, consider voice quality.

Quality of Service for Voice Traffic

Unlike much data traffic, voice traffic is highly latency-sensitive and drop-sensitive. Therefore, when a network experiences congestion due to a lack of bandwidth, the following symptoms can occur:

- **Delay:** *Delay* is the time required for a packet to travel from its source to its destination. You might have witnessed delay on the evening news, when the news anchor is talking via satellite with a foreign news correspondent. Due to the satellite delay, the conversation begins to feel unnatural.

- **Jitter:** *Jitter* is the uneven arrival of packets. For example, in a voice conversation, packet #1 arrives. Then, 20 minutes later, packet #2 arrives. After another 70 minutes, packet #3 arrives, and then packet #4 arrives 20 minutes behind packet #3. This variation in arrival times is not necessarily resulting in dropped packets. However, this jitter can make the conversation sound as if packets are being dropped.

■ **Drops:** Packet drops occur when a link is congested and a buffer overflows. Some types of traffic, such as UDP traffic (for example, voice and video traffic), are not retransmitted if packets are dropped.

Fortunately, Cisco offers a collection of quality of service (QoS) features that can recognize high-priority traffic (for example, voice and video) and treat that special traffic in a special way. To effectively configure QoS in a network, you should consider how traffic is treated end-to-end through the network. This implies not only configuring QoS on WAN routers, but also configuring QoS on multiple switches and routers along the traffic's path.

For example, even a wiring closet switch could benefit from a QoS configuration. Cisco recommends marking traffic as close to the source as possible. However, you typically do not want end users setting their own priority markings. Therefore, you can use Cisco Catalyst switches to create a *trust boundary*, which is a point in the network that does not trust incoming markings. An exception to having a wiring closet switch acting as a trust boundary would be a Cisco IP Phone connected to the switch. Because a Cisco IP Phone performs priority marking for voice traffic, you can extend the trust boundary to the phone.

High Availability for Voice Traffic

PBX administrators often boast about their telephone system having the *five nines* of availability, meaning that their network is up 99.999 percent of the time. This uptime percentage equates to only five minutes of down time per year. Unfortunately, a common perception about data networks is that they are not nearly as reliable. As a result, many organizations are reluctant to replace their PBX and its track record of high availability with a voice system that relies on what is perceived to be a less reliable data network.

To combat this somewhat-deserved stigma, today's network designers must focus on the redundancy and reliability of their designs. Fortunately, by using data components (for example, routers and switches) with a high mean time between failures (MTBF) and including redundant links with fast converging protocols, today's networks can also approach the five nines of availability.

Securing Voice Traffic

Similar to data traffic, voice traffic needs to be protected as it flows across a network. Beyond protecting voice traffic with traditional precautions such as firewalling, protecting voice traffic from potential eavesdroppers might include the following:

■ Separating voice and data traffic into different VLANs

■ Encrypting and authenticating voice media packets

■ Encrypting and authenticating voice signaling traffic

Other Services for Voice Traffic

In addition to QoS, availability, and security, introducing voice traffic into a data network brings with it several other design considerations:

Key Topic

■ **In-Line Power:** A Cisco IP Phone requires -48 Volts of direct current (DC) to boot up and operate. This voltage can be provided by an external power brick, which connects into a wall power outlet and converts the wall outlet's 120 Volts of alternating current (AC) into the phone's required -48 VDC. Alternately, power can be provided by a Cisco Catalyst switch. Specifically, the switch can apply the required voltage across the same leads used for Ethernet (that is, pins 1, 2, 3, and 6 in an RJ-45 connector). One approach for in-line power (also known as *Power over Ethernet* [*PoE*]) is a Cisco-proprietary approach, which uses a Fast Link Pulse (FLP) to determine if a switch port is connected to a device needing power. An industry-standard approach to providing in-line power, however, is IEEE 802.3af. The 802.3af approach looks for a 25,000 Ohm resistance attached to a switch port. The presence of this resistance on a switch port indicates that the port should provide power to the attached device. From a design and troubleshooting perspective, you should confirm that a Cisco Catalyst switch and its attached Cisco IP Phones support the same type of in-line power.

- **DHCP:** Chapter 10, "IP Services Troubleshooting," introduced DHCP operation and how an end station could obtain IP address information via DHCP. Beyond IP address, subnet mask, DNS server, and default gateway information, a Cisco IP Phone can also obtain via DHCP the IP address (that is, DHCP option 150) or DNS name (that is, DHCP option 66) of a TFTP server.

- **TFTP:** A Cisco IP Phone communicates with a TFTP server to receive some or all of its configuration information, in addition to firmware updates. This TFTP server might be a Cisco Unified Communications Manager (UCM) server if that server is acting as a call-processing agent for the Cisco IP Phone. Alternately, a Cisco IOS router might be acting as the TFTP server, if that router is configured as a Cisco UCME call agent.

- **NTP:** Cisco IP Phones can also benefit from Network Time Protocol (NTP). Most models of Cisco IP Phones obtain their time information from their call agent. This time is then displayed on the phone. However, having accurate time information goes well beyond the convenience of having the local time displayed on a phone. For example, a call agent might be configured to permit or deny certain calls (for example, international calls) based on office hours.

- **CDP:** Cisco Discovery Protocol (CDP) is used by a Cisco Catalyst switch to inform an attached Cisco IP Phone of the phone's VLAN.

- **VLAN:** Many Cisco IP Phones include a PC port, which allows a PC to connect to the Cisco IP Phone for its Ethernet network connectivity. The Cisco IP Phone then connects to a Cisco Catalyst switch in a wiring closet. To keep the voice and data traffic separate, the Cisco IP Phone can place the phone's voice traffic and the PC's data traffic in different VLANs. Traffic from these two VLANs is sent to the Cisco Catalyst switch over a single IEEE 802.1Q trunk connection, as seen in Figure 11-2. The voice VLAN is often referred to as an *auxiliary* VLAN, and the data VLAN is the native VLAN (that is, an untagged VLAN) on the 802.1Q trunk. Even though this connection between a Cisco IP Phone and the Cisco Catalyst switch is a trunk connection, many Cisco Catalyst switches allow the switch port to be configured as a multi-VLAN access port, rather than a trunk port. Specifically, even though a single connection supporting more than one VLAN is typically referred to as a *trunk connection*, a multi-VLAN access port is an access port that can send and receive untagged traffic (that is, the native VLAN traffic) in addition to traffic from an auxiliary VLAN.

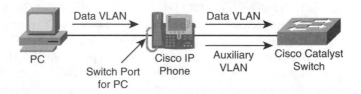

Figure 11-2   *IP Voice and Data VLAN Separation*

Cisco IP Phone Boot-Up Process

Understanding the steps involved in a Cisco IP Phone booting up can aid in troubleshooting a Cisco IP Phone that does not successfully register with its call agent. Recall that a call agent could be a Cisco UCM server or a Cisco UCME router. These call agents could also act as DHCP and TFTP servers.

As an example of a Cisco IP Phone's boot-up process, consider the steps illustrated in Figure 11-3. Assumptions for this example include the following:

■ The call agent is a UCME router.

■ The Cisco Catalyst switch and Cisco IP Phone both support the 802.3af PoE standard.

■ The UCME router is also acting as a DHCP server and TFTP server.

■ DNS services are not being used. Therefore, a Cisco IP Phone will obtain the IP address of the TFTP server via DHCP rather than the TFTP server's DNS name.

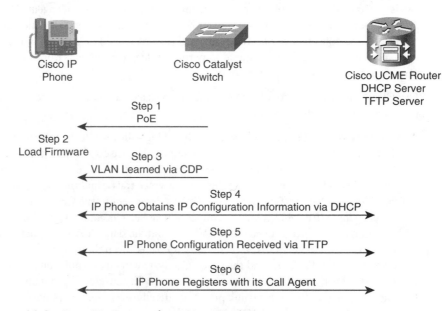

Figure 11-3   *Boot-Up Process for a Cisco IP Phone*

■ The Cisco IP Phone is using Skinny Client Control Protocol (SCCP) as its signaling protocol, as opposed to Session Initiation Protocol (SIP).

The following is the phone boot-up process:

Step 1.   The Cisco IP Phone receives power via PoE.

Step 2.   The Cisco IP Phone loads its firmware from its flash storage.

Step 3.   The Cisco Catalyst switch informs the Cisco IP Phone of the phone's VLAN.

Step 4.   The Cisco IP Phone requests and receives its IP configuration information (including DHCP option 150, which is the IP address of a TFTP server) via DHCP.

Step 5.   The Cisco IP Phone requests and receives a portion of its configuration information (including the IP address of the phone's call agent) from its TFTP server.

Step 6.   The Cisco IP Phone registers with its call agent and is now able to place and receive calls. Note that the protocol that carries voice calls between the two IP phones is *Real-time Transport Protocol* (RTP).

Common Voice Troubleshooting Issues

Because Cisco IP Phones rely on their underlying data network for communication, a troubleshooting issue on the data network could impact phone operation. Data networking troubleshooting targets should therefore be considered when troubleshooting a reported voice issue. Additionally, as a reference, Table 11-2 offers a collection of common voice troubleshooting targets and recommended solutions.

Table 11-2 *Common Voice Troubleshooting Targets*

Voice Troubleshooting Target	Recommended Solutions
IP Services	Check the configuration of the following IP services: CDP, DHCP, TFTP, NTP.
QoS	Check QoS configurations on routers and switches to confirm that voice traffic is being correctly classified, is being allocated a minimum amount of bandwidth, and is given priority treatment.
Security	Confirm voice and data VLAN separation. Additionally, check the encryption and authentication configurations for voice media and voice signaling traffic.
Power	In a modular Cisco Catalyst switch chassis (for example, a Cisco Catalyst 6500 chassis), the switch's power supply might not be sufficient to provide PoE to all attached Cisco IP Phones. Therefore, check the switch's power capacity and current utilization level.

Overview of Quality of Service

One of the biggest potential troubleshooting targets for voice traffic involves QoS. Although a comprehensive treatment of QoS is a study in itself and beyond the scope of the TSHOOT curriculum, this section introduces you to basic QoS configuration principles and commands used to monitor and troubleshoot a QoS configuration.

First, understand that QoS can classify traffic into different traffic classes. Cisco recommends that this classification be performed as close to the source as possible. When the traffic is classified, Cisco also recommends marking the traffic with a priority marking. One such marking is *Differentiated Services Code Point* (DSCP). A DSCP marking uses the six left-most bits in the Type of Service (ToS) byte in an IPv4 header. These six bits can be used to create as many as 64 different DSCP values (in the range 0–63). The Internet Engineering Task Force (IETF) selected a subset of these values and assigned names to those values. These names are called *Per-Hop Behaviors* (PHB), because these DSCP values can influence how traffic is treated at each hop (that is, router hop or switch hop) along the path from the traffic's source to its destination.

As an example, the DSCP numerical value of 46 also has the PHB name of *Expedited Forwarding* (EF). Cisco IOS accepts either DSCP numerical values or DSCP PHB names. A PHB of EF is the DSCP value that Cisco recommends you use to mark voice packets (specifically, voice payload traffic, not voice signaling traffic). Fortunately, a Cisco IP Phone, by default, marks voice frames leaving the phone with a PHB of EF. Therefore, if routers or switches in the topology are configured to classify traffic based on DSCP markings, they can easily recognize voice packets sourced from a Cisco IP Phone. If, however, you have analog phones in your network connected into voice gateways, realize that those voice packets are marked with a default DSCP value of zero (that is, a DSCP PHB of Default). Therefore, you might want to configure that voice gateway to mark those voice packets with a DSCP value of EF before transmitting those packets out of the router.

Once traffic has been classified and marked, routers and switches can examine those markings and make decisions based on those markings (for example, forwarding decisions or dropping decisions).

MQC

Cisco IOS offers a powerful three-step approach to QoS configuration, as illustrated in Figure 11-4. This approach is known as the *Modular Quality of Service Command Line Interface*, or *MQC* for short.

The following are the steps for the Modular Qos CLI:

Step 1. The first step of MQC is to create class maps, which categorize traffic types. The following command enters you into class map configuration mode:

```
Router(config)#class-map [match-any  match-all] class-name
```

Step 2. Once in class-map configuration mode, you can specify multiple match statements to match traffic, and all traffic meeting the criteria you specified with the **match** commands is categorized under the class map. If multiple match statements are specified, by default, all match statements must be met before a packet is classified by the class map. However, if you use the **match-any**

option, if any individual match condition is met, the packet is classified by the class map. After the class maps are defined, the first step of MQC is complete.

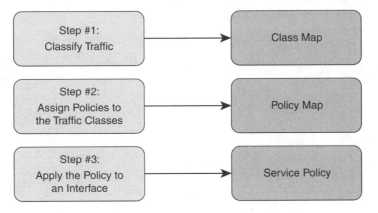

Figure 11-4 *Modular QoS CLI*

Step 3.   The second step is to create a policy map that defines how the classified traffic is to be treated. To enter policy map configuration mode, issue the following command:

```
Router(config)#policy-map policy-name
```

Step 4.   From policy map configuration mode, enter policy map class configuration mode, with the following command:

```
Router(config-pmap)#class class-name
```

Step 5.   From policy map class configuration mode, you can assign QoS policies to traffic classified by each class map. You might also have a situation where a packet matches more than one class map. In that case, the first class map identified in the policy map is used. Up to 256 class maps can be associated with a single policy map.

Step 6.   Finally, in the third step of MQC, the policy map is applied to an interface, Frame Relay map class, or ATM virtual circuit with the following command:

```
Router(config-if)#service-policy {input | output} policy-map-name
```

Example 11-1 provides an MQC sample configuration that classifies various types of e-mail traffic (for example, SMTP, IMAP, and POP3) into one class map. The KaZaa protocol, which is frequently used for music downloads, is placed in another class map. Voice over IP traffic is classified by yet another class map. Then, the policy map assigns bandwidth allocations or limitations to these traffic types.

Example 11-1 *MQC Sample Configuration*

```
R1# conf term
R1(config)# class-map match-any EMAIL
R1(config-cmap)# match protocol pop3
R1(config-cmap)# match protocol imap
R1(config-cmap)# match protocol smtp
```

```
R1(config-cmap)# exit
R1(config)# class-map MUSIC
R1(config-cmap)# match protocol kazaa2
R1(config-cmap)# exit
R1(config)# class-map VOICE
R1(config-cmap)# match protocol rtp audio
R1(config-cmap)# exit
R1(config)# policy-map TSHOOT-EXAMPLE
R1(config-pmap)# class EMAIL
R1(config-pmap-c)# bandwidth 128
R1(config-pmap-c)# exit
R1(config-pmap)# class MUSIC
R1(config-pmap-c)# police 32000
R1(config-pmap-c)# exit
R1(config-pmap)# class VOICE
R1(config-pmap-c)# priority 256
R1(config-pmap-c)# exit
R1(config-pmap)# exit
R1(config)# interface serial 0/1
R1(config-if)# service-policy output TSHOOT-EXAMPLE
```

Notice that the policy map named **TSHOOT-EXAMPLE** makes at least 128 kbps of bandwidth available to e-mail traffic. However, KaZaa version 2 traffic has its bandwidth limited to 32 kbps. Voice packets not only have access to 256 kbps of bandwidth, but they receive priority treatment, meaning that they are sent first (that is, ahead of other traffic), up to a 256-kbps limit.

The next logical question is, "What happens to all the traffic that was not classified by one of the configured class maps?" Interestingly, Cisco created a class map named **class-default**, which categorizes any traffic not matched by one of the defined class maps.

Finally in the example, the policy map is applied in the outbound direction on the Serial 0/1 interface.

Table 11-3 provides a listing of verification and troubleshooting commands for MQC configurations.

Key Topic

Table 11-3   *MQC Verification Commands*

Command	Description
show class-map [*class-map-name*]	Used to view what a class map is matching.
show policy-map [*policy-map-name*]	Used to view the policy applied to the classes within a policy map.
show policy-map interface *interface-identifier* [input	output]	Used to view policy map statistics for packets crossing a specific interface.

Example 11-2 provides sample output from the **show class-map** command. The output shows each class map, including the default class map of **class-default**. You can also see how traffic is classified in each class. For example, the **EMAIL** class is using **match-any** logic, where a packet is classified in the class if it is POP3, IMAP, or SMTP.

Example 11-2   show class-map *Command Output*

```
R1# show class-map
 Class Map match-any class-default (id 0)
   Match any

 Class Map match-all MUSIC (id 2)
   Match protocol kazaa2

 Class Map match-any EMAIL (id 1)
   Match protocol pop3
   Match protocol imap
   Match protocol smtp

 Class Map match-all VOICE (id 3)
   Match protocol rtp audio
```

Example 11-3 provides sample output from the **show policy-map** command. The output shows how each class of traffic is to be treated. For example, the **EMAIL** class has access to at least 128 kbps of bandwidth if it requires that much and more if it needs it and more is available. The **MUSIC** class of traffic has a maximum bandwidth utilization limit of 32 kbps. If traffic exceeds that 32-kbps limit, that excess traffic is dropped. The **VOICE** class of traffic guarantees the voice traffic has access to as much as 256 kbps of bandwidth if that much is required. This traffic is configured to have priority treatment, meaning this traffic is sent ahead of other traffic types. However, traffic from this class is not allowed to exceed 256 kbps, to prevent protocol starvation of other traffic classes.

Example 11-3   show policy-map *Command Output*

```
R1# show policy-map
  Policy Map TSHOOT-EXAMPLE
    Class EMAIL
      Bandwidth 128 (kbps) Max Threshold 64 (packets)
    Class MUSIC
     police cir 32000 bc 1500
        conform-action transmit
        exceed-action drop
    Class VOICE
```

```
      Strict Priority
      Bandwidth 256 (kbps) Burst 6400 (Bytes)
```

Example 11-4 provides sample output from the **show policy-map interface** *interface-identifier* command. The output in this example is from interface Serial 0/1. The output shows how traffic is classified in each class and how the policy map is treating each traffic class. Additionally, the output shows packet and byte counts for traffic matching each class.

Example 11-4 show policy-map interface interface-identifier *Command Output*

```
R1# show policy-map interface serial0/1
 Serial0/1

  Service-policy output: TSHOOT-EXAMPLE

    Class-map: EMAIL (match-any)
      0 packets, 0 bytes
      5 minute offered rate 0 bps, drop rate 0 bps
      Match: protocol pop3
        0 packets, 0 bytes
        5 minute rate 0 bps
      Match: protocol imap
        0 packets, 0 bytes
        5 minute rate 0 bps
      Match: protocol smtp
        0 packets, 0 bytes
        5 minute rate 0 bps
      Queueing
        Output Queue: Conversation 265
        Bandwidth 128 (kbps) Max Threshold 64 (packets)
        (pkts matched/bytes matched) 0/0
        (depth/total drops/no-buffer drops) 0/0/0

    Class-map: MUSIC (match-all)
      0 packets, 0 bytes
      5 minute offered rate 0 bps, drop rate 0 bps
      Match: protocol kazaa2
      police:
          cir 32000 bps, bc 1500 bytes
        conformed 0 packets, 0 bytes; actions:
          transmit
        exceeded 0 packets, 0 bytes; actions:
          drop
        conformed 0 bps, exceed 0 bps
```

```
    Class-map: VOICE (match-all)
      0 packets, 0 bytes
      5 minute offered rate 0 bps, drop rate 0 bps
      Match: protocol rtp audio
      Queueing
        Strict Priority
        Output Queue: Conversation 264
        Bandwidth 256 (kbps) Burst 6400 (Bytes)
        (pkts matched/bytes matched) 0/0
        (total drops/bytes drops) 0/0
    Class-map: class-default (match-any)
      23 packets, 1715 bytes
      5 minute offered rate 0 bps, drop rate 0 bps
      Match: any
```

AutoQoS

Optimizing a QoS configuration for VoIP can be a daunting task. Fortunately, Cisco added a feature called *AutoQoS VoIP* to many of its router and switch platforms to generate router-based or switch-based QoS configurations designed to ensure voice quality.

A few years after introducing AutoQoS VoIP, Cisco introduced AutoQoS Enterprise, which can automatically generate a QoS configuration on a router that seeks to provide appropriate QoS parameters for all of an enterprise's traffic types (that is, not just voice traffic).

Table 11-4 summarizes the platform support for these two versions of AutoQoS.

Table 11-4   *AutoQoS Platform Support*

Key Topic

AutoQoS Version	Platform Support
AutoQoS VoIP	Routers Catalyst Switches
AutoQoS Enterprise	Routers

First, consider the configuration of AutoQoS VoIP on a router. In interface configuration mode (or Frame Relay DLCI configuration mode), AutoQoS can be enabled with the following command:

```
Router(config-if)# auto qos voip [trust] [fr-atm]
```

The **trust** option indicates that Auto QoS should classify voice traffic based on DSCP markings, instead of using Network-Based Application Recognition (NBAR). The **fr-atm** option allows Frame Relay Discard Eligible (DE) markings to be converted into ATM Cell Loss Priority (CLP) markings, and vice versa.

Before enabling AutoQoS on a router interface, consider the following prerequisites:

Key Topic

- CEF must be enabled.

- A QoS policy must not be currently attached to the interface.

- The correct bandwidth should be configured on the interface.

- An IP address must be configured on an interface if its speed is equal to or less than 768 kbps.

Note that the interface's bandwidth determines which AutoQoS features are enabled. If an interface's bandwidth is equal to or less than 768 kbps, it is considered to be a low-speed interface. On a low-speed interface, AutoQoS might configure Multilink PPP (MLP), which requires an IP address on the physical interface. AutoQoS takes that IP address from the physical interface and uses it for a virtual multilink interface it creates.

To verify that AutoQoS is configured for a router interface, you can use the following command:

```
Router# show auto qos voip [interface interface-identifier]
```

This command displays global and interface (or optionally, only interface) configuration mode commands added by the AutoQoS VoIP feature.

Example 11-5 shows a sample of configuring and verifying AutoQoS VoIP on a router.

Example 11-5   *Configuring and Verifying AutoQoS VoIP on a Router*

```
R1# conf term
R1(config)# int s0/0
R1(config-if)# auto qos voip
R1(config-if)# end
R1# show auto qos
 !
  ip access-list extended AutoQoS-VoIP-RTCP
   permit udp any any range 16384 32767
 !
  ip access-list extended AutoQoS-VoIP-Control
   permit tcp any any eq 1720
   permit tcp any any range 11000 11999
   permit udp any any eq 2427
   permit tcp any any eq 2428
   permit tcp any any range 2000 2002
   permit udp any any eq 1719
   permit udp any any eq 5060
 !
  class-map match-any AutoQoS-VoIP-RTP-UnTrust
   match protocol rtp audio
   match access-group name AutoQoS-VoIP-RTCP
```

```
!
 class-map match-any AutoQoS-VoIP-Control-UnTrust
   match access-group name AutoQoS-VoIP-Control
!
 class-map match-any AutoQoS-VoIP-Remark
   match ip dscp ef
   match ip dscp cs3
    match ip dscp af31
!
  policy-map AutoQoS-Policy-UnTrust
   class AutoQoS-VoIP-RTP-UnTrust
    priority percent 70
    set dscp ef
   class AutoQoS-VoIP-Control-UnTrust
    bandwidth percent 5
    set dscp af31
   class AutoQoS-VoIP-Remark
    set dscp default
   class class-default
    fair-queue

  encapsulation ppp
  no fair-queue
  ppp multilink
  ppp multilink group 2001100114
!
 interface Multilink2001100114
  bandwidth 128
  ip address 10.1.1.1 255.255.255.0
  service-policy output AutoQoS-Policy-UnTrust
  ppp multilink
  ppp multilink fragment delay 10
  ppp multilink interleave
  ppp multilink group 2001100114
  ip rtp header-compression iphc-format
!
 rmon event 33333 log trap AutoQoS description "AutoQoS SNMP traps for Voice
   Drops" owner AutoQoS
 rmon alarm 33334 cbQosCMDropBitRate.1271.1273 30 absolute rising-threshold 1
   33333 falling-threshold 0 owner AutoQoS
```

Next, consider the configuration of AutoQoS VoIP on some models of Cisco Catalyst switches (for example, most new models of Cisco IOS-based Catalyst switches). To configure AutoQoS on these platforms, issue one of the following commands from interface configuration mode:

```
Switch(config-if)# auto qos voip trust
```

This command configures the interface to trust Class of Service (CoS) markings (that is, Layer 2 QoS priority markings on an Ethernet connection) for classifying VoIP traffic.

```
Switch(config-if)# auto qos voip cisco-phone
```

This command configures the interface to trust CoS markings only if those markings came from an attached Cisco IP Phone. CDP is used to detect an attached Cisco IP Phone.

Example 11-6 shows a sample of configuring and verifying AutoQoS VoIP on a switch.

Example 11-6   *Configuring and Verifying AutoQoS VoIP on a Switch*

```
Cat3550# conf term
Cat3550(config)# int gig 0/1
Cat3550(config-if)# auto qos voip cisco-phone
Cat3550(config-if)# end
Cat3550# show run
Building configuration...
...OUTPUT OMITTED...
mls qos map cos-dscp 0 8 16 24 32 46 48 56
mls qos
!
interface GigabitEthernet0/1
 mls qos trust device cisco-phone
 mls qos trust cos
auto qos voip cisco-phone
 wrr-queue bandwidth 10 20 70 1
 wrr-queue queue-limit 50 25 15 10
 wrr-queue cos-map 1 0 1
 wrr-queue cos-map 2 2 4
 wrr-queue cos-map 3 3 6 7
 wrr-queue cos-map 4 5
 priority-queue out
 spanning-tree portfast
...OUTPUT OMITTED...
```

Next, consider the configuration of AutoQoS Enterprise. This version of AutoQoS has the same collection of prerequisites shown earlier for AutoQoS VoIP. However, unlike AutoQoS VoIP, AutoQoS Enterprise targets all known applications on an enterprise network. Fortunately, you do not have to specify the individual applications and protocols you want to support. AutoQoS Enterprise instead dynamically learns the applications and protocols seen on an interface. Cisco recommends that this learning process, called the *discovery phase*, be conducted for at least two or three days. During this time, a router can use existing DSCP values (that is, Layer 3 QoS markings) or NBAR to classify traffic seen on an interface. Traffic can be classified into as many as ten classes by AutoQoS Enterprise. The following interface configuration mode command is issued to begin the discovery phase of AutoQoS Enterprise:

```
Router(config-if)# auto discovery qos [trust]
```

The **trust** keyword instructs the router to classify traffic based on existing DSCP markings, as opposed to using NBAR.

After the discovery phase runs for at least two or three days, you can issue the **show auto discovery qos** command to see what traffic has been classified and what behavior is specified in the recommended policy.

After examining the output of the **show auto discovery qos** command, if you are satisfied with the proposed configuration, you can apply the configuration by issuing the **auto qos** command in interface configuration mode for the interface that performed the discovery phase.

Example 11-7 shows these commands being issued for the Fast Ethernet 0/0 interface on a router named R4. The output of the **show auto discovery qos** command shows the ten classes of traffic that could be populated by the AutoQoS Enterprise feature, as indicated by the highlighted output.

Example 11-7   *Configuring AutoQoS Enterprise*

```
R4# conf term
R4(config)# int fa0/0
R4(config-if)# auto discovery qos
R4(config-if)# end
R4# show auto discovery qos
FastEthernet0/0
 AutoQoS Discovery enabled for applications
 Discovery up time: 1 minutes, 7 seconds
AutoQoS Class information:
 Class Voice:
  Recommended Minimum Bandwidth: 5 Kbps/<1% (PeakRate)
  Detected applications and data:
  Application/        AverageRate       PeakRate            Total
  Protocol            (kbps/%)          (kbps/%)            (bytes)
  ------              ------            ----                ------
  rtp audio           1/<1              5/<1                10138
 Class Interactive Video:
  No data found.
 Class Signaling:
  Recommended Minimum Bandwidth: 0 Kbps/0% (AverageRate)
  Detected applications and data:
  Application/        AverageRate       PeakRate            Total
  Protocol            (kbps/%)          (kbps/%)            (bytes)
  ------              ------            -----               ------
  skinny              0/0               0/0                 2218
 Class Streaming Video:
  No data found.
 Class Transactional:
   No data found.
```

```
Class Bulk:
  No data found.
Class Scavenger:
  No data found.
Class Management:
  No data found.
Class Routing:
  Recommended Minimum Bandwidth: 0 Kbps/0% (AverageRate)
  Detected applications and data:
  Application/      AverageRate       PeakRate          Total
  Protocol          (kbps/%)          (kbps/%)          (bytes)
  ---------         ---------         ---------         ---------
  eigrp             0/0               0/0               1110
  icmp              0/0               0/0               958
Class Best Effort:
  Current Bandwidth Estimation: 44 Kbps/<1% (AverageRate)
  Detected applications and data:
  Application/      AverageRate       PeakRate          Total
  Protocol          (kbps/%)          (kbps/%)          (bytes)
  ---------         ---------         ---------         ---------
  http              44/<1             121/1             372809
  unknowns          0/0               0/0               232


Suggested AutoQoS Policy for the current uptime:
 !
class-map match-any AutoQoS-Voice-Fa0/0
  match protocol rtp audio
 !
 policy-map AutoQoS-Policy-Fa0/0
  class AutoQoS-Voice-Fa0/0
   priority percent 1
   set dscp ef
  class class-default
   fair-queue
R4# conf term
R4(config)# int fa 0/0
R4(config-if)# auto qos
R4(config-if)# end
R4#
```

Video Troubleshooting

Like voice traffic, video traffic is latency-sensitive. Therefore, many of the same design and troubleshooting considerations for voice traffic (for example, QoS considerations) also apply to video traffic.

An additional consideration for video traffic, however, is multicasting. Specifically, a video server might send a single video stream to a multicast group. End-user devices wanting to receive the video stream can join the multicast group. Multicast configuration, however, needs to be added to routers and switches to support this type of transmission. With the addition of multicast configurations comes the potential of additional troubleshooting targets. This section describes the basic theory, configuration, and troubleshooting of a multicast network.

This section then concludes with a listing of potential video network troubleshooting targets.

Introduction to IP-Based Video

Figure 11-5 illustrates a sample IP-based video network.

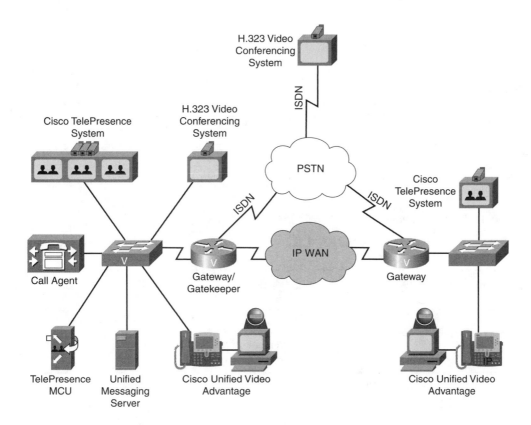

Figure 11-5 *IP-Based Video Network*

Many components in the figure are identical to components seen in a voice network. Three types of video solutions are shown, as follows:

- **H.323 Video Conferencing System:** Multiple third parties offer H.323 video conferencing systems, which can be used to set up a video conference over an IP or ISDN network.

- **Cisco Unified Video Advantage:** The Cisco Unified Video Advantage product uses a PC, a video camera, and a Cisco IP Phone as a video conferencing station. Specifically, the camera connects to a USB port on the PC. Software is loaded on the PC, and the PC is connected to the PC port on a Cisco IP Phone. Alternately, the Cisco IP Phone could be the software-based Cisco IP Communicator running on the PC. When a voice call is placed between two users running the Cisco Unified Video Advantage product, a video call can automatically be started, with the video appearing on each user's PC.

- **Cisco TelePresence:** The Cisco TelePresence solution uses CD-quality audio and High Definition (HD) video (that is, 1080p) displayed on large monitors to create life-like video conferences.

Design Considerations for Video

Due to the bandwidth-intensive and latency-sensitive nature of video, consider the following when designing or troubleshooting a video network:

- **QoS:** Like voice, video packets need to be allocated an appropriate amount of bandwidth and be treated with high priority. Table 11-5 shows the QoS metrics that Cisco recommends for various types of video applications.

Key Topic

Table 11-5 *Recommended QoS Metrics for Video*

QoS Metric	Cisco Unified Video Advantage	Cisco TelePresence	Video Surveillance
One-Way Delay	200 ms maximum	150 ms maximum	500 ms maximum
Jitter	10 ms maximum	10 ms maximum	10 ms maximum
Packet Loss	0.05 percent maximum	0.05 percent maximum	0.5 percent maximum

- **Availability:** Also like voice, video networks should be built on an underlying data network with reliable components and redundancy, such that the availability of the video network can approach an uptime of 99.999 percent.

- **Security:** Just as an eavesdropper could capture unencrypted voice packets and interpret the information contained in those packets, unencrypted video packets could also be captured and interpreted. Therefore, appropriate security measures, such as encryption and authentication, should be in place in a video network.

- **Multicasting:** More common in a video environment rather than in a voice environment is the use of multicasting technologies. Multicasting allows a multicast server to send traffic (for example, a video stream) to a destination Class D IP address known as a *multicast group*. End stations wanting to receive the traffic sent to the multicast group can join the group, thus allowing the multicast server (for example, a video server) to send a single stream of traffic, which is received by multiple recipients wishing to receive the traffic.

Multicasting

QoS, availability, and security considerations were discussed in the previous section. However, this chapter has not yet addressed multicasting in detail. Therefore, this section introduces you to multicasting operation, configuration, and troubleshooting.

Introduction to Multicasting

Consider a video stream that needs to be sent to multiple recipients in a company. One approach is to unicast the traffic. The source server sends a copy of every packet to every receiver. Obviously, this approach has serious scalability limitations.

An alternate approach is to broadcast the video stream, so that the source server only has to send each packet once. However, everyone within a broadcast domain of the network receives the packet, in that scenario, even if they do not want it.

IP multicast technologies provide the best of both worlds. With IP multicast, the source server only sends one copy of each packet, and packets are only sent to intended recipients.

Specifically, receivers join a multicast group, denoted by a Class D IP address (that is, in the range 224.0.0.0 through 239.255.255.255). The source sends traffic to the Class D address, and through switch and router protocols, packets are forwarded only to intended stations. These multicast packets are sent via UDP (that is, best effort). When doing a multicast design, also be aware of the potential for duplicate packets being received and the potential for packets arriving out of order.

Figure 11-6 shows a simple multicast network, where a multicast server is sending traffic to a destination IP address of 224.1.1.1. Notice that there are three workstations in this network. However, only two of the three workstations joined the multicast group. Therefore, only the two multicast group members receive traffic from the multicast server.

Internet Group Management Protocol

The protocol used between clients (for example, PCs) and routers to let routers know which of their interfaces have multicast receivers attached is Internet Group Management Protocol (IGMP). As an example, Figure 11-7 shows a PC sending an IGMP Join message to a multicast-enabled router. The router receives this IGMP Join message on its Fast Ethernet 0/0 interface. Therefore, the router knows that when it receives traffic destined for a particular multicast group (as identified in the IGMP Join message), that traffic should be forwarded out its Fast Ethernet 0/0 interface.

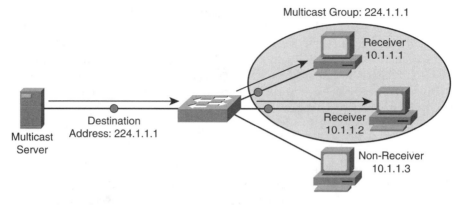

Figure 11-6 *Sample Multicast Topology*

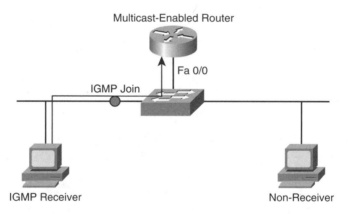

Figure 11-7 *Joining a Multicast Group*

There are three versions of IGMP. However, only two versions are in wide-scale deployment:

■ **IGMP Version 1:** When a PC wants to join a multicast group, it sends an IGMP Report message to the router, letting the router know that it wants to receive traffic for a specific group. Every 60 seconds, by default, the router sends an IGMP Query message to determine if the PC still wants to belong to the group. There can be up to a three-minute delay before the time the router realizes that the receiver left the group. The destination address of this router query is 224.0.0.1, which addresses all IP multicast hosts.

■ **IGMP Version 2:** IGMPv2 is similar to IGMP Version 1, except that IGMP Version 2 can send queries to a specific group, and a *Leave* message is supported. Specifically, a receiver can proactively send a Leave message when it no longer wants to participate in a multicast group, allowing the router to prune its interface earlier.

IGMP Version 1 and Version 2 hosts and routers do have some interoperability. When an IGMPv2 hosts sends an IGMPv2 report to an IGMPv1 router, the IGMP message type appears to be invalid, and it is ignored. Therefore, an IGMPv2 host must send IGMPv1 reports to an IGMPv1 router.

In an environment with an IGMPv2 router and a mixture of IGMPv1 and IGMPv2 receivers, the version 1 receivers respond normally to IGMPv1 or IGMPv2 queries. However, as illustrated in Figure 11-8, a version 2 router must ignore any leave message while IGMPv1 receivers are present because if the router processed the IGMPv2 leave message, it would send a group-specific query, which would not be correctly interpreted by an IGMPv1 receiver.

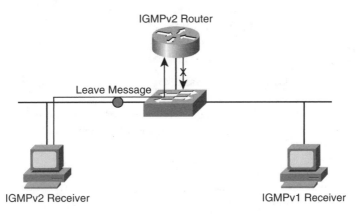

Figure 11-8   *Mixed IGMPv1 and IGMPv2 Topology*

As mentioned earlier, multicast routers can periodically send queries out of an interface to determine if any multicast receivers still exist off of that interface. However, there might be a situation where more than one multicast router exists on a broadcast media segment (for example, Ethernet). Therefore, one router must be designated as the *querier* for that segment. This IGMP designated *querier* is the router that has the lowest unicast IP address. To determine which router on a multi-access network is the querier, you can issue the following command:

`Router# show ip igmp interface [interface-id]`

The output from this command identifies the IP address of the IGMP querier. Additionally, the following command displays the IP multicast groups of which a router is aware:

`Router# show ip igmp group`

When a Layer 2 switch receives a multicast frame on an interface, by default, the switch floods the frame out all other interfaces. To prevent this behavior, the switch needs awareness of what interfaces are connected to receivers for specific multicast groups. *IGMP snooping* is a feature that can be enabled on many Cisco Catalyst switches, which allows a switch to autonomously determine which interfaces are connected to receivers for specific multicast groups by eavesdropping on the IGMP traffic being exchanged between clients and routers. To globally enable IGMP snooping on a Cisco Catalyst switch, issue the following command:

```
Switch(config)# ip igmp snooping
```

Once enabled globally, individual VLANs can be enabled or disabled for IGMP snooping with the following command:

```
Switch(config)# ip igmp snooping vlan vlan_id
```

Multicast Addressing

In a multicast network, the multicast source sends multicast packets with a Class D destination address. The 224.0.0.0 through 239.255.255.255 address range is the Class D address range, because the first four bits in the first octet of a Class D address are 1110. Some ranges of addresses in the Class D address space are dedicated for special purposes:

- **Reserved Link Local Addresses:** 224.0.0.0–224.0.0.255. These addresses are used, for example, by many network protocols. OSPF uses 224.0.0.5 and 224.0.0.6. RIPv2 uses 224.0.0.9, and EIGRP uses 224.0.0.10. Other well-known addresses in this range include 224.0.0.1, which addresses all multicast hosts, and 224.0.0.2, which addresses all multicast routers.

- **Globally Scoped Addresses:** 224.0.1.0–238.255.255.255. These addresses are used for general-purpose multicast applications, and they have the ability to extend beyond the local autonomous system.

- **Source-Specific Multicast (SSM) Addresses:** 232.0.0.0–232.255.255.255. These addresses are used in conjunction with IGMPv3, to allow multicast receivers to request not only membership in a group but also to request specific sources from which to receive traffic. Therefore, in an SSM environment, multiple sources with different content can all be sending to the same multicast group.

- **GLOP Addresses:** 233.0.0.0–233.255.255.255. These addresses provide a globally unique multicast address range, based on autonomous system numbers.

- **Limited Scope Addresses:** 239.0.0.0–239.255.255.255. These addresses are used for internal multicast applications (for example, traffic that doesn't leave an autonomous system), much like the 10.0.0.0/8 address space is a private IP address space.

In addition to Layer 3 addresses, multicast applications must also have Layer 2 addresses (that is, MAC addresses). Fortunately, these Layer 2 addresses can be constructed directly from the Layer 3 multicast addresses. A MAC address is a 48-bit address, and the first half (that is, 24 bits) of a multicast MAC address (in hex) is 01-00-5e. The 25th bit is always 0. The last 23 bits in the multicast MAC address come directly from the last 23 bits of the multicast IP address. Consider the following example:

Given a multicast IP address of 224.1.10.10, calculate the corresponding multicast MAC address.

Step 1. First, convert the last three octets to binary:

```
0000.0001.0000.1010.0000.1010
```

Step 2. If the right-most bit isn't already 0, it should be changed to a 0, because the 25th bit of a multicast MAC address is always 0:

`0000.0001.0000.1010.0000.1010`

Step 3. Convert each nibble (that is, each 4-bit section) into its hexadecimal equivalent:

`01-0a-0a`

Step 4. Prepend 01-00-5e to the calculated address to produce the multicast MAC address:

`01-00-5e-01-0a-0a`

Distribution Trees

To combat the issue of receiving duplicate packets, Cisco routers perform a Reverse Path Forwarding (RPF) check to determine if a multicast packet is entering a router on the appropriate interface. An RPF check examines the source address of an incoming packet and checks it against the router's unicast routing table to see what interface should be used to get back to the source network. If the incoming multicast packet is using that interface, the RPF check passes, and the packet is forwarded. If the multicast packet is coming in on a different interface, the RPF check fails, and the packet is discarded, as shown in Figure 11-9.

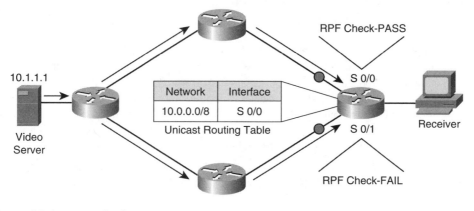

Figure 11-9 *RPF Check*

Only members of a multicast group receive packets destined for that group; however, the sender does not need to be a member of the group. Multicast traffic flows from a source to a destination over a *distribution tree*, which is a loop-free path. The two types of distribution trees are as follows:

- **Source Distribution Tree:** A source distribution tree, as depicted in Figure 11-10, creates an optimal path between each source router and each last-hop router (that is, a router connected to a receiver), at the expense of increased memory usage. Source distributions trees place (S, G) states in a router's multicast routing table to indicate the address of the source (S) and the address of the group (G).

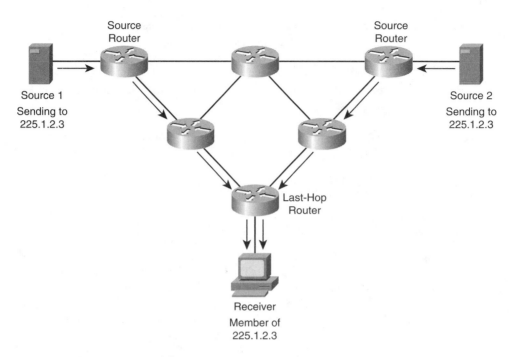

Figure 11-10   *Source Distribution Tree*

- **Shared Distribution Tree:** A shared distribution tree, as seen in Figure 11-11, creates a tree from a central *rendezvous point* (RP) router to all last-hop routers, with source distribution trees being created from all sources to the rendezvous point, at the expense of increased delay. Shared distribution trees place (*, G) states in a router's multicast routing table to indicate that any device could be the source (that is, using the wildcard * character) for the group (G). This (*, G) state is created in routers along the shared tree from the RP to the last-hop routers. Because each source for a group does not require its own (S, G), the memory requirement is less for a shared tree compared to a source tree.

PIM-DM Mechanics

Cisco routers can use the *Protocol Independent Multicast* (PIM) protocol to construct IP multicast distribution trees. PIM's protocol independence means that it can run over any IP network, regardless of the underlying unicast routing protocol (for example, OSPF or EIGRP). The two varieties of PIM are *PIM Dense Mode* (PIM-DM) and *PIM Sparse Mode* (PIM-SM). PIM-DM uses a source distribution tree, whereas PIM-SM uses a shared distribution tree.

A router is enabled for multicast routing with the following global configuration mode command:

```
Router(config)# ip multicast-routing
```

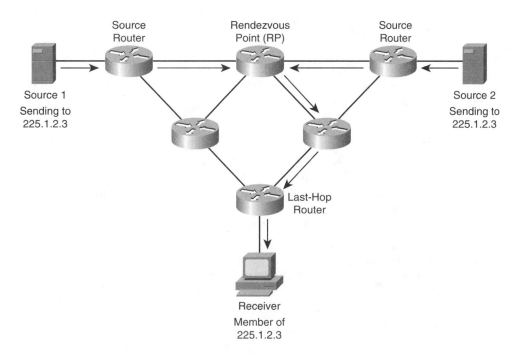

Figure 11-11   *Shared Distribution Tree*

Once IP multicast is globally enabled, individual interfaces need to be configured for PIM support. To configure an interface to participate in an IP multicast network, using PIM, issue the following interface configuration mode command:

```
Router(config-if)# ip pim {dense-mode | sparse-mode | sparse-dense-mode}
```

Cisco recommends sparse-dense-mode, which uses dense-mode to automatically learn the location of an RP, after which the interface runs in sparse-mode. First, consider the formation of a PIM Dense Mode distribution tree:

1. A multicast source comes up and begins flooding multicast traffic throughout the network.

2. If more than one router is forwarding over a common broadcast medium (for example, an Ethernet link), *Assert* messages are used to determine the PIM forwarder. The router with the better metric, or (by default) the highest IP address, wins the election.

3. Some routers might not have multicast receivers for the group whose traffic is currently being flooded. Those routers send a *Prune* message to their upstream router, requesting that their branch of the distribution tree be pruned off. However, if there is another router on the same broadcast medium as the router that sent the prune, and if that other router does have IP multicast receivers attached, the prune message is ignored. The reason that the prune message is ignored is because the router that is attached to IP multicast receivers sends a *Join Override* message.

4. If a receiver comes up on a router that was previously pruned from the tree, that router can rejoin the tree by sending a *Graft* message.

A major consideration for PIM-DM, however, is that this *flood-and-prune* behavior repeats every three minutes. Therefore, PIM-DM does not scale well. A better alternative to PIM-DM is PIM Sparse Mode (PIM-SM).

PIM-SM Mechanics

Next, consider the formation of a PIM Sparse Mode distribution tree:

1. A receiver sends an IGMP Report message to its router indicating that it wants to participate in a particular multicast group. The receiver's router (that is, the last-hop router) sends a *Join* message to the RP, creating (*, G) state along a shared tree between the RP and the last-hop router.

2. A source comes up and creates a source tree between its router (that is, the first-hop router) and the RP. (S, G) state is created in routers along this path. However, before the source tree is completely established, the source sends its multicast packets to the RP encapsulated inside of unicast *Register* messages.

3. After the RP receives the first multicast packet over the source tree, it sends a *Register Stop* message to the source, telling the source to stop sending the multicast traffic inside of Register messages. Two trees now exist: (1) a source tree from the first-hop router to the RP and (2) a shared tree from the RP to the last-hop router. However, this might not be the optimal path.

4. The last-hop router discovers from where the multicast traffic is arriving, and the last-hop router sends a *Join* message directly to the first-hop router to form an optimal path (that is, a source path tree) between the source and the receiver.

5. Because the last-hop router no longer needs multicast traffic from the RP, as it is receiving the multicast traffic directly from the first-hop router, it sends an (S, G) *RP-bit Prune* message to the RP, requesting the RP to stop sending multicast traffic.

6. With the shared tree to the last-hop router pruned, the RP no longer needs to receive multicast traffic from the first-hop router. So, the RP sends an *(S, G) Prune* message to the first-hop router. At this point, traffic flows in an optimal path from the first-hop router to the last-hop router. The process of cutting over from the path via the RP to the direct path is called *Shortest-Path Tree* (SPT) *Switchover*.

Comparing PIM-DM versus PIM-SM suggests that PIM-SM offers the benefits of PIM-DM (that is, optimal pathing) without PIM-DM's flood-and-prune behavior.

You can determine a distribution tree's topology by examining the multicast routing table of multicast routers in the topology. The **show ip mroute** command displays a router's multicast routing table, as demonstrated in Example 11-8.

Example 11-8 show ip mroute *Command Output*

```
Router# show ip mroute
IP Multicast Routing Table
Flags: D - Dense, S - Sparse, B - Bidir Group, s - SSM Group, C - Connected,
       L - Local, P - Pruned, R - RP-bit set, F - Register flag,
       T - SPT-bit set, J - Join SPT, M - MSDP created entry,
       X - Proxy Join Timer Running, A - Candidate for MSDP Advertisement,
       U - URD, I - Received Source Specific Host Report, Z - Multicast Tunnel,
       Y - Joined MDT-data group, y - Sending to MDT-data group
Timers: Uptime/Expires
Interface state: Interface, Next-Hop or VCD, State/Mode

(*, 224.0.100.4), 02:37:12, RP is 192.168.47.14, flags: S
  Incoming interface: Serial0, RPF neighbor 10.4.53.4
  Outgoing interface list:
    Ethernet1, Forward/Sparse, 02:37:12/0:03:42
    Ethernet2, Forward/Sparse, 02:52:12/0:01:23

(192.168.46.0/24, 224.0.100.4), 02:37:12, flags: RT
  Incoming interface: Ethernet1, RPF neighbor 10.4.53.4
  Outgoing interface list:
    Ethernet2, Forward/Sparse, 02:44:21/0:01:47
```

Notice the highlighted (*, G) and (S, G) entries. Other valuable information contained in the mroute table includes the incoming interface (IIF), which shows on which interface traffic is entering the router, and the outgoing interface list (OIL), which shows the router interfaces over which the multicast traffic is being forwarded.

Rendezvous Points

In a PIM-SM network, one or more routers need to be designated as a *rendezvous point* (RP). Non-RPs can be configured to point to a statically defined RP with the global configuration mode command **ip pim rp-address** *ip-address*. However, in larger topologies, Cisco recommends that RPs be automatically discovered. Cisco routers support two methods for automatically discovering an RP: Auto-RP and Bootstrap Router (BSR). Although Auto-RP is a Cisco approach, BSR is a standards-based approach to make the location of RPs known throughout a multicast network.

Common Video Troubleshooting Issues

As with voice networks, data networking troubleshooting targets should be considered when troubleshooting a reported video issue. Additionally, as a reference, Table 11-6 offers a collection of common video troubleshooting targets and recommended solutions.

Table 11-6 *Common Video Troubleshooting Targets*

Video Troubleshooting Target	Recommended Solutions
Bandwidth	Video streams can be bursty in nature and consume large quantities of bandwidth. Therefore, although sufficient bandwidth should be allocated for supported video applications, you should confirm that the video traffic is not consuming too much bandwidth (that is, an amount of bandwidth that would negatively impact other important traffic).
Pervasiveness of Video Applications	The volume of video traffic on a network might be somewhat unpredictable, because users might introduce their own video traffic on a network without the knowledge of network administrators. Therefore, your policy for network use should address the types of traffic a user is allowed to send and receive. Also, you might want to block video from portions of your network.
Security	In addition to protecting the content of your network's video streams, realize that security measures you have in place might be conflicting with your video applications. For example, if a video stream cannot be established, you might check your firewalls and router ACLs to confirm they are not blocking video media (that is, RTP) packets, video maintenance (for example, RTCP) packets, or video-signaling packets (for example, H.323).
QoS	Because video traffic is latency-sensitive, QoS mechanisms should be in place to ensure video packets are sent with priority treatment, and sufficient bandwidth should be allocated for your supported video applications.
Multicast	Because many video applications rely on multicast technologies to transmit a video stream to a multicast group, much of your video troubleshooting might be focused on multicast troubleshooting. For example, confirm that both routers and switches are properly configured with multicast protocols (for example, PIM-SM on a router and IGMP Snooping on a switch).

Trouble Tickets: Unified Communications

This section presents two trouble tickets based on Unified Communications issues. In the first trouble ticket (that is, Trouble Ticket #9), a Cisco IP Phone is failing to register with its Cisco Unified Communications Manager Express (UCME) router. Once that issue is resolved, the second trouble ticket (that is, Trouble Ticket #10) addresses poor voice quality on the network. In each of these trouble tickets, you are given sample **show** command output and are then challenged to identify a resolution for the issue described.

Trouble Ticket #9

You receive the following trouble ticket:

A Cisco IP Phone with directory number 3333 (connected to interface Fast Ethernet 5/45 on switch SW2) is unable to register with router R1, which is configured as a UCME call agent. This is a new installation and has never worked. Therefore, no baseline data is available.

This trouble ticket references the topology shown in Figure 11-12.

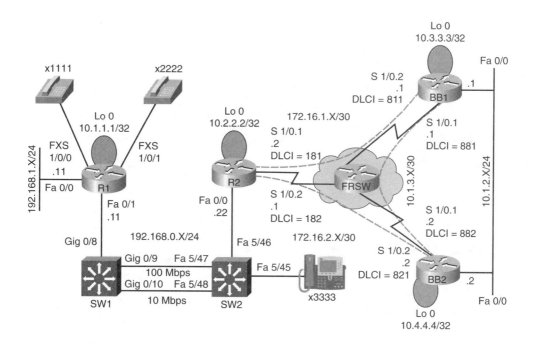

Figure 11-12 *Trouble Ticket #9—Topology*

Assume that you have already verified reachability between switch SW2 and router R1 and have decided to focus your efforts on the configuration of the Cisco Unified Communications Manager Express router (that is, router R1). Example 11-9 shows the running configuration for router R1.

Example 11-9 *Running Configuration of Router R1*

```
R1# show run
Building configuration...
...OUTPUT OMITTED...
hostname R1
!
ip cef
!
ip dhcp excluded-address 192.168.0.1 192.168.0.100
!
ip dhcp pool TSHOOT
   network 192.168.1.0 255.255.255.0
   option 150 ip 192.168.0.11
   default-router 192.168.0.11
!
interface Loopback0
 ip address 10.1.1.1 255.255.255.255
!
interface FastEthernet0/0
 ip address 192.168.1.11 255.255.255.0
!
interface FastEthernet0/1
 ip address 192.168.0.11 255.255.255.0
!
router ospf 1
network 0.0.0.0 255.255.255.255 area 0
!
voice-port 1/0/0
!
voice-port 1/0/1
!
dial-peer voice 1111 pots
 destination-pattern 1111
 port 1/0/0
!
dial-peer voice 2222 pots
 destination-pattern 2222
 port 1/0/1
!
telephony-service
 max-ephones 5
 max-dn 10
 ip source-address 192.168.0.11 port 2000
 create cnf-files version-stamp Jan 01 2002 00:00:00
 max-conferences 4 gain -6
```

```
!
ephone-dn   1
 number 1000
!
ephone   1
 mac-address  0008.A3D1.FBC4
 button   1:1
!
...OUTPUT OMITTED...
```

Assume you have confirmed that the MAC address configured for ephone 1 is correct. Although the TSHOOT curriculum does not cover the configuration of a UCME router, Table 11-7 offers a reference for some of the commands used in Example 11-9.

Table 11-7 *Sampling of Cisco UCME Configuration Commands*

Command	Description
telephony-service	Global configuration mode command that enters the configuration mode for setting up Cisco UCME parameters.
max-ephones *number*	Telephony service configuration mode command that specifies the maximum number of Ethernet phone directory numbers supported on the UCME system. (NOTE: The default is 0.)
max-dn *number*	Telephony service configuration mode command that specifies the maximum number of Ethernet phones supported on the UCME system. (NOTE: The default is 0.)
create cnf-files	Telephony service configuration mode command that creates .XML configuration files for configured ephones.
ephone-dn *tag*	Global configuration mode command that enters ephone-dn configuration mode for a locally significant ephone-dn tag.
number *directory-number*	Ephone-dn configuration mode command that specifies the directory number for an ephone-dn.
ephone *tag*	Global configuration mode command that enters ephone configuration mode for a locally significant ephone tag.

continues

Table 11-7   *Sampling of Cisco UCME Configuration Commands*   *(Continued)*

Command	Description
mac-address *MAC-address*	Ephone configuration mode command that specifies the MAC address for an ephone. (NOTE: The MAC address is entered in the following format: xxxx.xxxx.xxxx.)
button *button-number:ephone-dn-tag*	Ephone configuration mode command that associates a previously configured ephone-dn with a button on the ephone.
ip source-address *ip-address*	Global configuration mode command that specifies the IP address on the UCME router used to send and receive Skinny Client Control Protocol (SCCP) messages when communicating with Cisco IP Phones.
dial-peer voice *tag* pots	Global configuration mode command that creates a Plain Old Telephone Service (POTS) dial peer.
destination-pattern *pattern*	Dial peer configuration mode command that specifies the pattern of a dial string to be matched. (NOTE: Wildcards can be used.)
port *port-identifier*	Dial peer configuration mode command that specifies a voice port that a POTS dial peer references.

In an attempt to determine why the ephone registration is failing, you issue a **debug ephone** command on router R1. However, no debug output is generated.

Therefore, you decide to look through the running configuration of router R1, as previously presented in Example 11-9. On a separate sheet of paper, identify any misconfiguration you find and how you would correct that misconfiguration.

Suggested Solution: Trouble Ticket #9

In the running configuration of router R1, you might have noticed that the DHCP pool named THSOOT specified a network address space of 192.168.1.0 255.255.255.0. However, if you examine the topology provided in Figure 11-12, you can see that the IP phone (with directory number 3333) should be assigned an IP address in the 192.168.0.0 255.255.255.0 address space.

Example 11-10 shows the correction of this misconfiguration. Notice that after the configuration is corrected, the ephone successfully registers.

Example 11-10   *Correcting the DHCP Pool Misconfiguration on Router R1*

```
R1# conf term
R1(config)# ip dhcp pool TSHOOT
R1(dhcp-config)# no network 192.168.1.0 255.255.255.0
R1(dhcp-config)# network 192.168.0.0 255.255.255.0
```

```
R1(dhcp-config)# end
R1#
*Mar  3 15:19:24.304: %IPPHONE-6-REG_ALARM: 22: Name=SEP0008A3D1FBC4 Load=7.1(2.0)
Last=Reset-Reset
*Mar  3 15:19:24.308: %IPPHONE-6-REGISTER: ephone-1:SEP0008A3D1FBC4
IP:192.168.0.101 Socket:1 DeviceType:Phone has registered.
```

Trouble Ticket #10

Now that router R1 has been properly configured as a UCME router, the IP Phone (that is, directory number 3333) and the analog phones (that is, directory numbers 1111 and 2222) can call one another. Although the voice quality between these phones is fine on the LAN, the following trouble ticket indicates quality issues when placing calls over the Frame Relay WAN connections:

> When placing calls across the Frame Relay WAN, users are complaining that the voice quality is poor for calls originating on an analog phone, whereas the voice quality is fine for calls originating on an IP phone.

This trouble ticket references the previous topology (that is, Figure 11-12). Because the trouble ticket implies a QoS issue, you decide to investigate the configuration of router R2 sitting at the WAN edge. Example 11-11 shows the output from a collection of **show** commands.

Example 11-11   *Verifying Configuration on Router R2*

```
R2# show class-map
 Class Map match-any class-default (id 0)
   Match any
 Class Map match-all VOICE (id 1)
   Match    dscp ef (46)
R2# show policy-map
   Policy Map TSHOOT
     Class VOICE
       Strict Priority
       Bandwidth 256 (kbps) Burst 1600 (Bytes)
     Class class-default
       Flow based Fair Queueing
       Bandwidth 0 (kbps) Max Threshold 64 (packets)
R2# show policy-map interface s1/0
 Serial1/0
   Service-policy output: TSHOOT
     Class-map: VOICE (match-all)
       0 packets, 0 bytes
       5 minute offered rate 0 bps, drop rate 0 bps
       Match:  dscp ef (46)
       Queueing
         Strict Priority
```

```
        Output Queue: Conversation 264
        Bandwidth 64 (kbps) Burst 1600 (Bytes)
        (pkts matched/bytes matched) 0/0
        (total drops/bytes drops) 0/0
    Class-map: class-default (match-any)
      8 packets, 1010 bytes
      5 minute offered rate 0 bps, drop rate 0 bps
      Match: any
      Queueing
        Flow Based Fair Queueing
        Maximum Number of Hashed Queues 256
      (total queued/total drops/no-buffer drops) 0/0/0
```

Router R2's configuration appears to be classifying voice traffic based on a packet's DSCP values. Specifically, if a packet is marked with a DSCP PHB value of EF (that is, Expedited Forwarding, which has a decimal equivalent of 46), that packet is classified into the **VOICE** class. Traffic in this class has access to as much as 256 kbps of bandwidth and is given priority treatment.

Also provided as a reference, Example 11-12 shows the configuration of router R1.

Example 11-12 *Verifying Configuration on Router R1*

```
R1# show run
...OUTPUT OMITTED...
hostname R1
!
ip cef
!
ip dhcp excluded-address 192.168.0.1 192.168.0.100
!
ip dhcp pool TSHOOT
   network 192.168.0.0 255.255.255.0
   option 150 ip 192.168.0.11
   default-router 192.168.0.11
interface Loopback0
 ip address 10.1.1.1 255.255.255.255
interface FastEthernet0/0
 ip address 192.168.1.11 255.255.255.0
!
interface FastEthernet0/1
 ip address 192.168.0.11 255.255.255.0
!
router ospf 1
 network 0.0.0.0 255.255.255.255 area 0
!
```

```
dial-peer voice 1111 pots
 destination-pattern 1111
 port 1/0/0
!
dial-peer voice 2222 pots
ip nat inside
destination-pattern 2222
 port 1/0/1
!
telephony-service
 max-ephones 5
 max-dn 10
 ip source-address 192.168.0.11 port 2000
 create cnf-files version-stamp Jan 01 2002 00:00:00
 max-conferences 4 gain -6
!
ephone-dn  1
 number 1000
!
ephone  1
 mac-address 0008.A3D1.FBC4
 button  1:1
```

Based on the **show** command output, hypothesize how you could resolve the reported quality issue. You can then compare your recommended solution with the following suggested solution. Note that many possible solutions exist to solve this particular trouble ticket.

Suggested Solution: Trouble Ticket #10

Because router R2 is giving priority treatment to traffic marked with a DSCP PHB value of EF, you should ensure that all voice packets are being marked with that value. Cisco IP Phones, by default, mark voice packets with an EF. However, by examining the configuration of router R1 (that is, the router to which the two analog phones are attached), there does not seem to be any configuration that marks voice packets sourced from the analog voice ports with any DSCP value.

Therefore, router R1 should be configured to mark voice traffic with a DSCP PHB of EF. Although you could do this manually, using more than one approach, this suggested solution leverages the AutoQoS VoIP feature. By enabling AutoQoS VoIP on Router R1's Fast Ethernet 0/1 interface, voice packets will be automatically recognized (based on their use of RTP). Example 11-13 illustrates the application and verification of the AutoQoS VoIP feature to router R1.

Example 11-13   *Applying and Verifying AutoQoS VoIP on Router R1*

```
R1#conf term
R1(config)#int fa 0/1
R1(config-if)#auto qos voip
R1(config-if)#end
R1#show run
...OUTPUT OMITTED...
hostname R1
!
ip cef
!
ip dhcp excluded-address 192.168.0.1 192.168.0.100
!
ip dhcp pool TSHOOT
   network 192.168.0.0 255.255.255.0
   option 150 ip 192.168.0.11
   default-router 192.168.0.11
!
class-map match-any AutoQoS-VoIP-Remark
 match ip dscp ef
 match ip dscp cs3
match ip dscp af31
class-map match-any AutoQoS-VoIP-Control-UnTrust
 match access-group name AutoQoS-VoIP-Control
class-map match-any AutoQoS-VoIP-RTP-UnTrust
 match protocol rtp audio
 match access-group name AutoQoS-VoIP-RTCP
!
policy-map AutoQoS-Policy-UnTrust
 class AutoQoS-VoIP-RTP-UnTrust
  priority percent 70
  set dscp ef
 class AutoQoS-VoIP-Control-UnTrust
  bandwidth percent 5
```

```
  set dscp af31
 class AutoQoS-VoIP-Remark
  set dscp default
 class class-default
  fair-queue
!
interface Loopback0
 ip address 10.1.1.1 255.255.255.255
!
interface FastEthernet0/0
 ip address 192.168.1.11 255.255.255.0
!
interface FastEthernet0/1
ip address 192.168.0.11 255.255.255.0
 auto qos voip
 service-policy output AutoQoS-Policy-UnTrust
!
router ospf 1
 network 0.0.0.0 255.255.255.255 area 0
!
ip access-list extended AutoQoS-VoIP-Control
 permit tcp any any eq 1720
 permit tcp any any range 11000 11999
 permit udp any any eq 2427
 permit tcp any any eq 2428
 permit tcp any any range 2000 2002
permit udp any any eq 1719
 permit udp any any eq 5060
ip access-list extended AutoQoS-VoIP-RTCP
permit udp any any range 16384 32767
!
rmon event 33333 log trap AutoQoS description "AutoQoS SNMP traps for Voice Drops"
owner AutoQoS
```

```
rmon alarm 33333 cbQosCMDropBitRate.1081.1083 30 absolute rising-threshold 1 33333
falling-threshold 0 owner AutoQoS
!
voice-port 1/0/0
!
voice-port 1/0/1
!
dial-peer voice 2222 pots
 destination-pattern 2222
 port 1/0/0
!
dial-peer voice 3333 pots
 destination-pattern 3333
port 1/0/1
!
telephony-service
 max-ephones 5
 max-dn 10
 ip source-address 192.168.0.11 port 2000
 create cnf-files version-stamp Jan 01 2002 00:00:00
 max-conferences 4 gain -6
!
ephone-dn  1
 number 1000
!
ephone  1
mac-address 0008.A3D1.FBC4
 button  1:1
...OUTPUT OMITTED...
```

The highlighted commands in this example indicate the commands automatically entered by the AutoQoS VoIP feature. After AutoQoS VoIP is applied, router R1 begins to mark RTP audio packets (that is, voice packets) with a DSCP PHB of EF. Then, when those voice packets reach router R2, router R2 is able to classify them into the **VOICE** class, which receives priority treatment in being sent out over the Frame Relay WAN links, thus resolving the reported issue.

Exam Preparation Tasks

Review All Key Topics

Review the most important topics from inside the chapter, noted with the Key Topics icon in the outer margin of the page. Table 11-8 lists these key topics and the page numbers where each is found.

Key
Topic

Table 11-8   *Key Topics for Chapter 11*

Key Topic Element	Description	Page Number
List	IP telephony components	330
List	Symptoms of having a lack of bandwidth	331
List	Supporting services for voice traffic	332
Steps	Boot-up process for a Cisco IP Phone	335
Table 11-2	Common voice troubleshooting targets	335
List	MQC steps	336
Example 11-1	MQC sample configuration	337
Table 11-3	MQC verification commands	338
Table 11-4	AutoQoS platform support	341
List	AutoQoS configuration prerequisites	342
Table 11-5	Recommended QoS metrics for video	348
List	IGMP versions	350
Table 11-6	Common video troubleshooting targets	358

Complete Tables and Lists from Memory

Print a copy of Appendix B, "Memory Tables," (found on the CD) or at least the section for this chapter, and complete the tables and lists from memory. Appendix C, "Memory Tables Answer Key," also on the CD, includes completed tables and lists to check your work.

Define Key Terms

Define the following key terms from this chapter, and check your answers in the Glossary:

Voice over IP (VoIP), IP telephony, unified communications, IP phone, gatekeeper, gateway, multipoint control unit (MCU), call agent, application server, videoconference station, delay, jitter, drops, Differentiated Services Code Point (DSCP), Modular Quality of Service Command-Line Interface (MQC), AutoQoS VoIP, AutoQoS Enterprise, Cisco

Unified Video Advantage, Cisco TelePresence, multicasting, Internet Group Management Protocol (IGMP), Protocol Independent Multicast (PIM), rendezvous point (RP)

Command Reference to Check Your Memory

This section includes the most important configuration and EXEC commands covered in this chapter. To determine how well you have memorized the commands as a side effect of your other studies, cover the left side of the table with a piece of paper, read the descriptions on the right side, and see whether you remember the command.

Table 11-9   *Chapter 11 Configuration Command Reference*

Command	Description
class-map [match-any | match-all] *class-name*	Global configuration mode command that creates a class map and enters class map configuration mode.
policy-map *policy-name*	Global configuration mode command that creates a policy map and enters policy map configuration mode.
class *class-name*	Policy map configuration mode command that enters policy map class configuration mode.
service-policy {input | output} *policy-map-name*	Interface configuration mode command that applies a policy map in either the inbound or outbound direction.
auto qos voip [trust] [fr-atm]	Interface configuration mode command for a router that enables AutoQoS VoIP on an interface. (NOTE: The **trust** keyword indicates that traffic should be classified based on its DSCP value rather than being based on NBAR. The **fr-atm** keyword can cause a Frame Relay Discard Eligible (DE) bit to be translated into an ATM Cell Loss Priority (CLP) bit, and vice versa.)
auto qos voip trust	Interface configuration mode command for a switch that configures an interface to trust Class of Service (CoS) markings (that is, Layer 2 QoS priority markings on an Ethernet link) for classifying VoIP traffic.
auto qos voip cisco-phone	Interface configuration mode command for a switch that configures the interface to trust CoS markings only if those markings came from an attached Cisco IP Phone. (NOTE: CDP is used to detect an attached Cisco IP Phone.)
auto discovery qos [trust]	Interface configuration mode command on a router issued to begin the discovery phase on an interface for the Auto-QoS Enterprise feature. (NOTE: The **trust** keyword instructs the router to classify traffic based on existing DSCP markings, as opposed to using NBAR.)

Table 11-9   *Chapter 11 Configuration Command Reference   (Continued)*

Command	Description
auto qos	Interface configuration mode command on a router used to apply a policy map generated by AutoQoS Enterprise.
ip multicast-routing	Global configuration mode command used to enable IP multicast routing.
ip pim {dense-mode | sparse-mode | sparse-dense-mode}	Interface configuration mode command used to enable an interface to participate in a specified PIM mode.
ip pim rp-address *ip-address*	Global configuration mode command used to specify the IP address of a rendezvous point (RP) in a PIM Sparse Mode network.
ip igmp snooping	Global configuration mode command used on a Cisco Catalyst switch to globally enable IGMP snooping on the switch.
[no] ip igmp snooping vlan *vlan_id*	Global configuration mode command used on a Cisco Catalyst switch to enable (or disable, using the **no** option) IGMP snooping for a specific VLAN.

Table 11-10   *Chapter 11 EXEC Command Reference*

Command	Description
show class-map [*class-map-name*]	Used to view what a class map is matching.
show policy-map [*policy-map-name*]	Used to view the policy applied to the classes within a policy map.
show policy-map interface *interface-identifier* [**input** | **output**]	Used to view class map and policy map configuration and statistical information for packets crossing a specific interface.
show auto qos voip [**interface** *interface-identifier*]	Displays global and interface (or optionally, only interface) configuration mode commands added by the AutoQoS VoIP feature.
show auto discovery qos	Used to view how the AutoQoS Enterprise feature has classified traffic and the recommended policy generated by AutoQoS Enterprise.
show ip igmp interface [*interface-id*]	Can be used to identify the IP address of an IGMP querier.
show ip igmp group	Displays the IP multicast groups of which the router is aware.

This chapter covers the following subjects:

Reviewing IPv6: This section introduces the purpose and structure IP version 6 (IPv6) addressing. You consider the various types of IPv6 addresses, routing protocols supporting IPv6, and basic syntax for enabling a router to route IPv6 traffic. A sample configuration is provide to illustrate the configuration of a router to support IPv6. Additionall as an organization is migrating from IPv4 to IPv6, there might be portions of the network that are still running IPv4 with other portions of the network running IPv6. For IPv6 traffic to span an IPv4 portion of the network, one option is to create a tunnel spanning the IPv4 network. Then, IPv6 traffic can travel inside the tunnel to transit the IPv4 network. This section discusses the syntax and provides an example of tunneling IPv6 over an IPv4 tunnel.

OSPFv3 Troubleshooting: This section contrasts the characteristics of two versions of OSPF, specifically OSPFv2 and OSPFv3. OSPFv3 can support the routing of IPv6 networks, whereas OSPFv2 cannot. OSPFv3 configuration syntax is presented, along with a sample config uration. You are also provided with a collection of verification troubleshooting commands and a listing of common OSPFv3 issues.

Trouble Ticket: IPv6 and OSPF: This section presents you with a trouble ticket addressing a network experiencing OSPF adjacency issues. You are presented with a collection of **show** and **debug** commar output and challenged to resolve a series of misconfigurations. Suggested solutions are also provided.

RIPng Troubleshooting: This section contrasts the characteristics o RIP next generation (RIPng) with RIPv2. You are given a set of RIPng configuration commands along with a sample configuration. From a troubleshooting perspective, you compare RIPng troubleshooting co mands with those commands used to troubleshoot RIPv1 and RIPv2. Finally, this section identifies some of the more common RIPng troubleshooting issues you might encounter.

Trouble Ticket: IPv6 and RIPng: This section challenges you to resolve a couple of RIPng issues being observed in a network. Specifically, load balancing and default route advertisements are not behavin as expected. To assist in your troubleshooting efforts, you are armed with a collection of **show** and **debug** command output. Your propose solutions can then be compared with suggested solutions.

CHAPTER 12

IPv6 Troubleshooting

With the global proliferation of IP-based networks, available IPv4 addresses are rapidly becoming extinct. Fortunately, IPv6 provides enough IP addresses for many generations to come. This section introduces IPv6's address structure and discusses some of its unique characteristics. As part of an IPv4 to IPv6 migration, you might also need to update the IP routing protocol in use, because the existing IP routing protocol might not be compatible with IPv6. This chapter identifies a collection of IP routing protocols capable of routing IPv6 traffic. Additionally, you see how to tunnel IPv6 traffic across an IPv4 network.

After reviewing the fundamentals of IPv6, this chapter focuses on troubleshooting OSPF version 3 (OSPFv3), a routing protocol compatible with IPv6 routes. Troubleshooting OSPFv3 bears many similarities with troubleshooting OSPFv2, as discussed in Chapter 7, "OSPF and Route Redistribution Troubleshooting." Although you can certainly leverage many of your OSPFv2 troubleshooting strategies with OSPFv3, you do need to understand the subtle distinctions. Therefore, this section introduces you to the commonalities and differences in these two OSPF versions. OSPFv3 configuration, verification, and troubleshooting are also discussed.

To help you practice your OSPFv3 troubleshooting skills, this chapter challenges you with a trouble ticket addressing OSPFv3 issues present in a given network topology. Output from **show** and **debug** commands is provided to help you identify the underlying issues. Based on this collected information, you identify why the observed behavior is occurring and propose solutions. You can compare your solutions with suggested solutions.

Like OSPFv3, RIPng also supports IPv6 routes. This chapter contrasts RIPng with its predecessor, RIPv2. Configuration and troubleshooting syntax references are provided, in addition to a sample configuration. You are also given a listing of common RIPng troubleshooting issues you might encounter.

Finally, a trouble ticket addressing RIPng is presented. As with the OSPFv3 trouble ticket, you are challenged to resolve the identified issues, equipped with a collection of **show** and **debug** command output. Suggested solutions are provided.

"Do I Know This Already?" Quiz

The "Do I Know This Already?" quiz helps you determine your level of knowledge of this chapter's topics before you begin. Table 12-1 details the major topics discussed in this chapter and their corresponding quiz questions.

Table 12-1   *"Do I Know This Already?" Section-to-Question Mapping*

Foundation Topics Section	Questions
Reviewing IPv6	1–5
OSPFv3 Troubleshooting	6–8
RIPng Troubleshooting	9–11

1. Identify three IPv6 address types. (Choose the three best answers.)

   a. Unicast

   b. Broadcast

   c. Multicast

   d. Anycast

2. How can the following IPv6 address be condensed?
   0AA0:0123:4040:0000:0000:0000:000A:100B

   a. AA0::123:404:A:100B

   b. AA::123:404:A:1B

   c. AA0:123:4040::A:100B

   d. 0AA0:0123:4040::0::000A:100B

3. Identify three approaches for routing IPv6. (Choose the three best answers.)

   a. OSPFv2

   b. RIPng

   c. Static routes

   d. EIGRP

4. What command is used to enable IPv6 routing on a router?

   a. Router(config)# **ipv6 unicast-routing**

   b. Router(config)# **ipv6 routing**

   c. Router(config)# **ip routing ipv6**

   d. Router(config)# **ip routing unicast-ipv6**

5. You want to tunnel IPv6 traffic across an IPv4 portion of a network. In interface configuration mode for the tunnel you are configuring, what IP address would you enter after the tunnel source command?

   a. The IPv6 address assigned to the local tunnel interface

   b. The IPv4 address assigned to the local interface on which the tunnel is built

   c. The IPv6 address assigned to the remote tunnel interface

   d. The IPv4 address assigned to the remote interface on which the tunnel is built

6. Identify two OSPFv3 characteristics that are not characteristics of OSPFv2. (Choose the two best answers.)

    a. Uses a hierarchical structure divided into areas

    b. Requires direct connectivity from the backbone area to all other areas

    c. Uses link-local addresses to identify neighbors

    d. Allows communication between two nodes connected to a common link, even though the two nodes might not share a common subnet

7. In what configuration mode is the following OSPFv3 command issued?

```
ipv6 ospf process-id area area-id
```

    a. Router configuration mode

    b. Route-map configuration mode

    c. Global configuration mode

    d. Interface configuration mode

8. What command lists the state of a router's adjacency with all configured OSPFv3 neighbors? (Choose the best answer.)

    a. show ipv6 ospf

    b. show ipv6 ospf neighbor

    c. show ipv6 ospf interface

    d. debug ipv6 ospf adj

9. RIPng sends routing updates to what multicast address?

    a. 224.0.0.9

    b. FF02::9

    c. FE80::

    d. 224.0.0.5

10. What interface configuration mode command instructs an interface to participate in a specified RIPng routing process? (Choose the best answer.)

    a. ipv6 rip *process-name* **default-information** {only | originate}

    b. ipv6 interface *process-name*

    c. ipv6 router rip *process-name*

    d. ipv6 rip *process-name* **enable**

11. Which of the following commands shows the contents of an IPv6 routing table?

    a. show ipv6 rip [*process-name*] [database | next-hops]

    b. show ipv6 route

    c. show ripng route

    d. show rip route ipv6

Foundation Topics

Reviewing IPv6

With the worldwide depletion of IP version 4 (IPv4) addresses, many organizations have migrated, are in the process of migrating, or are considering migrating their IPv4 addresses to IPv6 addresses. IPv6 dramatically increases the number of available IP addresses. In fact, IPv6 offers approximately $5 * 10^{28}$ IP addresses for each person on the planet.

Beyond the increased address space, IPv6 offers many other features:

Key Topic

- Simplified header.
  - IPv4 header: Uses 12 fields.
  - IPv6 header: Uses 5 fields.
- No broadcasts.
- No fragmentation (performs MTU discovery for each session).
- Can coexist with IPv4 during a transition.
  - Dual stack (running IPv4 and IPv6 simultaneously).
  - IPv6 over IPv4 (tunneling IPv6 over an IPv4 tunnel).

This section reviews IPv6 address types, the IPv6 address structure, and routing options for IPv6. Subsequent sections in this chapter address troubleshooting IPv6 routing protocols, specifically OSPFv3 and RIPng.

IPv6 Address Types

IPv6 has three types of addresses:

Key Topic

- Unicast
- Multicast
- Anycast

Unicast

With unicast, a single IPv6 address is applied to a single interface, as illustrated in Figure 12-1. The communication flow can be thought of as a one-to-one communication flow.

In Figure 12-1, a server (that is, AAAA::1) is sending traffic to a single client (that is, AAAA::2).

Multicast

With multicast, a single IPv6 address (that is, a multicast group) represents multiple devices on a network, as seen in Figure 12-2. The communication flow is one-to-many.

In Figure 12-2, a server (that is, AAAA::1) is sending traffic to a multicast group (that is, FF00::A). Two clients (that is, AAAA::2 and AAAA::3) have joined this group. Those clients receive the traffic from the server, whereas any client that did not join the group (for example, AAAA::4) does not receive the traffic.

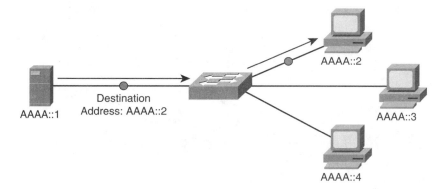

Figure 12-1   *IPv6 Unicast Example*

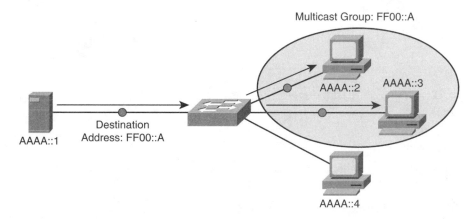

Figure 12-2   *IPv6 Multicast Example*

Anycast

With anycast, a single IPv6 address is assigned to multiple devices, as depicted in Figure 12-3. The communication flow is one-to-nearest (from the perspective of a router's routing table).

In Figure 12-3, a client with an IPv6 address of AAAA::1 wants to send traffic to a destination IPv6 address of AAAA::2. Notice that two servers (that is, Server A and Server B) have an IPv6 address of AAAA::2. In the figure, the traffic destined for AAAA::2 is sent to Server A, via router R2, because the network on which Server A resides appears to be closer than the network on which Server B resides, from the perspective of router R1's IPv6 routing table.

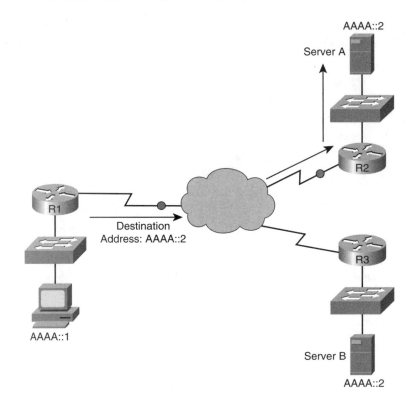

Figure 12-3 *IPv6 Anycast Example*

IPv6 Address Format

An IPv6 address has the following address format, where X equals a hexadecimal digit in the range of 0–F:

XXXX:XXXX:XXXX:XXXX:XXXX:XXXX:XXXX:XXXX

A hexadecimal digit is four bits in size (that is, four binary bits can represent sixteen values). Notice that an IPv6 address has eight fields, and each field contains four hexadecimal digits. The following formula reveals why an IPv6 address is a 128-bit address:

4 bits per digit * 4 digits per field * 8 fields = 128 bits in an IPv6 address

Key Topic

Because IPv6 addresses can be difficult to work with, due to their size, the following rules exist for abbreviating these addresses:

- Leading zeros in a field can be omitted.

- Contiguous fields containing all zeros can be represented with a double colon. (NOTE: This can only be done once for a single IPv6 address.)

As an example, consider the following IPv6 address:

ABCD:0123:4040:0000:0000:0000:000A:000B

Using the rules for abbreviation, the IPv6 address can be rewritten as

```
ABCD:123:4040::A:B
```

Also, the Extended Unique Identifier (EUI-64) format can be used to cause the router to automatically populate the low-order 64 bits of an IPv6 address based on an interface's MAC address.

IPv6 Routing Options

IPv6 maintains a separate routing table from IPv4. Following are methods of populating this IPv6 routing table:

- **Static routes:** Configured similar to IPv4 static routes.

- **RIP next generation (RIPng):** Has many of the same characteristics as RIPv2 (for example, a distance vector routing protocol with a 15 hop-count maximum).

- **OSPFv3:** Builds on OSPFv2 to add support for IPv6 network characteristics (for example, 128-bit network addresses and link-local addresses).

- **IS-IS for IPv6:** Similar to IS-IS for IPv4, with a few IPv6 extensions added (for example, new Type, Length, Value [TLV] attributes, and a new protocol ID).

- **Multiprotocol BGP:** Allows BGP to route protocols other than IPv4 (for example, IPv6).

- **EIGRP:** Configured on the interfaces with IPv6 addressing, similar to OSPFv3.

Configuring IPv6 Support

As a reference, Table 12-2 presents basic IPv6 configuration commands.

Table 12-2 *IPv6 Configuration Commands*

Command	Description
ipv6 cef	Global configuration mode command that configures Cisco Express Forwarding for IPv6.
ipv6 unicast-routing	Global configuration mode command that instructs a router to forward IPv6 traffic.
ipv6 address *ipv6-address/prefix-length* [eui-64]	Interface configuration mode command that assigns an IPv6 address to an interface. (NOTE: The **eui-64** option allows a router to complete the low-order 64 bits of an address, based on an interface's MAC address.)

Example 12-1 demonstrates how to enable a router to support IPv6 routing and how to assign IPv6 addresses to router interfaces.

Example 12-1   *IPv6 Configuration Example*

```
R1# show run
...OUTPUT OMITTED...
ipv6 unicast-routing
ipv6 cef
!
interface FastEthernet0/0
 ipv6 address B:B:B:B::2/64
!
interface FastEthernet0/1
 ipv6 address A:A:A:A::2/64
...OUTPUT OMITTED...
```

As Example 12-1 demonstrates, IPv6 unicast routing is enabled with the **ipv6 unicast-routing** command issued in global configuration mode. Cisco Express Forwarding support for IPv6 is then globally enabled using the **ipv6 cef** command. Finally, under interface configuration mode for both the Fast Ethernet 0/0 and 0/1 interfaces, IPv6 addresses are assigned with the **ipv6 address** *ipv6-address/prefix-length* command.

Tunneling IPv6 Through an IPv4 Tunnel

When an enterprise is migrating from an IPv4 to IPv6 environment, there might be times when IPv6 networks might be separated by one or more IPv4 networks. One option that allows these different address formats to peacefully coexist is to tunnel IPv6 traffic over an IPv4 tunnel.

Table 12-3 provides a command reference for setting up such a tunnel.

Table 12-3   *Commands Used to Tunnel IPv6 via IPv4*

Command	Description
interface tunnel *interface-id*	Global configuration mode command that creates a virtual IPv4 tunnel interface over which encapsulated IPv6 packets can flow.
tunnel source *ipv4-address*	Interface configuration mode command that identifies the IPv4 address of the local end of a tunnel.
tunnel destination *ipv4-address*	Interface configuration mode command that identifies the IPv4 address of the remote end of a tunnel.
tunnel mode ipv6ip	Interface configuration mode command that configures an interface to act as a manual IPv6 tunnel.
ipv6 address *ipv6-address/prefix-length*	Interface configuration mode command that specifies the IPv6 address assigned to a tunnel interface.

Table 12-3 *Commands Used to Tunnel IPv6 via IPv4   (Continued)*

Command	Description
ipv6 ospf *process-id* **area** *area-id*	Interface configuration mode command that allows the IPv6 address configured on a tunnel interface to participate in an OSPFv3 routing process.

Figure 12-4 depicts a topology tunneling IPv6 traffic over an IPv4 tunnel.

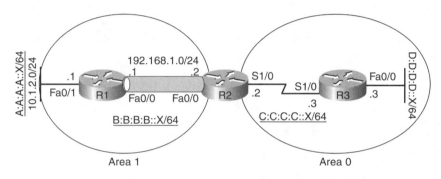

Figure 12-4 *IPv6 over IPv4 Tunnel*

Examples 12-2 and 12-3 show the configuration of the depicted IPv6 over IPv4 tunnel. Notice that each router specifies the source and destination IPv4 addresses of the tunnel, from the perspective of each router. The tunnel interface is then assigned an IPv6 address, told to participate in OSPF Area 1, and instructed to act as a manual IPv6 tunnel. The configuration and troubleshooting of OSPFv3, which is the version of OSPF that supports IPv6, is discussed in the next section.

Example 12-2 *Configuring IPv6 Parameters on Router R1's Tunnel Interface*

```
R1# show run
...OUTPUT OMITTED...
interface tunnel 1
 tunnel source 192.168.1.1
 tunnel destination 192.168.1.2
 ipv6 address b:b:b:b::1/64
 ipv6 ospf 1 area 1
 tunnel mode ipv6ip
```

> **Key Topic**

Example 12-3 *Configuring IPv6 Parameters on Router R2's Tunnel Interface*

```
R2# show run
...OUTPUT OMITTED...
interface tunnel 1
 tunnel source 192.168.1.2
```

```
tunnel destination 192.168.1.1
ipv6 address b:b:b:b::2/64
ipv6 ospf 1 area 1
tunnel mode ipv6ip
```

OSPFv3 Troubleshooting

As mentioned in the previous section, not all routing protocols (or all versions of some routing protocols) are compatible with IPv6. For example, although OSPFv2 is incompatible with IPv6, OSPFv3 can be used on IPv6 networks. This section discusses OSPFv3's characteristics and configuration. Additionally, you will learn some common OSPFv3 troubleshooting issues and commands.

Characteristics of OSPFv3

OSPFv3 builds on OSPFv2. Therefore, when you are working with OSPFv3, you will notice many similarities with OSPFv2. Following are some of these similarities:

■ Uses a hierarchical structure divided into areas.

■ Requires direct connectivity from the backbone area to all other areas.

■ Uses many of the same packet types (for example, Hello packets).

■ Adjacencies formed with neighbors.

Beyond the characteristics OPSFv3 has in common with OSPFv2, several enhancements have been made to provide support for IPv6 networks. Following is a sampling of some of OSPFv3's enhancements:

Key Topic

■ Routes over links rather than over networks.

■ Uses IPv6 link-local addresses to identify neighbors.

■ Can support multiple IPv6 subnets on a single link.

■ Allows communication between two nodes connected to a common link, even though the two nodes might not share a common subnet.

■ Supports multiple instances of OSPFv3 running over a common link.

■ Does not require the use of ARP.

Configuring OSPFv3

The primary difference in configuring OSPFv3, as opposed to OSPFv2, is that you go into interface configuration mode to tell an interface to participate in an OSPF routing process. In OSPFv2, you would go into router configuration mode for an OSPF process and specify network addresses and wildcard masks. These addresses and masks determined which of a router's interface would participate in the OSPF routing process.

Table 12-4 provides basic OSPFv3 configuration commands.

Table 12-4 *OSPFv3 Configuration Commands*

Command	Description
ipv6 ospf *process-id* **area** *area-id*	Interface configuration mode command that allows the IPv6 address configured on an interface to participate in an OSPFv3 routing process.
ipv6 router ospf *process-id*	Global configuration mode command that enables an OSPFv3 routing process on a router.
router-id *ipv4-address*	Router configuration mode command that specifies an IPv4 address to be used by OSPFv3 as a router's router ID.

Example 12-4 shows a sample OSPFv3 configuration on a router (that is, router R1), which is illustrated in Figure 12-5. Notice that an interface can simultaneously be configured with both IPv4 and IPv6 addresses. Also, notice the **ipv6 ospf 100 area 1** command issued in interface configuration mode for the Fast Ethernet 0/0 and 0/1 interfaces. This command causes both interfaces to participate in OSPFv3 routing process 100 as members of Area 1. The OSPFv3 process was started with the **ipv6 router ospf 100** command, and then in router configuration mode, an IPv4 address of 10.1.1.1 was specified as the address to use for the OSPF router ID.

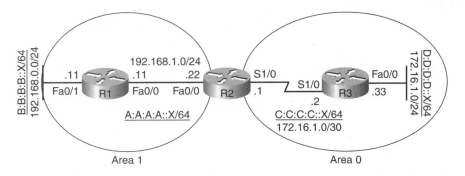

Figure 12-5 *OSPFv3 Sample Configuration Topology*

Example 12-4 *Sample OSPFv3 Configuration*

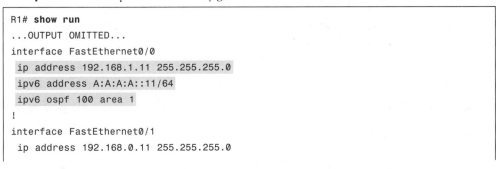

```
R1# show run
...OUTPUT OMITTED...
interface FastEthernet0/0
 ip address 192.168.1.11 255.255.255.0
 ipv6 address A:A:A:A::11/64
 ipv6 ospf 100 area 1
!
interface FastEthernet0/1
 ip address 192.168.0.11 255.255.255.0
```

```
   ipv6 address B:B:B:B::11/64
   ipv6 ospf 100 area 1
 !
ipv6 router ospf 100
 router-id 10.1.1.1
...OUTPUT OMITTED...
```

Troubleshooting OSPFv3

When troubleshooting an OSPFv3 issue, you can draw on your knowledge of troubleshooting OSPFv2, because many of the same troubleshooting issues arise in both environments. In fact, you do not need to relearn a completely different set of syntax for troubleshooting OSPFv3. In many cases, you can simply replace the **ip** keyword in a **show** command with a keyword of **ipv6**. For example, when troubleshooting OSPFv2, you might issue the **show ip ospf interface** command to view an interface's OSPF parameters. In an OSPFv3 environment, you could simply replace **ip** with **ipv6**, and give the **show ipv6 ospf interface** command. Table 12-5 provides a command reference of commonly used commands for troubleshooting OSPFv3 issues.

Key Topic

Table 12-5   *OSPFv3 Troubleshooting Commands*

Command	Description
show ipv6 ospf	Displays OSPFv3 routing process, router ID, various timers, and information about each area on a router.
show ipv6 ospf interface	Shows IPv6 link local address, area ID, process ID, router ID, and cost.
show ipv6 ospf neighbor	Lists the state of a router's adjacency with all configured OSPFv3 neighbors.
debug ipv6 ospf adj	Displays information about OSPFv3 adjacencies.
debug ip ipv6 ospf hello	Shows OSPFv3 HELLO packet information.

Many of the same root causes for an OSPFv2 issue could also result in an OSPFv3 issue. As just a few examples, consider the following list of potential reasons an OSPFv3 adjacency might not be formed:

Key Topic

- Mismatched HELLO parameters

- Mismatched IP MTU setting

- Interface configured as passive

- Mismatched area type

Although OSPFv2 and OSPFv3 do have many common characteristics, understanding the subtle differences between these OSPF versions can be valuable in your troubleshooting efforts. A listing of major differences was provided earlier in this section. To reinforce these OSPFv3 troubleshooting concepts, the next section in this chapter presents an OSPFv3 trouble ticket.

Trouble Ticket: IPv6 and OSPF

This section presents a trouble ticket based on an IPv6 and OSPF configuration. You are given sample **show** command output and are challenged to identify a resolution for the issue described.

Trouble Ticket #11

You receive the following trouble ticket:

Company A recently added IPv6 addressing to its existing IPv4 addressing. OSPFv3 is the protocol being used to route the IPv6 traffic.

Although the configuration was originally functional, now several OSPFv3 adjacencies are not forming. Full IPv6 reachability throughout the topology needs to be established.

This trouble ticket references the topology shown in Figure 12-6.

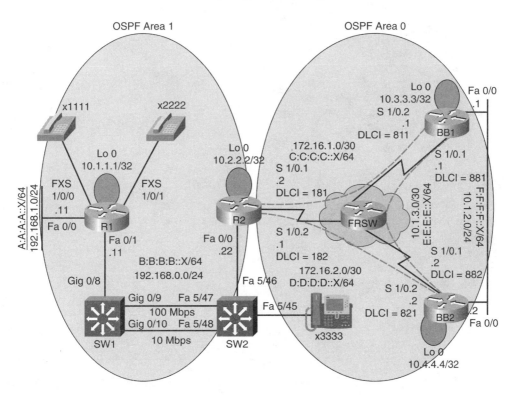

Figure 12-6 *Trouble Ticket #11 Topology*

Viewing Baseline Information

The routers in the topology were similarly configured for IPv6 and OSPFv3. The **show run** command was issued on router R2, the output of which is provided in Example 12-5. The configuration on the other routers in the topology was consistent with the configuration shown for router R2.

Example 12-5   *Working Configuration on Router R2*

```
R2# show run
Building configuration...

hostname R2
--- OUTPUT OMITTED ---
!
ipv6 unicast-routing
ipv6 cef

!
interface Loopback0
 ip address 10.2.2.2 255.255.255.255
!
interface FastEthernet0/0
 ip address 192.168.0.22 255.255.255.0
 ipv6 address B:B:B:B::22/64
 ipv6 ospf 1 area 1

!
interface Serial1/0.1 point-to-point
 ip address 172.16.1.2 255.255.255.252
 ipv6 address C:C:C:C::2/64
 ipv6 ospf 1 area 0

 frame-relay interface-dlci 181
!
interface Serial1/0.2 point-to-point
 ip address 172.16.2.1 255.255.255.252
 ipv6 address D:D:D:D::1/64
 ipv6 ospf 1 area 0

 frame-relay interface-dlci 182
!
!
--- OUTPUT OMITTED ---
ipv6 router ospf 1
```

Originally, all routers had full reachability throughout the topology, as verified in Examples 12-6, 12-7, 12-8, and 12-9.

Example 12-6 *Router R1's Initial IPv6 Routing Table*

```
R1# show ipv6 route
IPv6 Routing Table - 10 entries
Codes: C - Connected, L - Local, S - Static, R - RIP, B - BGP
       U - Per-user Static route
       I1 - ISIS L1, I2 - ISIS L2, IA - ISIS interarea, IS - ISIS summary
       O - OSPF intra, OI - OSPF inter, OE1 - OSPF ext 1, OE2 - OSPF ext 2
       ON1 - OSPF NSSA ext 1, ON2 - OSPF NSSA ext 2
C   A:A:A:A::/64 [0/0]
     via ::, FastEthernet0/0
L   A:A:A:A::11/128 [0/0]
     via ::, FastEthernet0/0
C   B:B:B:B::/64 [0/0]
     via ::, FastEthernet0/1
L   B:B:B:B::11/128 [0/0]
     via ::, FastEthernet0/1
OI  C:C:C:C::/64 [110/65]
     via FE80::C201:8FF:FE2C:0, FastEthernet0/1
OI  D:D:D:D::/64 [110/65]
     via FE80::C201:8FF:FE2C:0, FastEthernet0/1
OI  E:E:E:E::/64 [110/129]
     via FE80::C201:8FF:FE2C:0, FastEthernet0/1
OI  F:F:F:F::/64 [110/75]
     via FE80::C201:8FF:FE2C:0, FastEthernet0/1
L   FE80::/10 [0/0]
     via ::, Null0
L   FF00::/8 [0/0]
     via ::, Null0
```

Example 12-7 *Router R2's Initial IPv6 Routing Table*

```
R2# show ipv6 route
IPv6 Routing Table - 11 entries
Codes: C - Connected, L - Local, S - Static, R - RIP, B - BGP
       U - Per-user Static route
       I1 - ISIS L1, I2 - ISIS L2, IA - ISIS interarea, IS - ISIS summary
       O - OSPF intra, OI - OSPF inter, OE1 - OSPF ext 1, OE2 - OSPF ext 2
       ON1 - OSPF NSSA ext 1, ON2 - OSPF NSSA ext 2
O   A:A:A:A::/64 [110/11]
     via FE80::209:B7FF:FEFA:D1E1, FastEthernet0/0
C   B:B:B:B::/64 [0/0]
     via ::, FastEthernet0/0
L   B:B:B:B::22/128 [0/0]
```

```
        via ::, FastEthernet0/0
C    C:C:C:C::/64 [0/0]
        via ::, Serial1/0.1
L    C:C:C:C::2/128 [0/0]
        via ::, Serial1/0.1
C    D:D:D:D::/64 [0/0]
        via ::, Serial1/0.2
L    D:D:D:D::1/128 [0/0]
        via ::, Serial1/0.2
O    E:E:E:E::/64 [110/128]
        via FE80::C202:8FF:FE98:0, Serial1/0.1
        via FE80::C200:8FF:FE2C:0, Serial1/0.2
O    F:F:F:F::/64 [110/74]
        via FE80::C202:8FF:FE98:0, Serial1/0.1
        via FE80::C200:8FF:FE2C:0, Serial1/0.2
L    FE80::/10 [0/0]
        via ::, Null0
L    FF00::/8 [0/0]
        via ::, Null0
```

Example 12-8 *Router BB1's Initial IPv6 Routing Table*

```
BB1# show ipv6 route
IPv6 Routing Table - 11 entries
Codes: C - Connected, L - Local, S - Static, R - RIP, B - BGP
       U - Per-user Static route
       I1 - ISIS L1, I2 - ISIS L2, IA - ISIS interarea, IS - ISIS summary
       O - OSPF intra, OI - OSPF inter, OE1 - OSPF ext 1, OE2 - OSPF ext 2
       ON1 - OSPF NSSA ext 1, ON2 - OSPF NSSA ext 2
OI   A:A:A:A::/64 [110/75]
      via FE80::C201:8FF:FE2C:0, Serial1/0.2
OI   B:B:B:B::/64 [110/74]
      via FE80::C201:8FF:FE2C:0, Serial1/0.2
C    C:C:C:C::/64 [0/0]
      via ::, Serial1/0.2
L    C:C:C:C::1/128 [0/0]
      via ::, Serial1/0.2
O    D:D:D:D::/64 [110/74]
      via FE80::C200:8FF:FE2C:0, FastEthernet0/0
C    E:E:E:E::/64 [0/0]
      via ::, Serial1/0.1
L    E:E:E:E::1/128 [0/0]
      via ::, Serial1/0.1
C    F:F:F:F::/64 [0/0]
      via ::, FastEthernet0/0
```

```
L    F:F:F:F::1/128 [0/0]
       via ::, FastEthernet0/0
L    FE80::/10 [0/0]
       via ::, Null0
L    FF00::/8 [0/0]
       via ::, Null0
```

Example 12-9   *Router BB2's Initial IPv6 Routing Table*

```
BB2# show ipv6 route
IPv6 Routing Table - 11 entries
Codes: C - Connected, L - Local, S - Static, R - RIP, B - BGP
       U - Per-user Static route
       I1 - ISIS L1, I2 - ISIS L2, IA - ISIS interarea, IS - ISIS summary
       O - OSPF intra, OI - OSPF inter, OE1 - OSPF ext 1, OE2 - OSPF ext 2
       ON1 - OSPF NSSA ext 1, ON2 - OSPF NSSA ext 2
OI   A:A:A:A::/64 [110/75]
       via FE80::C201:8FF:FE2C:0, Serial1/0.2
OI   B:B:B:B::/64 [110/74]
       via FE80::C201:8FF:FE2C:0, Serial1/0.2
O    C:C:C:C::/64 [110/74]
       via FE80::C202:8FF:FE98:0, FastEthernet0/0
C    D:D:D:D::/64 [0/0]
       via ::, Serial1/0.2
L    D:D:D:D::2/128 [0/0]
       via ::, Serial1/0.2
C    E:E:E:E::/64 [0/0]
       via ::, Serial1/0.1
L    E:E:E:E::2/128 [0/0]
       via ::, Serial1/0.1
C    F:F:F:F::/64 [0/0]
       via ::, FastEthernet0/0
L    F:F:F:F::2/128 [0/0]
       via ::, FastEthernet0/0
L    FE80::/10 [0/0]
       via ::, Null0
L    FF00::/8 [0/0]
       via ::, Null0
```

Example 12-10 provides an additional sampling of baseline verification commands issued on router R2.

Example 12-10   *Additional Baseline Verification Commands on Router R2*

```
R2# show ipv6 ospf interface serial 1/0.2
Serial1/0.2 is up, line protocol is up
  Link Local Address FE80::C201:8FF:FE2C:0, Interface ID 14
  Area 0, Process ID 1, Instance ID 0, Router ID 10.2.2.2
  Network Type POINT_TO_POINT, Cost: 64
  Transmit Delay is 1 sec, State POINT_TO_POINT,
  Timer intervals configured, Hello 10, Dead 40, Wait 40, Retransmit 5
    Hello due in 00:00:04
  Index 1/2/3, flood queue length 0
  Next 0x0(0)/0x0(0)/0x0(0)
  Last flood scan length is 1, maximum is 2
  Last flood scan time is 0 msec, maximum is 0 msec
  Neighbor Count is 1, Adjacent neighbor count is 1
    Adjacent with neighbor 10.4.4.4
  Suppress hello for 0 neighbor(s)
R2# show ipv6 ospf
 Routing Process "ospfv3 1" with ID 10.2.2.2
 It is an area border router
 SPF schedule delay 5 secs, Hold time between two SPFs 10 secs
 Minimum LSA interval 5 secs. Minimum LSA arrival 1 secs
 LSA group pacing timer 240 secs
 Interface flood pacing timer 33 msecs
Retransmission pacing timer 66 msecs
Number of external LSA 0. Checksum Sum 0x000000
 Number of areas in this router is 2. 2 normal 0 stub 0 nssa
 Reference bandwidth unit is 100 mbps
    Area BACKBONE(0)
    Number of interfaces in this area is 2
    SPF algorithm executed 8 times
    Number of LSA 14. Checksum Sum 0x063F6C
    Number of DCbitless LSA 0
    Number of indication LSA 0
    Number of DoNotAge LSA 0
    Flood list length 0
    Area 1
    Number of interfaces in this area is 1
    SPF algorithm executed 5 times
    Number of LSA 11. Checksum Sum 0x0481E4
    Number of DCbitless LSA 0
    Number of indication LSA 0
    Number of DoNotAge LSA 0
```

```
      Flood list length 0
R2# show ipv6 ospf neighbor

Neighbor ID     Pri   State         Dead Time   Interface ID   Interface
10.4.4.4          1   FULL/  -      00:00:36    14             Serial1/0.2
10.3.3.3          1   FULL/  -      00:00:36    14             Serial1/0.1
10.1.1.1          1   FULL/BDR      00:00:39    4              FastEthernet0/0
```

Troubleshoot and Resolve the Identified OSPFv3 Adjacency Issue

The trouble ticket indicates that several adjacencies are not being formed. So, you decide to start your troubleshooting efforts on router R1 and check its adjacency with router R2, and then check the adjacencies between R2 and BB1 and BB2. Finally, you will check the adjacencies between BB1 and BB2.

Issue #1: Adjacency Between Routers R1 and R2

Example 12-11 shows the data collected from router R1.

Example 12-11   *Troubleshooting Data Collection on Router R1*

```
R1# show ipv6 ospf neighbor

R1# debug ipv6 ospf adj
OSPFv3 adjacency events debugging is on
R1# debug ipv6 ospf hello
OSPFv3 hello events debugging is on
R1# u all
All possible debugging has been turned off
R1# show run
...OUTPUT OMITTED...
hostname R1
!
ipv6 unicast-routing
ipv6 cef
!
interface Loopback0
 ip address 10.1.1.1 255.255.255.255
!
interface FastEthernet0/0
 ip address 192.168.1.11 255.255.255.0
ipv6 address A:A:A:A::11/64
 ipv6 ospf 100 area 1
!
interface FastEthernet0/1
 ip address 192.168.0.11 255.255.255.0
```

```
 ipv6 address B:B:B:B::11/64
 ipv6 ospf 100 area 1
!
ipv6 router ospf 100
...OUTPUT OMITTED...
R1# show ipv6 ospf interface fa 0/1
FastEthernet0/1 is up, line protocol is up
  Link Local Address FE80::209:B7FF:FEFA:D1E1, Interface ID 4
  Area 1, Process ID 100, Instance ID 0, Router ID 192.168.1.11
  Network Type BROADCAST, Cost: 1
  Transmit Delay is 1 sec, State DR, Priority 1
  Designated Router (ID) 192.168.1.11, local address FE80::209:B7FF:FEFA:D1E1
  No backup designated router on this network
  Timer intervals configured, Hello 10, Dead 40, Wait 40, Retransmit 5
    Hello due in 00:00:03
  Index 1/2/2, flood queue length 0
  Next 0x0(0)/0x0(0)/0x0(0)
  Last flood scan length is 1, maximum is 2
  Last flood scan time is 0 msec, maximum is 0 msec
  Neighbor Count is 0, Adjacent neighbor count is 0
  Suppress hello for 0 neighbor(s)
```

Notice that router R1 has not formed an adjacency with router R2. Therefore, as a first step in your troubleshooting efforts, you attempt to resolve the issue by preventing routers R1 and R2 from forming an adjacency. Example 12-12 shows the data collected from router R2.

Example 12-12 *Troubleshooting Data Collection on Router R2*

```
R2# show ipv6 ospf neighbor

R2# debug ipv6 ospf adj
  OSPFv3 adjacency events debugging is on
R2# u all
All possible debugging has been turned off
R2# show run
...OUTPUT OMITTED...
hostname R2
!
ipv6 unicast-routing
ipv6 cef
!
interface Loopback0
 ip address 10.2.2.2 255.255.255.255
```

```
!
interface FastEthernet0/0
ip address 192.168.0.22 255.255.255.0
 ipv6 address B:B:B:B::22/64
 ipv6 ospf hello-interval 60
 ipv6 ospf 1 area 1
!
interface Serial1/0
 no ip address
 encapsulation frame-relay
!
interface Serial1/0.1 point-to-point
 ip address 172.16.1.2 255.255.255.252
 ipv6 address C:C:C:C::2/64
ipv6 ospf 1 area 0
frame-relay interface-dlci 181
!
interface Serial1/0.2 point-to-point
 ip address 172.16.2.1 255.255.255.252
 ipv6 address D:D:D:D::1/64
 ipv6 ospf network point-to-multipoint
 ipv6 ospf 1 area 0
 frame-relay interface-dlci 182
!
ipv6 router ospf 1
 passive-interface default
...OUTPUT OMITTED...
```

Based on the output provided in Examples 12-11 and 12-12, hypothesize why routers R1 and R2 are not forming an adjacency. On a separate sheet of paper, write out your suggested solution to correct the issue.

Issue #1: Suggested Solution

Notice in Example 12-12 that router R2's HELLO timer on the Fast Ethernet 0/0 interface was set to a non-default value, whereas the other end of the link was still set to the default. Also, router R2 had its OSPFv3 process configured with the **passive-interface default** command, which prevented any of router R2's interfaces from forming OSPFv3 adjacencies. Example 12-13 shows the correction of these configuration issues on router R2.

Example 12-13 *Correcting Router R2's HELLO Timer and Passive-Interface Configuration*

```
R2# conf term
Enter configuration commands, one per line.  End with CNTL/Z.
R2(config)# int fa 0/0
R2(config-if)# no ipv6 ospf hello-interval 60
```

```
R2(config-if)# exit
R2(config)# ipv6 router ospf 1
R2(config-rtr)# no passive-interface default
```

Issue #2: Adjacency Between Routers R2 and BB2

After implementing the fix shown in Example 12-13, router R2 successfully forms OSPF adjacencies with routers R1 and BB1. However, an adjacency is not successfully formed with router BB2. Example 12-14 shows the output of the **show ipv6 ospf interface s1/0.2** command issued on router BB2. This command was issued to view the OSPFv3 configuration of router BB2's Serial 1/0.2 subinterface, which is the subinterface used to connect to router R2.

Example 12-14   *Viewing Router BB2's OSPFv3 Configuration on Subinterface Serial 1/0.2*

```
BB2# show ipv6 ospf interface s1/0.2
Serial1/0.2 is up, line protocol is up
  Link Local Address FE80::C200:8FF:FE2C:0, Interface ID 14
  Area 0, Process ID 1, Instance ID 0, Router ID 10.4.4.4
  Network Type POINT_TO_POINT, Cost: 64
  Transmit Delay is 1 sec, State POINT_TO_POINT,

R2# show ipv6 ospf neighbor

R2# debug ipv6 ospf adj
  OSPFv3 adjacency events debugging is on
R2# u all
All possible debugging has been turned off
R2# show run
...OUTPUT OMITTED...
hostname R2
!
ipv6 unicast-routing
ipv6 cef
!
interface Loopback0
 ip address 10.2.2.2 255.255.255.255
!
interface FastEthernet0/0
ip address 192.168.0.22 255.255.255.0
 ipv6 address B:B:B:B::22/64
 ipv6 ospf hello-interval 60
 ipv6 ospf 1 area 1
!
interface Serial1/0
 no ip address
```

```
 encapsulation frame-relay
!
interface Serial1/0.1 point-to-point
 ip address 172.16.1.2 255.255.255.252
 ipv6 address C:C:C:C::2/64
ipv6 ospf 1 area 0
  Timer intervals configured, Hello 10, Dead 40, Wait 40, Retransmit 5
    Hello due in 00:00:08
  Index 1/3/3, flood queue length 0
  Next 0x0(0)/0x0(0)/0x0(0)
  Last flood scan length is 2, maximum is 2
  Last flood scan time is 0 msec, maximum is 4 msec
  Neighbor Count is 0, Adjacent neighbor count is 0
  Suppress hello for 0 neighbor(s)
```

Based on router R2's configuration (shown in Example 12-12) and the output shown in Example 12-14, determine why an OSPF adjacency is not being formed between routers R2 and BB2. Again, on a separate sheet of paper, write out your suggested solution.

Issue #2: Suggested Solution

Router R2's OSPF network type on subinterface Serial 1/0.2 was set to point-to-multipoint, while the other end of the link was the default network type of point-to-point. Example 12-15 shows the correction of router R2's misconfiguration.

Example 12-15 *Correcting Router R2's OSPF Network Type*

```
R2# conf term
Enter configuration commands, one per line.  End with CNTL/Z.
R2(config)# int s1/0.2
R2(config-subif)# no ipv6 ospf network point-to-multipoint
R2(config-subif)# exit
```

At this point in the troubleshooting process, routers R1 and R2 have formed adjacencies. Additionally, router R2 has formed adjacencies with routers BB1 and BB2. The output in Example 12-16 confirms the establishment of these adjacencies.

Example 12-16 *Confirming Router R2's OSPF Adjacencies*

```
R2# show ipv6 ospf neighbor

Neighbor ID     Pri   State          Dead Time   Interface ID   Interface
10.4.4.4          1   FULL/  -       00:00:36    14             Serial1/0.2
10.3.3.3          1   FULL/  -       00:00:36    14             Serial1/0.1
192.168.1.11      1   FULL/DR        00:00:39    4              FastEthernet0/0
```

Issue #3: Adjacency Between Routers BB1 and BB2

As seen in the output provided in Example 12-17, router BB1 has formed an adjacency with router BB2 over router BB1's Fast Ethernet 0/0 interface. However, an adjacency has not been successfully formed with router BB2 over router BB1's Serial 1/0.1 subinterface.

Example 12-17   *Determining Router BB1's Adjacencies*

```
BB1# show ipv6 ospf neigh

Neighbor ID     Pri   State          Dead Time   Interface ID   Interface
10.2.2.2          1   FULL/  -       00:00:37    13             Serial1/0.2
10.4.4.4          1   DOWN/  -           -       13             Serial1/0.1
10.4.4.4          1   FULL/DR        00:00:34    4              FastEthernet0/0
```

To investigate why an OSPF adjacency is not forming with router BB2 via router BB1's Serial 1/0.1 subinterface, the **debug ipv6 ospf adj** and **debug ipv6 ospf hello** commands were issued on router BB1, as seen in Example 12-18.

Example 12-18   *Debugging OSPFv3 Adjacency and Hello Events on Router BB1*

```
BB1# debug ipv6 ospf adj
  OSPFv3 adjacency events debugging is on
BB1# debug ipv6 ospf hello
  OSPFv3 hello events debugging is on
BB1#
*Mar  1 00:19:24.707: OSPFv3: Rcv DBD from 10.4.4.4 on Serial1/0.1 seq 0x1AEF opt
  0x0013 flag 0x7 len 28  mtu 1500 state EXSTART
*Mar  1 00:19:24.707: OSPFv3: Nbr 10.4.4.4 has larger interface MTU
*Mar  1 00:19:25.015: OSPFv3: Rcv hello from 10.2.2.2 area 0 from Serial1/0.2
  FE80::C201:8FF:FE2C:0 interface ID 13
*Mar  1 00:19:25.019: OSPFv3: End of hello processing
*Mar  1 00:19:28.583: OSPFv3: Send hello to FF02::5 area 0 on Serial1/0.2 from
  FE80::C202:8FF:FE98:0 interface ID 14
*Mar  1 00:19:28.647: OSPFv3: Rcv hello from 10.4.4.4 area 0 from Serial1/0.1
  FE80::C200:8FF:FE2C:0 interface ID 13
*Mar  1 00:19:28.651: OSPFv3: End of hello processing
*Mar  1 00:19:28.983: OSPFv3: Send hello to FF02::5 area 0 on FastEthernet0/0
  from FE80::C202:8FF:FE98:0 interface ID 4
*Mar  1 00:19:29.215: OSPFv3: Rcv hello from 10.4.4.4 area 0 from FastEthernet0/0
  FE80::C200:8FF:FE2C:0 interface ID 4
*Mar  1 00:19:29.219: OSPFv3: End of hello processing
BB1# u all
All possible debugging has been turned off
```

Because your troubleshooting on router BB1 is focused on BB1's Serial 1/0.1 subinterface, the **show ipv6 interface s1/0.1** command was issued, the output for which appears in Example 12-19.

Example 12-19   *Viewing the IPv6 Configuration on Router BB1's Serial 1/0.1 Subinterface*

```
BB1# show ipv6 interface s1/0.1
Serial1/0.1 is up, line protocol is up
  IPv6 is enabled, link-local address is FE80::C202:8FF:FE98:0
  Global unicast address(es):
    E:E:E:E::1, subnet is E:E:E:E::/64
  Joined group address(es):
    FF02::1
    FF02::2
    FF02::5
    FF02::1:FF00:1
    FF02::1:FF98:0
  MTU is 1400 bytes
  ICMP error messages limited to one every 100 milliseconds
  ICMP redirects are enabled
  ND DAD is enabled, number of DAD attempts: 1
  ND reachable time is 30000 milliseconds
  Hosts use stateless autoconfig for addresses.
```

Based on the output provided in Examples 12-18 and 12-19, determine why router BB1 is failing to form an OSPF adjacency with router BB2, via router BB1's Serial 1/0.1 subinterface. On a separate sheet of paper, write out your proposed solution to this issue.

Issue #3: Suggested Solution

The debug output seen in Example 12-18 indicates that router BB1's neighbor (that is, 10.4.4.4) reachable over subinterface Serial 1/0.1 has a larger MTU than router BB1's Serial 1/0.1 subinterface. The output in Example 12-19 indicates that router BB1's Serial 1/0.1 subinterface has an MTU of 1400 bytes. This is less than the default value of 1500 bytes. Example 12-20 shows how this MTU value was reset to its default value.

Example 12-20   *Correcting the MTU on Router BB1's Serial 1/0.1 Subinterface*

```
BB1# conf term
Enter configuration commands, one per line.  End with CNTL/Z.
BB1(config)# int s1/0.1
BB1(config-subif)# ipv6 mtu 1500
*Mar  1 00:20:00.019: %OSPFv3-5-ADJCHG: Process 1, Nbr 10.4.4.4 on Serial1/0.1
from LOADING to FULL, Loading Done
BB1(config-subif)# end
```

Notice, in Example 12-20, that an adjacency with router BB2 (that is, 10.4.4.4) was formed over router BB1's Serial 1/0.1 subinterface after setting the subinterface's MTU size to the default of 1500 bytes. Examples 12-21 and 12-22 further confirm that routers BB1 and BB2 have formed all appropriate adjacencies with their OSPF neighbors.

Example 12-21 *Router BB1's OSPF Adjacencies*

```
BB1# show ipv6 ospf neighbor
Neighbor ID     Pri    State         Dead Time    Interface ID    Interface
10.2.2.2         1     FULL/         00:00:37     13              Serial1/0.2
10.4.4.4         1     FULL/         00:00:30     13              Serial1/0.1
10.4.4.4         1     FULL/DR       00:00:31     4               FastEthernet0/0
```

Example 12-22 *Router BB2's OSPF Adjacencies*

```
BB2# show ipv6 ospf neighbor
Neighbor ID     Pri    State         Dead Time    Interface ID    Interface
10.2.2.2         1     FULL/         00:00:37     14              Serial1/0.2
10.3.3.3         1     FULL/         00:00:37     13              Serial1/0.1
10.3.3.3         1     FULL/BDR      00:00:31     4               FastEthernet0/0
```

To confirm that full reachability has been restored in the network, a series of **ping** commands were issued from router BB2, with one ping to each router in the topology. As seen in Example 12-23, all of the pings were successful.

Example 12-23 *Confirming Reachability to All Routers*

```
BB2# ping a:a:a:a::11

Type escape sequence to abort.
Sending 5, 100-byte ICMP Echos to A:A:A:A::11, timeout is 2 seconds:
!!!!!
Success rate is 100 percent (5/5), round-trip min/avg/max = 88/124/164 ms
BB2# ping b:b:b:b::22
Type escape sequence to abort.
Sending 5, 100-byte ICMP Echos to B:B:B:B::22, timeout is 2 seconds:
!!!!!
Success rate is 100 percent (5/5), round-trip min/avg/max = 44/83/164 ms
BB2# ping f:f:f:f::1
Type escape sequence to abort.
Sending 5, 100-byte ICMP Echos to F:F:F:F::1, timeout is 2 seconds:
!!!!!
```

```
Success rate is 100 percent (5/5), round-trip min/avg/max = 40/79/128 ms
BB2# ping e:e:e:e::2


Type escape sequence to abort.
Sending 5, 100-byte ICMP Echos to E:E:E:E::2, timeout is 2 seconds:
!!!!!
Success rate is 100 percent (5/5), round-trip min/avg/max = 0/0/0 ms
```

RIPng Troubleshooting

Just as OSPFv3 supports IPv6 routes while OSPFv2 does not, RIPng supports IPv6 routes, whereas RIP versions 1 and 2 do not. This section reviews RIPng theory, provides a collection of RIPng configuration commands, shows a sample configuration, offers a collection of helpful RIPng troubleshooting commands, and lists common RIPng troubleshooting issues.

Review RIPng Theory

RIPng is an enhancement to RIPv2; however, RIPng does have several characteristics similar to RIPv2, as follows:

- Distance-vector routing protocol

- Hop count metric

- Maximum hop count of fifteen

- Sends routing updates via multicast:
    - RIPv2: 224.0.0.9
    - RIPng: FF02::9

The following characteristics are enhancements of RIPng over RIPv2:

- Supports the routing of 128-bit IPv6 network addresses.

- Link-local addresses used for next-hop addresses.

- Next-hop addresses stored in Routing Information Base (RIB).

- Interfaces added to a RIP routing process in interface-configuration mode (as opposed to router configuration mode).

RIPng Configuration Commands

Similar to OSPFv3, RIPng uses interface configuration mode to tell an interface to participate in a RIP routing process. This is as opposed to RIPv1's and RIPv2's approach to using the **network** command in router configuration mode to configure an interface to participate in a RIP routing process.

Table 12-6 provides basic RIPng configuration commands.

Key Topic

Table 12-6 *RIPng Configuration Commands*

Command	Description
ipv6 rip *process-name* **enable**	Interface configuration mode command that instructs an interface to participate in the specified RIPng routing process.
ipv6 rip *process-name* **default-information {only	originate}**	Interface configuration mode command that causes an interface to originate a default route advertisement (that is, an advertisement for network ::/0) and optionally suppress the advertisement of all other routes (using the **only** keyword).
ipv6 router rip *process-name*	Global configuration mode command that enters router configuration mode for the specified RIPng routing process.
maximum-paths *number*	Interface configuration mode command that specifies the number of equal-cost paths across which RIPng can load balance (defaults to 16 with a valid range of 1-64).

Example 12-24 shows a sample RIPng configuration on a router (that is, router R1), which is illustrated in Figure 12-7. Notice that an interface can simultaneously be configured with both IPv4 and IPv6 addresses. Also, notice the **ipv6 rip PROCESS1 enable** command issued in interface configuration mode. This command causes an interface to participate in the RIPng routing process named **PROCESS1**.

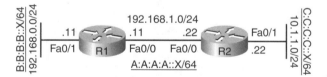

Figure 12-7 *RIPng Sample Configuration Topology*

Example 12-24   *Sample RIPng Configuration*

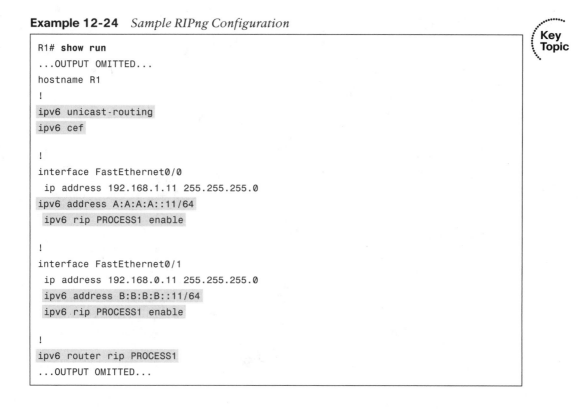

```
R1# show run
...OUTPUT OMITTED...
hostname R1
!
ipv6 unicast-routing
ipv6 cef

!
interface FastEthernet0/0
 ip address 192.168.1.11 255.255.255.0
ipv6 address A:A:A:A::11/64
 ipv6 rip PROCESS1 enable

!
interface FastEthernet0/1
 ip address 192.168.0.11 255.255.255.0
 ipv6 address B:B:B:B::11/64
 ipv6 rip PROCESS1 enable

!
ipv6 router rip PROCESS1
...OUTPUT OMITTED...
```

Troubleshooting RIPng

When troubleshooting a RIPng issue, you can take advantage of your RIPv1 and RIPv2 knowledge. Many commands used to troubleshoot RIPv1 and RIPv2 can be used for troubleshooting RIPng by simply replacing the **ip** keyword in a **show** command with a keyword of **ipv6**. For example, instead of using the RIPv2 **show ip rip database** command, you could use the **show ipv6 rip database** command in a network running RIPng. Table 12-7 provides a command reference of commonly used commands for troubleshooting RIPng issues.

Table 12-7   *RIPng Troubleshooting Commands*

Command	Description
show ipv6 rip [*process-name*] [**database** | **next-hops**]	Displays information about the specified RIPng routing process, and optionally the contents of the RIPng database and a listing of next-hop addresses.
show ipv6 route	Shows the contents of the IPv6 routing table.
debug ipv6 rip	Provides real-time information about RIPng messages.

Following is a listing of common RIPng issues you might encounter:

- RIPng routes not appearing in the IPv6 routing table

- RIPng not performing appropriate load balancing

- Interface not sending RIPng updates

- Individual network advertisements not suppressed when sourcing a default route

Trouble Ticket: IPv6 and RIPng

This section presents a trouble ticket based on an IPv6 and RIPng configuration. You are given sample **show** command output and are challenged to identify a resolution for the issue described.

Trouble Ticket #12

You receive the following trouble ticket:

Company A (that is, routers R1 and R2) is dual-homed to two Internet service providers (ISPs). The ISP routers are BB1 and BB2. However, router R2 only sees a single path to reach a default route (rather than one path from each ISP) in its IPv6 routing table. Also, router R2 is seeing other ISP-advertised routes (specifically, E:E:E:E::/64 and F:F:F:F::/64) rather than just a default route in its IPv6 routing table. All routes that router R2 receives from the ISP routers, except a default route, should be suppressed (see Figure 12-8).

Viewing Baseline Information

All routers in the shown topology have been configured with IPv6 addressing on their physical interfaces and subinterfaces. Routers R1 and R2 are considered to be enterprise routers, whereas routers BB1 and BB2 are considered to be Internet service provider (ISP) routers, with whom the enterprise is dual homed.

The backbone ISP routers are configured to only send IPv6 default route advertisements (that is, advertisements for route ::/0) to the enterprise routers. Therefore, routers R1 and R2 do not have entries for the E:E:E:E::/64 and F:F:F:F::/64 networks. Router R1's configuration, which is representative of the basic IPv6 and RIPng configuration present on all the routers in the topology, is presented in Example 12-25.

Example 12-25   *Running Configuration on Router R1*

```
R1# show run
...OUTPUT OMITTED...
hostname R1
!
ipv6 unicast-routing
ipv6 cef
```

```
!
interface Loopback0
 ip address 10.1.1.1 255.255.255.255
!
interface FastEthernet0/0
 ip address 192.168.1.11 255.255.255.0
 ipv6 address A:A:A:A::11/64
 ipv6 rip PROCESS1 enable

!
interface FastEthernet0/1
 ip address 192.168.0.11 255.255.255.0
 ipv6 address B:B:B:B::11/64
 ipv6 rip PROCESS1 enable

!
ipv6 router rip PROCESS1

...OUTPUT OMITTED...
```

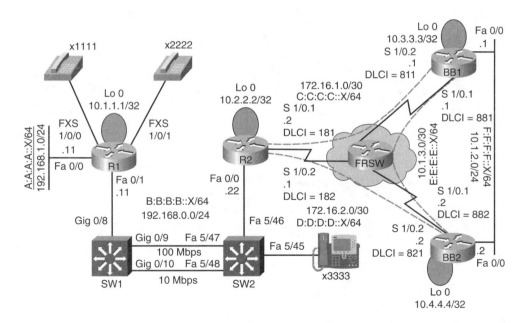

Figure 12-8 *Trouble Ticket #12 Topology*

Router R1's IPv6 routing table is shown in Example 12-26. Notice the absence of specific routes to the backbone IPv6 networks of E:E:E:E::/64 and F:F:F:F::/64. Instead, router R1 could reach these networks via the default route (that is, ::/0) in its routing table.

Example 12-26   *IPv6 Routing Table on Router R1*

```
R1# show ipv6 route
IPv6 Routing Table - 9 entries
Codes: C - Connected, L - Local, S - Static, R - RIP, B - BGP
       U - Per-user Static route
       I1 - ISIS L1, I2 - ISIS L2, IA - ISIS interarea, IS - ISIS summary
       O - OSPF intra, OI - OSPF inter, OE1 - OSPF ext 1, OE2 - OSPF ext 2
       ON1 - OSPF NSSA ext 1, ON2 - OSPF NSSA ext 2
R   ::/0 [120/3]
     via FE80::C201:EFF:FE64:0, FastEthernet0/1
C   A:A:A:A::/64 [0/0]
     via ::, FastEthernet0/0
L   A:A:A:A::11/128 [0/0]
     via ::, FastEthernet0/0
L   B:B:B:B::11/128 [0/0]
     via ::, FastEthernet0/1

R   C:C:C:C::/64 [120/2]
     via FE80::C201:EFF:FE64:0, FastEthernet0/1
R   D:D:D:D::/64 [120/2]
     via FE80::C201:EFF:FE64:0, FastEthernet0/1
L   FE80::/10 [0/0]
     via ::, Null0
L   FF00::/8 [0/0]
      via ::, Null0
```

Router R1's reachability to all IPv6 networks in the topology was confirmed by issuing a series of pings from R1, one to each IPv6 network in the topology. Example 12-27 shows the successful ping results.

Example 12-27   ping *Results for Router R1*

```
R1# ping a:a:a:a::11


Type escape sequence to abort.
Sending 5, 100-byte ICMP Echos to A:A:A:A::11, timeout is 2 seconds:
!!!!!
Success rate is 100 percent (5/5), round-trip min/avg/max = 1/1/1 ms
R1# ping b:b:b:b::22


Type escape sequence to abort.
```

```
Sending 5, 100-byte ICMP Echos to B:B:B:B::22, timeout is 2 seconds:
!!!!!
Success rate is 100 percent (5/5), round-trip min/avg/max = 20/54/88 ms
R1# ping c:c:c:c::1

Type escape sequence to abort.
Sending 5, 100-byte ICMP Echos to F:F:F:F::2, timeout is 2 seconds:
!!!!!
Success rate is 100 percent (5/5), round-trip min/avg/max = 64/145/337 ms
Type escape sequence to abort.
Sending 5, 100-byte ICMP Echos to C:C:C:C::1, timeout is 2 seconds:
!!!!!
Success rate is 100 percent (5/5), round-trip min/avg/max = 48/89/128 ms
R1# ping d:d:d:d::2

Type escape sequence to abort.
Sending 5, 100-byte ICMP Echos to D:D:D:D::2, timeout is 2 seconds:
!!!!!
Success rate is 100 percent (5/5), round-trip min/avg/max = 52/97/173 ms
R1# ping e:e:e:e::1

Type escape sequence to abort.
Sending 5, 100-byte ICMP Echos to E:E:E:E::1, timeout is 2 seconds:
!!!!!
Success rate is 100 percent (5/5), round-trip min/avg/max = 60/85/132 ms
R1# ping f:f:f:f::2
```

Router R2's routing table, provided in Example 12-28, shows that router R2 has two paths to reach the default network of ::/0: one path via router BB1 and one path via router BB2. These dual paths are made possible because RIPng (in addition to RIPv1 and RIPv2) can load balance across equal-cost paths. All versions of RIP use *hop count* as their metric.

Example 12-28 *IPv6 Routing Table on Router R2*

```
R2# show ipv6 route
IPv6 Routing Table - 10 entries
Codes: C - Connected, L - Local, S - Static, R - RIP, B - BGP
       U - Per-user Static route
       I1 - ISIS L1, I2 - ISIS L2, IA - ISIS interarea, IS - ISIS summary
       O - OSPF intra, OI - OSPF inter, OE1 - OSPF ext 1, OE2 - OSPF ext 2
```

```
          ON1 - OSPF NSSA ext 1, ON2 - OSPF NSSA ext 2
R    ::/0 [120/2]
     via FE80::C202:EFF:FEBC:0, Serial1/0.1
     via FE80::C200:EFF:FE64:0, Serial1/0.2
R    A:A:A:A::/64 [120/2]
     via FE80::209:B7FF:FEFA:D1E1, FastEthernet0/0
C    B:B:B:B::/64 [0/0]
     via ::, FastEthernet0/0
L    B:B:B:B::22/128 [0/0]
     via ::, FastEthernet0/0
C    C:C:C:C::/64 [0/0]

     via ::, Serial1/0.1
L    C:C:C:C::2/128 [0/0]
     via ::, Serial1/0.1
C    D:D:D:D::/64 [0/0]
     via ::, Serial1/0.2
L    D:D:D:D::1/128 [0/0]
     via ::, Serial1/0.2
L    FE80::/10 [0/0]
     via ::, Null0
L    FF00::/8 [0/0]
     via ::, Null0
```

Routers BB1 and BB2 both have listings for all of the topology's IPv6 networks in their IPv6 routing tables, as shown in Examples 12-29 and 12-30.

Example 12-29 *IPv6 Routing Table on Router BB1*

```
BB1# show ipv6 route
IPv6 Routing Table - 11 entries
Codes: C - Connected, L - Local, S - Static, R - RIP, B - BGP
       U - Per-user Static route
       I1 - ISIS L1, I2 - ISIS L2, IA - ISIS interarea, IS - ISIS summary
       O - OSPF intra, OI - OSPF inter, OE1 - OSPF ext 1, OE2 - OSPF ext 2
       ON1 - OSPF NSSA ext 1, ON2 - OSPF NSSA ext 2
R    A:A:A:A::/64 [120/3]
     via FE80::C201:EFF:FE64:0, Serial1/0.2
R    B:B:B:B::/64 [120/2]
     via FE80::C201:EFF:FE64:0, Serial1/0.2
C    C:C:C:C::/64 [0/0]
     via ::, Serial1/0.2
L    C:C:C:C::1/128 [0/0]
```

```
     via ::, Serial1/0.2
R    D:D:D:D::/64 [120/2]
       via FE80::C200:EFF:FE64:0, FastEthernet0/0
       via FE80::C200:EFF:FE64:0, Serial1/0.1
       via FE80::C201:EFF:FE64:0, Serial1/0.2
C    E:E:E:E::/64 [0/0]
       via ::, Serial1/0.1
L    E:E:E:E::1/128 [0/0]
       via ::, Serial1/0.1
C    F:F:F:F::/64 [0/0]
       via ::, FastEthernet0/0

L    F:F:F:F::1/128 [0/0]
       via ::, FastEthernet0/0
L    FE80::/10 [0/0]
       via ::, Null0
L    FF00::/8 [0/0]
       via ::, Null0
```

Example 12-30 *IPv6 Routing Table on Router BB2*

```
BB2# show ipv6 route
IPv6 Routing Table - 11 entries
Codes: C - Connected, L - Local, S - Static, R - RIP, B - BGP
       U - Per-user Static route
       I1 - ISIS L1, I2 - ISIS L2, IA - ISIS interarea, IS - ISIS summary
       O - OSPF intra, OI - OSPF inter, OE1 - OSPF ext 1, OE2 - OSPF ext 2
       ON1 - OSPF NSSA ext 1, ON2 - OSPF NSSA ext 2
R    A:A:A:A::/64 [120/3]
       via FE80::C201:EFF:FE64:0, Serial1/0.2
R    B:B:B:B::/64 [120/2]
       via FE80::C201:EFF:FE64:0, Serial1/0.2
R    C:C:C:C::/64 [120/2]
       via FE80::C201:EFF:FE64:0, Serial1/0.2
       via FE80::C202:EFF:FEBC:0, FastEthernet0/0
       via FE80::C202:EFF:FEBC:0, Serial1/0.1
C    D:D:D:D::/64 [0/0]
       via ::, Serial1/0.2
L    D:D:D:D::2/128 [0/0]
       via ::, Serial1/0.2
C    E:E:E:E::/64 [0/0]
       via ::, Serial1/0.1
L    E:E:E:E::2/128 [0/0]
       via ::, Serial1/0.1
C    F:F:F:F::/64 [0/0]
```

```
     via ::, FastEthernet0/0
L   F:F:F:F::2/128 [0/0]
     via ::, FastEthernet0/0
L   FE80::/10 [0/0]
     via ::, Null0
L   FF00::/8 [0/0]
     via ::, Null0
```

Notice that the IPv6 routing tables for routers BB1 and BB2 did not have a default route entry. The absence of the default route was because routers BB1 and BB2 were sourcing default route information to router R2, while suppressing more specific route information to router R2. Example 12-31 highlights the **ipv6 rip PROCESS1 default-information originate** command used on router BB1 to create its default route advertisement. Router BB2 was configured with an identical command.

Example 12-31   *Advertising Default Route Information on Router BB1*

```
BB1# show run | begin Serial1/0.2
interface Serial1/0.2 point-to-point
 ip address 172.16.1.1 255.255.255.252
 ipv6 address C:C:C:C::1/64
 ipv6 rip PROCESS1 enable
 ipv6 rip PROCESS1 default-information only
 frame-relay interface-dlci 811
```

Troubleshoot and Resolve the Identified RIPng Issue

The **show ipv6 route** command was issued on router R2 to confirm that the IPv6 routing table included only a single path to reach the default network of ::/0. Example 12-32 provides the output from this command, which also confirms the presence of the backbone routes E:E:E:E::/64 and F:F:F:F::/64 in the IPv6 routing table.

Example 12-32   *Confirmation of Troubleshooting Issues on Router R2*

```
R2# show ipv6 route
IPv6 Routing Table - 12 entries
Codes: C - Connected, L - Local, S - Static, R - RIP, B - BGP
       U - Per-user Static route
       I1 - ISIS L1, I2 - ISIS L2, IA - ISIS interarea, IS - ISIS summary
       O - OSPF intra, OI - OSPF inter, OE1 - OSPF ext 1, OE2 - OSPF ext 2
       ON1 - OSPF NSSA ext 1, ON2 - OSPF NSSA ext 2
R   ::/0 [120/2]
     via FE80::C200:EFF:FE64:0, Serial1/0.2
R   A:A:A:A::/64 [120/2]
     via FE80::209:B7FF:FEFA:D1E1, FastEthernet0/0
C   B:B:B:B::/64 [0/0]
```

```
        via ::, FastEthernet0/0
L   B:B:B:B::22/128 [0/0]
        via ::, FastEthernet0/0
C   C:C:C:C::/64 [0/0]
        via ::, Serial1/0.1
L   C:C:C:C::2/128 [0/0]
        via ::, Serial1/0.1
C   D:D:D:D::/64 [0/0]
        via ::, Serial1/0.2
L   D:D:D:D::1/128 [0/0]
        via ::, Serial1/0.2
R   E:E:E:E::/64 [120/2]
        via FE80::C200:EFF:FE64:0, Serial1/0.2
R   F:F:F:F::/64 [120/2]
        via FE80::C200:EFF:FE64:0, Serial1/0.2
L   FE80::/10 [0/0]
        via ::, Null0
L   FF00::/8 [0/0]
        via ::, Null0
```

The **show ipv6 rip database** command, as shown in Example 12-33, proves that router R2 received two default route advertisements; however, only one of those route advertisements was injected into the IPv6 routing table.

Example 12-33 *RIP Database on Router R2*

```
R2# show ipv6 rip database
RIP process "PROCESS1", local RIB
 A:A:A:A::/64, metric 2, installed
      FastEthernet0/0/FE80::209:B7FF:FEFA:D1E1, expires in 174 secs
 B:B:B:B::/64, metric 2
      FastEthernet0/0/FE80::209:B7FF:FEFA:D1E1, expires in 174 secs
D:D:D:D::/64, metric 2
      Serial1/0.2/FE80::C200:EFF:FE64:0, expires in 160 secs
E:E:E:E::/64, metric 2, installed
      Serial1/0.2/FE80::C200:EFF:FE64:0, expires in 160 secs
 F:F:F:F::/64, metric 2, installed
      Serial1/0.2/FE80::C200:EFF:FE64:0, expires in 160 secs
 ::/0, metric 2, installed
      Serial1/0.2/FE80::C200:EFF:FE64:0, expires in 160 secs
      Serial1/0.1/FE80::C202:EFF:FEBC:0, expires in 170 secs
```

Example 12-34 shows the running configuration on router R2.

Example 12-34   *Running Configuration on Router R2*

```
R2# show run
...OUTPUT OMITTED...
hostname R2
!
ipv6 unicast-routing
ipv6 cef
!
interface Loopback0
 ip address 10.2.2.2 255.255.255.255
!
interface FastEthernet0/0
 ip address 192.168.0.22 255.255.255.0
 ipv6 address B:B:B:B::22/64
 ipv6 rip PROCESS1 enable
!
interface Serial1/0
no ip address
 encapsulation frame-relay
 serial restart-delay 0
!
interface Serial1/0.1 point-to-point
 ip address 172.16.1.2 255.255.255.252
 ipv6 address C:C:C:C::2/64
 ipv6 rip PROCESS1 enable
 frame-relay interface-dlci 181
!
interface Serial1/0.2 point-to-point
 ip address 172.16.2.1 255.255.255.252
 ipv6 address D:D:D:D::1/64

ipv6 rip PROCESS1 enable
 frame-relay interface-dlci 182
!
ipv6 router rip PROCESS1
 maximum-paths 1
...OUTPUT OMITTED...
```

Issue #1: Router R2 Not Load Balancing Between Routers BB1 and BB2

The first issue you investigate is router R2 not load balancing between the ISP routers (that is, routers BB1 and BB2). Based on the **show** command output presented in Examples 12-32, 12-33, and 12-34, hypothesize why router R2's IPv6 routing table contains only a single entry for a default network (rather than having two entries, one for BB1 and one for BB2). On a separate sheet of paper, write out your proposed configuration change to resolve this issue.

Issue #1: Suggested Solution

A review of router R2's running configuration reveals the **maximum-paths 1** command in router configuration mode for the RIPng routing process. This command prevents two default route paths from appearing in router R2's IPv6 routing table. Example 12-35 shows how this command is removed from router R2's configuration in order to restore load balancing to a default route.

Example 12-35 *Restoring Load Balancing to a Default Route on Router R2*

```
R2# conf term
Enter configuration commands, one per line.  End with CNTL/Z.
R2(config)# ipv6 router rip PROCESS1
R2(config-rtr)# no maximum-paths 1
```

Issue #2: Backbone Routes Not Being Suppressed

The second issue you investigate is specific backbone routes (that is, E:E:E:E::/64 and F:F:F:F::/64) being advertized into Company A's enterprise network (that is, the network consisting of routers R1 and R2). The goal is to only advertise default route information into the enterprise network.

The **debug ipv6 rip** command was issued on router R2 to see if router BB2 was sending both default route information and specific route information. The output from this command, as presented in Example 12-36, confirms that router BB2 is not suppressing specific route information.

Example 12-36 *Debugging RIPng Traffic on Router R2*

```
R2# debug ipv6 rip
...OUTPUT OMITTED...
*Mar  1 00:33:30.747: RIPng: response received from FE80::C200:EFF:FE64:0 on
Serial1/0.2 for PROCESS1
*Mar  1 00:33:30.751:          src=FE80::C200:EFF:FE64:0 (Serial1/0.2)
*Mar  1 00:33:30.751:          dst=FF02::9
*Mar  1 00:33:30.755:          sport=521, dport=521, length=92
*Mar  1 00:33:30.755:          command=2, version=1, mbz=0, #rte=4
*Mar  1 00:33:30.755:          tag=0, metric=1, prefix=F:F:F:F::/64
*Mar  1 00:33:30.755:          tag=0, metric=1, prefix=E:E:E:E::/64
*Mar  1 00:33:30.755:          tag=0, metric=1, prefix=D:D:D:D::/64
*Mar  1 00:33:30.755:          tag=0, metric=1, prefix=::/0
...OUTPUT OMITTED...
```

Examples 12-37 and 12-38 show the RIPng configuration of the Serial 1/0.2 subinterface on routers BB1 and BB2. The Serial 1/0.2 subinterface on each router is the subinterface connecting to router R2.

Example 12-37 *Viewing the RIPng Configuration on Router BB1's Serial 1/0.2 Subinterface*

```
BB1# show run | begin Serial1/0.2
interface Serial1/0.2 point-to-point
 ip address 172.16.1.1 255.255.255.252
 ipv6 address C:C:C:C::1/64
 ipv6 rip PROCESS1 enable
 ipv6 rip PROCESS1 default-information only
 frame-relay interface-dlci 811
```

Example 12-38 *Viewing the RIPng Configuration on Router BB2's Serial 1/0.2 Subinterface*

```
BB2# show run | begin Serial1/0.2
interface Serial1/0.2 point-to-point
 ip address 172.16.2.2 255.255.255.252
 ipv6 address D:D:D:D::2/64
 ipv6 rip PROCESS1 enable
 ipv6 rip PROCESS1 default-information originate
 frame-relay interface-dlci 821
```

Based on the **debug** and **show** command output presented in Examples 12-36, 12-37, and 12-38, hypothesize why router R2 is receiving specific route information for networks E:E:E:E::/64 and F:F:F:F::/64. On a separate sheet of paper, write out your proposed configuration change to resolve this issue.

Issue #2: Suggested Solution

An inspection of router BB2's running configuration reveals the **ipv6 rip PROCESS1 default-information originate** command under subinterface configuration mode for Serial 1/0.2. The **originate** keyword in this command sources a default router advertisement, but it does not suppress the sending of more specific routes. Example 12-39 shows how this configuration was changed to use the **only** parameter. The **only** parameter causes the interface to only originate default route information, while suppressing more specific routes.

Example 12-39 *Suppressing Specific Route Information on Router BB2's Serial 1/0.2 Subinterface*

```
BB2# conf term
Enter configuration commands, one per line.  End with CNTL/Z.
BB2(config)# int s1/0.2
BB2(config-subif)# ipv6 rip PROCESS1 default-information only
```

After giving the E:E:E:E::/64 and F:F:F:F::/64 routes sufficient time to timeout of router R2's IPv6 routing table, the **show ipv6 route** was once again issued. The output, as shown in Example 12-40, confirms that the issues reported in the trouble ticket are resolved. Specifically, router R2 sees two paths across which it can load balance to reach a default route. Also, specific backbone routes (that is, E:E:E:E::/64 and F:F:F:F::/64) do not appear in router R2's IPv6 routing table.

Example 12-40   *Router R2's IPv6 Routing Table After Troubleshooting*

```
R2# show ipv6 route
IPv6 Routing Table - 10 entries
Codes: C - Connected, L - Local, S - Static, R - RIP, B - BGP
       U - Per-user Static route
       I1 - ISIS L1, I2 - ISIS L2, IA - ISIS interarea, IS - ISIS summary
       O - OSPF intra, OI - OSPF inter, OE1 - OSPF ext 1, OE2 - OSPF ext 2
       ON1 - OSPF NSSA ext 1, ON2 - OSPF NSSA ext 2
R   ::/0 [120/2]
     via FE80::C200:EFF:FE64:0, Serial1/0.2
     via FE80::C202:EFF:FEBC:0, Serial1/0.1
R   A:A:A:A::/64 [120/2]
     via FE80::209:B7FF:FEFA:D1E1, FastEthernet0/0
C   B:B:B:B::/64 [0/0]
     via ::, FastEthernet0/0
L   B:B:B:B::22/128 [0/0]
     via ::, FastEthernet0/0
C   C:C:C:C::/64 [0/0]
     via ::, Serial1/0.1
L   C:C:C:C::2/128 [0/0]
     via ::, Serial1/0.1
C   D:D:D:D::/64 [0/0]
     via ::, Serial1/0.2
L   D:D:D:D::1/128 [0/0]
     via ::, Serial1/0.2
L   FE80::/10 [0/0]
     via ::, Null0
L   FF00::/8 [0/0]
     via ::, Null0
```

Exam Preparation Tasks

Review All Key Topics

Review the most important topics from inside the chapter, noted with the Key Topics icon in the outer margin of the page. Table 12-8 lists these key topics and the page numbers where each is found.

Table 12-8 *Key Topics for Chapter 12*

Key Topic Element	Description	Page Number
List	IPv6 features	376
List	Three types of IPv6 addresses	376
List	Rules for abbreviating IPv6 addresses	378
List	Methods of populating an IPv6 routing table	379
Table 12-2	IPv6 configuration commands	379
Example 12-1	IPv6 configuration example	380
Table 12-3	Commands used to tunnel IPv6 via IPv4	380
Example 12-2	IPv6 over IPv4 tunnel configuration example	381
List	OSPFv3 enhancements	382
Table 12-4	OSPFv3 configuration commands	383
Example 12-4	OSPFv3 sample configuration	383
Table 12-5	OSPFv3 troubleshooting commands	384
List	Reasons an OSPFv3 adjacency might not be formed	384
List	RIPng enhancements	399
Table 12-6	RIPng configuration commands	400
Example 12-24	RIPng sample configuration	401
Table 12-7	RIPng troubleshooting commands	401

Complete Tables and Lists from Memory

Print a copy of Appendix B, "Memory Tables," (found on the CD) or at least the section for this chapter, and complete the tables and lists from memory. Appendix C, "Memory Tables Answer Key," also on the CD, includes completed tables and lists to check your work.

Define Key Terms

Define the following key terms from this chapter, and check your answers in the Glossary:

IPv6 over IPv4 tunnel, IPv6 unicast, IPv6 multicast, IPv6 anycast, OSPFv3, RIP next generation (RIPng)

Command Reference to Check Your Memory

This section includes the most important configuration and EXEC commands covered in this chapter. To determine how well you have memorized the commands as a side effect of your other studies, cover the left side of the table with a piece of paper, read the descriptions on the right side, and see whether you remember the command.

Table 12-9   *Chapter 12 Configuration Command Reference*

Command	Description
ipv6 cef	Global configuration mode command that configures Cisco Express Forwarding for IPv6.
ipv6 unicast-routing	Global configuration mode command that instructs a router to forward IPv6 traffic.
ipv6 address *ipv6-address/prefix-length* [**eui-64**]	Interface configuration mode command that assigns an IPv6 address to an interface. (NOTE: The eui-64 option allows a router to complete the low-order 64 bits of an address, based on an interface's MAC address.)
service-policy {**input** | **output**} *policy-map-name*	Interface configuration mode command that applies a policy map in either the inbound or outbound direction.
interface tunnel *interface-id*	Global configuration mode command that creates a virtual IPv4 tunnel interface over which encapsulated IPv6 packets can flow.
tunnel source *ipv4-address*	Interface configuration mode command that identifies the IPv4 address of the local end of a tunnel.

continues

Table 12-9   *Chapter 12 Configuration Command Reference   (Continued)*

Command	Description
tunnel destination *ipv4-address*	Interface configuration mode command that identifies the IPv4 address of the remote end of a tunnel.
tunnel mode ipv6ip	Interface configuration mode command that configures an interface to act as a manual IPv6 tunnel.
ipv6 address *ipv6-address/prefix-length*	Interface configuration mode command that specifies the IPv6 address assigned to a tunnel interface.
ipv6 ospf *process-id* **area** *area-id*	Interface configuration mode command that allows the IPv6 address configured on an interface to participate in an OSPFv3 routing process.
ipv6 router ospf *process-id*	Global configuration mode command that enables an OSPFv3 routing process on a router.
router-id *ipv4-address*	Router configuration mode command that specifies an IPv4 address to be used by OSPFv3 as a router's router ID.
ipv6 rip *process-name* **enable**	Interface configuration mode command that instructs an interface to participate in the specified RIPng routing process.
ipv6 rip *process-name* **default-information {only | originate}**	Interface configuration mode command that causes an interface to originate a default route advertisement (that is, an advertisement for network ::/0) and optionally suppress the advertisement of all other routes (using the **only** keyword).
ipv6 router rip *process-name*	Global configuration mode command that enters router configuration mode for the specified RIPng routing process.
maximum-paths *number*	Interface configuration mode command that specifies the number of equal-cost paths across which RIPng can load balance (defaults to 16 with a valid range of 1–64).

Table 12-10 *Chapter 12 EXEC Command Reference*

Command	Description
show ipv6 ospf	Displays OSPFv3 routing process, router ID, various timers, and information about each area on a router.
show ipv6 ospf interface	Shows IPv6 link local address, area ID, process ID, router ID, and cost.
show ipv6 ospf neighbor	Lists the state of a router's adjacency with all configured OSPFv3 neighbors.
debug ipv6 ospf adj	Displays information about OSPFv3 adjacencies.
debug ip ipv6 ospf hello	Shows OSPFv3 HELLO packet information.
show ipv6 rip [*process-name*] [database	next-hops]	Displays information about the specified RIPng routing process, and optionally, the contents of the RIPng database and a listing of next-hop addresses.
show ipv6 route	Shows the contents of the IPv6 routing table.
debug ipv6 rip	Provides real-time information about RIPng messages.

This chapter covers the following subjects:

Application Network Services Troubleshooting: This section introduces you to the Cisco Application Network Services (ANS) architecture. Cisco ANS includes multiple pieces of dedicated equipment aimed at optimizing the performance of network-based applications (for example, improving the response time of a corporate web server for users at a remote office). Although this section introduces a collection of Cisco ANS components, the primary focus of this section is on Cisco IOS features that can improve application performance. Specifically, the Cisco IOS features addressed are NetFlow, IP service-level agreements (SLA), Network-Based Application Recognition (NBAR), and quality of service (QoS).

Wireless Troubleshooting Targets: This section begins by contrasting autonomous and split-MAC wireless network architectures. Next, this section highlights wired network issues that can impact wireless networks. These include power, VLAN, security, DHCP, and QoS issues.

CHAPTER 13

Advanced Services Troubleshooting

Large enterprise networks carry multiple types of application traffic for their users. However, an inherent characteristic of large enterprise networks is that these networks are typically geographically dispersed. Separating these sites over an IP WAN can impact the performance of network-based applications. Fortunately, Cisco offers a collection of ANS devices that can help optimize the performance of network-based applications. In addition to dedicated hardware, however, Cisco IOS Software offers a collection of features that can help collect baseline information for these applications and then help improve application performance (for example, response time).

Although this chapter introduces you to a collection of Cisco ANS devices, the primary focus on application optimization is on Cisco IOS features. These features include baselining features such as NetFlow, IP SLA, and NBAR, in addition to QoS features. Beyond reviewing the theory and configuration of these Cisco IOS features, this chapter highlights common troubleshooting issues you might encounter when working with these features.

Another advanced service present in many networks is wireless network technology. Although troubleshooting the many aspects of a wireless network is an in-depth study, this chapter places the troubleshooting focus on wired network configurations, which can impact wireless network clients. For example, a Cisco Catalyst switch on a wired network might have an incorrect Power over Ethernet (PoE) configuration, preventing a wireless access point (WAP) from receiving power. As another example, the security configuration on a router might include an access control list (ACL) that blocks Lightweight Access Point Protocol (LWAPP) traffic that should flow between a WAP and a wireless LAN controller (WLC).

The "Wireless Troubleshooting Targets" section of this chapter begins by reviewing the components that comprise both autonomous and split-MAC wireless networks. Then the focus shifts to power, VLAN, security, DHCP, and QoS issues on a wired network that might impact wireless clients.

"Do I Know This Already?" Quiz

The "Do I Know This Already?" quiz helps you determine your level of knowledge of this chapter's topics before you begin. Table 13-1 details the major topics discussed in this chapter and their corresponding quiz questions.

Table 13-1   *"Do I Know This Already?" Section-to-Question Mapping*

Foundation Topics Section	Questions
Application Network Services Troubleshooting	1–6
Wireless Troubleshooting Targets	7–10

1. Which of the following Cisco ANS components enhances web applications by measuring response time and managing application layer security? (Choose the best answer.)

   a. Cisco Application Velocity System (AVS)

   b. Cisco Global Site Selector (GSS)

   c. Cisco Content Switching Module (CSM)

   d. Cisco Application Control Engine (ACE)

2. What are the four basic processes involved in optimizing an application? (Choose the four best answers.)

   a. Deploy

   b. Monitor

   c. Expand

   d. Baseline

   e. Optimize

3. Which of the following is a common NetFlow troubleshooting issue? (Choose the best answer.)

   a. A virtual interface has not been configured.

   b. The interface configured for NetFlow has an incorrect **bandwidth** command configured.

   c. The NetFlow collector is on the same subnet as the router configured for NetFlow.

   d. The configuration of the NetFlow collector is incorrect.

4. What is IP SLA's default frequency for sending probes?

   a. 30 seconds

   b. 60 seconds

   c. 90 seconds

   d. 120 seconds

5. In what configuration mode is the **ip nbar protocol-discovery** command issued?

   a.   Global configuration mode

   b.   Policy-map-class configuration mode

   c.   Interface configuration mode

   d.   Router configuration mode

6. Which three of the following steps should be performed prior to configuring Auto-QoS on a router interface? (Select the three best answers.)

   a.   Configure an IP address on the interface.

   b.   Enable Cisco Express Forwarding on the router.

   c.   Configure the **bandwidth** command on the interface.

   d.   Enable RSVP on the interface.

7. What wireless network mode of operation is characterized by having the functions of a traditional wireless access point divided between a lightweight access point and a wireless LAN controller?

   a.   Autonomous

   b.   Split horizon

   c.   Split-MAC

   d.   Split tunneling

8. Which two ports does LWAPP traffic use? (Choose the two best answers.)

   a.   TCP port 12222

   b.   UDP port 12222

   c.   TCP port 12223

   d.   UDP port 12223

9. What command can you use to display the VLANs that are permitted on the trunk ports of a switch?

   a.   **show interfaces trunk**

   b.   **show trunk interfaces**

   c.   **show switchport trunk**

   d.   **show trunk switchport**

10. What interface configuration mode command can you enter in a Cisco Catalyst switch to instruct the interface to trust incoming DHCP markings?

   a.   **wrr-queue dscp**

   b.   **wrr-queue bandwidth dscp**

   c.   **mls qos trust dscp**

   d.   **mls qos trust-device dscp**

Foundation Topics

Application Network Services Troubleshooting

Cisco Application Network Services (ANS) is a collection of Cisco solutions that fall under the Cisco Service-Oriented Network Architecture (SONA) framework. ANS technologies can, for example, enhance the performance of applications within a data center, for users at a remote site, and for a teleworker, as illustrated in Figure 13-1.

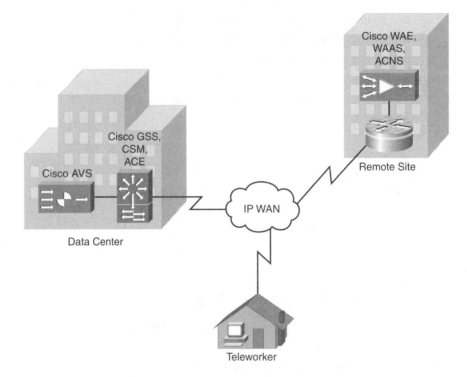

Figure 13-1 *ANS Sample Topology*

Table 13-2 describes some of the features offered by the ANS components seen in the topology.

Table 13-2 *ANS Network Components*

Component	Description
Cisco Application Velocity System (AVS)	Enhances web applications (for example, by measuring response time and by managing application layer security)
Cisco Global Site Selector (GSS)	Optimizes distributed data center environments

Table 13-2 *ANS Network Components*   (*Continued*)

Component	Description
Cisco Content Switching Module (CSM)	Performs load balancing across multiple devices (such as servers or firewalls)
Cisco Application Control Engine (ACE)	Performs intelligent load balancing and content switching to increase application availability
Cisco Wide Area Application Engine (WAAE)	Provides a platform on which users can run Cisco ACNS or Cisco WAAS software
Cisco Wide Area Application Software (WAAS)	Accelerates applications for remote office workers
Cisco Application and Content Networking System (ACNS)	Supports content distribution (for example, video streaming) to remote sites over an IP WAN

Keep in mind that the components presented are just a few examples of how application performance can be improved (or maintained) in a network. In addition to such specialized technologies, many Cisco IOS features can help ensure application performance. This section considers some of these Cisco IOS features and how they can be used to optimize application performance.

Application Optimization

The performance of network applications can be enhanced by gaining an understanding of the application traffic, followed by optimizing the network for those applications. After performing this optimization, you should again monitor the behavior of network traffic to determine what has changed as a result of your optimization. With your understanding of existing application traffic patterns, you can more efficiently deploy additional network applications.

This application optimization process can be summarized with the following four steps:

Step 1.   **Baseline:** The first step is to baseline the performance metrics of existing application traffic.

Step 2.   **Optimize:** After you understand the current behavior of the application traffic, you can optimize identified applications (for example, using QoS mechanisms).

Step 3.   **Monitor:** After implementing your optimization configuration, network traffic should again be monitored to determine how network traffic patterns are impacted by the new configuration.

Step 4.   **Deploy:** As a network evolves, new applications might be added, while existing applications might undergo multiple upgrades. Because the deployments of new applications or upgrades can affect the behavior of network applications, these steps should be repeated.

Not only do these steps help optimize network application performance, they can also aid in troubleshooting. For example, when troubleshooting an issue, you can compare data you collect against the baseline and monitoring data collected in the preceding steps. By identifying the difference in these data sets, you might be able to better determine the underlying cause for a troubleshooting issue.

NetFlow

The Cisco IOS NetFlow feature can be used when baselining network application performance. Recall from Chapter 3, "The Maintenance and Troubleshooting Toolbox," that NetFlow can distinguish between different traffic flows, where a *flow* is a series of packets, all of which share header information such as source and destination IP addresses, protocols numbers, port numbers, and Type of Service (TOS) field information. NetFlow can keep track of the number of packets and bytes observed in each flow. This information is stored in a *flow cache*. Also recall that the NetFlow feature can be used standalone on an individual router, or entries in the flow cache of a router can be exported to a *NetFlow collector* prior to the entries expiring. After the NetFlow collector has received flow information for a period of time, analysis software running on the NetFlow collector can produce reports detailing traffic statistics.

Figure 13-2 shows a sample NetFlow topology (originally presented in Chapter 3), where NetFlow is enabled on router R4, and a NetFlow collector is configured on a PC at IP address 192.168.1.50.

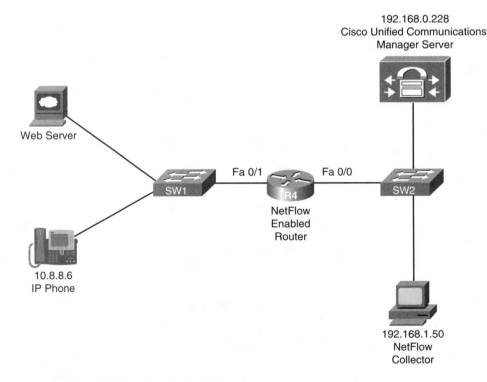

Figure 13-2 *NetFlow Sample Topology*

As a review, Example 13-1 shows the NetFlow configuration on router R4. The **ip flow ingress** command is issued for both the Fast Ethernet 0/0 and Fast Ethernet 0/1 interfaces, ensuring that all flows passing through the router, regardless of direction, can be monitored. Router R4 is configured to report its NetFlow information to a NetFlow collector at IP address 192.168.1.50. The **ip flow-export source lo 0** command indicates that all communication between router R4 and the NetFlow collector will be via interface Loopback 0. A NetFlow version of **5** was specified. Finally, the **ip flow-export destination 192.168.1.50 5000** command is issued to specify that the IP address of the NetFlow collector is **192.168.1.50**, and communication to the NetFlow collector should be done over UDP port **5000**. Because NetFlow does not have a standardized port number, please check the documentation of your NetFlow collector when selecting a port.

Example 13-1 *NetFlow Sample Configuration*

```
R4# conf term
R4(config)# int fa 0/0
R4(config-if)# ip flow ingress
R4(config-if)# exit
R4(config)# int fa 0/1
R4(config-if)# ip flow ingress
R4(config-if)# exit
R4(config)# ip flow-export source lo 0
R4(config)# ip flow-export version 5
R4(config)# ip flow-export destination 192.168.1.50 5000
R4(config)# end
```

Key Topic

Although an external NetFlow collector is valuable for longer-term flow analysis, you can issue the **show ip cache flow** command at the command-line interface (CLI) prompt of a router to produce a summary of flow information, as demonstrated in Example 13-2. Again, you can use this information in collecting baseline information for network applications.

Example 13-2 *Viewing NetFlow Information*

Key Topic

```
R4# show ip cache flow
...OUTPUT OMITTED...
Protocol      Total    Flows   Packets Bytes   Packets Active(Sec) Idle(Sec)
- - -         Flows    /Sec    /Flow   /Pkt    /Sec    /Flow       /Flow
TCP-Telnet       12    0.0        50    40      0.1       15.7       14.2
TCP-WWW          12    0.0        40   785      0.1        7.1        6.2
TCP-other       536    0.1         1    55      0.2        0.3       10.5
UDP-TFTP        225    0.0         4    59      0.1       11.9       15.4
UDP-other       122    0.0       114   284      3.0       15.9       15.4
ICMP             41    0.0        13    91      0.1       49.9       15.6
IP-other          1    0.0       389    60      0.0     1797.1        3.4
Total:          949    0.2        18   255      3.8        9.4       12.5
```

SrcIf	SrcIPaddress	DstIf	DstIPaddress	Pr	SrcP	DstP	Pkts
Fa0/0	10.3.3.1	Null	224.0.0.10	58	0000	0000	62
Fa0/1	10.8.8.6	Fa0/0	192.168.0.228	06	C2DB	07D0	2
Fa0/0	192.168.0.228	Fa0/1	10.8.8.6	06	07D0	C2DB	1
Fa0/0	192.168.1.50	Fa0/1	10.8.8.6	11	6002	6BD2	9166
Fa0/1	10.8.8.6	Fa0/0	192.168.1.50	11	6BD2	6002	9166
Fa0/0	10.1.1.2	Local	10.3.3.2	06	38F2	0017	438

If NetFlow is not behaving as expected, consider the following list of common NetFlow troubleshooting targets that could be investigated:

Key Topic

■ No network connectivity exists between a NetFlow router and its configured NetFlow collector.

■ The router's NetFlow configuration is incorrect.

■ The NetFlow collector's configuration is incorrect.

■ An ACL or a firewall is blocking NetFlow traffic.

IP SLAs

You can use the Cisco IOS IP SLA feature to measure how the network treats traffic for specific applications. IP SLA accomplishes this by synthetically generating traffic bearing similar characteristics to application traffic (for example, identical port numbers and packet sizes). This traffic, called *probes*, is sent to a destination router. This destination router is configured to respond to the received probes with time-stamp information, which can then be used to calculate performance metrics for the traffic. Like NetFlow, IP SLAs can be used for baselining network application performance.

Key Topic

Following are the steps to configure the IP SLA feature:

Step 1. Configure a router as an IP SLA responder.

Step 2. Configure the type of IP SLA operation.

Step 3. Determine the configuration options for the IP SLA operation.

Step 4. Specify any thresholds (which could trigger other events when exceeded).

Step 5. Specify when the IP SLA should run.

Step 6. View the results (for example, via the Cisco IOS CLI or a Simple Network Management Protocol [SNMP]-based network management system [NMS]).

To illustrate a basic IP SLA configuration, consider the topology shown in Figure 13-3. In this topology, which is the basic topology used for all trouble tickets presented in this book, router R1 is configured as the source IP SLA router, whereas router BB2 is configured as the IP SLA responder.

Example 13-3 shows the configuration of the IP SLA responder (that is, router BB2). The **ip sla monitor responder** command is used to make router BB2 act as a responder. The

ip sla monitor responder type tcpConnect ipaddress 10.4.4.4 port 80 command tells router BB2 to specifically act as a responder for tcpConnect probes sent to a destination address of 10.4.4.4 (that is, the loopback interface of router BB2) with a destination port of 80 (that is, the HTTP port).

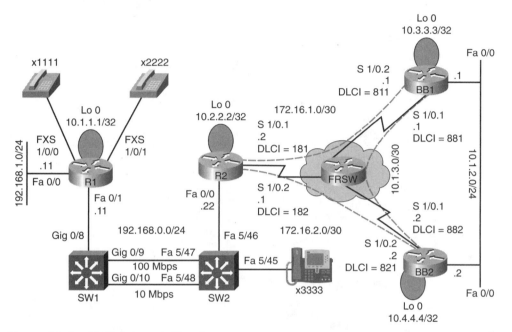

Figure 13-3 *IP SLA Sample Topology*

Example 13-3 *IP SLA Responder Configuration*

```
BB2# show run
...OUTPUT OMITTED...
!
ip sla monitor responder
ip sla monitor responder type tcpConnect ipaddress 10.4.4.4 port 80
!
... OUTPUT OMITTED...
```

Example 13-4 shows the configuration of the IP SLA source (that is, router R1). Notice that a specific SLA monitoring instance (numbered **1**) is created with the command **ip sla monitor 1**. The **type** keyword specifies the type of SLA probes (that is, tcpConnect probes with a destination IP address of 10.4.4.4 and a destination port number of 80 and a source port number of 17406). The **tos 64** command causes the TOS byte in the IP headers of the probes to be marked with a 64 (that is, 01000000 in binary, which equates to an IP Precedence value of 2, because IP Precedence only considers the three leftmost bits in a TOS byte). You also have the option of using the **frequency** *seconds* to specify how often the probes are to be sent (the default value is 60 seconds). Finally, the **ip sla monitor**

schedule 1 life forever start-time now command indicates that the IP SLA monitor 1 instance should begin immediately and run forever.

Example 13-4 *IP SLA Source Configuration*

```
R1# show run
...OUTPUT OMITTED...
!
ip sla monitor 1
 type tcpConnect dest-ipaddr 10.4.4.4 dest-port 80 source-port 17406
 tos 64
ip sla monitor schedule 1 life forever start-time now
!
...OUTPUT OMITTED...
```

Next, you can view the collected IP SLA information, as demonstrated in Example 13-5. The output indicates that the latest round trip time (RTT) measured for a probe was 168 ms. Also, you can see that 13 of the probes were responded to successfully, while one probe failed.

Example 13-5 *Viewing Information Collected on the IP SLA Source*

```
R1# show ip sla monitor statistics
Round trip time (RTT)     Index 1
    Latest RTT: 168 ms
Latest operation start time: *16:10:52.453 UTC Sun Mar 3 2002
Latest operation return code: OK
Number of successes: 13
Number of failures: 1
Operation time to live: Forever
```

You can also view the information collected by the IP SLA responder, as shown in Example 13-6. The output indicates that this responder received 15 messages, of which there was a single error. You can also see the IP addresses of IP SLA sources to which this responder recently responded. In this example, there was a single IP SLA source of 192.168.0.11.

Example 13-6 *Viewing Information Collected on the IP SLA Responder*

```
BB2# show ip sla monitor responder
IP SLA Monitor Responder is: Enabled
Number of control message received: 15 Number of errors: 1
Recent sources:
     192.168.0.11 [00:38:01.807 UTC Fri Mar 1 2002]
     192.168.0.11 [00:37:01.783 UTC Fri Mar 1 2002]
     192.168.0.11 [00:36:01.791 UTC Fri Mar 1 2002]
     192.168.0.11 [00:35:01.791 UTC Fri Mar 1 2002]
     192.168.0.11 [00:34:01.779 UTC Fri Mar 1 2002]
```

```
Recent error sources:
    192.168.0.11 [00:24:01.807 UTC Fri Mar 1 2002]    RTT_FAIL


tcpConnect Responder:
  IP Address         Port
  10.4.4.4
```

■   The source or destination IP addresses configured on the IP SLA source or responder is incorrect.

■   The frequency of the probes is set for a value that is too long.

■   The schedule is set to begin sending probes at some time in the future.

■   The probes are being filtered by an ACL or a firewall.

Network-Based Application Recognition

Network-Based Application Recognition (NBAR) can classify various traffic types by examining information at Layers 3 through 7. Protocols that change port numbers (that is, stateful protocols) can also be tracked. Although Cisco IOS comes with multiple NBAR application signatures, there is a continuing need for additional signature recognition capabilities. For example, although your router might be able to recognize KaZaa traffic, it might not be able to recognize Bit Torrent traffic. Fortunately, you can install a Bit Torrent Packet Description Language Module (PDLM) into the router's flash. This PDLM can be referenced by the router's Cisco IOS configuration, thus allowing the router to recognize Bit Torrent traffic. PDLMs are available for download from the following URL:

http://www.cisco.com/cgi-bin/tablebuild.pl/pdlm

Note that this site, as shown in Figure 13-4, requires appropriate login credentials.

In addition to usefulness of NBAR in classifying traffic, it can function as a protocol discovery tool. Therefore, like NetFlow and IP SLA, NBAR can serve as a useful baselining tool.

The protocol discovery feature of NBAR can be enabled on an interface to determine the applications consuming the most bandwidth on that interface (that is, the *top talkers*).

To enable NBAR protocol discovery, enter the following command in interface configuration mode:

```
Router(config-if)# ip nbar protocol-discovery
```

After NBAR has collected traffic statistics for an interface, you can use the **show ip nbar protocol-discovery** command to view the statistics, as demonstrated in Example 13-7. This output indicates that the top five protocols seen on the Fast Ethernet 0/0 interface on router R4 are RTP, HTTP, SKINNY, TELNET, and EIGRP. The output shows packet count, byte count, average bit rate, and maximum bit rate statistics for each of these protocols.

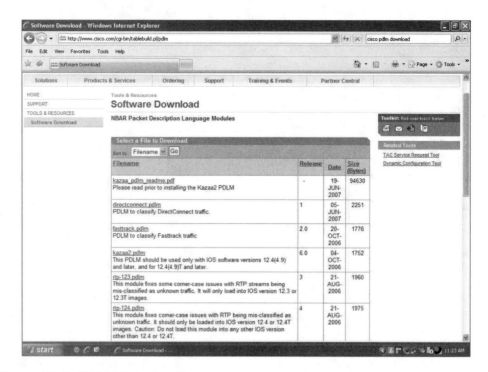

Figure 13-4   *PDLM Download Page*

Example 13-7   show ip nbar protocol-discovery *Command Output*

```
R4# show ip nbar protocol-discovery


FastEthernet0/0

                        Input               Output
                        -----               -----
    Protocol            Packet Count        Packet Count
                        Byte Count          Byte Count
                        5min Bit Rate (bps) 5min Bit Rate (bps)
                        5min Max Bit Rate (bps)  5min Max Bit Rate (bps)
    -----------------------------------------------------------------

    rtp                 922                 3923
                        65248               290302
                        6000                15000
                        9000                15000
    http                171                 231
                        11506               345647
                        0                   1000
                        3000                13000
    skinny              34                  42
                        3080                2508
```

```
                               0                    0
                               1000                 0
         telnet                92                   0
                               5520                 0
                               0                    0
                               0                    0
         eigrp                 44                   21
                               3256                 1554
                               0                    0
                               0                    0
...OUTPUT OMITTED...
```

Recall that a router's NBAR signature recognition capability can be expanded by adding one or more PDLM files to a router's flash. You can reference these PDLM files using the following command:

```
Router(config)# ip nbar pdlm pdlm_file
```

Also, for applications that are recognized based on TCP or User Datagram Protocol (UDP) port numbers, you can modify the ports the NBAR uses with the following command:

```
Router(config)# ip nbar port-map protocol {tcp  udp} port_number [port_number]
```

The following is a listing of common NBAR troubleshooting issues you might encounter:

Key Topic

- **NBAR is not correctly recognizing applications:** This can occur if an application is using a nonstandard port. You can use the **show ip nbar port-map** *protocol* command to see what port(s) is associated with a specified application. For example, perhaps a web server is using TCP port 8080 instead of port 80. You can issue the **show ip nbar port-map http** command and see that NBAR is only recognizing TCP port 80 as HTTP traffic. You can then use the **ip nbar port-map http tcp 80 8080** command in global configuration mode to cause NBAR to recognize either TCP port 80 or 8080 as HTTP traffic.

- **NBAR does not support a specific application:** If a PDLM file exists for an application, you can download it from Cisco.com, copy it to the flash of a router, and reference it with the **ip nbar pdlm** *pdlm-file* command in global configuration mode.

- **NBAR degrades router performance:** Depending on the underlying router platform, the performance of a router might suffer as a result of NBAR's inspection of multiple flows. You can use the **show processes cpu** command to determine the CPU utilization of a router.

QoS

In addition to baselining the application traffic for a network, a component of the Cisco ANS framework is ensuring appropriate levels of service for network applications. One approach to achieving and maintaining appropriate service levels is the use of QoS.

Chapter 11, "IP Communications Troubleshooting," introduced QoS technologies and how many of these technologies could be configured using the three-step Modular QoS

CLI (MQC) process. Also discussed was the AutoQoS Enterprise feature, which can, using NBAR, dynamically discover network traffic patterns and generate a recommended QoS policy.

As a review, AutoQoS Enterprise is configured via a three-step process:

Step 1.   Begin the AutoQoS Enterprise discovery phase with the **auto discovery qos** [**trust**] command in interface configuration mode.

Step 2.   After the discovery phase runs for a period of time (at least two or three days based on the Cisco recommendation), view the collected information and recommended policy with the **show auto discovery qos** command.

Step 3.   Apply the recommended policy using the **auto qos** command in interface configuration mode.

Originally presented in Chapter 11, Example 13-8 illustrates this three-step process. Notice that the AutoQoS Enterprise can recognize traffic in as many as ten different classes.

Example 13-8   *Configuring AutoQoS Enterprise*

```
R4# conf term
R4(config)# int fa0/0
R4(config-if)# auto discovery qos
R4(config-if)# end
R4# show auto discovery qos
FastEthernet0/0
 AutoQoS Discovery enabled for applications
 Discovery up time: 1 minutes, 7 seconds
 AutoQoS Class information:
 Class Voice:
  Recommended Minimum Bandwidth: 5 Kbps/<1% (PeakRate)
  Detected applications and data:
  Application/      AverageRate       PeakRate            Total
  Protocol          (kbps/%)          (kbps/%)            (bytes)
  -----------       -----------       --------            -----------
   rtp audio        1/<1              5/<1                10138
 Class Interactive Video:
  No data found.
 Class Signaling:
  Recommended Minimum Bandwidth: 0 Kbps/0% (AverageRate)
  Detected applications and data:
  Application/      AverageRate       PeakRate            Total
  Protocol          (kbps/%)          (kbps/%)            (bytes)
  -----------       -----------       --------            -----------
   skinny           0/0               0/0                 2218
 Class Streaming Video:
  No data found.
 Class Transactional:
```

```
        No data found.
  Class Bulk:
    No data found.
  Class Scavenger:
    No data found.
  Class Management:
    No data found.
  Class Routing:
    Recommended Minimum Bandwidth: 0 Kbps/0% (AverageRate)
    Detected applications and data:
    Application/        AverageRate        PeakRate          Total
    Protocol            (kbps/%)           (kbps/%)          (bytes)
    -----------         -----------        --------          ------------
    eigrp               0/0                0/0               1110
    icmp                0/0                0/0               958
  Class Best Effort:
    Current Bandwidth Estimation: 44 Kbps/<1% (AverageRate)
    Detected applications and data:
    Application/        AverageRate        PeakRate          Total
    Protocol            (kbps/%)           (kbps/%)          (bytes)
    -----------         -----------        --------          ------------
    http                44/<1              121/1             372809
    unknowns            0/0                0/0               232


Suggested AutoQoS Policy for the current uptime:
 !
 class-map match-any AutoQoS-Voice-Fa0/0
  match protocol rtp audio
 !
 policy-map AutoQoS-Policy-Fa0/0
  class AutoQoS-Voice-Fa0/0
   priority percent 1
   set dscp ef
  class class-default
   fair-queue
R4# conf term
R4(config)# int fa 0/0
R4(config-if)# auto qos
R4(config-if)# end
R4#
```

Following is a listing of common reasons that AutoQoS (both AutoQoS VoIP and Auto-QoS Enterprise) might not function correctly on a router:

Key Topic

- **Cisco Express Forwarding (CEF) is not enabled:** AutoQoS can use NBAR to recognize traffic types, and NBAR requires CEF to be enabled. You can enable CEF with the **ip cef** global configuration mode command.

- **An interface's bandwidth is not correctly configured:** Cisco IOS assumes the bandwidth of a serial interface to be 1.544 Mbps (that is, the bandwidth of a T1 circuit). Because serial interfaces often run at different speeds, you should configure these interfaces with the **bandwidth** *bandwidth-in-kbps* command in interface configuration mode. Some routing protocols (for example, Enhanced Interior Gateway Routing Protocol [EIGRP] and Open Shortest Path First [OSPF]) can reference this bandwidth amount when calculating a route metric. In addition, AutoQoS can reference this bandwidth amount to determine which QoS mechanisms should be enabled on an interface. Therefore, if the bandwidth value of an interface is left at its default setting, AutoQoS might not optimally configure QoS on an interface.

- **An interface has not been configured with an IP address:** One QoS mechanism that AutoQoS might configure is Multilink PPP (MLP), which is a link fragmentation and interleaving mechanism. Part of an MLP configuration involves the creation of a virtual multilink interface that needs to have an IP address assigned. AutoQoS takes the needed IP address from the physical interface being configured for AutoQoS. Therefore, an interface should be configured with an IP address prior to configuring the interface for AutoQoS.

- **Only one side of a link has been configured:** AutoQoS is enabled on an interface. However, the interface in the router at the other end of the link needs a complementary configuration. For example, consider two routers interconnected via a serial link running at a link speed of 512 kbps. If you configured AutoQoS for the interface at one end of the link, that interface might be configured for QoS mechanisms that include MLP and RTP header compression (cRTP). However, these mechanisms will not function correctly until the interface at the other end of the link is similarly configured.

- **The configuration created by AutoQoS has been modified:** AutoQoS configurations are based on QoS mechanisms available in Cisco IOS. Therefore, a configuration generated by AutoQoS can be customized. As a result, the underlying issue you are troubleshooting might be caused by the customization of AutoQoS' configuration.

Wireless Troubleshooting Targets

Troubleshooting wireless networks can require a variety of skill sets. For example, some troubleshooting scenarios might require an understanding of antenna theory and the radio frequency spectrum. Rather than focusing on such radio-specific troubleshooting targets, this section focuses on troubleshooting targets on a wired network that could impact a wireless network.

Specifically, after a review of the Cisco Unified Wireless Network operation, this section discusses such topics as how PoE, VLANs, security, DHCP, and QoS issues can result in issues for a wireless network.

Introducing the Cisco Unified Wireless Network

Wireless local-area networks (WLAN) offer network access via radio waves. Wireless clients (such as PCs or PDAs) access a *WAP* using half-duplex communication. The WAP allows a wireless client to communicate with the wired portion of a network.

Five primary components comprise the Cisco Unified Wireless Network architecture:

Key Topic

- **Wireless clients:** A wireless client device is typically an end-user device (such as a PC) that accesses a wireless network.

- **WAP:** WAPs offer network access for wireless clients.

- **Wireless network unification:** To offer wireless clients access to the resources of an organization, a wireless network needs to be integrated (that is, unified) with a wired LAN. This functionality is referred to as *network unification*.

- **Wireless network management:** Just as enterprise LANs benefit from network management solutions, a wireless LAN can use network management solutions to enhance security and reliability and offer assistance in WLAN deployments. An example of a wireless network management solution is the Cisco Wireless Control System (WCS).

- **Wireless Mobility:** Wireless mobility services include security threat detection, voice services, location services, and guest access.

Traditional WLANs use an access point in autonomous mode, where the access point is configured with a service set identifier (SSID), radio frequency (RF) channel, and RF power settings. However, having an autonomous access point tasked with all these responsibilities can limit scalability and hinder the addition of advanced wireless services.

Aside from autonomous mode, Cisco Unified Wireless Networks can alternatively operate in *split-MAC* mode. With split-MAC operation, an access point is considered a *lightweight access point*, which cannot function without a WLC.

Specifically, a WLAN client sending traffic to the wired LAN sends a packet to a lightweight access point, which encapsulates the packet using Lightweight Access Point Protocol (LWAPP). The encapsulated traffic is sent over an LWAPP tunnel to a WLC. LWAPP sends packets in a Layer 2 frame with an Ethertype of 0xBBBB. LWAPP data traffic uses a UDP destination port of 12222, whereas LWAPP control traffic uses a UDP destination port of 12223.

A lightweight access point, as shown in Figure 13-5, performs functions such as beaconing, packet transmission, and frame queuing, whereas the WLC assumes roles such as authentication, key management, and resource reservation.

Chapter 9, "Security Troubleshooting," introduced 802.1X as a means of authenticating users attempting to gain access to a network. Wireless networks often leverage 802.1X technologies to authenticate wireless clients.

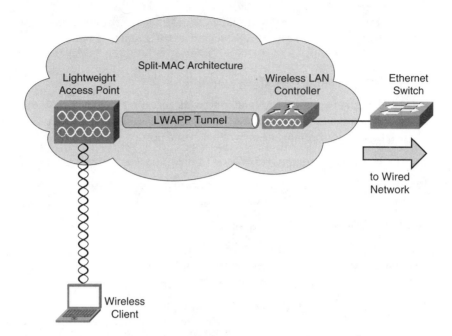

Figure 13-5   *Split-MAC Wireless Architecture*

Specifically, after a wireless client, such as a PC, associates with its access point, the access point only allows the client to communicate with the authentication server until the client successfully logs in and is authenticated, as illustrated in Figure 13-6. The WLC uses an Extensible Authentication Protocol (EAP) to communicate with the authentication server. Cisco Secure Access Control Server (ACS) can, for example, act as an authentication server.

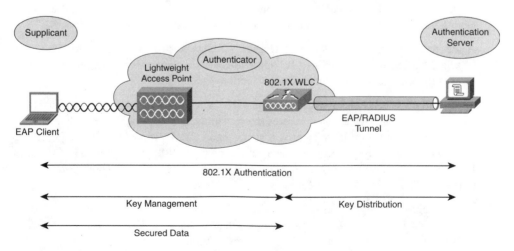

Figure 13-6   *Wireless Network Using 802.1X*

Supported EAP types include the following:

- **EAP-Transport Layer Security (EAP-TLS):** Wireless clients and authentication servers mutually authenticate using digital certificates.

- **EAP-Protected EAP (EAP-PEAP):** The authentication server (that is, a RADIUS server) is authenticated over a Transport Layer Security (TLS) tunnel using a digital certificate, whereas wireless clients are authenticated via Extensible Authentication Protocol—Generic Token Card (EAP-GTC) or Extensible Authentication Protocol—Microsoft Challenge Handshake Authentication Protocol version 2 (EAP-MSCHAPv2).

- **EAP Tunneled Transport Layer Security (EAP-TTLS):** The RADIUS server is authenticated over a TLS tunnel using the certificate of the server, and wireless clients authenticate using username and password credentials.

- **Cisco Lightweight Extensible Authentication Protocol (LEAP):** Cisco developed LEAP as an early and proprietary EAP method; however, LEAP's vulnerability to a dictionary attack represents a major LEAP weakness.

- **Cisco EAP-Flexible Authentication via Secure Tunneling (EAP-FAST):** Cisco proposed EAP-FAST to address weaknesses of LEAP.

Wireless network troubleshooters should also understand the following three WLAN controller components:

- **Ports:** A port on a WLAN controller physically connects the WLAN controller to the wired network (for example, to a Cisco Catalyst switch port).

- **Interfaces:** An interface of a WLAN controller logically maps to a VLAN on a wired network.

- **WLANs:** A WLAN can be configured with security features, QoS mechanisms, and other wireless network parameters. Also, a WLAN associates an SSID to a WLC interface.

Wired Network Issues Impacting Wireless Networks

Many issues that might be perceived as wireless problems result from underlying issues on the wired network. Examples of these issues include PoE, VLANs, security, DHCP, and QoS.

PoE

WAPs (in either an autonomous or split-MAC architecture) require power; however, these access points might need to be installed away from power outlets. For example, to provide appropriate coverage, an access point might be located in a drop ceiling. One option for providing power to such an access point is PoE (which was introduced in Chapter 11), where a Cisco Catalyst switch provides power to an attached device over the Ethernet leads in an unshielded twisted-pair (UTP) cable.

If the Cisco Catalyst switch is not appropriately configured to provide PoE, or if the switch has no additional power available, an attached WAP might fail to power on. In addition to verifying proper PoE configuration on the Cisco Catalyst switch, another troubleshooting aid is the Cisco Power Calculator, an online tool available at http://tools.cisco. com/cpc/launch.jsp. This tool can help determine the power capacity of a switch. Note that appropriate Cisco login credentials are required to access this tool.

VLANs

Traffic in a wireless network often belongs to its own VLAN; however, wireless users might experience connectivity issues if traffic from their wireless VLAN is not permitted over a trunk in the wired network. Therefore, trunk configurations on Cisco Catalyst switches might need to be inspected as part of troubleshooting wireless connectivity issues.

Chapter 4, "Basic Cisco Catalyst Switch Troubleshooting," introduced the troubleshooting of VLANs and trunks. As a review, Table 13-3 provides commands for gathering information about VLAN and trunk configuration information on a Cisco Catalyst switch.

Table 13-3   *VLAN and Trunk Troubleshooting Commands for a Cisco Catalyst Switch*

Command	Description
show vlan	Shows to which VLANs the ports of a switch belong
show interfaces trunk	Displays which VLANs are permitted on a switch's trunk ports, and which switch ports are configured as trunks
show interfaces switchport	Displays summary information for the ports on a switch, including VLAN and trunk configuration information

Security

Chapter 9 discussed how ACLs might inadvertently be configured to block traffic that should be permitted on a network. In the case of wireless networks configured in a split-MAC architecture, recall that UDP ports 12222 and 12223 (that is, the ports used by LWAPP) should be permitted between a WAP and a WLC. You can issue the **show access-lists** command to verify the access list configuration used on a router.

DHCP

Because an inherent characteristic of wireless networks is the mobility of wireless clients, those clients might need to roam from one subnet to another. In such an instance, a loss of wireless connectivity might result from a DHCP issue.

Chapter 10, "IP Services Troubleshooting," discussed troubleshooting DHCP; however, as a review, Table 13-4 offers a collection of **show**, **clear**, and **debug** commands useful in troubleshooting DHCP problems.

Table 13-4   *DHCP Troubleshooting Commands*

Command	Description
show ip dhcp conflict	Lists any IP address conflicts identified by a router, along with the method the router used to identify the conflicts (this is, via ping or gratuitous ARP)
show ip dhcp binding	Displays IP addresses assigned by an IOS DHCP server, their corresponding MAC addresses, and lease expirations
clear ip dhcp binding *	Releases all current DHCP leases
clear ip dhcp conflict *	Clears all currently identified DHCP conflicts
debug ip dhcp server events	Provides real-time information about DHCP address assignments and database updates
debug ip dhcp server packet	Displays real-time decodes of DHCP packets

QoS

Latency-sensitive traffic traveling over a wireless network (for example, Voice over Wireless LAN [VoWLAN]) might suffer from poor performance if QoS markings are not preserved as traffic crosses the boundary between the wireless and wired portions of a network.

You might want to review Chapter 11 for a more detailed discussion of QoS troubleshooting. The **mls qos trust dscp** interface configuration mode command, however, was not discussed in Chapter 11. You can issue this command on a Cisco Catalyst switch to cause an interface to trust incoming DSCP markings. To preserve priority markings on wireless traffic as it enters a wired network, you can issue this command on a Cisco Catalyst switch port that connects to a WLC.

Exam Preparation Tasks

Review All the Key Topics

Key Topic

Review the most important topics from inside the chapter, noted with the Key Topics icon in the outer margin of the page. Table 13-5 lists these key topics and the page numbers where each is found.

Table 13-5 *Key Topics for Chapter 13*

Key Topic Element	Description	Page Number
Table 13-2	ANS network components	422
Steps	Optimizing network applications	423
Example 13-1	NetFlow sample configuration	425
Example 13-2	Viewing NetFlow information	425
List	Common NetFlow troubleshooting issues	426
Steps	Configuring the IP SLA feature	426
Example 13-3	IP SLA responder configuration	427
Example 13-4	IP SLA source configuration	428
Example 13-5	Viewing information collected on the IP SLA source	428
Example 13-6	Viewing information collected on the IP SLA responder	428
List	Common IP SLA troubleshooting issues	429
List	Common NBAR troubleshooting issues	431
Steps	AutoQoS Enterprise configuration	432
Example 13-8	Configuring AutoQoS Enterprise	432
List	Common AutoQoS troubleshooting issues	434
List	Cisco Unified Wireless Network components	435
Table 13-3	VLAN and trunk troubleshooting commands for a Cisco Catalyst switch	438
Table 13-4	DHCP troubleshooting commands	439

Complete Tables and Lists from Memory

Print a copy of Appendix B, "Memory Tables" (found on the CD), or at least the section for this chapter, and complete the tables and lists from memory. Appendix C, "Memory Tables Answer Key," also on the CD, includes completed tables and lists to check your work.

Define Key Terms

Define the following key terms from this chapter, and check your answers in the Glossary:

Cisco Application Network Services (ANS), IP SLA, Network-Based Application Recognition (NBAR), Packet Description Language Module (PDLM), wireless client, wireless access point (WAP), wireless network unification, wireless network management, wireless mobility, autonomous mode, split-MAC mode, Lightweight Access Point Protocol (LWAPP), lightweight access point, wireless LAN controller (WLC), Extensible Authentication Protocol (EAP), Power over Ethernet (PoE)

Command Reference to Check Your Memory

This section includes the most important configuration and EXEC commands covered in this chapter. To determine how well you have memorized the commands as a side effect of your other studies, cover the left side of the table with a piece of paper; read the descriptions on the right side; and see whether you remember the command.

Table 13-6 *Chapter 13 Configuration Command Reference*

Command	Description
ip flow ingress	Interface configuration mode command used to enable NetFlow for that interface
ip flow-export source *interface-id*	Global configuration mode command used to specify the interface used to communicate with an external NetFlow collector
ip flow-export version {1 | 5 | 9}	Global configuration mode command used to specify the NetFlow version used by a device
ip flow-export destination *ip-address port*	Global configuration mode command used to specify the IP address and port number of an external NetFlow collector
ip sla monitor responder	Global configuration mode command that enables an IP SLA responder (Note: Some versions of Cisco IOS omit the **monitor** keyword in this command. Also note that this command is issued on the IP SLA responder router.)

continues

Table 13-6 *Chapter 13 Configuration Command Reference* *(Continued)*

Command	Description
ip sla monitor responder type *type* **ipaddress** *ip-address* **port** *port*	Global configuration mode command that specifies the type of IP SLA probe to be received by the responder router, including the destination IP address and port number of the probe (Note: Some versions of Cisco IOS would instead use the **ip sla responder** *type* **ipaddress** *IP_address* **port** *port* command.)
ip sla monitor *entry*	Global configuration mode command that defines an IP SLA monitor entry and enters IP SLA configuration mode (Note: Some versions of Cisco IOS omit the **monitor** keyword in this command. Also note that this command is issued on the IP SLA source router.)
type tcpConnect dest-ipaddr *dest-ip-address* **dest-port** *dest-port* **source-port source-port**	IP SLA configuration mode command that defines that the type of IP SLA probe to be sent is a TCP Connect probe (Note: Some versions of Cisco IOS use the **tcp-connect** *dest-ip-address dest-port* **source-port** *source-port* command. Also note that this command is issued on the IP SLA source router.)
tos value	IP SLA TCP configuration mode command that specifies the decimal equivalent of the eight binary bits in the TOS byte of an IPv4 header (Note: This command is issued on the IP SLA source router.)
ip sla monitor schedule *entry* **life forever start-time now**	Global configuration mode command that immediately starts a specified IP SLA entry, which then runs forever (Note: Some versions of Cisco IOS omit the **monitor** keyword in this command.)
ip nbar protocol-discovery	Interface configuration mode command that enables NBAR protocol discovery on the interface
ip nbar pdlm *pdlm-file*	Global configuration mode command that adds the specified PDLM file to the NBAR protocol recognition capability of the router
ip nbar port-map *protocol* {**tcp** | **udp**} *port-number* [*port-number*]	Specifies one or more TCP or UDP ports used by NBAR to recognize the specified protocol
auto discovery qos [trust]	Interface configuration mode command issued on a router to begin the discovery phase on an interface for the AutoQoS Enterprise feature (Note: The **trust** keyword instructs the router to classify traffic based on existing DSCP markings, as opposed to using NBAR.)

Table 13-6   *Chapter 13 Configuration Command Reference*   (*Continued*)

Command	Description
auto qos	Interface configuration mode command on a router used to apply a policy map generated by AutoQoS Enterprise
mls qos trust dscp	Interface configuration mode command used on a switch to instruct an interface to trust Differentiated Services Code Point (DSCP) markings on packets entering the interface

This chapter covers the following subjects:

Remote Office Troubleshooting: This section identifies a collection of technologies that might become troubleshooting targets for a remote office network. The primary technologies that this section focuses on are virtual private network (VPN) technologies. Sample syntax is provided for a VPN using IP security (IPsec) and Generic Routing Encapsulation (GRE). Also, several useful **show** commands are provided as a troubleshooting reference.

Complex Network Troubleshooting: This section identifies how multiple network technologies map to the seven layers of the Open Systems Interconnection (OSI) reference model. Also, you are given a list of resources that a troubleshooter should have prior to troubleshooting a complex enterprise network. Finally, this section reviews key points from all trouble tickets previously presented.

CHAPTER 14

Large Enterprise Network Troubleshooting

Most large enterprise networks connect to one or more remote office locations, typically accessible via an IP WAN. The introduction of a remote location into a network can pose additional troubleshooting targets. As a couple of examples, consider quality of service (QoS) and security issues. The relatively limited bandwidth available on an IP WAN might create quality issues for latency-sensitive applications such as streaming voice or video. Also, because the IP WAN might span an untrusted network (for example, the Internet), security mechanisms should be in place to secure the traffic flowing between the head-quarters and remote locations.

Although troubleshooting remote office network issues can involve several technologies (many of which have been discussed previously in this book), this chapter focuses on VPN technologies. Specifically, you will learn about the characteristics of site-to-site VPNs and remote-access VPNs, including common troubleshooting issues for those VPN types. You are also presented with a collection of commands useful in troubleshooting VPN-related issues.

Because troubleshooting a complex enterprise network requires understanding the operation of and the interaction between many networking technologies, this chapter reviews multiple network technologies discussed in previous chapters. Specifically, this chapter identifies at which layer(s) of the OSI model various networking technologies reside. Additionally, you are given a list of prerequisites a troubleshooter should have before troubleshooting a complex enterprise network. Finally, this chapter reviews each trouble ticket previously covered in this book. For each trouble ticket, this chapter reviews the reported symptoms, the Cisco IOS commands used to gather information, the identified issue, and the problem resolution.

"Do I Know This Already?" Quiz

The "Do I Know This Already?" quiz helps you determine your level of knowledge of this chapter's topics before you begin. Table 14-1 details the major topics discussed in this chapter and their corresponding quiz questions.

Table 14-1 *"Do I Know This Already?" Section-to-Question Mapping*

Foundation Topics Section	Questions
Remote Office Troubleshooting	1–4
Complex Network Troubleshooting	5–8

1. VPNs can generally be categorized as one of which two VPN types? (Choose the two best answers.)

   a. Centralized VPN

   b. Site-to-site VPN

   c. Remote-access VPN

   d. Distributed VPN

2. What VPN technology allows a VPN link between two remote offices to be dynamically created on an as-needed basis?

   a. ESP

   b. AH

   c. SHA-1

   d. DMVPN

3. Which of the following is generally true of a remote-access VPN but is generally not true of a site-to-site VPN? (Choose the best answer.)

   a. VPN client software needs to be installed on the remote-access VPN clients.

   b. IPsec is supported.

   c. User profiles are not supported.

   d. A router at the remote site terminates the VPN connection.

4. Which of the following commands displays IPsec security association settings? (Choose the best answer.)

   a. show crypto map

   b. show crypto engine connections active

   c. show ip protocols

   d. show crypto ipsec sa

5. If you are troubleshooting an EtherChannel issue, on which layer of the OSI model should you focus?

   a. Layer 1

   b. Layer 2

   c. Layer 3

   d. Layer 4

6. Which of the following symptoms are common results of a Spanning Tree Protocol issue? (Select the two best answers.)

   a. Routing protocols are not load balancing appropriately.

   b. A switch's MAC address table is corrupted.

   c. A switch's processor utilization is high.

   d. A switch's port experiences a security violation, resulting in the port entering the *errordisable* state.

7. Which of the following technologies can help provide default gateway redundancy for endpoints? (Choose the best answer.)

    a. NTP

    b. DHCP

    c. HSRP

    d. SRST

8. What feature can automatically deploy a QoS configuration on some router and switch platforms?

    a. AutoQoS

    b. NBAR

    c. CEF

    d. NetFlow

Foundation Topics

Remote Office Troubleshooting

Large enterprise networks often contain multiple remote offices connecting back to a network located at a corporate headquarters. Troubleshooting remote office network issues can require knowledge of a wide array of technologies, as illustrated in Figure 14-1.

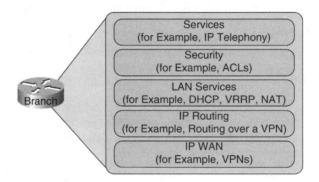

Figure 14-1   *Remote Office Troubleshooting Targets*

Each of the technology areas shown in the figure has previously been addressed in this book. Rather than reviewing each of these topics, this section primarily focuses on VPN issues that can impact remote office connectivity. For example, a VPN connection established through the Internet can be used as a backup to a private IP WAN connection, as shown in Figure 14-2.

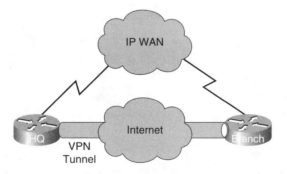

Figure 14-2   *Using a VPN Connection as a Backup Link*

VPN Types

As illustrated in Figure 14-3, most VPNs can be categorized as one of two types:

■ **Site-to-site VPNs:** A site-to-site VPN typically terminates in a router at the headquarters and a router at the remote site. Such an arrangement does not require the
clients at the remote site to have VPN client software installed.

■ **Remote-access VPNs:** A remote-access VPN requires VPN clients at the remote
site to run VPN client software. Although this approach might require more administrative overhead to install client software on all clients, remote-access VPNs do offer
more flexibility for mobile users. For example, clients can connect via their hotel's
Internet connection using VPN client software on their laptop computer.

Each VPN type has unique design considerations.

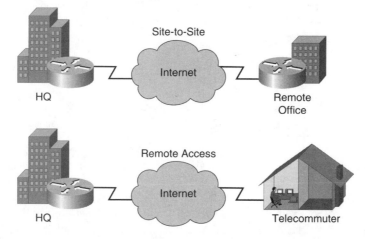

Figure 14-3   *Site-to-Site and Remote-Access VPNs*

Site-to-Site VPN Considerations

Figure 14-4 depicts a site-to-site VPN connection.

Following is a listing of potential issues that you should consider with site-to-site networks:

■ **Overlapping IP address spaces:** Notice that the Branch A and Headquarters locations have an overlapping IP address space (that is, 10.1.1.0/24). This overlap might
prevent these two networks from communicating successfully. A fix for such an issue
is to configure Network Address Translation (NAT) to support overlapping networks.

■ **Dynamic routing protocols:** Dynamic routing protocols (for example, Enhanced
Interior Gateway Routing Protocol [EIGRP], Open Shortest Path First [OSPF], and
Routing Information Protocol, version 2 [RIPv2]) typically send advertisements to a
multicast address; however, IPsec tunnels transport only unicast IP packets. A Generic
Routing Encapsulation (GRE) tunnel, however, can transport a variety of traffic
types. Therefore, all IP traffic (including multicast and broadcast traffic) can initially
be encapsulated within GRE packets, which are unicast IP packets. Those GRE packets can then be encapsulated inside IPsec packets to secure their transmission.

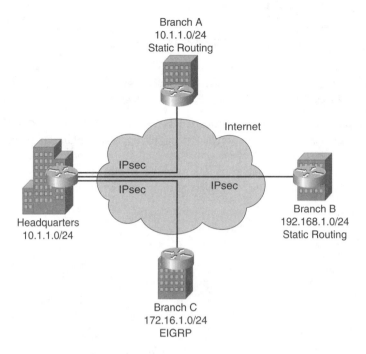

Figure 14-4   *Site-to-Site VPN Connection*

■   **Maximum transmission unit (MTU) size:** Most Cisco router interfaces default to
    an MTU size of 1500 bytes for packets (that is, not including a Layer 2 header). How-
    ever, when traffic is encapsulated inside a VPN tunnel, the tunnel header(s) add to the
    packet size. For example, a combined GRE and IPsec tunnel can add between 60 and
    80 bytes of overhead to a packet. As a result, the packet size might exceed its MTU
    setting. When an interface attempts to transmit a packet that exceeds the MTU of the
    interface, the interface attempts to fragment the packet. If successful, each fragment
    receives its own header creating a new packet, which is of an acceptable size. How-
    ever, fragmenting large packets can cause issues. First, the act of performing fragmen-
    tation increases the burden on a router processor. Additionally, some packets are
    marked with a Do Not Fragment (DF) bit, which can cause those packets to be
    dropped.

■   **Misconfiguration:** The configuration of IPsec tunnels can be quite complex. As a
    result, a common troubleshooting issue for site-to-site VPNs is a misconfiguration of
    the VPN endpoints (for example, the routers at each side of the VPN tunnel).

■   **Point-to-point nature of GRE tunnels:** Because GRE tunnels are point-to-point log-
    ical connections, suboptimal pathing might result. For example, consider Figure 14-5.

    Imagine that Branch B wants to communicate with Branch C. The GRE tunnels are
    configured in a hub-and-spoke topology, where the Headquarters location is func-
    tioning as the hub. Therefore, traffic travels from Branch B to Headquarters and then
    from Headquarters to Branch C. Because traffic is not flowing directly from Branch B
    to Branch C, excessive delay and poor performance might result.

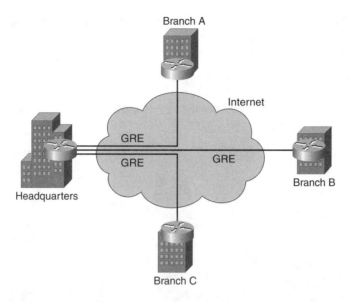

Figure 14-5 *Hub-and-Spoke GRE Tunnels*

Another option is to create a full mesh of VPN connections, as shown in Figure 14-6.

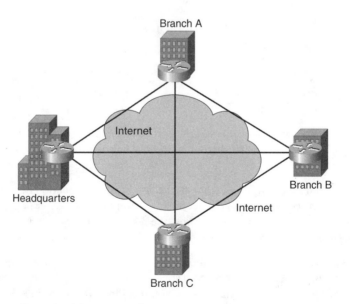

Figure 14-6 *Full Mesh of GRE Tunnels*

Full mesh networks, however, do not scale well. Specifically, the number of connections required to form a full mesh of connections between *n* sites equals $n(n-1)/2$. For example, if you had ten sites you wanted to interconnect in a full mesh topology, you would need to configure 45 (that is, $10(10-1)/2 = 45$) connections.

Rather than creating a full mesh of VPN connections between all sites in an enterprise network, you can alternatively use *Dynamic Multipoint VPN* (DMVPN) technology. DMVPM allows VPN connections to be dynamically created on an as-needed basis.

Figure 14-7 illustrates a DMVPN connection. In the figure, notice that when Branch B wants to communicate with Branch C, a dynamic VPN is formed between those two sites.

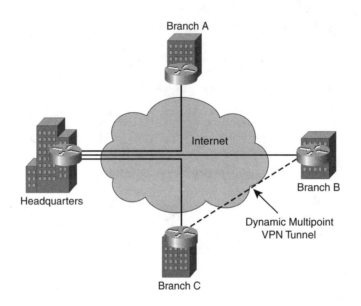

Figure 14-7   *DMVPN*

This DMVPN solution overcomes the performance issues of a hub-and-spoke topology, while simultaneously overcoming the scalability issues presented by a full mesh topology.

■ **Suboptimal routing:** Recall that a tunnel is a logical connection between two endpoints; however, that logical connection can span multiple router hops. If a portion of a tunnel spans a slow or unreliable link, the result can be poor performance for all tunnel traffic.

Another issue that can lead to suboptimal routing is *recursive routing*. For example, when configuring a GRE tunnel, you specify the IP address of the remote side of the tunnel. If the best route to that destination IP address (from the perspective of the IP routing table of the source router) is the source router's tunnel interface, the tunnel interface might experience flapping. Therefore, poor VPN performance can be linked to an inappropriate routing configuration on one or both of the VPN routers.

■ **Route processor overhead:** Depending on the security algorithms chosen to protect an IPsec tunnel, some router platforms might suffer from poor performance. Also, the number of VPN tunnels that can be terminated on a router depends on the underlying router platform. Table 14-2 contrasts the VPN tunnel capacity of various Integrated Services Router (ISR) platforms.

Table 14-2 *VPN Tunnel Capacity for Various ISR Platforms*

Router Platform	Maximum IPsec Speed and Number of Supported VPN Tunnels
Cisco 1841	95 Mbps IPsec VPN 800 tunnels
Cisco 2801	100 Mbps IPsec VPN 1500 tunnels
Cisco 2811	30 Mbps 1500 tunnels
Cisco 2821	140 Mbps 1500 tunnels
Cisco 2851	145 Mbps 1500 tunnels
Cisco 3825	175 Mbps 2000 tunnels
Cisco 3845	185 Mbps 2500 tunnels

Remote-Access VPN Considerations

Figure 14-8 depicts a remote-access VPN connection.

Following is a listing of potential troubleshooting issues that you should consider with remote-access networks:

- **Authentication:** Users connecting from their PC (running VPN client software) require user credentials (for example, username and password credentials) to gain access to a network. Therefore, one reason remote-access VPN users fail to establish a VPN tunnel is that they provide incorrect credentials. Alternatively, the users might provide correct credentials, but the authentication server might be configured incorrectly or might not be functioning.

- **User profiles:** Because users log into a remote-access VPN, different users can be assigned different policies through the use of user profiles. As a result, when remote-access VPN users are unable to connect to desired resources, the underlying issue might be their user profile.

- **MTU size:** Remote-access VPN clients have a similar issue with MTU sizes and fragmentation, as previously described for site-to-site VPNs. Fortunately, VPN client software often allows you to configure the MTU size of a tunnel.

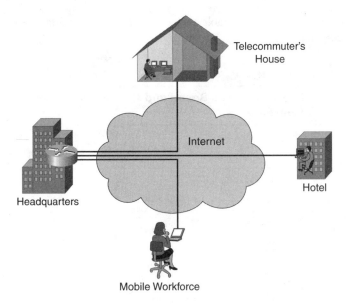

Figure 14-8   *Remote-Access VPN Connection*

- **Misconfiguration:** VPN software running on a client machine often has multiple configuration options. As a result, a common issue for remote-access VPNs is the misconfiguration of the VPN client software.

- **Client security software:** Security software running on a client machine might deny traffic required for VPN establishment. Therefore, firewall and anti-virus software running on a VPN client machine might result in the failure of a VPN connection.

Troubleshooting VPN Issues

VPNs involve multiple configuration elements. Therefore, as a troubleshooting aid, the following list provides a collection of questions to answer when troubleshooting a VPN issue:

- How is IP addressing assigned? (For example, do overlapping IP address ranges exist?)

- Is the VPN site-to-site or remote-access?

- How are the MTU values configured on the router interfaces transited by the VPN?

- What translations (if any) is NAT performing?

- Are routing protocols routing traffic over a GRE tunnel or over a physical interface?

- According to a router's IP routing table, is the best path to a tunnel destination's IP address the tunnel interface? (If so, a recursive routing issue might result.)

Table 14-3 lists a collection of Cisco IOS commands useful in troubleshooting VPN connections.

Table 14-3   *VPN Troubleshooting Commands*

Command	Description
show crypto ipsec sa	Displays IPsec security association settings
show crypto engine connections active	Displays configuration information for all active IPsec sessions
show crypto map	Displays the crypto map configuration of a router (for example, information about ACLs being referenced by the crypto map, the IP address of the IPsec peer, the security association lifetime, and the name of the crypto map transform set)
show ip route	Displays routes injected into a router's IP routing table, including next-hop IP address or exit interface information for IP routes
show ip protocols	Displays information about the active IP routing processes of a router
show interfaces tunnel *number*	Displays status and configuration information for a specified tunnel interface on a router

To illustrate the data collection process for a VPN using both IPsec and GRE technologies, consider Figure 14-9.

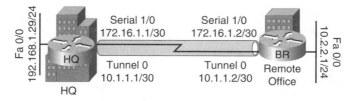

Figure 14-9   *IPsec and GRE Tunnel Topology*

Although the configuration of VPN tunnels is outside the scope of the TSHOOT curriculum, as a reference, Examples 14-1 and 14-2 illustrate the VPN configurations present on routers HQ and BR.

Example 14-1   *VPN Configuration on Router HQ*

```
HQ# show run
...OUTPUT OMITTED...
hostname HQ
!
crypto isakmp policy 1
```

```
 encr 3des
 authentication pre-share
 group 2
!
crypto isakmp policy 2
 encr aes
 authentication pre-share
 group 2
crypto isakmp key cisco address 172.16.1.2
!
crypto ipsec transform-set TSHOOT-TRANSFORM esp-aes esp-sha-hmac
!
crypto map SDM_CMAP_1 1 ipsec-isakmp
 description Tunnel to172.16.1.2
 set peer 172.16.1.2
 set transform-set TSHOOT-TRANSFORM
 match address 100
!
interface Tunnel0
 ip address 10.1.1.1 255.255.255.252
 ip mtu 1420
 tunnel source 172.16.1.1
 tunnel destination 172.16.1.2
 tunnel path-mtu-discovery
 crypto map SDM_CMAP_1
!
interface FastEthernet0/0
 ip address 192.168.1.29 255.255.255.0
!
interface Serial1/0
 ip address 172.16.1.1 255.255.255.0
 encapsulation ppp
 crypto map SDM_CMAP_1
!
ip route 0.0.0.0 0.0.0.0 Tunnel0
ip route 10.1.1.0 255.255.255.0 172.16.1.2
ip route 172.16.1.2 255.255.255.255 Serial1/0
!
!
access-list 100 remark SDM_ACL Category=4
access-list 100 permit gre host 172.16.1.1 host 172.16.1.2
!
...OUTPUT OMITTED...
```

Example 14-2   *VPN Configuration on Router BR*

```
BR# show run
...OUTPUT OMITTED...
hostname BR
!
crypto isakmp policy 1
 encr 3des
 authentication pre-share
 group 2
!
crypto isakmp policy 2
 encr aes
 authentication pre-share
 group 2
crypto isakmp key cisco address 172.16.1.1
!
crypto ipsec transform-set TSHOOT-TRANSFORM esp-aes esp-sha-hmac
!
crypto map SDM_CMAP_1 1 ipsec-isakmp
 set peer 172.16.1.1
 set transform-set TSHOOT-TRANSFORM
 match address SDM_1
!
interface Tunnel0
 ip address 10.1.1.2 255.255.255.252
 ip mtu 1420
 tunnel source 172.16.1.2
 tunnel destination 172.16.1.1
 tunnel path-mtu-discovery
 crypto map SDM_CMAP_1
!
interface FastEthernet0/0
 ip address 10.2.2.1 255.255.255.0
!
interface Serial1/0
 ip address 172.16.1.2 255.255.255.0
 encapsulation ppp
!
ip route 0.0.0.0 0.0.0.0 Tunnel0
ip route 10.1.1.0 255.255.255.0 172.16.1.1
ip route 172.16.1.1 255.255.255.255 Serial1/0
!
ip access-list extended SDM_1
 remark SDM_ACL Category=4
 permit gre host 172.16.1.2 host 172.16.1.1
...OUTPUT OMITTED...
```

Example 14-3 provides sample output from the **show crypto ipsec sa** command on router HQ. The output offers information about IPsec security association settings, including IP address information for the tunnel peers and information about the encryption and hashing algorithms being used to protect the tunnel traffic.

Example 14-3   show crypto ipsec sa *Command Output on Router HQ*

```
HQ# show crypto ipsec sa

interface: Serial1/0
    Crypto map tag: SDM_CMAP_1, local addr 172.16.1.1

    protected vrf: (none)
    local  ident (addr/mask/prot/port): (172.16.1.1/255.255.255.255/47/0)
    remote ident (addr/mask/prot/port): (172.16.1.2/255.255.255.255/47/0)
    current_peer 172.16.1.2 port 500
      PERMIT, flags={origin_is_acl,}
     #pkts encaps: 60, #pkts encrypt: 60, #pkts digest: 60
     #pkts decaps: 0, #pkts decrypt: 0, #pkts verify: 0
     #pkts compressed: 0, #pkts decompressed: 0
     #pkts not compressed: 0, #pkts compr. failed: 0
     #pkts not decompressed: 0, #pkts decompress failed: 0
     #send errors 4, #recv errors 0

      local crypto endpt.: 172.16.1.1, remote crypto endpt.: 172.16.1.2
      path mtu 1420, ip mtu 1420, ip mtu idb Tunnel0
      current outbound spi: 0x631F3197(1662988695)

      inbound esp sas:
       spi: 0x2441D1C7(608293319)
         transform: esp-aes esp-sha-hmac ,
         in use settings ={Tunnel, }
         conn id: 2002, flow_id: SW:2, crypto map: SDM_CMAP_1
         sa timing: remaining key lifetime (k/sec): (4451479/3185)
         IV size: 16 bytes
         replay detection support: Y
         Status: ACTIVE
```

```
        inbound ah sas:

        inbound pcp sas:

        outbound esp sas:
         spi: 0x631F3197(1662988695)
           transform: esp-aes esp-sha-hmac ,
           in use settings ={Tunnel, }
           conn id: 2001, flow_id: SW:1, crypto map: SDM_CMAP_1
           sa timing: remaining key lifetime (k/sec): (4451473/3183)
           IV size: 16 bytes
           replay detection support: Y
           Status: ACTIVE

        outbound ah sas:

        outbound pcp sas:

interface: Tunnel0
     Crypto map tag: SDM_CMAP_1, local addr 172.16.1.1

    protected vrf: (none)
    local  ident (addr/mask/prot/port): (172.16.1.1/255.255.255.255/47/0)
    remote ident (addr/mask/prot/port): (172.16.1.2/255.255.255.255/47/0)
    current_peer 172.16.1.2 port 500
      PERMIT, flags={origin_is_acl,}
     #pkts encaps: 60, #pkts encrypt: 60, #pkts digest: 60
     #pkts decaps: 0, #pkts decrypt: 0, #pkts verify: 0
     #pkts compressed: 0, #pkts decompressed: 0
     #pkts not compressed: 0, #pkts compr. failed: 0
     #pkts not decompressed: 0, #pkts decompress failed: 0
     #send errors 4, #recv errors 0

      local crypto endpt.: 172.16.1.1, remote crypto endpt.: 172.16.1.2
      path mtu 1420, ip mtu 1420, ip mtu idb Tunnel0
      current outbound spi: 0x631F3197(1662988695)

      inbound esp sas:
       spi: 0x2441D1C7(608293319)
         transform: esp-aes esp-sha-hmac ,
         in use settings ={Tunnel, }
         conn id: 2002, flow_id: SW:2, crypto map: SDM_CMAP_1
```

```
     sa timing: remaining key lifetime (k/sec): (4451479/3182)
     IV size: 16 bytes
     replay detection support: Y
     Status: ACTIVE

  inbound ah sas:

  inbound pcp sas:

  outbound esp sas:
   spi: 0x631F3197(1662988695)
     transform: esp-aes esp-sha-hmac ,
     in use settings ={Tunnel, }
     conn id: 2001, flow_id: SW:1, crypto map: SDM_CMAP_1
     sa timing: remaining key lifetime (k/sec): (4451473/3181)
     IV size: 16 bytes
     replay detection support: Y
     Status: ACTIVE

  outbound ah sas:

  outbound pcp sas:
```

Example 14-4 provides sample output from the **show crypto engine connections active** command on router HQ. The output shows local interface and IP address information for all active IPsec sessions. You can also see from the output the encryption and hashing algorithms being used.

Example 14-4   show crypto engine connections active *Command Output on Router HQ*

```
HQ# show crypto engine connections active
   ID Interface      IP-Address      State   Algorithm            Encrypt   Decrypt
    1 Serial1/0       172.16.1.1      set     HMAC_SHA+3DES_56_C        0         0
 2001 Serial1/0       172.16.1.1      set     AES+SHA                  28         0
 2002 Serial1/0       172.16.1.1      set     AES+SHA                   0         0
```

Example 14-5 provides sample output from the **show crypto map** command on router HQ. The output includes such information as the peer IP address, the ACL used to classify traffic to be sent over the tunnel, and the interfaces using a particular crypto map.

Example 14-5   show crypto map *Command Output on Router HQ*

```
HQ# show crypto map
Crypto Map "SDM_CMAP_1" 1 ipsec-isakmp
    Description: Tunnel to172.16.1.2
    Peer = 172.16.1.2
    Extended IP access list 100
        access-list 100 permit gre host 172.16.1.1 host 172.16.1.2
    Current peer: 172.16.1.2
    Security association lifetime: 4608000 kilobytes/3600 seconds
    PFS (Y/N): N
    Transform sets={
        TSHOOT-TRANSFORM,
    }
    Interfaces using crypto map SDM_CMAP_1:
        Serial1/0
        Tunnel0
```

Example 14-6 provides sample output from the **show ip route** command on router HQ. Notice that the route to the IP address of the tunnel destination is a physical interface and not a tunnel interface. This approach can help prevent the recursive routing issue previously discussed.

Example 14-6   show ip route *Command Output on Router HQ*

```
HQ# show ip route
Codes: C - connected, S - static, R - RIP, M - mobile, B - BGP
        D - EIGRP, EX - EIGRP external, O - OSPF, IA - OSPF inter area
        N1 - OSPF NSSA external type 1, N2 - OSPF NSSA external type 2
        E1 - OSPF external type 1, E2 - OSPF external type 2
        i - IS-IS, su - IS-IS summary, L1 - IS-IS level-1, L2 - IS-IS level-2
        ia - IS-IS inter area, * - candidate default, U - per-user static route
        o - ODR, P - periodic downloaded static route

Gateway of last resort is 0.0.0.0 to network 0.0.0.0

     172.16.0.0/16 is variably subnetted, 3 subnets, 2 masks
C        172.16.1.0/24 is directly connected, Serial1/0
C        172.16.2.0/24 is directly connected, FastEthernet0/1
C        172.16.1.2/32 is directly connected, Serial1/0
     10.0.0.0/8 is variably subnetted, 2 subnets, 2 masks
C        10.1.1.0/30 is directly connected, Tunnel0
S        10.1.1.0/24 [1/0] via 172.16.1.2
C    192.168.1.0/24 is directly connected, FastEthernet0/0
S*   0.0.0.0/0 is directly connected, Tunnel0
```

Example 14-7 provides sample output from the **show ip protocols** command on router HQ. The output normally displays information about routing protocols running on a router. However, in this example, the lack of any output indicates that no dynamic routing protocols are configured.

Example 14-7 show ip protocols *Command Output on Router HQ*

```
HQ# show ip protocols
```

Example 14-8 provides sample output from the **show interfaces tunnel 0** command on router HQ. From the output you can determine that the Tunnel 0 interface is operational at Layer 1 and Layer 2. You can also see the source and destination IP address of the tunnel and that the tunnel protocol in use is GRE.

Example 14-8 show interfaces tunnel 0 *Command Output on Router HQ*

```
HQ# show interfaces tunnel 0
Tunnel0 is up, line protocol is up
  Hardware is Tunnel
  Internet address is 10.1.1.1/30
  MTU 1514 bytes, BW 9 Kbit, DLY 500000 usec,
     reliability 255/255, txload 1/255, rxload 1/255
  Encapsulation TUNNEL, loopback not set
  Keepalive not set
  Tunnel source 172.16.1.1, destination 172.16.1.2
  Tunnel protocol/transport GRE/IP
    Key disabled, sequencing disabled
    Checksumming of packets disabled
  Tunnel TTL 255
  Fast tunneling enabled
  Path MTU Discovery, ager 10 mins, min MTU 92, MTU 0, expires never
  Tunnel transmit bandwidth 8000 (kbps)
  Tunnel receive bandwidth 8000 (kbps)
  Last input never, output 00:06:48, output hang never
  Last clearing of "show interface" counters never
  Input queue: 0/75/0/0 (size/max/drops/flushes); Total output drops: 4
  Queueing strategy: fifo
  Output queue: 0/0 (size/max)
  5 minute input rate 0 bits/sec, 0 packets/sec
  5 minute output rate 0 bits/sec, 0 packets/sec
     0 packets input, 0 bytes, 0 no buffer
     Received 0 broadcasts, 0 runts, 0 giants, 0 throttles
     0 input errors, 0 CRC, 0 frame, 0 overrun, 0 ignored, 0 abort
     60 packets output, 7216 bytes, 0 underruns
     0 output errors, 0 collisions, 0 interface resets
     0 output buffer failures, 0 output buffers swapped out
```

Complex Network Troubleshooting

Previous chapters in this book have addressed a wide array of networking technologies. Because many of these technologies can be found in the typical enterprise network, a successful troubleshooter of large enterprise networks needs a broad understanding of each of these technologies. In addition, a troubleshooter needs to understand how these technologies interoperate and impact one another. In some cases the troubleshooter might not have the depth of knowledge required in a specific technology. In such a situation, the troubleshooter should know how to obtain the required knowledge or identify who can provide the required expertise.

This section categorizes major networking troubleshooting areas based on the layers of the OSI model. Fundamental requirements for enterprise network troubleshooting are presented. Finally, this chapter reviews each of the trouble tickets presented in this book. Specifically, the symptoms of each trouble ticket are presented, along with the troubleshooting commands used and the suggested solution to the underlying issue or issues.

Troubleshooting Complex Networks

Complex enterprise networks are composed of multiple technologies that might reside at various layers of the OSI model. Knowing which technologies correspond to which OSI layers can help a troubleshooter better understand how issues with one technology can impact other technologies.

Table 14-4 identifies the OSI layer (or layers) that correspond to a variety of network technologies.

Table 14-4   *OSI Layers of Various Networking Technologies*

Technology	Layer 1	Layer 2	Layer 3	Layer 4	Layer 5	Layer 6	Layer 7
Security	X	X	X	X	X	X	X
Performance	X	X	X	X	X		
Packet Forwarding			X				
Routing Protocols			X				
Mapping Layer 2 QoS Markings to Layer 3	X	X					
Spanning Tree Protocol		X					
Frame Forwarding		X					
EtherChannel		X					
Physical Interfaces	X	X					
Cabling	X						

Key Topic

The following list identifies important prerequisites for troubleshooters to possess before they troubleshoot a complex enterprise network.

- A high-level understanding of multiple network technologies that might be encountered and access to specialized knowledge as needed

- An understanding of how network technologies impact one another

- An understanding of the architectural planes of a router (for example, the data plane and control plane) and the functions of each plane

- A familiarity with troubleshooting tools (for example, appropriate Cisco IOS commands and packet capture software)

- Previously collected baseline information, against which newly collected data can be compared

Case Study Review

Because troubleshooting large enterprise networks requires knowledge of multiple network technologies, this chapter concludes by reviewing each of the previously presented trouble tickets, highlighting the reported symptom(s), troubleshooting commands used to diagnose the issue, and presenting the underlying issue along with the implemented solution.

Trouble Ticket #1 Review

Trouble ticket #1 is presented in Chapter 4, "Basic Cisco Catalyst Switch Troubleshooting."

Symptom: Users were experiencing latency when attempting to reach a remote network.

Troubleshooting commands used:

- **show spanning-tree vlan** *vlan-id*

- **show spanning-tree summary**

- **show spanning-tree summaryinterface** *interface-id* **detail**

Issue: Spanning Tree Protocol (STP) was not configured on two switches, resulting in a Layer 2 topological loop that caused MAC address table corruption and a high CPU utilization on the Cisco Catalyst switches.

Resolution: STP was properly configured on the switches, eliminating the CPU utilization and MAC address table corruption issues.

Trouble Ticket #2 Review

Trouble ticket #2 is presented in Chapter 5, "Advanced Cisco Catalyst Switch Troubleshooting."

Symptom: Hot Standby Routing Protocol (HSRP) was not working properly. Specifically, an inappropriate router was the active HSRP router.

Troubleshooting commands used:

- **show standby brief**
- **debug standby**
- **ping ip-address**

Issue: The *preempt* feature was not enabled on the router that should be acting as the active HSRP router. Therefore, after that router rebooted, it did not regain its active status.

Resolution: The preempt feature was enabled on the router that should have been acting as the active HSRP router, resulting in that router regaining its active status.

Trouble Ticket #3 Review

Trouble ticket #3 is presented in Chapter 6, "Introduction to Troubleshooting Routing Protocols."

Symptom: A router configured for EIGRP was not load balancing appropriately.

Troubleshooting commands used:

- **show ip route**
- **show ip eigrp topology**
- **show run | begin router**

Issue: The paths across which the router should have load-balanced had different costs.

Resolution: EIGRP's *variance* feature was configured to enable load balancing across unequal cost paths.

Trouble Ticket #4 Review

Trouble ticket #4 is presented in Chapter 7, "OSPF and Route Redistribution Troubleshooting."

Symptom: Routers in a multiarea OSPF topology did not have full reachability to all networks.

Troubleshooting commands used:

- **show run | begin router**
- **show ip ospf neighbor**
- **show ip route**
- **show ip ospf**
- **show ip ospf interface** *interface-id*
- **show ip ospf virtual-links**

Issue #1: A virtual link configuration was incorrect. Specifically, the transit area (that is, the area between area 0 and the area that is not physically adjacent to area 0) configured in the **area** *number* **virtual-link** command was incorrect.

Resolution #1: The virtual link configuration was corrected by specifying the appropriate transit area in the **area** *number* **virtual-link** command.

Issue #2: One of the routers had nondefault Hello and Dead timers configured for a subinterface. These parameters did not match the parameters at the far end of the Frame Relay link, preventing an OSPF adjacency from forming over that link.

Resolution #2: The OSPF Hello and Dead timers were returned to their default settings, after which an OSPF adjacency formed between the routers at each end of the Frame Relay link.

Issues #3 and #4: Two of the routers had interfaces configured with incorrect OSPF network types.

Resolution #3 and #4: The interfaces with the incorrect OSPF network types were configured to use their default OSPF network types, after which OSPF adjacencies formed between the routers at each end of the links.

Trouble Ticket #5 Review

Trouble ticket #5 is presented in Chapter 7.

Symptom: Two companies merged, and they used different routing protocols (that is, OSPF and EIGRP). Route redistribution was not correctly performing mutual route redistribution between these two autonomous systems.

Troubleshooting commands used:

- **show ip route**
- **show run | begin router**

Issue #1: The EIGRP routing process configured on the router performing the redistribution lacked a default metric that would be assigned to routes being redistributed in the EIGRP routing process.

Resolution #1: The **default-metric 1500 100 255 1 1500** command was issued in router configuration mode for the EIGRP routing process. This made redistributed routes appear to have a bandwidth of 1500, a delay of 100, a reliability of 255, a load of 1, and an MTU of 1500.

Issue #2: The OSPF routing process configured on the router performing the redistribution lacked the **subnets** parameter at the end of the **redistribute** command. The **subnets** parameter is required to allow nonclassful networks to be redistributed into OSPF.

Resolution #2: The existing **redistribute** command in router configuration mode for the OSPF routing process was replaced with the **redistribute eigrp 100 metric 64 subnets** command, which instructed OSPF to redistribute routes from EIGRP AS 100 with a metric of 64 and to redistribute nonclassful networks (that is, subnets).

Trouble Ticket #6 Review

Trouble ticket #6 is presented in Chapter 8, "Troubleshooting BGP and Router Performance Issues."

Symptom: An enterprise is dual homed to the Internet using two service providers. The dual homing is configured using BGP. However, BGP selected the slower of the two links going out to the Internet.

Troubleshooting commands used:

- **show ip route**
- **show run | begin router**
- **show ip bgp summary**
- **show ip bgp**

Issue: The enterprise router was pointing to the service provider reachable over the slower link, because the router of that service provider had the lowest BGP router ID.

Resolution: The enterprise router was configured to assign local preference attributes to routes being advertised by the service provider routers. BGP prefers higher local preference values. Higher local preferences were applied to routes being advertised by the service provider reachable over the higher-speed link. Therefore, outbound traffic used the optimal path.

To influence inbound path selection (that is, traffic coming in from the Internet), the enterprise router was configured to prepend multiple instances of its AS on route advertisements sent over the slower-speed link. This caused the service provider routers to prefer the higher-speed link when sending traffic into the enterprise, because it appeared to require fewer AS hops.

Trouble Ticket #7 Review

Trouble ticket #7 is presented in Chapter 9, "Security Troubleshooting."

Symptom: The enable secret password for a router was forgotten. Also, a Telnet session to one of the routers in the topology timed out after only 1 second. Finally, an ACL was not preventing Telnet sessions as expected.

Troubleshooting command used:

- **show running-config**

Issue #1: The administrator forgot the enable secret password for a router. Therefore, the administrator was not able to access the privileged mode of the router.

Resolution #1: Password recovery was performed, which involved rebooting the router, entering ROMMON configuration mode, changing the configuration register to ignore the startup configuration, and rebooting the router. Privileged mode could then be entered, because the router booted up without a startup configuration. The startup configuration was copied to the running configuration, and the enable secret password was changed. Interfaces in the shutdown state were administratively brought up, and the configuration register was changed to use the startup configuration upon a reboot. Finally, the router was rebooted, and the router booted up using the startup configuration, which had the newly configured enable secret password.

Issue #2: The **exec-timeout** parameter for the VTY lines of a router was configured to **0 1**, which meant that a Telnet session would time out after only 1 second.

Resolution #2: The **exec-timeout** parameter for the VTY lines of the router was reconfigured to **0 0**, meaning that a Telnet session would never time out. However, the challenge was to perform this reconfiguration without timing out in the process. The solution was to repeatedly tap the down arrow on the keyboard (which did not enter characters in the CLI but still reset the idle timer of the VTY line) with one hand while typing the reconfiguration commands with the other hand.

Issue #3: An ACL was applied in the outbound direction on an interface, when it should have been applied in the inbound direction on the interface.

Resolution #3: The **ip access-group** command that applied the ACL in the incorrect direction was removed and replaced with an appropriate **ip access-group** command.

Trouble Ticket #8 Review

Trouble ticket #8 is presented in Chapter 10, "IP Services Troubleshooting."

Symptom: NAT was partially working on a router; however, only two NAT translations could simultaneously be set up. Additionally, NAT translations failed.

Troubleshooting commands used:

- **show ip nat translations**
- **debug ip nat**
- **ping ip-address**

Issue: The **ip nat translation max-entries 2** command was preventing more than two simultaneous NAT translations.

Resolution: The **ip nat translation max-entries 2** command was removed, which allowed additional NAT translations to be created.

Trouble Ticket #9 Review

Trouble ticket #9 is presented in Chapter 11, "IP Communications Troubleshooting."

Symptom: A Cisco IP Phone was failing to register with a Cisco Unified Communications Manager Express (UCME) router.

Troubleshooting command used:

- **show running-config**

Issue: The DHCP server configured on one of the routers in the topology was misconfigured. Specifically, the **network** command in DHCP configuration mode for the DHCP pool of the IP phones specified an incorrect IP address space.

Resolution: The incorrect **network** command in DHCP configuration mode was removed and replaced with a **network** command that specified the appropriate address space.

Trouble Ticket #10 Review

Trouble ticket #10 is presented in Chapter 11.

Symptom: Voice calls placed across a Frame Relay WAN link were suffering from poor voice quality if the call originated from an analog phone, whereas calls that originated from a Cisco IP Phone did not experience quality issues.

Troubleshooting commands used:

- **show class-map**
- **show running-config**

Issue: A Cisco IP Phone automatically marks voice packets with a DSCP value of Expedited Forwarding (EF). However, by default, calls originated from an analog phone are not marked with a DSCP value of EF.

Resolution: The AutoQoS VoIP feature was configured on a router, which caused voice traffic to be recognized (using NBAR) and marked with a DSCP value of EF.

Trouble Ticket #11 Review

Trouble ticket #11 is presented in Chapter 12, "IPv6 Troubleshooting."

Symptom: Routers in a topology were configured with IPv6 addressing, and OSPFv3 was chosen as the routing protocol. However, some of the OSPFv3 routers were not forming appropriate adjacencies.

Troubleshooting commands used:

- **show running-config**
- **show ipv6 route**
- **show ipv6 ospf interface** *interface-id*
- **show ipv6 ospf neighbor**

Issue #1: The HELLO timer on an interface on one of the routers was set to a nondefault value, whereas the other end of the link was configured for its default HELLO timer value. This prevented an adjacency from forming between these two routers.

Resolution #1: The router interface with a nondefault HELLO timer was configured to use the default HELLO timer value, after which an adjacency was formed between these two routers.

Issue #2: The OSPF network type on the subinterface of a router was set to point-to-multipoint, whereas the other end of the link was a default OSPF network type of point-to-point.

Resolution #2: The router subinterface with a nondefault OSPF network type was configured to use the default network type of point-to-point, after which an adjacency was formed between the routers at each end of the link.

Issue #3: Subinterfaces at opposite sides of a link had different MTU values. Specifically, one subinterface had a default MTU of 1500 bytes, whereas the other subinterface had a nondefault MTU of 1400 bytes.

Resolution #3: The subinterface with the nondefault MTU of 1400 bytes was reconfigured to have a default MTU of 1500 bytes, after which an adjacency formed between the routers at each end of the link.

Exam Preparation Tasks

Review All the Key Topics

Key Topic

Review the most important topics from inside the chapter, noted with the Key Topics icon in the outer margin of the page. Table 14-5 lists these key topics and the page numbers where each is found.

Table 14-5 *Key Topics for Chapter 14*

Key Topic Element	Description	Page Number
List	Potential site-to-site network issues	449
List	Potential remote-access network issues	453
List	Questions to answer when troubleshooting a VPN issue	454
Table 14-3	VPN troubleshooting commands	455
Table 14-4	OSI layers of various networking technologies	463
List	Prerequisites for troubleshooting a complex enterprise network	464

Complete Tables and Lists from Memory

Print a copy of Appendix B, "Memory Tables" (found on the CD), or at least the section for this chapter, and complete the tables and lists from memory. Appendix C, "Memory Tables Answer Key," also on the CD, includes completed tables and lists to check your work.

Define Key Terms

Define the following key terms from this chapter, and check your answers in the Glossary:

virtual private network (VPN), site-to-site VPN, remote-access VPN, Generic Routing Encapsulation (GRE), IP security (IPsec), Dynamic Multipoint VPN (DMVPN)

Command Reference to Check Your Memory

This section includes the most important configuration and EXEC commands covered in this chapter. To determine how well you have memorized the commands as a side effect of your other studies, cover the left side of the table with a piece of paper; read the descriptions on the right side; and see whether you remember the command.

Table 14-6   *Chapter 14 EXEC Command Reference*

Command	Description
show crypto ipsec sa	Displays IPsec security association settings
show crypto engine connections active	Displays configuration information for all active IPsec sessions
show crypto map	Displays the crypto map configuration of a router (for example, information about ACLs being referenced by the crypto map, the IP address of the IPsec peer, the security association lifetime, and the name of the transform set of the crypto map)
show ip route	Displays routes injected into a router's IP routing table, including next-hop IP address or exit interface information for IP routes
show ip protocols	Displays information about a router's active IP routing processes
show interfaces tunnel *number*	Displays status and configuration information for a specified tunnel interface on a router

The first 14 chapters of this book cover the technologies, troubleshooting strategies, and commands required to be prepared to pass the 642-832 TSHOOT exam. Although these chapters supply detailed information, most people need more preparation than simply reading the first 14 chapters of this book. This chapter details a set of tools and a study plan to help you complete your preparation for the 642-832 TSHOOT exam.

This short chapter has two main sections, as follows:

- The first section lists information about the 642-832 TSHOOT exam and the exam preparation tools useful at this point in your study.

- The second section lists a suggested study plan now that you have completed all the earlier chapters in this book.

Note: This chapter makes reference to many of the chapters and appendixes included with this book, as well as tools available on the enclosed CD. Some of the appendixes, beginning with Appendix B, "Memory Tables," are included only on the CD that comes with this book. To access those, just insert the CD and make the appropriate selection from the opening interface.

CHAPTER 15

Final Preparation

Tools for Final Preparation

This section lists some information about the exam, available tools, and how to access those tools.

Information About the TSHOOT Exam

The TSHOOT exam number is 642-832. At the time of this writing, Cisco estimates that approximately ten percent of the TSHOOT exam will consist of multiple choice questions, with approximately ninety percent of exam questions being questions where you actively troubleshoot a trouble ticket.

Cisco has constructed questions on the TSHOOT exam in a way to combat brain dump sites on the Internet. For example, more than one troubleshooting scenario might have the same topology and challenge you with the same trouble ticket. However, the correct answer is dependent upon the underlying issue (for example, mismatched EIGRP AS numbers or auto summarization being turned on) that you need to discover. This approach prevents exam candidates from simply memorizing a response to a given trouble ticket.

Also, check the TSHOOT exam blueprint at Cisco.com in order to identify any topics or areas that you will not be tested on. Specifically, this book mirrors the topics covered in the TSHOOT course. However, at the time of this writing, not every topic covered in the TSHOOT course was on the TSHOOT exam blueprint (for examples, firewalls and multicast). Because Cisco can update this blueprint at any time, check the blueprint to ensure that you are studying relevant exam topics.

Exam Engine and Questions on the CD

The CD in the back of this book includes the Boson Exam Environment (BEE). The BEE is the exam-engine software that delivers and grades a set of free practice questions written by Cisco Press. The BEE supports multiple-choice questions, drag-and-drop questions, and many scenario-based questions that require the same level of analysis as the questions on the CCNP TSHOOT 642-832 exam. The installation process has two major steps. The first step is installing the BEE software—the CD in the back of this book has a recent copy of the BEE software, supplied by Boson Software (www.boson.com). The second step is activating and downloading the free practice questions. The practice questions written by Cisco Press for the CCNP TSHOOT 642-832 exam are not on the CD; instead, the practice questions must be downloaded from www.boson.com.

Note: The CD case in the back of this book includes the CD and a piece of paper. The paper contains the activation key for the practice questions associated with this book. *Do not lose this activation key.*

Install the Software from the CD

The following are the steps you should perform to install the software:

Step 1.   Insert the CD into your computer.

Step 2.   From the main menu, click the option to install the Boson Exam Environment (BEE). The software that automatically runs is the Cisco Press software needed to access and use all CD-based features, including the BEE, a PDF of this book, and the CD-only appendixes.

Step 3.   Respond to the prompt windows as you would with any typical software installation process.

The installation process might give you the option to register the software. This process requires you to establish a login at the www.boson.com website. You need this login to activate the exam; therefore, you should register when prompted.

Activate and Download the Practice Exam

After the Boson Exam Environment (BEE) is installed, activate the exam associated with this book.

Step 1.   Launch the BEE from the Start menu.

Step 2.   The first time you run the software, you should be asked to either log in or register an account. If you do not already have an account with Boson, select the option to register a new account. You must register to download and use the exam.

Step 3.   After you have registered or logged in, the software might prompt you to download the latest version of the software, which you should do. Note that this process updates the BEE, not the practice exam.

Step 4.   From the Boson Exam Environment main window, click the Exam Wizard button to activate and download the exam associated with this book.

Step 5.   From the Exam Wizard dialog box, select Activate a Purchased Exam and click the Next button. Although you did not purchase the exam directly, you purchased it indirectly when you bought the book.

Step 6.   In the EULA Agreement window, click Yes to accept the terms of the license agreement, and then click Next. If you do not accept the terms of the license agreement, you will be unable to install or use the software.

Step 7.   In the Activate Exam Wizard dialog box, enter the activation key from the paper inside the CD holder in the back of the book, and then click Next.

Step 8. Wait while the activation process downloads the practice questions. When the exam has been downloaded, the main BEE menu should list a new exam. If you do not see the exam, click the My Exams tab on the menu. You might also need to click the plus sign icon (+) to expand the menu and see the exam.

At this point, the software and practice questions are ready to use.

Activating Other Exams

You need to install the exam software and register only once. Then, for each new exam, you will need to complete only a few additional steps. For example, if you bought this book along with *CCENT/CCNA ICND1 Official Exam Certification Guide* or *CCNA ICND2 Official Exam Certification Guide*, you would need to perform the following steps:

Step 1. Launch the BEE (if it is not already open).

Step 2. Perform Steps 4 through 7 under the section "Activate and Download the Practice Exam," earlier in the chapter.

Step 3. Repeat Steps 1 and 2 for any exams in another Cisco Press book.

You can also purchase Boson ExSim-Max practice exams that are written and developed by Boson Software's subject-matter experts at www.boson.com. The ExSim-Max practice exams simulate the content on the actual certification exams, enabling you to gauge whether you are ready to pass the real exam. When you purchase an ExSim-Max practice exam, you receive an activation key. You can then activate and download the exam by performing Steps 1 and 2 above.

The Cisco CCNP Prep Center

Cisco provides a wide variety of CCNP preparation tools at a Cisco Systems website called CCNP Prep Center. CCNP Prep Center includes such resources as the following:

■ Practice exam questions

■ Quick learning modules

■ CCNP discussion forums

■ CCNP news and information

■ CCNP TV

To use CCNP Prep Center, point your browser to http://www.cisco.com/go/prep-ccnp. Once there, you can explore its many features.

Study Plan

You could simply study using all the available tools, as mentioned earlier in this chapter; however, this section suggests a particular study plan, with a sequence of tasks that might work better than just randomly using the tools. Feel free to use the tools in any way and at any time to help you get fully prepared for the exam.

The suggested study plan separates the tasks into two categories:

- **Recall the Facts:** Perform recommended activities that help you remember all the necessary details from the first 14 chapters of the book.

- **Use the Exam Engine:** The exam engine on the CD can be used to study using a bank of unique questions available only with this book.

Recall the Facts

As with most exams, there are many facts, concepts, and definitions that must be recalled in order to do well on the test. This section suggests a couple of tasks that should help you remember the necessary information:

Step 1.   **Review and repeat, as needed, the activities in the "Exam Preparation Tasks" section at the end of each chapter.** Most of these activities help refine your knowledge of a topic while also helping you to memorize the facts.

Step 2.   **Using the Exam Engine, answer all the questions in the book database.** This question database includes all the questions printed in the beginning of each chapter. Although some of the questions might be familiar, repeating the questions will help improve your recall of the topics covered in the questions.

Use the Exam Engine

The exam engine includes two basic modes:

- **Study mode:** Study mode is most useful when you want to use the questions for a comprehensive review. In study mode, you can select options such as whether you want to randomize the order of the questions or the order of the answers, whether you want to automatically see answers to the questions, and many other options.

- **Simulation mode:** Simulation mode can either require or allow a set number of questions and a set time period. These timed exams not only enable you to study the TSHOOT exam topics, they also help you simulate the time pressure that can occur on the actual exam.

Choosing Study or Simulation Mode

Both study mode and simulation mode are useful for exam preparation. The following steps show how to move to the screen from which to select study or simulation mode:

Step 1.   Click the Choose Exam button, which should list the exam under the title ExSim for Cisco Press TSHOOT ECG.

Step 2.   Click the name of the exam once, which should highlight the exam name.

Step 3.   Click the Load Exam button.

The engine should display a window. Here you can choose Simulation Mode or Study Mode using the radio buttons.

Passing Scores for the TSHOOT Exam

When scoring your simulated exam using this book's exam engine, you should strive to get a score of 85 percent or better. However, the scoring on the book's exam engine does not match how Cisco scores the actual TSHOOT exam. Interestingly, Cisco does not publish many details about how they score their exams, with the result being that you cannot reasonably deduce which questions you missed or how many points are assigned to each question.

Cisco does publish some specific guidance about how they score the exam, whereas other details have been mentioned by Cisco personnel during public presentations about their exams. Some of the key facts about scoring are as follows:

■   Cisco does give partial credit on simulation questions. So, complete as much of a simulation question as you can.

■   Cisco might give more weight to some questions.

■   The test does not adapt based on your answers to early questions in the test. For example, if you miss a BGP troubleshooting question, the test does not start giving you more BGP troubleshooting questions.

■   Cisco scores range from 300 to 1000, with a passing grade usually (but not always) around 849.

■   The 849 out of 1000 does not necessarily mean that you got 84.9% of the questions correct.

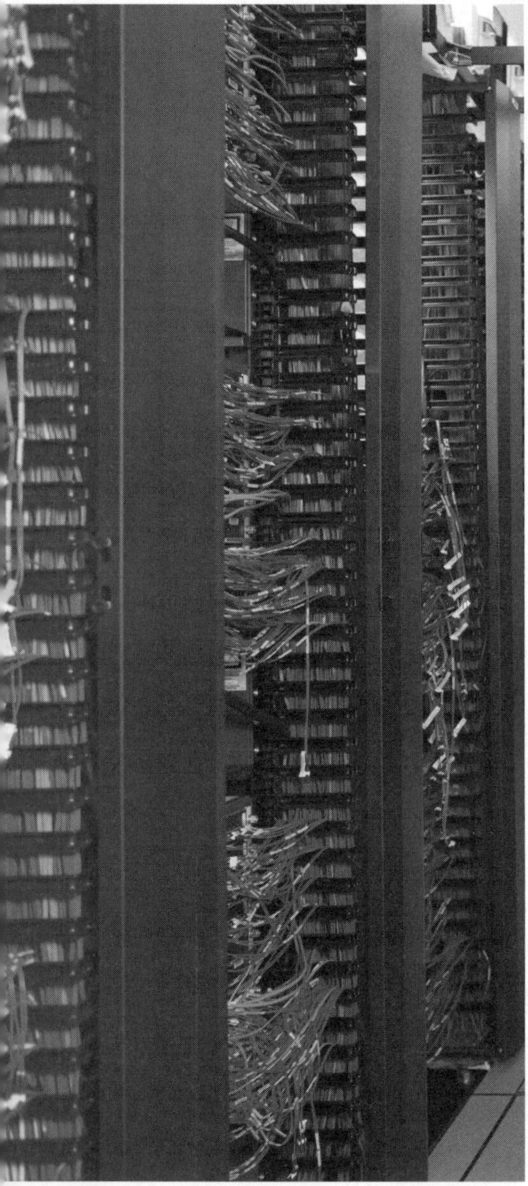

Answers to the "Do I Know This Already?" Quizzes

Chapter 1

1. A, C, and D
2. B and C
3. C
4. C
5. D
6. A
7. C and D
8. A, B, and D
9. A, C, and D
10. D
11. B
12. C
13. A
14. B

Chapter 2

1. B, C, and D
2. B
3. D
4. C
5. D
6. B
7. B and D
8. A
9. B
10. B and C
11. C and D
12. B
13. A, C, and D
14. A
15. A, C, and D
16. A and C

Chapter 3

1. B
2. C
3. A
4. A, B, and D
5. C
6. A and D
7. B

Chapter 4

1. A and D
2. A and C
3. A
4. A and C
5. B and D
6. B

Chapter 5

1. B and D
2. B
3. C
4. B
5. C
6. B
7. A and C
8. B and C
9. A, B, and D
10. B

Chapter 6

1. A and C
2. C and D
3. C
4. A, C, and D
5. A and D
6. C

Chapter 7

1. B
2. A
3. C
4. D
5. C
6. B
7. C
8. A

Chapter 8

1. A and D
2. B
3. B
4. D
5. A and B

Chapter 9

1. A, C, and D
2. C
3. D
4. A and D
5. B
6. C
7. B and C
8. A and B

Chapter 10

1. A
2. B
3. A, C, and D
4. B and D
5. B
6. A, B, C, and E
7. A and C
8. B
9. B

Chapter 11

1. B
2. C
3. D
4. A, B, C, and E
5. B, C, and D
6. C
7. D
8. A
9. A, B, D, and E

Chapter 12

1. A, C, and D
2. C
3. B, C, and D
4. A
5. B
6. C and D
7. D
8. B
9. B
10. D
11. B

Chapter 13

1. A
2. A, B, D, and E
3. D
4. B
5. C
6. A, B, and C
7. C
8. B and D
9. A
10. C

Chapter 14

1. B and C
2. D
3. A
4. D
5. B
6. B and C
7. C
8. A

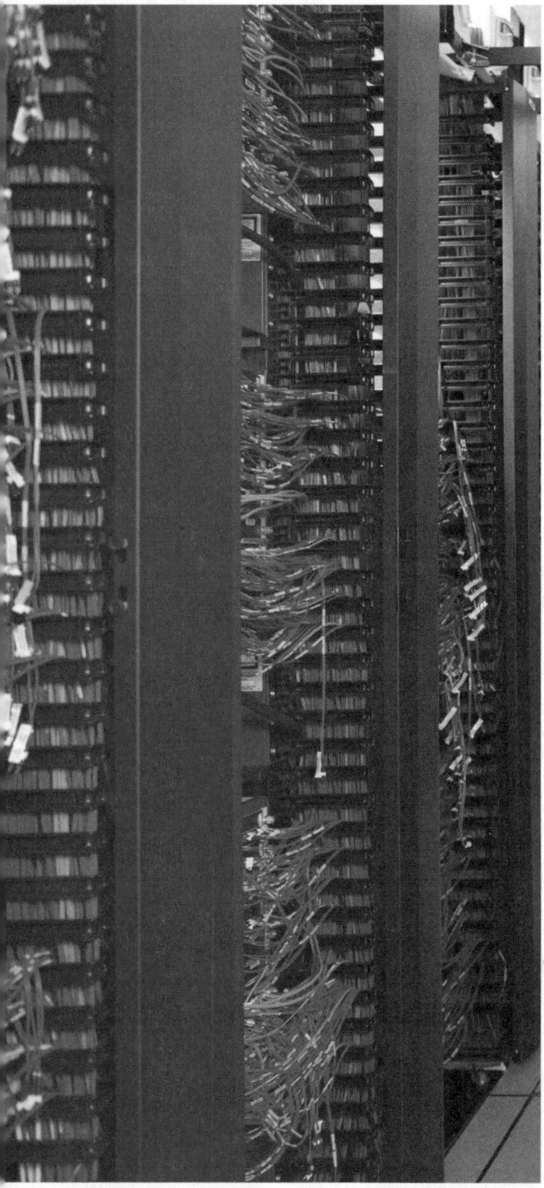

GLOSSARY

access control list (ACL) An ACL is a set of rules applied to a router that dictate what traffic is allowed or not allowed to enter or exit an interface.

accounting The accounting service can collect and store information about a user login. This information can be used, for example, to keep an audit trail of what was performed on a network.

Address Resolution Protocol (ARP) A network device that knows the IP address of a destination can send out an ARP request in an attempt to dynamically learn the MAC address of the destination device (or the MAC address of the next-hop gateway used to reach that device).

adjacency table When a router is performing a route lookup using Cisco Express Forwarding (CEF), the Forwarding Information Base (FIB) references an entry in the adjacency table. The adjacency table entry contains the frame header information required by the router to properly form a frame. Therefore, an egress interface and a next-hop IP address would be in an adjacency entry for a multipoint interface, whereas a point-to-point interface would only require egress interface information.

administrative distance An administrative distance is a measure of the believability of a routing protocol, with lower administrative distances being more believable. For example, Routing Information Protocol (RIP) has an administrative distance of 120, whereas Open Shortest Path First (OSPF) has an administrative distance of 110. Therefore, if a router ran both RIP and OSPF, and if both routing protocols knew of a route to reach a destination network, the router would install the OSPF-learned route into its IP routing table because of the preferable administrative distance of OSPF.

application server An application server provides services such as voice mail, unified messaging, and presence information (which can show the availability of another user).

ARP Input process The ARP Input process is in charge of sending ARP requests on a router.

ASPATH ASPATH is a Border Gateway Protocol (BGP) attribute that contains a listing of the autonomous systems (AS) that must be transited to reach a specific destination network.

authentication The authentication service can check user credentials to confirm that users are who they claim to be.

authorization   When authenticated, the authorization service determines what a user is allowed to do.

autonomous mode   Autonomous mode is a wireless network mode of operation in which an access point is configured with a service set identifier (SSID), radio frequency (RF) channel, and RF power settings. Having an autonomous access point tasked with all these responsibilities can limit scalability and hinder the addition of advanced wireless services.

autonomous system (AS)   An autonomous system is a network under a single administrative control.

AutoQoS Enterprise   AutoQoS Enterprise is a feature supported on some models of Cisco routers that learns current network traffic patterns and recommends a policy that could enforce the observed traffic behavior for as many as ten classes of traffic.

AutoQoS VoIP   AutoQoS VoIP is a Cisco IOS feature supported on some models of Cisco routers and switches that optimizes a router or switch port for voice quality.

backplane   The backplane of a switch physically interconnects a switch's ports. Therefore, depending on the specific switch architecture, frames flowing through a switch enter via a port (that is, an ingress port), flow across the switch's backplane, and are forwarded out of another port (that is, an egress port).

baseline   A baseline is a collection of network measurements taken when the network is functioning properly. Measurements taken during a troubleshooting scenario could be contrasted with baseline information.

BGP neighbor table   A BGP neighbor table contains a listing of all BGP neighbors configured for a router, including each neighbor's IP address, the autonomous system (AS) number, the state of the neighborship, and several other statistics.

BGP table   The BGP table, sometimes referred to as the BGP Routing Information Base (RIB), contains routes learned from Border Gateway Protocol (BGP) peers and routes locally injected into a router's BGP table.

blocking   Blocking is one of four Spanning Tree Protocol (STP) forwarding states for a port. A port remains in the blocking state for 20 seconds by default. During this time a nondesignated port evaluates bridge protocol data units (BPDUs) in an attempt to determine its role in a spanning tree.

bottom-up method   The bottom-up method of troubleshooting starts at the bottom (that is, Layer 1) of the OSI model and works its way up.

boundary router   A boundary router is a router that sits at the boundary of the routing domains to be redistributed.

BPDU Guard   The BPDU Guard feature is enabled on Cisco Catalyst switch ports configured with the Cisco PortFast feature. The PortFast feature is enabled on ports that connect to end-user devices, such as PCs, and reduces the time required for the port to transition into the forwarding state after being connected. The logic of PortFast is that a port connecting to an end-user device does not have the potential to create a topology loop. Therefore, the port can go active sooner by skipping the STP Listening and Learning states, which by default take 15 seconds each. Because PortFast ports are connected to end-user devices, these ports should never receive a bridge protocol data unit (BPDU). Therefore, if a port enabled for BPDU Guard receives a BPDU, the port is disabled.

buffer leak   A buffer leak occurs when a process does not return a buffer to the router when the process has finished using the buffer.

call agent   A call agent provides call control for IP phones, call admission control (CAC), bandwidth control and management, and address translation. Although a call agent can be server based, Cisco also supports a router-based call agent, known as Cisco Unified Communications Manager Express (UCME).

Cisco Application Network Services (ANS)   Cisco ANS is a collection of Cisco solutions that fall under the Cisco Service-Oriented Network Architecture (SONA) framework. ANS technologies can, for example, enhance the performance of applications within a data center, for users at a remote site, and for a teleworker.

Cisco Express Forwarding (CEF)   CEF maintains two tables in the data plane. Specifically, the Forwarding Information Base (FIB) maintains Layer 3 forwarding information, whereas the Adjacency Table maintains Layer 2 information for next-hops listed in the FIB. These sources of packet switching information can be used to efficiently make packet forwarding decisions.

Cisco Lifecycle Services   The Cisco Lifecycle Services maintenance model defines distinct phases in the life of a Cisco technology in a network. These phases are Prepare, Plan, Design, Implement, Operate, and Optimize. As a result, the Cisco Lifecycle Services model is often referred to as the PPDIOO model.

Cisco TelePresence   The Cisco TelePresence solution uses CD-quality audio and high-definition (HD) video (that is, 1080p) displayed on large monitors to create lifelike video conferences.

Cisco Unified Video Advantage   The Cisco Unified Video Advantage product uses a PC, a video camera, and a Cisco IP Phone as a video conferencing station. Specifically, a camera connects to a USB port on the PC. Software is loaded on the PC, and the PC is connected to the PC port on a Cisco IP Phone. Alternatively, the Cisco IP Phone could be the software-based Cisco IP Communicator product running on the PC. When a voice call is placed between two users running the Cisco Unified Video Advantage product, a video call can automatically be started, with video appearing on the PC of each user.

Classic Cisco IOS Firewall   The Classic Cisco IOS Firewall was previously known as Context-Based Access Control (CBAC). The Classic Cisco IOS Firewall inspects traffic flowing from a trusted network to an untrusted network. Returning flows from the untrusted network can be permitted into the trusted network. However, if someone attempts to initiate a session from the untrusted network into the trusted network, that session is denied by default.

comparing configurations   The comparing configurations method of troubleshooting compares a known good configuration with a current configuration. The difference in those configurations might give the troubleshooter insight into the underlying cause of a problem.

component swapping   The component swapping method of troubleshooting replaces individual network components (for example, a cable, switch, or router) in an attempt to isolate the cause of a problem.

control plane   The control plane of operation encompasses protocols used between routers and switches. These protocols include, for example, routing protocols and Spanning Tree Protocol (STP). Also, a router or switch's processor and memory reside in the control plane.

Data Link Connection Identifier (DLCI)   A DLCI is a locally significant identifier for a Frame Relay virtual circuit (VC).

data plane   The data plane is the plane of operation in charge of forwarding data through a router or switch.

delay   Delay is the time required for a packet to travel from its source to its destination.

designated port   Every network segment in a spanning tree has a single designated port, which is the port on that segment closest to the root bridge, in terms of cost. Therefore, all ports on a root bridge are designated ports.

DHCP snooping   The DHCP snooping feature on Cisco Catalyst switches can combat a DHCP server spoofing attack. With this solution, Cisco Catalyst switch ports are configured in either the trusted or untrusted state. If a port is trusted, it is allowed to receive DHCP responses (for example, DHCPOFFER, DHCPACK, or DHCPNAK). Conversely, if a port is untrusted, it is not allowed to receive DHCP responses, and if a DHCP response does attempt to enter an untrusted port, the port is disabled.

Differentiated Services Code Point (DSCP)   A DSCP marking uses the six leftmost bits in the Type of Service (TOS) byte in an IPv4 header. You can use these six bits to create as many as 64 different DSCP values (in the range 0–63). The Internet Engineering Task Force (IETF) selected a subset of these values and assigned names to those values. These names are called per-hop behaviors (PHBs) because these DSCP values can influence how traffic is treated at each hop (that is, each router hop or switch hop) along the path from the traffic source to its destination.

Dijkstra shortest path first (SPF) algorithm   Dijkstra's algorithm, which Open Shortest Path First (OSPF) uses, takes the information contained in the LSAs to determine the shortest path to any destination within an area of the network.

divide and conquer method   The divide and conquer method of troubleshooting begins in the middle (for example, Layer 3) of the OSI model and radiates out from that layer.

drops   Packet drops occur when a link is congested and a buffer overflows. Some types of traffic, such as UDP traffic (for example, voice traffic), are not retransmitted if packets are dropped.

Dynamic ARP Inspection (DAI)   The DAI feature can help prevent Address Resolution Protocol (ARP) spoofing attacks. DAI works similarly to DHCP snooping by using trusted and untrusted ports. ARP replies are allowed into the switch on trusted ports. However, if an ARP reply enters the switch on an untrusted port, the contents of the ARP reply are compared against the DHCP binding table to verify their accuracy. If the ARP reply is not consistent with the DHCP binding table, the ARP reply is dropped, and the port is disabled.

Dynamic Host Configuration Protocol (DHCP)   DHCP serves as one of the most common methods of assigning IP address information to a network host. Specifically, DHCP allows a client to obtain an IP address, subnet mask, default gateway IP address, Domain Name System (DNS) server IP address, and other types of information from a server.

Dynamic Multipoint VPN (DMVPN)   DMVPN is a technology that allows spoke sites, in a hub-and-spoke topology, to dynamically form a direct VPN tunnel between themselves, on an as-needed basis.

dynamic NAT   Dynamic NAT is a dynamic mapping of private internal IP addresses to a pool of public external IP addresses.

EIGRP interface table   All the router interfaces that have been configured to participate in an Enhanced Interior Gateway Routing Protocol (EIGRP) routing process are listed in this table. However, if an interface has been configured as passive (that is, an interface that does not send routing information), it does not appear in this table.

EIGRP neighbor table   This table lists the Enhanced Interior Gateway Routing Protocol (EIGRP) neighbors of a router (that is, neighboring routers from whom an EIGRP Hello message has been received). A neighbor is removed from this table if it has not been heard from for a period defined as the hold-time. Also, if an interface off of which a neighbor is known is removed from the EIGRP interface table because it goes down, the neighbor is removed from this table.

EIGRP topology table   This table contains routes learned by an Enhanced Interior Gateway Routing Protocol (EIGRP) routing process. The best route for a network in this table becomes a candidate to be injected into the router's IP routing table. If multiple routes in this table have an equal metric, or if EIGRP's variance feature is configured, more than one route might become a candidate for injection into the IP routing table.

Embedded Event Manager (EEM)   The EEM feature can create custom event definitions on a router and specify actions the router can take in response to these events.

EtherChannel   An EtherChannel logically combines the bandwidth of multiple physical interfaces into a logical connection between switches.

Extensible Authentication Protocol (EAP)   An EAP is an 802.1X protocol used to communicate between an 802.1X authenticator (for example, a wireless LAN controller) and an 802.1X authentication server (for example, a RADIUS server).

fast switching   Fast switching is a router packet switching mode that makes use of a Fast cache maintained in a router's data plane. The Fast cache contains information about how traffic from different data flows should be forwarded. The first packet in a data flow is process switched by a router's CPU. Once the router determines how to forward the first frame of a data flow, that forwarding information is then stored in the Fast cache. Subsequent packets in that same data flow are then forwarded based on information in the Fast cache, as opposed to being process switched. As a result, Fast switching reduces a router's CPU utilization, as compared to process switching.

FCAPS   FCAPS is a network management model defined by the ISO, where the acronym FCAPS stands for Fault management, Configuration management, Accounting management, Performance management, and Security management.

following the traffic path   Following the traffic path is a method of troubleshooting that checks components (for example, links and devices) over which traffic flows on its way from source to destination.

forwarding   Forwarding is one of four STP forwarding states for a port. A port moves from the learning state to the forwarding state and begins to forward frames.

Forwarding Information Base (FIB)   The FIB contains Layer 3 information, similar to the information found in an IP routing table. Additionally, an FIB contains information about multicast routes and directly connected hosts.

gatekeeper   A gatekeeper provides call admission control (CAC), bandwidth control and management, and address translation in an H.323 network.

gateway   A gateway provides translation between VoIP and non-VoIP networks, such as the Public Switched Telephone Network (PSTN). A gateway also provides physical access for local analog and digital voice devices, such as telephones, fax machines, key systems, and Private Branch Exchanges (PBX).

Gateway Load Balancing Protocol (GLBP)   GLBP can load-balance traffic destined for a next-hop gateway across a collection of routers, known as a GLBP group. Specifically, when a client sends an Address Resolution Protocol (ARP) request, in an attempt to determine the MAC address corresponding to a known IP address, GLBP can respond with the MAC address of one member of the GLBP group. The next such request would receive a response containing the MAC address of a different member of the GLBP group.

Generic Routing Encapsulation (GRE)   GRE is a tunnel encapsulation protocol that can encapsulate a variety of traffic, including unicast, multicast, and broadcast IP traffic, in addition to non-IP protocols such as Internetwork Packet Exchange (IPX) and AppleTalk. GRE, however, does not natively offer security for traffic traveling over the tunnel.

Hot Standby Routing Protocol (HSRP)   HSRP uses virtual IP and MAC addresses. One router, known as the active router, services requests destined for the virtual IP and MAC addresses. Another router, known as the standby router, can service such requests in the event the active router becomes unavailable.

input errors   The input errors value shown in the output of a **show interfaces** command indicates frames were not received correctly (for example, a cyclic redundancy check [CRC] error occurred), perhaps indicating a cabling problem or a duplex mismatch.

input queue drops   The input queue drops value shown in the output of a **show interfaces** command indicates that a router received information faster than the router could process it.

Internet Group Management Protocol (IGMP)   IGMP is a protocol used between clients (for example, PCs) and routers to let routers know which of their interfaces have multicast receivers attached.

interrupt driven task   An interrupt driven task is a network maintenance task that arises in response to a reported network issue.

intrusion detection system (IDS)   An IDS device receives a copy of traffic to be analyzed and can send an alert when it identifies traffic as malicious. Some IDS devices can dynamically configure a firewall or a router to block the malicious traffic.

intrusion prevention system (IPS)   An IPS device sits inline with the traffic that it analyzes and can drop traffic identified as malicious.

IP Background process   When an interface changes its state, the IP Background process handles that state change.

IP phone   An IP phone is an Ethernet device that provides IP voice to the desktop.

IP security (IPsec)   IPsec is a collection of VPN technologies that have the ability to secure traffic traveling over a virtual private network (VPN). IPsec by itself, however, supports only unicast IP traffic flowing over an IPsec tunnel.

IP SLA   The Cisco IOS IP SLA feature can measure how the network treats traffic for specific applications. IP SLA accomplishes this by synthetically generating traffic bearing similar characteristics (for example, port numbers and packet sizes). This traffic, called probes, is sent to a destination router configured to respond to the received probes with time-stamp information, which can then be used to calculate performance metrics for the traffic.

IP telephony   IP telephony refers to a telephony solution that uses IP phones and a call processing server (for example, Cisco Unified Communications Manager).

IPv6 anycast   An IPv6 anycast transmission can be thought of as a one-to-nearest communication flow, where a single IPv6 source address sends traffic to a single IPv6 destination address, and that single IPv6 destination address is assigned to multiple devices. The communication flow is one-to-nearest from the perspective of a router's IPv6 routing table.

IPv6 multicast   An IPv6 multicast transmission can be thought of as a one-to-many communication flow, where a single IPv6 source address sends traffic to an IPv6 multicast group. Devices needing to receive traffic destined for the multicast group can join the group.

IPv6 over IPv4 tunnel   An IPv6 over IPv4 tunnel allows IPv6 traffic to be transported over an IPv4 tunnel. Although the source and destination of the IP tunnel are defined as IPv4 addresses, IPv6 addresses can be assigned to the virtual tunnel interfaces, which allows the IPv6 traffic to be transmitted over the IPv4 tunnel.

IPv6 unicast   An IPv6 unicast transmission can be thought of as a one-to-one communication flow, where a single IPv6 source address sends traffic to a single IPv6 destination address.

IT Infrastructure Library (ITIL)   An ITIL defines a collection of best practice recommendations that work together to meet business goals.

jitter   Jitter is an uneven arrival of packets that can, for example, impact voice quality.

Layer 3 switch   A Layer 3 switch can act as a Layer 2 switch (that is, making forwarding decisions based on MAC addresses), or it can make forwarding decisions based on Layer 3 information (for example, IP address information).

learning   Learning is one of the four Spanning Tree Protocol (STP) states for a port. A port moves from the listening state to the learning state and remains in this state for 15 seconds by default. During this time, the port begins to add entries to its MAC address table.

lightweight access point   A lightweight access point is a wireless network device that performs functions such as beaconing, packet transmission, and frame queuing.

Lightweight Access Point Protocol (LWAPP)   LWAPP is a protocol used to communicate between a lightweight access point and a wireless LAN controller (WLC). LWAPP sends packets in a Layer 2 frame with an Ethertype of 0xBBBB. LWAPP data traffic uses a User Datagram Protocol (UDP) destination port of 12222, whereas LWAPP control traffic uses a UDP destination port of 12223.

link-state advertisement (LSA)   A link-state advertisement is a message sent and received by OSPF routers to educate routers about a network topology. Various LSA types exist.

listening   Listening is one of the four STP forwarding states for a port. A port moves from the blocking state to the listening state and remains in this state for 15 seconds by default. During this time, the port sources bridge protocol data units (BPDU), which inform adjacent switches of the port intent to forward data.

local preference   Local preference is a Border Gateway Protocol (BGP) attribute that can be applied to routes coming into a router. This might cause the router to make its outbound routing decisions based on those local preference values. Higher local preference values are preferred over lower local preference values.

management plane   The management plane of operation is used to manage a router or a switch. This management involves, for example, accessing and configuring a device.

Media Access Control (MAC) address   A MAC address is a 48-bit address assigned to various types of network hardware (for example, network interface cards in PCs). A Layer 2 switch can learn which MAC addresses reside on specific switch ports and make forwarding decisions based on that information.

memory allocation failure   A memory allocation failure (which produces a MALLOC-FAIL error message) occurs when a process attempts to allocate a block of memory and fails to do so.

memory leak   When a router starts a process, that process can allocate a block of memory. When the process completes, the process should return its allocated memory to the router's pool of memory. If not all the allocated memory is returned to the router's main memory pool, a memory leak occurs.

Modular Quality of Service Command-Line Interface (MQC)   MQC is a three-step process for configuring a variety of QoS mechanisms. These steps are (1) Create one or more class maps. (2) Create a policy map that specifies how traffic in the class maps is to be treated. (3) Apply the policy map (typically to an interface) in either the incoming or outgoing direction.

multicasting   Multicasting technology allows a multicast source (for example, a video server) to send a single stream of traffic to a Class D address, which represents a multicast group. Devices wishing to receive the stream can join the multicast group.

multipoint control unit (MCU)   An MCU mixes audio and/or video streams, thus allowing participants in multiple locations to attend the same conference.

NAT overloading   NAT overloading allows multiple private internal IP addresses to use a single public external IP address by keeping track of Layer 4 port numbers, which make each session unique (that is, Port Address Translation [PAT]).

Net Background process   An interface has a certain number of buffers available to store packets. These buffers are sometimes referred to as an interface's queue. If an interface needs to store a packet in a buffer but all the interface's buffers are in use, the interface can pull from a main pool of buffers that its router maintains. The process that allows an interface to allocate one of these globally available buffers is the Net Background process.

NetFlow   The NetFlow feature collects detailed information about traffic flows on routers and high-end switches. Collected information can optionally be sent to a NetFlow collector, which can produce reports about the traffic flows.

Network Address Translation (NAT)   NAT allows private IP addresses (as defined in RFC 1918) to be translated into Internet-routable IP addresses (that is, public IP addresses).

Network-Based Application Recognition (NBAR)   NBAR can classify various traffic types by examining information at Layers 3–7. Protocols that change port numbers (that is, stateful protocols) can also be tracked. You can expand the NBAR recognition capability by using Protocol Description Language Modules (PDLMs).

Network Management System (NMS)   A Network Management System (NMS) collects information from managed agents via Simple Network Management Protocol (SNMP).

nondesignated port   Nondesignated ports in a spanning tree block traffic to create a loop-free topology.

OSPF area border router (ABR)   An OSPF ABR connects to more than one OSPF area and therefore maintains multiple link-state databases (one for each connected area). A primary responsibility of an ABR is to exchange topological information between the backbone area and other connected areas.

OSPF autonomous system boundary router (ASBR)   An OSPF ASBR has at least one connected route participating in an OSPF area and at least one connected route participating in a different autonomous system. The primary role of an ASBR is to exchange information between an OSPF autonomous system and one or more external autonomous systems.

OSPF backbone router   An OSPF backbone router has at least one of its connected networks participating in OSPF area 0 (that is, the backbone area). If all the connected networks are participating in the backbone area, the router is also considered an internal router. Also, if a backbone router has one or more connected networks participating in another area, the backbone router is also considered an area border router (ABR).

OSPF interface table   All the router interfaces that have been configured to participate in an OSPF routing process are listed in the OSPF interface table.

OSPF internal router   All the networks directly connected to an OSPF internal router belong to the same OSPF area. Therefore, an OSPF internal router has a single link-state database.

OSPF link-state database   The OSPF link-state database is an OSPF data structure that contains topology information for all areas in which a router participates, in addition to information about how to route traffic to networks residing in other areas or autonomous systems.

OSPF neighbor table   OSPF neighbors learned via Hello packets are present in an OSPF neighbor table. A neighbor is removed from this table if Hellos have not been heard from the neighbor within the dead time interval. Additionally, a neighbor is removed from this table if the interface associated with the neighbor goes down.

OSPF Routing Information Base (RIB)   The OSPF RIB stores the results of OSPF's shortest path first (SPF) calculations.

OSPFv3   OSPFv3 is a version of the OSPF routing protocol that can support the routing of IPv6 traffic.

output errors   The output errors value shown in the output of a **show interfaces** command indicates frames were not transmitted correctly, perhaps due to a duplex mismatch.

output queue drops   The output queue drops value shown in the output of a **show interfaces** command indicates that a router received information faster than the information could be sent out of the outgoing interface (perhaps due to an input/output speed mismatch).

overlapping NAT   Overlapping NAT can allow communication between two subnets containing overlapping IP addresses.

Packet Description Language Module (PDLM)   A PDLM is a file (typically downloaded from the Cisco website and installed in a router's flash) that contains signature information for a specific protocol. A router's Cisco IOS configuration can be configured to reference a PDLM file to extend the Network-Based Application Recognition (NBAR) capability of the router.

Port Address Translation (PAT)   *See* NAT overloading.

Power over Ethernet (PoE)   PoE is a technology that allows an Ethernet switch (for example, a Cisco Catalyst switch) to provide power to an attached device (for example, an IP phone or a wireless access point) over the Ethernet leads in an unshielded twisted-pair (UTP) cable.

process switching   Process switching is a router packet switching mode in which the CPU of the router becomes directly involved with all packet-switching decisions.

Protocol Independent Multicast (PIM)   PIM is a multicast protocol used to construct IP multicast distribution trees. Protocol independence in PIM means that it can run over an IP network, regardless of the underlying unicast IP routing protocol (for example, Open Shortest Path First [OSPF] or Enhanced Interior Gateway Routing Protocol [EIGRP]). The two varieties of PIM are PIM Dense Mode (PIM-DM) and PIM Sparse Mode (PIM-SM). PIM-DM uses a source distribution tree, whereas PIM-SM uses a shared distribution tree.

remote-access VPN   A remote-access VPN requires virtual private network (VPN) clients at a remote site to run VPN client software. Although this approach might require more administrative overhead to install client software on all clients, remote-access VPNs do offer more flexibility for mobile users than site-to-site VPNs do. For example, clients can connect via the Internet connection at their hotel, using VPN client software on their laptop computer.

Remote Switch Port Analyzer (RSPAN)   The RSPAN feature of a Cisco Catalyst switch allows a port to receive a copy of traffic seen on a port or a VLAN on another switch.

rendezvous point (RP)   An RP is a centralized point in a PIM-SM multicast network. Clients wanting to receive a particular multicast stream initially receive the stream from the RP.

RIP next generation (RIPng)   RIPng is a version of the RIP routing protocol that can support the routing of IPv6 traffic.

root bridge   A root bridge is a switch that is elected as a reference point for a spanning tree.

Root Guard   The Root Guard feature can be enabled on all switch ports in a network off of which a root bridge should not appear. If a port configured for Root Guard receives a superior BPDU instead of believing the BPDU, the port goes into a root-inconsistent state. While a port is in the root-inconsistent state, no user data is sent across the port. However, after the superior BPDUs stop, the port returns to the forwarding state.

root port   Every nonroot bridge in a spanning tree has a single root port, which is the port on the switch that is closest to the root bridge, in terms of cost.

route redistribution   Route redistribution allows routes learned via one method (for example, statically configured, locally connected, or learned via a routing protocol) to be injected into a different routing protocol.

service-level agreement (SLA)   An SLA is an agreement between a service provider and the customer that specifies minimum service-level guarantees for various performance metrics. For example, an SLA might guarantee that 90 percent of the time, the customer will have 256 kbps of bandwidth available to the service provider cloud.

shoot from the hip   The shoot from the hip troubleshooting method occurs when a troubleshooter bypasses examined information and eliminates potential causes, based on the troubleshooter's experience and insight.

Simple Network Management Protocol (SNMP)   SNMP is the protocol used to communicate between an SNMP agent running on a network device and a network management station (NMS). SNMP allows an NMS to query a managed device. Also, if a managed device detects a defined event, the occurrence of that event can be reported to the NMS in the form of an SNMP trap.

site-to-site VPN   A site-to-site VPN typically terminates in a router at a headquarters and a router at the remote site. Such an arrangement does not require clients at the remote site to have VPN client software installed.

Spanning Tree Protocol (STP)   STP allows physically redundant links in a Layer 2 topology, while logically breaking any topological loops that could cause issues such as broadcast storms.

split-MAC mode   Split-MAC mode is a wireless network mode of operation whereby an access point is considered to be a lightweight access point, which cannot function without a wireless LAN controller (WLC). Specifically, a wireless LAN client sending traffic to the wired LAN sends a packet to a lightweight access point, which encapsulates the packet using the Lightweight Access Point Protocol (LWAPP). The encapsulated traffic is sent over an LWAPP tunnel to a WLC.

static NAT   Static NAT is one-to-one mapping of private internal IP addresses to public external IP addresses.

structured maintenance task   A structured maintenance task is a network maintenance task that is performed as part of a predefined plan.

Switched Port Analyzer (SPAN)   The SPAN feature of a Cisco Catalyst switch allows a port to receive a copy of traffic seen on another port or VLAN.

switched virtual interface (SVI)   You can configure the IP address for a collection of ports belonging to a VLAN under a virtual VLAN interface. This virtual VLAN interface is called a switched virtual interface (SVI).

TCP Timer process   The TCP Timer process runs for each of the TCP connections for a router. Therefore, a router with many simultaneous TCP connections could have a high CPU utilization due to the resources being consumed by the TCP Timer.

Telecommunications Management Network (TMN)   The TMN network management model is the Telecommunications Standardization Sector (ITU-T) variation of the FCAPS model. Specifically, TMN targets the management of telecommunications networks.

Ternary Content Addressable Memory (TCAM)   TCAM is a special type of memory that uses a mathematical algorithm to quickly look up forwarding information. The forwarding information in the TCAM comes from the routing processes and traffic policies residing in the control plane of the switch.

top-down method   The top-down method of troubleshooting starts at the top (that is, Layer 7) of the OSI model and works its way down.

trap   An SNMP trap is an event notification sent from a managed network device to a Network Management System (NMS).

trunk   A trunk is a type of link that can be used to interconnect switches. A trunk has the unique property of being able to carry traffic for multiple VLANs over a single connection.

unified communications   Unified communications is an IP communications framework that encompasses more than just voice. Unified communications includes a collection of applications and technologies that enhance user collaboration.

variance   Variance is an Enhanced Interior Gateway Routing Protocol (EIGRP) feature that supports load balancing over unequal-cost paths.

videoconference station   A videoconference station provides access for end-user participation in videoconferencing. The videoconference station contains a video capture device for video input and a microphone for audio input. A user can view video streams and hear the audio that originates at a remote user station. Cisco targets its Unified Video Advantage product at desktop videoconferencing applications.

virtual link   Non-backbone Open Shortest Path First (OSPF) areas (that is, areas other than area 0) must be adjacent to the backbone area. If, however, an OSPF area is not physically adjacent to area 0, a virtual link can be constructed to interconnect the discontiguous area to area 0. A virtual link spans a transit area, which is adjacent to area 0.

Virtual Path Identifier/Virtual Circuit Identifier (VPI/VCI)   A VPI/VCI is a pair of numbers identifying an ATM virtual circuit (VC).

virtual private network (VPN)   A VPN is a logical connection established through a network. That network can be an untrusted network. However, if the VPN is configured for appropriate security protocols, traffic can securely be sent over that untrusted network within the protection of the VPN tunnel.

Virtual Router Redundancy Protocol (VRRP)   VRRP, similar to Hot Standby Routing Protocol (HSRP), allows a collection of routers to service traffic destined for a single IP address. Unlike HSRP, the IP address serviced by a VRRP group does not have to be a virtual IP address. The IP address can be the address of a physical interface on the virtual router master, which is the router responsible for forwarding traffic destined for the IP address of the VRRP group.

VLAN   A VLAN is analogous to a subnet, in that traffic needs to be routed to go from one VLAN to another. Ports on many Layer 2 switches can be logically grouped into different VLANs, thus creating multiple broadcast domains on a switch.

VoIP   VoIP is a technology that transmits voice over an IP network using voice-enabled routers.

wiki   A wiki (which is the Hawaiian word for fast) can act as a web-based collaborative documentation platform.

wireless access point   Wireless access points offer network access for wireless clients.

wireless client   A wireless client device is typically an end-user device (such as a laptop) that accesses a wireless network.

wireless LAN controller (WLC)   A WLC is a wireless network device that assumes roles such as authentication, key management, and resource reservation.

wireless mobility   Wireless mobility services include security threat detection, voice services, location services, and guest access.

wireless network management   Just as enterprise LANs benefit from network management solutions, a wireless LAN can use network management solutions to enhance security and reliability and offer assistance in WLAN deployments. An example of a wireless network management solution is the Cisco Wireless Control System (WCS).

wireless network unification   To offer wireless clients access to the resources of an organization, a wireless network needs to be integrated (that is, unified) with a wired LAN. This functionality is referred to as network unification.

Zone-Based Policy Firewall   The Zone-Based Policy Firewall feature allows various router interfaces to be assigned to a zone. Interzone policies can then be configured to dictate what traffic is permitted between these defined zones.

Index

Numerics

N

O

T

You've Studied, But Are You Ready?

ExSim-Max™
PRACTICE EXAMS

Know you can pass.

Even if you read this book five times, can you really be sure you're ready to take the exam? With ExSim-Max practice exams, you can. ExSim-Max simulates the content and difficulty of the actual exam so accurately that if you can pass the ExSim-Max exam, you can pass the real exam, guaranteed*. Know you can pass with Boson.

Save time

Knowing the topics you need to focus on is important. That's why ExSim-Max provides a score report, which shows the topics that need additional attention. This allows you to go back and study exactly what you need to learn, pass our practice exam and know you are ready to take the real exam.

Be confident

Thinking you can pass is different than knowing you can. ExSim-Max simulates the complete exam experience, including topics covered, question types, question difficulty and time allowed, so you know what to expect. Most importantly, you'll know whether or not you are ready. Take the exam with confidence with ExSim-Max.

Pass the exam

If you can pass an ExSim-Max practice exam, you can pass the real exam. We are so sure of this that we guarantee it. That's right; you are guaranteed to pass the exam, or you get your money back with Boson's No Pass, No Pay guarantee*.

Get ExSim-Max and know you can pass.

*See website

Special Offer!

As the original purchaser of this book, you are eligible for a special offer for ExSim-Max. Get your special offer at www.boson.com/ready.

Boson®
boson.com

GO FURTHER, FASTER.
BECOME CERTIFIED.

Stop thinking about your potential. Realize it. Take your training, skills and knowledge to the next level. Get Cisco Certified through Pearson VUE.

Take your Cisco Career Certification exam at one of more than 4,400 conveniently located Pearson VUE® Authorized Test Centers worldwide to experience a no-hassle test experience. To register at a test center near you, simply visit PearsonVUE.com/Cisco.

FREE Online Edition

Your purchase of **CCNP TSHOOT 642-832 Official Certification Guide** includes access to a free online edition for 45 days through the Safari Books Online subscription service. Nearly every Cisco Press book is available online through Safari Books Online, along with more than 5,000 other technical books and videos from publishers such as Addison-Wesley Professional, Exam Cram, IBM Press, O'Reilly, Prentice Hall, Que, and Sams.

SAFARI BOOKS ONLINE allows you to search for a specific answer, cut and paste code, download chapters, and stay current with emerging technologies.

Activate your FREE Online Edition at
www.informit.com/safarifree

> **STEP 1:** Enter the coupon code: GKPUOXA.

> **STEP 2:** New Safari users, complete the brief registration form.
> Safari subscribers, just log in.

If you have difficulty registering on Safari or accessing the online edition, please e-mail customer-service@safaribooksonline.com